JANE'S

AMERICAN FIGHTING SHIPS
OF THE 20TH CENTURY

JANE'S

AMERICAN FIGHTING SHIPS
OF THE 20TH CENTURY

COMPILED AND EDITED BY CAPTAIN JOHN MOORE RN
PREFACE BY VICE ADMIRAL M. STASER HOLCOMB, US NAVY (RET)

MALLARD PRESS

PUBLISHER'S NOTE

With such a vast mass of information we have had to be very selective. Some may find their favourite ship has been omitted, and to those we can only offer our apologies in advance.

Over the years the shape and format of Jane's has changed, sometimes a minor matter, and at others, like the post-war shift from the landscape to the horizontal book format, a major but necessary change. These variations have given rise to a certain amount of re-organization of entries and to alterations in the type used, while old age has caused the loss of clarity in some of the photographs. Other variations, particularly in class names, are sometimes the result of changes in official practice and, at other times, due to the idiosyncrasies of the editors. In the latter case, when dealing with five individualistic enthusiasts, such differences are probably excusable.

A final word on the General Information section, which deals with flags, ensigns, charts and similar items. This was an entry which was much curtailed after World War II and finally discontinued in the interests of space. The same restriction explains our decision to provide only representative entries for the Tenders, Gunboats and Coast Guard. The limited space afforded them is not intended to denigrate their importance in any way.

MALLARD PRESS
An Imprint of BDD Promotional Company
666 Fifth Avenue
New York, N.Y. 10103.

Mallard Press and its accompanying design and logo
are trademarks of BDD Promotional Book Company, Inc.

Jane's American Fighting Ships of the 20th Century.
Originally published by Jane's Publishing Company in
Jane's All The World's Ships 1898 – 1980.

This edition first published by Studio Editions, London.
First published in the United States of America
in 1991 by The Mallard Press.

By arrangement with the proprietor.

ISBN 0-7924-5626-2

Printed and bound in Hong Kong.

CONTENTS

PREFACE

At the turn of the century, the United States Navy had a great many supporters and few detractors.

Flush with two widely dispersed victories against the Spanish fleet in 1898 – one in Santiago, Cuba, the other in Manila Bay – the U.S. Navy enjoyed a position on center stage, and seemed unlikely to lose its celebrity any time soon.

Not all Navy supporters had the same clear vision of the maritime imperatives in national security. There were ardent fans of a particular ship, or of a class of ships, or even of the specific weapons warships carried . . . support was often more focused on means than on ends.

In 1900, the 40-year reign of the steel battleship with rifled guns had just begun and the navies of the world were scrambling to outdo each other. Traditional wisdom held that the main business of a navy was to defeat other navies, and the line-of-battle ship remained the consummate expression of the naval art. Keeping track of changes in the characteristics of such ships in the major navies of the world had become a serious pursuit, giving birth to the renowned standard reference, *Jane's Fighting Ships*, in 1898.

During this period, one of the Navy's more effective supporters was President Theodore Roosevelt, an unabashed naval buff who brought both strategic vision and determination to his championship of the Navy. Having served as Assistant Secretary of the Navy during a period filled with reforms in the late 1890s, he had long embraced Alfred Thayer Mahan's views regarding the influence of seapower on history. During his tenure (1901–1909), the fleet grew in both capability and relevance to national power.

As commander-in-chief, Roosevelt sent the "Great White Fleet" of 16 coal-burning, steel battleships around the world in 1907–09. He intended to make a statement that the United States had a fleet with global reach, a navy that could and would operate anywhere on the world's oceans where national interests might require it.

By the beginning of World War I in 1914, there was every reason to expect that major battles at sea, pitting fleets of battleships against each other in tests of naval supremacy, would contribute significantly to the outcome of the conflict. But no such confrontations had occurred by war's end in 1918, German and British battle fleets having managed to avoid each other. Meanwhile, Germany's submarines effectively defied Britain's control of the seas. In its brief year at war, the United States Navy played mainly a convoying and logistics role.

In the aftermath of that "war to end wars", naval arms control became a serious international policy issue for the first time. Naval build-ups that had begun during the war were an obvious concern, leading to the Washington Naval Conference of 1921 and a series of follow-up negotiations. Battleships were the primary focus, the aim being to fix the relationship between the sizes of the major navies and end the race to build bigger and more powerful ships. Nothing really meaningful came out of these efforts, largely because of changes in the ingredients of seapower – in particular, the advent of aircraft carriers and the proliferation of submarines – that had been obscured by such intense scrutiny of the tonnage of battleships and cruisers and the size of their guns. Circumvention of treaty limitations was more common in the 1930s than was their observance.

Franklin Delano Roosevelt, president of the United States from 1933 to 1945, turned to a naval build-up to accelerate recovery from the Great Depression as well as to help draw the nation out of the isolationism that had set in after World War I. He, too, had served as Assistant Secretary of the Navy (1913–1918) and he recognized the potential of the Navy in the conflict then developing in Europe. In securing passage of the Naval Expansion Act of 1940, Roosevelt achieved a 70 per cent increase in the size of the fleet and established the concept of a "Two-Ocean Navy" for the United States.

Those actions, combined with modification of the Neutrality Act of 1937 and the Lend Lease Act of 1941, gave the nation a running start on what was to become World War II, and built the foundation for a naval posture that would change very little in the next 40 years.

In World War II, naval operations in both Atlantic and Pacific Ocean areas were central to the outcome. Carrier-based aviation quickly succeeded battleship gunnery as the primary striking power of the fleet. The U.S. submarine force came of age in the interdiction of sea lines of communication as well as in the destruction of enemy warships. Assault from the sea on heavily defended positions – amphibious warfare – triumphed again and again. Logistics took on unprecedented dimensions and prompted the construction and use of an incredible variety of ships and capabilities.

World War II ended with the United States Navy supreme on the seas. Demobilization of many U.S. wartime naval capabilities quickly followed, but there was to be no lessening of the nation's involvement on the international scene.

As the Cold War set in, squaring off NATO allies with the USSR-centered Warsaw Pact, America's response was a policy of containment. Attempting to counter Soviet expansionism, permanent forward deployment of naval forces – in the form of ships assigned to the Sixth Fleet in the Mediterranean and to the Seventh Fleet in the Western Pacific and a small Middle East Force – became de rigueur.

Deployment or repositioning of carriers and marines in response to crisis in one of the world's trouble spots (which occurred an average of six times a year between 1945 and 1980), as often as not directly sparked by Soviet adventurism, became a way of life for the U.S. fleet.

By the mid-1950s, the Soviet Navy had grown to the point that it began to constitute a threat to the use of certain ocean areas by the Western powers. With more than 300 submarines and steadily increasing numbers of warships, the Soviets had begun to tailor their four fleets to the task of holding NATO naval forces at bay.

Meanwhile, sizeable portions of the strategic nuclear capabilities of both sides were put to sea in the form of long-range ballistic missiles in submarines. Employment of submarines to seek out and destroy other submarines became a preoccupation for both Warsaw Pact and NATO navies.

Against this background of Cold War polarization and the growing Soviet maritime threat, the United States had found itself engaged in two lengthy wars – the war in Korea (1950–53) and the conflict in Vietnam (1964–1973) – in which the increasingly sophisticated threat posed by the Soviet Navy played no part. Projection of power against targets ashore, from sea areas in which there proved to be little or no opposition, had become the Navy's dominant real-world mission.

With no alternative but to build a fleet capable of overcoming Soviet naval power in the NATO–Warsaw Pact context, the United States found itself having to use its naval forces repeatedly for quite different purposes. Huge budget demands for ballistic missile submarines and nuclear attack submarines, as well as for surface combatants necessary to defend power projection forces in situations where they might have to confront the Soviet Navy, came at the expense of simpler forces and weapons more frequently called for. The result was a Navy considerably smaller than what might be necessary to carry out the demands of a war at sea in a NATO conflict, and a Navy ill-prepared for a prolonged period of power projection.

Looking backward in 1980, some ambivalence about the force structure that had evolved in 80 years was understandable, but the U.S. Navy could certainly take pride in conspicuous success across the spectrum of maritime challenges.

M. Staser Holcomb
Vice Admiral, US Navy (Ret)

FOREWORD

BATTLESHIPS

By 1900, the starting-point of this book, the US Navy was undergoing a very rapid expansion with all the problems which attend such events. Public support had been engendered by the naval successes of the Spanish–American war, not least by the epic 15,000 mile voyage of the battleship *Oregon* from Puget Sound to the Caribbean. The year 1901 brought a turning point for the USN. President McKinley had been in power during the war with Spain and was returned for a second term. Secretary Long continued in office and, with hostilities two years past, there were all the signs of post-war indecision and compromise. The assassination of McKinley in September 1901 brought a totally new direction for the navy. Theodore Roosevelt entered the White House where he stayed for the next eight years. Grasping the essential fact that foreign and naval policies were essential and inextricable elements of the nation's strategy, he looked forward to the place of the USA amongst the great nations.

By 1905 the naval building programme was absorbing 20.7 per cent of the total Federal budget. The main emphasis during the Roosevelt/Taft administrations of 1901–13 was on the construction of battleship which, in the earlier years, took anything from three to four years to build. The smaller ships, it was argued, could be built in short order.

The 14 month, 46,000 mile cruise of the Great White Fleet in 1909–1911 caused the naval planners to give deep consideration to the logistic problems of long range operations; the provision of colliers and supply vessels, the establishment of support bases and coaling stations, the improvement of fleet communications. Admiral Evans and his fleet were safe home well before the combined efforts of Roosevelt, his successor as President, William Howard Taft (1909–13) and senior naval officers prised sufficient funds from Congress to establish a base at Guantanamo in Cuba, to progress the base at Pearl Harbor and to provide minimal facilities at Olongapo (Subic Bay) and Cavite in the Philippines. These distant areas were of little interest to the majority of Washington's politicians – there were no votes to be gained from their development.

During the war with Spain the actions of the US squadrons, though successful, demonstrated the lamentable inefficiency of ships' gunnery. Great names like Dahlgren there may have been in the past but a score of some three per cent hits from the 8,000 rounds fired in the action off Santiago on 3 July 1898 was not only inefficient but also wasteful. No 13 inch shells registered and only two 12 inch were successful. Such standards were unacceptable to a small number of dedicted and enthusiastic young officers in both the USN and Britain's Royal Navy. Captain Percy Scott RN put the matter succinctly – "Trying to conduct a fight at long range without the necessary tools for doing it is a useless expenditure of ammunition." What was needed was the ability to engage the enemy at increasingly longer ranges than the 2–3,000 yards of the Spanish war and the 5,000 yards employed by the Japanese at Tsushima in September 1905.

The influence which Captain William (the new Inspector of Target Practice) Sims exerted was evident in the design of the first US battleships built to what was to become the 'Dreadnought' design, ships mounting a main armament of large calibre guns with an anti-torpedo-boat battery all of one smaller calibre. The design was begun in 1904 by the Bureau of Construction and, had there been less procrastination, the first of the class of two, *South Carolina*, would

have been a near contemporary of the British *Dreadnought*. The consideration of the latter's particulars was begun in January 1905, she was laid down on 2 October of that year and carried out basin trials on 3 October 1906. She was ready for sea before Christmas. *South Carolina*, although design began in 1904, was not laid down until December 1906 and completed in March 1910. Although her armament was basically similar to that of *Dreadnought* she had reciprocating engines and lacked the turbine power and speed of the British ship and, partly because of the 16,000 ton limit imposed by Congressional interference, had 1,600 miles less range.

The next class, *Delaware* and *North Dakota*, was delayed by Congressional requirements that private designs were to be considered in competition with those of the Bureau of Construction and Repair. None of the private entries was satisfactory and both ships were completed to the C and R design in under two and a half years. *Delaware* had reciprocating engines while *North Dakota* was driven by turbines and the difference between the two ships was a startling reversal of expectations. While both exceeded 21 knots on trials *North Dakota* with her Curtis turbines had a notable increase in her fuel consumption at 14 knots. As the distance from San Diego to the recently acquired Philippines was 6,600 miles this was far from satisfactory, a situation resulting from current problems with turbine construction in the USA.

These turbine deficiencies did not come to light until mid-1910 when *North Dakota*'s trials showed that she would need refuelling 1,000 miles short of the Philippines while *Delaware* would still have 500 miles in hand on arrival. By this time both ships of the 'Florida' class had been launched and the two 'Wyomings' were on the slips – all with Parsons turbines. The General Board, which had taken over responsibility for ship design from the Bureau of Construction and Repair soon after the latter's dismal showing with the 'South Carolinas', decided to revert to triple expansion machinery for the next class, the 'New Yorks'. This cautious move was proved unnecessary when, in 1912, the two ships of the 'Wyoming' class of 27,200 tons full load exceeded 21 knots on trials and had a range of 8,000 miles at 10 knots, nearly 1,000 miles in excess of the two 'New Yorks' who were completed two years later.

However *New York* and *Texas* had several distinctive points. Although reverting to the old 'up and down' machinery their gunnery arrangement was a very new departure – ten 14-inch guns in five twin turrets – their fuel system allowed for both coal and oil, their armour protection was improved and their tonnage was increased beyond the 'Wyomings' by over 1,000 tons. Later in her life *New York* achieved further distinction as the first USN ship to mount radar, the XAF prototype fitted in December 1938.

While the previous classes of battleships had been, on the whole, expansions of their predecessors, the two ships of the 'Nevada' class showed marked differences. The use of oil fuel allowed for considerable changes in design, the armour protection was much improved, they carried only one funnel, the use of two triple 14 inch turrets gave a handier layout, while the complement was reduced by 178 men. From this time on design was primarily a matter of steady increase in armament and protection although the propulsion was little altered until the post-war 'Colorado' class which carried turbo-electric drive. Their full load displacement of 33,600 tons was little more than their immediate predecessors but their main armament was far more capable – eight 16-inch guns replaced the twelve 14-inch guns of previous classes.

In 1916 the Navy Act authorized six ships of an entirely new design. The first of the 'South Dakotas' was laid down in New York Navy Yard on 15 March 1920, a giant of a ship which was to displace some 43,200 tons, mount twelve 16-inch guns in triple turrets and sixteen 6-inch guns in the superstructure and, with four shafts on turbo-electric drive, achieve 23 knots with a range of 8,000 miles at 10 knots. The building of this impressive class was brought to a halt by the Washington Naval Treaties and none were ever completed. The same fate awaited the six ships of the 'Lexington' class battle-cruisers. Nearly 200 feet longer than the 'South Dakotas' and with a somewhat greater displacement they were to have a shaft horse-power of 180,000 compared to *South Dakota*'s 50,000, the result being a designed speed of 33.5 knots. The planned armament was eight 16-inch guns, sixteen 6-inch guns and 8 torpedo tubes. They would have required 100 more men than *South Dakota* and 200 more than *Colorada* but their complement of 1,297 was dwarfed by the 1,900 men in the ships' companies of *Lexington* and *Saratoga* when those two of the class, saved from scrapping, were converted into aircraft carriers.

From 8 February 1922 when work stopped on the 'South Dakota' and 'Lexington' classes over fifteen years supervened before the next US battleship was laid down. On 27 October 1937 construction of *North Carolina* was begun at New York Navy Yard to a design which had passed through many vicissitudes before reaching its final shape. Originally accepted as that of a 30 knot ship with nine 14-inch guns protected against fire of ships with a similar armament the plans were changed to those of a 27 knot ship with 11 (later 12) 14-inch guns. When Japan refused to accept the 14-inch limit laid down in the 1936 London Treaty the USN changed the main armament to three triple 16-inch turrets. World War II saw many things happen to this class. *Washington* was the only US battleship to sink an enemy capital ship, the Japanese *Kirishima* on 14 November 1942. Both were heavily engaged in the Western Pacific where their original anti-air armament of sixteen 1.1-inch guns and twelve 0.5-inch single machine guns proved totally inadequate against guided missile (Kamikaze) attacks. By VJ day *North Carolina* carried sixty 40mm guns in quadruple mounts, and thirty six 20mm in single and twin mounts, a strong support for the argument that the best way to combat such attacks is to fill the sky with lead.

Two more classes were to complete the USN's record of battleship building, the four ships of the 'South Dakota' class and six 'Iowas'. The design of the first of these had begun in 1936/37 but it was not until 17 May 1939 that Congress approved their construction. All were completed within 30–34 months, a powerful recommendation for their builders. With the same main armament as the 'North Carolinas', they had an improved armour protection, were half a knot slower and had, at 15,000 miles at fifteen knots, 2,500 miles less range than their predecessors.

As the finale of the battleship building programme came the magnificent 'Iowa' class, surely the pinnacle of capital ship development. Only four of the original planned total of six were completed; *Iowa, New Jersey, Missouri* and *Wisconsin*. The first, *Iowa*, entered service on 22 February 1943 being completed in 32 months, a clear indication of the drive and efficiency in the US naval shipbuilding programme at that time. This class, whose full load tonnage was 57,540, were remarkable ships in many ways. They were improvements on the 'South Dakotas', their increase of 13,000 tons displacement allowing, amongst other things, for the use of the more effective 16-inch 50 calibre gun, and their original fit of eighty 40mm guns and forty nine 20mm. Like the 'South Dakotas' they carried three

aircraft but in the engine rooms all similarity ceased. Their General Electric turbines produced 212,000 shp. compared with the 'South Dakotas' 130,000. Their much increased size (over 200 feet longer) was clearly to their advantage; their designed speed was increased by five knots to 32.5. Their armour was increased in many areas although this in no way approached that fitted in the Japanese 'Yamato' class.

Although the 'Iowa' class was the last to be built for the USN, a further five ships of the 'Montana' class of 70,500 tons full load, suspended in April 1942, were not finally cancelled until July 1943. But the 'Iowas' were not to be lost to the fleet. Their battle honours speak of a wealth of valuable service. From January 1944 ships of the class were engaged in pretty well every carrier and amphibious operation in the Western Pacific. Off Korea all four were operating at various times from 1950–53 while in 1968–69 *New Jersey* was once again in action off Vietnam. From 1970 on many looked on these "dinosaurs", "mastodons from another era" as space-wasters in reserve. Then, in 1980, came the first of the Soviet 'Kirov' class battle-cruisers. There was a need for big ships as counters, for command and control ships which were well protected against missiles. The Falklands campaign of 1982 showed an urgent need for heavy artillery for gunfire support of amphibious operations. On 1 October 1981 *New Jersey* was taken in hand for modernization, to be followed by the other three until *Wisconsin* completed fitting-out in February 1989. Their full load displacement was little changed, their speed in service had been shown to be 35 knots but their complement had been reduced from a war figure of some 2,800 to 1,518. They retained their nine 16-inch guns and twelve of their original twenty 5-inch guns. There the similarity stopped. 32 Tomahawk cruise missiles and 16 Harpoon missiles were backed by a self-protection kit of four Vulcan Phalanx. Great ships who could carry out bombardment at 21 miles were not great ships who could strike targets 1,400 miles away and engage other ships with Tomahawk at 250 miles or with Harpoon at 70 miles. The 'Iowas', far from being "mastodons of another era" had ushered in a new era when they entered their claim during the 1991 Gulf War. They worked.

MISSOURI

AIRCRAFT CARRIERS

In September 1922 the US Navy's first aircraft carrier, USS *Langley*, put to sea. Converted from the collier *Jupiter* she had a flight deck of some 530 feet with an aircraft lift from the hangar deck to which disassembled aircraft were raised by crane from what had once been the coal holds. She was propelled at 15.5 knots by turbo-electric drive, the funnels for her three boilers being hinged down during flying operations. Although this was the USN's first sight of carrier operations and the arresting gear consisted of fore and aft wires there were no fatalities amidst the various accidents on the flight deck. After three years of experiments and trials *Langley* embarked the first shipborne squadrons in January 1925 and was soon involved in her first fleet exercise.

Encouraged by the success of this small ship the General Board pressed ahead with the conversion of two battle-cruiser hulls made redundant by the Washington Treaty. Work had stopped on 8 February 1922, a little over a year after keel-laying and with both ships about a third complete. On 1 July 1922 authorization had been forthcoming for *Lexington* and *Saratoga* to be completed, using much of the aircraft carrier designs previously put in hand. Both were completed in November/December 1927, huge ships of 43,000 tons full load and a flight deck 888 feet long. Their enormous power of 180,000 shp generated a speed of 33.25 knots. The most eye-catching element in these two ships was the island structure with its huge funnel which replaced the original seven funnels of the battle-cruiser design needed to serve the sixteen boilers. With the need to operate a large number of aircraft at long range from base, the aircraft complement in *Lexington* was raised to 120 by 1929 although this was soon reduced to a variable figure for both ships of 63–87. Their range of 10,500 miles at fifteen knots was a lot less than the 12–15,000 miles of later fleet carriers but these were fine ships despite the drawbacks inherent in conversions.

The first custom-built carrier for the US Navy, USS *Ranger*, was commissioned in June 1934 and the benefit of a dedicated design was immediately evident – she carried 76 aircraft. She was, however, too small (769 feet overall), too slow (29 knots) and her movement in heavy seas frequently precluded flying operations. The result was the construction of the two sisters *Yorktown* and *Enterprise*, both laid down in mid-1934. Of 19,875 tons standard they helped the General Board keep within the letter of the treaty though their full load displacement was almost 25,500 tons. They had three aircraft lifts to cope with their complement of 96 although, in December 1941, they carried only 72/69 machines, a mix of fighters, dive bombers and torpedo bombers, a similar outfit to those in *Lexington* and *Saratoga*. Armour protection for these ships was mooted, including an armoured flight deck, but lack of sufficient plate limited this to a small side belt and the main deck. Three catapults were provided, two on the flight deck and one athwartships on the hangar deck. Four shafts and 120,000 shp gave a speed of at least 32.5 knots with a range increased to 12,000 miles at 15 knots.

When *Yorktown* and *Enterprise* were commissioned in 1937–38 the second small carrier, *Wasp*, was under construction. Built to modified 'Ranger' design she packed 16,500 more shp which made no difference to her speed but, by a mathematical inversion, increased her range by 2,500 miles at fifteen knots to 12,500. She was thirty feet shorter than *Ranger*, had only two lifts in order to save cost but had a primordial deck-edge lift on the port side forward.

In 1940 Congress approved a new 40,000 ton carrier but, to avoid delays while a new design was completed, a third and improved 'Yorktown' was ordered, USS *Hornet*. It was after the loss of *Hornet* in the Solomons that the argument over the advisability of operating two carrier forces together came to the fore. It had been a pre-war aim and over the months the cogent and favourable arguments of Rear-Admiral Kinkaid, founded on basic principles of war, won the day. But in October 1942 such matters were largely academic – *Lexington*, *Yorktown*, *Wasp* and *Hornet* had been sunk, *Enterprise*, the only carrier in the South Pacific, was damaged and *Saratoga* was under repair after a torpedo hit. In May 1943 two carriers were once again available in the South West Pacific – a repaired *Saratoga* and the British carrier HMS *Victorious*, detached from the Home Fleet to help out.

But the astonishing capabilities of the US shipyards were now being proved. Two new classes of carriers were in hand 'Essex' at Newport

News and 'Independence' at New York SB. The name ships of these two classes were completed within a day of each other as 1942 became 1943. *Essex*, built to a design which was an enlarged, improved and better protected 'Yorktown' was a 34,880 deep load ship which was completed in twenty months from keel-laying while her sister *Lexington* was only seventeen months in Bethlehem's yard. The 14,750 ton *Independence* and her eight sisters were, on President Roosevelt's order, conversions of 'Cleveland' class cruisers.

Various other yards, particularly in the North West, were producing escort carriers at an astounding rate. By the end of 1943 thirty six of these ships had been completed. Seventeen were converted merchant ship hulls while the other 19 were those designed and built by that amazing ship man, Henry J. Kaiser, whose merchant ships were being completed at an unexampled rate. The building time for this, the 'Casablanca' class, was 8–9 months for the earlier ships but, as Kaiser's men and women got into the swing, this period was cut to 4–4½ months. The fifty 'Casablancas' completed by Kaiser, Vancouver had a total capacity of 1,350 aircraft – fighters, bombers and torpedo bombers. The last of the war-time 'Casablancas' commissioned in July 1944, by which time the first of Todd-Pacific's 21,397 ton 'Commencement Bay' class was nearing completion. These were conversions from tanker hulls and thus had a very large range – 23,900 miles at 15 knots. Ten of this class had been commissioned by the end of World War II, nine were completed in 1945–46 and four were cancelled. 77 escort carriers joined the US Navy before the cessation of hostilities.

The final results at sea off Leyte in October 1945 were decisive. Although the US fleets lost a fleet carrier, two escort carriers, three destroyers and a PT boat these were all replaceable at a very early date. The Japanese losses of one fleet carrier, 3 light carriers, 3 battleships, 9 cruisers and 8 destroyers were irreplaceable. The might of American industry provided an unending supply of the tools with which the navy did the job. On VJ-day, 2 September 1945, the US Navy had in commission 20 fleet carriers, 8 light fleets and 71 escort carriers. In addition there were 21 carriers of various categories in the yards while 18 others were cancelled.

A new design class, *Midway*, *Franklin D. Roosevelt* and *Coral Sea*, was completed between 1945–47. These were the largest warships in service with an overall length of 968 feet and a full load displacement of 55,000 tons. They were the first US carriers to follow the British plan of having an armoured flight deck, both the lead ships carried eighteen 5-inch guns and, with the Pacific experience to build on, a mass of close range weapons.

In the spring of 1946 President Truman signed the National Defense Act which provided, for the first time, for an overall Secretary of Defense, a cabinet post. The Secretaries of the Navy and Army were joined by a third, the Secretary of the newly created Air Force, all being subordinate to the Secretary of Defense. Under this reorganization the demands of the extremists were ignored – the navy retained its own air arm, both carrier and land based, and the Marine Corps. The creation of the Department of Defense was a logical move in view of the lessons of tri-service operations in World War Two and there was a reasonably peaceful atmosphere for the first couple of years. The 1948 budget, in which $16 billion was projected for defense, was the cause of an unholy row and what became known as the "Great Debate". The navy had designed the 83,250 ton full load carrier *United States* for one major purpose, the operation of nuclear attack aircraft and their escorting fighters. This raised the temperature in the three year old Air Force to dangerous levels. Their complaint was simple – the navy was trying to horn in on their strategic bombing strategy. The Navy's response was that the Air Force plans for the use of the B-36 bombers was inflexible and unlikely to succeed. Back

ENTERPRISE

in the Mediterranean and carrying nuclear weapons, embarked AJ-1 Savage heavy strike aircraft. This was the first move in the incorporation of a nuclear capability into the US carrier force. With the evidence of the Korean war to buttress their arguments the navy ordered the four ships of the 'Forrestal' class. These were completed between October 1955 (*Forrestal*) and January 1959 (*Independence*), the first carriers designed to operate jet aircraft. They were vastly different from the 'Essex' class despite the reconstruction which was undertaken in some of those ships and more effective than the reconstructed *Midway*. With an overall length of 1,039 feet and a full load displacement of 78,500 tons these four ships incorporated a ten and a half degree angled deck, an idea imported from Britain, and four of the British type steam catapults. This meant that, of her 90–100 aircraft, eight could be launched every minute. To cope with these gas-guzzlers *Forrestal* carried three times as much aviation fuel as *Essex*. These were a new generation of carriers and their successors, the four ships of the 'Kitty Hawk' class, though differing ship from ship (apart from *Kitty Hawk* and *Constellation*), were slightly enlarged and improved versions of the earlier design. They were all completed between April 1961 (*Kitty Hawk*) and September 1968 (*John F. Kennedy*) but another and mightier vessel joined the fleet seven months after *Kitty Hawk*. This was the new *Enterprise*, at that time the largest warship ever built, nuclear powered with a hangar capacity of 216,000 square feet for some 80–100 aircraft.

The need for underwater protection provides storage for a much increased load of 8,500 tons of aircraft fuel, sufficient to enable her to carry out twelve days of intensive flying without replenishment. Her eight A2W nuclear reactors with today's improved cores need refuelling only every dozen years or so but there is still the need for replenishment of spares, stores, munitions and victuals. With a complement as a flagship of 3,285 (ship) and 2,480 (aircrew) the call on the commissariat is considerable and continuous from the first breakfast to the last of mid-rats.

Enterprise was originally designed without armament, a cost cutting exercise which was over-ridden in later years. In 1979–82 she underwent a major overhaul and now carriers three Vulcan Phalanx CIWs and three octuple Sea Sparrow launchers. From 1993 for a scheduled forty two months she will again be under "complex overhaul" (the CVN equivalent of Service Life Extension programme) and refuelling. As a sidelight on the inflation of warship prices it should be noted that the building cost for *Enterprise* was $445 million – $1.4 billion has been provided in the FY 1990 budget for her next overhaul.

The value of nuclear propulsion was demonstrated in 1964 when, on July 31, Task Force One left the Mediterranean and, having passed south of Africa they visited Pakistan, Australia and Brazil reaching the East Coast of the USA on 3 October. *Enterprise*, *Long Beach* and *Bainbridge*, the first all-nuclear task force, covered 30,500 miles in 57 days steaming at an average speed of 22 knots without embarking any stores or victuals.

At 23.40 on 4 August 1964 (Washington time) President Johnson announced that, following torpedo boat attacks on US destroyers in the Gulf of Tonkin, he had ordered "the military forces of the United States to take action in reply". This "action" was to continue for the best part of nine years, involving every type of warship and aircraft in the US Navy. The war off Vietnam had an unfortunate after-effect in some quarters. Attention was focussed on the fleet's activities in that conflict in the same way as the general public's viewpoint, amongst those who thought about it, was concentrated on that small area of South East Asia. The use of the various task forces had been primarily in support of a land campaign at a time when there was no threat of submarine opposition or air intervention. For over three years these

came the Air Force – carriers, they claimed, were out of date and vulnerable. This ungentlemanly slanging match was further exacerbated when the new Secretary of Defense, Louis Johnson, ordered the cancellation of the construction of *United States*. She was laid down at Newport News on April 18 1949 and cancelled five days later. The Chief of Naval Operations was relieved of his post and the Air Force chalked up a victory. The early and sulphurous effects of unification rumbled on until, on 25 June 1950, the battle lines were transferred from the Pentagon to Korea.

At the start of the Korean War the US Seventh Fleet was based on Japan and, within two days of the North Korean invasion, they were taking up positions to neutralize Taiwan, to evacuate refugees and to attack North Korean landings. The transport of US troops from Japan was carried out in LSTs and by air-lift while two carriers, USS *Valley Forge* and HMS *Triumph* flew close support and interdiction missions.

For those who had eyes to see, the events of 15 September 1950 were of great significance. That was the day when the most hastily planned and most brilliantly successful small scale amphibious assault in history took place. Three weeks in gestation the landings at Inchon achieved everything that had been hoped for. After a two day bombardment by cruisers and destroyers the first landings were one minute late on schedule while those on the main city were on time. The Marine Corps, carrying out the first attack on a city in their long history, had their headquarters ashore in 24 hours and a day later began to advance on Seoul.

On All Saints' Day (1 November) 1952 the United States detonated the first hydrogen bomb and demolished a whole island in Eniwetok Atoll. In August 1953 the Soviet Union carried out a similar test. The Korean war was over – was the world facing what many called "a nuclear holocaust"?

In this environment the shape and size of the US Navy was slowly beaten out. The expanding navy of the USSR was the prime threat. By 1955 over 90 per cent of major US naval ships were up to or past their tenth birthdays. Alterations and additions of new equipment could go only so far before habitability and efficiency were affected. Conversions were not enough – new ships were needed.

In March 1951 the carriers *Franklin D. Roosevelt* and *Coral Sea*, then tasks had overlaid the fact which should have been foremost in people's minds, that such employment was secondary to the primary role of the US Navy; control of the seas.

However, the activities of the carriers off Vietnam did prove one thing to McNamara's mathematicians. As he put it: "Total costs to procure, support and defend overseas land-based tactical air forces are comparable to total costs of carrier task forces of equal capability". Whether he considered three other facets of shore-based air operations – the need to find friendly air space through which to deploy in an emergency, the need for tanker aircraft during such a deployment and the need for a suitable airfield on arrival – is difficult to assess. The result of this unexpected approbation was that McNamara revised his decision to cut to 13 carriers. The number of ships was to remain at 15 while the air wings were to be reduced to 12. In June 1968 USS *Nimitz* was laid down at Newport News where she was completed in May 1975, a majestic vessel of 91,487 tons full load.

The estimated cost of *Nimitz*, $544 million, caused a lot of people a lot of concern. With President Ford in the White House from 1974 a new plan was hatched – the Tentative Conceptual Baseline (T-CBL) for a 60,000 ton full load carrier with a conventional power plant and a speed of about 28 knots. Studies of this design were dropped when the Navy requested nuclear propulsion and approval was given for a second 'Nimitz'.

SUBMARINES

The first submarine class to embody all the latest advances was the two boat 'E class', both of which were launched in 1911. Their surface speed of 13.5 knots was an improvement on previous classes and they were fitted with bow planes, a reasonable move as their underwater speed was increased to 11.5 knots and many of the crews were inexperienced. The emphasis on a comparatively high underwater speed was maintained until after World War I and reflected the

current thinking that a submarine was, primarily, an underwater craft. This was much at variance with German practice which required the U-boats to operate on the surface until required to dive for an attack or if danger threatened. As a result the German boats were more seaworthy on the surface than their American counterparts and marginally slower underwater. When the U-boat campaign on merchant shipping showed startling and previously unexpected dividends the size of their boats increased markedly.

This tendency was not reflected in the US Navy until the three boats of the 'AA(T)' class were launched in 1918–19. Of 1,480 tons with 6 tubes and two 3-inch guns they were the first "fleet boats" and generally unsuccessful. Their surface speed of 20 knots was insufficient to keep up with the fleet and their diving depth of 150 feet was 50 feet less than their predecessors. The somewhat earlier British experiments with the 'J' class and the steam-driven 'K' class were also failures.

The US Navy had completed 27 boats of the 'R' class and 51 of the five 'S' class variants in the period 1918–24 but they lacked the range necessary for trans-Pacific operations. In the first post-war design, the 'Barracuda' class, this need was not adequately addressed. Like the earlier 'AA(T)' boats they were too slow to operate with the fleet and their range was only 6,000 miles at 11 knots. The 2,500 tons dived displacement of the 'Barracudas' was increased in *Argonaut* (launched November 1927), who carried her two 6-inch guns on 4,050 tons. She was the one and only minelayer ever built for the USN and was soon followed by the two cruiser submarines *Narwhal* and *Nautilus*. These were sisters of 3,960 tons dived and armed with 6 torpedo tubes and two 6-inch guns. All three of these monsters at least had a notable range on the surface – 18,000 miles at 10 knots.

In the late 1920s the next design, *Dolphin*, was a single boat of 2,200 tons dived with a maximum surface speed of 17 knots and 8 knots dived. Herself unsuccessful due to a range of only 6,000 miles, she was a first move towards the enormously successful classes which

CARL VINSON

followed. By the early 1930s War Plans Division was working on the assumption that submarines would be carrying out thirty five day patrols 3,900 miles from base with a total time on passage and patrol of seventy five days.

In the next three classes diesel-electric drive was preferred, in the following two direct-drive diesels were re-instituted but, from the "Seadragon" class of 1939 onwards, the far more flexible and reliable diesel-electric system became standard. By the beginning of 1941 the 12 boats of the "Tambor" class were in the water. At last a Trans-Pacific submarine was at hand with a 48 hour underwater capability, air-conditioning, a huge food storage and a peacetime complement of 60. The last six of the "Tambors" were the immediate progenitors of the immensely successful "fleet boats" of the "Gato", "Balao" and "Tench" classes which were to bear the main weight of the Pacific war. On 12 May 1941 USS *Drum* was launched at Portsmouth Navy Yard, the precursor of 217 similar boats to be launched before the war's end. Their astonishing record has been so often recorded in other places that it is probably sufficient to say here that well over 50 per cent of Japanese merchant shipping sunk in World War II was credited to these submarines.

In the post-war years there was a similar re-appraisal of submarine capabilities as that which followed World War I. The German Type XXI boats showed how a streamlined hull containing exceptional battery power, could out-run conventional designs. The US Navy took immediate note of these changes and combined them with the introduction of the Dutch snorkel system which had been adopted by the Germans. As the two boats of "GUPPY I" (Greater Underwater Propulsive Power), without snorkels, were overtaken by the GUPPY IA, II, IIA and III, which were all snorkel boats, as well as the Fleet Snorkel boats, the US Navy was becoming adjusted to greater underwater speeds up to 17 knots. Speeds somewhat greater were designed into the "Tang" class which were all six completed in 1951–52. These were good, fast boats but, in December 1953, came the acme of all diesel/electric driven submarines, *Albacore*. The "Albacore hull", in its later stages, achieved 33 knots. Other diesel

SEAWOLF (model)

designs followed her, more conventional in design but some, of the 'Barbel' class showing a high speed capability.

Then, on 17 January 1955, came a signal from USS *Nautilus* which changed the whole story of underwater operations. That signal "Underway on nuclear power" was the culmination of seven years of design work and fabrication resulting from the Manhattan Project. *Nautilus* was not particularly fast by modern standards (21+ knots), nor was her shape very different from the GUPPY boats. But in her initial trials she steamed long distances (1,300–1,380 miles) at average speeds of 18 to 20 knots. It was a time of urgent re-appraisal, not only of submarine tactics but also of A/S warfare as a whole. The arrival of the "Skipjack" class compounded these problems. Using the "Albacore" hull pattern these six boats were capable of over 30 knots based on the new S5W reactor which, with two exceptions, was to

PITTSBURGH

remain standard until the arrival of the "Los Angeles" class. The fifty one boats of the "Thresher/Sturgeon" classes were completed between 1962 and 1975 but, by the time the later boats were commissioning, the first ten boats of the SSN 688 "Los Angeles" class, were on the slips. Their only slightly increaed speed was due to the increase in dived displacement from 4,960 tons to 6,930 tons. From 1972 for the next 20 years the basic "Los Angeles" design was used for all the US Navy's SSNs. Some alleviation of the "Los Angeles" tube loading problem was achieved after the thirty first of class when vertical launch missile tubes were fitted external to the pressure hull abaft the BQQ-5 sonar array forward. Improved sensors, navigation and communications equipment were installed while the forward hydroplanes were moved from the fin to the normal British position on the forward hull and made retractable.

The latest USN design of the "Seawolf" class is a shorter, stubbier boat than the "Los Angeles" class but of well over an additional 2,000 tons dived displacement. The number of torpedo tubes has been doubled to eight allowing for the deletion of the external VLS for missiles as fitted in the later "Los Angeles" class. The internal load of weapons is 50 compared to "Los Angeles" 26. *Seawolf* is to have a higher tactical speed, improved sonar and a diving depth of 2,000 feet, over 500 feet more than "Los Angeles". This is a large, multi-role and effective submarine but, at over $1.5 billion, a very expensive one which can be in only one place at any one time. To an outsider this policy appears to be very limiting in numbers, whereas the construction of smaller, cheaper and more specialised submarines would provide a larger force for deployment.

MISSILE SUBMARINES

There is no more specialized submarine than the nuclear propelled ballistic missile SSBNs. In 1949 *Carbonero*, a converted fleet boat, was the first missile firing submarine but the large Regulus was a cruise missile requiring its submarine to surface for launching. While this programme was underway Admiral Raborn's Polaris programme was rapidly taking shape. Begun in 1955 so much progress had been made by 1958 that authority was given for the construction of the first three of what was to be the five boat "George Washington" class. All entered service between December 1959 and March 1961. By 1967 they had been joined by the five "Ethan Allens" and the thirty one of the "Lafayette/Benjamin Franklin" classes. In 12 years 41 SSBNs with their missiles had been planned, designed and completed, a truly amazing record. Development and improvements followed swiftly over the next three years. The 1,300 mile Polaris was superseded by the 1,500 mile A-2 version which, in 1968, gave way to the 2,500 mile A-3. Two years later the Poseidon C-3 was introduced with a similar range but an improved capability. From 1970 to 1977 twenty six boats were fitted with Poseidon and from 1978 to 1982 twelve of these were further converted to launch the Trident 1 (C-4) missiles. These have a 4,000 mile range with either eight MIRVs or six MARVs and were the original weapons of the "Ohio" class of 18,700 tons dived. With 24 missile tubes and a complement of 155 these huge boats are second only in size to the Soviet "Typhoon" class. The

completion of *Ohio* did not take place until 11 November 1981, over seven years since ordering. In the next ten years a further 11 boats will have joined the fleet, those from number nine onwards carrying the 6,500 mile Trident II (D-5) which out-ranges the current Soviet ballistic missiles by 2,000 miles and has a more capable and more accurate load. Thus by the end of 1991 there will be twelve "Ohios" in commission with four more building, provided the savage defence cuts currently under discussion do not affect the SSBNs.

MICHIGAN

CRUISERS

Doubt about the US Navy's cruisers' ability to carry out their tasks could have resulted from the disastrous Battle of Savo Island on 9 August 1942 when, in less than an hour, without any damage to the numerically inferior enemy, three American heavy cruisers and one Australian were sunk and *Chicago* lost her bow. However, such doubt about the cruisers would have been premature. At Savo the Allied cruiser force was in two groups too far apart for rapid mutual support while the destroyer screen was not far enough out to give adequate warning. The fault was in the orders, not the ships.

The Okinawa operations lasted from 14 March to 30 June 1945, a period when kamikaze attacks reached their peak. In this time ten major mass attacks took place as well as many individual runs. In all there were some 1,900 suicide sorties made on naval forces and possibly over 5,000 by conventional naval and army aircraft. During the whole of this time only 3 cruisers were hit, *Indianapolis*, Admiral Spruance's flagship, *Biloxi* and *Birmingham*, sixth ship of the "Cleveland" class. As there were, at various times, 38 cruisers present off Okinawa, these figures suggest that the cruisers were lucky or were very capable of protecting themselves and those in their vicinity.

That greatest peril of the sea, a tight-knit tornado, was to bring into question the basic structure of the new cruisers. On 5 June 1945, TF38 with carriers, cruisers and destroyers was overtaken by a typhoon with winds gusting up to 100 knots and 50 to 60 feet seas. At 0640 the "Baltimore" class cruiser *Pittsburgh* lost her bow. More accurately she lost the forward 104 feet of her hull, which set off on its own. Six days later the cruiser reached Guam, followed the next day by her bow under tow by a destroyer. In the same mighty seas which had wrecked *Pittsburgh*'s appearance her sister *Baltimore* was seriously twisted and the "Cleveland" class *Duluth* had her bow buckled upwards with consequent flooding, distortion and cracking. The subsequent court of inquiry reported that "our new cruisers are weak structurally".

The design of US cruisers had been much hampered by the various treaty restrictions. The "Atlanta" class ships which began commissioning in 1942 were, in effect, made a virtue from a necessity. While the "Atlantas" were under construction so, also, were the "Clevelands". The advent of war in 1939 had caused their design to be radically altered; the planned treaty-limited 8,000 tonners gave way to ships of over 14,000 tons full load — what seems to be a modified form of the last "Brooklyns".

By the time *Baltimore* was laid down there were, therefore, three classes of cruisers under construction some with 5-inch, some with 6-inch and *Baltimore* with 8-inch guns. The "Baltimores" were 63 feet

MISSISSIPPI

BUNKER HILL

longer than the "Clevelands" and over 4 feet greater in the beam with a 3,000 ton increase in full load displacement. This gave a measure of veer and haul in the filling of additional top-weight, particularly close-range weapons.

Alaska and *Guam*, the first pair of what was planned to be a class of six 34,250 ton ships carrying nine 12-inch guns, twelve 5-inch guns, fifty six 40mm and thirty four 20mm close range weapons were approved in July 1940. Their triple 12-inch guns were enormously expensive, the ships were the size of battleships with less clout than their contemporaries and poorer protection. There was, at the time of their completion in mid-1944, no requirement for a heavily armed raiding cruiser, although in July 1945 both were part of a force which searched the East China and Yellow Seas for mercantile targets with little result. Both were paid off in 1961.

In the immediate post-war years decisions came as fast as their cancellation. From this welter of discussion came the three ships of the 21,000 ton "Des Moines" class and the two "Worcester" class,

so-called "light cruisers" of 18,000 tons full load carrying twelve 6-inch DP, 24 3-inch and twelve 20mm guns. Modifications of "Cleveland" and "Baltimore" class cruisers took place to provide platforms for Talos and Terrier surface-to-air missiles (SAM). A Talos from *Chicago* performed satisfactorily off Haiphong in 1972, shooting down a MiG at 48 miles range.

On July 1 1975 order was once again restored to what had been a confused listing. The "guided missile frigates" became "cruisers". Of the ships then listed as "cruisers", five were nuclear powered (*Long Beach*, *Bainbridge*, *Truxton* and the "California" class). Eight more were missile cruiser conversions of World War II ships and four of the same vintage remained as all-gun ships in reserve. With the addition of three "Virginia" class of generally similar characteristics to the "Californias" the ship count nevertheless declined as the older ships were deleted. But in the modern ships the A/A capability was being reinforced by a surface-to-surface armament — Harpoon and, later, Tomahawk were added. By 1991 the latter was fitted in the

LONG BEACH

"Virginias", *Long Beach* and the latest class, "Ticonderoga" (after the first five).

The "Ticonderogas" are a generation ahead of their predecessors, apart from their gas-turbine propulsion. All ships carry modern data systems, sonar and communications, the SPY 1A phased array radar and the Aegis control system. Aegis has revolutionized surface and air warfare with the long range of SPY 1A, the system's own swift reaction time and its multi-target capability. Already proven against aircraft, missiles and surface attackers its capabilities in the twenty ships of this class which will be commissioned through 1991 must greatly enhance the Navy's capabilities. With this force of 29 cruisers the formation of several carrier groups is possible. One great advantage conferred by Aegis is that, though it cannot identify the type of aircraft detected, its coverage is such that combat air patrols can be much reduced.

DESTROYERS AND FRIGATES

Unfortunately sonar has no counterpart to the SPY 1A radar. As a result ASW still requires maximum effort from own submarines, ships and aircraft, both fixed and rotary winged and the SOSUS system. The diesel submarine and the earlier nuclears are susceptible to passive detection but there are strong indications that current Soviet nuclears have rapidly achieved a high degree of silencing which will only improve in the future. This puts the highest priority on ASW research, development and training. The first two will be greatly influenced by the provision of funds, often a tricky subject to explain to the financial managers. The third, no less important, depends to a large degree on the availability of ships, submarines and aircraft to work together under all conditions. With very little diminution of overseas tasks and the continuing danger of more intervention activity the rumours of an energetic pursuit of the "peace dividend" suggest that such training will become progressively more difficult with a consequent drop in efficiency. A building programme of 10 ships a year suggests a navy of some 250 major modern vessels in 25 years

SPRUANCE

time. This may sound simplistic but at the current rate of technical development retrofitting and modernization will become extremely expensive, if even possible.

By the end of 1991 the destroyer/frigate force of the US Navy will, at present rates, number 161. Of the 61 destroyers, two will be the new Aegis fitted "Arleigh Burkes" (with another eleven building or authorized), thirty five "Spruance/Kidd" classes, eight of the 30 year old "Coontz" class and sixteen "Charles F. Adams" class of about the same vintage. Amongst this group only the "Spruance/Kidd" classes carry a helicopter; of the remainder ten have a platform and some form of facilities. The *Seahawk* LAMPS III helicopters carry dipping sonar, radar and other search and attack equipment. Towed arrays and sonars of the SQS-53 family are fitted in the 37 modern destroyers while the remainder have no towed arrays and the more elderly SQS-23.

The ASW story is more promising amongst the frigate force. The fifty one "Oliver Hazard Perry" class carry SQS-53 or 56, a towed array and two LAMPS helicopters while the forty six ships of the 20 year old "Knox" class have SQS-26, SQS-35 variable depth sonar (VDS), a towed array and a LAMPS helicopter. The remaining three frigates carry SQS-26, one has a VDS and none a helicopter. The reinforcement

ARLEIGH BRUCE (artist's impression)

CURTIS

CALLAGHAN

of these ships would come from the US Coast Guard's twelve "Hamilton" class cutters with sonar, A/S torpedo tubes and a large helicopter.

Allowing for a fairly high peace-time availability of 50 per cent the destroyer/frigate force is surely fully stretched to meet its commitments. In the event of a major war when availability should rise a few notches and the "Hamiltons" would be included, the story would be very similar to that in the rest of the NATO allies. Once the needs of carrier battle groups, amphibious forces, underway replenishment groups and supply forces had been met there would be nothing left to

escort the merchant shipping on which both the domestic and military sectors rely entirely for their supply.

There is no simple answer to the future requirements of navies. It will as always be a matter of assessing priorities and apportioning slender resources. If previous planners have made mistakes in their choice of the shape and size of the fleet, disaster will very soon be at the door. A similar result will be at hand if the necessary financial resources are denied the forces charged with the country's defence. The Constitution of the USA is very clear about the responsibilities of the nation's leaders in this respect.

AMPHIBIOUS AFFAIRS

One of the sure stays of America's success over the last two centuries has been the US Marine Corps. For some 120 years after President Henry Adams inaugurated the Corps on 11 July 1798 the Marines were basically a colonial intervention force delivered by sea. The brutal years of 1917–18 on the Western Front proved them to be capable of standing beside the finest infantry in the world, but change was on the horizon.

Prompted by the energetically held views of a remarkable Marine staff officer, Pete Ellis, the USMC began studies of island warfare in the Pacific under the broad title of "Orange Plan". In 1921 came the handbook "Advanced Base Operations in Micronesia" and over the next four years a series of amphibious exercises showed the ideas to be right but the material totally inadequate. In 1932 the new handbook "Marine Corps Landing Operations" was distributed, followed in 1934 by "Tentative Manual for Landing Operations". This latter volume, refined and expanded, was the basis for all US amphibious operations in World War II.

From 1933 onwards annual fleet landing exercises were carried out by the newly formed Fleet Marine Force. These covered all aspects of amphibious landings, the earlier ones pointing the need for specialized landing craft. From 1936 new types of these craft were under trial, amongst them the amphibian amtrac, developed from an Everglades rescue boat. By 1940–41 the main types had been tested, including the ubiquitous LCVP and LCM to Andrew Higgin's design and the British LCT. These were the assault craft – assault ships and transports were needed to take the men and the craft to the beaches. In addition there was a pressing requirement to transport and land the tanks and artillery which any amphibious force would need. In January 1942 the British had ordered 200 Landing Ships Tank (LST) in the USA; in May all forms of landing ships and craft were given priority over every other naval craft. At this time even a carrier's keel was removed from the slip to make way for LSTs, the first of which were completed in October 1942. The Landing Craft Tank (LCT) were capable of carrying up to 160 tons of tanks or cargo to a radius of about 1,000 miles at 10 knots. The first of these was also available in October 1942 at a time when the 158 feet Landing Craft Infantry (Large) (LCI(L)) was in production. (LCI(L) to distinguish them from the British 105 feet LCI(S).) The LCI(L), unlike the LST and LCT, had no bow door/ramp but a sharp bow with hinged gangways for disembarkation of the 205 men carried. With these new additions arriving in growing numbers it was possible to carry out direct "shore-to-shore" operations instead of using

WASP

the more hazardous "ship-to-shore" method in which the smaller landing craft were loaded with men, tanks and guns from transports anchored off shore.

In mid-December 1942 the first flotilla of LCIs was formed at Little Creek, Virginia and from then on matters advanced with spectacular speed. In six weeks LCI(L)s were being despatched to the South-West Pacific where they were greeted by the redoubtable "Uncle Dan the Amphibious Man" – Rear-Admiral Daniel E. Barbey.

In June the first amphibious landings with the new ships and craft took place. On 11 June British forces occupied Pantelleria in the Mediterranean and from 23 June Uncle Dan's VII Amphibious Force of twenty four LSTs, twelve LCI(L)s and seven LCMs (Material) with a group of destroyer transports took over the Trobriand Islands off new Guinea. From then on numerous suffixes were added to the basic LCI label – LCI(R) carried rockets, LCI(G) guns and so forth – and the many island landings in the South-West Pacific and Central Pacific benefited.

The prime Allied aim was the destruction of Germany; with that accomplished the full weight of Allied power was to be turned on Japan. As things turned out these twin aims ran almost in parallel. Just over four months after Normandy a huge force descended on the Japanese held Philippines and the battles for Leyte lasted from 17–25 October 1944.

In the forefront of this operation by the US Third and Seventh Fleets was Uncle Dan Barbey commanding the Northern Attack Force of the Seventh Fleet, TF 78, while Vice-Admiral T.S. Wilkinson commanded the Southern Attack Force, TF 79. These two task forces covered huge areas of ocean – 168 landing ships, 92 major landing craft, 16 destroyer transports, 33 attack transports, 10 transports, 10 attack cargo ships, 3 cargo ships and 47 merchant ships as compared with the 250 landing ships and 2,000 landing craft used in Normandy.

The difference between Normandy and Leyte is underlined by these figures. In the first case there had to be a continuous injection of troops and stores into the bridgehead over a short distance – by 30 May 1944 there were 1,526,965 US troops and 5,297,306 long tons of US stores in Great Britain, a high proportion awaiting shipment to Europe. In Leyte a complete and adequate re-occupation force was

delivered whose requirements after landing were normal stores and victuals delivered from long range. In Normandy the job had been started, in Leyte it was very soon done.

In the post-war years a further element other than ships, craft and fixed-wing aircraft was inserted in the amphibious equation – the helicopter. In 1931 trials of OP-1 autogiros were carried out in USS *Langley* and with the US Marine Corps detachments in the Nicaraguan jungles. The germ was planted. British and Italian tests followed and by 1944 a production order for 1,000 German FC282 helicopters was approved, although only 24 were completed. The US Coast Guard had, in 1943, recommended the use of helicopters from ships and the USN ordered 23 training machines and 150 operational machines. Sixty seven were purchased by the Royal Navy and the RAF at the same time. In December 1947 Marine Helicopter Experimental Squadron One was commissioned to develop the principles of amphibious assault by helicopter, later known as "vertical envelopment". In August 1950 the first Marine Brigade in Korea had 6 helicopters and a year later a squadron of HRS-2, each capable of lifting 8 men, had joined and occasionally operated from the escort carriers. In November 1956, 22 helicopters from the British carriers *Ocean* and *Theseus* carried out the first "vertical envelopment" at Port Said during the Suez engagement, landing 415 Royal Marines and 23 tons of equipment in one and a half hours. This proof of the value of such operations coincided with the early trials of USS *Thetis Bay*, an escort carrier converted to carry 1,000 Marines and 20 HRS helicopters. In 1959–61 the three "Essex" class carriers *Boxer*, *Princeton* and *Valley Forge* followed the same path but with an increased capacity of 1,650 Marines, up to 24 HUS helicopters each carrying 12 troops and a couple of HR2S with space for 20 troops or three jeeps.

The show was on the road. On 26 August 1961 the Navy's first from-the-keel-up helicopter carrier *Iwo Jima* was commissioned. Of 18,000 tons full load and 602 feet overall she had space for 2,057 Marines, nine HR2S helicopters or twenty HUS. By July 1969 seven of this class were in service, *Iwo Jima* herself having proved the value of a joint amphibious/helicopter assault at the battle of Chu Lai in Vietnam in August 1965.

The "Terrebonne Parish" class of LSTs was built at a time when the

LCAC 12

FORT McHENRY

Korean War had shown the continued advantage of amphibious operations. Larger than the war-time LSTs and incorporating a number of improvements they were, at 15 knots from 6,000 bhp, a somewhat disappointing investment. The "De Soto County" class, over 2,000 tons more full load displacement at 7,854 tons, appeared in 1957 and had several points in their favour – air-conditioning, accommodation for 634 troops in place of their predecessors" 391, space for 4 landing craft and an LCU as well as deck space for 5 helicopters. However an increase to 15,000 shp raised their speed to only 17½ knots.

A much larger and, therefore, more effective class joined the fleet in the mid-1950s. The "Thomaston" class of LSDs is of 11,270–12,150 tons full load with 24,000 shp, a speed of up to 24 knots and, major blessing, a range of 10,000 miles at 20 knots. Their dock can hold three LCUs or nine LCM-8s or fifty LVT amphibians while there is accommodation for 340 troops. Three more classes of LSD followed, the "Raleighs", "Austins" and "Anchorages", 18 ships with the same general tasks although of varying sizes and capabilities. One limitation which is shared by all three classes is the lack of a hangar for a significant number of helicopters while the "Raleighs" and "Anchorages" have no air maintenance facilities.

In 1969 the first of twenty "Newport" class LSTs commissioned and at last a 20 knot speed was achieved for this type of ship. New LSDs were needed but it was not until 1985 that the first of eight "Whidbey Island" class commissioned after a period of shilly-shallying during the Carter administration which seriously delayed their construction. Although these ships and their near sisters of the "Harpers Ferry" class (a cargo version of the "Whidbeys") are large at 15,726/16,695 tons full load there is no space other than the flight deck for embarked aircraft. The increase in size compared with the "Anchorages" is due to the staff requirement for the "Whidbeys" to carry four LCACs (Landing Craft Air Cushion). These craft of 200 tons full load can carry 25 troops, a main battle tank or 75 tons of cargo at 40 knots fully laden.

The USMC is currently the largest and the best equipped in the world. Its 61 air squadrons include fighter/attack, attack, reconnaissance, and observation fixed wing aircraft, helicopter gunships and 25 squadrons of helicopter transports. The presence of AV-8B Harriers, CH-53E Super Stallions carrying 56 Marines and the LCACs has provided a rapid "over-the-horizon" capability which would be much enhanced if the USMC's request for the MV-22A Osprey were approved in full. This aircraft with its rotary/fixed wing capabilities can deliver twenty four Marines to a range of 200 miles in half an hour – it would give an even newer meaning to "vertical envelopment".

The sea bases for the USMC have been much improved since the "Iwo Jima" class LPHs and the two "Blue Ridge" class command ships. The five "Tarawa" class amphibious assault ships (LHA) which entered service between 1976 and 1980 are of 39,000 tons full load with a full length flight deck, large docking well and garages. The final class, of which the name ship *Wasp* commissioned on 6 July 1989, is longer than *Tarawa* and of 1,200 tons greater displacement. In this very considerable hull she can carry a mixed load of aircraft such as 6-8 AV-8B Harriers and 42 Sea Knight helicopters, 3 LCACs or a mix of smaller craft such as 12 LCM6s. There are 20,000 square feet of garage space, 101,000 cubic feet of cargo space, stowage for 1,232 tons of aviation fuel and accommodation for 1,873 Marines. With a speed of 23 knots and a range of 9,500 miles at 18 knots this is a formidable, self-contained ship with full command and control facilities.

MINE WARFARE

In the order of battle of the vast armada gathered around Okinawa in early 1945 was TG 52.2, the "Mine Warfare Flotilla". This force of 122 ships included several types from destroyer minesweepers and layers, ocean minesweepers, motor minesweepers down to the small carft which patrolled the swept areas and channels. Their motto was simple and significant – "No sweep, no invasion". In the event they were almost completely successful against a somewhat scattered threat of floating contact mines. They swept 510 of these and of the four ships lost by mining only one did not belong to TG 52.2.

AVENGER

OSPREY (model)

In the post-war years mine counter measures (MCM) received little attention. It was too easy to forget that the convoys would never have reached their destinations, the great amphibious forces would never have got ashore, the huge fleets would have been at risk had the MCM forces not carried out their tasks effectively. Some idea of the scope and size of their operations may be gauged from a few simple figures. During World War II the Royal and Commonwealth Navies commissioned 2,242 minesweepers of all types and the US Navy 962, a grand total of 3,204. In comparison the same navies in 1991 can muster a grand total of 135. Of these 57 belong to the US Navy; 8 modern ships, 27 of an average age of 36, seven of 39 tons and 22 converted training and fishing craft. The Soviet Navy has clearly taken matters more seriously. Their total is today 354. Although this is an ageing fleet it shows a realization of a continuing need. Admiral Gorshkov pointed the lesson several times in "The Seapower of the State". Maybe the victims of mine warfare in the Gulf in 1991 will do the same.

CONCLUSION

There was insufficient space in this book to give full coverage to that huge number of ships which have, over the last 90 years, supported, provisioned, fuelled and repaired the fighting ships of the US Navy. These deserve a book to themselves for, without them, no fleet could keep the seas. To revert to the Okinawa campaign of 1945, the Fast Carrier Force was absent from any form of base for over two months. The figures of stores, fuel and ammunition supplied under what were frequently the most arduous and dangerous conditions might amaze even a modern logistics man with his computer and carefully racked stores. Like the minesweepers the Servrons were vital members of a great team.

Jane's Fighting Ships did all it could over the years to present an accurate statement of the strength and development of the US Navy. What will be displayed in its pages over the next decades depends on the citizens of the USA and their elected representatives. In the introduction to Volume 15 of Samuel Eliot Morison's magnificent *History of the United States Navy in World War II* there is a quotation from Patrick Henry — "I have but one lamp by which my feet are guided and that is the lamp of experience. I know of no way of judging the future but by the past".

Captain John Moore, R.N.
May 1991

JANE'S

AMERICAN FIGHTING SHIPS
OF THE 20TH CENTURY

Uniforms, Flags, Guns.—U.S.A.

UNITED STATES FLEET.

Revised from Official Handbook, "Ships' Data, U.S. Naval Vessels," and from information furnished by courtesy of the Navy Department, Washington, D.C., 1924.

UNIFORMS. (1924)

Admiral of the Navy.   Rear-Admiral.   Captain.   Commander.   Lieut-Commander.   Lieutenant.   Ensign.

Note.—Lieutenants, junior grade, have 1½ stripes. Chief Warrant Officers one stripe broken with blue. Line Warrant Officers star without any stripe. Staff Warrant Officers under Chiefs have no sleeve mark. Engineers same as Line Officers (interchangeable). Other branches than executive wear no sleeve star, but have badge of branch over top stripe.

UNIFORMS. (1931)

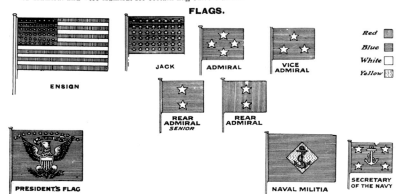

As Rear-Admiral, but with two and one extra thin stripes respectively.

Admiral.   Vice-Admiral.   Rear-Admiral.   Captain.   Commander.   Lieut-Commander.   Lieutenant.   Ensign.

The rank of Admiral has been provided for the Chief of Naval operations, Navy Dept., also the ranks of Admiral and Vice-Admiral for certain flag officers afloat.

FLAGS.

ENSIGN   JACK   ADMIRAL   VICE ADMIRAL

Red   Blue   White   Yellow

REAR ADMIRAL SENIOR   REAR ADMIRAL

PRESIDENT'S FLAG   NAVAL MILITIA   SECRETARY OF THE NAVY

Principal Guns in the U. S. Fleet.

(Official Details of New Marks added, 1920.)

Built at Washington Gun Factory, proved at Indian Head, Dahlgren, Va., and Potomac Range.

	Notation	Nominal Calibre.	Mark or Model.	Length in Calibres.	Weight of Gun.	Weight of A.P. Shot.	*Service* Initial Velocity.	*Maximum* penetration firing *capped* A.P. direct impact against K.C. armour.			Muzzle Energy
								9000	6000	3000	
		inch.			tons.	lbs.	ft. secs.	in.	in.	in.	ft-tons.
HEAVY		16	...	50	130	2100	2800	...	...	...	98,406
		16	I	45	105	2100	2800	...	...	...	76,087
		14	IV	50	81	1400	2800	...	...	...	...
		14	...	45	63½	1400	2600	18	...	...	...
		12	VII	50	56·1	870	2950	11·0	13·9	17·5	52,483
		12	VI	45	53·6	870	2850	10·6	13·3	16·6	48,984
		12	V	45	52·9	870	2700	9·8	12·3	15·5	43,964
		10	III	40	34·6	510	2700	6·9	9·0	11·9	25,772
MEDIUM		8	VI	45	18·7	260	2750	4·4	6·1	8·6	13,630
		8	V	40	18·1	260	2500	4·0	5·3	7·5	11,264
		6	XII	53	10	105	3000	...	...	...	6,551
		6	VIII	50	8·6	105	2800	2·3	3·2	5·2	5,707
		6	VI	50	8·3	105	2600	2·2	2·9	4·7	4,920
		6*	IX	45	7·0	105	2250	2·1	2·5	3·8	3,685
		6*	IV, VII	40	6·0	105	2150	2·1	2·4	3·6	3,365
		5*	VII	51	5·0	50	3150	1·4	1·8	3·4	3,439
		5	VII	50	4·6	50	3000	1·4	1·7	3·2	3,122
		5	V & VI	50	4·6	60	2700	1·6	2·0	3·5	3,032
		5*	II, III, IV	40	3·1	50	2300	1·4	1·7	2·6	1,834
LIGHT and AA.		4°	VIII	50	2·9	33	2800	1·2	1·5	2·6	1,794
		4°	VII	50	2·6	33	2500	1·2	1·4	2·2	1,430
		4°	III,IV,V,VI	40	1·5	33	2000	...	1·2	1·7	915
		3§	X	50	1·15	13	2700	...	...	...	657
		3	V, VI, S-A	50	1·0	13	2700	...	0·8	1·2	658
		3°	II, III	50	1·0	13	2700	...	0·8	1·2	658

* = Brass cartridge case.

Guns of 1899 and later have Vickers breech, etc. All guns use nitro-cellulose.

§ Anti-aircraft gun.

Senior officer when of or below rank of captain flies a blue triangular flag. Assistant-Secretary of Navy has a flag same as Secretary's with colours reversed, *i.e.*, white ground and blue anchor and stars. Correction to Ensign and Jack : Stars should number 48, in six rows of eight.

I.—Ordnance, &c. (Also v. Special Memoir, V (b) 1.) 1921.

DIRECTORS.—In all Battleships and New Light Cruisers Type of Director : Sperry-Ford. Range Clocks on masts and Deflection Scales on gunhouses, as in British Navy.

***RANGE FINDERS.*—Made in various sizes from short 3-feet base range finders for navigation to 30-feet base range finders for use in turrets. Standard practice in U.S. Navy is now to mount one range finder in each turret.

***HIGH EXPLOSIVES.*—T.N.T. standard high explosive for U.S. Navy. Some Amatol used. A new explosive, known as T.N.X. or Tri-Nitro-Xylol, almost identical with T.N.T. in properties, was developed during the War to eke out production of T.N.T.

***NON-RICOCHET SHELLS.*—Flat-nosed type ; does not ricochet from surface when fired at elevation of over 2°. Made in 3 inch, 4 inch, 5 inch and 6 inch sizes for guns of equivalent bores. Delay action fuze commences on impact with water. Use of this shell converts gun into what is practically a long range depth charge thrower, the flat-nosed shell acting as depth charge.

***STAR SHELLS.*—Range, three to six land miles. Made for 3 inch, 4 inch and 5 inch guns. Time fuze lights lamp and expels parachute and burner through base of shell. Normally, shell detonates at 1000 feet. Burner, 800,000 candle power, burning for 30 seconds, and illuminating sea for one mile diameter.

II.—Torpedoes. (Also v. Special Memoir, V (b) 2.) 1921.

***Torpedoes in U.S. Navy are all turbine-driven. Manufactured in 18 inch and 21 inch sizes, 21 inch for Battleships and Destroyers, and 18 inch and 21 inch for Submarines. (No official details available of marks, ranges, speeds, charges and types of heater.) Hammond radio-dynamic (distance-controlled) torpedo, reported under test.

III.—Mines. (Also v. Special Memoir, V (b) 3.) 1921.

***Made in various sizes and of constructions particularly adapted for work they are expected to perform. Anchor similar to British type.

Unofficial Notes.—Mk. VI anti-submarine type of mine is reported to weigh 1400 lbs. and to have 300 lbs. T.N.T. charge. Body of mine, spherical, 3 feet diameter. Form of detonation uncertain ; said to consist of antennae fitted with the Earle Patent Magnetic Pistol. Sinker is box-shaped and has wheels to gauge of laying ship's mine-discharging rails. Mine and sinker float together immediately after laying, while a 90 lb. plummet (attached to ¼ inch steel wire) sinks. The " plummet cord " is measured off to same depth at which mine is to float below surface. When plummet cord is spun full out, latch is unlocked and mine and sinker separate. Mine still floats on surface, while mine-mooring cable begins to spin off drum and sinker descends. Immediately the plummet touches bottom, the running-out of mine-mooring cable is stopped and cable is locked. Sinker (or anchor) then comes down to bottom, drawing down the mine to the desired depth below the surface. Soluble safety plug used. Antennae said to consist of thin conducting wires and magnetic pistols, floating out in a star pattern all round body of mine and giving a contact diameter of 50 feet. Has been found effective against large surface ships. Being light and easily handled, it has been adopted for laying by Light Minelayers.

IV.—Aircraft Bombs.

***(a) 18 lb. (modified 3 inch shell). Explosive charge, T.N.T.
(b) 20 lb. Cooper. Explosive charge, Amatol (to be replaced by T.N.T.)
(c) 163 lb.* Explosive charge, 117 lbs. T.N.T.
(d) 215 lb.* Explosive charge, 172 lbs. T.N.T.
(e) 230 lb. (British design).* Explosive charge, T.N.T.
(f) 270 lb.* Explosive charge, 217 lbs. T.N.T.
(g) 520 lb. (British design).* Explosive charge, T.N.T.
(h) 1650 lb. (British design.) Explosive charge, 900 lbs. Amatol.
(i) 2000 lb.
(j) 3000 lb. reported under test.

Note.—Types marked * for Anti-Submarine use. Excepting 230 lb. type, all fitted with U.S. Mark VI fuse. Mark VI fuse (and fuse of 230 lb. type) both armed by revolving of aerial propeller. Delay action feature consists of burning powder train.

V.—Anti-Submarine.

***DEPTH CHARGES. Mk. IV.*—Charge 600 lbs. of T.N.T. Dimensions : 24 inch diameter, 28 inches long. 100 feet effective radius, hydrostatic firing valve, similar to Mks. II and III Depth Charges.

***Depth Charge, Mks. II and III. Charge : 300 lbs. of T.N.T. Dimensions : 18 inch diameter, 28 inches long. Effective within a radius of 70 feet from point of detonation. Limit of detonation adjustable between 36 and 300 feet. Safety device prevents detonation due to gun blast, etc., detonation above six fathoms, or when thrown overboard with firing device in the off position. Detonation by hydrostatic pressure only. During War, destroyers carried from 30 to 50 depth charges and vessels on submarine patrols up to 100 depth charges.

***Y-GUN OR DEPTH CHARGE PROJECTOR.*—Two barrels set at an angle of 90°, each barrel 3 feet long and 6 inch bore. 300 lb. depth charges fastened to arbors, inserted in barrels of Y and common powder charge exploded at junction of barrels ; range of about 30 yards obtained.

HYDROPHONES.—K-tube fish type, 30 miles acoustic radius, but operating vessel must stop engines and auxiliaries while listening. SC- and MB-tube types, 3 miles acoustic radius ; built into hull and insulated against noise ; can be used without stopping ship.

(Also v. Non-Ricochet Shells ; Aircraft Bombs, Sweeping Gear.)

VI.—Sweeping Gears.

PV's as British Navy of H.S.S.S. and H.S.M.S. types, but with slight modification of inhaul gear. Methods of attachment also same as British Navy. During War, U.S. Sweepers also used the French Ronar'ch form of sweep (a combination of kites and " explosive knives "), which may have been adopted by U.S. Navy and improved.

VII.—Searchlights.

No details known, but in latest ships are of controlled type, as in British Navy.

VIII.—General.

All battleships and light cruisers being fitted with catapults for launching seaplanes. Reported that Battleships of NEW YORK and later classes are to be fitted with bulges. Certain battleships are also to have deck armouring extended.

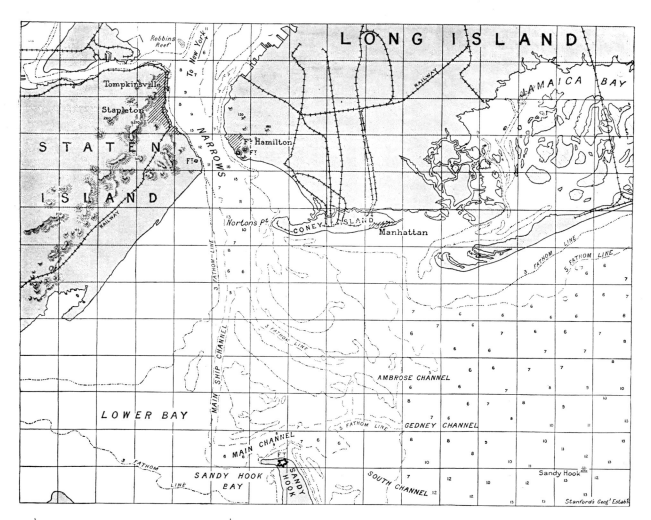

NEW YORK (& BROOKLYN).—3rd Naval District. Depôt and shipbuilding yard. Slip No. 1 to be re-built. Slip No. 2 suitable for building largest types of Dreadnoughts and Battle-Cruisers built 1917-21. New plant also installed, workshops re-arranged and renovated, new offices and general stores built and magazine stores greatly enlarged, 1917-18.

Dry docks :

(1) granite, $330 \times 66 \times 25$ feet.

(2) concrete, $440 \times 90 \times 26$ feet.

(3) wood $613 \times 105\frac{3}{4} \times 29\frac{1}{2}$ feet.

(4) granite and concrete, $700 \times 120 \times 35$ feet.

Naval hospital here. Admiralty Chart No. 3204, 2491. Rise of Spring Tide, $4\frac{3}{4}$ feet. On Long Island : Naval Diving School, Bay Shore and Rockaway Aviation Stations.

Note.—Private docks : Altogether there are nearly 100 privately owned docks in the neighbourhood of New York and adjoining districts, the majority being floating docks or patent slips. The Morse Dry Dock & Repair Co. have a dock capable of taking a ship of 30,000 tons and 725 feet in length, and there are 11 others of 10,000 tons capacity or over.

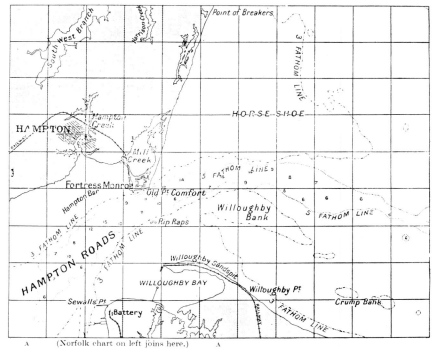

(Norfolk chart on left joins here.)

(HAMPTON ROADS AS ABOVE MAP.)

NORFOLK, VA.—5th Naval District. To be the dockyard section of the Hampton Roads Navy Operating Base. Depôt and ship-building yard. Naval hospital here. One or more slips for building Battleships or Battle-Cruisers. (1) Wood dock, $460 \times 85 \times 25\frac{1}{4}$ feet ; (2) granite, $303 \times 60 \times 25\frac{1}{4}$ feet ; (3) granite dock, $713 \times 97 \times 34$ feet ; (4) concrete dock, $1000 \times 110 \times 43\frac{1}{2}$ feet, divisible into 2 sections, about 650 and 350 feet long ; has electric towing gear, 50-ton electric crane, and hydraulic lifts for rapid handling of repair materials, etc. Capable of being emptied in 30 mins. ; floating pontoon crane 150 tons, and auxiliary 25 tons on hoist. (5) and (6) two concrete docks, each $455 \times 62 \times 20$ feet. In 1917 new foundry, workshops, and plant for making mines installed and old plant renovated. Three patent slips here, each 1500 tons. Admiralty Chart No. 2818,2843a.

HAMPTON ROADS NAVY OPERATING BASE (continuation to N. and N.W. of Norfolk Chart).—5th Naval District. Site on ground of Jamestown Exposition was purchased here in 1917, where it is intended that in conjunction with the Norfolk N.Y., a Naval Base shall be established which will eventually become the principal warship port on the Atlantic coast. Plans as laid down during 1917 by the Navy Department, contemplated the following works : Submarine and Aviation Bases ; Training Station for 10,000 men ; Fuel Station (for coal and oil) ; Depôts for fleet stores, mines, torpedoes and anti-submarine nets, etc.

U. S. YARDS, HARBOURS, ETC.—ATLANTIC.

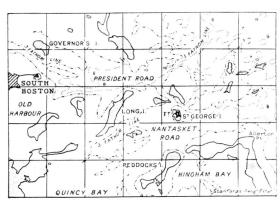

Admiralty Chart No. 1227,2482.   Rise of Spring Tide, 5 feet (Charlestown Naval Yard).

LEAGUE ISLAND.
Admiralty Chart No. 2564.

PORTSMOUTH N.H.
Admiralty Chart No. 2482,2487.
Rise of Spring Tide, 8½ feet.

Navy Yards (ATLANTIC COAST).

BOSTON, MASS.—1st Naval District. Depôt. One granite dock, 389×46×26 feet ; one granite and concrete dock, 729×101½×30½ feet. Commonwealth Dock (completed 1920), concrete, granite and rock, 1171×120×46 feet, divisible into 635 feet (inner) and 490 feet (outer) sections. Naval hospital here. Also two wooden private docks and four patent slips 1000—2300 tons.

SQUANTUM, MASS. Late Destroyer Plant operated by Bethlehem Co. Repair Base for T.B.D. and S/M. 10 building slips with electric bridge cranes and three wet slips. Maximum length of slips 310 feet (p.p.). One 20-ton stiff leg derrick ; one 10-ton guy derrick ; wet slips have one 25-ton and two 10-ton bridge cranes. Yard covers 60 acres approximately. Water-front about 3600 feet.

LEAGUE ISLAND, PHILADELPHIA PA.— 4th Naval District. Depôt. Slips Nos. 2 and 3 can build Dreadnoughts or Battle-Cruisers. New workshops, foundry and Marine Barracks, 1917-18. One wooden dock, 420×89×25½ feet ; second dock, granite and concrete, 680 ×95×30 feet. New dock, 1005×114×43½ feet, divisible into two sections, viz., 675 feet outer section and 330 feet inner section. Pier 1000 feet long, with 350-ton crane. Aircraft base and flying ground ; also Government seaplane factory. Naval hospital here.

WASHINGTON. No docks. Yard devoted to ordnance and torpedo construction. Naval hospital here.

PORTSMOUTH, N.H.—1st Naval District. One granite and concrete, 720×101½×30⅔ feet. Naval hospital here.

CHARLESTON, S.C.—6th Naval District. 2nd class Navy yard. Dry dock, 503×113× 34½ feet. 2000-ton patent slip finished 1920. Also a private floating dock (1919-20), 440× 88×22½ feet (10,500 tons).

Naval Stations, &c.

ANNAPOLIS. Naval Academy.

NARRAGANSET BAY, R.I.

NEWPORT, R.I.—2nd Naval District. Chief torpedo station. Manufactory of torpedoes, etc. Naval war college and apprentice-training station. Naval hospital and coal depôt.

CAPE MAY, N.J.—4th Naval District. Base for Submarines and Navy Airships. 349 acres bought 1919 for developing this Station.

NEW LONDON, CONN.—2nd Naval District. Submarine Training Station.

NORTH CHICAGO. Training Station for Great Lakes.

SOUTH CHARLESTON (W.VA.). U.S. naval ordnance plant, 207 acres site. Equipped for producing 20-inch shells and 20-inch armour plate. Building Mk. XII 6-inch guns, 1920.

ALEXANDRIA (Va.). U.S. Navy Torpedo Factory. Output, 8 torpedoes per day. Testing range on Potomac River near Piney Point. Employees, 1500.

Note.—Charleston, Norfolk, and Bradford, R.I., are stations for petrol and oil fuel.

PRIVATE DOCKS, &c.

(exclusive of those in New York and Brooklyn districts.)

NEW LONDON (CONN.), three patent slips, 1000–2000 tons.   PHILADELPHIA, one floating dock (3500 tons) and two patent slips (1000 and 2300 tons). CAMDEN (N.J.), three patent slips, 1200–1500 tons. BALTIMORE (MD.), Wm. Skinner & Sons dry dock, 600×80×22½ feet. Columbian Ironworks Dock (wood), 437×80×21 feet. Maryland Steel Co., Sparrow Point. wood and steel floating dock, 20,000 tons. Also one 3000-ton floating dock and two patent slips (2000 and 1500 tons). At Portland (Me.), Savannah (Ga.), Jacksonville (Fla.), small patent slips of 1200 tons (Jacksonville, one 4500 ton floating dock).

U.S. NAVY YARDS, STATIONS, &c.—GULF COAST, CARIBBEAN, &c.

SAN JUAN, PUERTO RICO.
Admiralty Chart No. 478,3408.   Rise of Spring Tide, 1 foot.

NEW ORLEANS, LA.—8th Naval District. Floating dock, 525×100×28¼ feet (18,000 tons).

PENSACOLA, FLA.—8th Naval District. 2nd class yard. 8th Naval District. Big new Aviation Station for seaplanes, dirigibles, kite-balloons, &c. Floating dock, 450×82×27 feet (12,000 tons), ordered by Shipping Board to be stationed here, when ready.

KEY WEST.—7th Naval District. No docks. Submarine and Aircraft Station.

Small Naval Stations may also exist at San Juan (Porto Rico) and St. Thomas (Virgin Islands).

Principal Private Docks.

NEW ORLEANS : Two floating docks, 10,000 and 8000 tons, and 3 smaller.

MOBILE (ALA.) : Two floating docks, 10,000 and 9000 tons, and several smaller.

GALVESTON : Floating dock, 10,000 tons.

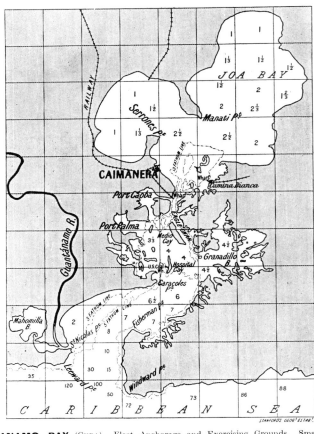

GUANTANAMO BAY (CUBA). Fleet Anchorage and Exercising Grounds. Small repairs undertaken here. Fuel Depôt. Admiralty Chart No. 904.

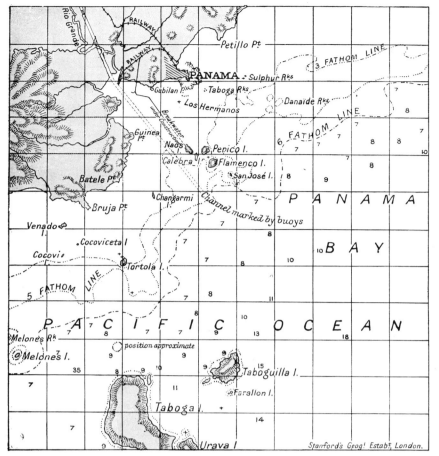

PACIFIC ENTRANCE TO PANAMA CANAL. Heavily fortified. Terminal Graving Dock, No. 1, Balboa. $1000 \times 110 \times 41\frac{1}{2}$ feet. Also fuel depôt for 300,000 to 350,000 tons of coal at Balboa. 2—250 ton floating cranes. U.S. warships are stationed in the Canal Zone, where facilities exist for repairing ships.

ATLANTIC ENTRANCE TO PANAMA CANAL. Heavily fortified. Dock and Fuel Depôt at Cristobal same size as Balboa (see opposite). In the Canal, Gatun, San Miguel and Miraflores Locks (over $1000 \times 110 \times 41\frac{1}{2}$ feet) can be used as docks.

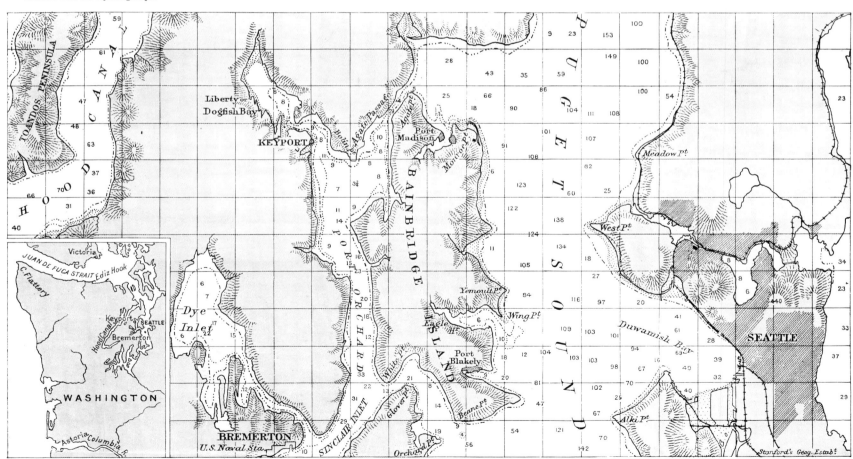

Sketch map of district. **BREMERTON, PUGET SOUND.**—13th Naval District. Navy Yard and Station. For Ediz Hook and Keyport in this vicinity, v. Naval Stations on a later page. Slips for building Scout Cruisers or Auxiliaries begun here during 1917. Dry docks: (1) Wood, $618 \times 73 \times 27\frac{1}{4}$ feet; (2) Granite and concrete, $801\frac{3}{4} \times 113 \times 35\frac{1}{4}$ feet; (3) Concrete, $927\frac{1}{2} \times 124 \times 23\frac{1}{2}$ feet. Two slips, 440×48 feet. Recommended that the yard, &c., be developed into a 1st class Fleet Base, with two 1000 feet and two 472 feet graving docks, &c., at a cost of 44 million dollars.

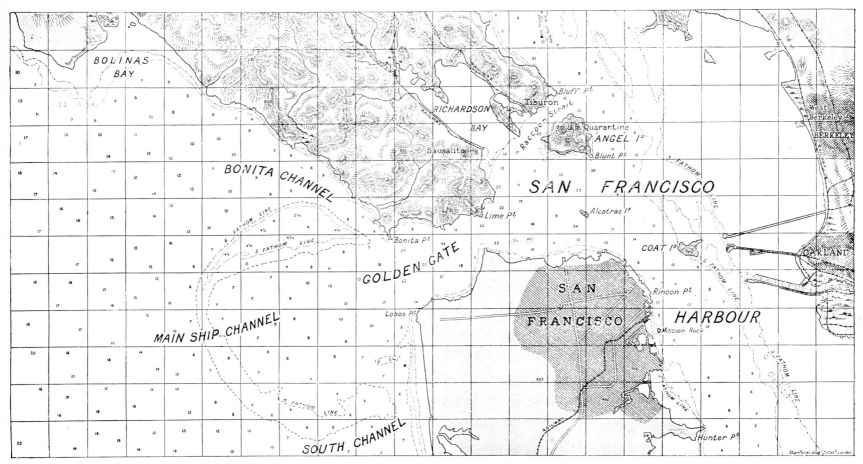

SAN FRANCISCO FLEET OPERATING BASE.—Site secured by free gift at ALAMEDA, within Bay and opposite Hunters Point. No details available, but cost estimated at fifty million dollars. No work begun yet. Recommended that South, Bonita and Main Ship Channels be dredged and protected by breakwaters to allow safe and rapid passage of Battle Squadrons (comprising ships 1000 feet long and drawing 40 feet) at all states of tides.

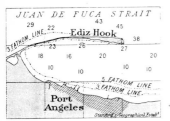

Ediz Hook.
Admiralty Chart No. 1717.

ASTORIA. Admiralty Chart No. 2839.

Minor Naval Stations.—PACIFIC.

EDIZ HOOK (or FALSE NESS). Recommended that a Naval Station be created here, to operate 18 torpedo boat destroyers and 12 submarines in peace time and double these numbers in war. Also Naval Air Station for coastal airships, K.B., flying-boats, seaplanes, aeroplanes also recommended. Credits for commencing work not yet secured.

KEYPORT (Bainbridge Island, Puget Sound). Sub-Base to Bremerton Navy Yard. Torpedo station. Recommended that a submarine station be located here, to operate 12 boats (peace), 24 (war).

ASTORIA (Columbia River, Oregon). At Tongue Point, establishment of Naval Station for 12 submarines and 8 torpedo destroyers (double these numbers for war time) and aircraft recommended. Also anchorage recommended for 8 super-dreadnoughts. No work begun yet, but $280,000 voted to commence torpedo boat destroyer and submarine station, 1920.

*For Keyport, c. Bremerton Chart on an earlier page.

SAN DIEGO. Admiralty Chart No. 2885.

MARE ISLAND.—12th Naval District. Depôt and Navy Yard (22 miles N. of San Francisco), of which small Map is given on next page. Slip to build Dreadnoughts of 600 feet length, or above. Destroyers also built.

Dry Docks : (1) Granite......418 × 88 × 27½ feet.
(2) Concrete ....683 × 102 × 31½ „

MARE ISLAND. Admiralty Chart No. 2887.
(For Docks, see previous page.)

(RISDON, San Francisco. Temporary plant for building torpedo boat destroyers erected here during war and operated by Bethlehem Co. Believed to have reverted to control of Navy Department, but will probably be sold).

LAS ANIMAS, Cal. Naval Hospital.*

SAN DIEGO, Cal. About two million dollars voted 1920 for Marine Barracks, Naval Station, Fuel Depôt, Repair and Training Stations. Is Supply, Repair and Fuel Base for torpedo boat destroyers and submarines. North Island Air Station (1200 acres) is jointly used by U.S. Navy and Army Air Services. Very large projects, involving an outlay of 30½ million dollars have been prepared, to convert San Diego into a Fleet Operating Base, Fleet, Fuel, Supply and Repair Station, but no credits have been secured for this work.

SAN PEDRO, Cal. Station for Submarines exists here. No details known. (For Chart, v. next page.)

*A new and very large Central Naval Hospital has been projected at Balboa, near San Diego, but credits not allowed for this scheme yet.

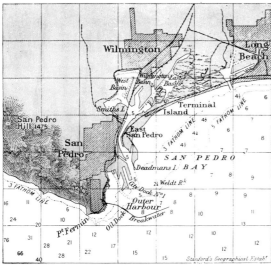

SAN PEDRO (*v. preceding page*). Admiralty Chart No. 108.

Private Shipyards.—PACIFIC COAST.

(Warship Builders only.)

Bethlehem Union Plant.

BETHLEHEM UNION PLANT (SAN FRANCISCO). 38 acres. Three dry docks (Hunters Point) : (1) $716 \times 86 \times 29$ feet (28,000 tons), (2) $1000 \times 110 \times 40$ feet. Three small floating docks of 2500 and 1800 tons and two of 12,000 tons. Six slips of 600 feet long, fully equipped with electric cranes, etc., and 4 smaller. Five wharves 585×50 feet, berthing for 15 average sized vessels. One sheer leg 100 tons, one 40 tons. 2 marine railways. All plant dates from 1910 or later. *Employees* : Average 2300. Enlarged 1917. Also yard for mercantile construction at Alameda.

California S.B. Co.

CALIFORNIA SHIPBUILDING CO. (LONG BEACH, CAL.). Submarine builders.

Todd Shipyards Corporation.

SEATTLE YARDS. Floating dock, (1) $521 \times 98\frac{1}{2} \times 30$ feet, for 15,000 tons ; (2) $468 \times 85 \times 27\frac{1}{2}$ feet (12,000 tons) ; (3) floating dock for 2500 tons ; one patent slip, 3000 tons.

TACOMA YARD. No details available. Is building Cruisers.

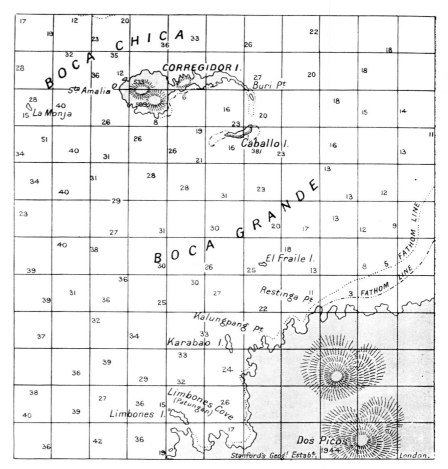

ENTRANCE TO MANILA BAY. (Asiatic Station.)   (*Continued on next page.*)

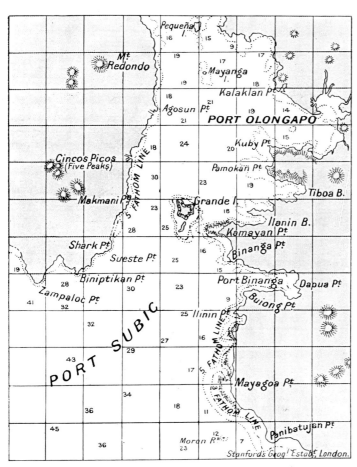

OLONGAPO & PORT SUBIC.

Naval Stations.—2ND CLASS, PACIFIC.

PEARL HARBOUR. (1) Honolulu. (2) Pearl Harbour, on S. side of Island of Oahu, about 10–15 miles west of Honolulu. Large dock here, $1001 \times 114 \times 34\frac{3}{4}$ feet. Recommended that Pearl Harbour be developed into a 1st Class Fleet and Submarine Base, with extra dry docks and extended fuel and fleet stores. Credits not secured for this work.

TUTUILA (SAMOA).

Recommended that GUAM be developed as a Fuel and Repair Station for U.S. Naval and Mercantile vessels bound for Far East. Credits not approved for this work yet.

Alaska.

Fuel and Supply Base recommended.

Asiatic Naval Stations.

CAVITE (P.I.) Small dry dock at Manila. Map of entrance on preceding page.

OLONGAPO (P.I.) Dewey Floating dock, 18,500 tons, $501' 0\frac{3}{4}'' \times 100' \times 37' 0''$.

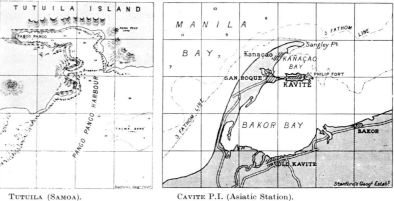

TUTUILA (SAMOA).
Admiralty Chart No. 1730.

CAVITE P.I. (Asiatic Station).
Admiralty Chart No. 975.976.

BATTLESHIPS

THE first true battleships of what is generally known as the "New Navy" of the USA were authorized in August 1886 – *Texas* and *Maine*. Both were comparatively small with the usual mix of armament consonant with the current theories of naval engagement. During the next twenty years nine further classes were built, none with a speed exceeding 18 knots and none with more than four large calibre guns in their main armament. The standard of gunnery in the US Navy was, at this time and in common with many other navies, at a desperately low ebb. However the appointment of Captain William Sims as Inspector of Target Practice in 1902 had a rejuvenating effect on the fleet's efficiency. By the time that the first of the single-calibre battleships (*South Carolina*) was laid down in December 1906 (largely as the result of Sims' enthusiasm) the standards of gunnery firings were among the best in the world. Had the design staff of the Bureau of Construction and Repair been less dilatory over the design of this class and had Cramp's Shipyard been more speedy in her construction (they took five and a quarter years while Britain's contemporary *Dreadnought* was fourteen months in the yard), the USN would have had a ship whose armament was fit to accept this new-found efficiency.

Nine classes of battleships followed and were completed before the requirements of the Washington Naval Treaties of 1921–22 called a halt to such building. During these years the size of the ships had grown at an impressive rate. *South Carolina*, completed in March 1910, was, as a result of Congressional restrictions, 453 feet long with a displacement of 17,617 tons full load. *West Virginia*, completed in December 1923, had a length of 624 feet and a displacement of 33,590 tons. With the increase in size, increased armour protection was provided in the last five classes while the armament was much improved. Instead of *South Carolina*'s eight 12-inch and twenty two 3-inch guns *West Virginia* mounted eight 16-inch and fourteen 5-inch guns.

Propulsion was a problem in the years up to 1913. The American turbine industry took some time to come to grips with the high standards and low tolerances needed in such engines. As a result fuel consumption was unacceptably high and it was not until the "Pennsylvania" class (laid down in 1913–14) that the General Board approved the universal fitting of turbines. Twenty one knots was the normal maximum speed for all post-"South Carolina" classes.

Three classes of battleships followed the expiration of the Washington Treaty restrictions – "North Carolina", "South Dakota" and "Iowa". Although the first two varied considerably in internal arrangements and appearance they were both of about 45,000 tons with a speed of around 28 knots and a similar armament of nine 16-inch and twenty 5-inch guns. Their successors, the four "Iowas", were a great advance on the "South Dakotas". Lengthened by over 200 feet, with improved armour and a power output of 212,000 shp in place of 130,000, their speed was increased to 35 knots. Although their armament appears identical to their predecessors the increased size of the ships allowed the introduction of the more capable 16-inch 50-calibre guns.

Ships of this class served in the majority of the major West Pacific actions of World War II, were deployed off Korea, and *New Jersey* served off Vietnam before all four were retired to reserve. In 1981 *New Jersey* was taken in hand for modernization and in the succeeding eight years all were brought up to date. Modern radar, EW systems and communications were needed in ships which, in addition to their gun armament, carried 32 Tomahawk missiles with a range out to 1,400 miles, and 16 Harpoons reaching out to strike ships 70 miles away. The new-look battleships' day was far from done. With a complement of 1,518 (almost half their previous war complement) they proved the efficacy of their new control systems off Lebanon and the capability of their Tomahawks in the Gulf War of early 1991.

J.M.
May 1991

U. S. MONITORS (slow).

MONTEREY (April, 1891).

Displacement 4084 tons. Complement 203.

Length, 256 feet. Beam, 59 feet. *Maximum* draught, 17 feet.

Guns :	Armour (Harvey) :
2—12 inch, 35 cal. (A).	13" Belt (amidships) .... aa
2—10 inch, 35 cal. (B).	6" Belt (ends) c
6—6 pdr.	2" Deck (flat) ....
4—1 pdr.	Protection to vitals .... aa
2 Colts.	14" Fore barbette (A)......... aa
Torpedo tubes :	11½" After barbette (B) ...... aa
none.	8" Hoods to both.............. b
	10" Conning tower .... a

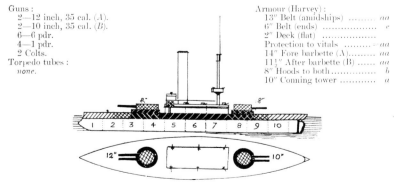

Machinery : 2 sets vertical inverted triple expansion. 2 screws. Boilers (1904) : Babcock and Wilcox. Designed H.P. 5400 = 13·6 kts. (exceeded on *trial* under favourable circumstances). Coal : *normal* 200 tons.

SOLD 2/22

Signal letter : HY.

PURITAN (1882).

Displacement 6060 tons. Complement 230.

Length, 289 feet. Beam, 60 feet. *Maximum* draught, 20 feet.

Guns :	Armour (Harvey) :
4—12 inch, 35 cal. (A).	14" Belt (amidships) .... aa
6—4 inch, 40 cal. (F).	6" Belt (ends) c
4—3 pdr.	2" Deck (flat) ....
4—1 pdr.	Protection to vitals is .... aa
4 Gatlings.	14" Barbettes .... aa
Torpedo tubes :	8" Turrets to these .... b
none.	8" Conning tower.............. b

Machinery : 2 sets horizontal compound. 2 screws. Boilers : 8 cylindrical. Designed H.P. *natural* 3700 = 12·4 kts. Coal : *normal* 400 tons ; *maximum* 580 tons.

Notes.—*Puritan* was not completed till 1895 or thereabouts. See notes to *Terror*, all of which apply to *Puritan*.

TARGET- SOLD 1/22

MIANTONOMOH.

AMPHITRITE. (1906)   *Photo, copyright, Rau.*

TERROR, MIANTONOMOH, MONADNOCK, AMPHITRITE. 3990 tons. Guns: 4—10 inch, 35 cal. (B) in *Terror.* 30 cal. (D) in others. Last two also carry a couple of 4 inch. Belts (iron): 7″ in first two, with 11½″ steel low turrets; in second two 9″ iron belts, with 11½″ steel barbettes and 7½″ turrets. Nominal speeds: 10—12 knots. Coal: 330 tons *maximum.*

SOLD 3/21   SOLD 1/22   SOLD 8/23   SOLD 1/20 HULK

TERROR.   *Photos, copyright, William H. Rau.*

MONADNOCK. (1906)   *Photo, copyright, Taber.*

Signal letter: GK.

TEXAS (June, 1892).

& MAINE — SUNK HAVANA.

Displacement 6300 tons. Complement 380.

Length *(waterline),* 301 feet. Beam, 64 feet. *Maximum* draught, 24 feet.

Guns :
2—12 inch, L, 35 cal. (A).
6—6 inch, 35 cal. RF (F).
12—6 pdr.
10—1 pdr.
2 Colts.
1 Field gun.
Torpedo tubes :
2 *above water*
(bow & stern).

Armour (compound) :
12″ Belt .... *a*
3″ Deck .... *d*
[Deck flat on belt.]
Protection to vitals .... *a*
12″ Bulkheads (under deck) *a*
12″ Redoubt.................. *a*
12″ Turrets (2).............. *a*
6″ Hoists to redoubt (2) ... *d*
12″ Conning tower .... *a*

Ahead :
2—12 in.
3—6 in.

Astern :
2—12 in.
3—6 in.

TEXAS.

Broadside : 2—12 in., 4—6 in.

Machinery : 2 sets vertical inverted direct acting triple expansion. 2 screws. Boilers : cylindrical (4 double ended). Designed H.P. 8000 *f.d.*=17 kts. Coal : *normal* 500 tons : *maximum* 950 tons.

General Notes.—Changes have been made in the 12 in. gun mountings; they can now fire every two minutes. Laid down at Norfolk Navy Yard, June, 1889. Completed 1895. Burns a great deal of coal and is a poor steamer.

SAN MARCOS   SUNK AS TARGET

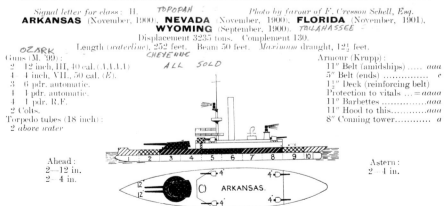

Signal letter for class : H.   TOPOPAH   *Photo by favour of F. Cresson Schell, Esq.*
ARKANSAS (November, 1900). **NEVADA** (November, 1900). **FLORIDA** (November, 1901).
WYOMING (September, 1900).   TALLAHASSEE
Displacement 3235 tons. Complement 130.

OZARK   Length *(waterline),* 252 feet. Beam 50 feet. *Maximum* draught, 12¼ feet.

Guns (M. '99) :   CHEYENNE
2—12 inch, III, 40 cal. (AAAA)   ALL SOLD
4—4 inch, VII., 50 cal. (E).
3—6 pdr. automatic.
4—1 pdr. automatic.
4—1 pdr. R.F.
2 Colts.
Torpedo tubes (18 inch) :
2 *above water*

Armour (Krupp) :
11″ Belt (amidships) ..... *aaa*
5″ Belt (ends) .... *a*
1½″ Deck (reinforcing belt)
Protection to vitals ...= *aaaa*
11″ Barbettes .... *aaa*
11″ Hood to this........... *aaa*
8″ Conning tower........... *a*

Ahead :
2—12 in.
2—4 in.

ARKANSAS.

Astern :
2—4 in.

Broadside : 2—12 in., 2—4 in.

Machinery : 2 sets vertical inverted 3 cylinder triple expansion. 2 screws. Boilers : *Arkansas,* 4 Thornycroft ; *Nevada,* 4 Niclausse ; *Florida,* 4 Normand ; *Wyoming,* 4 Babcock & Wilcox. Designed H.P. 2400=12 kts. Coal : *normal* tons ; *maximum* 400 tons.

Name.	Builders.	Laid down.	Completed.	Differences.
Arkansas	Newport News	Nov., '99	1902	As photo
Nevada	Bath Ironworks	April, '99	1903	Topmast abaft
Florida	Elizabeth Port	Jan., '99	1903	Smaller s. l. platform
Wyoming	Union I. W. 'Frisco	April, '99	1903	

24 pneumatic watertight doors.

(INDIANA CLASS—3 Ships.)

INDIANA (February, 1893), **MASSACHUSETTS** (June, 1893), **OREGON** (October, 1893).

Displacement 10288 tons. Complement 470.

SUNK AS TARGET Length (*waterline*), 358 feet. Beam, 69½ feet. *Maximum* draught, 28 feet. *SCRAPPED 1956*

SUNK AS TARGET

Guns:
4—13 inch, I, (A.A.A.).
8—8 inch, 30 cal. (F).
4—6 inch, 40 cal. (F).
20—6 pdr.
6—1 pdr.
4 Colts.
Torpedo tubes:
removed.

Armour (Harvey):
18″–15″ Belt (amidships) ... *aaaa-aaa*
17″ Bulkheads .... *aaaa*
3″ Deck (flat on belt).
Protection to vitals is ... *aaaa*
17″ Barbettes .... *aaaa*
8½″ Turrets .... *a*
5″ Turret bases .... *d*
5″ Lower deck side .... *d*
6″ Secondary turrets .... *c*
8″ Barbettes to these ... *b*
3″ Hoist .... *e*
5″ Sponsons to 6″ guns .. *d*
10″ Conning tower ...... *a*

Ahead:
2—13 in.
4—8 in.

Astern:
2—13 in.
4—8 in.

Broadside: 4—13 in., 4—8 in., 2—6 in.

Machinery: 2 sets vertical inverted triple expansion 3 cylinder. 2 screws. Boilers: *Indiana*, Babcock, others, Cylindrical, 4 horizontal return tube, 2 single ended. Designed H. P. *natural* 8000 = 15 kts., *forced* 9500 = 17 kts. Coal: *normal* 400 tons; *maximum* 1800 tons.

Armour Notes.—Belt is 7½ feet wide by 200 feet long.

Gunnery Notes.—Loading positions, big guns: end on. Electric hoists. Arcs of fire: Big guns, 265°; secondary turrets, 135°.

Torpedo Notes.—Whitehead torpedoes. Tubes being removed or reduced in number. Complete electric installation.

Engineering Notes.—

Name.	Builder.	Laid down.	Completed.	Mean of 62 kt. trial 1895-96.
Indiana	Cramp	May, '91	1895	9500 = 15·61
Massachusetts	Cramp	June, '91	1895	= 16·15
Oregon	Union Co., 'Frisco	Nov., '91	1896	= 16·78

Consumption: At 11 kts. 3 7/10 tons per hour. At 9500 H.P. (15-16 kts.), 10¼ tons per hour.

IOWA (1896).

Displacement 11,410 tons. Complement 486.

Length (*waterline*), 360 feet. Beam, 72 feet. *Maximum* draught, 28 feet.

SUNK AS TARGET

Guns:
4—12 inch, I, 35 cal. (A).
8—8 inch, 30 cal. (F).
4—4 inch, (F).
22—6 pdr.
4—1 pdr.
4 Colts.
2 Field guns (3 inch.)
Torpedo tubes (18 inch):
3 above water—now removed.

Armour (Harvey):
14″—11″Belt(amidships) *aa-a*
12″ Bulkheads .... *aa*
3″ Deck (flat on belt).
Protection to vitals is ... *aa*
14″ Turrets .... *aa*
5″ Turret bases .... *d*
5″ Lower deck side .... *d*
6″ Secondary turrets .... *c*
8″ Barbettes to these ... *b*
10″ Conning tower ...... *a*

Ahead:
2—12 in.
4—8 in.
2—4 in.

Astern:
2—12 in.
4—8 in.
2—4 in.

Broadside: 4—12 in., 4—8 in., 2—4 in.

Machinery: 2 sets vertical inverted triple expansion. 2 screws. Boilers: cylindrical. Designed H.P. *forced* 11,000 = 16·5 kts. Coal: *normal* 625 tons; *maximum* 1780 tons.

Armour Notes: Belt is 7½ feet wide by 200 feet long; 5 feet of it below waterline; lower edge is 9½″ thick amidships. Main belt is reinforced by coal bunkers 10 feet thick.

Gunnery Notes: Loading positions, big guns: all round. Big guns manœuvred, hydraulic gear; secondary turrets, steam.
Arcs of fire: Big guns, 265°; 8 in., 135° from axial line.
Ammunition carried: 12 in., 60 rounds per gun; 8 in., 125 rounds per gun.

Torpedo Notes: Howell torpedoes; broadside tubes, section 8.

Engineering notes: Designed speed reached on trial.

General notes: Laid down at Cramp's, August, 1893; completed 1897.

Cost *complete*, nearly £1,000,000.

(Top gallant masts now fitted to all).   INDIANA. (1906)   *Photo, Rau.*

Signal letter for class: M.   OREGON (taken 1904).   *Photo, S. Ballou, Esq.*

Differences:—

Name.	Steampipes.	At after bridge.
Indiana	Both sides of funnels	Big cowl
Massachusetts	Both sides of funnels	Ensign staff
Oregon	Abaft funnel only	No cowl and no staff

The *Oregon* is also distinguished from the other two by 2 searchlights aft, shields to all the 6 pdr. guns, and by the U.S. flag on her bow instead of the usual scroll-work ornament.

Signal letter: L.   (Lower yard now removed, and top gallant mast fitted).   *Photo, copyright, W. Rau.*

IOWA. (1911)   *Photo, Abrahams.*

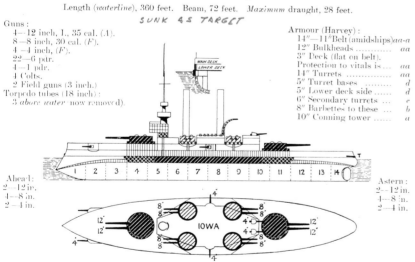

KEARSAGE & KENTUCKY (*both* March, 1898).

Normal displacement 11,500 tons. *Full load* displacement 12,320 tons. Complement 520 (586 as flag ship).
Length (*waterline*), 368 feet; Beam, 72 feet; *Mean draught*, 23½ feet; Length over all, 376 feet.

ALL SCRAPPED

Guns :
4—13 inch, II. (.1.1.1.)
4—8 inch, III., 40 cal. (D.)
14—5 inch, 40 cal. (F.)
20—6 pdr.
4—1 pdr. (R.F.)
4—1 pdr., (automatic.)
4 Colts.
2 Field guns (3 inch.)
Torpedo tubes (18 inch) :
had 4 above water (remored.)
(Total weight with ammunition,
1077 tons).

Armour (Harvey-nickel) :
16½″ Belt (amidships) *aaaa*
4″ Belt (bow) .... *d*
2½″ Deck (flat on belt)
10″ Fore bulkhead ...... *aa*
12″ After bulkhead ... *aaa*
Protection to vitals is *aaaa*
4″ Deck (aft) ....
17″-15″Turrets(for13in.) *aaaa*
15″-12½″Tret bases *aaaa-aaa*
9″ Turrets (for 8 inch)
5½″ Lower deck side ... *c*
5½″ Battery .... *c*
2″ Battery (bulkheads) *f*
10″ Conning tower...... *aa*
(Total weight 3419 tons.)

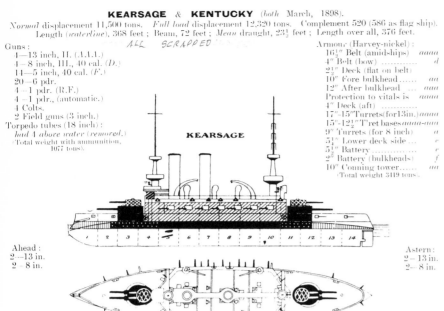

KEARSAGE

Ahead :
2—13 in.
2—8 in.

Astern :
2—13 in.
2—8 in.

Broadside : 4—13 in., 4—8 in., 7—5 in.

Machinery : 2 sets vertical triple expansion 3 cylinder. 2 screws. Boilers : cylindrical (6 double ended and 4 single ended). Designed H.P. 10,500 = 16 kts. Coal : *normal* 410 tons ; *maximum* 1210 tons.

Armour Notes.— Belt is 7½ feet wide by 290 feet long from bow. Lower edge is 9½″ thick amidships. Upper belt (lower deck side), 190 feet long. 2″ screens in battery.
Gunnery Notes.— Loading positions, big guns : all round. Hoists : electric for all guns. Big guns manœuvred electrically.
Arcs of fire : 13 in. and 8 in. guns 255 ; battery guns 100.
Ammunition carried : 13 in., 60 rounds per gun ; 8 in., 150 per gun.
Height of guns above water : Big guns 18 feet ; 8 in. 25 feet, 5 in. 11 feet.
Torpedo Notes. Whiteheads.
Engineering Notes.— Machinery, &c., weight 1100 tons.

Name.	Builders.	Laid down.	Completed.	40 hours n.d.	4 hours forced.
Kearsage	Newport News	June 96	1900	—11·1	16·81
Kentucky	Newport News	June 96	1900	—11·9	16·89

Kentucky at full displacement (12996 tons), made a four hours forced trial and reached 16·33 kts.
Coal consumption : 12 tons an hour at 10,500 H.P. (16 kts.) ; 9 tons an hour at 8,000 H.P. (15 kts.)
General Notes.—Cost complete, about £900,000.
Differences :

Name.	After bridge.
Kearsage	2 bridges
Kentucky	Only 1

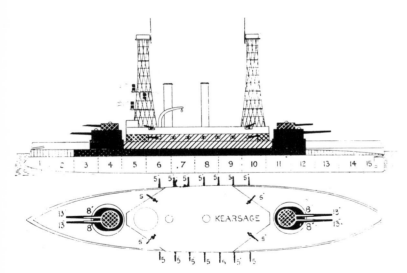

KEARSAGE (taken 1903). *Photo, Symonds.*

KENTUCKY turrets (port side) (1906) *Photo, Loeffler.*

KEARSAGE after refit 1909–11

KENTUCKY after refit 1911

(ALABAMA CLASS—3 SHIPS).

ALABAMA (May, 1898), **ILLINOIS** (October, 1898), **WISCONSIN** (November, 1898).

Normal displacement 11,552 tons. *Full load displacement* 12,150 tons. Complement 490.

Length (*waterline*), 368 feet. Beam, 72 feet. *Mean draught*, 23½ feet.

SUNK AS TARGET   SCRAPPED   SCRAPPED

Guns :	Armour (Harvey-nickel) :
4—13 inch, 35 cal. (*A.A.A.*).	16½—14″ Belt .... *aaaa-aaa*
14—6 inch, 40 cal. (*F*).	4″ Belt (bow) .... *d*
6—6 pdr.	4″ Deck (slopes) ....
6—6 pdr. (semi-automatic).	12″ Bulkhead .... *aaa*
4—1 pdr.	Protection to vitals ...... =*aaaaa*
4—1 pdr. (automatic).	14″ Turrets .... *aaaa*
4 Colts.	15″—10″ Turret bases ...*aaaaa*
2 Field guns (3 inch).	5¼″ Lower deck .... *c*
Torpedo tubes (18 inch) :	5¼″ Battery .... *c*
4 *above water* (armoured).	6″ Casemates .... *b*
(Removed in *Illinois*).	10′ Conning tower .... *aa*
	(Total *circa* 3,500 tons).

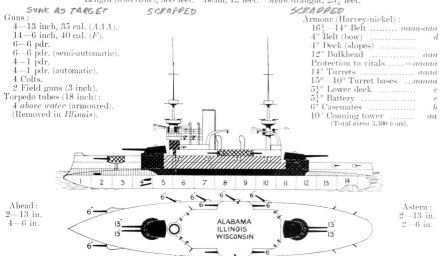

ALABAMA. (1906)   *Photo, copyright, W. Rau.*

Ahead :
2—13 in.
4—6 in.

Astern :
2—13 in.
2—6 in.

Broadside : 4—13 in., 7—6 in.

Machinery : 2 sets vertical triple expansion. 3 cylinders. 2 screws. Boilers : Cylindrical ; 8 single ended. Designed H.P. *forced* 10,000=16 kts. Coal : *normal* 850 tons ; *maximum* 1,450 tons.

Armour Notes.—Main belt is 7½ feet wide by about 178 feet long, continued to bow with 4″ plates ; lower edge is 9½″ thick, and only top strake is full thickness. Armour, without deck, weighs 2800 tons. 3 feet cofferdam behind waterline belt. 1½″ screens in battery.

Gunnery Notes.—Loading positions, big guns : all round. Big guns manœuvred, electric gear. Arcs of fire : Big guns, 270° ; casemate guns, 135° ; battery guns, 110°.

Engineering Notes.—

Name.	Built at	Laid down	Completed	Full power on 33 kt. course.
Alabama	Cramp's	December, '96	1900	=17·45
Illinois	Newport News	February, '97	1901	11,920=16·20
Wisconsin	Union Works, 'Frisco	February, '97	1901	12,322=17·17

Wisconsin also did a 48 hours trial, I.H.P. 7,700=15·8 kts. *mean*. Coal consumption : somewhat large.

Cost, *complete, per ship about* £950,000.

WISCONSIN. (1906)   *Photo, S. Ballou, Esq.*

Differences.—

Name.	Cranes.	Lower part of fore mast.	Yards per mast.	Shields to 6 pdrs. on bridges.
Alabama	4	stout	1	......
Illinois	2	slight	1	......
Wisconsin	2	stout	2	none

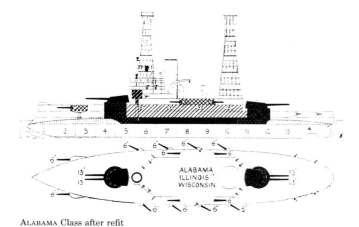

ALABAMA Class after refit

WISCONSIN. (1911)

(MAINE CLASS.—3 SHIPS).

OHIO (May, 1901), **MAINE** (July, 1901), **MISSOURI** (December, 1901).

Normal displacement 12,500 tons. *Full load* displacement 13,500 tons. Complement 551.
Length (*waterline*), 388 feet ; Beam, 72¼ feet ; *Mean* draught, 24 feet ; Length over all, 394 feet.

Guns (M. '99) :   ALL SCRAPPED
  4—12 inch, III. (*AAAA*).
  16—6 inch, VI., 50 cal. (*C*).
  6—14 pdr.
  8—3 pdr.
  6—1 pdr. (automatic)
  2—1 pdr. (R.F.)
  2 Colts.
  4 Machine.
Torpedo tubes (18 inch) :
  2 *submerged.*
  (Total weight with ammunition,
  1058 tons).

Armour (Krupp) :
  11″ Belt (amidships) ... *aaa*
  4″ Belt (bow) .... *d*
  10″ Bulkhead (aft) ...... *aaa*
  2½″ Deck (on slopes) ...
  Protection to vitals = *aaaa*
  4″ Deck (aft) ....
  12″ Turrets (H.N.)...... *aaa*
  12″—8″ Turret bases...*aaa-a*
  6″ Lower deck side ...... *a*
  6″ Battery (*see notes*)... *a-b*
  6″ Casemates (forward) ... *b*
  10″ Conning tower..... *aa*
  (Total weight 3053 tons).

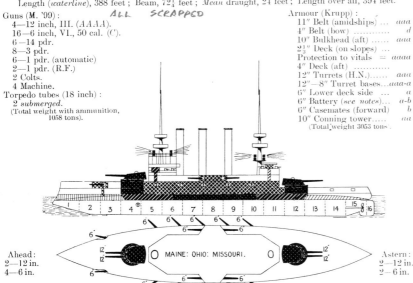

MISSOURI.   *Photo by favour of H. Reuterdahl, Esq.*

Maine has a white after turret ; *Missouri* a buff one.   (1906)

Ahead :
2—12 in.
4—6 in.

 MAINE: OHIO: MISSOURI.

Astern :
2—12 in.
2—6 in.

Broadside : 4—12 in., 8—6 in.

Machinery : 2 sets vertical inverted triple expansion 3 cylinder, except *Missouri* which is 4 cylinder.
2 screws. Boilers : 12 Thornycroft, except *Maine*, 12 Babcock. Designed H.P. 16,000 = 18 kts.
Coal : normal 1,000 tons ; maximum 2,000 tons.
Armour Notes.—Belt is 7½ feet wide by 300 feet long from bow. Lower edge is 7½ in. amidships at
1 foot below water. Armour without deck weighs 2453 tons. Deck 600 tons. Cornpith belt
along water line. Battery K.C. to sills of ports ; above that K.N.C. (*b*).
Gunnery Notes.—Loading positions, big guns : all round. Hoists : electric for all guns. Big guns
manœuvred electrically.
  Arcs of fire : Big guns 270° ; 6 in. 110°.
  Ammunition carried : 12 in., 60 rounds per gun ; 6 in., 200 per gun (only ⅔ of this normally carried).
  Height of guns above water : Bow turret 26½ feet ; After turret guns 19 feet ; Conning tower 34½ feet.
Engineering Notes.—Machinery, &c. (with water) weighs 1396 tons. Trials :—

OHIO   *Photo by favour of S. Ballou, Esq.*

Name.	Where built.	Laid down.	Completed.	33 kt. sea trial, 125 revolutions.	Mean speeds :	Boilers.
Maine	Cramp's	Feb. '99	1902	16,000=18·3 (*max.* 18.9).		Niclausse
Missouri	Newport News	Feb. '00	1903	=18·22 (*max.* 18.75).		Thornycroft
Ohio	Union Works, Frisco	April '99	Sept. '01	16,498=17·82		Thornycroft

Coal consumption at 10,000 H.P. about 9¾ tons per hour ; at 16,000 H.P. about 16¾ tons per hour (18 kts.)
General Notes : Hull weighs 4836 tons ; stores 677. Displacement with full stores, coal and ammunition
is 13,500 tons. All joiners work fireproof wood. Pneumatic w.t. doors fitted.

Differences:

Name.	Funnels.	Steam pipes, fore funnel.	
Maine	Very high	Very conspicuous	Big hawse pipes.
Missouri	Very high	Not conspicuous	2 very high ventilators aft, small and high hawse pipes
Ohio	Much shorter	Not conspicuous	Small hawse pipes.

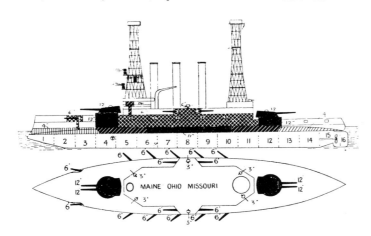

MAINE Class after refit

OHIO.
Shorter funnels.
Round top on main.
Small hawse pipes.
High cowls close aft of
main mast on super-
structure.

MAINE
Prominent steam pipes
to fore funnel.
Big hawse pipes.

MISSOURI
Small hawse pipes.

MISSOURI. (1911)   *Photo by favour of Collier's Weekly*

SUNK AS TARGET   SUNK AS TARGET
(New Jersey Class—5 Ships).

VIRGINIA (April, 1904), **NEW JERSEY** (November, 1904), **GEORGIA** (October, 1904),
NEBRASKA (October, 1904), **RHODE ISLAND** (May, 1904).
SCRAPPED   SCRAPPED   SCRAPPED

Normal displacement 14,948 tons. *Full load* displacement 16,094 tons. Complement 703.
Length (*waterline*), 435 feet. Beam, 76½ feet. *Maximum* draught, 26 feet. Length *over all* 441 feet.

Guns—(Model, '99) :
4—12 inch, 40 cal. (*AAAA*).
8—8 inch, 45 cal. (*A*).
12—6 inch, 50 cal. (*C*).
20—14 pdr.
12—3 pdr.
4—1 pdr. (automatic).
4—1 pdr. (R.F.)
8 Colts.
Torpedo tubes (21 inch) :
4 *submerged*.
(Total weight without ammunition,
805 tons).
(Two-thirds ammunition 408 tons).

Armour—(Krupp and H N.) :
11″ Belt (amidships) ... *aaa*
4″ Belt (ends) .... *d*
3″ Deck (flat on belt amidships)
Protection to vitals ...... *aaa*
10″—7″ Barbettes (H.N.) *aaa*
12″—8″ Turrets (H.N.) ...*aaa*
6″ Secondary turrets ... *b*
6″ Lower deck side (H.N.) *b*
6″ Battery (H.N.) .... *b*
2″ on 14 pdr. guns ...... *f*
9″ Conning tower (K.N.C.) *aa*
(Total weight 3,690 tons).

(1906)   *Photo by favour of H. Reuterdahl, Esq.*

Ahead :
2—12 in.
6—8 in.
2—6 in.

NEW JERSEY CLASS

Astern :
2—12 in.
6—8 in.
2—6 in.

Broadside : 4—12 in., 6—8 in., 6—6 in.

Machinery : 2 sets 4 cylinder vertical inverted triple expansion. 2 screws. Boilers : 12 Babcock
or 24 Niclausse. Designed H.P. 25,463=19 kts. Coal : *normal* 900 tons ; *maximum* 1,967 tons.

Armour Notes.—Belt is 8 feet wide, 7 feet of it below waterline (at *maximum* draught) ; lower edge
is 25% thinner than at waterline, except at bow and stern. Protective deck flat on belt amidships,
but reinforces sides at ends.

Gunnery Notes.—Loading positions, big guns : all round. Hoists : electric, to all guns : serve : 12 in., 1 in
30 seconds ; 8 in., 1 in 20 seconds ; 6 in., 3 per minute. Big guns manœuvred electrically.
Secondary turrets electrically.
Arcs of fire : 12 in., 270° ; superposed 8 in., 270° ; beam 8 in., 180° ; battery 6 in., 110° (55° before
and abaft).
Ammunition carried : 12 in., 60 per gun ; 8 in., 125 per gun ; 6 in., 200 per gun (only ⅔ normally
carried).
Height of guns above water : 12 in., 26½ feet ; axial, 8 in., 32 feet ; side 8 in., 26 feet ; battery
guns, 12 feet.

Engineering Notes.—Machinery weighs 1,730 tons + 100 tons reserve water.

Name.	Builders.	Laid down	Completed	Trials	Boilers.
New Jersey	Fore River Co.	April, '02	Mar. '06	—	Babcock
Georgia	Bath Ironworks	April, '02	Mar. '06	—	Babcock
Nebraska	Moran Bros.	July, '02	Sept. '06	—	Babcock
Rhode Island	Fore River Co.	May, '02	Feb. '06	—19·4 (*Max*).	Babcock
Virginia	Newport News	May, '02	Feb. '06	—	Babcock

General Notes.—Stores carried : 970 tons. Cost, *complete,* per ship, estimated at £1,300,000 or more.

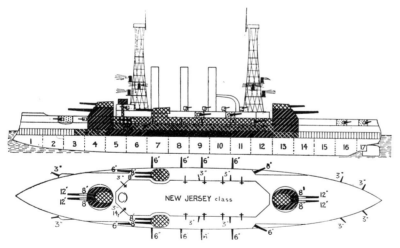

New Jersey Class after refit

Differences: Georgia has windsails instead of cowls. *N. Jersey* and *V.* have s.l. platform between the funnels.
Virginia, Nebraska and *Rhode Island* have round main tops. *N.J.* & *G.* rectangular.

Nebraska (1914)

(LOUISIANA CLASS. 2 SHIPS).

LOUISIANA (August, 1904) & **CONNECTICUT** (September, 1904).

Normal displacement 16,000 tons. *Full load* 17,570 tons. Complement 916 as flagship.

Length (*waterline*), 450 feet. *Beam*, 76¾ feet. *Maximum draught*, 26½ feet. *Length over all*, 456½ feet.

ALL SCRAPPED

Guns :
4—12 inch, 45 cal. (A.A.A.A.)
8—8 inch, 45 cal. (A).
12—7 inch, 50 cal. (B).
20—14 pdr.
12—3 pdr.
4—1 pdr. S.A.
2—·30 (automatic).
2—·30 (machine).
2—Field guns, 3 inch.
Torpedo tubes (21 in.) :
4 submerged.
(Total weight with ⅔ ammunition, 1536 tons).

Armour (Krupp) :
11″ Belt (amidships) ...... *aaa*
4″ Belt (ends) .... *d*
3″ Deck (flat on belt) ..... *aaa*
Protection to vitals is ...
10″—8″ Turrets (N.S.) ... *aaa-a*
12″ Turret bases (N.C.) ... *aaa*
7″ Lower deck redoubt ... *a*
2″ Battery .... *a*
7″ Casemates (14 pdr.) ... *f*
6″ Secondary turrets (N.C.) *b*
9″ Conning tower .... *aa*
5″ Signal tower .... *c*
(Total weight 3992 tons.)

(1906)   *Photo by favour of "Collier's Weekly."*

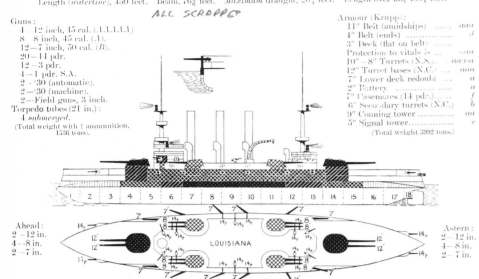

Ahead :
2—12 in.
4—8 in.
2—7 in.

LOUISIANA

Astern :
2—12 in.
4—8 in.
2—7 in.

Broadside : 4—12 in., 4—8 in., 6—7 in.

Machinery : 2 sets vertical 4 cylinder triple expansion. 2 screws (outward turning). Boilers : 12 Babcock (1906 model) in 3 compartments. Designed H.P. 16,500 = 18.5 kts. Coal : *normal* 900 tons ; *maximum* 2380 tons.

Notes.—All notes to *Kansas* class apply to these which differ only in disposition of the armour deck and belt thickness

	Name.	Builder.	Laid down.	Completed.	Trials.	Boilers.
Authorized 1902	Louisiana	Newport News	Feb., '03	June '06		Babcock
	Connecticut	New York Yard	April, '03	June '06		Babcock

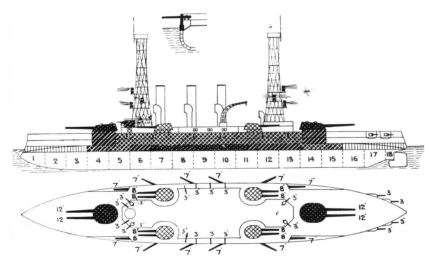

LOUISIANA. (1911)   *Photo, J. Romanes, Esq.*

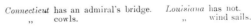

Connecticut has an admiral's bridge.   *Louisiana* has not.
     „   cowls.   „   wind sails.

CONNECTICUT. (1914)   *Photo, Silk.*

Connecticut has an admiral's bridge.   *Louisiana* has not.
Connecticut has at present black painted waterline like British ships.

U. S. BATTLESHIPS (18 knot). First of class laid down 1904

(Kansas Class—4 Ships).

KANSAS (Sept., 1905), **VERMONT** (Aug., 1905), **MINNESOTA** (April, 1905), & **NEW HAMPSHIRE** (–1906).

Normal displacement 16,000 tons. *Full load* displacement, 17,650 tons. Complement 916 (as flagship).

Length (*waterline*), 450 feet. Beam, 76¾ feet. *Maximum* draught, 26¾ feet. Length *over all*, 456⅓ feet.

ALL SCRAPPED

Guns :
4—12 inch, 45 cal. (A⁵).
8—8 inch, 45 cal. (A).
12—7 inch, 50 cal. (B).
20—3 inch, 14 pdr.
2—3 pdr. S.A.
4—1 pdr. S.A.
2 Machine ·30
2 Automatic ·30
2 Field guns, 3 inch.
Torpedo tubes (21 inch) :
4 *submerged*.
(Total weight with ⅔ ammunition 1468½ tons).
(Armament only, 1063 tons).

Armour (Krupp) :
9″ Belt (amidships) .... aa
4″ Belt (ends) .... d
3″ Deck (slopes) ....
Protection to vitals .... = aaa
7″ Lower deck side .... a
10″ Barbettes .... aa
12-8″ Turrets to these ....aaa-a
7″ Battery ....
2″ Casemates (for 14 pdrs.).
6″-4″ Small turrets .... b-d
9″ Conning tower .... a
5″ Director station (near C.T.) c
(Total weight 3920½ tons).

Vermont (1911)   *Photo, J. Romanes, Esq.*

New Hampshire (1911)

Differences.—*New Hampshire* has peculiar funnels (*see photo*).
M. has low cowls : V. & K. high ones.
M. has round top to main mast : all the others have rectangular.

Ahead :
2—12 in.
4—8 in.
2—7 in.

KANSAS class

Astern :
2 12 in.
4 8 in.
2 7 in.

Broadside : 4 —12 in., 4 —8 in., 6 —7 in.

Machinery : 2 sets vertical 4 cylinder triple expansion. 2 screws (outward turning). Boilers : 12 Babcock. Designed H.P. 16,500 = 18 kts. Coal : *normal* 900 tons ; *maximum* 2388 tons (2592 in *N. Hampshire*).

Armour Notes.—Main belt is 9½ feet wide, thick part 285 feet long, gradually thinning to 1′ armour 8 feet wide at ends ; lower edge always 25% less thick than waterline. Belt is K.C. up to sills of main deck gun ports, above that H.N. or K.N.C.

Gunnery Notes.—Loading positions, big guns : all round. Hoists, electric big guns. Big guns manœuvred electrically. Secondary turrets electric control. Arcs of fire : Big guns, 270° ; Secondary turrets, 135° ; 7 inch guns, 110°. Ammunition carried : *normal* 12 inch, 40 rounds per gun ; 8 inch, 100 per gun ; 7 inch, 100 per gun ; full supply ⅓ more. Hand hoists to 8 inch and 7 inch guns, also hand loading.

Torpedo Notes.—21 inch tubes fitted 190s.

Engineering Notes.—Machinery weighs 1500 tons ; ⅔ stores 26½ tons ; reserve water 66 tons. Heating surface 46,750 sq. feet. Grate area 1100 sq. ft. Working pressure, 265lbs. Funnels 100 feet high. Water carried 17,000 gallons. 33 Blowers for forced ventilation. Coal consumption at 10 kts. is 3⅓ tons an hour. Economical ships.

Name.	Builders	Machinery	Laid down	Completed	Refit	Trials	Boilers	Best recent speed
Kansas	Camden N.J.		'04	Apr., '07		19,302 = 18·09	Babcock	18·96
Vermont	Fore River Co.		'04	May, '07		17,624 = 18·33	Babcock	18·96
Minnesota	Newport News		'04	Dec. '06		19,896 = 18·85	Babcock	18·42
New Hampshire	Camden N.J.		'05	'08			Babcock	18·52

General Notes.—Boats, etc., weigh 51½ tons. Masts and spars 31 tons. ‡ Miscellaneous stores 81½ tons. ‡ Small stores, provisions, etc., 144½ tons. Crew, etc., 110 tons. 35 Sliding water-tight doors, and 6 armoured hatches. Freeboard 20½ feet. Authorised 1903 and 1904. These ships are excellent seaboats.

FUNNELS.

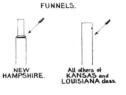

NEW HAMPSHIRE.   All others of KANSAS and LOUISIANA class.

Kansas. (1914)   *Photo, J. H. Hare, Collier's Weekly.*

Vermont.   (Note to photo : Main deck battery now removed.)   *Photo, U.S. Naval Air Service.* (1919)

(IDAHO CLASS—2 SHIPS.)

IDAHO (December, 1905), & **MISSISSIPPI** (September, 1905).

Normal displacement 13,000 tons. *Full load* displacement 14,465 tons. Complement 720.

Length (*waterline*), 375 feet. Beam, 77 feet. *Mean* draught, 24¾ feet. Length *over all*, 382 feet.

KILKIS   TO GREECE   LEMNOS

SUNK 1941

Guns :
4—12 inch, 45 cal. (A⁵).
8—8 inch, 45 cal. (A).
8—7 inch, 45 cal. (B).
12—3 inch, 14 pdr.
6—3 pdr.
4—1 pdr.
6—·30 (automatic).
2—·30 (machine).
2 Field guns.
Torpedo tubes (21 inch) :
2 *submerged*.

Armour (Krupp) :
9″—7″ Belt (amidships)   *aa-a*
4″ Belt (ends) ....   *d*
3″ Armour deck ....
Protection to vitals ... = *aaa*
12″—8″ Turrets ...... = *aaa-a*
10″—7½″ T'ret bases(NC) *aa-a*
6″ Secondary turrets (N.C.)   *b*
7″ Lower deck (redoubt) ...   *a*
7″ Battery (redoubt) ...   *a*
9″ Conning tower ......   *aa*
(Total weight 3377 tons).

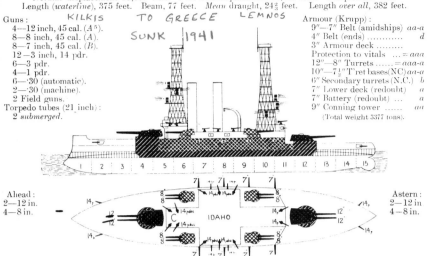

Ahead :
2—12 in.
4—8 in.

Astern :
2—12 in
4—8 in.

Broadside : 4—12 in., 4—8 in., 4—7 in.

Machinery : 2 sets vertical 4 cylinder triple expansion. 2 screws. Boilers : 8 Babcock. Designed H.P. 10,000=17 kts. Coal : *normal*, 750 tons ; *maximum*, 1841 tons.

Armour Notes.—Main belt is 9¼ feet wide by 244 feet long ; lower edge is 7″ amidships, 5″ at turret bases. Turret bases only 10″ where exposed ; only faces of turrets are 12″. 3″ tubes to 8″ turrets.

Gunnery Notes.—Loading positions, big guns : all round. Hoists, electric all guns. Big guns manœuvred electrically ; secondary guns, electric and hand gear.
Arcs of fire : 12 in., 270° ; 8 in., 135° ; 7 in., 110°.
Ammunition carried : 12 in., 60 rounds per gun ; 8 in. and 7 in., 125 per gun. (Only ⅔ of this carried normally.)
Height of guns above water : Bow turret, 26½ feet ; after turret, 19 feet ; 8 inch guns, 26 feet ; 7 in. guns, 11 feet. *Idaho* has trunked-in hoists to 12 inch guns.

Torpedo Notes.—Whitehead torpedoes.

Name	Builder	Machinery	Laid down	Com-pleted	Trials (mean)	Boilers	Best recent speed
Idaho	Cramp's	Cramp	May,'04	1908	= 17·25	Babcock	17·15
Mississippi	Cramp's	Cramp	May,'04	Jan., '08	= 16·75	Babcock	17·02

Idaho reached a maximum of 18·4 on trial.

General Notes.—Estimated cost *complete*, was about £900,000 per ship. Authorised, 1903. They are particularly interesting ships as they put into practice the "moderate dimensions" theory. These ships have experimental fire controls on top of the conning tower.

(S. CAROLINA CLASS—2 SHIPS.)

SOUTH CAROLINA (1908), & **MICHIGAN** (May, 1908).

Normal displacement 16,000 tons. *Full load* displacement 17,617 tons. Complement 869.

Length (*waterline*), 450 feet. Beam, 80¼ feet. *Mean* draught, 24½ feet. Length *over all*,   feet.

ALL SCRAPPED

Guns :
8—12 inch, 45 cal. (A⁵).
22—3 inch. 14 pdr.
2—3 pdr. (semi-automatic).
8—1 pdr. (semi-automatic).
4—·30 (automatic).
2 Field guns (3 inch).
Torpedo tubes (21 inch).
2 *submerged*.
(Total about 1150 tons.)

Armour (Krupp) :
12″—10″ Belt (amidships)........ *aaa*
1½″ Belt (ends) .... *f*
3″ Armour deck (slopes)
Protection to vitals .... = *aaaa*
10″ Bulkheads ....*aaa*
12″—8″ Turrets (N.C.) ....*aaa-a*
10″—8″ Turret bases (N.C.) ......*aa*
10″—8″ Lower deck, redoubt *aaa-aa*
12″ Conning tower (N.C.).........*aaaa*
9″ tube .... *aa*
(about 4000 tons).

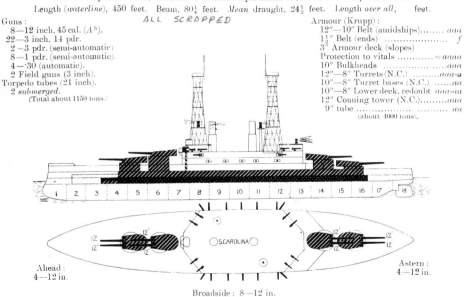

Ahead :
4—12 in.

Astern :
4—12 in.

Broadside : 8—12 in.

Machinery : 2 sets vertical 4 cylinder triple expansion. 2 screws (outward turning). Boilers : 12 Babcock (1906 model) in 3 compartments. Designed H.P. 16,500=18.5 kts. Coal : *normal* 900 tons ; *maximum* 2380 tons.

Armour Notes.— Main belt, 8 feet wide ; 6¾ feet of it below waterline ; lower edge, 10″. Amidships it is 12″, under the turrets 11½″. Redoubt belt 8″ at upper edge, 10″ lower. Low turrets with small bases. Fronts of turrets, 12″, sides, 8″. Redoubt, 300 ft. long.

Gunnery Notes.—Loading positions, big guns : all round. Special sights. Hoists, electric. Big guns manœuvred electrically. Arcs of fire, 270° each turret. Fore Turret guns 24 ft. above water, "after fore turret" guns 32 feet. Barbette of this rises 12 feet above the deck. Twelve hoists for 14 pdr.

Engineering Notes.—Pressure, 265 lbs. Revolutions full power=121. Machinery, etc., weighs 1600 tons.

Name	Builder	Laid down	Completed	Trials (mean)		Boilers	Best recent speed
S. Carolina	Cramp	Nov., '06	Sept., '09			Babcock	19
Michigan	N.Y. Ship Bldg. Co.	Dec., '06	Oct., '09	13,253 = 17·95	16,016 = 18·78	Babcock	20·01

General Notes.—Authorised 1905. These ships, though laid down after, were projected *before* the British *Dreadnought* : and so may be considered as the first "Dreadnoughts" (*i.e.* all big gun ships). They are good sea boats but roll heavily.

(1911)

Differences :—None. Both these ships have fore top round and main top rectangular.

U. S. DREADNOUGHTS.   (First of class laid down, Nov., 1906)   Nos **1** & **2**

SOUTH CAROLINA (1911)   *Photo by favour of Collier's Weekly. Copyright, Stebbins.*

MICHIGAN (1911)

Differences.—*Michigan* carries steam launch athwart ships abaft after funnel. S. C. has emergency cabin in base of main mast, M. has not. Both have old type platforms to masts.

(Delaware Class—2 Ships).

DELAWARE (February, 1909), & **NORTH DAKOTA** (November, 1908). U. S. DREADNOUGHTS. (First of class laid down November, 1907.) Nos. **4 & 3**

Normal Displacement, 20,000 tons. Full load, 22,000 tons. Complement, 930.
Length (*waterline*), 510 feet. Beam, 85¼ feet. *Mean* draught, 27 feet. Length *over all*, 518¾ feet.

ALL SCRAPPED

Guns :
  10—12 inch, 45 cal. (A⁵)
  14—5 inch, R.F.
  2—3 pdr.
  4—1 pdr., S.A.
  2 Machine, 30 cal.
  2 Field guns (3 inch).
Torpedo tubes (21 inch).
  2 submerged.

Armour (Krupp) :
  11″ Belt (amidships) ....aaa
  ″ Belt (ends)................
  ″ Deck (slopes)..............
  Protection to vitals ......= aaaa
  10″ Upper belt (amidships) aaa
  12″-8″ Turrets (N.C.) = aaaa-aaa
  Turret bases (N.C.).........
  5″ Battery (amidships) (N.C.)...c

DELAWARE, 1911, with forward sponson removed.

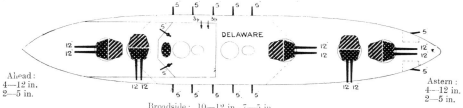

Ahead :
4—12 in.
2—5 in.

DELAWARE

Astern :
4—12 in.
2—5 in.

Broadside : 10—12 in., 7—5 in.

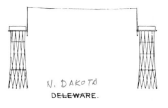

N. DAKOTA
DELAWARE.

Machinery : *Delaware*, 2 sets triple expansion. 2 screws. *N. Dakota*, Curtis turbines. screws. Boilers : 14 Babcock. Designed H.P. 25,000 = 21 kts. Coal: *normal* 1016 tons ; *maximum* 2650 tons. Also 380 tons oil.
Gunnery Notes.—Magazines fitted with refrigerators. 3 pdrs. mounted extreme aft of superstructure on starboard side.
Armour Notes.—Main belt 8 feet wide, 6¾ feet of it below waterline at full load displacement, 11″ thick amidships, upper belt, 7¾ feet wide. Splinter-proof armour on uptakes and ventilators within citadel and in battery and upper deck.
Engineering Notes.—Full speed, *Delaware* = 128 revs. *N. Dakota*, 263 r.p.m. for 21 kts., 229 for 19 kts ., 142½ for 12 kts. Trial consumption: 1·83 lbs. per H.P. all purposes. At 12 kts. *Delaware* burned 100 tons per 24 hours, *N. Dakota* 140 tons.
Nominal Radii : About 6500 at 12 kts., 4600 at 18 kts., 3000 at 21·5 kts. for *N. Dakota*. Somewhat more for *Delaware*.
These ships have especially large boilers. The grates are 7ft. long by 11¾ft. wide = about 100 sq. ft. per boiler.
General Notes.—*N. Dakota* has now a torpedo defence control platform abaft after funnel. She has wooden yards instead of steel ones. Authorised 1906. Cost, without armament, £789,200.

Name.	Builder.	Laid down	Completed	Refit	Trials	Boilers	Best recent speed
Delaware	Newport News	Nov., 1907	Oct., 1909		28,578 = 21·56	Babcock	21·98
North Dakota	Fore River Co.	Dec., 1907	Nov., 1909		28,578 = 21·56	Babcock	22·25

These ships are splendid sea-boats and successful in every way.

1914 rig. NORTH DAKOTA.
Photo. H. Reuterdahl, Esq.

DETAILS OF DELAWARE.
Photo, Miller. (1914)

DELEWARE
N. DAKOTA.

1909 U. S. DREADNOUGHTS Nos. **6** & **5**

(Utah Class—2 Ships.)

UTAH (Dec. 1909), & **FLORIDA** (May, 1910).

Normal displacement 21,825 tons. *Full load*, 23,033 tons. Complement, 940 (as flagship, 995).

Length (*waterline*), 510 feet. *Beam*, 88¼ feet. *Mean* draught, 28½ feet. Length *over all*, 521½ feet.

[handwritten: SUNK 12/7/41 PEARL HARBOR / SCRAPPED]

Guns :
10—12 inch, 45 cal. (A⁵).
16—5 inch, 51 cal.
4—6 pdr.
2—1 pdr.
2 machine.
2—3 inch Ldg. guns.
Torpedo tubes (21 inch) :
2 submerged.

Armour (Midvale) :
11″ Belt (amidships)............ *aaa*
3″ Belt (ends) .... *e*
″ Deck (slopes) ....
Protection to vitals............ *=aaaa*
10″ Upper belt (amidships)... *aaa*
12″—8″ Turrets (N.C.) = *aaaa-aaa*
Turret bases ....
6½″ Battery amidships ...... *a*
6½″ Casemates .... *a*

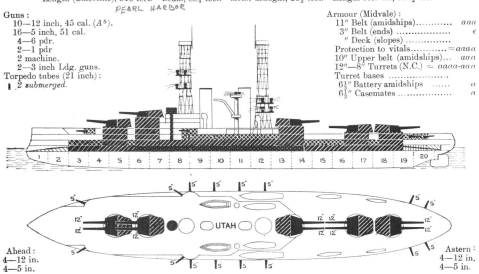

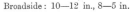

Ahead :
4—12 in.
4—5 in.

Astern :
4—12 in.
4—5 in.

Broadside : 10—12 in., 8—5 in.

FLORIDA, 1914.   *Photo, H. Reuterdahl, Esq.*

Differences.—*Florida* has lattice yards
Utah „ solid „

Machinery : Parsons turbine. 4 screws. Boilers : 12 Babcock. Designed H.P. 28,000=20·75 kts.
Coal : *normal* 1667 tons ; *maximum* 2520 tons. Oil, 400 tons. *Nominal* radius, 6720 miles at 10 kts.

Armour Notes.—Main belt 8¼ feet wide ; upper belt 8 feet wide. 2″ splinter bulkheads between all 5 inch battery guns, ¼″ wall in rear. Special subdivision and powerful pumping system against damage by mines or torpedoes.

Gunnery Notes.—Height of guns above water : in fore fore-turret, 33 feet ; after fore-turret, 40 feet ; amidship turret, 32 feet ; in after pair of turrets, 25 feet.

Engineering Notes.—Grate area : 1428 sq. feet. Heating surface : 64,234 sq. feet. Weight of machinery : 2060 tons. Electrical installation : 4 sets, each 300 k.w., 125 volts, 2400 amps., by General Electric Co. *Florida* on trials developed 41,004 shaft h.p. In *Utah* 192 r.p.m.=12 kts. ; 313=21 kts. Searchlights : 16.

Name	Builders	Machinery	Laid down	Completed	Trials	Turbines	Boilers	Best recent speed
Florida	N.Y.Shipbld.Co New York Y.	N.Y. Shipbld. Co. New York Yard	Mar.,'09	Aug.,'11	=22·08	Parsons	Babcock	
Utah			Mar.,'09	Aug.,'11	27,445=21·04	Parsons	Babcock	

General Notes.—Authorised 1908. Contracts awarded, 1908. *Florida* fitted as flagship.
Between 1924–26 both ships were refitted and modernised. The mainmast was replaced by a pole mast, a catapult was fitted on the midships' turret and aircraft cranes fitted either side of the single remaining funnel. The bridgework was much altered.

UTAH. (1914)   *Photo, Müller.*

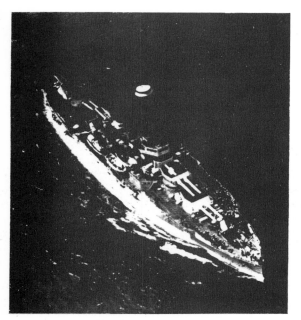

FLORIDA   Aircraft View from starboard bow. (1924)

1934 *Photo.*

UTAH (New York S.B. Corpn., Dec. 23, 1909). Ex-battleship employed as wireless controlled target ship. *Standard* displacement : 19,800 tons. Dimensions : 512 (*w.l.*) × 106 × 22½ feet (*mean* draught). Parsons turbines. White-Forster boilers. Speed originally was 21 kts.

1910 U. S. DREADNOUGHTS Nos. **8 & 7**

(ARKANSAS CLASS—2 SHIPS.)
ARKANSAS (Jan., 1911), & **WYOMING** (May, 1911).
Normal displacement, 26,000 tons. *Full load,* 27,243 tons. Complement, 1036 (as flagship, 1091).
Length (*waterline*), 554 feet. Beam, 93¼ feet. *Mean draught,* 28½ feet. Length *over all,* 562 feet.

SUNK AS TARGET   SCRAPPED
BIKINI

Guns :
12—12 inch, 50 cal. (A⁶).
21—5 inch, 51 cal.
4—3 pdr. (saluting)
Torpedo tubes (21 inch) :
2 *submerged.*

Armour (Midvale) :
11″ Belt amidships ...... *aaa*
5″ Belt (ends) .... *c*
12″ Turrets .... = *aaaa*
11″ Turret bases .... *aa*
6½″ Battery .... *a*

WYOMING. (1914)   *Photo by favour of H. Reuterdahl, Esq.*

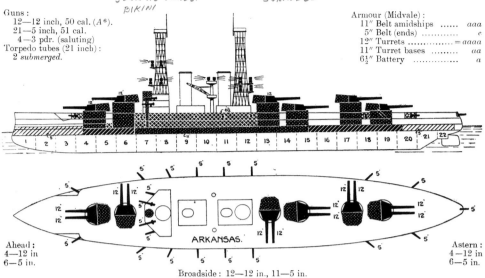

Ahead :
4—12 in
6—5 in.

Astern :
4—12 in
6—5 in.

Broadside : 12—12 in., 11—5 in.

FORE TURRETS, ETC., ARKANSAS. (1914)   *Photo, H. Reuterdahl, Esq.*

Machinery : Parsons turbine. 4 screws. Boilers : 12 Babcock. Designed H.P. 28,000 = 20·5 kts.
Coal : *normal* 1669 tons ; *maximum* 2500 tons. Oil, 400 tons.
Gunnery Notes.—Height of guns above water: No. 1 turret, 28½ feet; No. 2, 36¼ feet; No. 3, 33 feet; No 4, 25 feet; No. 5, 31¼ feet; No. 6, 23¼ feet.
Arcs of training: (1) 300°, (2) 270°, (3) 280°, (4) 260°, (5) 330°, (6) 300°.
Armour Notes.—Main belt 400 feet long, goes 6 feet below l.w.l.
Engineering Notes.—Approximately 148 r.p.m. = 10·5 kts., 215 = 15 kts., 300 = 20 kts., 320 = 22 kts. Grate area: 1428 sq. feet. Heating surface: 64,234 sq. feet Weight of machinery: 2177 tons. Electrical installation: 4 sets each 300 k.w., 125 volts, 2400 amps. by General Electric Co. Searchlights: 16.

Name	Builder	Machinery	Laid down	Completed	Trials (mean) 24 hrs. at 19	4 hrs. f.p.	Boilers	Best recent speed
Arkansas	N.Y.Shipbld. Co	N.Y. Shipbld. Co.	Jan.,'10	Sept.,'12	=	28,697 = 21·05	Babcock	21·15
Wyoming	Cramp	Cramp	Feb.,'10	Sept.,'12	20,784 = 19·21	31,601 = 21·22	Babcock	22·45

General Notes.—Authorised 1909. Contracts awarded Sept. & Oct., 1909. Both fitted as flagships. Freeboard: Forward, 25′; amidships, 19′ 2″; at No. 6 turret, 18′; at stern, 16′ 3″.

Between 1925–7 both ships were modified. The bridgework was much altered, the after funnel and mainmast were removed, a catapult was fitted on No 3 turret, two aircraft cranes rigged abreast the funnel and a small tripod mast stepped between Nos 4 and 5 turrets.

WYOMING   Aircraft View from starboard bow. (1924)

Gunnery Training Ship.

(12 inch guns no longer mounted.)   1938, *Wright & Logan.*

WYOMING (May 25, 1911). Displacement : 19,700 tons. Dimensions : 555½ (*w.l.*) × 93 × 23½ feet (*mean* draught). Guns vary according to circumstances, but ship recently mounted a number of 5 inch, 54 cal., with various small AA. Machinery: Parsons turbines. S.H.P.: 28,000 = 21 kts. (present best speed 18 kts.). Boilers of White-Forster type. Distinctive number is *A G* 17.

Notes.—Was built by Cramps as a sister ship to battleship *Arkansas,* described on an earlier page, but was demilitarised under the terms of the London Naval Treaty of 1930, bulges being removed and boiler power reduced. Employed as an anti-aircraft gunnery training ship. Another ex-battleship, the *Utah* (used as a target vessel) was lost at Pearl Harbour, Dec. 7, 1941.

SUNK AS TARGET
BIKINI

(TEXAS CLASS— 2 SHIPS.)

NEW YORK (Oct. 30th, 1912) and **TEXAS** (May 18th, 1912).

MEMORIAL

Displacement $\begin{cases} Normal, 27,000 \text{ tons.} \\ Full\ load, 28,367 \text{ tons.} \end{cases}$ Complement, 1507.

Length (*waterline*) : 565 feet. } Beam 95ft. 2½ins. { *Mean* draught, 28½ feet. }
Length (*over all*) : 573 feet. }   { *Max.* .... 29ft. 7ins. }

Guns (**Dir. Con.** :
    10 —14 inch, 45 cal.
    16 —5 inch, 51 cal.
    8 —3 inch A.A., Mk. III.
    4 —3 pdr. (saluting)
    2 —1 pdr.
    2 M.G.
    2 landing.
Torpedo tubes (21 inch):
    4 submerged.

Armour (Midvale) :
    12" Belt (amidships) .....
    " Belt (ends) ....
    3" Deck ....
    9"–6" Upper Belt
    14"–8" Turrets ....
    12" Barbettes ....
    6" Battery ... .
    12" C.T. ....

Note to Plans.—Corrected to 1921.

Gunnery Notes.—Maximum elevation of 14 inch guns being increased to 30°.

Engineering Notes.—Builders of turbine engines in the U.S. refused to adopt the standards laid down by the Navy Department. Accordingly, in these ships, reciprocating engines were reverted to, to show the turbine builders that the Navy Department was determined to have turbines built to official specification, or else the older type of engines would be taken up again. Cylinders: H.P. 39", I.P. 63", L.P. (2) 83". Stroke: 48". Grate area: 1554 sq. feet. Heating surface: 62,213+3267 sq. feet (superheaters). Weight of machinery: 2375 tons. Electrical installation: 4 sets each of 300 k.w., 125 volts, 2400 amps., by General Electric Co.

Name	Builder	Machinery	Laid down	Completed	Trials:* Full Power.	Boilers	Best recent speed
Texas	Newport News	Newport News	Apl.,'11	Mar.,'14	28,373 = 21·05	Babcock	22
New York	New York Yard	New York Yard	Sept.,'11	Apl.,'14	29,687 = 21·47	Babcock	

* Both ships were light on trials—about 750 tons under normal displacement.

General Notes.—Authorised 1910 as *No. 34 (N.Y.)* and *35 (Texas)*. Both ships fitted as flagships. First design for these ships is said to have included 15—12 inch guns in five triple turrets. Are very economical ships and most successful steamers. *Texas* cost *about* £2,194,000. Big refit, Spring, 1921.

To distinguish.—From *Arkansas* class, only 3 turrets aft ; 2nd funnel set well forward of cage mainmast. From *Utah* class, No. 5 turret superfires over No. 6 ; also upper deck level unbroken and with strong sheer from stern to amidships.

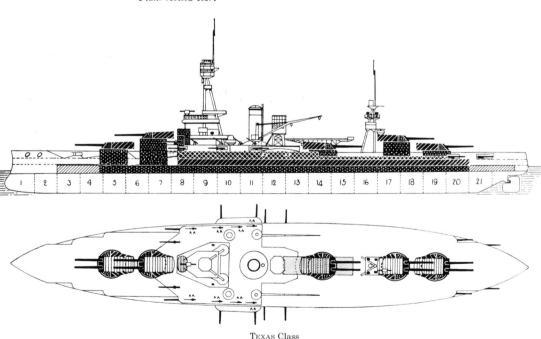

Ahead :
4 —14 in.
2 to 4—5 in.

Broadside : 10 —14 in., 8—5 in. ; 2—21 in. torpedo tubes.

Astern :
4 —14 in.
2 to 4 - 5 in.

Machinery : Vertical triple expansion, 4 cylinder. 2 screws. Boilers : 14 Babcock (8 with superheaters).* Designed H.P. 28,100 = 21 kts. Coal : *normal* tons ; *maximum*, 2918 tons in *New York* ; 2960 tons in *Texas*. Oil : 400 tons in both ships.

* Coal and Oil burning. To be converted to burn oil only.

Plans revised 1927.

(1924)

Aircraft View from starboard quarter. New tops and S.L. positions added to this Class, 1920, as illustration on later page.

TEXAS Class

NEW YORK.
1934 *Photo, Mr. L. Sprague de Camp.*

TEXAS. (No ⟨-faced forebridge in New York).　　　　　　　　　　　　　　1921 *Copyright Photo, O. W. Waterman.*

NEW YORK.　　　　　　　　　　　　　　1936 *Photo, O. W. Waterman.*

TEXAS　　　　(To distinguish from *New York*, note forward control top.)　　　　1938, *Wright & Logan.*

TEXAS. (To distinguish from *New York*, note forward control top and mainmast platforms.)　　1942, *Official.*

TEXAS. (To distinguish from *New York*, note forward control top and mainmast platforms.) 1944, *U.S. Navy Official.*

(NEVADA CLASS—2 SHIPS).

OKLAHOMA (March 23rd, 1914) & **NEVADA** (July 11th, 1914).

SUNK *SUNK AS TARGET*
12/1/41 Displacement { Normal, 27,500 tons. } *SUNK BIKINI* Complement, both 1384.
PEARL HARBOR { Full load, 28,400 tons. }

Length { waterline, 575 feet. } Beam, 95 ft. 2½ ins. { Mean draught 28½ feet.
{ over all, 583 feet. } { Max. ,, 29 ft 7½ ins.

War : Nevada, 1598, Oklahoma, 1628.

Guns (Dir. Con.) :
10—14 inch, 45 cal.
12—5 inch, 51 cal.
8—3 inch (AA.) Mk. III.
4—6* or 3† pdr. (saluting).
2—1 pdr.
2 machine.
1 landing.

Torpedo tubes (21 inch) :
2 submerged
*In Nevada. †In Oklahoma.

Armour :
13½″ Belt (amidships) ....
8″ Belt (aft).........................
13½″ Bulkheads ....
13½″ Funnel base ....
3″ Deck (ends) ....
18″—9″ Triple turrets ..
16″—9″ Double turrets... }
16″ Conning tower and tube ......
(Total weight, 7664 tons.)

Note to Plans.—Revised to 1921.

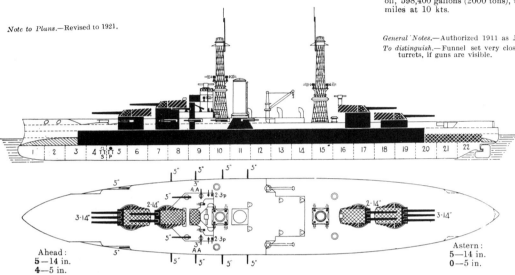

Ahead :
5—14 in.
4—5 in.

Astern :
5—14 in.
0—5 in.

°*Armour Notes.*—Main belt is 400 feet long by 17½ feet wide; 8½ feet of it being below l.w.l. Lower edge is 8″. The ends are unarmoured; the battery also. Plates are applied in vertical strakes. Two protective decks, upper 3″ flat, lower 1½″ flat, 2″ on slopes. Barbette bases are 13½″ thick, but turrets are only 4½″ where below protective deck and behind belt. Barbette shields; 18″ port plate for triple positions, 16″ port plate for twin positions, 10″ sides, 9″ back, 5″ roof. Sighting slits in conning tower closed by splinter-proof shutters. There is a signalling station protected by 16″ armour behind conning tower. These ships mark a new era in naval construction, being the first to embody the "everything or nothing" idea in the matter of protection. No bulkhead between 14 inch guns in this or any newer ships.

°*Gunnery Notes.*—Guns in the triple turrets in one sleeve, can be fired as one piece. Proposed to increase maximum elevation of 14-inch guns to 30°.

Engineering Notes.—Nevada has 2 H.P. and 2 L.P. Curtis turbines. Cylinders of Oklahoma are H.P. 35″, I.P. 59″, L.P. (2) 78″. Stroke, 48″. Total heating surface, 48,000 sq. feet. Weight of machinery, Nevada, 1880 tons : Oklahoma, 1998 tons. Electric installation in both is 4 generating sets of 300 k.w., 125 volts, 2400 amp. each. Boilers are in 6 compartments and occupy less than 80 feet of length. Boilers are large tube "Express" type, those specially designed by Messrs. Babcock & Wilcox for Oklahoma proving most satisfactory. No superheaters. Electric-driven f.d. blowers proved too unreliable, and were replaced by steam turbine-driven blowers. All oil fuel carried in double bottom ; no wing tanks.

Name	Builder	Machinery	Laid down	Completed	Trials : (Full Power—12 hrs.)	Tons fuel per day: 10 kts.	15 kts.	19 kts.
Oklahoma	N.York S.B.Co	N.Y. S.B. Co.	Oct. '12	May,'16	21,703 = 20·58	77	143	278
Nevada	Fore River Co.	Fore River	Nov.'12	Mar. '16	23,312 = 20·53	{ 50·5‡	132·5†	—
						{ 77§	149§	210§

Broadside : **10**—14 in., **6**—5 in., **1**—21 in. torpedo tube.

Machinery: *Oklahoma*, Triple expansion, 4 cylinder; *Nevada*, Curtis (geared cruising) turbines. 2 screws in both. Boilers: O, 12 Babcock; N, 12 Yarrow. Designed H.P. 24,800 = 20·5 kts. Fuel: oil, 598,400 gallons (2000 tons), *maximum capacity*. Radius of action : 4000 miles at full speed, 10,000 miles at 10 kts.

†Cruising turbines. §Main turbines.

General Notes.—Authorized 1911 as No. 36 (Nevada), 37 (Oklahoma).

To distinguish.—Funnel set very close to fore cage mast ; derrick-posts about *half* funnel height. Also by twin turrets, if guns are visible.

*Unofficial Notes.

OKLAHOMA (*Nevada* same appearance).   1921 *Copyright Photo, O. W. Waterman.*

OKLAHOMA.   1930 *Official photo.*

NEVADA.   (To distinguish from *Oklahoma*, observe mainmasthead.)   *1935, O. W. Waterman.*

OKLAHOMA.   *1936, Wright & Logan.*

OKLAHOMA   *1936, Wright & Logan.*

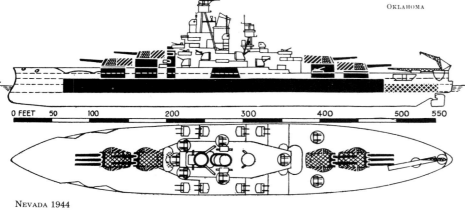

0 FEET 50   100   200   300   400   500   550

NEVADA 1944

NEVADA.   *1944, U.S. Navy Official.*

(Pennsylvania Class—2 Ships).

PENNSYLVANIA (16th March, 1915) & **ARIZONA** (19th June, 1915)·
Standard Displacement, 33,100 and 32,600 tons respectively·

[handwritten: SUNK AS TARGET BIKINI] *[handwritten: SUNK 12-7-41 PEARL HARBOR]*

Length $\begin{cases} w.l. \text{ 600 feet} \\ o.a. \text{ 608 feet} \end{cases}$ Beam, 106 feet, 3 in. $\begin{cases} \text{Mean draught, 28 feet in } Penn- \\ sylvania; \text{ 5 ins. less in} \\ Arizona. \\ Maximum \text{ draught, } 33\frac{1}{2} \text{ feet.} \end{cases}$

Complement, 1358.

Guns:
12—14 inch, 45 cal.
12—5 in., 51 cal.
8—5 in. (AA.), 25 cal.
4—3 pdr. (saluting).
(Torpedo tubes removed).

Aircraft: 3

Catapults:
1 on "X" Turret
1 on quarter deck.

Armour:
14″ Belt (amidships) .... ▅
8″ Belt (aft) .... ▨
3″ Deck (ends) .... ▨
15″–9″ Funnel base .... ▅
18″–9″ Turrets ▅▅ ▨▨
(Total, 8072 tons.)
16″ Conning tower & tube ... ⬚
6″ deck amidships (4″ upper,
2″ lower).

Armour Notes.—Generally as for *Nevada* class. Increase of armour weight due to increased internal protection against submarine explosions and greater length of belt. Armour for each triple barbette, 226½ tons. *Arizona* has cement backing to belt, instead of teak, and armoured fire-control tops.

Gunnery and Fire Control Notes.—14 inch guns mounted in single sleeve, and can be fired as one piece. *Max.* range at 15° elevation reported to be 21,000 yards. Triple positions weigh about 650 tons each (guns, mountings and armour). Turrets are capable of putting 2—3 salvoes a minute through a target at short range practice. Breech blocks worked by hand power. Interior of the shields to 14 inch guns very roomy and well arranged.

Name	Builder	Machinery	Laid down	Completed	Trials Full Power : 12 hrs.	Tons Fuel per day		
						10—	15—	19—kts.
Pennsylvania	Newport News	Newport News	Oct.'13	June,'16	29,366 = 21·05	65/—	90/—	—/—
Arizona	New York Yard	New York Yard	Mar.'14	Oct. '16	33,376 = 21	76/—	167/174	—/509

General Notes.—*Pennsylvania* authorised 1912, as *No. 38*, *Arizona* 1913, as *No. 39*. Both ships are enlarged and improved *Nevadas*. They have proved excellent sea boats, very steady gun platforms, and have proved to be very economical ships. Both ships have undergone extensive reconstruction which has cost $14,800,000. Battery raised a deck and AA. armament increased ; tripods fitted, funnel moved further aft ; bulges and increased internal protection ; additional bridges, and catapults fitted. In appearance differ from *Nevada* and *Oklahoma* in having higher conning tower and bridge which reaches funnel level.

Machinery : *Pennsylvania*, Curtis turbines, L.P. ahead and astern, H.P. astern. *Arizona*, Parsons turbines, L.P. ahead and astern, H.P. astern. In both ships: Westinghouse geared turbines, H.P. ahead and cruising. 4 shafts. Boilers : *Arizona*, 6 Bureau Express. *Pennsylvania*, 1 Bureau Express, 5 White-Forster. Designed H.P. 32,000 = 21 kts. (unaffected by modernisation). Fuel : Oil only, *normal* 2,322 tons (694,830 gallons).

Pennsylvania. Aircraft View. (1924)

Pennsylvania. Aircraft and Detail View, looking forward, and showing new type of tops and SL. positions on cage masts (1920 alterations). Port 5 inch director tower appears at break of deck levels ; W/T. tower abaft funnel. Note these details on No. 3 gunhouse :—(a) aeroplane, (b) 3 inch AA. guns mounted in angles formed by wings and fuselage of aeroplane, (c) small-base R.F. protected by shield. In turrets Nos. 1, 2, 3, ends of large-base R.F. will be seen projecting beyond and through sides of gunhouses—a R.F. position normal to various U.S. Dreadnought types. It is said to be unsatisfactory, on account of "shimmer effect," created by confusing light rays being reflected off sides of gun-houses into lenses of the R.F. (1924)

Pennsylvania, showing heightened funnel.   1939, *Bear Photo Service.*

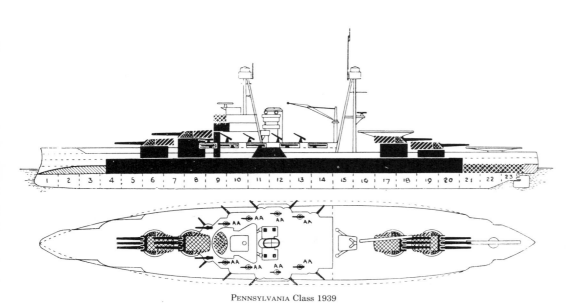

Pennsylvania Class 1939

Pennsylvania.
1934 Photo, Mr. L. Sprague de Camp.

PENNSYLVANIA. (Funnel since heightened.)   1933 *O. W. Waterman.*

ARIZONA.   (Observe difference in height of C.T. compared with *Pennsylvania*.)   1935, *O. W. Waterman*

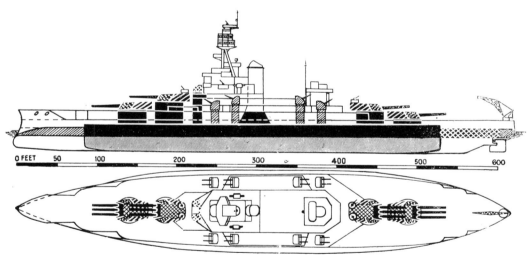

O FEET   50   100   200   300   400   500   600

PENNSYLVANIA 1943

PENNSYLVANIA.   1944, *U.S. Navy Official.*

(NEW MEXICO class—3 ships).

NEW MEXICO (ex-*California*, April 23rd, 1917), **IDAHO** (June 30th, 1917),

MISSISSIPPI (January 25th, 1917).

ALL SCRAPPED

Displacement { Normal, 32,000 tons. } { Full load, 33,000 tons. }   Complements { N.M., 1476. } { I., } 1434. { Missi., }

Length { waterline, 600 feet. } { over all, 624 feet. }   Beam, 97½ft. 4½in. { Mean draught, 30 feet. } { Max. ,, 31ft. 0½in. }

Guns (Dir. Con.):
12—14 inch, 50 cal., Mk. IV.
12—5 inch, 51 cal.
8—3 inch (A.A.), Mk. III.
4—6 or 3† pdr. (saluting)
2—1 pdr.
2 machine
1 landing
Torpedo tubes (21 inch):
2 submerged.

† In *Idaho* only.
Note to Plans.—Renewed 1921.

2—5 inch guns removed 1922, and 4—3 inch A.A. added.

Armour :
14″ Belt (amidships) .... ▓
8″ Belt (aft) .... ▨
″ Deck ends .... ▧
15″—9″ Funnel base ...... ▨
18″—9″ Turrets ▦
16″ Conning tower & tube

Name.	Builder and Machinery.	Laid down.	Completed	Trials. (4 hrs.)	Tons Fuel per day.†			Best recent speed.
					10—	15—	19—kts.	
New Mexico	New York Yard§	Oct., '15	May, '18	31,397=21·08	—	132	263	21
Idaho	N. York S.B. Co.	Jan., '15	Mar., '19	33,100=21·29	—/74	165/194	—/510	21·92
Mississippi	Newport News	Apl., '15	Dec., '17	31,804=21·09	77	—/168	—/305	

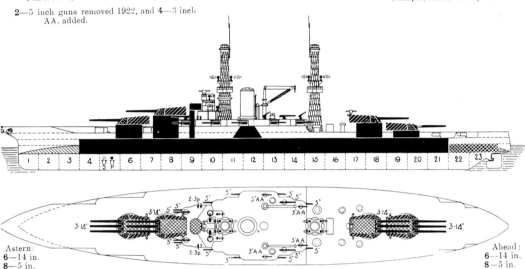

Astern:
6—14 in.
8—5 in.

Ahead:
6—14 in.
8—5 in.

Broadside : **12—14 in., 7—5 in., 1—21 in. torpedo tube.**

Machinery : *New Mexico :* G.E. turbines with electric drive (see *Notes*). *Idaho :* Parsons 4-shaft (geared cruising) turbines. *Mississippi :* Curtis 4-shaft (geared cruising) turbines. 4 screws in all three ships Boilers : 9 Babcock & Wilcox. Designed H.P., *New Mexico* 27,500, others 32,000 = 21 knots. Fuel : Oil only, 2200 tons.

To distinguish. Easily separated from the *Pennsylvania* and *Nevada* classes by yacht bow, and 5 inch battery amidships on forecastle deck level. Derrick posts *higher* than funnel. Also funnel looks small and short.

* Unofficial Notes. †Stated as tons burnt running on cruising turbines/main turbines. §Machinery by G. E. Co. in *N.M.*

NEW MEXICO. Aircraft View (from starboard bow). (1924)

NEW MEXICO.

Added 1944, U.S. Navy Official.

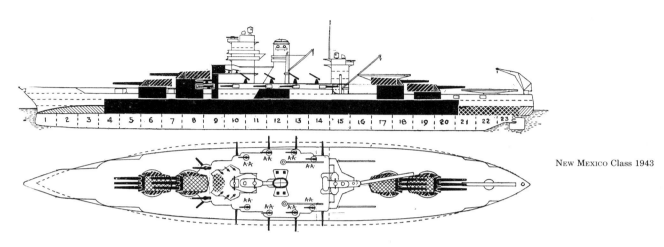

NEW MEXICO Class 1943

IDAHO

1936, O. W. Waterman

MISSISSIPPI.

Added 1935, courtesy of U.S. Naval Institute, Annapolis, Md.

IDAHO.

1944, U.S. Navy Official.

Guided Missile Ship.

MISSISSIPPI (equipped with guided missile launchers aft).

1954 ,U.S. Navy, Official.

EAG
128 MISSISSIPPI

Displacement :	29,700 tons (36,000 tons *full load*)
Dimensions :	600 (*w.l.*) 626 (*o.a.*) × 106 × 29¼ (*mean*), (*max.*) feet
Guns :	2 Guided missile projectors, 2—6 inch d.p. 47 cal., 2—5 inch, 54 cal. (new type twin mount), 4—3 inch 50 cal. (new type twin mounts), Rockets. Also 6 standard 5-inch, 38 cal., for instructional purposes
Machinery :	Westinghouse geared turbines. 4 shafts. S.H.P. : 40,000 = 21·5 kts. (*max.* now 19 kts.)
Boilers :	6 Bureau Express
Oil fuel :	2,200 tons

Notes.—Built by Newport News S.B. Co. Laid down 5 Apr. 1951. Launched 25 Jan. 1917. Completed 18 Dec. 1917. Built as a battleship (BB 41) of *New Mexico* class, but converted into an Experimental Gunnery Ship at Norfolk Navy Yard, 1947. No longer carries 14-inch turret aft. Now fitted to carry and launch rockets and missiles. Launchers for " Terrier " guided missiles located in stern.

MISSISSIPPI.

1944, U.S. Navy Official.

Notes.—These three ships were not at Pearl Harbour when the Japanese made their surprise attack on December 7, 1941, but have been modernised to a certain extent. *New Mexico* may differ slightly from others, as she undewent further alterations after a severe bomb hit on the bridge, Jan. 6, 1945.

(CALIFORNIA *class*—2 ships).

CALIFORNIA (Nov. 20th, 1919) and **TENNESSEE** (April 30th, 1919).

Displacement { *Normal*, 32,300 tons.
{ *Full load*, 33,190 tons.

Complement, 1407.°

Length { (*w.l.*) 600 feet. }
{ (*o.a.*) 624 feet. } Beam, 97 feet 3½ inches { *Mean* draught, 30 feet }
{ *Max.* ,, 31 feet }

° As Fleet Flagship, 1469.

ALL SCRAPPED

Guns (Dir. Con.) :
- 12—14 inch, 50 cal., Mk. IV.
- 12—5 inch, 51 cal.
- 8—3 inch (anti-aircraft), Mk. III.
- 4—6 pdr. (saluting).
- 2—1 pdr.
- 2 M.G.
- 2 landing.

Torpedo tubes (21 inch) :
- 2 *submerged*.

Armour :
- 14″ Belt ....
- 8″ Belt (aft) ....
- 3″ Deck (ends) ... ...
- 15″—9″ Funnel bases ..
- 18″—9″ Turrets ....
- 16″ Conning tower and tube ....

Gunnery Notes.—The 14 inch mounted in separate sleeves ; elevation, up to 30°. Main guns controlled from upper storey and 5 inch from lower storey of masthead tops.

Armour Notes.—Generally as *New Mexico*, *Pennsylvania* and *Nevada* classes on subsequent pages. Internal subdivision by unpierced bulkheads developed to the utmost degree below waterline.

Engineering Notes.—Generally as those relating to *New Mexico* on next page, but (*a*) current generated is 3-phase, (*b*) turbine speed is controlled by hydraulic governors instead of mechanical, (*c*) controls are located in one small room. Four alternating current motors, one to each propeller shaft, supplied by current at 3400 volts, from 2 turbo-generators. Motors are wound for 36 and 24-pole connections, operating on former as squirrel-cage machines, and on latter as wound-rotor machines. Oil for trials : 1467 tons and 187 tons feed water. Estimated weight of machinery : *California*, 1805 tons ; *Tennessee*, 1983 tons. Heating surface : 50984 sq. ft. for Express Bureau boilers in *California* ; 41,768 sq. ft. + 4168 sq. ft. (superheated) for Babcock boilers in *Tennessee*. Each boiler is in a separate w.t. compartment. Boiler rooms are abeam of engine rooms (4 to port, 4 to starboard), and boilers are under central control. Turbines are in tandem on centre line. On *trials*, *Tennessee* brought to rest from full speed within 3 minutes ; tactical diameter : 700 yards (full helm, both screws turning forward).

Appearance Notes.—General build most peculiar and quite distinctive. Hull is not recessed for any secondary guns. Forward cage mast is embedded in a perfect skyscraper of bridges. Funnels look "pushed back" towards stern ; they are small and insignificant. Seen from angles well round towards bow, they vanish and these ships appear to be funnel-less.

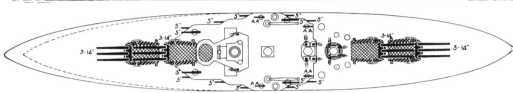

Name	Builder	Machinery	Laid down	Completed	Refit	Trials	Boilers	Best recent speed
California	Mare Island Y.	G. E. Co.	Oct.,'16	Aug.'21		21·75	Express	
Tennessee	New York Yard	Westinghouse Co.	May,'17	June'20		30,908 = 21·378″	Babcock	

General Notes.—Authorised 1915 as No. 43 (*Tennessee*) and 44 (*California*). The above design is practically identical with *New Mexico* class on next page. *California* fitted as Fleet Flagship.

Ahead :
6—14 in.
6—5 in.

Broadside : **12**—14 in. **6**—5 in. ; **1**—21 in. torpedo tube.

Astern :
6—14 in.
6—5 in.

CALIFORNIA Class 1924

Machinery : *California*, G. E. turbines with electric drive. *Tennessee*, Westinghouse turbines with electric drive. 4 screws in both ships. Boilers : 8 Express Bureau type in *California*, 8 Babcock in *Tennessee*. Designed H.P. 28,500 = 21 kts. Fuel (oil only) : *normal* 2200, *maximum* 3328 tons.

Corrections to Plans.—(*a*) Only fore half of C.T. base is armoured. (*b*) Armoured uptakes to funnels do not rise above the forecastle deck level. (*c*) The shallow 8″ belt at stern extends further aft to a little distance beyond the rudder pintle. Two of 5-inch guns shown on plan removed and four 3-inch substituted.

TENNESSEE.

1921 *Copyright Photo, O. W. Waterman.*

CALIFORNIA.

1930, *Official Photo*

CALIFORNIA.

1939

CALIFORNIA CLASS 1943

0 FEET 50 100   200   300   400   500   600

0 FEET 50 100   200   300   400   500   600

CALIFORNIA.

1943, *U.S. Navy, Official.*

TENNESSEE.

Added 1949, U.S. Navy. Official.

(MARYLAND CLASS—3 SHIPS.)

COLORADO (March 22nd, 1921), **MARYLAND** (March 20th, 1920), and **WEST VIRGINIA** (Nov. 19th, 1921).

Normal displacement, 32,600 tons. *Full load*, 33,590 tons. Complement, 1407.

Length (*w.l.*), 600 feet. Beam, 97 feet 3½ inches. { *Mean* draught, 30½ feet. { *Max.* „ 31 ft. 3½ in.

Length (*o.a.*), 624 feet. Complement, as fleet flagship, 1486.

Guns (Dir. Con.) : *ALL SCRAPPED*
- 8—16 inch, 45 cal. Mk. I.
- 12—5 inch, 51 cal.
- 8—3 inch (AA.) Mk.III
- 4—6 pdr. (saluting).
- 2—1 pdr.
- 2 M.G.
- 2 landing

Torpedo tubes (21 inch) :
- 2 *submerged*.

Armour :
- 16"—14" Belt............
- 8" Belt (aft) ....
- 3" Deck (ends)..........
- 16"—9" Funnel bases .
- 18"—9" Turrets ....
- 16" Conning tower and tube...................

Armour Notes. } *Appearance Notes.* } As next page.

Anti-Torpedo Protection.—Ferrati type triple hull and minute internal subdivision by longitudinal and transverse unpierced bulkheads.

Engineering Notes.—" Electric Drive " is identical with that for *California* Class (next page), but, in these ships, electric installation has been extended. Part of steam generated in boilers is diverted for running six auxiliary turbo-generators, supplying current to anchor gear, workshop lathes, refrigerating plant, bakeries, &c. Guns are also electrically manœuvred, ammunition hoists are electric. In fact, every possible item of equipment, even down to potato peelers and ice-cream freezers, is run by electric power. Estimated weight of machinery, 2002 tons. Heating surfaces as *Tennessee* on next page.

Name	Builder	Machinery	Laid down	Completed	Trials	Boilers	Best recent speed
Colorado	New York S.B. Co.	Westinghouse Co	May '19	Aug., '23	........=21·37	Babcock	}
Maryland	Newport News	Gen. Elec. Co.	Apl., '17	July '21	36,673=21·07	Babcock	} 21
W. Virginia	Newport News	Gen. Elec. Co.	Apl., '20	Dec. '23		Babcock	}

General Notes.—Authorised 1916 as No. 46 (*Colorado*), No. 47 (*Maryland*), and No. 49 (*W. Virginia*). *Maryland* and *W. Virginia* fitted as Fleet Flagships. Except for change in primary armament, and slight increase in displacement, they are identical in nearly all respects with *California* class, described on next page. *Washington* scrapped under Naval Treaty.

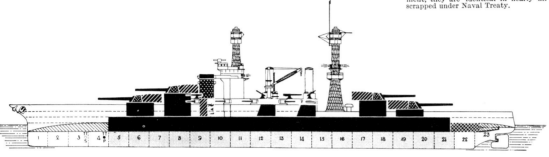

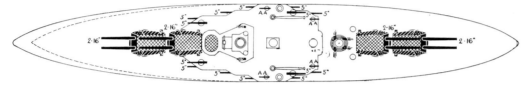

Ahead :
4—16 in.
8—5 in.

Broadside : **8**—16 inch, **7**—5 inch, **1**—21 inch torpedo tube.

Astern :
4—16 in.
6—5 in.

(1924)

W. VIRGINIA.—bow view.

1924 *Photo, Abrahams.*

Machinery : In *Colorado* Westinghouse turbines and electric drive ; in *Maryland* and *W. Virginia*, G.E. turbines with electrical drive. Designed S.H.P. 28,900 = 21 kts. 4 screws. Boilers : 8 Babcock & Wilcox. Fuel (oil only) : *normal* tons ; *maximum* tons.

Gunnery Notes.—16 inch are a new model, successfully proved at Indian Head, 1917. Maximum elevation, 30°; Maximum range at this elevation unofficially stated to be 33,300 yards. Turrets electrically manœuvred and with electric hoists. Excepting increase of calibre to 16 inch, otherwise as Notes for *Tennessee* Class on next page. 2—5 inch guns removed 1922, and 4—3 inch guns added. Now reported to be mounted on turret tops. New director system installed, 1923. Main control is at a height of 140 feet above sea level.

WEST VIRGINIA.

1924 *Photo, Abrahams.*

MARYLAND.

1922 *Photo.*

COLORADO. (MARYLAND similar.)

1944, *U.S. Navy, Official.*

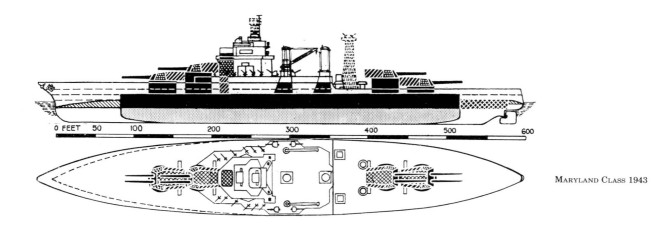

0 FEET 50   100   200   300   400   500   600

MARYLAND CLASS 1943

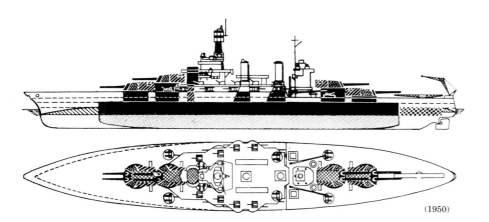

(1950)

WEST VIRGINIA as rebuilt.

1943, *U.S. Navy, Official.*

MARYLAND.

Added 1949, *U.S. Navy, Official.*

WEST VIRGINIA.

Added 1949, *U.S. Navy, Official.*

(WASHINGTON CLASS—2 Ships)

NORTH CAROLINA (June 13, 1940) —MEMORIAL
WASHINGTON (June 1, 1940) SCRAPPED

Standard displacement: 35,000 tons. (*About* 41,000 tons, *full load.*)
Complement: 2,500

Length: 704 ft. (*w.l.*); 729 ft. (*o.a.*). Beam: 108 ft.
Draught: 26 ft. 8 in. (*mean*).

Aircraft: 4   Catapults: 2

Guns:	Armour: (Unofficial)
9—16 inch, 50 cal.	16″ Side amidships.
20—5 inch, 38 cal. (dual purpose).	6″ Upper Deck.
Over 100—40 mm. and 20 mm.	4″ Lower Deck.
	Triple hull below *w.l.* and internal bulges.

WASHINGTON.

1945. *courtesy Commander P. A. Morgan, R.N.R.*

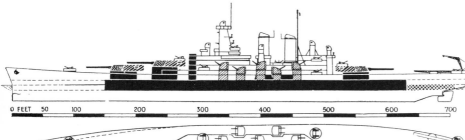
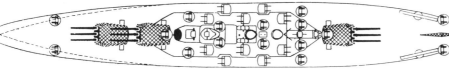

0 FEET 50 100 200 300 400 500 600 700

NORTH CAROLINA (1949)

Added 1950, U.S. Navy, Official.

Machinery: Geared turbines. 4 shafts. S.H.P.: 115,000 = over 27 kts. Babcock and Wilcox boilers of a new pattern (working pressure reported to be 600 lb. per sq. inch, with 400° of superheat). Oil fuel.

General Notes.—Delays in laying down these ships were due to changes in design, late delivery of materials and necessity for extending and strengthening building slips. Ships are fully 35 per cent. welded. Engine room is arranged on a novel plan to save weight.

Gunnery Notes.—16 inch are a new model, reported to weigh 125 tons. Each turret weighs 650 tons complete.

Engineering Notes.—Weight of machinery has been reduced in comparison with earlier battleships. Steam pressures and temperatures are reported to be greater than in any other battleship afloat.

Programme	Name and No.	Builder	Machinery	Laid down	Completed	Cost
1936	N. Carolina (55)	New York Navy Yard	Gen. Electric Co.	Oct. 27, 1937	Aug., 1941	$76,885,750 each
	Washington (56)	Philadelphia Navy Yard	Gen. Electric Co.	June 14, 1938	March, 1942	

WASHINGTON.

1941, *U.S. Navy Official.*

NORTH CAROLINA

1941, *Associated Press.*

NORTH CAROLINA.

1944, *U.S. Navy Official.*

(SOUTH DAKOTA CLASS—4 SHIPS)

SCRAPPED

ALABAMA (Feb. 16, 1942), **INDIANA** (Nov. 21, 1941), **MASSACHUSETTS** (Sept.
MEMORIAL
23, 1941), **SOUTH DAKOTA** (June 7, 1941). *FOR DISPOSAL 1962*
SCRAPPED

Standard displacement: 35,000 tons (42,000 tons *full load*).   Complement: 2,500.

Length: 680 feet (*o.a.*).   Beam: 108 feet 2 inches.   Draught: 26 feet 9 inches.

Guns: Aircraft: Armour:

    9—16 inch, 50 cal.   **4** or more.   Understood that these ships

    20—5 inch, 38 cal., dual purpose.   have enhanced protection

    (*S. Dakota* has only 16.)   as compared with *Wash-*

Over **100**—40 mm. and 20 mm.   Catapults: *ington* type.

    2

ALABAMA.   1943, *Keystone.*

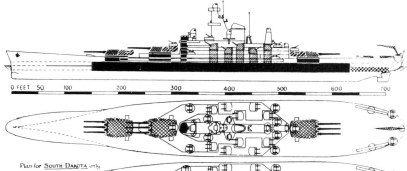

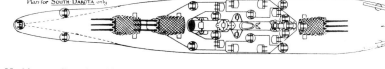

MASSACHUSETTS.   1942, *U.S. Navy, Official.*

Plan for SOUTH DAKOTA only

Machinery: Geared turbines. 4 shafts. S.H.P.: 130,000 = 30 kts. Boilers: Babcock &
Wilcox in *S. Dakota* and *Massachusetts*; Foster Wheeler in *Indiana* and *Alabama*. Working
pressure reported as 600 lb. per sq. inch with 400° of superheat. Oil fuel.

General Notes.—These ships are a modification of *Washington* design with increased freeboard and reduced length,
embodying sundry improvements. *Alabama* was built in 2¾ years from date of laying keel. *S. Dakota* played a
prominent part in naval victory over Japanese squadron in Battle of Guadalcanal, Nov. 13-15, 1942.

Gunnery Notes.—Outstanding feature of these ships is the very large number of 40 mm. Bofors and 20 mm. Oerlikon
guns included in AA. armament. 5 inch are mounted at a higher level than in *N. Carolina* and *Washington.*

Programme	Name and No.	Builder	Machinery	Laid down	Completed	Cost
1938	*S. Dakota* (57)	New York S.B. Corpn.	Gen. Electric Co.	July 5, 1939	Aug., 1942	$77,000,000 each
	Indiana (58)	Newport News Co.	Westinghouse Co.	Nov. 20, 1939	Oct., 1942	
	Massachusetts (59)	Bethlehem Steel Co. (Quincy)	Gen. Electric Co.	July 20, 1939	Sept., 1942	
	Alabama (60)	Norfolk Navy Yard	Westinghouse Co.	Feb. 1, 1940	Nov., 1942	

SOUTH DAKOTA.   Added 1949, *U.S. Navy, Official.*

MASSACHUSETTS.   Added 1949. *U.S Navy, Official.*

MASSACHUSETTS (1959)   *United States Navy, Official*

"Iowa" Class.
4 + 1 SHIPS.

IOWA (Aug. 27, 1942)   **NEW JERSEY** (Dec. 7, 1942)

MISSOURI (Jan. 29, 1944)   **WISCONSIN** (Dec. 7, 1943)

KENTUCKY (Jan. 20, 1950). Suspended

MEMORIAL-HAWAII

ALL RESERVE

IOWA.   1944, U.S. Navy, Official.

Standard displacement:	45,000 tons (57,600 tons *full load*)
Dimensions:	Length: 861½ (*pp.*), 867¼ (*o.a.*) feet. Beam: 108 feet. Draught: 38 feet (*max.*)
Guns:	9—16 inch, 50 cal., 20—5 inch, 38 cal., 80—40 mm. AA., 50—20 mm.
Armour:	19"–16" side
Machinery:	Geared turbines. 4 shafts. S.H.P.: 200,000 → 33 kts. (35 kts. reached in service)
Boilers:	12 Babcock & Wilcox
Oil fuel:	8,800 tons
Complement:	2,700 (war). *Missouri*, 1,470.

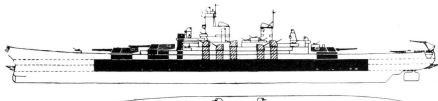

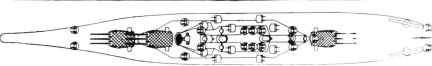

NEW JERSEY.   1947, Wright & Logan.

WISCONSIN.   1947, Wright & Logan.

Note to Plan.—Catapults now removed.

General Notes.—Inclusive cost officially stated to exceed $100,000,000 each. *Iowa* and *New Jersey* were each built in 2⅗ years. same period as occupied by the *Alabama*, a smaller ship. Construction of *Kentucky*, after being suspended for a time, was resumed in Dec., 1944, only to be arrested again in Aug., 1946, and resumed once more on Aug. 17, 1948; while the *Illinois* (65), authorised in 1940 and ordered from Philadelphia Navy Yard in Dec., 1942, was cancelled when 22% complete, on Aug. 11, 1945. *New Jersey*, at Naval Shipyard Annexe at Bayonne as part of Atlantic Reserve Fleet, may be "reactivated", *Iowa* "mothballed", *Missouri*, the only U.S. battleship now in commission, carries two helicopters. She went aground Jan. 7, 1950, and was not refloated until Feb. 1, 1950. Subsequently used as Training Ship.

Armour Note.—Not reported, other than belt, but more extensive than in "Alabama" class.

Appearance Note.—While serving as Third Fleet flagship, *New Jersey* had a lattice mainmast stepped against her after-funnel to accommodate flag-hoists. *Missouri* has been similarly equipped.

Special Note.—*Kentucky's* armament was to have been modified to include a number of guided missiles, but work has been at a standstill, and although construction has been intermittently resumed, this was merely to free the dry dock in which she was built. As a battleship she is 70% complete with machinery installed. She was floated out from her building dock on Jan. 20, 1950, to be laid up in Norfolk, and is being retained in her present condition for eventual completion if a future emergency arises. She may not be scrapped without the approval of Congress or the House Armed Services Committee. No work is being done on her.

Programme	Name and No.	Builders	Machinery	Laid down	Completed
1940	*Iowa* (61)	New York Navy Yard	General Electric Co.	27 June '40	22 Feb. '43
	New Jersey (62)	Philadelphia Navy Yard	Westinghouse Co.	16 Sept. '40	23 May '43
	Missouri (63)	New York Navy Yard	General Electric Co.	6 Jan. '41	11 June '44
	Wisconsin (64)	Philadelphia Navy Yard	Westinghouse Co.	25 Jan. '41	16 April '44
	Kentucky (66)	Norfolk Navy Yard	do.	6 Dec. '42	

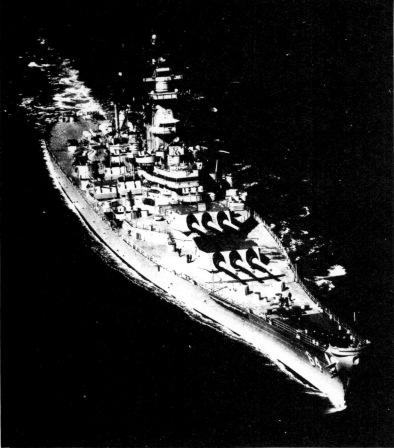

WISCONSIN (1980)   USN

NEW JERSEY (off Viet-Nam)   4/1969, USN

IOWA

Added 1959, United States Navy, Official

NEW JERSEY (BB 62)

1968, United States Navy by PHC Harold Wise

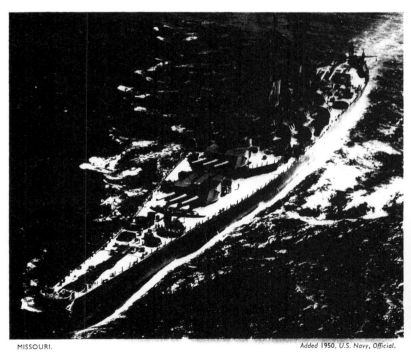

MISSOURI.

Added 1950, U.S. Navy, Official.

NEW JERSEY (BB 62)

1968, United States Navy

AIRCRAFT CARRIERS

DESPITE the fact that the first aircraft to take off from a ship had been launched from a platform on the bow of USS *Birmingham* on 14 November 1910, with Eugene Ely as pilot, the USN's first carrier, *Langley*, did not complete her conversion from being a collier until 1922.

In spite of her slow speed, *Langley*'s performance demonstrated the value of the aircraft carrier. Further conversions, this time of two battle-cruiser hulls, were completed in 1927 – *Lexington* and *Saratoga*. These were huge ships by current standards with a length of 888 feet, a full load tonnage of 43,000, a speed of over 33 knots and a peacetime aircraft complement of 63. They were the last conversions, the inefficiency of such designs becoming apparent when *Ranger* commissioned in 1934. Although only of 17,600 tons and with a speed of 29 knots, the fact that she was designed from the keel up as a carrier allowed her to carry a peacetime complement of 76 aircraft.

Two months before *Ranger* commissioned the first of the three "Yorktown" class was laid down. These embodied the experience gained over the previous twelve years but, although the possibility was discussed, the flight deck was unarmoured. *Wasp* was laid down in 1936, the last US carrier designed under treaty inhibitions on tonnage. Over 100 feet shorter than the "Yorktowns" and with a speed of 29.5 knots, her maximum aircraft complement was 76–80.

Thus, by the time of Pearl Harbor in December 1941, the US Navy had seven carriers and three new ships of the "Essex" class were building, forerunners of a class of 24. They were basically enlarged "Yorktowns" with twice the full load displacement of *Wasp* and able to handle up to 110 machines. As before, their flight decks were not armoured, yet not one was sunk.

Nine ships of the "Cleveland" class cruisers then on order were converted into the "Independence" class of 15,000 tons full load with a speed of 31.6 knots and carrying a maximum of 45 aircraft.

The British HMS *Audacity* was the first conversion from a merchant ship hull for twenty years, followed in June 1941 by USS *Long Island*. From then on there emerged a string of escort carriers, 86 in total. None was fast (maximum 19 knots), they carried a light armament but they embarked anything up to 36 aircraft. All but nine were completed before Japan capitulated.

While this activity was at its peak three much larger ships (of an originally planned six) were laid down, the "Midway" class. Of 968 feet overall and nigh on 60,000 tons full load they had a speed of 33 knots and, with three lifts and an armoured flight deck, could carry 137 aircraft. In 1991, having had extensive modernizations in her 45 year life, *Midway* is the last USN ship built during World War II to be in front line service.

After the Korean War (1950–53) came the construction of the four "Forrestal" class, whose tonnage has crept upwards with various changes, including the Service Life Extension Programme (SLEP), until, in 1991, all are around 80,000 tons full load. The four "Kitty Hawks", which followed in the 1960s, vary one from the other in dimensions, tonnage and, particularly in *John F. Kennedy*, internal arrangements. They were the last of the conventionally propelled carriers as the first nuclear powered carrier *Enterprise* was simultaneously building at Newport News. The power plant called for a larger ship – 1,123 feet overall – and, after modifications, of 93,970 tons full load. Her aircraft complement was much the same as her predecessors, but her unlimited range and steady speed of 33 knots were of inestimable value. Her cost had many politicians running scared and a series of designs for smaller, conventionally propelled carriers, were put forward. None reached fruition and in 1975 the first of the "Nimitz" class commissioned. With two reactors in place of the eight in *Enterprise*, these huge ships have increased internal space. Five were in commission in 1991 with three more building.

J.M.
May 1991

AIRCRAFT TRANSPORTS

LANGLEY.

1925 *Photo*.

LANGLEY (ex-Fleet Collier *Jupiter*, 1912, launched Aug. 24th, 1912, converted 1920-21).

SUNK

Displacement, { *Normal*, 12,700 tons. } { *Full load*, tons. }   Complement, 341 (excluding flying personnel).

Length, { *p.p.* 520 feet. } { *o.a.* 542 feet. }   Beam, 65 feet.   Draught { *Mean*, 18 feet 10½ in. } { *Full load*, feet. }

SUNK 2/42

Guns :
4—5 inch, 51 cal.
(Carries 275 bombs for aircraft,
also 24 torpedoes).

Armour :
Nil.

Note to Plan.—Now has 2 funnels.

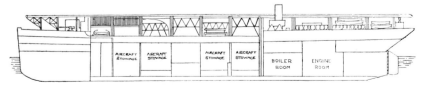

Machinery.—G.E. turbines and electric drive.   2 screws.   Boilers : 3 double-ended cylindrical.
S.H.P. (on first trials as Fleet collier) 7152 = 14·99 kts.   *Max.* fuel capacity : oil only.

Engineering Notes.—First large ship of U.S.N. built with the Melville-McAlpine electric drive.   This system of propulsion proved so successful, it has been adopted for Capital Ships.   Two horizontal smoke ducts, inter-connected so that smoke can be discharged on lee side.   One duct has a hinged extension, which can be lowered close to waterline ; smoke from the other duct can be discharged through water spray.   Fitted with Sperry gyro-stabiliser.

Note.—Now has 2 funnels, as in 1st photo.   *Photo added* 1924.

W/T. Notes.—Masts stow flat along hangar deck. Auxiliary radio carried for communicating with 'planes when main W/T. masts are housed down.

Aircraft Capacity.—Maximum capacity reported as 55 planes, but at present carries :—
   (a) 12 single-seater chasing 'planes (3 hours endurance at 100 kts.).
   (b) 12 two-seater spotting 'planes (4 hours endurance at 100 kts.)
   (c) 4 torpedo-dropping 'planes (2 hours endurance at 100 kts.).   (24 torpedoes carried for these).
   (d) 6 80-kt. torpedo-seaplanes.

Aircraft Stores, Repairs, &c.—For planes, all stores, spare parts, accessories, and magazines built for bombs, torpedoes, &c.   Petrol capacity : 578 tons, with elaborate plant for pumping petrol and lubricating oil to hangar and flying decks.   Repair plant ; machine shop ; wing-repair shop ; metal working shop ; kite balloon filling station, etc.

Handling of Aircraft.—Original cargo holds altered to give max. space for housing 'planes.   Runways below flight deck carry travelling cranes for hoisting 'planes from hold and moving them fore and aft, or to lifts for hoisting to flying deck.   Electric lift raises 'planes from hangar to flying deck.

Flying-off.—Flight deck : 534 × 64 feet and 56 feet over w.l.   Launching catapults fitted which can deliver torpedo planes into air at 60 m.p.h. with 60 feet run.

Flying-on and Landing Alongside.—Mantlets rigged to check speed. 2 cranes on each beam, with wide radii to pick seaplanes from water and place them on deck.   Can receive planes at 60 m.p.h. and stop in 40 feet without injury to machine or pilot.   It is considered safe for planes to alight on deck in a moderate sea.

General Notes.—Begun at Mare Island N. Yd., October, 1911, and completed as Fleet Collier, 1913.   So served till March, 1920, when she was placed out of commission for conversion by Norfolk Navy Yd.   For training purposes a complete and full-sized replica of LANGLEY'S flight deck, with landing net, has been erected at the Long Beach Aerodrome.

Aircraft Tenders (AV).

Note.—Minelayer *Aroostook*, Destroyers *Harding* and *Munford*, Minesweepers *Gannet*, *Pelican*, *Teal* and *Sandpiper*, and Miscellaneous Auxiliary *Ajax* have been serving for some time past as Seaplane Tenders.

WRIGHT   1924, *Official Photo.*

WRIGHT (ex-Emergency Fleet Corporation Hull *No. 180*, "Type B," launched at Hog Island, April 28th, 1920). Conversion effected by Tietjen & Lang Dry Dock Co., Hoboken, 1920-22. 11,500 tons. Dimensions : 448 (*p.p.* and *o.a.*) × 58 × 27¾ feet *max.* draught. Guns : 2—5 inch, 51 cal., 2—3 inch, 50 cal. AA. Designed S.H.P. 6000 = 15 kts. G.E. geared turbines and 6 Babcock & Wilcox boilers. Oil: 1630 tons. Complement, 311. Fitted as flagship, and will be attached to Asiatic Squadron on completion of 1st Line Carriers.

Special Notes.—This ship now serves as Tender to Seaplanes, a large space forward with a big hatchway in weather deck being provided for stowage of spare seaplane wing sections. Other spare parts also carried for Seaplanes. Conversion work carried out allows the landing by means of booms of seaplanes in the space aft on the main deck. Foundry, smithy, carpentry, and machine shops, motor erecting shop, fabric and dope shops for repairs and maintenance of aircraft material.

(Classed as Seaplane Tender.)   1939, *O. W. Waterman*

AIRCRAFT CARRIERS

LEXINGTON (3rd Oct., 1925.) *SUNK*
SARATOGA (7th April, 1925.) *SUNK AS TARGET - BIKINI*

Displacement, 33,000 tons.   *Full load* about 40,000 tons.
Complement (including flying personnel) : 1,899, of whom 169 are Commissioned Officers.
Length (*w.l.*) 830 ; (*pp.*) 850 ft.; (*o.a.*) 888 ft.
Beam, 105½ ft. (*extreme*).
Draught, 24 feet 2 inches (*mean*). 32 feet (*max.*)

Guns :
8—8 inch, 55 cal.
12—5 inch AA., 25 cal.
4—6 pdr. saluting.
8—50 cal. M.G.

Aircraft :
Lexington 90.
Saratoga 79.
Catapult, 1.

Armour :
Unofficially reported to have 6" Belt, 600 feet in length, and 3" deck. Triple hull and bulge protection.

LEXINGTON.   (Platform added around funnel top)   1936, *O. W. Waterman*

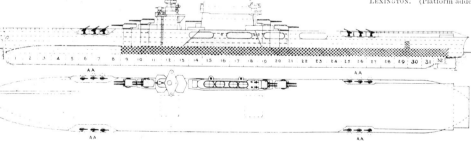

Machinery : G.E. turbines, electric drive. Designed S.H.P. : 180,000   33·25 kts. Boilers : *Lexington*, 16 Yarrow ; *Saratoga*, 16 White-Forster. 4 shafts. Oil fuel : 7,000 tons.

Name	Builder	Machinery	Laid down	Completed	Trials	Boilers
Lexington	Fore River S.B. Co.	} Gen. Elec. Co.	8 1/21	Dec '27	153,600 = 33·91	Yarrow
Saratoga	New York S.B. Co.		25 9 20	Nov.'27	138,375 = 33·42	White-Forster

Special Note.—It is intended to reconstruct these 2 ships at a cost of $15,000,000 for the two. They will be modernised as regards AA. and gas defence, damage control and aircraft operation. Flight deck to be widened at the bow by 60 ft. A bulge to be built along port side, nearly the full length of the ship and adding 2½ feet to the beam, to balance the weight of the island superstructure. This will make it possible to utilise the full quantity of oil fuel carried, instead of retaining some as ballast. This will increase deadweight by 450-500 tons but decrease displacement by about 2,000 tons, as ship will stand higher out of water.

General Notes.—These two ships were originally authorised in 1916 for construction as Battle Cruisers of 35,300 tons, with *seven* funnels and boilers disposed on two deck levels. After the War, plans were to a large extent re-cast, v. F.S. 1919-1921 Editions. Total cost, with aircraft, was over $45,000,000 each.

As Aircraft Carriers it is believed the waterline protection is retained and that deck protection has been heavily reinforced. The general lines of the hull remain unaltered, and the special system of underwater protection is also adhered to. Flight deck is 880 feet long, from 85 to 90 feet in width, and 60 feet above waterline. 8-inch guns have 30° elevation and range to 28,000 yards. Depth of hull from keel to flight deck is 74½ feet, and funnel rises 79 feet above flight deck.

Handling of Aircraft.—The Landing Net is placed just before the recessed stern portion of the Flight Deck ; it is about 100 feet long. Before it is a large T-shaped lift for moving aircraft from Flight to Hangar Deck. There is another and similar T-shaped lift abeam of the mast and C.T. At the bow is a catapult, 155 feet in length, capable of launching the heaviest aircraft into the air at flying speed with a travel of 60 feet. Before the C.T. and abaft the Navigating Officers' Deck House, and right over to starboard beam, are powerful derricks for lifting seaplanes and flying boats from the water. As a result of experiments with *Langley*, certain modifications were made enabling planes to land safely on deck in any weather.

SARATOGA.   1928 *Photo, by favour of H. C. Bywater, Esq.*

SARATOGA. (Appearance has since been altered, vide photo below.) 1936, *O. W. Waterman*

SARATOGA. 1928 *Photo, by favour of H. C. Bywater, Esq.*

Handling of Aircraft.—The Landing Net is placed just before the recessed stern portion of the Flight Deck ; it is about 100 feet long. Before it is a large T-shaped lift for moving aircraft from Flight to Hangar Deck. There is another and similar T-shaped lift abeam of the mast and C.T. At the bow is a catapult, 155 feet in length, capable of launching the heaviest aircraft into the air at flying speed with a travel of 60 feet. Before the C.T. and abaft the Navigating Officers' Deck House, and right over to starboard beam, are powerful derricks for lifting seaplanes and flying boats from the water. As a result of experiments with *Langley,* certain modifications were made enabling planes to land safely on deck in any weather.

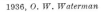

LEXINGTON, showing altered shape of bow. 1939.

SARATOGA. 1944, *U.S. Navy Official.*

NEW
LEXINGTON.

SARATOGA. 1943, *U.S. Navy Official.*

NEW
LEXINGTON. (1944)

RANGER (Newport News S.B. & D.D. Co., Feb. 25, 1933).

Displacement : 14,500 tons.   *SCRAPPED*

Complement (including flying personnel) : 1,788, of whom 162 are
commissioned officers.

Dimensions :   728 (*w.l.*), 769 (*o.a.*) × 80¹⁄₂ × 19³⁄₄ ft. (*mean*).

Guns :	Aircraft :	Armour :
8—5 inch 38 cal. dual purpose.	**72** (peace-time complement).	1″ Flight Deck
40 smaller	**86** can be carried.	Double Hull and internal subdivision, but no side armour beyond small patch shown.

Added 1937, O. W. Waterman.

Note to Plan.—Guns shown on forecastle and q.d. now mounted on superstructure over sections
6 and 26—27, as shown in 2 lower photos dated 1936, 1937.

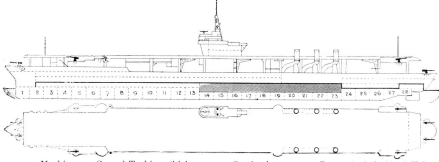

Machinery : Geared Turbines (high pressure Curtis ; low pressure Parsons). 2 shafts. S.H.P. :
53,500 = 29¼ kts.   Trials : 58,700 = 30·35 kts. (*max.*).   Boilers : 6 Babcock & Wilcox sectional Express.

General Notes.—Laid down Sept. 26 1931. Completed June 4, 1934.   Is officially numbered CV 4.   The six funnels can
be lowered to horizontal position, as shown in photo.   Cost approached $20,000,000.   *Ranger* was first U.S. aircraft
carrier designed as such.   War loss : *Wasp*, of similar displacement, but differing appearance.

With funnels lowered.   *1936, O. W. Waterman.*

Ranger.   *Added 1935, courtesy U.S. Naval Institute.*

1944, U.S. Navy Official.

ENTERPRISE (Oct. 3, 1936). *SCRAPPED* **HORNET** (building).
YORKTOWN (April 4, 1936). *LOST*
LOST + SUNK
Displacement : 19,900 tons. Complement, 2,072 (including flying
personnel).

Length : 761 feet (*w.l.*), 809½ feet (*o.a.*). Beam, 83¼ feet.
Draught, 21¾ feet (*mean*).

Guns :   Aircraft :
8—5 inch 38 cal. AA.   83 (space for over 100).
16—1·1 inch M.G. A.A.   Armour : A patch of side
16 smaller M.G.   armour over machinery
and boiler spaces, and
a heavy protective deck.

Machinery : Geared turbines. S.H.P.: 120,000
= 34 kts. (exceeded on trials). Boilers : 9
Babcock & Wilcox Express type.

ENTERPRISE.   *1938, Official, courtesy " Our Navy."*

Name	Builder	Laid down	Completed
Enterprise	Newport	16 July, 1934	18 July, 1938
Yorktown	News Co	21 May, 1934	1938
Hornet		Sept. 1939	1942

General Notes.—Owing to serious mechanical defects,
involving replacement of the reduction gearing and
over 1,200 boiler tubes, completion of *Yorktown* was
postponed until late in 1938. *Enterprise* was
similarly delayed. Cost over $21,000,000 apiece,
without armament. *Hornet* ordered end March, 1939.
To cost $31,800,000.

Aircraft Notes.—Aircraft can be catapulted from hangar
deck as well as from flight deck, thus increasing the
number that can be put into the air at short notice.

Note to Plan.—This shows starboard beam to illustrate details of funnel, etc.

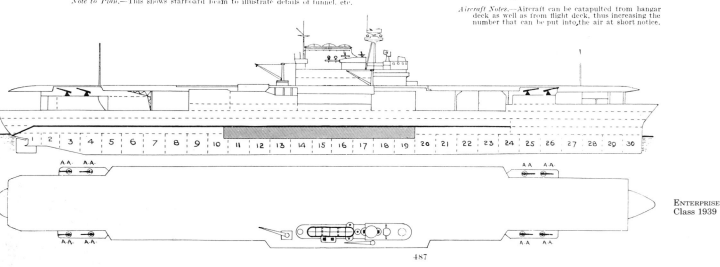

ENTERPRISE
Class 1939

487

YORKTOWN (Note " Y " on funnel).   *1939.*

ENTERPRISE.   *1944, U.S. Navy, Official.*

ENTERPRISE.   *Added 1950, U.S. Navy, Official.*

(Essex Class—24 ships.)

ANTIETAM (Aug. 20, 1944), **BENNINGTON** (Feb. 26, 1944), **BON HOMME RICHARD** (April 29, 1944), **BOXER** (Dec. 14, 1944), **BUNKER HILL** (Dec. 7, 1942), **ESSEX** (July 31, 1942), **FRANKLIN** (Oct. 14, 1943), **HANCOCK** (ex-*Ticonderoga*, Jan. 24, 1944), **HORNET** (ex-*Kearsarge*, Aug. 29, 1943), **INTREPID** (April 26, 1943), **KEARSARGE**, (May 5, 1945), **LAKE CHAMPLAIN**, (Nov. 1944), **LEXINGTON** (ex-*Cabot*, Sept. 26, 1942), **LEYTE** (ex-*Crown Point* Aug. 23, 1943), **ORISKANY** (Oct. 13, 1945), **PHILIPPINE SEA** (ex-*Wright*, Sept. 5, 1945), **PRINCETON** (ex-*Valley Forge*, July 8, 1945), **RANDOLPH** (June 28, 1944), **SHANGRI-LA** (Feb. 24, 1944), **TARAWA** (May 12, 1945), **TICONDEROGA** (ex-*Hancock*, Feb. 7, 1944), **VALLEY FORGE** (Nov. 18, 1945), **WASP** (ex-*Oriskany*, Aug. 17, 1942), **YORKTOWN** (ex-*Bon Homme Richard*, Jan. 21, 1943),.

Displacement : 27,100 tons (33,000 tons *full load.*)   Complement : 2,900.

Length : 874 feet (*pp.*). 888 feet (*o.a.*).   Beam : 93 feet.   Draught : 29 feet (*max.*).
(First 8 ships built are only 855 feet 10 in. *o.a.*)

Guns:
12—5 inch, 38 cal.
72—40 mm. AA.
52—20 mm.
(quadruple mounts).

Aircraft :
Ca. 100 (officially, over 80).

Armour :
Similar to *Enterprise.*

BOXER.   1945, U.S. Navy Official.

Machinery : Geared turbines.   4 shafts.   S.H.P.: 150,000 = 33 kts.

No.	Name	Builders	Machinery	Laid down	Completed
CV 9	Essex			28/4/41	12/42
10	Yorktown			1/12/41	16/5/43
11	Intrepid	Newport News S.B. &	Builders.	1/12/41	1943
12	Hornet	D.D. Co.		1942	1943
13	Franklin			7/12/42	31/1/44
14	Ticonderoga			1942	1944
15	Randolph			15/7/41	1944
16	Lexington	Bethlehem Steel Co.,		15/9/41	1943
17	Bunker Hill	Quincy	do.	1941	1943
18	Wasp			1942	24/11/43
19	Hancock			1942	1944
20	Bennington	New York Navy Yard	Not reported.	15/12/42	8/44
21	Boxer	Newport News Co.	Builders.	1943	16/4/45
31	B. H. Richard	New York Navy Yard	Not reported.	2/1/43	26/11/44
32	Leyte	Newport News Co.	Builders.	1944	1945
33	Kearsarge	New York Navy Yard	Not reported.	1/3/44	1945
34	Oriskany	do.	do.	1944	
36	Antietam	Philadelphia Navy Yard	do.	1943	28/1/45
37	Princeton	do.	do.	1944	1945
38	Shangri-La.	Norfolk Navy Yard.	do.	1942	15/4/44
39	Lake Champlain	do.	do.	1944	3/6/45
40	Tarawa	do.	do.	1943	1945
45	Valley Forge	Philadelphia Navy Yard	do.	1944	
47	Philippine Sea	Bethlehem Co., Quincy	Builders.	1944	1945

Notes.—First 11 of class ordered 1940. Inclusive cost officially estimated to average $68,932,000 each. *Essex* was built in 20 months, *Yorktown* in 17½ months Contracts were changed from original assignments in some instances. Later ships of this class are of improved design, with stronger flight decks and are more thoroughly sub-divided. Two ships under construction at New York Navy Yard (*Reprisal*) and Newport News (*Iwojima*, ex-*Crown Point*) were cancelled in August, 1945, and 10 others in March, 1945.

BOXER.   1945, U.S. Navy Official.

RANDOLPH (note deck-edge elevator).   Added 1949, U.S. Navy, Official.

ANTIETAM. (1944)

LEYTE.   1946, U.S. Navy, Official.

PHILIPPINE SEA (note deck-edge elevator)   1954, U.S. Navy, Official

PHILIPPINE SEA modified with united mast and funnel and twin clinker screen. Six helicopters flying in formation above the carrier.

1957, U.S. Navy, *Official*

VALLEY FORGE

1957, courtesy " *Our Navy* "

VALLEY FORGE

1962, courtesy Mr. W. H. Davis

YORKTOWN (port quarter oblique aerial view)

(1959) *United States Navy, Official*

Support Aircraft Carriers (CVS)
Amphibious Assault Ships (LPH)
Auxiliary Aircraft Transports (AVT)
19 "Essex" Class

ANTIETAM	LEXINGTON (ex-Cabot)
BENNINGTON	LEYTE (ex-Crown Point)
BOXER	PHILIPPINE SEA (ex-Wright)
BUNKER HILL	PRINCETON
ESSEX	RANDOLPH
FRANKLIN	TARAWA
HORNET (ex-Kearsarge)	VALLEY FORGE
INTREPID	WASP (ex-Oriskany)
KEARSARGE	YORKTOWN (ex-Bon Homme Richard)
LAKE CHAMPLAIN	

Displacement:	30,800 tons standard (38,500 tons *full load*)
Dimensions:	Length: 786 (pp.), 840 (w.l.), 888 (o.a.). Franklin 878 (o.a.), Bunker Hill, 879 (o.a.) Bennington, Lexington, Tarawa Valley Forge, 889 (o.a.) Essex 898 (o.a.) Hornet, Lake Champlain, Wasp 899 (o.a.) feet. Flight deck: 876 feet. Hangar: 720 feet
	Beam: 93 Hornet, Lake Champlain, Wasp 101 (hull), 113 feet (over sponsons). Width: Hangar 93 (max.), Ship 136 feet (extreme). Wasp Antietam 154 feet (including angled deck). Draught: 30¾ (max.) feet
Guns:	12—5 inch, 38 cal: 44 to 72—40 mm. AA., 52—20 mm. (quadruple mounts). Some active ships have 3-inch guns in place of 40 mm. mounts, 36 to 52—20 mm. (twin) mounts (see Gunnery)
Aircraft:	35 (more or fewer, according to size and type). CVS carry 20 fixed wing aircraft, 16 ASW helicopters. (see General). Boxer and Princeton carry 30 to 40 RH2S helicopters
Armour:	3"—2" side amidships, 3" hangar deck, 1⅜" flight deck, 1¼" upper deck
Machinery:	Geared turbines, 4 shafts. S.H.P.: 150,000=33 kts.
Boilers:	8 Babcock & Wilcox
Complement:	CVS Allowance: 87 officers, 1,430 men (excluding air group personnel). Accommodation for 340 officers, 2,890 men

WASP

1964. *United States Navy. Official*

General

The first ship of this class was ordered in 1940. The designed displacement was 27,100 tons. The original capacity, with smaller aircraft, was 85 to 100, and 107 were carried by close stowage. Essex was built in 20 months, Yorktown in 17½ months. Later ships of this class were of improved design, with stronger flight decks, and more thoroughly sub-divided. Princeton launched the "Regulus" guided missile at sea. CVSs underwent conversion for anti-submarine warfare. Conversion of Leyte was completed with aircraft reduced to 50 and operating crew to 1,300 (half previous complement). As Amphibious Assault Ships Boxer and Princeton were adapted to carry 30 HR2S helicopters and a Marine detachment of 10 officers and 323 men, with accommodation for 1,650 troops, but no structural alterations were made. Bunker Hill, Franklin, Leyte and Tarawa (all declassified to AVT) may be scrapped in the near future.

Sonar

Randolph was fitted with sonar, the first of its type in any aircraft carrier. Other CVSs are also now fitted with sonar.

Engineering

In Nov. 1945, Lake Champlain made Atlantic crossing from Gibraltar to Newport News in 4 days, 8 hours, 51 minutes, an average speed of 32·048 kts. Philippine Sea made Pacific crossing from Yokohama to San Francisco in 7 days, 13 hours, an average speed of 25·2 kts.

Marine Complements

In addition to their ship's companies of 1,000 officers and men Boxer, Princeton and Valley Forge are capable of carrying a Marine Battalion Landing Team of 1,200 to 1,500 officers and men, plus the crews for 30 to 40 helicopters.

BON HOMME RICHARD (before conversion).   1954, U.S. Navy, Official.

LAKE CHAMPLAIN (CVS 39)   United States Navy

ANTIETAM.   1954, U.S. Navy, Official.

KEARSARGE   1958, courtesy "Our Navy"

ANTIETAM (showing new angled or "canted" deck).   1953, U.S. Navy, Official.

WASP   1953, U.S. Navy, Official.

15 "Oriskany" (Improved "Essex") Class.

ORISKANY

No. :	CVA 34
Builders :	New York Navy Yard
Ordered :	7 Aug. 1942
Laid down :	1 May 1944
Launched :	13 Oct. 1945
Completed :	25 Sep. 1950

BENNINGTON	**LAKE CHAMPLAIN**
BON HOMME RICHARD	**LEXINGTON** (ex-*Cabot*)
ESSEX	**RANDOLPH**
HANCOCK (ex-*Ticonderoga*)	**SHANGRI-LA**
HORNET (ex-*Kearsarge*)	**TICONDEROGA** (ex-*Hancock*)
INTREPID	**WASP** (ex-*Oriskany*)
KEARSARGE	**YORKTOWN**
	(ex-*Bon Homme Richard*)

Displacement :	33,100 tons *standard* (40,800 to 42,600 tons *full load*).
	(Displacement of 27c conversions : 41,434 tons *full load*)
Dimensions :	Length : 786 (pp.), 840 (w.l.), 888 (o.a.) feet. (Oriskany 904 feet (o.a.).
	Flight deck : 876 feet. Hangar : 720 feet. Beam : 103 feet (hull), 129
	feet (over sponsons). Width : Hangar 93 feet (max.), ship 152 feet
	(extreme). Draught : 32 (max.) feet. (Dimensions of 27c conversions :
	Length : 830 feet. Width : 164 feet (extreme)
Guns :	8—5 inch, 38 cal. ; 28—3 inch, 50 cal. in twin mounts
Aircraft :	100
Catapults :	2 steam (Bon Homme Richard, Hancock, Intrepid,
	Lexington, Shangri-La, Ticonderoga
Armour :	3" sides, 3" decks
Machinery :	Geared turbines. 4 shafts. S.H.P.: 150,000 = 33 kts.
Boilers :	8 Babcock & Wilcox
Complement :	About 2,100 (peacetime), 2,800 to 3,300 (wartime)

BENNINGSTON (port bow aerial view showing canted deck and hurricane bow) *1959, U.S. Navy, Official*

SHANGRI-LA (enclosed bow, angled deck, steam catapults). *1955, U.S. Navy, Official.*

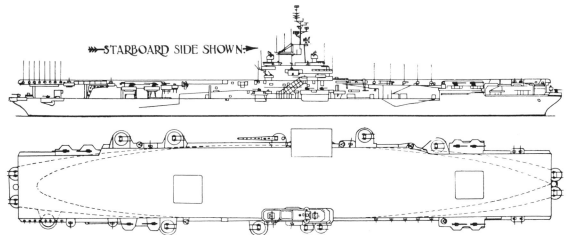

➤➤ STARBOARD SIDE SHOWN ➤

Notes.—Oriskany was the first of a new type to which modified " Essex " class carriers subsequently conformed ; her construction was delayed with a view to recasting of plans and she was completed to a modified design with a smaller island, heavier decks and handling gear to operate bigger aircraft, larger lifts, more powerful catapults, a stronger runway and increased stowage for petrol as compared with " Essex " class. Bulges offset the extra weight thus added. For builders and construction dates of above modernised ships of the " Essex " class see next page. All will eventually be fitted with the angled deck. Hancock completed catapult conversion Jan. 1954 : first to have new steam catapults and starboard deck-edge elevator ; first of 27c conversions, has one-foot wider blister than 27a conversions. Recent catapult conversions completed as follows :—Intrepid Apr. 1954, Ticonderoga Apr. 1954. Angled deck and enclosed bow conversion completed in Bennington and planned for Essex, Hancock, Hornet, Intrepid, Kearsarge, Lake Champlain, Oriskany, Randolph, Ticonderoga, Wasp and Yorktown. Angled deck, steam catapult and enclosed bow conversion completed in Shangri-La Feb. 1955, Lexington Sep. 1955, Bon Homme Richard Nov. 1955. Several, including Hancock, fitted to launch " Regulus " guided missiles.

RANDOLPH (CVS 15) (1968) *United States Navy*

INTREPID (CVS 11) 1966, United States Navy

ESSEX (port bow oblique aerial view, showing aircraft park and angled deck) 1959, U.S. Navy, Official

RANDOLPH (port quarter overhead aerial) 1958, U.S. Navy Official

BON HOMME RICHARD (port bow view at hangar deck level) Refuelling of two destroyers. 1958, U.S. Navy, Official

ORISKANY (CVA 34)

1970, United States Navy

ORISKANY (CVA 34)
Drawing by A. D. Baker

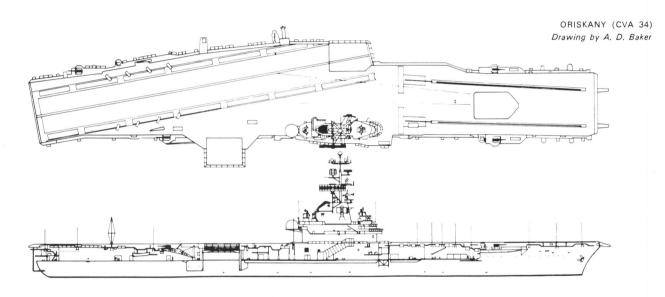

MODERNISATION. The completion of the *Oriskany* was delayed after World War II, allowing her to be completed with heavier catapults, improved elevators, reinforced flight deck, increased aviation fuel storage, and other features for operating jets. The table on the following page shows major "Essex" class modernisations. These ships are capable of operating high-performance fighters and attack aircraft including the Mach 1·7 Crusader fighter and 35-ton KA-3B Skywarrior aerial tanker.

ORISKANY (CVA 34)

1970 United States Navy

ORISKANY (CVA 34)   *1966, US Navy*

ORISKANY (CVA 34)   *1966. United States Navy*

INTREPID (CVS 11)   *1969, United States Navy*

TICONDEROGA (CVA 14)   *1965, US Navy*

TICONDEROGA (CVA 14)   *1967, United States Navy*

2 MODERNISED "ESSEX" CLASS: ASW AIRCRAFT CARRIERS (CVS)

Name	No.	Builders	Laid down	Launched	Commissioned	F S
HORNET	CVS 12	Newport News Shipbuilding & Dry Dock Co	3 Aug 1942	29 Aug 1943	29 Nov 1943	PR
BENNINGTON	CVS 20	New York Navy Yard	15 Dec 1942	26 Feb 1944	6 Aug 1944	PR

Displacement, tons: 33 000 standard; 40 600 full load
Dimensions, feet (metres): 899 × 101 × 31 *(274 × 30·7 × 9·4)*
Flight deck width, feet (metres): 172 *(52·4)*
Catapults: 2 hydraulic (H-8)
Aircraft: 45 (including 16 to 18 helicopters)
Guns: 4—5 in *(127 mm)*/38 (single Mk 24)
Main engines: 4 geared turbines (Westinghouse);
150 000 shp; 4 shafts
Boilers: 8 (Babcock & Wilcox)
Speed, knots: 30+
Complement: 1 615 (115 officers, approx 1 500 enlisted men)
plus approx 800 assigned to ASW air group for a total of
2 400 per ship

The two above ships and the previously listed "Hancock" and
"Intrepid" classes are the survivors of the 24 "Essex" class
carriers built during World War II (with one ship, *Oriskany*, not
completed until 1950). Both of the above ships were extensively modernised during the 1950s; however, they lack the
steam catapults and other features of the "Hancock" and
"Intrepid" classes.
Bennington was decommissioned on 15 January 1970 and
Hornet on 26 June 1970. Both laid up at Bremerton. Wash.

Classification: These ships originally were designated as Aircraft Carriers (CV): reclassified as Attack Carriers (CVA) on
1 October 1952. Subsequently they became ASW Support Aircraft Carriers (CVS): *Hornet* on 27 June 1958, and *Bennington*
on 30 June 1959.

Design: All 24 "Essex" class ships were built to the same basic
design except for the delayed *Oriskany*. Standard displacement as built was 27 100 tons, full load displacement was
36 380 tons, and overall length 888 or 872 ft.

Fire control: One Mk 37 and three Mk 56 GFCS.

Modernisation: These ships have been modernised under
several programmes to increase their ability to operate
advanced aircraft and to improve sea keeping. Also modernised to improve anti-submarine capabilities under the Fleet
Rehabilitation and Modernisation (FRAM II) programme.

Radar: Search: SPS 10, 30 and 43; Tacan.

Sonar: SQS 23 (bow-mounted).

BENNINGTON (starboard lift raised during replenishment)   *1968, USN*

HORNET   *1968, USN*

3 "Midway" Class

CORAL SEA (April 2, 1946)
FRANKLIN D. ROOSEVELT (ex-*Coral Sea*, April 29, 1945)
MIDWAY (March 20, 1945) MEMORIAL - SAN DIEGO

Displacement:	45,000 tons (55,000 tons *full load*)
Dimensions:	Length: 968 (*o.a.*) feet. Beam: 113 feet (hull); Width: 136 (*max.*) feet. Draught: 32¾ feet
Guns:	14—5 inch, 54 cal., 84—40 mm. AA. (quadrupled), 82—20 mm. AA.
Aircraft:	137 (including large bombers of latest type)
Machinery:	Geared turbines. 4 shafts. S.H.P.: 20,000 33 kts.
Boilers:	12
Complement:	Over 3,000 (war)

General Notes.—Are the most extensively welded ships in U.S. Navy, and cost $90,000,000 each. On Sept. 6, 1947, the first carrier-borne guided missile was launched from the flight deck of the *Midway*. On March 7, 1949, a Lockheed PV2 long-range bomber which can handle atomic bombs took off with rocket assistance from the *Coral Sea* with a load of 37 tons on a 2,000-mile flight. Three more ships of this class (CVB 44, 56, 57) were projected, but cancelled in 1945.

Armour Notes.—Officially stated that these ships are protected by heavy armour, intricate water-tight compartments and an improved system of damage control. Armoured flight deck is 932 × 113 feet, covered with non-skid surface material; it was strengthened in all 3 ships during 1947–48, to enable heavier aircraft to be handled.

Gunnery Notes.—*Midway* and *Franklin D. Roosevelt* originally had eighteen 5 inch. They now mount fourteen 5 inch, 38 cal. and 5 inch, 54 cal. d.p. and 21 quadruple 40 mm.

Appearance Note.—*Coral Sea* differs in her gun layout from other two; there were four 5-inch guns abaft funnel on starboard side instead of 6.

MIDWAY.   1945, *U.S. Navy Official.*

MIDWAY.   1946, *Mr. Wm. H. Davis.*

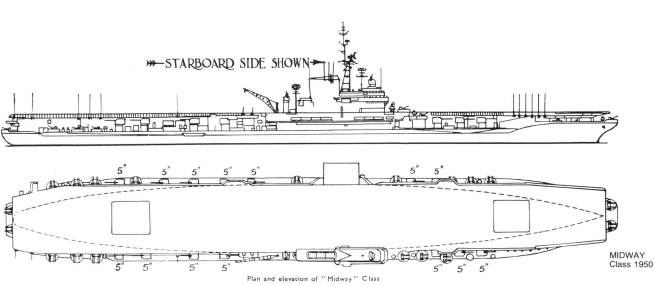

→ STARBOARD SIDE SHOWN →

MIDWAY
Class 1950

Plan and elevation of "Midway" Class

FRANKLIN D. ROOSEVELT.   Added 1950, *U.S. Navy, Official.*

CORAL SEA.   1950, *U.S. Navy, Official.*

MIDWAY (after conversion with angled deck and enclosed bow).   Starboard quarter aerial view.

1958, U.S. Navy, Official

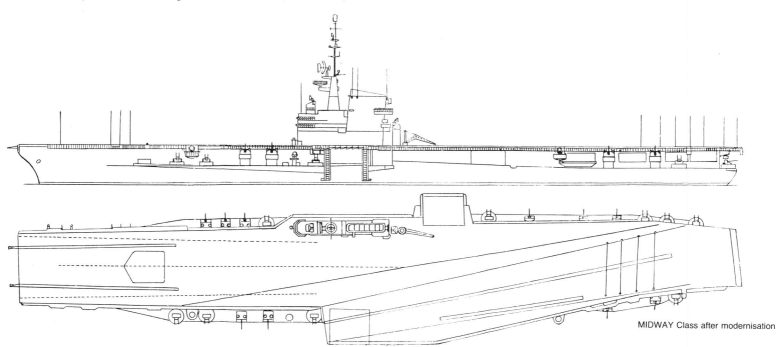

MIDWAY Class after modernisation

Gunnery Notes

Midway and *Franklin D. Roosevelt* originally had eighteen 5 inch. They subsequently mounted fourteen 5 inch, 54 cal. d.p. and now have only ten, four on the port side and six on the starboard side. They and *Coral Sea* now have twin-3-inch mountings in place of the former quadruple 40 mm. mountings.

Armour Notes

Officially stated that these ships are protected by heavy armour, intricate water-tight compartments and an improved system of damage control. Armoured flight deck is 932 × 113 feet, covered with non-skid surface material; it was strengthened in all 3 ships during 1947-48, to enable heavier aircraft to be handled.

flight Deck Notes

The angled deck arrangement installed in the " Midway " class aircraft carriers requires only half the arresting gear for normal operations and eliminates crash barriers, releasing considerable topside weight and gallery deck space.

Elevator Notes

The triangular section on the forward end of the forward elevators of these ships (and some modernised " Essex " class) increases the length of the elevators 12 feet along the centreline. The additional length permits easier handling of larger aircraft.

Following modernisation the *Midway* and *Roosevelt* each have two deckedge and one centreline elevator. The *Coral Sea* will have three deck-edge elevators.

Disposition Notes

Coral Sea and *Midway*, Pacific Fleet; *Franklin D. Roosevelt*, Atlantic Fleet.

Modernisation and Conversion Notes

Franklin D. Roosevelt was modernised at Puget Sound Naval Shipyard under the 1954 conversion programme. Now has angled deck, enclosed bow, 3 higher capacity catapults (steam), increased aviation fuel capacity, and broader hull. Remodelling enables her to handle faster and heavier jet aircraft.   Conversion completed 6 Apr. 1956 and cost $48,000,000. 53 per cent of ship's original cost.

Modernisation and conversion of *Midway*, including installation of the angled deck, as authorised in the 1954 Fiscal appropriations commenced in Autumn 1955 at Puget Sound Naval Shipyard and was completed on 30 Sep. 1957 when she was recommissioned for duty with the Pacific Fleet. Modernisation and conversion of *Coral Sea* was authorised in Fiscal 1957 appropriations.   Conversion at Puget Sound Naval Shipyard in two years commencing Apr. 1957 (to Bremerton, Wash., 26 Feb. 1957; placed in the status of "out of commission, in reserve " 24 May 1957). The forward centreline elevator has been replaced by a deck-edge elevator on the starboard side forward, while the port side elevator originally installed has been moved aft. Arresting gear and barricades have been relocated, and extensive changes made in the hangar bay area.   The beam at the waterline has been increased by approximately 8 feet.

Estimated completion date is 15 Mar. 1960. This ship was designed during the Second World War on the basis of experience with the " Essex " class, but was completed too late to see service. This is the first major conversion she has had, and consists of a completed modernisation, including angled deck, hurricane bow and replacement of two hydraulic catapults by three steam catapults. Estimated commissioning date is 25 Jan. 1960.

Classification Notes

All originally designated as CVB's but were reclassified as Attack Aircraft Carriers, CVA, in Oct. 1952

Class Notes

Three more ships of this class (CVB 44, 56, 57) projected were cancelled in 1945.

Notes to Drawing

Port elevation and plan. Drawn in 1957.
Scale : 128 feet = 1 inch.
This represents *Franklin D. Roosevelt* See *Modernisation and Conversion Notes*, and *Appearance Notes*.

No.	Name	Builders	Machinery	Laid down	Launched	Completed
CVA 43	*Coral Sea*	Newport News Co.	Westinghouse	10 July 1944	2 Apr. 1946	1 Oct. 1947
CVA 42	*Franklin D. Roosevelt*	New York Navy Yard	General Electric	1 Dec. 1943	29 Apr. 1945	27 Oct. 1945
CVA 41	*Midway*	Newport News Co	Westinghouse	27 Oct. 1943	20 Mar. 1945	11 Sep. 1945

FRANKLIN D. ROOSEVELT (CVA 42)

United States Navy

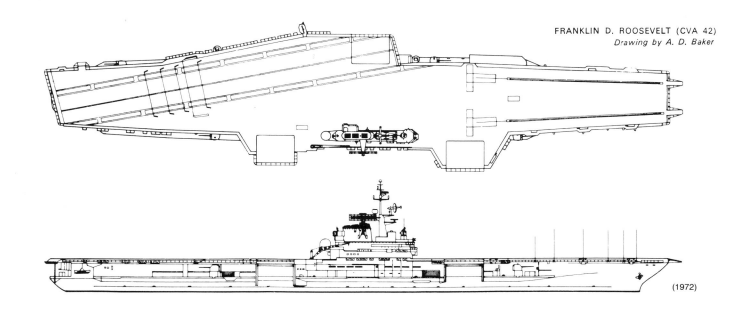

FRANKLIN D. ROOSEVELT (CVA 42)
Drawing by A. D. Baker

(1972)

FRANKLIN D. ROOSEVELT (CVA 42)

1970, United States Navy

MIDWAY

1959, United States Navy, Official

MIDWAY (CVA 41)

1965, United States Navy

MIDWAY

1/1975, USN

CORAL SEA (CVA 43)   *United States Navy*

CORAL SEA   *4/1976, USN*

CORAL SEA (CVA 43)   *1971, United States Navy*

2 "MIDWAY" CLASS: MULTI-PURPOSE AIRCRAFT CARRIERS (CV)

Name		No.
MIDWAY	MEMORIAL	CV 41
CORAL SEA	SAN DIEGO	CV 43

Displacement, tons: *Midway:* 51 000 standard;
   Coral Sea: 52 500 standard; 62 200 full load
Dimensions, feet (metres): 979 × 121 × 35·3
   (298·4 × 36·9 × 10·8)
Flight deck width, feet (metres): 238 *(72·5)* maximum
Catapults: 2 steam in *Midway* (C 13); 3 in *Coral Sea* (C 11)
Aircraft: Approx 75
Missiles: See note
Guns: See notes
Main engines: 4 geared turbines (Westinghouse); 212 000 shp;
   4 shafts
Boilers: 12 (Babcock & Wilcox)
Speed, knots: 30+
Complement: *Midway* 2 615 (140 officers, approx 2 475
   enlisted men); *Coral Sea* 2 710 (165 officers, approx 2 545
   enlisted men) plus approx 1 800 assigned to air wing

The original three carriers of this class were the largest US
warships constructed during World War II. Completed too late
for service in that conflict, they were the backbone of US naval
strength for the first decade of the Cold War. The entire class
has been in active service (except for overhaul and modernisation) since the ships were completed. *F. D. Roosevelt* deleted in
1977.
Midway was homeported at Yokosuka, Japan, in October 1973;
she is the only US aircraft carrier to be based overseas.
Midway will probably be retained in service until 1985 to provide a 13 carrier force level. *Coral Sea* is currently active but has
no regular air wing and is used for contingencies. She will be
replaced in the active fleet by *Carl Vinson*.
Coral Sea relieved *Kitty Hawk* in the Indian Ocean late 1979.
The unnamed CVB 44, 56 and 57 of this class were cancelled
prior to the start of construction.

Classification: These ships were initially classified as large
Aircraft Carriers (CVB); reclassified as Attack Aircraft Carriers
(CVA) on 1 October 1952. Both ships reclassified as Aircraft
Carriers (CV) on 30 June 1975.

Design: These ships were built to the same design with a
standard displacement of 45 000 tons, full load displacement of
60 100 tons, and an overall length of 968 feet. They have been
extensively modified since completion (see *Modernisation*
note). These ships were the first US aircraft carriers with an
armoured flight deck and the first US warships with a designed
width too large to enable them to pass through the Panama
Canal.

Electronics: Naval Tactical Data System (NTDS); Tacan.
Fitted with OE-82 satellite communications antenna.

Fiscal: Construction cost of *Midway* was $85·6 million and
Coral Sea $87·6 million.

Gunnery: As built, these ships mounted 18 5-in guns (14 in
Coral Sea), 84—40 mm guns, and 28—20 mm guns. In 1978 the
last 5-in guns were removed.
Both are to be fitted with three 20 mm Mk 15 CIWS in near
future.
Both ships carry two 40 mm saluting guns.

Missiles: *Midway* is to be fitted with two Mk 25 Sea Sparrow
launchers (BPDMS) in near future as well as two Mk 115 Missile
FC systems.

Modernisation: Extensively modernised. Their main conversion gave them angled flight decks, steam catapults, enclosed
bows, new electronics, and new lift arrangement *(Midway*
from 1955 to 1957, and *Coral Sea* from 1958 to 1960; both at
Puget Sound Naval Shipyard). Lift arrangement was changed
in *Midway* to one centreline lift forward, one deck-edge lift aft
of island on starboard side, and one deck-edge lift at forward
end of angled deck on port side. *Coral Sea* has one lift forward
and one aft of island on starboard side and third lift outboard
on port side aft. *Midway* began another extensive modernisation at the San Francisco Bay Naval Shipyard in February 1966;
she was recommissioned on 31 January 1970 and went to sea
in March 1970.
Her modernisation included widening the flight deck, provisions for handling newer aircraft, new catapults, new lifts
(arranged as in *Coral Sea*), and new electronics.
Midway is now the more capable of the two ships *Coral Sea*
had an extensive refit in 1979.

MIDWAY   *1979, Dr. Giorgio Arra*

MIDWAY   *1979, Dr. Giorgio Arra*

Radar: Low angle air search: SPS 58.
Search: SPS 10, 30 and 43.
Navigation: SPN 6 and 10.

MIDWAY (with Sea Sparrow lattice abaft island)   *8 1979, Dr. Giorgio Arra*

2 "Kitty Hawk" Class

CONSTELLATION   **KITTY HAWK**

4 "Forrestal" Class

FORRESTAL   **RANGER**
INDEPENDENCE   **SARATOGA**

Displacement:	60.000 tons *standard* (76.000 tons *full load*) except *Forrestal*, 59.650 tons (75.900 tons *full load*), *Constellation* and *Kitty Hawk* 76.700 tons *full load*
Dimensions:	Length: 990 (*pp.*), 1,039 (*o.a.*) *Forrestal*, 1,045 (*o.a.*) *Saratoga*, 1,046 (*o.a.*) *Ranger*, *Independence*, 1,047 (*o.a.*) *Kitty Hawk*, *Constellation*, 1,047½ (*o.a.*) feet. Beam: 129¼ (*hull*), 252 (*o.a.*) feet Draught: 37 (*max.*) feet Area of flight deck: 4·1 acres
Guns:	4—5 inch. 54 cal. dual purpose (no guns in *Constellation* and *Kitty Hawk*) see *Gunnery*
Guided missiles:	2 twin "Terrier" launchers in *Kitty Hawk* and *Constellation* ("*Forrestal*" class have "Regulus" capability)
Aircraft:	80 to 60 (more or fewer according to size and type)
Catapults:	4 steam
Machinery:	4 geared turbines. 4 shafts. S.H.P.: 260.000 (in *Forrestal*) = 33 kts. All others 280.000 = 35 kts.
Boilers:	8 Babcock & Wilcox (Foster Wheeler in *Constellation* and *Kitty Hawk*)
Oil fuel	7,828 tons
Aviation fuel:	5,882 tons
Complement:	Allowance: 119 officers, 2,540 men excluding air group personnel). Accommodation for 428 officers, 4,155 men (*Kitty Hawk* class); 442 officers, 3,360 men (*Forrestal* class) See *Complement* notes

General

Four deck edge elevators and three separate launching areas for aircraft. *Forrestal* (contract awarded on 12 July 1951) was named after the Secretary of Defence who was in office when the subsequently cancelled Heavy Carrier *United States* (CVA 58) was named in 1949. *Ranger* authorised 1954 Fiscal year: contract awarded 2 Feb. 1954. *Independence* authorised in 1955 Fiscal year. *Kitty Hawk*, named for the site where the Wright brothers made their historic flights, was first tentatively to have been named *Congress*. Cost $218,000,000 (*Forrestal*), $209,700,000 (*Saratoga*), $182,000,000 (*Ranger*), $189,311,000 (*Independence*) and $200,000,000 (*Constellation*). *Independence* commissioned on 10 Jan. 1959, *Kitty Hawk* on 2 Apr. 1961 and *Constellation* on 27 Oct. 1961. During a 6-months overhaul of *Ranger* in 1963-64 eight feet was added to angled deck width to accommodate newer aircraft.

Construction

Flight deck about 80 feet longer than that in the "Midway" class to operate larger, heavier carrier-based naval aircraft of the newest designs. Increased catapult and arresting capacity, larger elevators, higher hangar decks, mirror sight to aid in landing on aircraft, added armour and improved underwater protection. The flight deck is a strength deck by reduction of the openings in the hangar sides, bow enclosed up to the flight deck for seaworthiness in all types of weather, island acoustically constructed to block out external noise, air-conditioned berthing quarters, three rudders. *Independence* has sponsons streamlined from below, which is a refinement over other "Forrestal" class carriers. Additional electronic equipment was installed in *Kitty Hawk*.

Elevators

The aircraft elevators in *Kitty Hawk* and *Constellation* are located differently from those in the four ships of the "Forrestal" class, the island structure being sited more aft (see *Appearance*). Largest elevators ever installed in a ship, each capable of lifting 89,000 lbs.

Engineering

Two propellers are 4-bladed and two 5-bladed. *Kitty Hawk* has four 5-bladed propellers. *Saratoga* has machinery arrangements to produce somewhat higher speeds *Independence*, *Kitty Hawk* and *Constellation* have substantially the same characteristics, but with somewhat more powerful propelling machinery.

Complement

The complement is being increased by 400 to 800 men per ship for support of new aircraft maintenance.

Gunnery

The forward gun sponsons were removed from *Forrestal*, *Independence*, *Ranger* and *Saratoga*. The sponsons interfered with operations during heavy weather, tending to slow the ship down. The sponsons contained 2—5 inch guns each, thus the armament has been halved, only 4—5 inch mounts remaining in the two after sponsons. Sponsons were not built in *Constellation* and *Kitty Hawk*.

Appearance

Mast configurations differ. Two masts in *Forrestal*, one in others. In the last two ships, *Kitty Hawk* and *Constellation*, the island is smaller and further aft than the superstructure in the first four, and the lifts are disposed two before the island and one abaft the island on the starboard side, and one on the after quarter on the port side, compared with two abaft the island on the starboard side, and one before the island on the starboard side, and one on the forward quarter on the port side in the first four ships.

Photographs

Port bow aerial view of *Ranger* in 1957-58 to 1961-62 editions. Port bow aerial view of *Independence* in 1959-60 to 1962-63 editions. Port bow oblique aerial view of *Kitty Hawk* in 1961-62 and 1962-63 editions. Starboard bow aerial view of *Forrestal* in 1958-59 to 1963-64 editions. Counter aerial view of *Kitty Hawk* showing mast hinged down in 1961-62 to 1963-64 editions.

CONSTELLATION   1963, *United States Navy, Official*

SARATOGA   1958, *courtesy Dr. Ian S. Pearsall*

No.	Name	Builders	Laid down	Launched	Completed
CVA 59	Forrestal	Newport News S.B. Co.	14 July 1952	11 Dec. 1954	1 Oct. 1955
CVA 60	Saratoga	New York Naval Shipyard	16 Dec. 1952	8 Oct. 1955	14 Apr. 1956
CVA 61	Ranger	Newport News S.B. Co.	2 Aug. 1954	29 Sep. 1956	10 Aug. 1957
CVA 62	Independence	New York Naval Shipyard	1 July 1955	6 June 1958	3 Apr. 1959
CVA 63	Kitty Hawk	New York S.B. Corp., N.J.	27 Dec. 1956	21 May 1960	9 June 1961
CVA 64	Constellation	New York Naval Shipyard	14 Sep. 1957	8 Oct. 1960	19 Jan. 1962

INDEPENDENCE (starboard broadside aerial view)   1959, *United States Navy, Official*

FORRESTAL (starboard bow aerial view)

1958 .U.S. Navy, Official

Drawing
Starboard elevation and plan of U.S.S. *Forrestal*.
Scale: 128 feet=1 inch.

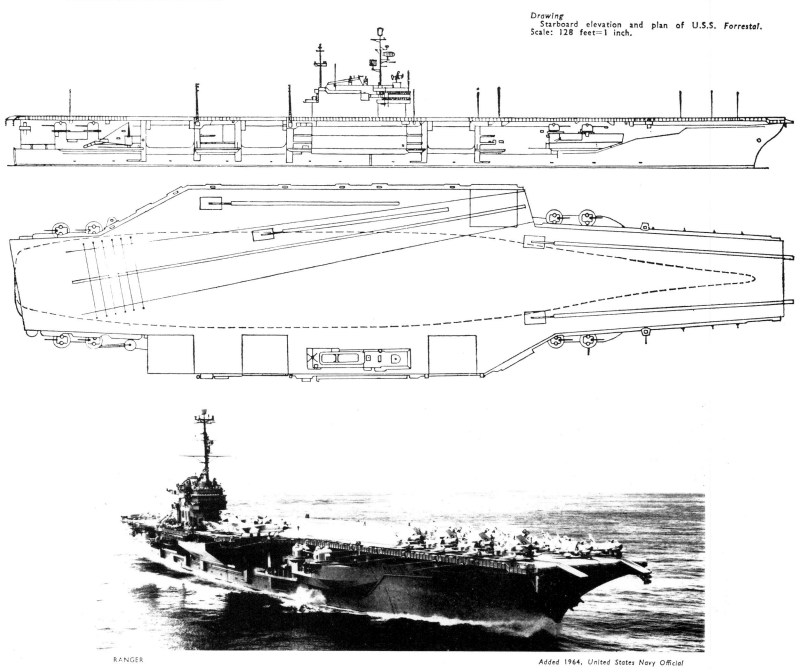

RANGER

Added 1964, United States Navy Official

KITTY HAWK

1963. United States Navy, Official (direct from U.S.S. Kitty Hawk, courtesy of Commanding Officer)

INDEPENDENCE (port bow aerial view)

1959, United States Navy, Official

SARATOGA (CVA 60)

1967, United States Navy

ENGINEERING. The *Saratoga* and later ships have an improved steam plant; increased machinery weight of the improved plant is more than compensated by increased performance and decreased fuel consumption.

GUNNERY. All four ships initially mounted 8—5 inch guns in single mounts, two mounts on each quarter. The forward sponsons carrying the guns interfered with ship operations in rough weather, tending to slow the ships down. The forward sponsons and guns were subsequently removed, reducing armament to four guns per ship. The guns are 5 inch/54 calibre, rapid-fire, dual-purpose weapons.

MODERNISATION. During an overhaul in 1963-1964 the width of the *Ranger's* angled flight deck was extended eight feet to accommodate newer aircraft.

FORRESTAL (CVA 59)

1968, United States Navy

RANGER (CVA 61)

1966, United States Navy

INDEPENDENCE (CV 62)   1970, United States Navy

RANGER (CVA 61) (Retains Forward Sponsons)   1967, United States Navy

RANGER (CVA 61)   1968, United States Navy

SARATOGA (CV 60)   1970, United States Navy, PH1 R. D. Williams

FORRESTAL (CVA 59)

1971, United States Navy

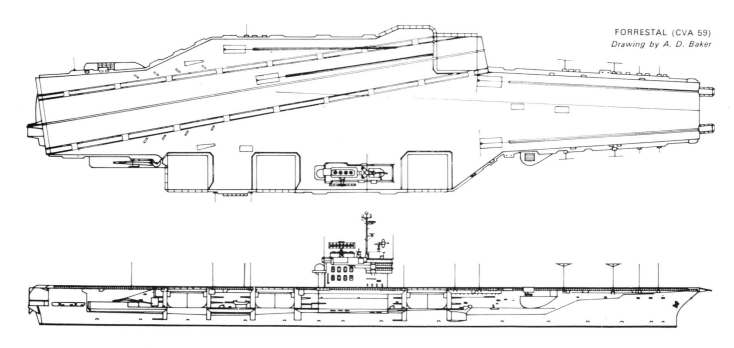

FORRESTAL (CVA 59)
Drawing by A. D. Baker

FORRESTAL

7/1976, A. D. Baker III

Missiles: The four after 5-in guns were removed from *Forrestal* late in 1967 and a single BPDMS launcher for Sea Sparrow missiles was installed forward on the starboard side. An additional launcher was provided aft on the port side in 1972. Two BPDMS launchers fitted in *Independence* in 1973; *Saratoga* in 1974; *Forrestal* in 1976. These are soon to be replaced by three Mk 29 BPDMS launchers—the same type fitted in *Ranger*.

Names: *Forrestal* is named after James V. Forrestal, Secretary of the Navy from 1944 until he was appointed the first US Secretary of Defense in 1947.

Radar: Low angle air search: SPS 58.
Search: SPS 30 and 43 (*Saratoga* —to be replaced by SPS 48 and 49 during SLEP); SPS 48 and 49 in remainder.
Navigation: SPN 10.

Rockets: One Mk 28 rocket launching system fitted in all but *Ranger.* Mk 36 Chaffroc RBOC to be fitted in all ships.

Service Life Extension Programme (SLEP): Owing to current building costs this programme is intended to extend carriers' lives from 30 to 45 years. The "Forrestal" class will be the first to undergo this modernisation—*Saratoga* first under FY 1981, *Forrestal* in FY 1983, *Independence* in FY 1985 and *Ranger* in FY 1987.
Each modernisation will last 18-24 months and include extensive re-cabling and renovation. Cost approx $496 million each (FY 1980 dollars). $32·2 million advance funding approved in FY 1979 for first SLEP which will be *Saratoga* at Philadelphia NY. Protests at this choice from Newport News resulted in Congress deciding to make their own decision and finally approved Philadelphia in late 1979. *Saratoga* will decommission in October 1980 and will then enter the Navy Yard to begin her SLEP. In FY 1981 dollars this will cost about 40 per cent of the building price of a large-deck carrier.

SARATOGA

1975, USN

INDEPENDENCE

11/1979, Michael D. J. Lennon

RANGER

7/1979, Dr. Giorgio Arra

4 Attack Aircraft Carriers (CVA): Improved "Forrestal" Class

Name	No.	Builder	Laid down	Launched	Commissioned
*KITTY HAWK	CVA 63	New York SB Corp NJ	27 Dec 1956	21 May 1960	29 Apr 1961
*CONSTELLATION	CVA 64	New York Naval Shipyard	14 Sep 1957	8 Oct 1960	27 Oct 1961
*AMERICA	CVA 66	Newport News SB & DD Co	9 Jan 1961	1 Feb 1964	23 Jan 1965
*JOHN F. KENNEDY	CVA 67	Newport News SB & DD Co	22 Oct 1964	27 May 1967	Sep 1968

Displacement, tons
Kitty Hawk — 60 100 standard ; 75 200 full load
Constellation — 60 100 standard ; 75 200 full load
America — 60 300 standard ; 78 250 full load
John F. Kennedy — 61 000 standard ; 83 000 full load

Length, feet (metres) — 990 (301·8) wl
Kitty Hawk — 1 062·5 (323·9) oa
Constellation — 1 072·5 (326·9) oa
America, J.F.K. — 1 047·5 (319·3) oa

Beam, feet (metres)
Kitty Hawk,
Constellation — 129·5 (38·5)
America, J.F.K. — 130 (39·6)

Flight deck width, feet (metres)
Constellation — 260 (79·2) maximum
Others — 252 (76·8) maximum

Catapults — 4 steam
Aircraft — 70 to 90, according to type
Missiles — 2 twin Terrier surface-to-air launchers in *Kitty Hawk, Constellation, America* ; 2 twin Tartar surface-to-air launchers in *John F. Kennedy*
Main engines — 4 geared turbines (Westinghouse) ; 280 000 shp ; 4 shafts
Boilers — 8 — 1 200 psi (83·4 kg/cm²) (Foster Wheeler)
Speed — 35 knots
Complement — 2 700 (120 officers, approx 2 600 enlisted men) plus approx 2 000 assigned to attack air wing for a total of 4 700 to 5 000 officers and enlisted men per ship

These ships were built to an improved "....al" design and are easily recognised by their .... nd structure ......s set further aft than the .... ure in the four .....tal" class ships. Lift arrangement also differs (see .... notes). The *Kitty Hawk* was authorised in Fiscal .. 1956 new construction programme, the *Constellation* in FY 1957, the *America* in FY 1961, and the *John F. Kennedy* in FY 1963. Completion of the *Constellation* was delayed because of a fire which ravaged her in the New York Naval Shipyard in December 1960. Construction of the *John F. Kennedy* was delayed because of debate over whether to provide her with conventional or nuclear propulsion.
Estimated construction costs were $217 963 000 for *Kitty Hawk* and $247 620 000 for *Constellation*.

DESIGN. These ships are officially considered to be of a different design than the "Forrestal" class by the Navy's Ship Characteristics Board. The island structure is smaller and set further aft in the newer ships with two deck-edge lifts forward of the superstructure, a third lift aft of the structure, and the port-side left on the after quarter (compared with two lifts aft of the island and the port-side lift at the forward end of the angled deck in the earlier ships). This lift arrangement considerably improves flight deck operations. All four of these ships also have a small radar mast aft of the island structure.

ELECTRONICS. All four ships of this class have highly sophisticated electronic equipment and the Naval Tactical Data System (NTDS). The *America* and *John F. Kennedy* have bow-mounted SQS-23 sonar, the first US attack carriers with anti-submarine sonar (several ASW carriers have been fitted with sonar during modernizations).

MODERNISATION. The *Constellation* was extensively modified during her 1965 overhaul with her displacement and overall length being increased to the dimensions noted above.

KITTY HAWK (CVA 63)   *1968, United States Navy by PH 1 K. H. Thompson*

KITTY HAWK (CVA 63)   *United States Navy by PHC R. C. Moen*

NOMENCLATURE. US aircraft carriers are generally named after battles and old ships. However, the *Kitty Hawk* better honours the site where the Wright brothers made their historic flights than the converted aircraft ferry of that name which served in World War II. The *Constellation* remembers a frigate built in 1797 which is still afloat at Baltimore, Maryland, although no longer in Navy commission. The name "America" was previously carried by a 74-gun ship-of-the-line launched in 1782 and presented to France, by the racing schooner which gave her name to the America's Cup, and by the German liner *Amerika* which was taken over by the US Navy in World War I, renamed, and used as a troop transport. The *John F. Kennedy* remembers the martyred president who was assassinated in 1963. The destroyer *Joseph P. Kennedy Jr.* (DD 850) honours his older brother who was killed in a bomber explosion over England in World War II.

AMERICA (CVA 66)   *1972, United States Navy, PH3 G. R. Stromquist*

CONSTELLATION (CVA 64)

United States Navy

KITTY HAWK

8/1979, Dr. Giorgio Arra

CONSTELLATION

10/1975, USN

CONSTELLATION

3/1980, Dr. Giorgio Arra

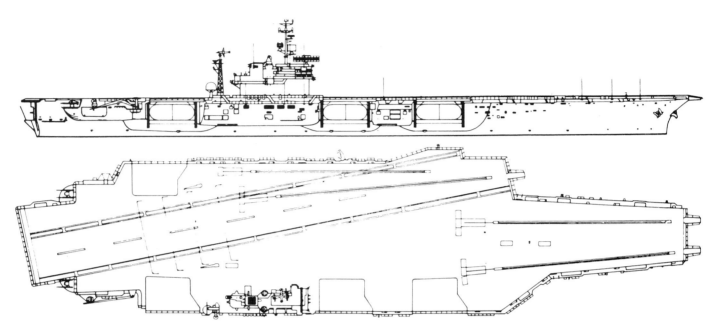

AMERICA (1980)

Drawing by A. D. Baker III

AMERICA
(CVA 66), *1964*

KITTY HAWK
(CVA 63), *1961*

Classification: As completed, all four ships were classified as attack aircraft carriers (CVA); first two changed to multi-mission aircraft carriers (attack and anti-submarine) when modified with A/S command centres and facilities for S-3 Viking fixed-wing aircraft and SH-3 Sea King helicopters. *Kitty Hawk* from CVA to CV on 29 April 1973; *John F. Kennedy* from CVA to CV on 1 December 1974; *Constellation* and *America* from CVA to CV on 30 June 1975, prior to A/S modifications.

Design: They have two deck-edge lifts forward of the super-structure, a third lift aft of the structure, and the port-side lift on the after quarter. This arrangement considerably improves flight deck operations. Four C13 catapults (with one C13-1 in each of later ships). *John F. Kennedy* and *America* have stern anchors as well as bower anchors because of their planned bow sonar domes (see *Sonar* notes). All have a small radar mast abaft the island.

Electronics: All four ships of this class have highly sophisticated electronic equipment including the Naval Tactical Data System (NTDS). Tacan in all ships. Fitted with OE-82 satellite communications antenna.

Fire control: *Kitty Hawk:* Two Mk 91 MFCS for Mk 29 BPDMS.
Constellation: Four Mk 76 MFCS for Terrier.
America: Four Mk 76 MFCS for Terrier.
John F. Kennedy: Three Mk 115 MFCS for Mk 25 BPDMS.
It is planned to replace Mk 76 and Mk 115 systems with Mk 91 in *Constellation* and *John F. Kennedy.*

Fiscal: Construction costs were $265·2 million for *Kitty Hawk,* $264·5 million for *Constellation,* $248·8 million for *America,* and $277 million for *John F. Kennedy.*

Gunnery: Planned to mount three 20 mm Mk 15 CIWS in each ship. All currently have only 40 mm saluting guns (two in 63 and 64, four in 66 and one in 67).

Missiles: The two Terrier-armed ships have a Mk 10 Mod 3 launcher on the starboard quarter and a Mod 4 launcher on the port quarter.
America has updated Terrier launchers and guidance system

that can accommodate Standard missiles; *Constellation* retains older Terrier HT systems which will be replaced by three NATO Sea Sparrow launchers (Mk 29).
Three Sea Sparrow BPDMS launchers were fitted in *John F. Kennedy* early in 1969. It is planned to replace *John F. Kennedy's* Mk 25 with Mk 29 BPDMS. *America* is to retain her Terrier until 1980.

Radar: 3D search: SPS 52 (3 ships).
Search: SPS 43.
Search: SPS 30 (3 ships).
Search: SPS 48 and 58 (*John F. Kennedy*).

Rockets: Mk 28 Mod 5 rocket launching systems fitted in *America* and *John F. Kennedy.*

Sonar: SQS 23 (*America* only).
This is the only US attack carrier so fitted, although it was planned also for *John F. Kennedy.*

JOHN F. KENNEDY (CVA 67)

1969, United States Navy

JOHN F. KENNEDY (CVA 67)

1973, United States Navy, PH1 D. D. Deverman

JOHN F. KENNEDY

1976, Michael D. J. Lennon

JOHN F. KENNEDY

1974, USN

JOHN F. KENNEDY

8/1978, USN (PH1. Osborne)

AMERICA (CVA 66)

1970, United States Navy, PH3 L. J. Lafeir

JOHN F. KENNEDY
(CVA 67), 1967

1 NUCLEAR-POWERED ATTACK AIRCRAFT CARRIER (CVAN): "ENTERPRISE" TYPE

Name	No.	Builder	Laid down	Launched	Commissioned
*ENTERPRISE	CVAN 65	Newport News Shipbuilding & Dry Dock Co	4 Feb 1958	24 Sep 1960	25 Nov 1961

Displacement, tons	75 700 standard; 89 600 full load
Length, feet (*metres*)	1 040 (*317·0*) wl; 1 123 (*341·3*) oa
Beam, feet (*metres*)	133 (*40·5*)
Draft, feet (*metres*)	35·8 (*10·8*)
Flight deck width, feet (*metres*)	257 (*78·3*) maximum
Catapults	4 Steam
Aircraft	approx 95
Missile launchers	3 Basic Point Defence Missile System (BPDMS) launchers with Sea Sparrow missiles (see *Armament* notes)
Main engines	4 geared steam turbines (Westinghouse); approx 280 000 shp; 4 shafts
Nuclear reactors	8 pressurised-water cooled A2W (Westinghouse)
Speed, knots	35
Complement	3 100 (162 officers, approx 2 940 enlisted men) plus 2 400 assigned to attack air wing for a total of 5 500

ENTERPRISE (CVAN 65)

1969, United States Navy

The *Enterprise* was the largest warship ever built at the time of her construction and will be rivalled in size only by the nuclear-powered "Nimitz" class ships. The *Enterprise* was authorised in the Fiscal Year 1958 new construction programme. She was launched only 19 months after her keel was laid down.

The *Enterprise* was flagship of Task Force One during Operation Sea Orbit when the carrier, the nuclear-powered cruiser *Long Beach* (CGN 9), and the nuclear-powered frigate *Bainbridge* (DLGN 25) circumnavigated the world, in 1964, cruising more than 30 000 miles in 64 days (underway 57 days) without refuelling.

The cost of the *Enterprise* was $451 300 000.

The Fiscal Year 1960 budget provided $35 000 000 to prepare plans and place orders for components of a second nuclear-powered carrier, but the project was deferred.

ARMAMENT. The *Enterprise* — "the world's largest warship"—was completed without any armament in an effort to hold down construction costs. Space for Terrier missile system was provided. Short-range Sea Sparrow BPDMS subsequently was installed.

DESIGN. Built to a modified "Forrestal" Class design. The most distinctive feature is the island structure. Nuclear propulsion eliminated requirement for smoke stack and boiler air intakes, reducing size of superstructure, and reducing vulnerability to battle damage, radioactivity and biological agents. Rectangular fixed-array radar antennas ("billboards") are mounted on sides of island; electronic countermeasures (ECM) antennas ring cone-shaped upper levels of island structure. Fixed antennas have increased range and performance (see listing for cruiser *Long Beach*). The *Enterprise* has four deck-edge lifts, two forward of island and one aft on starboard side and one aft on port side (as in "Kitty Hawk" class).

ELECTRONICS. Fitted with the Naval Tactical Data System (NTDS). In addition to SPS-32 and SPS-33 "billboard" radar systems, the *Enterprise* has SPS-10 and SPS-12 search radars and various navigation radar antennas atop her island structure; SPS-58 radar fitted to detect low-flying aircraft and missiles. TACAN navigation pod caps mast.

ENGINEERING. The *Enterprise* is the world's second nuclear-powered warship (the cruiser *Long Beach* was completed a few months earlier). Design of the first nuclear powered aircraft carrier began in 1950 and work continued until 1953 when the programme was deferred pending further work on the submarine reactor programme. The large ship reactor project was reinstated in 1954 on the basis of technological advancements made in the previous 14 months. The Atomic Energy Commission's Bettis Atomic Power Laboratory was given prime responsibility for developing the nuclear power plant. The first of the eight reactors installed in the *Enterprise* achieved initial criticality on 2 Dec 1960, shortly after the carrier was launched. After three years of operation during which she steamed more than 207 000 miles, the *Enterprise* was overhauled and refuelled from November 1964 to July 1965. Her second set of cores provided

ENTERPRISE (CVAN 65)

Drawing by A. D. Baker

(1970)

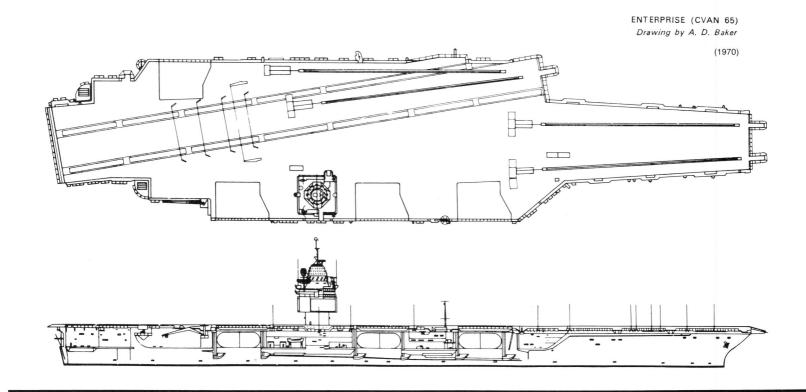

ENTERPRISE
1962, courtesy Newport News Shipbuilding and Dry Dock Company

ENTERPRISE (CVAN 65)
United States Navy

ENTERPRISE
1964, courtesy Newport News Shipbuilding and Dry Dock Company

ENTERPRISE (CVAN 65)
1968, United States Navy

ENTERPRISE (CVAN 65) (see following page)
United States Navy

ENTERPRISE (CVAN 65)   *1969, United States Navy*

ENTERPRISE (CVAN 65)   *1968, United States Navy*

ENTERPRISE   *1978, Michael D. J. Lennon*

3 + 1 "NIMITZ" CLASS: MULTI-PURPOSE AIRCRAFT CARRIERS (nuclear propulsion) (CVN)

Name	No.	Builders	Laid down	Launched	Commissioned	F/S
NIMITZ	CVN 68	Newport News Shipbuilding & Dry Dock Co	22 June 1968	13 May 1972	3 May 1975	AA
DWIGHT D. EISENHOWER	CVN 69	Newport News Shipbuilding & Dry Dock Co	15 Aug 1970	11 Oct 1975	18 Oct 1977	AA
CARL VINSON	CVN 70	Newport News Shipbuilding & Dry Dock Co	11 Oct 1975	Mar 1980	1982	Bldg
	CVN 71	Newport News Shipbuilding & Dry Dock Co	—	—	1988	Ord

[handwritten: ABRAHAM LINCOLN / T. ROOSEVELT / R. REAGAN / GEORGE W. BUSH]

Displacement, tons: 72 700 light (condition A);
81 600 standard; 91 487 full load (96 351, CVN 71)
Dimensions, feet (metres): 1 092 × 134 × 37
(332 × 40·8 × 11·3)
Flight deck width, feet (metres): 252 *(76·8)* (257 *(78·4,* CVN 71)
Catapults: 4 steam (C13-1)
Aircraft: 90+
Missiles: 3 Basic Point Defence Missile System (BPDMS) launchers with Sea Sparrow missiles (see notes)
Guns: See notes
Main engines: Geared steam turbines; 280 000 shp; 4 shafts
Nuclear reactors: 2 pressurised-water cooled (A4W/A1G)
Speed, knots: 30+
Complement: 3 300 plus 3 000 assigned to air wing for a total of 6 300 per ship

The lead ship for this class and the world's second nuclear-powered aircraft carrier was ordered 9½ years after the first such ship, *Enterprise* (CVN 65). *Nimitz* was authorised in the FY 1967 new construction programme; *Dwight D. Eisenhower* in the FY 1970 programme; *Carl Vinson* in the FY 1974 programme and CVN 71 in the FY 1980 programme. The builders are the only US shipyard now capable of constructing large, nuclear-propelled warships.
The completion of the first two ships was delayed almost two years because of delays in the delivery and testing of nuclear plant components. *Eisenhower* was contracted for delivery to the Navy 21 months after *Nimitz*.
Originally it was planned to procure two more ships of this class (CVN 71 and 72). Long lead items for CVN 71 were requested under FY 1977 and $350 million were authorised.

President Ford's request to cancel CVN 71 was backed by President Carter but Congress allowed $268·4 million of the original authorisation to stand, a sum already contractually agreed. The stipulation was made that this sum should be used for spare components for CVN 68/70 or for long lead items for CVN 71 should the Administration decide to go ahead with her. This all came about at a time when Congress and the Pentagon were debating the future Carrier programme in the light of increasing cost, size and building time of the CVNs. After examining all the alternatives, including the Aircraft Carrier, Medium (CVV), a majority of Congress decided that the nuclear-powered aircraft carrier was the most cost effective platform even with the long period of time necessary for construction. After the President had vetoed the Congressional appropriation of $2 000 million for a fourth "Nimitz" class on 17 August 1978 a series of studies followed with various groups of partisans for the three main contenders—CVV, modified "J. F. Kennedy" class or CVN 71. In the end, after a series of compromises, the majority of the members of Congress won their way and CVN 71 was approved.

Classification: *Nimitz* and *Eisenhower* were ordered as attack aircraft carriers (CVAN): reclassified CVN on 30 June 1975. First two ships will be refitted with A/S control centre and facilities for A/S aircraft and helicopters for their new multi-mission role (attack/ASW). *Vinson* and CVN 71 will be completed with these facilities.

Electronics: These ships have the Naval Tactical Data System (NTDS). All are or are to be fitted with OE-82 satellite communications antenna.

Endurance: 13 years for reactors, 16 days for aviation fuel (steady flying).

Engineering: These carriers have only two nuclear reactors compared with the eight reactors required for *Enterprise*. The nuclear cores for the reactors in these ships are expected to provide sufficient energy for the ships each to steam for at least 13 years, an estimated 800 000 to 1 million miles between refuelling.

Fiscal: A number of cost growth factors have had an impact on these ships, including delays in schedule. The cost of *Nimitz* in FY 1976 dollars was equivalent to $1 881 million; the three later ships will cost in excess of $2 000 million each in equivalent dollars.

Gunnery: It is planned to add three 20 mm Mk 15 CIWS in *Nimitz* and *Eisenhower* and four in *Vinson* and CVN 71. The first two at present have only two 40 mm saluting guns.

Missiles: *Nimitz* and *Eisenhower* will shortly receive Mk 29 Sea Sparrow in place of Mk 25.

Protection: Sides with system of full and empty compartments. Full compartments can contain aviation fuel. Approximately 2·5-in plating over certain areas of side shell. Box protection over magazine and machinery spaces.

Radar: 3D air search: SPS 48.
Air search: SPS 43A.
Surface search: SPS 10.
Navigational: SPN 42, 43 and 44.

Sonar: None.

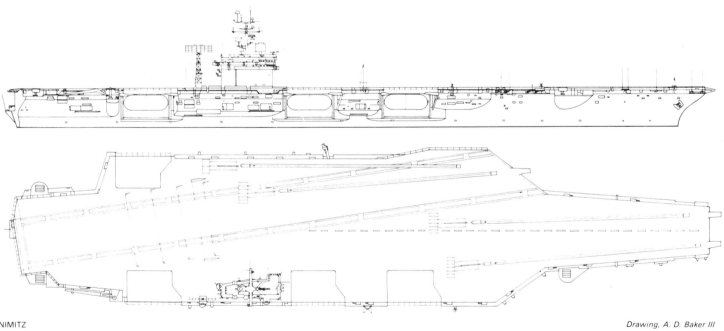

NIMITZ

Drawing, A. D. Baker III

NIMITZ

7/1979, Dr. Giorgio Arra

NIMITZ

9/1976, USN

NIMITZ (with *California* CGN 36 and *South Carolina* CGN 37)

9/1976, USN

NIMITZ

9/1976, USN

9 1976, USN

Small Aircraft Carriers (CVL).

2 "Saipan" Class.

SAIPAN (July 8, 1945)   **WRIGHT** (Sept. 1, 1945)

Displacement:	14,500 tons (20,000 tons *full load*)
Dimensions:	Length: 683½ (*o.a.*) feet. Beam: 76¾ feet (*hull*). Width: 115 (*extreme*) feet. Draught: 25 (*max.*) feet.
Guns:	40—40 mm. AA., 32—20 mm. AA.
Aircraft:	Over 50
Machinery:	Geared turbines. 4 shafts. S.H.P.: 120,000 33 kts.
Boilers:	8 Babcock & Wilcox
Fuel:	2,400 tons
Complement:	1,400 (war)

WRIGHT.   *Added 1950, U.S. Navy, Official.*

SAIPAN.   *Added 1950, U.S. Navy, Official.*

SAIPAN.   *1952, courtesy Godfrey H. Walker Esq.*

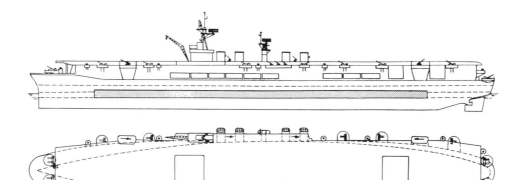

SAIPAN Class 1950

Note to Plan.—Wright now has only three funnels.

General Notes.—Hulls of these ships were laid down with intention of completing them as heavy cruisers of the "Baltimore" type. *Saipan* is employed as an experimental ship for testing jet-propelled aircraft, as well as improvements in radar equipment. She recently operated successfully a squadron of McDonnell Phantom fighters. *Wright* has recently been used for training purposes. Has had fore funnel removed.

No.	Name	Builders and Machinery	Laid down	Completed
CVL 48	Saipan }	New York S.B. Corpn.	(10 July '44	14 July '46
49	Wright }		(21 Aug. '44	9 Feb. '47

SAIPAN.   *1953 U.S. Navy, Official.*

WRIGHT

1957, United States Navy, Official

Rated as
Auxiliary Aircraft Transports (AVT)
Former Aircraft Carriers (CVL)

2 " Saipan " Class

SAIPAN		WRIGHT
Name:	Saipan	Wright
No.:	AVT 6 (ex-CVL 48)	AVT 7 (ex-CVL 49)
Builders:	New York Shipbuilding Corporation, New Jersey	New York Shipbuilding Corporation, New Jersey
Laid down:	10 July 1944	21 Aug. 1944
Launched:	8 July 1945	1 Sep. 1945
Completed:	14 July 1946	9 Feb. 1947

Displacement: 14,500 tons *standard* (20,060 tons *full load*)
Dimensions: Length: 683½ *(o.a.)* feet. Beam: 76¾ feet *(hull)*. Width: 115 *(extreme)* feet. Draught: 28 *(max.)* feet
Guns: 40—40 mm. AA., 32—20 mm. AA.
Aircraft: Over 50
Machinery: General Electric geared turbines. 2 shafts. S.H.P.: 120,000=33 kts
Boilers: 8 Babcock & Wilcox
Fuel: 2,400 tons
Complement: 1,821 (243 officers and 1,578 men) in wartime. Only 775 of 1,007 enlisted men retained in *Saipan* as training carrier

General Notes
Modifications of the "Baltimore" class heavy cruiser design laid down and built as aircraft carriers (CVLs). The hull below the main (hangar) deck duplicates that of the Camden-built heavy cruisers *Bremerton, Fall River, Macon* and *Toledo. Saipan* was employed as an experimental ship for testing jet propelled aircraft, as well as improvements in radar equipment. She recently operated successfully a squadron of McDonnell Phantom fighters. She was the training ship for student pilots at Pensacola until replaced by the *Antietam.* Both are now decommissioned. Both ships had four funnels but have had fore funnel removed (see two photos of *Saipan* and another photo of *Wright* in the 1957-58 edition.)

Notes to Drawing
Both *Saipan* and *Wright* now have only three funnels as shown in port elevation and plan drawn in 1957. Scale: 128 feet=1 inch.

Reclassification Notes
Both ships were reclassified from aircraft carriers (CVL) to aircraft transports (AVT) on 15 May 1959.

The *Wright* was originally completed as a light aircraft carrier (CVL 49). Although her hull design is that of the "Baltimore" class heavy cruisers, she was ordered as a carrier and not changed during construction as with previous US Light Carriers. She served for a decade as an experimental and training carrier before being decommissioned on 15 Mar 1956. She was converted to a national emergency command ship at the Puget Sound Naval Shipyard, 1962-1963.
She was decommissioned on 27 May 1970 and placed in reserve.

Classification: While in reserve, as a carrier, she was reclassified on 15 May 1959 as an auxiliary aircraft transport (AVT 7). She was reclassified as CC 2 on 1 Sep 1962.

Conversion: She was converted to a command ship under the Fiscal Year 1962 authorisation at a cost of $25 000 000. She is fitted with elaborate communications, data processing, and display facilities for use by national authorities. The command spaces include presentation theatres similar to those at command posts ashore. The *Wright* has the most powerful transmitting antennae ever installed in a ship. They are mounted on plastic-glass masts to reduce interference with electronic transmissions. The tallest mast is 83 feet high and is designed to withstand 100-mph winds.

WRIGHT

1968, USN

Escort Aircraft Carriers (CVE).

CHARGER (ex-H.M.S. *Charger*, ex-*Rio de la Plata*) (March 1, 1941), **LONG ISLAND** (ex-*Mormacmail*) (Jan. 11, 1940). Of slightly differing type. Displacement : *ca.* 12,000 tons. Dimensions : $492 \times 69\frac{1}{2} \times 25\frac{1}{4}$ (*Charger*), $25\frac{3}{4}$ (*Long Island*) feet, *max.* draught. Guns : 1—5 inch 51 cal., several smaller. Machinery : Sun-Doxford Diesels in *Long Island*, Busch-Sulzer in *Charger*. B.H.P. : 8,500 = 16 kts.

Notes.—All are named after sounds, except *Charger*. Builders : *Long Island*, Sun S.B. Co., conversion from merchantman to aircraft carrier being carried out by Newport News Co. in 77 days. Other ships all by Seattle-Tacoma S.B. Corpn. These vessels are equipped with derricks for retrieving seaplanes. Flight deck is 450 feet long. *Long Island* is numbered CVE 1; *Bogue*, 9; *Card*, 11; *Copahee*, 12; *Core*, 13; *Nassau*, 16; *Altamaha*, 18; *Barnes*, 20; *Breton*, 23; *Croatan*, 25; *Charger*, 30; *Prince William*, 31.

LONG ISLAND. (Flight deck since extended beyond forward gun position.)   1941, *U.S. Navy Official*

CHARGER.   1942, *U.S. Navy Official.*   LONG ISLAND.   1944, *U.S. Navy Official.*

CHARGER.   1942, *U.S. Navy Official.*

---

9 '' Bogue '' Class.

ALTAMAHA. (Observe funnel.)

ALTAMAHA	BRETON	CORE
BARNES	CARD	CROATAN
BOGUE (ex-Steel Advocate)	COPAHEE (ex-Steel Architect)	NASSAU

Displacement: 9,800 tons (15,700 tons *full load*)
Dimensions: Length: 465 (*pp.*), 496 (*o.a.*) feet. Beam: 69½ feet (*hull*). Width: 112 feet (*extreme*). Draught: 26 (*max.*) feet
Guns: 1 or 2—5 inch, 51 cal., 16—40 mm. Bofors, 20—20 mm. Oerlikon
Aircraft: 30
Machinery: Westinghouse geared turbines. S.H.P.: 8,500 × 18 kts.
Boilers: Foster Wheeler type
Complement: 800

Notes.—All converted from mercantile hulls built by Seattle-Tacoma S.B. Corpn., and vary slightly in appearance. Flight deck is 450 feet long. All are named after sounds. These vessels are equipped with derricks for retrieving seaplanes. Out of commission, in reserve.

No.	Name	Laid down	Launched	Completed
CVE 9	Bogue	1 Oct. 1941	15 Jan. 1942	26 Sept. 1942
11	Card	27 Oct. 1941	21 Feb. 1942	8 Nov. 1942
12	Copahee	18 June 1941	21 Oct. 1941	2 Sept. 1942
13	Core	2 Jan. 1942	15 May 1942	10 Dec. 1942
16	Nassau	27 Nov. 1941	4 Apr. 1942	20 Aug. 1942
18	Altamaha	19 Dec. 1941	22 May 1942	15 Sept. 1942
20	Barnes	19 Jan. 1942	22 May 1942	20 Feb. 1943
23	Breton	25 Feb. 1942	27 June 1942	12 Apr. 1943
25	Croatan	15 Apr. 1942	3 Aug. 1942	28 Apr. 1943

BOGUE.   Added 1951, *U.S. Navy, Official.*

COPAHEE.   1942, *U.S. Navy Official.*

ALTAMAHA. (Observe funnel.)   1944, *U.S. Navy Official.*

1 "Prince William" Class.

PRINCE WILLIAM (Aug. 23, 1942)

Displacement:	8,333 tons (14,000 tons *full load*)
Dimensions:	Length: 496 (*o.a.*) feet. Beam: 69½ feet (*hull*). Width: 112 feet (*extreme*). Draught: 26 (*mean*) feet.
Guns:	2—5 inch, 38 cal.
Aircraft:	30
Machinery:	Geared turbines. 1 shaft. S.H.P.: 8,500. 18 kts.
Complement:	Over 800

Notes.—CVE 31. Laid down May 18, 1942, and completed April 9, 1943. Converted from mercantile hull by Seattle-Tacoma S.B. Corporation. Same type as "Ruler" class, which served in Royal Navy during the war. Can carry up to 90 aircraft when used as a ferry carrier.

PRINCE WILLIAM.   Added 1950, U.S. Navy, Official.

BRETON   1964. United States Navy, Official.

CHENANGO (ex-*Esso New Orleans*, Jan. 4, 1939), **SANGAMON** (ex-*Esso Trenton*, Nov. 4, 1939), **SANTEE** (ex-*Seakay*, March 4, 1939). **SUWANEE** (ex-*Markay*, March 4, 1939). Ex-oilers converted into Aircraft Carriers.

Displacement: 12,000 tons.   Complement: Over 1,000.

Dimensions (prior to conversion): 525 (*w.l.*), 556 (*o.a.*) × 75 × 30 feet. Guns: 2—5 inch, 51 cal., many smaller. Machinery: Geared turbines. 2 shafts. S.H.P.: 13,500 = 18 kts.

Note.—*Sangamon* built by Federal S.B. & D.D. Co., *Santee* by Sun S.B. Co. On May 4, 1945, *Sangamon* was heavily damaged by suicide aircraft attack; repairs are reported to have been deferred pending decision as to her disposal.

SANGAMON.   1942, *Associated Press.*

(SANGAMON CLASS—4 SHIPS, CVE 26–29.)

SANGAMON   Added 1944, U.S. Navy Official.

SUWANEE.   Added 1950, U.S. Navy, Official.

(INDEPENDENCE CLASS—8 SHIPS.)

BATAAN (ex-*Buffalo*), (Aug. 1, 1943), **BELLEAU WOOD** (ex-*New Haven*, Dec. 6, 1942), **CABOT** (ex-*Wilmington*, April 4, 1943), **COWPENS** (ex-*Huntington*, Jan. 17, 1943), **INDEPENDENCE** (ex-*Amsterdam*, Aug. 22, 1942), **LANGLEY** (ex-*Crown Point*, ex-*Fargo*, May 22, 1943), **MONTEREY** (ex-*Dayton*, Feb. 28, 1943), **SAN JACINTO** (ex-*Reprisal*, ex-*Newark*, Sept. 26, 1943).

Displacement: 11,000 tons (13,000 tons *full load*).   Complement: 1,400.

Length: 600 feet (*w.l.*), 618 feet (*o.a.*).   Beam: 71½ feet.   Draught: 20 feet.

Guns: Aircraft:
4—5 inch, 38 cal. (May not still be mounted).   45.
Many 40 mm. and 20 mm. AA.

No.	Name.	Builders and Machinery.	Laid down.	Completed.
CVL 22	Independence		1/5/41	14/1/43
24	Belleau Wood		11/8/41	31/3/43
25	Cowpens		17/11/41	28/5/43
26	Monterey	New York S.B. Corpn.	29/12/41	17/6/43
27	Cabot		11/4/42	31/8/43
28	Langley		16/8/42	24/7/43
29	Bataan		31/8/42	17/11/43
30	S. Jacinto		26/10/42	15/12/43

Note.—These vessels were all laid down as cruisers of the *Cleveland* class, described on a later page, but were ordered to be completed as aircraft carriers. *Princeton* (CVL 23), ex-*Tallahassee*, lost in action.

BATAAN.   1944, U.S. Navy, Official.

S. JACINTO.   1944, U.S. Navy Official.

COWPENS.   1944, U.S. Navy, Official.

CABOT.   Added 1950, U.S. Navy, Official.

INDEPENDENTE Class
1944

Machinery: Geared turbines. 4 shafts. S.H.P.: 100,000 = 33 kts.

MONTEREY.   1955, U.S. Navy, Official.

Gunnery Notes
    Were originally designed to include 4—5 inch in armament.

Experimental Notes
    Independence. CVL 22, utilized for Bikini atom-bomb experiments, 1946, was retained by the Navy, although a hulk, as part of the radiological laboratory at the San Francisco Naval Shipyard until 30 Jan. 1951 when she was towed to sea and sunk on an experimental weapon test.

Reclassification Notes
    All these ships were reclassified from small aircraft carriers (CVL) to aircraft transports (AVT) on 15 May 1959.

BATAAN.   1951, U.S. Navy, Official.

CABOT

Added 1957, United States Navy, Official

34 "Casablanca" Class.

ANZIO (ex-*Coral Sea*, ex-*Alikula Bay*, May 1, 1943)
BOUGAINVILLE (ex-*Didrickson Bay*, May 16, 1944)
CAPE ESPERANCE (ex-*Tananek Bay*, March 3, 1944)
CORREGIDOR (ex-*Atheling*, ex-*Anguilla Bay*, May 12, 1943)
FANSHAW BAY (Nov. 1, 1943)
GUADALCANAL (ex-*Astrolabe Bay*, June 5, 1943)
HOGGATT BAY (Dec. 4, 1943)
HOLLANDIA (ex-*Astrolabe Bay*, April 28, 1944)
KADASHAN BAY (Dec. 11, 1943)
KASAAN BAY (Oct. 24, 1943)
KWAJALEIN (ex-*Bucareli Bay*, May 4, 1944)
LUNGA POINT (ex-*Alazon Bay*, April 11, 1944)
MAKASSAR STRAIT (ex-*Ulitaka Bay*, March 23, 1944)
MANILA BAY (ex-*Bucareli Bay*, July 10, 1943)
MARCUS ISLAND (ex-*Kanalku Bay*, Dec. 16, 1943)
MATANIKAU (ex-*Dolomi Bay*, May 22, 1944)
MISSION BAY (ex-*Atheling*, May 26, 1943)
MUNDA (ex-*Tonowek Bay*, June 8, 1943)
NATOMA BAY (ex-*Begum*, July 20, 1943)
NEHENTA BAY (ex-*Khedive*, Nov. 28, 1943)
PETROF BAY (Jan. 5, 1944)
RUDYERD BAY (Jan. 12, 1944)
SAGINAW BAY (Jan. 19, 1944)
SARGENT BAY (Jan. 31, 1944)
SAVO ISLAND (ex-*Kaita Bay*, Dec. 22, 1943)
SHAMROCK BAY (Feb. 3, 1944)
SHIPLEY BAY (Feb. 12, 1944)
SITKOH BAY (Feb. 19, 1944)
STEAMER BAY (Feb. 26, 1944)
TAKANIS BAY (March 10, 1944)
THETIS BAY (March 16, 1944)
TRIPOLI (ex-*Didrickson Bay*, Sept. 2, 1943)
WHITE PLAINS (ex-*Elbour Bay*, Sept. 27, 1943)
WINDHAM BAY (March 29, 1944)

No.		Name	Laid down	Launched	Completed
CVE	57	Anzio	12 Dec. 1942	1 May 1943	27 Aug. 1943
	58*	Corregidor	17 Nov. 1942	12 May 1943	31 Aug. 1943
	59	Mission Bay	28 Dec. 1942	26 May 1943	13 Sept. 1943
	60	Guadalcanal	5 Jan. 1943	5 June 1943	25 Sept. 1943
	61	Manila Bay	15 Jan. 1943	10 July 1943	5 Oct. 1943
	62	Natoma Bay	17 Jan. 1943	20 July 1943	14 Oct. 1943
	64*	Tripoli	1 Feb. 1943	2 Sept. 1943	31 Oct. 1943
	66	White Plains	11 Feb. 1943	27 Sept. 1943	15 Nov. 1943
	69	Kasaan Bay	11 May 1943	24 Oct. 1943	4 Dec. 1943
	70	Fanshaw Bay	18 May 1943	1 Nov. 1943	9 Dec. 1943
	74	Nehenta Bay	20 July 1943	28 Nov. 1943	3 Jan. 1944
	75	Hoggatt Bay	17 Aug. 1943	4 Dec. 1943	11 Jan. 1944
	76	Kadashan Bay	2 Sept. 1943	11 Dec. 1943	18 Jan. 1944
	77	Marcus Island	15 Sept. 1943	16 Dec. 1943	26 Jan. 1944
	78	Savo Island	27 Sept. 1943	22 Dec. 1943	3 Feb. 1944
	80	Petrof Bay	15 Oct. 1943	5 Jan. 1944	18 Feb. 1944
	81	Rudyerd Bay	24 Oct. 1943	12 Jan. 1944	25 Feb. 1944
	82	Saginaw Bay	1 Nov. 1943	19 Jan. 1944	2 Mar. 1944
	83	Sargent Bay	8 Nov. 1943	31 Jan. 1944	9 Mar. 1944
	84	Shamrock Bay	15 Nov. 1943	4 Feb. 1944	15 Mar. 1944
	85	Shipley Bay	22 Nov. 1943	12 Feb. 1944	21 Mar. 1944
	86*	Sitkoh Bay	23 Nov. 1943	19 Feb. 1944	28 Mar. 1944
	87	Steamer Bay	4 Dec. 1943	26 Feb. 1944	4 Apr. 1944
	88*	Cape Esperance	11 Dec. 1943	3 Mar. 1944	9 Apr. 1944
	89	Takanis Bay	16 Dec. 1943	10 Mar. 1944	15 Apr. 1944
	90	Thetis Bay	22 Dec. 1943	16 Mar. 1944	21 Apr. 1944
	91	Makassar Strait	29 Dec. 1943	22 Mar. 1944	27 Apr. 1944
	92*	Windham Bay	5 Jan. 1944	29 Mar. 1944	3 May 1944
	94	Lunga Point	19 Jan. 1944	11 Apr. 1944	14 May 1944
	97	Hollandia	12 Feb. 1944	28 Apr. 1944	1 June 1944
	98	Kwajalein	19 Feb. 1944	4 May 1944	7 June 1944
	100	Bougainville	3 Mar. 1944	16 May 1944	18 June 1944
	101	Matanikau	10 Mar. 1944	22 May 1944	24 June 1944
	104	Munda	29 Mar. 1944	8 June 1944	8 July 1944

Cape Esperance, Corregidor, Sitkoh Bay, Tripoli, and *Windham Bay* are assigned to Military Sea Transportation Service, and serve as Aircraft Ferry Ships. Others out of commission, in reserve.

Standard displacement: 6,700 tons (10,200 tons *full load*)
Dimensions: Length: 487 (*pp.*), 498 (*w.l.*), 512 (*o.a.*) feet. Beam: 65 feet (*hull*). Width: 108 feet (*extreme*). Draught: 19⅝ (*max.*) feet.
Guns: 1—5 inch, 38 cal., 24—20 mm. AA. (Later ships have 8—40 mm. AA., 24—20 mm. AA.)
Aircraft: 30
Machinery: Skinner Unaflow (reciprocating) engines. 2 shafts. I.H.P.: 11,200 – 18 kts.
Complement: Over 800 (*war*)

Notes.—CVE 57–104. Designed as aircraft carriers, all these ships were built by the Henry J. Kaiser Co., Inc., at Vancouver, Wash. or by the Oregon S.B. Corpn. at Portland, Oregon. They are of an improved design, differing from converted ships of "Bogue" class, which were found difficult to land upon in light airs. *Bougainville* took only 76 days to build. War losses: *Bismarck Sea* (CVE 95), *Gambier Bay* (73), *Liscome Bay* (56), *Ommaney Bay* (79), *St. Lo* (63). Sold or scrapped since: *Admiralty Islands, Attu, Casablanca, Kalinin Bay, Kitkun Bay, Makin Island, Roi, Salamaua, Solomons, Tulagi, Wake Island.*

1946, Ted Stone.

CASABLANCA.

1943, U.S. Navy, Official.

TRIPOLI.

1953, Skyfotos.

CORREGIDOR.

Added 1950, U.S. Navy, Official.

THETIS BAY (showing new LPH number)

1959, *Hajime Fukaya*

Rated as **Aircraft Ferrys** (AKV)
and **Amphibious Assault Ship** (LPH)
Former Escort Aircraft Carriers
(CVE, CVHE, CVU, CVHA)
17 " Anzio " Class

BOUGAINVILLE (ex-*Didrickson Bay*)
CAPE ESPERANCE (ex-*Tananek Bay*)
HOGGATT BAY
HOLLANDIA (ex-*Astrolabe Bay*)
KADASHAN BAY
KWAJALEIN (ex-*Bucareli Bay*)
LUNGA POINT (ex-*Alazon Bay*)
MARCUS ISLAND (ex-*Kanalku Bay*)
MATANIKAU (ex-*Dolomi Bay*)
NEHENTA BAY (ex-*Khedive*)
RUDYERD BAY
SAVO ISLAND (ex-*Kaita Bay*)
SITKOH BAY
TAKANIS BAY
THETIS BAY
TRIPOLI (ex-*Didrickson Bay*)
WINDHAM BAY

THETIS BAY (starboard quarter showing open lift aft)

1957, *U.S. Navy, Official*

Displacement:	7,800 tons *standard* (10,400 tons *full load*)
Dimensions:	Length: 487 (pp.), 498 (w.l.). 512 (o.a.) feet. Beam: 65 feet (hull). Width: 108 feet (extreme). Draught: 19⅔ (max.) feet
Guns:	1—5 inch, 38 cal., 24—20 mm. AA. (Later ships have 8—40 mm. AA., 24—20 mm. AA.)
Aircraft:	30 (20 to 40 helicopters in *Thetis Bay*)
Machinery:	Skinner Unaflow (reciprocating) engines. 2 shafts. I.H.P.: 11,200 = 19·5 kts.
Boilers:	2
Complement:	643 (peace). Over 800 (war). *Thetis Bay* (complement of 40 officers and 500 men plus accommodation for 1,600 troops) carries 390 troops (capacity over 1,000 marines)

General Notes

Designed from the start as aircraft carriers, all these ships were built by the Henry J. Kaiser Co., Inc., at Vancouver, Wash., or by the Oregon S. B. Corpn. at Portland, Oregon. They are of an improved design, differing from the converted ships of the " Bogue " class, which were found difficult to land upon in light airs.

Conversion Notes

The Fiscal 1955 program authorised the conversion of one CVE to an Assault Helicopter Transport for use by the Marine Corps in amphibious landings. Accordingly CVE 90 *Thetis Bay*, entered San Francisco Naval Shipyard in June 1955 for conversion and was commissioned on 20 July 1956. Redesignated CVHA 1 on 25 Feb. 1955. She will not only provide coverage for helicopters but will also take care of the assault troops. She carries at least 15 helicopters. Conversion included elimination of catapults and arrester gear, enlarging and resiting of elevators and accommodation for marine troops. The conversion of another CVE to CVHA, requested in the Fiscal 1957 appropriations, was subseuqently cancelled.

Seaplane Notes

One escort carrier was to have been converted into a sea-plane carrier (tender) in the Fiscal Year 1958 appropriations, but although requested by the Navy, Congress did not pro-vide funds for such a conversion.

CORREGIDOR

1956, *Skyfotos*

Reclassification Notes

Of the 34 former Escort Aircraft Carriers (CVE) of the " Anzio " Class, 10 were reclassified as Escort Helicopter Aircraft Carriers (CVHE) and 23 reclassified as Utility Aircraft Carriers (CVU) on 12 June 1955. The remaining vessel had been reclassified as an Assault Helicopter Aircraft Carrier previously (see *Conversion Notes*). Thirteen surviving ships of the class were reclassified as AKV on 7 May 1959. The *Thetis Bay* was reclassified as LPH 6 on 28 May 1959. The remaining 17 ships were stricken from the list, see *Recent Disposals*.

19 "Commencement Bay" Class.

MINDORO.

1953, Skyfotos.

COMMENCEMENT BAY.

1944, U.S. Navy Official.

BADOENG STRAIT (ex-*San Alberto Bay*)
BAIROKO (ex-*Portage Bay*)
BLOCK ISLAND (ex-*Sunset Bay*)
CAPE GLOUCESTER (ex-*Willapa Bay*)
COMMENCEMENT BAY (ex-*St. Joseph's Bay*)
GILBERT ISLANDS (ex-*St. Andrew's Bay*)
KULA GULF (ex-*Vermilion Bay*)
MINDORO
PALAU

POINT CRUZ (ex-*Trocadero Bay*)
PUGET SOUND (ex-*Hobart Bay*)
RABAUL
RENDOVA (ex-*Mosser Bay*)
SAIDOR (ex-*Saltery Bay*)
SALERNO BAY (ex-*Winjah Bay*)
SIBONEY (ex-*Frosty Bay*)
SICILY (ex-*Sandy Bay*)
TINIAN
VELLA GULF (ex-*Totem Bay*)

Displacement:	11,373 tons (24,275 tons *full load*)
Dimensions:	Length: 557 (*o.a.*) feet. Beam: 75 feet (*hull*). Width: 105 feet (*extreme*). Draught: 30⅝ (*max.*) feet
Guns:	1—5 inch, 38 cal., 24—40 mm. AA., 24—20 mm. AA., 4 rocket launchers
Aircraft:	34
Machinery:	Geared turbines. 2 shafts. S.H.P.: 16,000 — 19 kts.
Complement:	924 (*peace*). Over 1,000 (*war*)

General Notes.—All built by Todd Pacific Shipyards, Tacoma. Design modelled on that of " Suwanee " class, see later page. Sixteen more ships of this class, *Bastogne, Eniwetok, Lingayen, Okinawa*, and CVE 128-139, were cancelled in Aug. 1945.

Gunnery Notes.—After starboard 5 inch gun has been or will be removed. No. I Bofors 40 mm. mounting removed. 12 Oerlikon 20 mm. twin mounts now instead of former total of 30. Four rocket launchers now located amidships, two on each side.

CAPE GLOUCESTER.

Added 1950, U.S. Navy, Official.

No.	Name	Laid down	Launched	Completed
CVE 105	Commencement Bay	23 Sept. 1943	9 May 1944	27 Nov. 1944
106	Block Island	25 Oct. 1943	10 June 1944	30 Dec. 1944
107	Gilbert Islands	29 Nov. 1943	20 July 1944	5 Feb. 1945
108	Kula Gulf	16 Dec. 1943	15 Aug. 1944	12 May 1945
109	Cape Gloucester	10 Jan. 1944	12 Sept. 1944	5 Mar. 1945
110	Salerno Bay	7 Feb. 1944	26 Sept. 1944	19 May 1945
111	Vella Gulf	7 Mar. 1944	19 Oct. 1944	9 Apr. 1945
112	Siboney	1 Apr. 1944	9 Nov. 1944	14 May 1945
113	Puget Sound	12 May 1944	30 Nov. 1944	18 June 1945
114	Rendova	15 June 1944	28 Dec. 1944	22 Oct. 1945
115	Bairoko	25 July 1944	25 Jan. 1945	16 July 1945
116	Badoeng Strait	18 Aug. 1944	15 Feb. 1945	14 Nov. 1945
117	Saidor	29 Sept. 1944	17 Mar. 1945	4 Sept. 1945
118	Sicily	23 Oct. 1944	14 Apr. 1945	27 Feb. 1945
119	Point Cruz	4 Dec. 1944	18 May 1945	16 Oct. 1945
120	Mindoro	2 Jan. 1945	27 June 1945	22 Dec. 1945
121	Rabaul	29 Jan. 1945	14 July 1945	30 Aug. 1946
122	Palau	19 Feb. 1945	6 Aug. 1945	15 Jan. 1946
123	Tinian	20 Mar. 1945	5 Sept. 1945	30 July 1946

SICILY.

1948, Mr. W. H. Davis.

RENDOVA.

1953, U.S. Navy, Official.

SICILY.

Added 1951, U.S. Navy, Official.

Reclassification Notes

Seven Escort Aircraft Carriers (CVE) of this class were reclassified as Escort Helicopter Aircraft Carriers (CVHE) on 12 June 1955. *Block Island* was reclassified as LPH on 22 Dec. 1957. Her conversion to Helicopter Amphibious Assault Ship under the Fiscal Year 1957 Shipbuilding and Conversion Program was being undertaken at Philadelphia Navy Shipyard and her officially estimated completion date was 30 July 1960, but in 1958 her conversion was cancelled as a measure of economy and she was reclassified as an AKV on 7 May 1959 when all the remaining 18 ships of the class were also reclassified as AKVs.

SIBONEY

1956, Wright & Logan

11 rated as **Aircraft Ferrys** (AKV)

1 rated as **Major Communications**

Relay Ship (AGMR)

Former Escort Carriers (CVE, CVHE)

12 " Commencement Bay " Class

ANNAPOLIS (ex-*Gilbert Islands*, ex-*St. Andrew's Bay*)
BADOENG STRAIT (ex-*San Alberto Bay*)
COMMENCEMENT BAY (ex-*St. Joseph's Bay*)
CAPE GLOUCESTER (ex-*Willapa Bay*)
KULA GULF (ex-*Vermilion Bay*)
RABAUL
POINT CRUZ (ex-*Trocadero Bay*)
RENDOVA (ex-*Mosser Bay*)
SAIDOR (ex-*Saltery Bay*)
SIBONEY (ex-*Frosty Bay*)
TINIAN
VELLA GULF (ex-*Totem Bay*)

Displacement:	11,373 tons standard (24,275 tons *full load*) *Annapolis* 22,500 tons *full load*)
Dimensions:	Length: 557 (o.a.) feet. Beam: 75 feet (*hull*). Width: 105 feet (*extreme*). Draught: 30¼ (*max.*) feet
Guns:	1—5 inch, 38 cal., 24—40 mm. AA. 24—20 mm. AA., 4 rocket launchers (*Annapolis*: 8—3 inch, 50 cal. (4 twin)
Aircraft:	See *General*
Machinery:	Geared turbines 2 shafts. S.H.P.: 16,000=19 kts.
Boilers:	2
Complement:	*Annapolis*: 704 (37 officers and 667 men). See *General*

Conversion

Gilbert Islands was converted into a Major Communications Relay Ship (AGMR) in the Fiscal Year 1963. Conversion Programme by New York Naval Shipyard, the contract being awarded on 22 Aug. 1962 and she recommissioned on 7 Mar. 1964, equipped with 24 radio transmitters. *Vella Gulf* was to have been converted to AGMR in the Fiscal Year 1964 Conversion Program; but her conversion was never commenced (she was to have been renamed *Arlington*), and instead *Saipon*, see next page was selected for the second AGMR. The AGMR type will be capable of supplying vital communications services in any sea area in the world.

ANNAPOLIS   1964, "Our Navy" Photo

SIBONEY   Added 1961. *Official*

BADOENG STRAIT   Added 1957, *United States Navy, Official*

CRUISERS

THE difference between "armoured cruisers" and "cruisers" as they were in the first 20 years of the century is self-evident from their type names. The former were, in a sense, a half-way house between a battleship and a cruiser. Their armament was less formidable than the battleship, their armour less extensive, and their speed less than that of the newer cruisers. The first US armoured cruiser was the 9021 ton full load *New York* laid down in 1890. Eighteen years later, when the first British battle-cruiser with a battleship's main armament and a speed of 25 knots was commissioned, the armoured cruiser was obsolete as a warship, though still useful in foreign squadrons in peace-time.

The US Navy's building programmes before 1916 concentrated very largely on battleship construction on the principle that lesser ships could be built in a shorter time when required. Fifteen armoured cruisers were completed between 1890 and 1908 but no clear pattern of cruiser building emerged. Thus, by 1918, there were only the three "Chester" class, then ten years old, which could be classified as reasonably modern. Under the 1916 programme, ten "Omahas" were built, much larger than the "Chesters", with twelve, 6-inch guns and a speed of 34 knots. There was a five year gap between the commissioning of the last

"Omaha" and the arrival of *Salt Lake City* ("Pensacola" class), the first of 17 ships in four classes armed with 8-inch guns, a speed of 32.5 knots, a range of 10,000 miles at 15 knots and with up to four aircraft in covered hangars. The "Brooklyn" class reverted to a 6-inch gun armament to be followed by *Wichita*, once more carrying 8-inch guns and the forerunner of the "Baltimore" class. A further change in armament was made in the "Atlantas" who carried sixteen 5-inch guns and were chiefly employed as AA cruisers. In July 1940 the first "Cleveland" class was laid down, the beginning of the longest planned cruiser programme. Of the 52 ships ordered only 29 were completed to the original design, nine being converted into "independence" class carriers and the remainder cancelled. Instead of carrying twelve of the 6-inch guns like the "Cleveland", the next class, "Baltimore", carried nine guns of 8-inches on a displacement of some 17,000 tons, 3,000 more than the "Cleveland". This removed much of the topweight problem which plagued the latter class when it was necessary to fit increased close range armament.

Only two of the six "Alaska" class were completed, the name ship being laid down in December 1941. Giants of 34,250 tons full load, they carried nine 12-inch guns, and were outmoded before completion.

The post war programme began with the completion of four of the "Des Moines" class and two "Worcester" class vessels. It was a time of fluctuating decisions and the introduction of the new surface-to-air missiles brought a crop of conversions. In September 1961 the world's first nuclear propelled surface warship, *Long Beach*, was completed and there followed a mixture of conventional and nuclear powered cruisers. The 7,590 ton "Leahys" had their nuclear counterpart in *Bainbridge*. The next class, the "Belknaps", were somewhat larger than the "Leahys" while *Truxtun*, again slightly bigger, was the nuclear counterpart. From 1974 to 1980 six nuclear cruisers were completed, the two "California" vessels and four "Virginias", carrying SAM and ASW missiles, and in addition, a helicopter in the "Virginia" craft. As they were completed "Ticonderogas" was laid down, proving on commissioning to be the greatest advance in warship capability for generations. On an enlarged "Spruance" class hull, this class carries the SPYIA phased array radar and the Aegis control system which provides a unique capacity for long-range detection and defence. With two helicopters, the 27 ships of this class planned by 1993 will be a major reinforcement to the US fleet.

J.M.
May 1991

U. S. BELTED CRUISER (19 knot).

NEW YORK (December, 1891).

Displacement 8200 tons. Complement 566.

Length (*waterline*), 380 feet. Beam, 64 feet. *Maximum* draught, 28 feet.

Guns (Old Models):
  6—8 inch, 35 cal. (E).
  12—4 inch, 40 cal. (F).
  8 - 6 pdr.
  4 - 1 pdr.
  4 Colts.
Torpedo tubes:
  4 *above water* (broadside).
  1 *above water* (bow).

Armour (Harvey):
  4" Belt .... d
  6" Deck (amidships)
  [Cofferdam and cellulose.]
  Protection to vitals... —a
  10" Barbettes .... a
  7" Turrets (2) .... b
  5" Hoists............. d
  4" on 4" guns .... d
  7" Conning tower ... b

Ahead:
4—8 in.
4 - 4 in.

Astern:
4 - 8 in.
4 - 4 in.

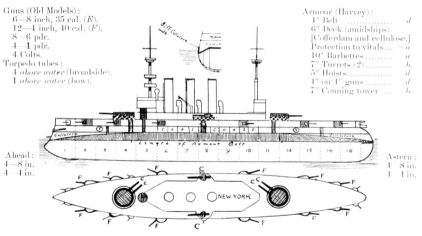

NEW YORK

Broadside: 5—8 in., 6 - 4 in.

Machinery: 4 sets vertical triple expansion. 2 screws. Boilers: cylindrical; 6 double-ended, 2 single-ended; 50 furnaces. Designed H.P. *forced* 16,500 - 21 kts. Coal: *normal* 750 tons; *maximum* 1150 tons.

Armour Notes.— Belt is 200 feet long.

Gunnery Notes.— The 8 inch turrets are electrically manoeuvred with electric hoists. Amidship 8 inch guns, hand gear only. One electric hoist at each end of battery for the 4 inch guns. Ammunition goes to individual guns by manual power only.

Engineering Notes.— On first trials she made 21 kts. with I.H.P. 17,400. She has always been a good steamer.

General Notes.—Good sea boat. Laid down at Philadelphia, September, 1890. Completed 1893.

Name changed to *Saratoga* in 1911 and then to *Rochester* in 1917.

Photo, copyright 1900, W. H. Rau.

(Fore funnel removed, 1927.)
ROCHESTER (ex-*Saratoga*, ex-*New York*). (1891). (Reconstructed 1907-08 and 1927).

SUNK AS BLOCKSHIP - SUBIC BAY

103

BROOKLYN (1895).

Displacement 9215 tons. Complement 500.

Length, 400 feet. Beam, 65 feet. *Maximum draught, 28 feet.*

Guns :
  8—8 inch, 35 cal. (*E*).
  12—5 inch, old (*F*).
  12—6 pdr.
  4—1 pdr.
  4—Gatlings.
Torpedo tubes (Howell) :
  5 *above water* (bow and broadside).

Armour (Harvey) :
  3" Belt .... *ϵ*
  6" Deck (amidships) = *aa*
  3" Deck (ends)..........
  [Cofferdam and cellulose belt.]
  Protection to vitals = *aa*
  8" Barbettes .... *b*
  8" Hoods to barbettes... *b*
  6" Hoists ...... *c*
  4" Shields (fixed) 5" guns *ϵ*
  7½" Conning tower...... *b*

SOLD

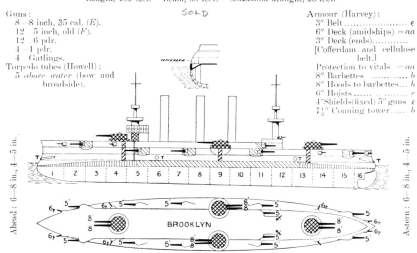

BROOKLYN

Ahead : 6—8 in., 4—5 in.
Astern : 6—8 in., 4—5 in.

Broadside : 6—8 in., 6—5 in.

Photo, Rau.

Machinery : 4 sets vertical triple expansion. 2 screws. Boilers : cylindrical ; 20 2-ended and 8 1-ended. Designed H.P. *forced* 18,000 = 21 kts. Coal : *normal* 900 tons ; *maximum* 1650 tons.

Armour Notes.—The belt is 8 feet wide, and 267 feet long. There are no bulkheads.

Engineering Notes.—On first *trial* (4 hours) she made *mean* I.H.P. 18,769 = 21·9 knots (138-140 revolutions). She was very light, and has not since equalled this performance. At Santiago, however, she made 16 knots without her forward engines.

U. S. ARMOURED CRUISERS (22 knot*j.*)

(CALIFORNIA CLASS—6 SHIPS)
WEST VIRGINIA (April, 1903), **COLORADO** (April, 1903), **PENNSYLVANIA** (Aug., 1903), **MARYLAND** (Sept., 1903), **CALIFORNIA** (April, 1904) & **SOUTH DAKOTA** (1904).
13,400 tons. Complement 822.
Length, 502 feet. Beam, 70 feet. *Maximum draught, 26½ feet at normal displacement.*

Guns—(model 1899) :
  4—8 inch, 45 cal. (*A*).
  14—6 inch, 50 cal. (*C*).
  18—14 pdr., 50 cal. (*F*).
  12—3 pdr.
  8—1 pdr.
  8 Colts, etc.
  2 Field guns, 3 in.
Torpedo tubes (18 in.) :
  2 *submerged.*
  (700 tons with two-thirds ammunition).

Armour (Krupp) :
  6" Belt........................ *a*
  3½" Belt (ends) .... *dϵ*
  4" Deck (on slopes) .....
  Protection to vitals ......= *aa*
  5" Upper belt .... *b*
  4" Bulkheads .... *d*
  6" Turrets (N.C.) .... *b*
  6½" fronts to these .... *b*
  4" Hoists to these .... *d*
  5" Battery .... *b*
  2½" Screens in battery .....
  6" Casemates (N.C.)........ *b*
  9" Conning tower (N.C.)... *aa*
  5" Signal tower (aft) ...... *c*
  (Total 2219 tons).

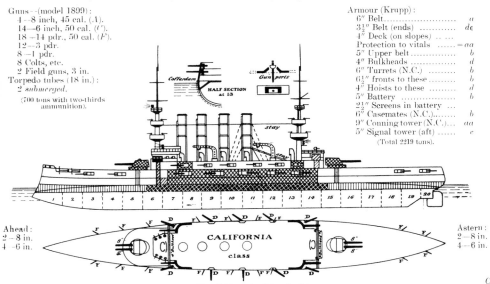

CALIFORNIA class

Ahead :
2—8 in.
4—6 in.

Astern :
2—8 in.
4—6 in.

Broadside : 4—8 in., 7—6 in.

(1906)   *Photo, copyright, by favour of E. Scholl, Esq.*

Machinery : 2 sets 4 cylinder triple expansion. 2 screws. Boilers : 30 Babcock or 32 Niclausse.
Designed H.P. 23,000 = 22 kts. Coal : *normal* 900 tons ; *maximum* 2000 tons.

Gunnery Notes.—8 inch manœuvred electrically and by hand ; electric hoists supply 1 round per 50 seconds.
  6 " " by hand ; " " " 3 " " minute.
Rounds per gun : 8 inch, 125 ; 6 inch, 200 ; 14 pdr., 250 ; lesser guns, 500 per gun.
  (At normal displacement only two-thirds of this ammunition is on board).
Arcs of fire : 8 inch, 270° ; casemate and angles of battery, 6 inch, 150° ; remaining *starboard*, 6 inch, 75° before the beam and 55° abaft ; remaining *port guns,* 55° before only, and 75° abaft ; 14 pdrs., all about 135°.
Armour Notes.—Main belt amidships 244 feet long by 7½ feet wide, 6½ feet below water, 1 foot above. Lowest strake of it is 5" thick. Deck behind belt amidships is only about 2½" on slopes. Cellulose belt. Upper belt, 232 feet long and 7½ feet wide, forming redoubt with 4" bulkheads.
Engineering Notes.—Grate area 1,600 square feet. Heating surface 68,000 square feet. Weight of machinery and boilers, with water, 2,100 tons.

Class distinction.—Rig of main mast and big cowl abaft fore mast.

Distinctions between the ships.—

Name.	Where built.	Laid down.	Completed.	4 hours full power trial. I.H.P.		Kts.	Boilers.
California ...	Union Ironworks	7/5/02	1906	—	=	—	Babcock
Pennsylvania	Cramp's	7/8/01	1905	29,843	=	22·48	Niclausse
West Virginia	Newport News	16/9/01	1905	—	=	22·14	Babcock
Colorado ...	Cramp's	25/4/01	1905	—	=	22·24	Niclausse
Maryland ...	Newport News	24/10/01	1906	—	=	—	Babcock
South Dakota	Union Ironworks	7/5/02	1906	—	=	—	Babcock

Average consumption :—Niclausse boilered ships burn about 22½ tons an hour at full speed.
Babcock boilered ships about 30 tons an hour.

General Notes.—Authorised 1899 and 1900. Average cost, *complete,* about £1,200,000 per ship.

WEST VIRGINIA & MARYLAND.   *Photos, G. Parrott, Esq.*
(Note different position of foremast).   (1911)

PENNSYLVANIA & COLORADO, also (but without big cowl abaft foremast) CALIFORNIA & S. DAKOTA.
(All fitting with skeleton foremasts.)   (1911)

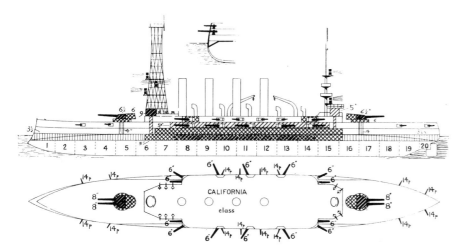

CALIFORNIA
class

Photo. Müller.

California and *S. Dakota* are without the big cowl abaft foremast.   (1914)

Class distinction.—Smaller turrets than *Washingtons*.

Over the years names were changed – *West Virginia* to *Huntington*, *Colorado* to *Pueblo*, *Pennsylvania* to *Pittsburgh*, *Maryland* to *Frederick*, *California* to *San Diego*, *South Dakota* to *Huron*. *San Diego* was mined and lost July 1918.

ALL OTHERS SCRAPPED

PITTSBURGH. (1919)

HUNTINGTON.*   1919 *Photo.*

Frederick is the same, *i.e.*, cage mast close to fore funnel; no high ventilator between forward cage mast and first funnel; no ventilators just before mainmast; only two tops to mainmast.   Compare these details with *Pittsburgh* below.

HURON. Resembles *Charlotte* class, ventilators being abeam of funnels, and not between funnels, as ships below. Distinguish from *Charlotte* class by smaller turrets and position of cranes abeam of second funnel.

PUEBLO. (*Pittsburgh* similar, but without first funnel.)   1921 *Photo, M. Bar, Toulon.*

First funnel set well abaft cage mast. Also note high ventilator just abaft cage mast.

(St. Louis Class.—3 Ships.)

CHARLESTON (1904), **MILWAUKEE** (1904), **ST. LOUIS** (1905).

Sheathed and coppered.

Displacement 9700 tons. Complement 564.

Length, 423 feet. Beam, 65 feet. *Maximum draught*, 23¼ feet.

SCRAPPER

Guns : *SCRAPPED*

LOST

14—6 inch, 50 cal. (C).

18—14 pdr. (F).

EUREKA, CA

12—3 pdr.

12—1 pdr.

8—Colts.

Torpedo tubes (18 inch) :

  2 submerged

Armour (Krupp) :

4″ Belt .... *d*

3″ Deck ... .

Protection to vitals... = *b*

4″ Lower deck redoubt *d*

4″ Battery .... *d*

4″ Casemates .... *d*

5″ Conning tower ...... *d*

3″ Tube ....

(Total 854 tons, including cellulose..)

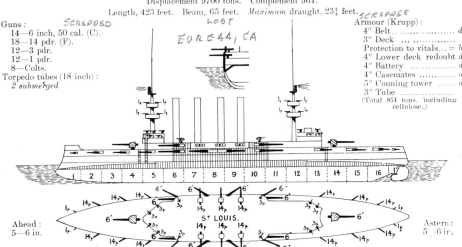

St. Louis. (1906)   *Photo by favour of H. Reuterdahl, Esq.* (1906)

Ahead :

5—6 in.

Astern :

5—6 in.

Broadside fire : 8—6 in.

Machinery : 2 sets vertical 4 cylinder triple expansion. 2 screws. Boilers : 16 Babcock and Wilcox. Designed H.P. 21,000 = 21·5 kts. Coal : *normal* 650 tons ; *maximum* 1500 tons.

Armour Notes—The belt is partial ; 197 feet long, by 7½ feet wide. Armour weighs 854 tons.

Gunnery Notes—All guns fitted with electric hoists, which will serve 6 rounds per minute to 6 inch guns, and 15 per minute to the 3 inch 14-pounder guns.

Arcs of fire : Fore and aft 6 inch, 270° ; upper casemate guns 145° from axial line ; end guns main deck 130° (85° ahead and 55° astern for fore ones, *vice versâ* for after) : other guns 110°.

Weight of ammunition *normal* 519 tons.

Engineering Notes.—

Name.	Builders.	Laid down.	Completed.	Trials.	4 hrs. f.p. at 143 revs.	Boilers
Charleston	Newport News	Jan., 1902	1905	=	= 22·03	Babcock
Milwaukee	Union I.W., 'Frisco	1903	1906	=	=	Babcock
St. Louis	Neafie & Levy	1903	1906	=	=	Babcock

St. Louis. (1919)   *Photo, O. W. Waterman.*

(*Officially rated as First Class Cruisers.*)

General Notes—Hull and armour deck weigh 5346 tons. These ships which are officially known as " semi-armoured " have comparatively small fighting value, being inferior even to the British *County* class.

St. Louis. (1914)   *Photo, Müller*

Charleston.   (Note new gun positions).   1921 *Photo, O. W. Waterman.*

(WASHINGTON CLASS.—4 SHIPS).

NORTH CAROLINA (7th Oct., 1906), **MONTANA** (December, 1906), **WASHINGTON** (March, 1905), and **TENNESSEE** (December, 1904).

Normal Displacement 14,500 tons. *Full load* displacement 15,950 tons. Complement 861 (as flagship).
Length (*waterline*), 502 feet. Beam, 73 feet. *Maximum* draught, 26¼ feet. Length *over all*, 504½ feet.

Guns (M. '99):
4—10 inch, 40 cal. (A.A.A.).
16—6 inch, 50 cal.
23—3 inch, 14 pdr.
12—3 pdr., semi aut.
2—1 pdr., aut.
2—1 pdr., R. F.
2 machine.
2 Colt.
2 field guns, (12 pdr.)
Torpedo tubes (21 inch) :
4 *submerged.*
(Total, with ½ ammunition
961½ tons.)

Armour (Krupp) :
5"—3" Belt .... b-c
3" Deck (ends) ....
Protection to vitals ...... a
5" Lower deck side ...... b
6" Lower deck bulkheads a
7" Barbettes (N.C.) ...... a
9"—5" Turrets ...... aaa-b
5" Battery .... b-c
2" Battery for 14 pdrs.... f
9" Conning tower (fore) aa
5" Tube (N.C.) ....
5" After C. T. (N.C.) ... c
(Total: 2516½ tons.)

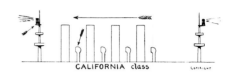

WASHINGTON class

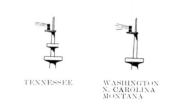

CALIFORNIA class

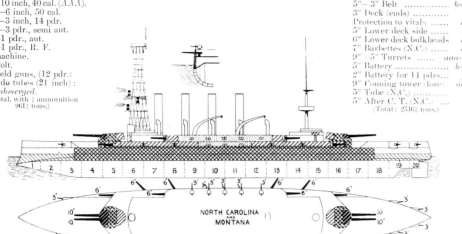

NORTH CAROLINA
AND
MONTANA

Ahead :
2—10 in.,
4—6 in.

Broadside : 4—10 in., 8—6 in.

Astern :
2—10 in.,
4—6 in.

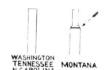

TENNESSEE   WASHINGTON
N. CAROLINA
MONTANA

Difference.

WASHINGTON
TENNESSEE   MONTANA
N. CAROLINA

Tennessee has one band on fore funnel ; *Washington* one on second funnel.

Machinery : 2 sets 4 cylinder triple expansion. 2 screws, outward turning. Boilers : 16 Babcock. Designed H.P. 23,000 = 22 kts. Coal : *normal* 900 tons ; *maximum* 2000 tons.

Armour Notes.—Belt is 17¼ feet wide, and of uniform thickness. It reaches to 5 feet below *normal* waterline. 2½" N.S. tops to turrets. 1¼" screens in battery ; 2" bulkheads. Prot. Deck amidships, 2½" on slopes ; the flat part thickened over magazines. 3" teak backing to all side armour ; 2" to turrets.

Gunnery Notes.—Turrets electrically manoeuvred. Electric and hand hoists. 16 for 6 inch guns, 14 for small guns. 6 inch hoists deliver 8 rounds per minute. All round loading positions to big guns. Arcs of fire : big guns, 270°.

Torpedo Notes.—Electric plant, 600 kilowatt capacity (in 100 K.W. units). Generators, 125 volts.

Engineering Notes :—120 revs.= full speed. 1570 sq. feet grate surface ; 68,000 feet heating surface. Boiler pressure, 265 lbs., reduced to 250 lbs. at engines. Machinery weighs 2060 tons. ⅔ stores, 26 tons. Water reserve, 66 tons.

Name.	Builder.	Machinery.	Laid down.	Completed.	Refit.	Trials (mean).	Boilers.	Best recent speed.
N. Carolina*	Newport News		1905	1908		29,225 = 22·48		
Montana	Newport News	By	1905	1908		= 22·26	Babcock	
Washington	N. York Shipbuilding	Builders	1903	1907		26,862 = 22·27	in all.	
Tennessee	Cramp		1903	1907		26,540 = 22·16		

*N. Carolina did 24 hours 19,800 = 20·556 knots.

General Notes.—Freeboard forward, 24 feet ; amidships, 18 feet. Boats carried : one 50 ft. cutter, 20 smaller and two patent rafts.

TENNESSEE. (1911)   *Photo, Brown & Shaffer.*
(All fitting with skeleton foremasts.)

Some are fitted with high searchlight platforms around the funnels.   *Photo, Spairali.*

Over the years names were changed as follows: *Washington* to *Seattle, Tennessee* to *Memphis,— LOST*
North Carolina to *Charlotte, Montana* to *Missoula. Memphis* was converted to a seaplane carrier
and then, in 1922-23, refitted as an administrative flagship.

ALL SCRAPPED

SEATTLE (as Seaplane Carrier—main deck battery now removed). (1919)   *Photo, O. W. Waterman.*

Note.—SEATTLE is now serving as Administrative Flagship of the U.S. Fleet, for which purpose she was extensively overhauled and refitted, 1922-23, and has had 12 of her 6 inch guns removed (from main deck).

MISSOULA.   *Photo added 1923.*

(OMAHA CLASS—10 SHIPS.)

OMAHA (Dec. 14th, 1920), **MILWAUKEE** (Mar 24th, 1921), **CINCINNATI** (May 23rd, 1921),
RALEIGH (Oct. 25th, 1922), **DETROIT** (July 12th, 1922), **RICHMOND** (Sept 29th, 1921), **CONCORD**
(Dec. 15th, 1921), **TRENTON** (1923), **MARBLEHEAD** (Oct. 9th, 1923), **MEMPHIS** (1923).

Normal displacement, 7500 tons; *full load*, —— tons. Complement, 466.

Length (*waterline*), 550 feet.　Beam, 55 feet.　{ *Mean* draught, 14′ 3″ }　Length *over all*, 555½ feet.
{ *Max.* ,,　—— }

ALL SCRAPPED

Guns : (**Dir. Con.**)　　　　　　　　　　　　　　　　　Armour :
　12—6 inch, 53 cal. Mk. XII.　　　　　　　　　　　　　,, Belt ....
　4—3 inch, 50 cal. AA.　　　　　　　　　　　　　　　,, Deck ... .
　2—3 pdr. (saluting) :
Torpedo tubes (21 inch) :
　4 in two twin deck mountings
　6 in two triple ,,　,,

DETROIT.　　　　　　　　　　　　*1923 Photo, by courtesy of the Bethlehem Corporation (Builders).*

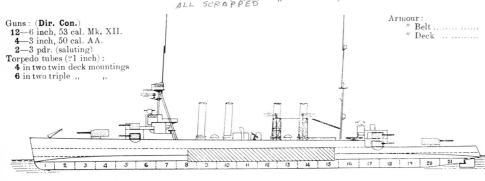
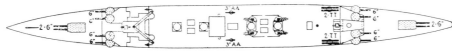

Ahead :　　　　　　　　　　　　　　　　　　　　　　　　　　　　　Astern :
　6—6 inch.　　　Broadside : **8—6 inch, 2—21 inch T.T.**　　　　6—6 inch.

Machinery : Turbines (see Table for types), with reduction gears.　Designed S.H.P. 90,000 = 33·7 kts. 4 screws.　Boilers : see Table.　Fuel : oil only : *about* 2000 tons.　Radius of action reported as 10,000 miles at 15 knots, 7200 at 20 kts.

Name.	Built and Engined by	Laid down	Com-pleted	Trials	Turbines.	Boilers	Heating Surface (sq. ft.)
Omaha	Todd Co., Tacoma	6 Dec. '18	Feb. '23		Westghs. Parsons	12 Yarrow	
Milwaukee	,,　　,,	13 Dec. '18	May '23		,,	12 Yarrow	
Cincinnati	,,　　,,	15 May '20	July, '23		,,	12 Yarrow	90276
Raleigh	Bethlehem Co., Quincy	16 Aug. '20	Sept. '23		Curtis	12 Yarrow	
Detroit	,,　　,,	10 Nov. '20	June '23	97,375 = 35·05	,,	12 Yarrow	
Richmond	Wm. Cramp & Sons	26 Feb. '20	May '23	95,000 = 34·5	Parsons	12 White-F	
Concord	,,　　,,	29 Mar. '20	Nov. '23		,,	12 White-F	90840
Trenton	,,　　,,	18 Aug. '20	1924		,,	12 White-F	
Marblehead	,,　　,,	1 Aug. '20	1924		,,	12 White-F	
Memphis	,,　　,,	14 Oct. '20	1924		,,	12 White-F	

RALEIGH.　　　　　　　　　　　　　　　　　　　*1929 Photo, R. Perkins, Esq.*

Gunnery Notes.—Originally designed with 8—6 inch guns, but about October-November, 1920, design was modified by addition of 4—6 inch in 2 twin mounts on forecastle and quarter deck.　This alteration estimated to add (*a*) 400 tons to normal displacement, (*b*) 9 inches to *mean* draught and (*c*) to reduce designed *max.* speed by 1.3 kts., for which corrections have been effected in figures given opposite.　The "turrets" on forecastle and quarter-deck are neither turrets nor barbettes in reality.　The guns are not protected, but on either side of them is a light splinter-proof "shed" to protect gunlayers, sightsetters, etc.　Loading party and ammunition supply do not appear to have any protection at all.　There are 6 ammunition hoists, delivery rate 10 r.p.m. each.

Aircraft Notes.—2 Seaplanes stowed between 4th funnel and mainmast.　2 catapults fitted for launching, while running with, against or across wind.

General Notes.—Estimated cost (without guns) in 1916, five to six million dollars each ; revised estimate 1919, 7½ million dollars each.　Reported that in some cases even this has been exceeded by over a million dollars.　Authorized (in order of names as given above) as *Nos.* 4—7 (1916), *Nos.* 8—10 (1917 and *Nos.* 9—13 (1918).

Torpedo Notes and Corrections to Plans.—Two sets of triple revolving deck tubes are mounted (one P., one S.) on upper deck, behind lidded ports, between 4th funnel and mainmast, in position as shown for *Twin TT* in 1920 edition of "Fighting Ships."

War Losses:

Marblehead damaged in Java Sea 4 February 1942. *Raleigh* refitted after damage at Pearl Harbor. *Milwaukee* transferred to USSR 1944, renamed *Murmansk*, returned 1949.

DETROIT.　　　　　　　　　　　　　　　　　　　*1927 Photo, F. J. Parsons, Esq.*

MEMPHIS, showing starboard catapult and plane.   *Photo added* 1927.

MARBLEHEAD.   (Showing alterations to after battery.)   1930 *Photo, Mr. L. Opdycke.*

RICHMOND. (Showing alterations to after battery.)   1931 *Photo, Mr. L. Opdycke.*

MARBLEHEAD.   *Added* 1940, *B. R. Goodfellow, Esq.*

CINCINNATI.   1937, *O. W. Waterman.*

Appearance Note.—Foretopmast removed in some to provide for 4 AA. M.G. in control top.

MARBLEHEAD (Now mounts only 10—6 inch).   1935, *Official.*   MARBLEHEAD.   1944, *U.S. Navy Official.*

(Pensacola Class).

PENSACOLA (April 25th, 1929), **SALT LAKE CITY** (Jan. 23rd, 1929).

Standard displacement, 9,100 tons.   (Estimated *normal* displacement, 11,568 tons.)

Complement, 612.

Length (*p.p.*), 570 feet ; *o.a.*, 585½ feet.   Beam, 64 ft.

Mean draught (at *normal* displacement), 17 ft. 5 in.

Guns :
10—8 inch, 55 cal.
4—5 inch, 25 cal. AA.
2—3 pdr.
Torpedo tubes (21 inch) : **6** (tripled).
Catapults, **2**.
4 planes.

Armour :
3″ side.
1″ deck.
1½″ gunhouses.

Name	Builders	Machinery	Laid down	Completed	Trials
Pensacola Salt Lake City	New York N. Yd, Am. Brown Boveri Cpn.	Am. B. B. Cpn.	Oct. 1926 June 1927	Nov. 1929	107,746 = 32·78

SALT LAKE CITY.   1930 *Photo.*

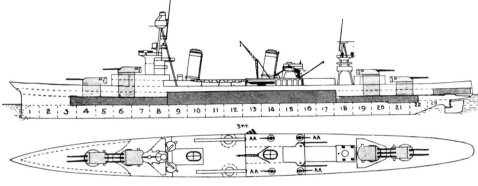

Machinery : 4 sets of Parsons geared turbines. Cramp type, with de Laval single reduction gearing. Designed S.H.P., 107,000 = 32.5 kts. (more expected). 8 White-Forster boilers, working pressure reported as 300 lbs. to square inch. 4 screws. Radius of action : 13,000 miles at 15 kts.

General Notes.—Laid down under Act of December 18, 1924. Tons per inch immersion, 60·7. Utmost economy in weights practised in design and construction. Aluminium alloy fittings replacing steel and aluminium paint is used internally. Welding has been employed wherever possible instead of rivetting. They suffer from lack of freeboard, vibration is excessive, mainly due to the shape of their sterns, and they roll considerably. Anti-rolling tanks are being tried out in *Pensacola.*

Gunnery Notes.—These ships are the first to carry 8 in. 55 cal. guns.   The fore control station at the mast head is about 120 feet above w.l.: the after control is abaft second funnel, and AA. control on fore bridge.

Engineering Notes.—Heating surface, 95,000 square feet. Machinery weighs 2,161 tons. Can steam at 30 kts. with 60 per cent H.P. There are 2 engine and 2 boiler rooms, the outboard shafts coming from the foremost engine rooms.

SALT LAKE CITY   Official Photo added 1930

PENSACOLA. To distinguish, note position of main topmast.   1935 *Photo, O. W. Waterman.*

PENSACOLA.   1944, *U.S. Navy Official.*

(AUGUSTA *class* 6—ships).

AUGUSTA (Feb. 1st, 1930). **CHESTER** (July 3rd, 1929). **CHICAGO** (Apr. 10th, 1930). **HOUSTON** (Sept. 7th, 1929). **LOUISVILLE** (Sept. 1st, 1930). **NORTHAMPTON** (Sept. 5th, 1930).

Standard displacement, 9,050 tons.* Complement, 611.
Dimensions, 582 (*p.p.*), 600 (*o.a.*) × 65 × 17 feet 7 inches (*mean*).

Guns :
10—8″, 55 cal.
4—5″ AA.
2—3 pdr.
Torpedo tubes (21″)
  6 in. 2 triple mountings
Catapults : 2
  4 planes.

* **Chester** 9,200 tons.
Chicago 9,300 tons.

Armour :
  3″ Belt.
  1″ Deck.
  1½″ Gunhouses.

HOUSTON.   1931 *Official Photo.*

(*Note extension of forecastle to catapult base.*)

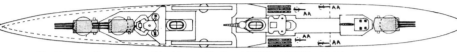

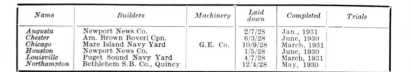

Machinery : Parsons geared turbines. Designed S.H.P. 107,000 = 32·7 kts. 8 White-Forster boilers, excepting in *Northampton* (8 Yarrow). 4 screws. Radius :

General Notes.—Authorised 1926–27 under Act of December, 1924, as Nos. 26–31. Although this class are considerably improved editions of the *Pensacola,* they have not proved particularly successful. The previous class having worked out at 9,100 tons only, the dimensions were increased and a forecastle deck added. Weight was saved by reducing and re-grouping the armament, while a certain amount of extra protection was worked in. Because of vibration in the *Pensacola* the hull was stiffened to try and overcome this defect. Owing to the centre of gravity being placed too low, they roll considerably and *Northampton* has been fitted with bigger bulge keels. If the anti-rolling tanks in *Pensacola* are more successful in overcoming this defect, these will be fitted to the remainder of the class. Some have developed cracked stern posts due to weight-saving and/or vibration. Four planes are carried, two on top of and two inside the large hangars amidships. *Houston, Augusta* and *Chicago* are fitted as flagships and extra accommodation has been secured by extending the forecastle aft to the catapult.

Gunnery Notes.—

Engineering Notes.—Heating surface, 95,040 sq. feet. Machinery weighs 2,161 tons. 4 Turbo-generator sets ; 250 kilo-watts each ; 120—240 volts ; built by General Electric Co.
There are 4 boiler rooms

Name	Builders	Machinery	Laid down	Completed	Trials
Augusta	Newport News Co.		2/7/28	Jan., 1931	
Chester	Am. Brown Boveri Cpn.		6/3/28	June, 1930	
Chicago	Mare Island Navy Yard	G.E. Co.	10/9/28	March, 1931	
Houston	Newport News Co.		1/5/28	June, 1930	
Louisville	Puget Sound Navy Yard		4/7/28	March, 1931	
Northampton	Bethlehem S.B. Co., Quincy		12/4/28	May, 1930	

CHICAGO (*Augusta* similar ; *Houston* has a small clinker screen.)   1938, *O. W. Waterman.*

AUGUSTA.   1931 *photo. Mr. L. Opdycke.*

NORTHAMPTON.   1930 *Photo, favour of Bethlehem Steel Co.*

War Losses:

Chicago torpedoed by Japanese naval aircraft nr Rennell Is 29 January 1943, sunk following day; *Houston* sunk by gunfire of two Japanese cruisers Sunda Straits 1 March 1942; *Northampton* torpedoed by Japanese destroyer off Lunga Point 1 December 1942.

NORTHAMPTON. (Observe raised fore funnel and short foretopmast.) (*Chester, Louisville,* similar.)   1935, *O. W. Waterman.*

(PORTLAND CLASS—2 SHIPS).

PORTLAND (May 21, 1932). (Bethlehem S.B. Co., Quincy.)

INDIANAPOLIS (Nov. 7, 1931). (New York S.B. Co.)
Standard Displacement : 9,800 and 9,950 tons respectively. Complement : 551.

Dimensions : *Indianapolis*, 584 (*w.l.*), 610¼ (*o.a.*) × 66 × 17½ feet (*mean*). *Portland*, 582 (*w.l.*), 610¼ (*o.a.*) × 66 × 17½ feet (*mean*).

PORTLAND.   1934 *Photo.*

(The funnel raised and AA guns mounted on foremast platforms.)

Guns :
  9—8 inch, 55 cal.
  8—5 inch AA.
  2—3 pdr.
  10—Smaller
Torpedo tubes :
  None.

Aircraft :
  4 and **5**, respectively.
Catapults : **2**.

Armour :
  3″—4″ Vert. Side ⎫
  2″+2″ Decks.   ⎬ Not Official.
  1½″—3″ Turrets. ⎭

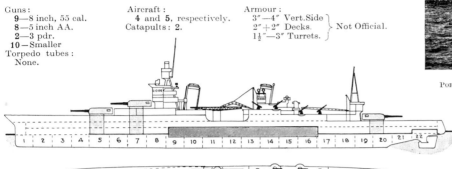

War Losses :

Indianapolis sunk by Japanese submarine NE of Leyte 7 July 1945.
CA 33 *Portland* placed on the disposal list after World War II, but restored to the Navy List in 1952.

Machinery : Parsons geared turbines. 4 shafts. S.H.P. 107,000 = 32·7 kts. 8 White-Forster boilers in *Indianapolis*, 8 Yarrow in *Portland*.

General Notes.—These ships follow the general design of the *Augusta* class with alterations in weight distribution to improve stability. Some 40 tons of plating has been spread over the bridge work, which is higher than in *Augusta*, with a 30 feet reduction in the height of the masthead control top. *Portland* laid down Feb. 17, 1930, completed Feb. 23, 1933. *Indianapolis* laid down March 31, 1930, and completed November 15, 1932.

Portland said to be a bad roller ; *Indianpolis* unaccountably is not. Machinery of both ships supplied by builders.

PORTLAND. (Fore funnel since heightened).   1933 *Photo, Official.*

PORTLAND.   1944, *U.S. Navy Official.*

PORTLAND.   Added 1954, *U.S. Navy, Official.*

(MINNEAPOLIS CLASS—7 SHIPS)

ASTORIA (Dec. 16, 1933).
MINNEAPOLIS (Sept. 6, 1933).
NEW ORLEANS (April 12, 1933).
TUSCALOOSA (Nov. 15, 1933).
SAN FRANCISCO (March 9, 1933).
QUINCY (June 19, 1935).
VINCENNES (May 21, 1936).

Displacement: 9,950 tons, except *Tuscaloosa*, 9,975, *Vincennes*, 9,400 and *Quincy*, 9,375 tons.

Complement, 551.

Dimensions: 574 (w.l.), 588 (o.a.) × 61¾ × 19½ feet (mean), 23½ (max.).

Quincy and *Vincennes*: 569 (w.l.), 588 (o.a.) × 61¾ × 18¾ feet (mean).

TUSCALOOSA.

(For particulars of these ships, see preceding page.)

1942, Associated Press.

Guns:
9—8 inch, 55 cal.
8—5 inch AA.
2—3 pdr.
10—Smaller.

Torpedo Tubes: None
Aircraft: 4.
Catapults: 2.

Armour
1½″ Side (fore and aft).
5″ Side (amidships between sections 10–17).
3″+2″ Decks.
5″—6″ Turret faces.
3″ Turret sides and backs.
8″ Conning Tower.

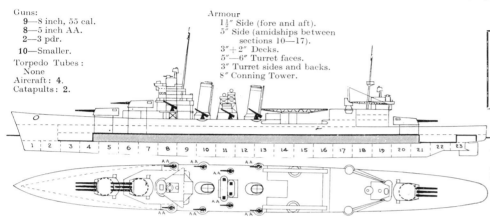

Name	Builders	Machinery	Laid down	Completed
Astoria	Puget Sound Navy Yard	Westinghouse Co.	1/9/30	1/6/34
Minneapolis	Philadelphia Navy Yard	Do.	27/6/31	20/6/34
New Orleans	New York Navy Yard	Do.	14/3/31	18/4/34
Tuscaloosa	New York S.B. Corp.	N.Y.S.B. Corp.	3/9/31	17/8/34
San Francisco	Mare Isld. Navy Yard	Westinghouse Co.	9/9/31	23/4/34
Quincy	Bethlehem Fore River	Bethlehem Corp.	15/11/33	9/6/36
Vincennes	Bethlehem, Fore River	Do.	2/1/34	24/2/37

War Losses:

Astoria, *Quincy* and *Vincennes* sunk by gunfire of Japanese cruisers at Battle of Savo 8–9 August 1942.

Machinery: Parsons geared turbines in *Tuscaloosa*, *Quincy*, *Vincennes*; Westinghouse in others. 4 shafts. S.H.P.: 107,000 = 32·7 kts. (32 kts. in 2 later ships). 8 Babcock & Wilcox boilers. Fuel: 1,650 tons.

General Notes.—In this class, the forecastle deck has been extended to the second funnel with a slight lowering of the freeboard; the bow form altered and overhang dispensed with; bridges raised and pole rig substituted for tripods; AA. guns re-distributed; hangars moved aft and extended to shelter deck, all the boats excepting the lifeboats being stowed on top to avoid interference with the AA. guns. These ships possess better protection than the *Portland* class as armour has been distributed to better advantage on the new design. The utmost economy has been effected in construction, electric welding having been employed extensively and weight saved in every direction even to the extent of using aluminium paint internally. 8 inch guns and mountings are of a lighter model and the weight so saved has been put into armour. Cost, $15,000,000 apiece. There is a certain amount of plating on the bridgework, not shown in the plan.

Gunnery Notes.—8 inch guns elevate to 45°

NEW ORLEANS

1934 Photo, Wright & Logan.

ASTORIA.

1934 Photo. Official.

SAN FRANCISCO.

1942, Associated Press.

NEW ORLEANS.   1934 *Photo, Hr. Registrator Ossi Janson.*   TUSCALOOSA.   1940, *Theo. N. Stone.*

TUSCALOOSA.   Observe petrol pipe line extended outboard to reduce fire risk.   1944 , *U.S. Navy Official.*

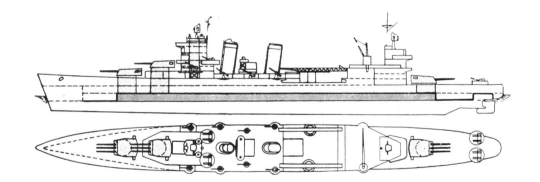

MINNEAPOLIS Class 1955

SAN FRANCISCO.   Added 1950, *U.S. Navy, Official.*

BROOKLYN CLASS (9 SHIPS)
BROOKLYN (Nov. 30, 1936), **PHILADELPHIA** (Nov. 17, 1936), **SAVANNAH** (May 8, 1937), **NASHVILLE** (Oct. 2, 1937), **PHOENIX** (March 12, 1938), **BOISE** (Dec. 3, 1936),
HONOLULU (Aug. 26, 1937), **HELENA** (Aug. 27, 1938), **ST. LOUIS** (April 15, 1938).

Displacement : 9,700 tons (*Brooklyn* and *Philadelphia*), 9,475 tons (*Savannah*), 9,650 tons (*Honolulu*), others estimated as 10,000 tons.
Complement : 868 (*Helena* and *St. Louis*, 888).   Dimensions : 600 (*w.l.*) × 61½ × 19¾ feet (*mean*).

Name	Builders	Machinery	Laid down	Completed
Brooklyn	New York Navy Yd.		12/3/35	18/7/38
Philadelphia	Philadelphia Navy Yd.		28/5/35	28/7/38
Savannah	New York S.B. Corp.		31/5/34	30/8/38
Nashville	Do.	Builders	24/1/35	25/11/38
Phœnix	Do.	in each	15/4/35	18/3/39
Boise	Newport News Co.	case	1/4/35	1/2/39
Honolulu	New York Navy Yd.		10/9/35	7/9/38
Helena	New York Navy Yd.		9/12/36	/39
St. Louis	Newport News Co.		10/12/36	/39

HONOLULU.

1938, *Theo. N. Silberstein.*

HONOLULU.

1938, *Wright & Logan.*

Guns : **15**—6 inch, 47 cal.
      8—5 inch, 25 cal. AA.
      4—3 pdr.
      5—1 pdr.
      3 M.G.
(*Helena* and *St. Louis* will mount 5-in.
guns in pairs behind shields.)
Aircraft : **4** (see *Notes*).

Armour : (Unofficial)
  1½″—4″ Side.
  3″ + 2″ Decks.
  3″—5″ Gunhouses.
  8″ C.T.

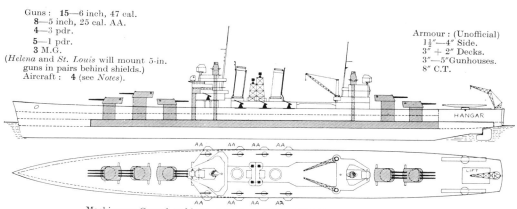

Machinery : Geared turbines. 4 shafts. S.H.P. : 100,000 = 32·5 kts. Boilers : 8 Babcock &
Wilcox Express type. Oil fuel : 2,100 tons. Radius : 14,500 miles at 15 kts.

Note.—The first four of this class were ordered under the Emergency Programme of 1933 : the next three under the
provisions of the " Vinson Bill "; and the last pair under the 1935–36 Programme. They are a reply to the Japanese
" Mogami " class. Cost approaches $17,000,000 apiece. *Helena* and *St. Louis* are of a slightly modified design.
Aircraft Note—The hangar included in hull right aft is a completely new departure. It is provided with a lift and can
accommodate 8 aircraft, though 4 is normal peace complement. Presence of this hangar accounts for very wide flat
counter and high freeboard aft, which is also utilised to give after guns higher command. The two catapults are
mounted as far outboard as possible and the revolving crane is placed at the extreme stern.

General Notes.—*Honolulu* was severely damaged by a bomb at Pearl Harbour on Dec. 7, 1941 ; and on Oct. 20, 1944, off Leyte, she
was again badly damaged by a torpedo from a Japanese aircraft. *Honolulu* and *Savannah*, when refitted, had anti-torpedo bulges
added, increasing beam by 8 feet. Both out of commission, in reserve.

War Losses:

Helena sunk at Battle of Kula Gulf 6 July 1943. *St. Louis* differed from rest in mounting paired
5-in guns (following entry).

Class Notes.—*Brooklyn* and *Nashville* of this class were transferred to Chile ; *Philadelphia* and *St. Louis* (latter ship was of slightly
modified type) were transferred to Brazil : and *Boise* and *Phoenix* (of this class) transferred to Argentina, all Jan. 22-25, 1951.
Two last-named ships (also *Nashville* and *St. Louis*) had been in Philadelphia with the Reserve Fleet but not a part of it, having
been designated as excess to the needs of the U.S. Navy and already earmarked for disposal to South American countries.
Philadelphia, which originally cost $14,750,000, actually commissioned in Brazilian Navy 21 Aug., 1951.

BROOKLYN.

Added 1940, *O. A. Tunnell, courtesy " Our Navy ".*

PHILADELPHIA.

Added 1950, U.S. Navy, Official.

SAVANNAH.

Added 1950, U.S. Navy, Official.

ST. LOUIS (April 15, 1938).

Displacement: 9,700 tons.   Complement: 888.

Length: 600 feet (*w.l.*).   Beam: 61½ feet.   Draught: 19¾ feet (*mean*)

St. Louis.   1940, *Official.*

Guns:	Aircraft:	Armour:
15—6 inch, 47 cal.	**4**	1½″—5″ Side.
8—5 inch, **38** cal. dual purpose.		3″+2″ Decks.
4—3 pdr.	Catapults:	3″—5″ Gunhouses.
5—1 pdr.	**2**	8″ C.T.
3 M.G.		

Machinery: Geared turbines. 4 shafts. S.H.P.: 100,000 = 32·5 kts. Boilers: 8 Babcock & Wilcox Express type. Oil fuel: 2,100 tons. Radius: 14,500 miles at 15 kts.

General Notes.—Laid down by Newport News S.B. Co.' under 1934 Programme on Dec. 10, 1936, and completed in December 1939. Differs from *Brooklyn* class in having 5 inch guns mounted in pairs behind shields on high bases; a different scheme of boat stowage; a small tripod mast immediately abaft second funnel and after gunnery control arrangements redistributed. Distinctive number is CL 49. War loss: *Helena.*

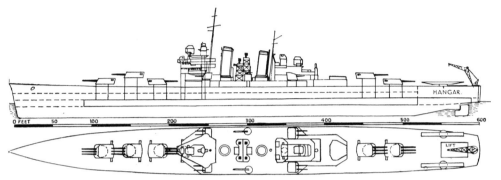

St. Louis 1943

St. Louis.   1940, *Theo. N. Stone.*

St. Louis.   1944, *U.S. Navy Official.*

WICHITA (Nov. 16, 1937).

Displacement : 10,000 tons (*estimated*).   Complement : 551.

Length, 600 feet (*w.l.*), 614 feet (*o.a.*).   Beam, 61¾ feet.   Draught, 19⅜ feet (*mean*).

Guns :	Aircraft :	Armour :
9—8 inch, 55 cal.	4	1½″ Side (fore and aft)
8—5 inch AA.	Catapults :	5″ Side (amidships)
2—3 pdr.	2	3″ + 2″ Decks
10 smaller		5″—6″ Turret faces
		3″ Turret sides and backs
		8″ C.T.

Name	Builder	Machinery	Laid down	Completed
Wichita	Philadelphia Navy Yard	Westinghouse Co.	Oct. 28, 1935	March, 1939

Appearance Note.—5 inch guns had not all been mounted when above photos were taken.   A more recent view will be found in Addenda.

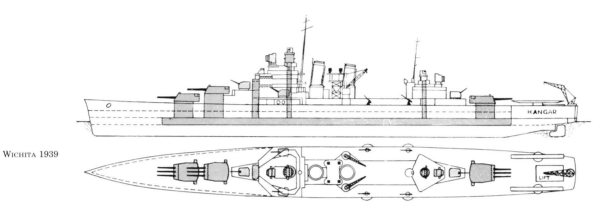

Wichita 1939

Machinery : Westinghouse geared turbines. 4 shafts. S.H.P. : 100,000 = 32·5 kts. Boilers : 8 Babcock & Wilcox. Fuel : 1,650 tons.

Notes.—Though originally to have been a unit of *Minneapolis* class, this ship was completed as a modified *Brooklyn* with 8 inch guns.

WICHITA.   1939.

WICHITA   1942, *Official.*

WICHITA.   1944, *U.S. Navy Official.*   WICHITA.   Added 1950, U.S. Navy, *Official.*

(CLEVELAND CLASS—29 SHIPS.)

AMSTERDAM (April 25, 1944), **ASTORIA** (ex-*Wilkes-Barre*, (March 6, 1943), **ATLANTA** (Feb. 6, 1944), **BILOXI** (Feb. 23, 1943), **BIRMINGHAM** (March 20, 1942), **CLEVELAND** (Nov. 1, 1941), **COLUMBIA** (Dec. 17, 1941), **DAYTON** (March 19, 1944), **DENVER** (April 4, 1942), **DULUTH** (Jan. 13, 1944), **FARGO** (Feb. 25, 1945), **GALVESTON** (April 22, 1945), **HOUSTON** (ex-*Vicksburg*, June 19, 1943), **HUNTINGTON** (April 8, 1945), **LITTLE ROCK** (Aug. 27, 1944), **MANCHESTER** (1945), **MIAMI** (Dec. 8, 1942), **MOBILE** (May 15, 1942), **MONTPELIER** (Feb. 12, 1942), **OKLAHOMA CITY** (Feb. 20, 1944), **PASADENA** (Dec. 28, 1943), **PORTSMOUTH** (Sept. 20, 1944), **PROVIDENCE** (Dec. 28, 1944), **SANTA FE** (June 10, 1942), **SPRINGFIELD** (March 9, 1944), **TOPEKA** (Aug. 19, 1944), **VICKSBURG** (ex-*Cheyenne*, Dec. 14, 1943), **VINCENNES** (ex-*Flint*), (July 17, 1943), **WILKES-BARRE** (Dec. 24, 1943).

WILKES-BARRE.

Added 1949, *Abrahams*.

Displacement: 10,000 tons (12,000 tons *full load*). Complement: 900/1,200. Length: 600 feet (*w.l.*); 608½ feet *o.a.* Beam: 63 feet. Draught: 20 feet (*mean*).

Guns :
12—6 inch, 47 cal.
12—5 inch 38 cal. (dual purpose), paired.
Many 40 mm. and 20 mm. AA.

Aircraft : 2

Catapults: 2

Armour :
1¼"—5" Side.
3"+2" Decks.
3"—5" Gunhouses.

Appearance Note.—Fargo and *Huntington* have only one funnel.

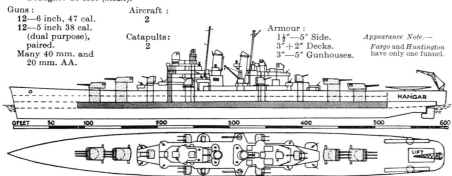

No. and Name	Builders & Machinery	Laid down	Completed	No. and Name	Builders & Machinery	Laid down	Completed
55 Cleveland	New York S.B. Corp.	1/7/40	15/6/42	89 Miami	Cramp S.B. Co.	2/8/41	28/12/43
56 Columbia		19/8/40	29/6/42	90 Astoria		6/9/41	17/5/44
57 Montpelier		2/12/40	9/9/42	91 Oklahoma City		8/12/42	22/12/44
58 Denver		26/12/40	15/10/42	92 Little Rock		6/3/43	17/6/45
60 Santa Fe		7/6/41	24/11/42	93 Galveston		20/2/44	
103 Wilkes-Barre		14/12/42	1/7/44	64 Vincennes	Bethlehem Co., Quincy	7/3/42	21/1/44
104 Atlanta		25/1/43	3/12/44	65 Pasadena		6/2/43	8/6/44
105 Dayton		8/3/43	7/1/45	66 Springfield		13/2/43	9/8/44
106 Fargo		23/8/43	} 1945	67 Topeka		21/4/43	23/12/44
107 Huntington		4/10/43		82 Providence		27/7/43	15/5/45
62 Birmingham	Newport News Co.	17/2/41	29/1/43	83 Manchester		25/9/44	
63 Mobile		14/4/41	24/3/43				
80 Biloxi		9/7/41	31/8/43				
81 Houston		4/8/41	20/12/43				
86 Vicksburg		26/10/42	12/6/44				
87 Duluth		9/11/42	18/9/44				
101 Amsterdam		3/3/43	8/1/45				
102 Portsmouth		28/6/43	25/6/45				

*Note.—*Cancelled ships 11/8/45: *Youngstown* (94), *Newark* (108), *New Haven* (109), *Buffalo* (110), *Wilmington* (111), *Tallahassee* (116), *Cheyenne* (117), *Chattanooga* (118).

Machinery : Geared turbines. 4 shafts. S.H.P.: 100,000=33 kts.

*Notes.—*This is the largest group of cruisers of a single design ever put in hand. Several originally ordered from New York S.B. Corpn. were converted into aircraft carriers of the *Independence* class (vide an earlier page). Names first assigned to these have in some instances been transferred to later ships of class. Official estimate of average cost of earlier ships is $31,090,000, and it has also been stated officially that *Houston* cost $42,000,000. *Duluth* and *Vicksburg* were originally to have been built by Federal S.B. & D.D. Co., but contracts were transferred.

Birmingham was torpedoed 8/11/43; again severely damaged when *Princeton* blew up alongside her in Oct. 1944; and nearly sunk by a Japanese suicide aircraft whose bomb penetrated three of her decks off Okinawa on 4/5/45. *Houston* was heavily damaged by a torpedo from a Japanese aircraft off Formosa in Oct. 1944.

BIRMINGHAM.

Added 1950. *U.S. Navy, Official.*

HOUSTON.

1944, *U.S. Navy Official.*

MANCHESTER.

1955, *U.S. Navy, Official.*

2 " Fargo " Class.

FARGO   **HUNTINGTON**

Displacement :   10,000 tons (13,755 tons *full load*)
Dimensions :   Length : 600 (*w.l.*), 610 (*o.a.*) feet. Beam : 66 feet. Draught (at *normal* displacement) : 20 (*mean*),
                  25 (*max.*) feet
Guns :   12—6 inch, 47 cal. 12—5 inch, 38 cal., d.p., 24—40 mm. AA., 19—20 mm. AA.
Aircraft :   3 seaplanes
Catapults :   2
Armour :   Similar to *Cleveland* class
Machinery :   Geared turbines. 4 shafts. S.H.P. :100,000 = 32·5 kts.
Boilers :   8 Babcock & Wilcox
Complement :   916 (peace), 1,200 (war)

Notes.—These two ships are modified *Clevelands*, with single funnels and simplified superstructures, intended to enlarge the area
of fire of AA. armament. Cancelled units : *Newark* (108), *New Haven* (109), *Buffalo* (110), *Wilmington* (111) ; Nos. 112-115 ;
Tallahassee (116), *Cheyenne* (117), *Chattanooga* (118). Hull of *Newark* was sold for scrap in 1949 after being used for trials of
torpedoes and mines.

FARGO.   *1946, London Studio.*

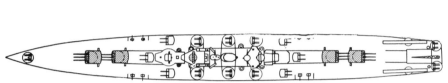

No.	Name	Builders and Machinery	Laid down	Launched	Completed
106	*Fargo*	New York S.B. Corpn.	23 Aug. 1943	25 Feb. 1945	9 Dec. 1945
107	*Huntington)*		4 Oct. 1943	8 Apr. 1945	23 Feb. 1946

FARGO.   *Added 1949, Marius Bar.*

FARGO.   *1954, U.S. Navy, Official.*

The *Fargo* was one of two modified "Cleveland" class
cruisers completed shortly after World War II. She was
mothballed in 1949 ; her sister ship *Huntington* (CL 107)
was stricken on 1 Sep 1962.

AIRCRAFT. The *Fargo* and *Huntington* were completed
with two stern catapults and carried four floatplanes.

GUNNERY. The 40 mm weapons are mounted in six
quad and two twin mounts, the latter in stern "tubs".
As built 19—20 mm AA guns were also installed ; they
were removed after completion.

HUNTINGTON   *United States Navy, Official*

Guided Missile Light Cruisers (CLG)

6 Converted "Cleveland" Class

GALVESTON
LITTLE ROCK
OKLAHOMA CITY

PROVIDENCE
SPRINGFIELD
TOPEKA

Displacement:	10,670 tons *standard* (14,600 tons *full load*)
Dimensions:	Length: 600 (w.l.), 610 (o.a.) feet Beam: 66 feet. Draught: 25 (*max.*) feet
Guns:	*Cleveland* and others: 6—6 inch, 47 cal.; 16—5 inch, 38 cal. d.p. *Little Rock, Oklahoma City*: 3—6 inch, 47 cal.; 2—5 inch, 38 dal. d.p.
Guided Missiles:	*Galveston, Little Rock, Oklahoma City*: One "Talos" twin launcher aft, with 46 missiles. *Providence, Springfield, Topeka*: One "Terrier" twin launcher aft with 120 missiles.
A/S weapons:	Launchers for ASW torpedoes
Armour:	5" belt, 5" decks, 5"—3" gunhouses
Machinery:	General Electric geared turbines. 4 shafts. S.H.P.: 100,000=33 kts.
Boilers:	8 Babcock & Wilcox
Oil fuel:	2,100 tons
Radius:	7,500 miles at 15 kts.
Complement:	1,070 (70 officers and 1,000 enlisted men)

GALVESTON (aerial view off starboard quarter)

1959, *United States Navy, Official*

General Notes

These six former light cruisers of the "Cleveland" class (CL) were converted into guided missile light cruisers (CLG), *Galveston* under the 1956 Fiscal program and the other five under the 1957 Fiscal program. They have a conventional armament forward, and amidships, and guided missile launchers aft, three being armed with "Terrier" missiles and three with "Talos" missiles.

Flagship Notes

Little Rock, Oklahoma City, Providence and *Springfield* are being refitted as flagships, the navigating bridge and forward superstructure being reconstructed to provide for flag spaces and to include high frequency radio systems with side band capability. Other work, such as improvement of habitability, is also being done in conjunction with the installation of missile capabilities.

Construction Notes

For builders and dates of laying down, launch, and original completion, see table on next page under "Vincennes" class

Guided Missile Notes

The Bendix "Talos" ramjet-powered surface-to-air missile, the principal armament in the *Galveston*, has a range of more than 65 miles and is able to carry a nuclear warhead. See full notes under "Long Beach", the nuclear powered guided missile cruiser under construction, on a previous page.

Torpedo Notes

The guided missile conversions are to be fitted with torpedo launchers for anti-submarine warfare torpedoes.

Conversion Notes

Galveston, formerly CL 93, was converted to a guided missile light cruiser at Philadelphia Naval Shipyard. She was re-classified CLG 93 on 4 Feb. 1956, and CLG 3 on 23 May 1957. Conversion began on 15 Aug. 1956 and was completed on 5

Sep. 1958 (commissioned 28 May 1958). *Topeka* is being converted at New York Naval Shipyard; *Springfield* at Bethlehem Steel Company, Quincy, Mass.; *Oklahoma City* at Bethlehem Pacific Coast Steel Corp., San Francisco, Calif.; *Little Rock* at New York Shipbuilidng Corp., Camden, N.J.; and *Providence* at Boston Naval Shipyard. *Providence, Springfield* and *Topeka* will carry "Terrier" guided missiles and *Little Rock* and *Oklahoma City* will carry "Talos" guided missiles. *Providence* conversion began on 1 June, 1957, and were completed on 30 Sept. 1959 (commissioning date 17 Sep. 1959). *Topeka* conversion began on 19 Aug. 1959 and will be completed on 13 Mar. 1960 (commissioning date 4 Jan. 1960). *Little Rock* conversion began on 30 Jan. 1957 and estimated commissioning date is Mar. 1960. *Oklahoma* began conversion on 21 May 1957. *Springfield* conversion began on 1 Aug. 1957 and estimated commissioning date is Mar. 1960.

Photograph Notes

Photographs of *Providence* (after conversion) and *Little Rock* (artist's impression) appear on page 477 (Addenda) of this edition.

GALVESTON (starboard bow view)

1959, *United States Navy, Official, courtesy "Our Navy"*

GALVESTON (surface view off port beam)

1959, *United States Navy, Official*

PROVIDENCE

1960, United States Navy, Official

OKLAHOMA CITY (CLG 5)

United States Navy

GALVESTON (CLG 3)

United States Navy

SPRINGFIELD

1973, USN

SPRINGFIELD (CLG 7)

United States Navy

14 "Baltimore" Class.

BALTIMORE
G BOSTON
BREMERTON
G CANBERRA (ex-Pittsburgh)
CHICAGO
COLUMBUS
FALL RIVER

HELENA (ex-Des Moines)
LOS ANGELES
MACON
PITTSBURGH (ex-Albany)
QUINCY (ex-St. Paul)
ST. PAUL (ex-Rochester)
TOLEDO

Displacement :	13,600 tons (17,070 tons *full load*)
Dimensions :	Length : 673½ (*o.a.*) feet. Beam : 71 feet. Draught : 26 (*max.*) feet
Guns	9—8 inch 55 cal., 12—5 inch, 38 cal., 52—40 mm. AA., (3-inch guns replace 40 mm. in active units)
Aircraft :	All ships carry a helicopter
Armour :	6" side, 3" — 2" decks
Machinery :	Geared turbines. 4 shafts. S.H.P. : 120,000 = 34 kts.
Boilers :	8 Babcock & Wilcox
Fuel :	2,500 tons
Complement :	1,700 (war)

Boston and *Canberra* were converted in early 1950s to carry two twin Terrier missile launchers in place of the after turret.

ST. PAUL.

1953, U.S. Navy, Official.

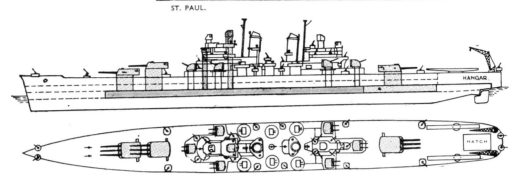

Note to Plan.—Only one crane now at stern. Catapults discarded.

General Notes.—*Boston* was built in two years. Are much enlarged and improved editions of *Wichita*. Last 6 ships belong to War Programme. *Canberra* was named in commemoration of H.M.A.S. *Canberra*, sunk in 1st Battle of Savo Island, Aug. 9, 1943.

Gunnery Note.—8-inch guns are a new model, firing a heavier shell than those mounted in earlier cruisers. *Bremerton, Columbus, Helena, Los Angeles* and *St. Paul* are to undergo armament conversion (improved rapid-firing 3-inch 50 cal. AA. guns replacing 40 mm. AA. guns.

No.		Name	Builders and Machinery	Laid down	Launched	Completed
	CA 68	Baltimore	⎫	26 May 1941	28 July 1942	15 Apr. 1943
CAG 1 (ex-CA 69)		Boston	⎪	30 June 1941	26 Aug. 1942	30 June 1943
CAG 2 (ex-CA 70)		Canberra	⎪	3 Sept. 1941	19 Apr. 1943	14 Oct. 1943
	CA 71	Quincy	⎬ Bethlehem Steel Co.,	9 Oct. 1941	23 June 1943	15 Dec. 1943
	CA 72	Pittsburgh	Quincy	3 Feb. 1943	22 Feb. 1944	10 Oct. 1944
	CA 73	St. Paul	⎪	3 Feb. 1943	16 Sep. 1944	17 Feb. 1945
	CA 74	Columbus	⎪	28 June 1943	30 Nov. 1944	8 June 1945
	CA 75	Helena	⎭	9 Sep. 1943	28 Apr. 1945	4 Sep. 1945
	CA 130	Bremerton	⎫	1 Feb. 1943	2 July 1944	29 Apr. 1945
	CA 131	Fall River	⎬ New York S.B. Corpn.	12 Apr. 1943	13 Aug. 1944	1 July 1945
	CA 132	Macon	⎪	14 June 1943	15 Oct. 1944	25 Aug. 1945
	CA 133	Toledo	⎭	13 Sep. 1943	6 May 1945	27 Oct. 1946
	CA 135	Los Angeles	⎱ Philadelphia Navy Yard	28 July 1943	20 Aug. 1944	22 July 1944
	CA 136	Chicago	⎰	28 July 1943	20 Aug. 1944	10 Jan. 1945

CHICAGO.

1944, U.S. Navy Official.

COLUMBUS.

1950, Wright & Logan.

Guided Missile Cruisers (CAG)

2 Converted " Baltimore " Class

Name:	BOSTON	CANBERRA (ex-Pittsburgh)
	Boston	Canberra
No.:	CAG 1 (ex-CA 69)	CAG 2 (ex-CA 70)
Builders:	Bethlehem-Steel Co., Quincy	Bethlehem-Steel Co., Quincy
Laid down:	30 June 1941	3 Sep. 1941
Launched:	26 May 1942	19 Apr. 1943
Completed:	30 June 1943	14 Oct. 1943
Converted:	1 Nov. 1955	15 June 1956

Displacement:	13,600 tons standard (17,200 tons full load)
Dimensions:	Length: 673½ (o.a.) feet. Beam: 71 feet. Draught: 26 (max.) feet
Guns:	6—8 inch 55 cal.; 10—5 inch 38 cal.; 12—3 inch, 50 cal. AA.
G.M. Launchers:	2 twin mountings for " Terriers " (aft only)
Armour:	6 inch side belts, 3 inch decks
Machinery:	General Electric geared turbines. 4 shafts. S.H.P.: 120,000=34 kts.
Boilers:	8 Babcock & Wilcox
Oil fuel:	2,500 tons
Complement:	1,635 (Boston 110 officers, 1,620 men)

General Notes

The world's first guided missile cruisers and first operational combat ships capable of firing supersonic anti-aircraft guided weapons. These ships with their associated radars and guidance systems for the " Terrier " and other anti-aircraft missiles represent a completely new naval weapons system specifically designed to further the U.S. Navy's policy of countering aircraft. Formerly classified as Heavy Cruisers (CA). *Boston* was originally built in exactly two years. *Canberra*, just before completion, was renamed in commemoration of H.M.A.S. *Canberra* which was sunk in the 1st Battle of Savo Island, 9 Aug., 1942.

Conversion Notes

Both ships were converted to Guided Missile Heavy Cruisers (CAG) by the New York Shipbuilding Corporation, Camden, New Jersey, at a cost of $30,000,000 for both. The after 143-ton 8 inch triple gun turret and the after 5 inch twin gun mounting were removed and two twin guided missile launchers mounted in " X " and " Y " positions in their place. Both ships have undergone other drastic changes to prepare them for their new role of defence against aircraft. The ships' superstructure was entirely remodelled to accommodate the new weapons. One of the two funnels was entirely removed which vastly alters the appearance of the vessels.

Guided Missile Notes

A slim needle-nosed supersonic anti-aircraft weapon, with a length of 27 feet and a speed of 1,500 m.p.h., the " Terrier," developed by the U.S. Navy's Bureau of Ordnance is designed to intercept aircraft under any weather conditions at a longer range and higher altitudes than conventional anti-aircraft guns. Stowage of the " Terrier " is below decks in two magazines, dubbed the " coke machines," which are completely automatic loading devices. Radar and electronic equipment for detecting targets and for guiding the missiles represent the most drastic change. This equipment is the most modern available and is designed for a maximum degree of automatic operation. Each of the two twin launchers is capable of firing two " Terriers " simultaneously. Can launch four missiles in

eight-tenths of a second. Two missiles per launcher every 30 seconds. Automatic loading. 144 " Terrier " missiles carried in each ship. The " Terrier " was fired experimentally in

fleet operations in Nov. 1954, from the U.S.S. *Mississippi*, the Navy's oldest battleship, which had been converted into a test ship for this purpose; she was scrapped in 1957.

BOSTON   1959, Ted Stone

BOSTON   1956, U.S. Navy, Official

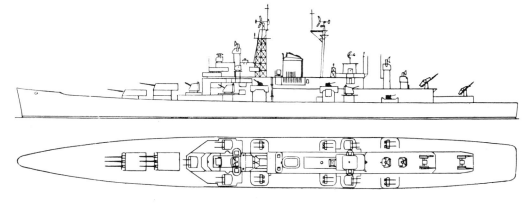

Notes to Drawing
Port elevation and plan.
Scale: 128 feet=1 inch.

CANBERRA   1958, courtesy Ian S. Pearsall, Esq.

Guided Missile Cruisers (CG) and Heavy Cruisers (CA)

12 "Baltimore" Class

BALTIMORE	LOS ANGELES
BREMERTON	MACON
CHICAGO	PITTSBURGH (ex-*Albany*)
COLUMBUS	QUINCY (ex-*St. Paul*)
FALL RIVER	ST. PAUL (ex-*Rochester*)
HELENA (ex-*Des Moines*)	TOLEDO

Displacement:	13,600 tons *standard* (17,200 tons *full load*)
Dimensions:	Length: 673½ (o.a.) feet. Beam: 71 feet. Draught: 26 (*max.*) feet
Guns:	9—8 inch, 55 cal., 12—5 inch, 38 cal., 52—40 mm. AA. (20—3 inch 50 cal. guns replace 40 mm. in active units except *Baltimore*)
Aircraft:	All ships carry a helicopter
Armour:	6" side, 3" + 2" decks.
Machinery:	General Electric geared turbines. 4 shafts. S.H.P.: 120,000 = 34 kts.
Boilers:	8 Babcock & Wilcox
Oil Fuel:	2,500 tons
Radius:	9,000 miles at 15 kts.
Complement:	1,700 (war)

ST. PAUL

1959, U.S. Navy, Official, courtesy " Our Navy "

HELENA

1957, U.S. Navy, Official

General Notes

Pittsburgh was built in 20 months. All others except *Toledo* were built in two years. Are much enlarged and improved editions of *Wichita*. Last 6 ships belong to War Programme. *Baltimore* and *Pittsburg* were decommissioned in 1956. Only one crane now at stern except *Baltimore* and *Quincy* which have two cranes on stern as shown in photograph of *Baltimore* in 1958-59 edition. Catapults discarded. Active units have twin 3 inch, 50 cal. guns on starboard quarter only, except those fitted as guided missile cruisers which have none on quarter. The classification and hull numbers of *Chicago* (CA 136 to CG 11) and *Fall River* (CA 131 to CG 12) were officially changed to become effective on 1 Nov. 1958, but the classification of *Fall River* as CG 12 was cancelled on 9 Oct. 1958.

St. Paul was designated as the permanent flagship of the 7th Fleet in 1959, her home port being at Yokosuka, Japan. She now has a tower foremast, and improved radar, see photograph.

Gunnery Notes

8-inch guns are a new model, firing a heavier shell than those mounted in earlier cruisers. *Bremerton, Columbus, Helena, Los Angeles, Macon, St. Paul* and *Toledo* have undergone armament conversion (improved rapid-firing 3 inch 50 cal. AA. guns replacing 40 mm. AA. guns).

Guided Missile Notes

Boston and *Canberra* have been converted to guided missile ships (CAG), see earlier page. (Fitted with surface-to-air " Terrier " missile installations.) *Los Angeles* was converted to carry " Regulus " guided missiles at Mare Island Naval Shipyard during 3 months of 1954 with little change in previous armament. *Helena, Macon* and *Toledo* also fitted for " Regulus " guided missiles. These four ships are not classified as guided missile cruisers, however.

Conversion Notes

The *Chicago* and *Fall River* of this class were to have been converted into guided weapon cruisers under the Fiscal 1958 cruiser conversion program, but the conversion of *Fall River* was subsequently cancelled. *Fall River* was to have been converted at Puget Sound Naval Shipyard, and *Chicago* at San Francisco Naval Shipyard. Two ships of this class are being converted to guided missile cruisers under the Fiscal 1959 program. The conversions of *Chicago* and *Columbus* are now being proceeded with, *Chicago* at San Francisco Naval Shipyard and *Columbus* at Puget Sound Naval Shipyard. *Chicago*

Recent Disposals

The heavy cruisers *Augusta*, CA 31, *Chester*, CA 27 and *Louisville*, CA 28, of the " Chester " class; the *Portland*, CA 33; the *New Orleans*, CA 32, *Minneapolis*, CA 36, *Tuscaloosa*, CA 37 and *San Francisco*, CA 38, of the " New Orleans " class; and the *Wichita*, CA 45, were scrapped in 1959 (stricken from the Navy List on 1 Mar. 1959).

No.	Name	Builders	Laid down	Launched	Completed
CA 68	Baltimore		26 May 1941	28 July 1942	15 Apr. 1943
CA 71	Quincy		9 Oct. 1941	23 June 1943	15 Dec. 1943
CA 72	Pittsburgh	Bethlehem Steel Co. Quincy	3 Feb. 1943	22 Feb. 1944	10 Oct. 1944
CA 73	St. Paul		3 Feb. 1943	16 Sep. 1944	17 Feb. 1945
CG 12 (ex-CA74)	Columbus		28 June 1943	30 Nov. 1944	8 June 1945
CA 75	Helena		9 Sep. 1943	28 Apr. 1944	4 Sep. 1945
CA 130	Bremerton		1 Feb. 1943	2 July 1944	29 April 1945
CA 131	Fall River	New York S.B. Corpn.	12 Apr. 1943	13 Aug. 1944	1 July 1945
CA 132	Macon		14 June 1943	15 Oct. 1944	26 Aug. 1945
CA 133	Toledo		13 Sep. 1943	6 May 1945	27 Oct. 1946
CA 135	Los Angeles	Philadelphia Navy Yard	28 July 1943	20 Aug. 1944	22 July 1945
CG 11 (ex-CA 136)	Chicago		28 July 1943	20 Aug. 1944	10 Jan. 1945

conversion began on 1 Apr. 1959, *Columbus* on 1 May, and it is estimated that they will be commissioned in Nov. and Dec. 1961, respectively.

They are to have a combination of " Talos " and " Tartar " surface-to-air missile systems with " Talos " mounted on twin launchers fore and aft, and " Tartar " launchers installed amidships. " Regulus " launchers can be installed as required. All superstructure and gun mountings are being removed, and they are to be rebuilt to provide for ASW weapons in addition to missiles.

Photograph Notes

Photograph of " Regulus " guided missile being launched from *Helena*, and port broadside view of *Macon* in the 1957-58 edition. Port quarter view of *Baltimore* in 1954-55 to 1958-59 editions.

Notes to Drawing

Port elevation and plan of "Baltimore" class not converted.

Scale: 128 feet = 1 inch.

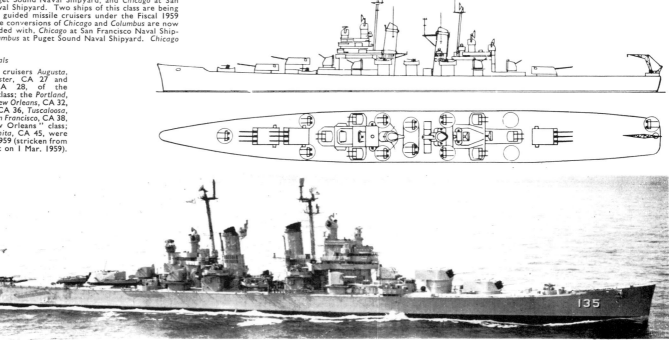

LOS ANGELES (catapults now removed, fitted for " Regulus " guided missiles)

1958, U.S. Navy, Official

Heavy Cruisers (CA).

3 " Oregon City " Class.

ALBANY   **OREGON CITY**   **ROCHESTER**

Displacement:	13,700 tons, *Rochester* 13,000 tons *standard* (17,070 tons *full load*)
Dimensions:	Length: 673½ (*o.a.*) feet. Beam: 71 feet. Draught: 26 (*max.*) feet
Guns:	9—8 inch, 55 cal., 12—5 inch, 38 cal., 52—40 mm. AA., 24—20 mm. AA.
Aircraft :	I helicopter
Armour:	6″ side, 3″ + 2″ decks
Machinery:	General Electric geared turbines. 4 shafts. S.H.P.: 120,000 = 33 kts.
Boilers:	8 Babcock & Wilcox
Fuel:	2,500 tons
Complement:	1,700 (war)

ALBANY.

Added 1951 U.S. Navy, Official.

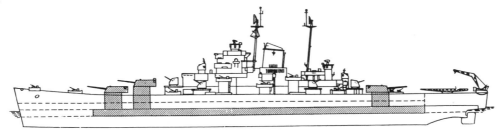

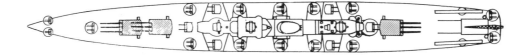

Note to Plan.—Catapults now discarded in *Albany* and *Rochester*. Armour does not cover the 8-inch magazines (on the side only).

General Notes.—These ships are modified *Baltimores*, with a single funnel and simplified superstructure. Bridge is further aft than in *Baltimore* class. Six more units of this class were cancelled, CA 126–129 (*Cambridge, Bridgeport, Kansas City, Tulsa*), CA 137 and CA 138 (*Norfolk, Scranton*).

Engineering Notes.—Cruising turbines are not included in engine design. In event of port or starboard fuel tanks being ruptured, change-over of suction to other side could be accomplished in a minute, oil burner lines being divided at boiler face.

No.	Name	Builders and Machinery	Laid down	Launched	Completed
CA 122	Oregon City	⎰	8 Apr. 1944	9 Apr. 1945	16 Feb. 1946
123	Albany	Bethlehem Steel Co., Quincy	6 Mar. 1944	30 June 1945	15 June 1946
124	Rochester	⎱	29 May 1944	28 Aug. 1945	20 Dec. 1946

ROCHESTER.   1947, U.S. Navy, Official.   OREGON CITY.   1946, U.S. Navy, Official.

OREGON CITY

Added 1954, U.S. Navy, Official.

2 "ALBANY" CLASS (GUIDED MISSILE CRUISERS (CG))

Name	No.	Builders	Laid down	Launched	Commissioned
*ALBANY	CG 10 (ex-CA 123)	Bethlehem Steel Co (Fore River)	6 Mar 1944	30 June1945	15 June 1946
*CHICAGO	CG 11 (ex-CA 136)	Philadelphia Navy Yard	28 July 1943	20 Aug 1944	10 Jan 1945

Displacement, tons: 13 700 standard; 17 500 full load
Length, feet (metres): 664 *(202·4)* wl; 674 *(205·4)* oa
Beam, feet (metres): 70 *(21·6)*
Draught, feet (metres): 30 *(9·1)*
Missile launchers:
  2 twin Talos surface-to-air launchers (Mk 12 Mod 1)
  2 twin Tartar surface-to-air launchers (Mk 11 Mod 1 and Mod 2)
Guns: 2—5 inch *(127 mm)* 38 calibre (Mk 24) (single)
A/S weapons: 1 ASROC 8-tube launcher; 2 triple torpedo tubes (Mk 32)
Helicopters: Deck for utility helicopters
Main engines: 4 geared turbines (General Electric); 120 000 shp; 4 shafts
Boilers: 4 (Babcock & Wilcox)
Speed, knots: 32
Complement: 1 222 (72 officers, 1 150 enlisted men)
Flag accommodations: 68 (10 officers, 58 enlisted men)

These ships were fully converted from heavy cruisers, the *Albany* having been a unit of the "Oregon City" class and the *Chicago* of the "Baltimore" class. Although the two heavy cruiser classes differed in appearance they had the same hull dimensions and machinery. These ships form a new, homogeneous class.
The cruiser *Fall River* (CA 131) was originally scheduled for missile conversion, but was replaced by the *Columbus* (now deleted). Proposals to convert two additional heavy cruisers (CA 124 and CA 130) to missile ships (CG 13 and CG 14) were dropped, primarily because of high conversion costs and improved capabilities of newer missile-armed frigates.

Conversion: During conversion these ships were stripped down to their main hulls with all cruiser armament and superstructure being removed. New superstructures make extensive use of aluminium to reduce weight and improve stability. The *Albany* was converted at the Boston Naval Shipyard between January 1959 and new commissioning on 3 Nov 1962; *Chicago* at San Francisco Naval Shipyard from July 1959 to new commissioning on 2 May 1964.

Electronics: Naval Tactical Data System (NTDS) is fitted.

Fire control: Two Mk 77 Mod 3 missile fire control systems, four Mk 74 Mod 1 missile fire control systems, two Mk 56 Mod 43 gunfire control systems, one Mk 6 Mod 2 or Mod 3 weapon direction system, four SPG-49B and four SPG-51C weapon control radars.

Gunnery: No guns were fitted when these ships were converted to missile cruisers. Two single open-mount 5 inch guns were fitted subsequently to provide low-level defence. Phalanx 20 mm CIWS to be fitted.

Missiles: One twin Talos launcher is forward and one aft, a twin Tartar launcher is on each side of the main bridge structure. During conversion, space was allocated amidships for installation of eight Polaris missile tubes, but the plan to install ballistic missiles in cruisers was cancelled in mid-1959. Reportedly 92 Talos and 80 Tartar missiles are carried.
Harpoon to be fitted.

Modernisation: The *Albany* underwent an extensive anti-air warfare modernisation at the Boston Naval Shipyard, including installation of NTDS, a digital Talos fire-control system and improved radars. This began in February 1967 and was completed in August 1969. She was formally recommissioned on 9 Nov 1968. The *Chicago* will not have AAW modernisation.

Radar: *Albany*
3D Search; SPS 48
Search; SPS 10, 30 and 43
Chicago
Search; SPS 10, 30, 43 and 52

Rockets: Mk 28 Chaffroc to be fitted.

Sonar: SQS-23 (bow mounted)

ALBANY   *8/1975, USN*

ALBANY   *1976, Michael D. J. Lennon*

ALBANY   *9/1975, Reinhard Nerlich*

Large Cruisers (CB).

2 + 1 " Alaska " Class.

ALASKA **GUAM** **HAWAII**

Displacement : 27,500 tons (34,250 tons *full load*)
Dimensions : Length : 808½ (o.a.) feet. Beam : 91 feet.
  Draught : 31½ (max.) feet
Guns : (*Alaska* and *Guam*) 9—12 inch, 50 cal., 12—5 inch,
  38 cal., 56—40 mm. AA., 34—20 mm. A.A.
Aircraft : 4
Catapults : 2
Armour : 9″-5″ side, 12¾″ turret faces, 5″ turret sides and
  crowns, 4½″-3¾″ decks
Machinery : General Electric geared turbines. 4 shafts.
  S.H.P. : 150,000 = 33 kts. (30 kts. *designed*)
Boilers : 8 Babcock & Wilcox
Complement : 1,370 (peace). 1,900 (war)

ALASKA *U.S. Navy, Official*

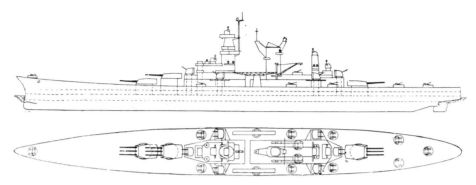

Note to Plan.—Stern is actually of more rectangular form than shown here.

General Notes.—All ordered in Sep., 1940, and officially described as " Large Cruisers." In fact, they were the first vessels with the characteristics of battle cruisers to be ordered by any Navy since the Washington Conference met in 1921; and although they have cruiser lines their length and displacement exceed those of many battleships. *Guam* proved her worth in nearly six months of Pacific operations. Made her debut on March 18, 1945, in the historic carrier attack against the Ryukyas and steamed for 61 consecutive days. *Alaska* and *Guam* are at Naval Shipyard Annex at Bayonne as part of the inactivated Reserve Fleet. Inclusive cost is officially estimated at $74,066,000 per ship. Three more ships of this type, *Philippines, Puerto Rico* and *Samoa,* authorised in 1940, were cancelled on June 24, 1943. Construction of *Hawaii* was held up awaiting final decision concerning armament, which it had been proposed to modify by fitting rocket projectors, and ship was laid up in naval shipyard 82 per cent. complete. After work was suspended, it is officially stated, there was discussion that she might be completed as a guided missile ship.

Gunnery Notes.—The 12-inch guns are of a new and powerful model. Anti-aircraft batteries very efficient.

Armour Notes.—Protection generally is on the lines of an armoured cruiser rather than of a battleship. Officially stated that their compartmentation makes them some of the most combat-worthy ships in the world.

Special Note.—The classification of *Hawaii* was in 1952 changed from CB 3 to CBC 1 and she was to have been completed as a Large Tactical Command Ship. The conversion was to have included the installation of a great deal of radar, communications, and headquarters equipment to fit her for being an operations command ship and to act as such for a carrier task force or similar large fleet or group of ships. The largest guns mounted were to have been of 5 inch calibre. The conversion was authorised but the contract was not awarded and no work has been undertaken. The ship was again reclassified as CB 3 on 9 Sep., 1954, with conversion plans cancelled. Laid up in Reserve Fleet, Philadelphia Naval Shipyard.

ALASKA. [1944, *U.S. Navy Official.*

No.	Name	Builders	Machinery	Laid down	Launched	Completed
CB 1	Alaska	} New York Shipbuilding Corpn.	Gen. Electric Co.	16 Dec. 1941	15 Aug. 1943	17 June 1944
CB 2	Guam			2 Feb. 1942	21 Nov. 1943	17 Sep. 1944
CB 3	Hawaii			20 Dec. 1943	11 Mar. 1945	

GUAM. 1944, *U.S. Navy Official.*

GUAM. Added 1949, *U.S. Navy, Official.*

GUAM *United States Navy, Official*

Heavy Cruisers (CA)

Heavy Cruisers (CA).

3 " Des Moines " Class.

DES MOINES	NEWPORT NEWS	SALEM

Displacement :	17,000 tons (21,500 tons *full load*)
Dimensions :	Length : 716½ (*o.a.*) feet. Beam : 75½ feet.
	Draught : 26 (*max.*) feet
Guns :	9—8 inch, 55 cal., triple turrets,
	12—5 inch, 38 cal., d.p., twin mounts, 24—3 inch AA., 50 cal.
Aircraft :	1 helicopter
Armour :	8″-6″ side, 3″ + 2″ decks
Machinery :	Geared turbines. 4 shafts. S.H.P. : 120,000 = 33 kts.
Boilers :	4 Babcock & Wilcox
Fuel :	2,600 tons
Complement :	1,860 (war)

NEWPORT NEWS. 1955, U.S. Navy, Official.

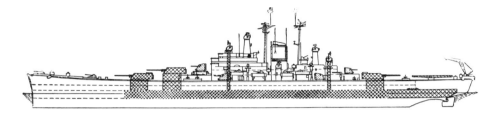

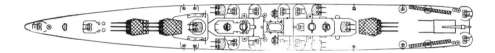

Note to Plan.—Catapults now discarded, seaplane units having been disbanded.

General Notes.—The heaviest cruisers in the world, and the first vessels to mount completely automatic rapid-fire 8-inch guns, these ships represent an expansion of *Oregon City* design. Much of extra tonnage is absorbed by rapid loading gear and extra magazine space, though part of this is made up by saving in complement. *Newport News* is completely air-conditioned and similar equipment will be installed in the *Salem*. The *Des Moines* is not air-conditioned. All assigned to Atlantic Fleet.

Gunnery Notes.—All guns are of fully automatic type. Cartridge cases have replaced wrapped charges and shells have automatic fuse setting. 8-inch guns are said to be capable of firing four times more rapidly than any previous model. The 24—3 inch AA. guns are in 12 twin mountings : 2 twin mountings abreast funnel are not installed in peacetime.

Appearance Note.—As completed have single funnels, thus resembling " Oregon City " class in appearance.

No.	Name	Builders and Machinery	Laid down	Launched	Completed
CA 134	*Des Moines*	Bethlehem Steel Co., Quincy	28 May 1945	27 Sep. 1946	17 Nov. 1948
139	*Salem*	Bethlehem Steel Co., Quincy	4 June 1945	25 Mar. 1947	9 May 1949
148	*Newport News*	Newport News Co.	1 Oct. 1945	6 Mar. 1947	29 Jan. 1949

SALEM. 1950, U.S. Navy, Official.

DES MOINES 1957, U.S. Navy, Official

DES MOINES. Added 1954, U.S. Navy, Official.

NEWPORT NEWS

10/1974, USN

NEWPORT NEWS (CA 148)

1967, United States Navy,

SALEM (midship details)

Added 1959, A. & J. Pavia

These ships were the largest and most powerful 8-in gun cruisers ever built. Completed too late for World War II, they were

employed primarily as flagships for the Sixth Fleet in the Mediterranean and the Second Fleet in the Atlantic. *Salem* was decommissioned on 30 January 1959 and *Des Moines* on 14 July 1961. Both laid up at Philadelphia.

Design: These ships are an improved version of the previous "Oregon City" class. The newer cruisers have automatic main batteries, larger main turrets, taller fire control towers, and larger bridges. *Des Moines* is fully air-conditioned.
Additional ships of this class were cancelled: *Dallas* (CA 140) and the unnamed CA 141-142, CA 149-153.

Electronics: Tacan.

Fire control: Four Mk 56 gunfire control systems, two Mk 54 gunfire control directors and four Mk 37 GFCS.

Gunnery: These cruisers were the first ships to be armed with fully automatic 8-in guns firing cased ammunition. The guns can be loaded at any elevation from −5 to +41 degrees; rate of fire is four times faster than earlier 8-in guns. Mk 16 8-in guns in these ships.
As built, these ships mounted 12 5-in guns, 24 3-in guns (in twin mounts), and 12—20 mm guns (single mounts). The 20 mm guns were removed almost immediately and the 3-in battery was reduced gradually as ships were overhauled. With full armament the designed wartime complement was 1 860.

DES MOINES

USN

Light Cruisers (CL).

2 " Worcester " Class.

ROANOKE   **WORCESTER**

Displacement : 14,700 tons (18,500 tons *full load*)
Dimensions : Length : 668 (w.l.) 679½ (o.a.) feet. Beam : 70½ feet. Draught : 25 (*max.*) feet
Guns : 12—6 inch, 47 cal., d.p. (semi-automatic), 24—3 inch, 50 cal., d.p. (rapid fire)
Aircraft : 1 helicopter
Armour : 6"—3" side, 4" turrets, 3" + 2" decks
Machinery : Geared turbines. 4 shafts. S.H.P. : 120,000 = 32 kts.
Boilers : 4 Babcock & Wilcox
Oil fuel : 3,300 tons
Complement : 1,170 (70 officers, 1,100 men) (peace), 1,700 (war)

ROANOKE.

Added 1951 ,U.S. Navy, Official, courtesy " Our Navy."

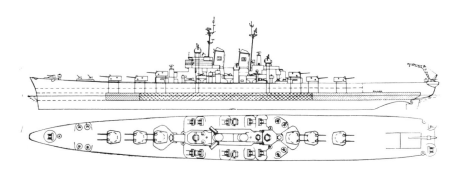

General Notes.—Both ordered June 15, 1943. *Roanoke* commissioned at Philadelphia Navy Yard. Both in Atlantic Fleet. These ships, which are larger than most heavy cruisers, are nevertheless rated as light cruisers by Treaty definitions. Two incomplete sister ships, *Vallejo* (146) and *Gary* (147), were cancelled on 11 Aug., 1945. Six additional ships, CL 154-159, were cancelled in 1945.

Gunnery Notes.—Have 6 inch dual purpose guns of a new automatic model in six twin turrets, and 3 inch in eleven twin mounts of a new type, and two single mounts.

Conversion Notes.—The Fiscal 1956 shipbuilding and conversion programme requests funds for the conversion of one light cruiser to a guided missile cruiser.

No.	Name	Builders	Laid down	Launched	Completed
CL 145	Roanoke	New York S.B. Corpn.	15 May 1945	16 June 1947	4 Apr. 1948
144	Worcester	New York S.B. Corpn.	29 Jan. 1945	4 Feb. 1947	25 June 1948

These ships are amongst the largest cruisers ever constructed and are ranked as "light" cruisers only because of their 6 inch main battery. They served in the active fleet for a decade, often paired to an 8 inch-gunned "Salem" class cruiser in two-ship cruiser divisions. Both the *Worcester* and *Roanoke* were decommissioned and placed in mothballs late in 1958, giving them the distinction of being the last all-gun light cruisers to serve in the United States Navy.

DESIGN. These ships are similar in arrangement to the twin-funnel "Cleveland" class light cruisers but with their 12—6 inch guns arranged in six twin turrets vice 12 guns in four triple turrets of the earlier ships. The *Worcester* and *Roanoke* are also the only US cruisers of World War II design without twin 5 inch gun mounts.

Eight additional ships of this class were cancelled : the *Vallejo* (CL 146), *Gary* (CL 147), and the unnamed CL 154-159.

WORCESTER.

1955, U.S. Navy, Official.

WORCESTER (starboard broadside)

B. L. Devenish-Meares

ROANOKE

1958, U.S. Navy, Official

9 Anti-Aircraft Cruisers (CLAA).

3 "Juneau" Class.

FRESNO (March 5, 1946)   **SPOKANE** (Sept. 22, 1945)
JUNEAU (July 15, 1945)

4 "Oakland" Class.

FLINT (ex-*Spokane*, Jan. 25, 1944)   **RENO** (Dec. 23, 1942)
OAKLAND (Oct. 23, 1942)   **TUCSON** (Sept. 3, 1944)

2 "San Diego" Class.

SAN DIEGO (July 26, 1941)   **SAN JUAN** (Sept. 6, 1941)

Displacement:	6,000 tons (8,000 tons *full load*)
Dimensions:	Length: 541 feet. Beam: 52¼ feet. Draught: 20 (*mean*), 24 (*max.*) feet
Guns:	12—5 inch, 38 cal. (d.p.), 24 to 32—40 mm. AA., 12 to 16—20 mm. AA. (*San Diego, San Juan*: 16—5 inch, 38 cal., 10—40 mm. AA., 15—20 mm. AA.)
Armour:	3½" side, 2" deck
Tubes:	Removed
Machinery:	Geared turbines. 2 shafts. S.H.P.: 75,000 = 35 kts. (designed) Rated speed in service is not above 32 kts.
Complement:	597 (peace), 700 (war)

SAN DIEGO.   1944, *U.S. Navy Official*.

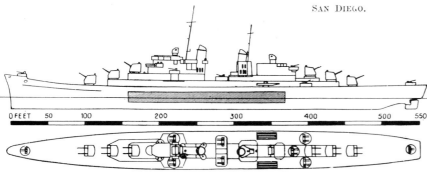

FRESNO.   1947, *Mr. L. L. v. Münching*.

Notes to Plan.—*San Diego* and *San Juan* had two wing turrets mounted abreast the after superstructure. In *Juneau, Spokane* and *Fresno*, "B" and "X" turrets were placed a deck lower than in earlier ships, and T.T. were omitted, to improve stability.

General Notes.—Originally light cruisers (CL). All reclassified as anti-aircraft cruisers (CLAA). Cost averages $23,261,500 each, inclusive. Arrangement of main armament forward and aft is reminiscent of British "Dido" class. Bridges are reported to be armoured. Seven earlier ships had 8—21 inch torpedo tubes in quadruple deck mountings which were removed in 1945. All laid up except *Juneau*. War losses: *Atlanta, Juneau*. Two new ships of these names have been built, of which the former belongs to 10,000-ton "Cleveland" class.

OAKLAND.   1944, *U.S. Navy Official*

SPOKANE.   1952, *Ted Stone*.

RENO.   1944, *U.S. Navy Official*

JUNEAU   1952, *Photo, U.S. Navy, Official*

JUNEAU

Added 1957, Ted Stone

FRESNO

Added 1957, U.S. Navy, Official

Formerly rated as
Cruiser, Task Fleet Command Ship

1 " Northampton " Type

NORTHAMPTON

No.:	CLC 1
Builders:	Bethlehem Co., Quincy, Mass.
Laid down:	31 Aug. 1944
Launched:	27 Jan. 1951
Completed:	7 Mar. 1953
Displacement:	14,700 tons *standard* (17,200 tons *full load*)
Dimensions:	Length: 676 (o.a.) feet. Beam: 71 feet. Draught: 29 (*max.*) feet
Guns:	4—5 inch, 54 cal. as main armament, 8—3 inch, 70 cal. AA. (see *Gunnery Notes*)
Aircraft:	2 helicopters
Armour:	6″ side, 3″ + 2″ decks
Machinery:	General Electric geared turbines. 4 shafts. S.H.P.: 120,000=33 kts.
Boilers:	8 Babcock & Wilcox
Oil fuel:	2,500 tons
Complement:	1,675 (war), 1,251 (peace)—56 officers, 1,195 men

General Notes

This vessel was originally designed as a heavy cruiser of the modified " Oregon City " class numbered CA 125. She was 57 per cent constructed as such when she was cancelled on 11 August 1945. She was re-ordered 1 July 1948, and re-designed as a Task Force (now Tactical) Command Ship with the new rating of CLC 1, for the exclusive use of Task Force commanders in conducting either operations of fast moving carrier task forces or an amphibious assault. Accommodation and equipment were modified accordingly. She is fully air-conditioned with an installation at least as extensive as that of the largest heavy cruiser *Salem* to which she now approximates in displacement. She was commissioned on 7 Mar. 1953, to fulfil the same functions as an AGC., i.e. as Operations-Communications-Headquarters Ship, but has more speed, manoeuvrability, armament, and anti-aircraft fire than an AGC. Reported to have been designed to resist atomic attack. Has large installation of newly developed electronic equipment, a vast communications network, an imposing array of electronic antennae, and features one of the largest seaborne radar aerials in the world. She is one deck higher than a normal cruiser to provide for additional office space, and has the tallest unsupported mast afloat (125 feet). Seven months trials to Nov. 1954. First operational assignment was to Atlantic Fleet Amphibious Force as temporary flagship in Nov. 1954. Now serves as Second Fleet flagship.

Gunnery Notes

The main armament comprises four 5 inch dual purpose guns of a new model disposed in single turrets, two forward and two aft, " B " and " X " superfiring over " A " and " Y " respectively. They are reported to have a rate of fire of 54 rounds per minute. The anti-aircraft battery includes eight 3 inch weapons, also of a new pattern, disposed in twin turrets, two on each side amidships abreast the funnel.

Photograph Notes

A starboard bow oblique aerial view of *Northampton* appears in the 1957-58 edition.

Notes to Drawing

Port elevation and plan of *Northampton* drawn 1954 to a scale of 128 feet=1 inch. The forward 5 inch gun is actually off the centre line to starboard.

NORTHAMPTON (As CLC 1)

1960. United States Navy

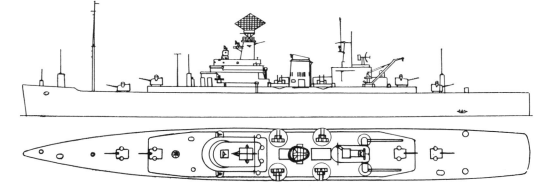

NORTHAMPTON.

1955, U.S. Navy, Official.

NORTHAMPTON.

1954, U.S. Navy, Official.

NORTHAMPTON

1957, U.S. Navy, Official

NORTHAMPTON (port quarter view showing radar arrays)

1959, Ted Stone

NORTHAMPTON (broadside silhouette)

1958, courtesy Ian S. Pearsall, Esq.

NORTHAMPTON (CC 1)

United States Navy

NORFOLK

1957, courtesy "Our Navy"

Officially rated as **Frigate** (DL)
(Formerly rated as
Cruiser, Hunter Killer Ship, CLK)
1 " Norfolk " Type

NORFOLK

No.:	DL 1 (ex-CLK 1)
Builders:	New York Shipbuilding Corporation, Camden, New Jersey
Ordered:	17 Nov. 1948
Laid down:	1 Sep. 1949
Launched:	29 Dec. 1951
Completed:	4 Mar. 1953

Displacement:	5,600 tons *standard* (7,300 tons *full load*)
Dimensions:	Length: 520 (*w.l.*), 540$\frac{1}{4}$ (*o.a.*) feet. Beam: 54$\frac{1}{4}$ feet. Draught: 26 (*max.*) feet
Guns:	8—3 inch, 70 cal. (twin mounts);
Tubes:	4 Mark 24
A/S weapons:	4 Mark 108 A.S.W. rocket launchers. 8—21 inch fixed torpedo tubes
Machinery:	2 sets General Electric geared turbines. 2 shafts. S.H.P.: 80,000 = 32 kts. (34 kts. *max.*)
Boilers:	4 Babcock & Wilcox 2 drum, 1,200 lb. per sq. in. pressure, 950 deg. F.
Oil fuel:	1,400 tons
Radius:	7,000 miles at 15 kts.
Complement:	480

General Notes

Designed as a special category of anti-submarine vessel of cruiser size and entirely novel type to engage in hunter killer operations even in the worst weather, and incorporates lessons learned at Bikini in her construction. Built on a true cruiser hull. Cost, exclusive of armament, reported to be $44,000,000. Re-rated in 1951 as a Destroyer Leader (DL), a category new to the U.S. Navy, but reclassified as a Frigate (DL) on 1 Jan. 1955. Fitted with newly developed communications equipment including radar, sonar, and electronics gear. Will serve as flagship for destroyer screens attached to fast carrier forces.

Gunnery Notes

The 8—20 mm. AA. guns (twin mounts) have been removed.

Engineering Notes

The trial speed is reported to have exceeded 34 knots. (35 knots reached.) Shafts fitted with six-bladed propellers.

Anti-Submarine Notes

Used primarily as a test ship for new anti-submarine warfare equipment. The largest and heaviest sonar dome (39,500 lbs., or nearly 18 tons) was installed at Norfolk Naval Shipyard in 1958.

In the early 1960s *Norfolk* carried out the first ASROC trials.

Photograph Notes

Stern cleared for anti-submarine helicopter operations.

Class Notes

Two Hunter Killer Ships were authorised in 1947. *Norfolk* (originally CLK 1), subsequently DL-1 (Destroyer Leader), was commissioned for service on 4 March 1956. The construction of her sister ship, CLK 2, was deferred in 1949.

NORFOLK (oblique aerial view off starboard bow)

1959, United States Navy, Official

NORFOLK

1957, U.S. Navy, Official

1 NUCLEAR-POWERED GUIDED MISSILE CRUISER (CGN): "LONG BEACH" TYPE

Name	No.	Builder	Laid down	Launched	Commissioned
•LONG BEACH	CGN 9 (ex-CGN 160, CLGN 160)	Bethlehem Steel Co, (Quincy, Massachusetts)	2 Dec 1957	14 July 1959	9 Sep 1961

Displacement, tons	14 200 standard, 17 350 full load
Length, feet (metres)	721 2 (220) oa
Beam, feet (metres)	73 2 (22 3)
Draft, feet (metres)	29 (8 8)
Missile launchers	1 twin Talos surface-to-air launcher (Mk 12 Mod 0) 2 twin Terrier surface-to-air launchers (Mk 10 Mod 1 and 2)
Guns	2—5 in (127 mm) 38 calibre dual-purpose (see Gunnery notes)
A/S weapons	1 ASROC 8-tube launcher 2 triple torpedo tubes (Mk 32)
Helicopter	utility helicopter carried
Main engines	2 geared turbines (General Electric), approx 80 000 shp, 2 shafts
Reactors	2 pressurised-water cooled C1W (Westinghouse)
Speed, knots	approx 35
Complement	1 000 (60 officers approx 950 enlisted men)

The *Long Beach* was the first ship to be designed and constructed from the keel up as a cruiser for the United States since the end of World War II. She is the world's first nuclear-powered surface warship and the first warship to have a guided missile main battery. She was authorised in the Fiscal Year 1957 new construction programme. Estimated construction cost was $332 850 000. Construction was delayed because of shipyard strike.
No additional new-construction cruisers are planned because of the capabilities of new guided-missile frigates (DLG and DLGN) which are approaching the size of World War II-era light cruisers.

CLASSIFICATION. The *Long Beach* was ordered as a Guided Missile Light Cruiser (CLGN 160) on 15 Oct 1956; reclassified as a Guided Missile Cruiser (CGN 160) early in 1957 and renumbered (CGN 9) on 1 July 1957.
DESIGN. The *Long Beach* was initially planned as a large destroyer or "frigate" of about 7 800 tons (standard displacement) to test the feasibility of a nuclear powered surface warship. Early in 1956 the decision was made to capitalise on the capabilities of nuclear propulsion and her displacement was increased to 11 000 tons and a second Terrier missile launcher was added to the design. A Talos missile launcher was also added to the design which, with other features, increased displacement to 14 000 tons by the time the contract was signed for her construction on 15 October 1956.

ELECTRONICS. The *Long Beach* has fixed-array ("billboard") radar which provides increased range over rotating antennas. Horizontal antennas on bridge superstructure are for SPS-32 bearing and range radar; vertical antennas are for SPS-33 target tracking radar. The SPS-33 uses an "S" band frequency and the SPS-32 is VHF; both frequency scan in elevation. Developed and produced by Hughes Aircraft, they are believed the first operational fixed-array radar systems in the Western world. Also installed in the nuclear-powered aircraft carrier *Enterprise* (CVAN 65).
SPS-12 and SPS-10 search radars are mounted on the forward mast.

The SPS-32,33 "Scanfar" radars and the associated computers were modified in 1970 to improve performance. She is equipped with Naval Tactical Data System (NTDS) and SQS-23 sonar.

LONG BEACH (CGN 9)

1968, United States Navy

ENGINEERING. The reactors are similar to those of the nuclear-powered aircraft carrier *Enterprise* (CVAN 65). The *Long Beach* first got underway on nuclear power on 5 July 1961. After four years of operation and having steamed more than 167 000 miles she underwent her first overhaul and refuelling at the Newport News Shipbuilding and Dry Dock Company from August 1965 to February 1966.

GUNNERY. Completed with an all-missile armament. Two single 5 inch mounts were fitted during 1962-1963 yard period to provide defence against low flying subsonic aircraft and torpedo boats.

MISSILES. Initial plans provided for installation of the Regulus II surface-to-surface missile, a transonic missile which carried a nuclear warhead and had a 1 000-mile range. Upon cancellation of the Regulus II programme, provision was made for providing eight Polaris missile tubes, but they were never installed. Plans to provide Polaris were dropped early in 1961 in an effort to reduce construction costs.
Reportedly, the *Long Beach* carries 40 Talos and 240 Terrier missiles.

NOMENCLATURE. Cruisers are named for American cities. Since 1971 the Navy also has named attack submarines for cities, beginning with the SSN 688 (*Los Angeles*).

OPERATIONAL. Talos missiles fired from the *Long Beach* have downed Communist aircraft in what are believed to have been the first surface-to-air "kills" in combat with ship-launched missiles.
While operating in the Tonkin Gulf, the ship's Talos missiles shot down one supersonic MiG fighter on May 23, 1968, and a second MiG in June 1968; both aircraft were over North Vietnam at the time of their destruction.

LONG BEACH

1964, United States Navy, Official

LONG BEACH (CGN 9)   1968, United States Navy

LONG BEACH (CGN 9)   1963, United States Navy

LONG BEACH (CGN 9)   1963, United States Navy

LONG BEACH (after 1980-82 modernisation)   1980, USN

1 "BAINBRIDGE" CLASS: GUIDED MISSILE CRUISER (nuclear propulsion) (CGN)

Name	No.	Builders	Laid down	Launched	Commissioned	F S
BAINBRIDGE	CGN 25	Bethlehem Steel Co, Quincy, Mass	15 May 1959	15 Apr 1961	6 Oct 1962	PA

Displacement, tons: 7 600 standard; 8 592 full load
Dimensions, feet (metres): 565 × 57·9 × 25·4
(172·3 × 17·6 × 7·7)
Missiles: SSM; Harpoon;
SAM; 80 Standard-ER (SM-1) (2 twin Mk 10 launchers)
Guns: 2—20 mm Mk 67 (twin)
A/S weapons: 1 ASROC 8-tube launcher;
2 triple torpedo tubes (Mk 32)
Main engines: 2 geared turbines, approx 60 000 shp; 2 shafts
Nuclear reactors: 2 pressurised-water cooled D2G (General Electric)
Speed, knots: 30
Complement: 470 (34 officers, 436 enlisted men)
Flag accommodations: 18 (6 officers, 12 enlisted men)

Bainbridge was the US Navy's third nuclear-powered surface warship (after the cruiser *Long Beach* and the aircraft carrier *Enterprise*). Authorised in the FY 1959 shipbuilding programme. Construction cost was $163·61 million.

Classification: *Bainbridge* was originally classified as a guided missile frigate (DLGN); reclassified as a guided missile cruiser (CGN) on 30 June 1975.

Electronics: Fitted with OE-82 satellite communications antenna, SSR-1 receiver and WSC-3 transceiver.

Engineering: Development of a nuclear power plant suitable for use in a large "destroyer type" warship began in 1957. The Atomic Energy Commission's Knolls Atomic Power Laboratory undertook development of the destroyer power plant (designated D1G/D2G).

Fire control: Four Mk 76 missile control systems, one Mk 14 weapons direction system, four SPG 55A weapon control radars.

Gunnery: Four 3-in *(76 mm)* in twin mountings removed during modernisation. Two 40 mm saluting guns carried.

Missiles: Has Terrier Mk 10 Mod 5 launcher forward and a Mk 10 Mod 6 launcher aft. The 80 missiles are evenly split between the two rotating magazines.

Modernisation: *Bainbridge* underwent an Anti-Air Warfare (AAW) modernisation at the Puget Sound Naval Shipyard from 30 June 1974 to 24 September 1976. The ship was fitted with the Naval Tactical Data System (NTDS) and improved guidance capability for missiles. Estimated cost of modernisation $103 million.

Radar: 3D search: SPS 52.
Search: SPS 10 and 37.

Rockets: Mk 36 Chaffroc RBOC to be fitted.

Sonar: SQS 23 (bow-mounted).

BAINBRIDGE (DLGN 25)   1971, United States Navy

BAINBRIDGE   3 1978, USN (PH1 A. E. Legare)

9 "LEAHY" CLASS: GUIDED MISSILE CRUISERS (CG)

Name	No.	Builders	Laid down	Launched	Commissioned	F/S
LEAHY	CG 16	Bath Iron Works Corporation	3 Dec 1959	1 July 1961	4 Aug 1962	PA
HARRY E. YARNELL	CG 17	Bath Iron Works Corporation	31 May 1960	9 Dec 1961	2 Feb 1963	AA
WORDEN	CG 18	Bath Iron Works Corporation	19 Sep 1960	2 June 1962	3 Aug 1963	P.
DALE	CG 19	New York S.B. Corporation	6 Sep 1960	28 July 1962	23 Nov 1963	AA
RICHMOND K. TURNER	CG 20	New York S.B. Corporation	9 Jan 1961	6 Apr 1963	13 June1964	AA
GRIDLEY	CG 21	Puget Sound Bridge & Dry Dock Co	15 July 1960	31 July 1961	25 May 1963	PA
ENGLAND	CG 22	Todd Shipyards Corporation	4 Oct 1960	6 Mar 1962	7 Dec 1963	PA
HALSEY	CG 23	San Francisco Naval Shipyard	26 Aug 1960	15 Jan 1962	20 July 1963	PA
REEVES	CG 24	Puget Sound Naval Shipyard	1 July 1960	12 May 1962	15 May 1964	PA

Displacement, tons: 5 670 standard; 7 800 full load
Dimensions, feet (metres): 533 × 54·9 × 24·8 sonar—19·6 keel
(162·5 × 16·6 × 7·6—6)
Missiles: SSM; Harpoon to be fitted (already in CG 20, 21, 23 and 24);
SAM; 80 Standard-ER (SM-2) (Mk 10 launcher)
Guns: 4—3 in *(76 mm)*/50 (twin Mk 33)
A/S weapons: 1 ASROC 8-tube launcher;
2 triple torpedo tubes (Mk 32)
Main engines: 2 geared turbines (see *Engineering* notes); 85 000 shp; 2 shafts
Boilers: 4 (Babcock & Wilcox in CG 16-20, Foster-Wheeler in 21-24)
Speed, knots: 32·7
Fuel, tons: 1 800
Range, miles: 8 000 at 20 knots
Complement: 377 (18 officers, 359 enlisted men) (16, 17, 21, 23); 413 (32 officers, 381 men) (18-20, 22, 24)
Flag accommodations: 18 (6 officers, 12 enlisted men)

These ships are "double-end" missile cruisers especially designed to screen fast carrier task forces. They are limited in only having 3-in guns. Authorised as DLG 16-18 in the FY 1958 new construction programme and DLG 19-24 in the FY 1959 programme.

Classification: These ships were originally classified as guided missile frigates (DLG); reclassified as guided missile cruisers (CG) on 30 June 1975.

Design: These ships are distinctive in having twin missile launchers forward and aft with ASROC launcher between the forward missile launcher and bridge on main deck level.
There is a helicopter landing area aft but only limited support facilities are provided; no hangar.

Electronics: Naval Tactical Data System (NTDS) fitted during AAW modernisation.
Fitted with OE-82 satellite communications antenna, SSR-1 receiver and WSC-3 transceiver.

Engineering: General Electric turbines in CG 16-18, De Laval turbines in CG 19-22, and Allis-Chalmers turbines in CG 23 and CG 24.

Fire control: Four Mk 76 missile control systems, one Mk 11 weapon direction system, (to be replaced by Mk 14 WDS) and four SPG 55 radars. Mk 114 ASW fire control system.

Gunnery: Two Phalanx 20 mm CIWS Mk 15 to be fitted.
Two 40 mm saluting guns fitted.

Modernisation: These ships were modernised between 1967 and 1972 to improve their Anti-Air Warfare (AAW) capabilities. Superstructure enlarged to provide space for additional electronic equipment, including NTDS; improved Tacan fitted and improved guidance system for Terrier/Standard missiles installed, and larger ship's service turbo generators provided.
All ships modernised at Bath Iron Works except *Leahy* at Philadelphia Naval Shipyard.
Cost of *Leahy* modernisation was $36·1 million.

Radar: 3D search: SPS 48 (replacing SPS 39 or 52 in some ships).
Search: SPS 10, 37.

Rockets: Mk 36 Chaffroc RBOC to be fitted.

Sonar: SQS 23 bow-mounted.

LEAHY   *1962, United States Navy, Official*

GRIDLEY (DLG 21)   *1970, United States Navy*

HARRY E. YARNELL (DLG 17)   *1972, Giorgio Arra*

ENGLAND   1978, Dr. Giorgio Arra

DALE   10/1979, Michael D. J. Lennon

HARRY E. YARNELL   1971, USN

HALSEY   9/1975, USN

GRIDLEY (DLG 21)   1963, United States Navy

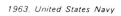

HALSEY (with Harpoon)   12/1979, Dr. Giorgio Arra

9 "BELKNAP" CLASS: GUIDED MISSILE CRUISERS (CG)

Name	No.	Builders	Laid down	Launched	Commissioned	F/S
BELKNAP	CG 26	Bath Iron Works Corporation	5 Feb 1962	20 July 1963	7 Nov 1964	AA
JOSEPHUS DANIELS	CG 27	Bath Iron Works Corporation	23 Apr 1962	2 Dec 1963	8 May 1965	AA
WAINWRIGHT	CG 28	Bath Iron Works Corporation	2 July 1962	25 Apr 1964	8 Jan 1966	AA
JOUETT	CG 29	Puget Sound Naval Shipyard	25 Sep 1962	30 June 1964	3 Dec 1966	PA
HORNE	CG 30	San Francisco Naval Shipyard	12 Dec 1962	30 Oct 1964	15 Apr 1967	PA
STERETT	CG 31	Puget Sound Naval Shipyard	25 Sep 1962	30 June 1964	8 Apr 1967	PA
WILLIAM H. STANDLEY	CG 32	Bath Iron Works Corporation	29 July 1963	19 Dec 1964	9 July 1966	PA
FOX	CG 33	Todd Shipyard Corporation	15 Jan 1963	21 Nov 1964	8 May 1966	PA
BIDDLE	CG 34	Bath Iron Works Corporation	9 Dec 1963	2 July 1965	21 Jan 1967	AA

Displacement, tons: 6 570 standard; 7 900 full load
Dimensions, feet (metres): 547 × 54·8 × 28·8, sonar—19, keel
(166·7 × 16·7 × 8·8—5·8)
Aircraft: 1 SH-2D LAMPS helicopter
Missiles: SSM; Harpoon to be fitted (fitted in CG 27);
SAM; 60 Standard-ER/ASROC (1 twin Mk 10 launcher)
Guns: 1—5 in (127 mm)/54 (Mk 42)
2—3 in (76 mm)/50 (single Mk 34)
A/S weapons: ASROC (see above); 2 triple torpedo tubes (Mk 32)
Main engines: 2 geared turbines (General Electric except De Laval in CG 33): 85 000 shp; 2 shafts
Boilers: 4 (Babcock & Wilcox in CG 26-28, 32-34; Combustion Engineering in CG 29-31)
Speed, knots: 32·5
Complement: 418 (31 officers, 387 enlisted men) including squadron staff
Flag accommodations: 18 (6 officers; 12 enlisted men)

These ships were authorised as guided missile frigates; DLG 26-28 in the FY 1961 shipbuilding programme; DLG 29-34 in the FY 1962 programme.
Belknap was severely damaged in a collision with the carrier *John F. Kennedy* (CV 67) on 22 November 1975 near Sicily; the cruiser was towed back to the USA for rebuilding at Philadelphia Naval Shipyard. Placed "Out of Commission—Special" 20 December 1975. Repair and modernisation began 9 January 1978. Estimated cost is $213 million and includes new improved 5-in gun, up-dated missile armament, sonar communications and radar suites as well as improvements in habitability. Recommissioned May 1980.

Ammunition: 60 missiles for Mk 10 launcher of which only 20 can be ASROC.

Classification: These ships were originally classified as guided missile frigates (DLG); reclassified as guided missile cruisers (CG) on 30 June 1975.

Design: These ships are distinctive by having their single missile launcher forward and 5-in gun mount aft. This arrangement allowed missile stowage in the larger bow section and provided space aft of the superstructure for a helicopter hangar and platform. The reverse gun-missile arrangement, preferred by some commanding officers, is found in *Truxtun*.

Electronics: Naval Tactical Data System (NTDS); Tacan. Fitted with OE-82 satellite communications antenna, SSR-1 receiver and WSC-3 transceiver.

Fire control: Two Mk 76 missile control systems, one Mk 68 gunfire control system, one Mk 11 weapon direction system (Mk 7 in *Josephus Daniels* and *Belknap*), one SPG 53A and two SPG 55B weapon control radars. (Mk 14 WDS to be fitted in place of Mk 11 WDS).

Gunnery: All of this class will be fitted with two Phalanx 20 mm Mk 15 CIWS as will *Belknap* during rebuilding.

Helicopters: These ships are the only conventionally powered US cruisers with a full helicopter support capability. All fitted with the Light Airborne Multi-Purpose System, now the SH-2D helicopter. *Belknap* embarked the first operational SH-2D/LAMPS in December 1971.

Missiles: A "triple-ring" rotating magazine stocks both Standard anti-craft missiles and ASROC anti-submarine rockets, feeding either weapon to the launcher's two firing arms. The rate of fire and reliability of the launcher provide a potent AAW/ASW capability to these ships.
This class will be fitted with Tomahawk cruise missiles, *Fox* having carried the experimental version since 1977.

Radar: 3D search: SPS 48.
Search: SPS 10 and 37 (26-28) or 40 (remainder).

Rockets: Mk 36 Chaffroc RBOC to be fitted in place of Mk 28.

Sonar: SQS 26 (bow-mounted).

Torpedoes: As built, these ships each had two 21-in tubes for anti-submarine torpedoes installed in the structure immediately forward of the 5-in mount, one tube angled out to port and one to starboard; subsequently removed.

BELKNAP (DLG 26)   1964, United States Navy

JOSEPHUS DANIELS (DLG 27)   1965, United States Navy

JOSEPHUS DANIELS (DLG 27)   1972, Giorgio Arra

WAINWRIGHT (DLG 28)

1966, United States Navy

WILLIAM H. STANDLEY

4/1976, USN

BIDDLE

11/1978, Leo van Ginderen

HORNE

6/1979, Dr. Giorgio Arra

WILLIAM H. STANDLEY

9/1976, Dr. Giorgio Arra

WAINWRIGHT

1979, L. and L. van Ginderen

1 ''TRUXTUN'' CLASS: GUIDED MISSILE CRUISER (nuclear propulsion) (CGN)

Name	No.	Builders	Laid down	Launched	Commissioned	F/S
TRUXTUN	CGN 35	New York SB Corp (Camden, New Jersey)	17 June 1963	19 Dec 1964	27 May 1967	PA

Displacement, tons: 8 200 standard; 9 127 full load
Dimensions, feet (metres): 564 × 58 × 31 *(171·9 × 17·7 × 9·4)*
Aircraft: 1 helicopter
Missiles: SSM; Harpoon; SAM/ASW; 60 Standard-ER/ASROC
    (1 twin Mk 10 launcher)
Guns: 1—5 in *(127 mm)*/54 (single Mk 42)
    2—3 in *(76 mm)*/50 (single Mk 34)
A/S weapons: ASROC (see above);
    4 fixed torpedo tubes (Mk 32)
Main engines: 2 geared turbines; 60 000 shp; 2 shafts
Nuclear reactors: 2 pressurised-water cooled D2G (General
    Electric)
Speed, knots: 29
Complement: 528 (36 officers, 492 enlisted men)
Flag accommodations: 18 (6 officers, 12 enlisted men)

Truxtun was the US Navy's fourth nuclear-powered surface warship. The Navy had requested seven oil-burning frigates in the FY 1962 shipbuilding programme; Congress authorised seven ships, but stipulated that one ship must be nuclear-powered.
Although the *Truxtun* design is adapted from the ''Belknap'' class design, the nuclear ship's gun-missile launcher arrangement is reversed from the non-nuclear ships.
Construction cost was $138·667 million.

Ammunition: Of the 60 rounds for the missile launcher no more than 20 can be ASROC.

Classification: *Truxtun* was originally classified as a guided missile frigate (DLGN); subsequently reclassified as a guided missile cruiser (CGN) on 30 June 1975.

Electronics: Naval Tactical Data System (NTDS); Tacan.
Fitted with OE-82 satellite communications antenna, SSR-1 receiver and WSC-3 transceiver.

Engineering: Power plant is identical to that of the cruiser *Bainbridge*.

Fire control: Two Mk 76 missile control systems, one Mk 68 gunfire control system, one Mk 11 weapon direction system, one SPG 53A and two SPG 55B weapon control radars (Mk 11 WDS to be replaced by Mk 14).

Gunnery: 2 Phalanx 20 mm systems (Mk 15) to be fitted.
Two 40 mm saluting guns fitted.

Name: *Truxtun* is the fifth ship to be named after Commodore Thomas Truxton *(sic)* who commanded the frigate *Constellation* (38 guns) in her successful encounter with the French frigate *L'Insurgente* (44) in 1799.

Radar: 3D search: SPS 48.
Search: SPS 10 and 40.

Rockets: Mk 36 Chaffroc RBOC will be fitted soon replacing the Mk 28 system.

Sonar: SQS 26 (bow-mounted).

Torpedoes: Fixed Mk 32 tubes are below 3-in gun mounts, built into superstructure.

TRUXTUN (with Harpoon)   *3/1980, Dr. Giorgio Arra*

TRUXTUN (with Harpoon)   *3/1980, Dr. Giorgio Arra*

TRUXTUN   *8/1978, Dr. Giorgio Arra*

2 "CALIFORNIA" CLASS: GUIDED MISSILE CRUISERS (nuclear propulsion) (CGN)

Name	No.	Builders	Laid down	Launched	Commissioned	F/S
CALIFORNIA	CGN 36	Newport News Shipbuilding Co	23 Jan 1970	22 Sep 1971	16 Feb 1974	AA
SOUTH CAROLINA	CGN 37	Newport News Shipbuilding Co	1 Dec 1970	1 July 1972	25 Jan 1975	AA

Displacement, tons: 9 561 standard; 11 100 full load
Dimensions, feet (metres): 596 × 61 × 31·5
  (181·7 × 18·6 × 9·6)
Missiles: SSM; Harpoon to be fitted in near future;
  SAM; 80 Standard-MR (two single Mk 13 launchers)
  (see note)
Guns: 2—5 in (127 mm)/54 (single Mk 45)
A/S weapons: 4 torpedo tubes (Mk 32);
  1 ASROC 8-tube launcher (Mk 16)
Main engines: 2 geared turbines; 60 000 shp; 2 shafts
Nuclear reactors: 2 pressurised-water cooled D2G (General
  Electric)
Speed, knots: 30+
Complement: 540 (28 officers, 512 enlisted men)

California was authorised in the FY 1967 new construction programme and *South Carolina* in the FY 1968 programme. The construction of a third ship of this class (DLGN 38) was also authorised in FY 1968, but the rising costs of these ships and development of the DXGN/DLGN 38 design (now "Virginia" class) caused the third ship to be cancelled.

Classification: These ships were originally classified as guided missile frigates (DLGN); subsequently reclassified as guided missile cruisers (CGN) on 30 June 1975.

Design: These ships have tall, enclosed towers supporting radar antennae in contrast to the open lattice masts of the previous nuclear frigates *Truxtun* and *Bainbridge*. No helicopter support facilities provided.

Electronics: Fitted with the Naval Tactical Data System (NTDS). Fitted with OE-82 satellite communications antenna, SSR-1 receiver and WSC-3 transceiver.

Engineering: Estimated nuclear core life for these ships provides 700 000 miles range; estimated cost is $11·5 million for the two initial nuclear cores in each ship.

Fire control: Two Mk 74 MFCS; one Mk 86 GFCS; one Mk 11 weapons direction system (to be replaced by Mk 13).

Fiscal: Estimated cost is $200 million for *California* and $180 million for *South Carolina*.

Gunnery: Two Phalanx 20 mm CIWS (Mk 15) to be fitted. Each ship carries two 40 mm saluting guns.

Missiles: Reportedly, these ships carry some 80 surface-to-air missiles divided equally between a magazine beneath each launcher.

Radar: 3D air search: SPS 48.
Search: SPS 10 and 40.
Fire control: SPG 51D, SPG 60 and SPQ 9A.

Rockets: Mk 36 Chaffroc RBOC to be fitted in place of Mk 28 system.

Sonar: SQS 26CX (bow-mounted).

CALIFORNIA

1979, L. and L. van Ginderen

SOUTH CAROLINA

9/1976, USN

CALIFORNIA

6/1977, C. and S. Taylor

3 + 1 "VIRGINIA" CLASS: GUIDED MISSILE CRUISERS (nuclear propulsion) (CGN)

Name	No.	Builders	Laid down	Launched	Commissioned	F/S
VIRGINIA	CGN 38	Newport News S.B. and D.D. Co	19 Aug 1972	14 Dec 1974	11 Sep 1976	AA
TEXAS	CGN 39	Newport News S.B. and D.D. Co	18 Aug 1973	9 Aug 1975	10 Sep 1977	AA
MISSISSIPPI	CGN 40	Newport News S.B. and D.D. Co	22 Feb 1975	31 July 1976	5 Aug 1978	AA
ARKANSAS	CGN 41	Newport News S.B. and D.D. Co	17 Jan 1977	21 Oct 1978	Nov 1980	Bldg

Displacement, tons: 10 000 full load
Dimensions, feet (metres): 585 × 63 × 29·5 (178·4 × 19·2 × 9)
Aircraft: 2 (see *Helicopter* notes)
Missiles: SSM; Harpoon to be fitted;
 SAM/ASW; Standard-MR/ASROC (2 twin Mk 26 launchers)
Guns: 2—5 in (127 mm)/54 (single Mk 45)
A/S weapons: ASROC (see above);
 2 triple torpedo tubes (Mk 32)
Main engines: 2 geared turbines; 60 000 shp; 2 shafts
Reactors: 2 pressurised-water cooled D2G (General Electric)
Speed, knots: 30+
Complement: 472 (27 officers, 445 enlisted men)

Virginia was authorised in the FY 1970 new construction programme, *Texas* in the FY 1971, *Mississippi* in the FY 1972, and *Arkansas* in the FY 1975.
CGN 42 was proposed in the FY 1976 new construction programme but was not funded by the Congress.
Construction of this class has been delayed because of a shortage of skilled labour in the shipyard. Newport News S.B. & D.D. Co (Virginia) is the only shipyard in the USA now engaged in the construction of nuclear surface ships. The first three ships of the class were more than one year behind their original construction schedules.

Classification: These ships were originally classified as guided missile frigates (DLGN); subsequently reclassified as guided missile cruisers (CGN) on 30 June 1975.

Design: The principal differences between the "Virginia" and "California" classes are the improved anti-air warfare capability, electronic warfare equipment, and anti-submarine fire control system. The deletion of the separate ASROC Mk 16 launcher permitted the "Virginia" class to be 10 ft shorter.

Electronics: Naval Tactical Data System (NTDS).
Fitted with OE-82 satellite communications antenna, SSR-1 receiver and WSC-3 transceiver.

Fiscal: The cost of these ships have increased noticeably during their construction. Fiscal data on the earlier ships were in the 1974-75 and earlier editions.

Fire control: Mk 74 missile control directors.
Digital Mk 116 ASW FCS.
Mk 86 WCS for forward missile channel and gun fire.

Gunnery: Mk 86 gunfire control directors. Two 20 mm Mk 15 CIWS will be fitted in each ship.
Each ship has two 40 mm saluting guns.

Helicopters: A hangar for helicopters is installed beneath the fantail flight-deck with a telescoping hatch cover and an electro-mechanical elevator provided to transport helicopters between the main deck and hangar. These are the first US post-World War II destroyer/cruiser ships with a hull hangar.

Missiles: The initial design for this class provided for a single surface-to-air missile launcher; revised in 1969 to provide two Mk 26 launchers that will fire the Standard-Medium Range (MR) surface-to-air missile and the ASROC anti-submarine missile. "Mixed" Standard/ASROC magazines are fitted for each launcher.
It is planned to fit the Tomahawk cruise missile.

Radar: 3D search: SPS 48A.
Search: SPS 40B and 55.

Rockets: Mk 36 Chaffroc RBOC (Rapid Bloom Overhead Chaff) to be fitted.

Sonar: SQS 53A (bow-mounted).

VIRGINIA   9/1978, J. L. M. van der Burgh

MISSISSIPPI   8/1978, USN (PM3 J. Swanstrom)

VIRGINIA   9/1978, Michael D. J. Lennon

0 + 2 + 26 "TICONDEROGA" CLASS GUIDED MISSILE CRUISERS (CG) (AEGIS) (ex-DDG)

Name	No.	Builder/Programme	Laid down	Launched	Commissioned	F/S
TICONDEROGA	CG 47 (ex-DDG 47)	Ingalls Shipbuilding Corp	21 Jan 1980	Mar 1981	Jan 1983	Bldg
—YORKTOWN -49	CG 48 (ex-DDG 48)	Ingalls Shipbuilding Corp	—	—	—	Ord
—VINCENNES -49	CG 49/50	Requested FY 1981				Proj
—VALLEY FORGE -50	CG 51/53	Proposed FY 1982				Proj
—THOMAS S. GATES -51	CG 54/56 LEYTE GULF -55	Proposed FY 1983				Proj
—BUNKER HILL -52	CG 57/60	Proposed FY 1984				
—MOBILE BAY -53	CG 61/64 SAN JACINTO -56	Proposed FY 1985				
ANTIETAM -54						

Displacement, tons: 9 055 full load
Dimensions, feet (metres): 563·3 × 55 × 31
(171·7 × 16·8 × 9·5)
Aircraft: 2 LAMPS helicopters
Missiles: SSM; 16 Harpoon (8-tube launchers);
SAM/ASW; 88 Standard-MR/ASROC
(2 twin Mk 26 launchers) (see notes)
Guns: 2—5 in (127 mm)/54 (single Mk 45);
2—20 mm/76 Phalanx (6-barrelled Mk 15 CIWS)
A/S weapons: ASROC; torpedo tubes (Mk 32)
Main engines: 4 General Electric LM 2500 gas turbines;
80 000 shp; 2 shafts
Speed, knots: 30+
Complement: 316 (27 officers, 289 enlisted men)

The "Ticonderoga" class fulfills the proposal for a non-nuclear Aegis armed ship as proposed in the early 1970s, but subsequently dropped to avoid conflict with the Navy's nuclear propelled cruiser programme.
The original programme class force level was 18 which was increased to 28 in February 1980.

Design: The "Ticonderoga" class design is a modification of the "Spruance" class. The same basic hull will be used, with the same gas turbine propulsion plant. The design calls for 1-in steel armour plate to protect the magazines.

Classifications: Originally rated as Guided Missile Destroyers (DDG). Rerated as Guided Missile Missile Cruisers (CG) on 1 January 1980. At the same time DDG 47/48 were reclassified CG 47/48.

Electronics: Aegis is described under "Shipboard Systems" in the tables in the introduction of the US section. This class will be equipped with the full Aegis system and also with the OE-82 Satellite Navigation System antenna, the WSC-3 transceiver and the SSR-1 receiver.

Fire control. Aegis Weapons Control System Mk 7 with UYK-7 computers to control radar phasing, Mk 86 gunfire control system, four Mk 99 missile guidance illuminators, Mk 116 Underwater FCS.

Fiscal: CG 47 was approved under the FY 1978 programme at a cost of $930 million; CG 48 under the FY 1980 programme at a cost of $820 million. CG 49/50 are requested under the FY 1981 programme at a cost of $1 613·7 million for both.

Nomenclature: The class is reportedly to be named after famous battles in US military history.

Radar: SPY 1A paired arrays (one forward, one aft).
Search: SPS 49.
Weapons: SPQ 9.

Sonar: SQS 53 (bow-mounted) and TACTAS towed array.

"TICONDEROGA" Class

A. D. Baker III

"TICONDEROGA" Class

1979, USN

TORPEDO BOATS, DESTROYERS, ESCORT DESTROYERS AND FRIGATES

BETWEEN 1887 and 1905 the US Navy built 31 torpedo boats, but the reason for their construction, like that of the early destroyers, is not at all clear. The torpedo boats were all restricted to coastal operations by their size and range and, at that time, no navy threatened United States' shores.

By 1910 a more reasoned approach had produced the 900 ton "Smith" class. These vessels had a high forecastle and five 3-inch guns and, despite their low range of 2,800 miles at 10 knots, they were the first likely fleet escorts. From then on, five more classes were built, with the 1225 ton "Sampson" class as the last of the pre-World War I designs. The "Caldwells" were flush-deckers, the lead ships of the huge group built under the 1916 Navy Act. These were the theoretically similar ships of the "Wickes" and "Clemson" classes though there was much variation in range and fittings. In an attempt to even out this range, the "Clemsons" carried 35 per cent more fuel than the "Wickes". In all, 265 ships of the two classes were completed as World War I came to an end.

With this huge stock of modern ships available, it was not until 1930 that the first of the eight ship "Farragut" class was laid down. At 2,604 tons these vessels were much larger than the flush-deckers and faster at 36.5 knots; in addition, their range was increased to 6,500 miles at 12 knots. Then came the "Porters" with their eight 5-inch guns, the somewhat smaller "Mahans", the "Gridleys" and the "Bagleys".

During this period, machinery was steadily improving; speeds up to 38.5 knots were achieved, and the new classes carried heavier torpedo armament. This armament would have been of more use had the torpedoes themselves performed with any sort of consistency. The "Somers" were followed by the "Benhams", with 16 torpedo tubes, and the overweight "Sims". The last pre-war classes were the "Benson/Gleaves" and between 1939 and 1943, ninety-six of these were completed and 17 sunk in the war. An even more numerous class, the "Fletchers", began commissioning in May 1942. In all, 175 of these fine 3,000 ton design were completed.

But these were all ships primarily intended for the fleet. War had found the US Navy as deficient of convoy A/S escorts as the British and had been in 1939, but with no similar plans for their construction. Thus it was not until April 1943 that the first of the destroyer escorts, the 1,360 ton "Evarts" were commissioned. In total, 97 of these "short" (290 feet) ships were completed. The next five classes of "long" (306 feet) ships varied mainly in their propulsion – the astonishing fact was that 468 were completed during the war.

While this extraordinary programme was in full swing, 56 fleet destroyers of the "Allen M. Sumner" class were completed, to be followed by an amazing 116 ship order of the 3,460 ton "Gearing" class. After 1945, there was a spate of conversions of many of the later wartime designs; the four "Mitscher" class were completed and from 1953 the 18 "Forrest Shermans" were laid down. By 1957 the first missile destroyers, the "Coontz" class of some 6,000 tons were being laid down, to be followed by the "Charles F. Adams" class, smaller at 4825 tons. The armament of all these later ships has changed much over the years, but it still shows a preponderance of surface and AA action capability. The same is true of the later "Spruance" and "Kidd" classes of over 8,000 tons, as well as the newest of all, the "Arleigh Burke" with her SPY ID radar and Aegis control system.

The anti-submarine problem, the most intractable today, is mainly in the hands of the frigates. With the earlier "Garcia" and "Brooke" classes now deleted, the whole burden of this task is borne by the 46 ships of the "Knox" class (18 of whom are more than 20 years old), and the 51 ships of the more modern "Oliver Hazard Perry" class. The latter, with two A/S helicopters, hull-mounted sonar and towed array, are valuable ships with one major problem: a speed of only 29 knots.

J.M.
May 1991

2 *Dahlgren class*: **Dahlgren** ('96) (T.A.M.), **Craven** ('96) (Built at Bath Ironworks). 146 tons. Designed H.P. 4200=22.5 kts. Normand boilers. Armament: 4—1 pdr., 2—18 inch tubes (single) aft. Coal: 32 tons. Complement, 26.

1 **Dupont** ('96) (Built by Herreshoff Co.). 165 tons. Designed H.P. 3800=27.5 kts. did over 28 on trial. Boilers: 3 Normand. Armament: 4—1 pdr., 3—18 inch tubes. Coal: 36 tons. Complement 30.

Davis.

Morris type: **Morris** ('96), 105 tons. (Herreshoff Co.). **Davis** ('98), 154 tons. Designed H.P. 1750=22.5 kts. (23.54 trial). Boilers: 2 Thornycroft, except Morris, 2 Normand. Armament: 3—1 pdr., 3—18 inch tubes. Coal: max. 40 tons. Complement, 27.

1 **Bailey** ('99) (Built by Gas Engine Co. and Seabury). 280 tons. H.P. 5600=30 kts. Seabury boilers. Armament: 4—6 pdr., S.A. 2—18 inch tubes. Coal: 39 tons. Complement, 57.

Morris. *(see below)*.

All illustrations JFS 1914

19 + 4 *(Subsidiary)* **Torpedo Boats.**

No.	Type.	Date.	Displacement.	H.P.	Max. speed.	Fuel.	Complement.	T. Tubes.	Max. draug't
	1st Class					tons			
3	*Barney*	'01–'00	175	3920	28·5	40/80	27	3	...
7	*Shubrick*	'02–'99	196	3000	26	40/72	29	3	...
1	*Stringham*	'99	340	7200	30†	96/120	55	2	...
1	*Goldsborough*	'99	255	6000	30†	—/89	61	2	...
1	*Farragut*	'98	273	5600	30	44/95	62	2	...
1	*Bailey*	'99	280	5600	30	50/99	57	2	...
2	*Dahlgren*	'96	146	4200	22·5	32	26	2	...
1	*Dupont*	'95–'96	165	3800	28	*max.* 60	25	3	...
2	*Morris*	'96	105	1750	24	*max.* 28	24	3	...
	2nd Class								
1	*Mackenzie*	'96	65	850	20	15	16	2	6
	3rd Class								
1	*Gwin*	'98–'96	46	850	20	9	16	2	4½

3 others assigned to Naval Militia, and one to special service. † Nominal only : never made.

BARNEY, BAGLEY, BIDDLE CLASS.

Farragut

1 **Stringham** ('99) (Built by Harland & Hollingsworth). 340 tons. Designed H.P. 7200 30 kts. Boilers: Thornycroft. Armament: 7 6 pdrs. S.A. 2 18 inch tubes aft. Coal: 96 tons; *max.* 120 tons. Max. draught: 8 feet.

SOLD

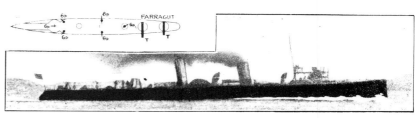

1 **Farragut** '98. Union Ironworks. 273 tons. H.P. 5600 30 kts. made 31·7 on trial. Thornycroft boilers. Armament: 6 6 pdr. 2 18 inch tubes aft. Coal: 44 tons, *max.* 76 tons.
1 **Goldsborough** '99. Wolff & Zwicker. 247 tons. Designed H.P. 6000 30 kts. Seabury boilers. Armament 4 6 inch tubes aft. Coal; *max.* 131 tons. Reengined 1903.

ALL SOLD

GWIN.

3 *Barney class* (Built by Bath Ironworks).—**Barney** '00, **Biddle** '01, **Bagley** '00. 175 tons. Designed H.P. 3920 28·5 kts. Normand boilers. Armament: 5 3 pdr. 3 18 inch tubes (one amidship, one abaft funnels, one aft). Coal: 43 tons. Complement 27. *Max.* draft: about 6 feet.

ALL SOLD

7 *Shubrick class*: **Shubrick** '99, **Thornton** '00, **Stockton** '99. (Built by Trigg), **De Long** '00, **Blakely** '00. (Built by Lawley, Boston), **Wilkes** '01 (Gas Engine Co. and Seabury), and **Tingey** '02. (Columbian Ironworks). 196 tons. H.P. 3000 26 kts. (*Shubrick* did 28 on trial). Thornycroft boilers except *Wilkes*, which has Seabury. Armament: 3 1 pdr. 3 18 inch tubes (two of them between funnels, the other right aft). Coal: *max.* 72 tons. Complement: 29. Max. draught: about 6 feet.

SOLD & TARGETS

2 *Cramp.* **Lamson** 1910, **Smith** 1910. Parsons turbine. 3 screws. Machinery: 250 tons. Boilers: 4 Mosher. Coal: *Lamson*, 284 tons; *Smith*, 298. Trials: *Lamson*, 32·27; *Smith*, 28·35 kts.

ALL SOLD

1 *New York Shipbuilding.* **Preston** 1910. Parsons turbines. 3 screws. Machinery: 255 tons. Boilers: 4 Thornycroft. Coal: 283 tons.

SOLD

Old Destroyers.
BAINBRIDGE class (**9**).
420 tons (*full load* 592 tons). Dimensions: 245 *w.l.* × 23·6 feet *mean*. Armament: 2—3 inch, 5—6 pdr., 2—18 inch tubes.

LOST

1 *Gas Engine Co.* **Stewart** 1902. Machinery, 205 tons. Boilers: 4 Seabury. Coal, 181 tons. Trial speed: 29·69 kts.
3 *Neafie and Levy.* **Bainbridge** 1901, **Barry** 1902, **Chauncey** 1901. Machinery, 209 tons. Boilers: 4 Thornycroft. Coal: 181 tons. Trials: *Bainbridge*, 28·45; *Barry*, 28·45; *Chauncey*, 28·64 kts.
2 *Trigg.* **Dale** 1900, **Decatur** 1900. Machinery, 201 tons. Boilers: 4 Thornycroft. Coal: 186 tons. Trials: *Dale*, 28; *Decatur*, 28·10 kts.
3 *Union Iron Works.* **Paul Jones** 1902, **Perry** 1900, **Preble** 1901. Machinery, 206 tons. Boilers: 4 Thornycroft. Coal: 179 tons. Trials: *Paul Jones*, 28·91; *Perry*, 28·32; *Preble*, 28·05 kts.

ALL SOLD EXCEPT ↑

PAULDING class (**21**).
All 742 tons, 883 (*full load*). Dimensions: 289 *w.l.* × 26·8 *mean*. Armament: 5—3 inch, 50 cal., 6—18 inch tubes (in pairs).

Photo, Müller.

Trials: *Drayton*, 30·83; *Jouett*, 32·27; *Jenkins*, 31·27; *Paulding*, 32·80; *Trippe*, 30·89 kts.

FLUSSER class (**5**).
All 700 tons (*full load*, 902 tons). Dimensions: 289 *w.l.* × 26·8 (*mean*). Armament: 5—3 inch, 50 cal., 3—18 inch tubes.

Photo, Commander Williams, U.S.N.

2 *Bath I.W.* **Flusser** 1910, **Reid** 1910. Parsons turbines. 3 screws. Machinery, 228 tons. Boilers: 4 Normand. Coal: 316 tons. Trials: *Flusser*, 30·41; *Reid*, 31·82 kts.

ALL SOLD

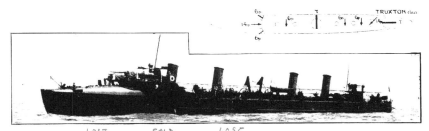

LOST   SOLD   LOST

5 *Truxton class:* **Truxton** 1901, **Whipple** 1902, **Worden** 1902. 486 tons. H.P. 8300—29 kts. Armament: 2—3 inch fore and aft, 6—6 pdr., 2—18 inch tubes. Coal: 175 tons. Complement 75.

4 funnels like Truxton's, but higher.

Hull class:— **Hopkins** 1901 and **Hull** 1902. 408 tons. H.P. 8456—29 kts. Armament: 2—3 inch, 5—6 pdrs. 2—18 inch tubes (amidships and aft.). Coal: 150 tons. Complement 64.

ALL SOLD

2 *Lawrence class:* **Lawrence** 1900, **Macdonough** 1900. 400 tons. H.P. 8100—30 kts. Armament: 7—6 pdr. 2—18 inch tubes. Coal: 123 tons. Complement 75.
General Note. *Lawrence* is the worst of the lot; but all are good sea boats. None of these older boats can maintain more than 25 kts.

ALL SOLD

Photo by favour of Lieut. Comdr. H. C. Woodward, U.S.N.

1 *Cramp.* **Beale** 1912, **Mayrant** 1910, **Patterson** 1911, **Warrington** 1910. *Mayrant* and *Warrington* have Zoelly turbines. 2 screws. Weight of machinery, 284 tons. Oil, 246 tons. Boilers: 4 White-Forster, *Beale* and *Patterson* have Parsons turbines. 3 screws. Machinery, 273 tons. Oil fuel, 239 tons. Boilers: 4 White-Forster. Trials: *Beale*, 29·65; *Mayrant*, 30·22; *Patterson*, 29·69; *Warrington*, 30·12 kts.
4 *Fore River.* **Henley** 1912, **Perkins** 1910, **Sterrett** 1910, **Walke** 1911. *Henley* has Curtis turbines and reciprocating 285 tons, other three Curtis turbines only 300 tons. 2 screws. Boilers: 4 Yarrow. Oil fuel, 217 t'ns. Trials: *Henley*, 29·50; *Perkins*, 29·76; *Sterrett*, 30·37; *Walke*, 29·76 kts.
1 *Newport News.* **Fanning** 1912, **Monaghan** 1811, **Roe** 1910, **Terry** 1910. Parsons turbines. 3 screws. Machinery, 276 tons. Boilers: 4 Thornycroft. Oil fuel: 225 in *Fanning*, 234 in other three. Trials: *Fanning*, 29·99; *Monaghan*, 30·15; *Roe*, 29·60; *Terry*, 30·24 kts.

ALL SCRAPPED

Photo, Müller.

4 *New York Shipbuilding.* **Ammen** 1911, **Burrows** 1910, **Jarvis** 1912, **McCall** 1910. Parsons turbine. 3 screws. Machinery averages 280 tons. Boilers: 4 Thornycroft. Oil fuel, 227 tons in *Ammen* and *Jarvis*, 255 in other two. Trials: *Ammen*, 30·48; *Burrows*, ——; *Jarvis*, 30·01; *McCall*, 30·66 kts.

ALL SCRAPPED

TUCKER (of *Conyngham* class). *Copyright Photo, O. W. Waterman.*

6 Cushing Class.

NICHOLSON. *Copyright Photo, O. W. Waterman.*

1 *Fore River:* **Cushing** (1912). 1050 tons (1071 *full load*). Parsons (geared cruising) turbines. Machinery: weighs 360 tons. Boilers: 4 Yarrow—21,500 sq. feet heating surface. Trials: 29·18 kts.
1 *New York S.B. Co.:* **Ericsson*** (1914). 1090 tons (1211 *full load*). 3 sets Parsons turbines with reciprocating machinery weighs 364 tons. Boilers: 4 Thornycroft—26,936 sq. ft. heating surface. Trials: 29·29 kts.
1 *Bath I.W.:* **McDougal** (1914). 1025 tons (1139 *full load*). Two sets Parsons turbines and two reciprocating. Machinery weighs 325 tons. Boilers: 4 Normand—21,509 sq. feet heating surface. Trials: 30·7 kts
3 *Cramp:* **Nicholson** (1914), **O'Brien*** (1914), **Winslow** (1915). 1050 tons (1171 *full load*). 2 Cramp-Zoelly turbines with 2 reciprocating. Machinery weighs 351 tons. Boilers: 4 White-Forster—21,600 sq. feet heating surface. Trials: *Nicholson* 29·08 kts, *O'Brien* 29·17 kts., *Winslow* 29·05 kts.
General Notes.—Dimensions are about 300 (*w.l.*) × $30\frac{1}{3}$ × 9 feet 4 inches to 9 feet 9 inches (*mean*). *Full load* draught: 9 feet 8 inches to 10 feet 9 inches. Armament: 4—4 inch (50 cal.), 8—21 inch tubes in 4 twin-deck mountings. Designed H.P. 16,000 = 29 kts. Oil fuel: 309 tons, but *McDougal* carries 327 tons. Complement: 101, (war 132.) Built to guaranteed radius at 15 kts.

* Have very low mainmasts.

ALL SCRAPPED

6 Allen class.

SAMPSON. *Davis* has after S.L. *before* mainmast on high lattice tower. *Photo, O. W. Waterman.*

2 *Bath I.W.:* **Allen** (1916), **Davis** (1916). 1071 tons (1185 *full load*). Designed H.P. 17,500 = 30 kts. Parsons (geared cruising) turbines. Machinery weighs 350 tons. Boilers: 4 Normand—22,500 sq. ft. heating surface. Trials: *Allen*, 30·29; *Davis*, 30·36 kts.

2 *Fore River:* **Rowan** (1916), **Sampson** (1916). 1110 tons (1125 *full load*.) Designed H.P. 17,000 = 29·5 kts. Curtis (geared cruising) turbines. Machinery averages 385 tons. Boilers: 4 Yarrow—21,500 sq. ft. heating surface. Trials: *Rowan*, 29·57 kts.; *Sampson*, 29·52 kts.

1 *Mare Island Navy Yard:* **Shaw** (1916). Displacement, H.P. and speed as *Rowan*. Parsons (geared cruising) turbines. Boilers: 4 Thornycroft.

1 *Cramp:* **Wilkes** (1916). 1110 tons (1124 *full load*). Designed H.P. 17,000 = 29·5 kts. Parsons (geared cruising) turbines. Machinery weighs 367 tons. Boilers: 4 White-Forster. Trials: 29·58 kts.

General Notes.—Dimensions: 310 (*w.l.*) × $29\frac{5}{8}$ × $9\frac{1}{4}$ to $9\frac{1}{2}$ feet *mean* draught. *Full load* draught of first two: 9 ft. $9\frac{1}{4}$ in. Others, 10 ft. $8\frac{1}{4}$ in. Armament: 4—4 inch (50 cal.), 2—1 pdr. auto. anti-aircraft, 12—21 inch deck tubes in 4 triple deck mountings. Designed H.P. 17,000 = 29·5 kts. Oil fuel: 290 tons (estimated). Complement: 103 136 war.

Davis, Shaw and *Wilkes* transferred to the Coast Guard in mid-1920s.

5 Conyngham Class.

CONYNGHAM. *Photo, U.S. Navy Recruiting Bureau.*

2 *Cramp:* **Conyngham** (1915), **Porter** (1915). 1090 tons (1205 *full load*.) Designed H.P. 18,000 = $29\frac{1}{2}$ kts. Parsons (geared cruising) turbines. Machinery weighs 375 tons. Boilers: 2 White-Forster—24,000 sq. ft. heating surface. Trials: *Conyngham*, 29·63 kts.; *Porter*, 29·58 kts.

1 *New York S.B. Co.:* **Wainwright** (1915). 1050 tons (1265 *full load*). Designed H.P. 17,000 = $29\frac{1}{2}$ kts. Parsons (geared cruising) turbines. Machinery averages 369 tons. Boilers: 4 Normand—21,500 sq. ft. heating surface. Trials: 29·67 kts. (*Jacob Jones* of this type lost during war.)

1 *Fore River:* **Tucker** (1915). Displacements as *Conyngham*. Designed H.P. 17,000 = $29\frac{1}{2}$ kts. Curtis (geared cruising) turbines. Machinery weighs 369 tons. Boilers: 4 Yarrow—21,500 sq. ft. heating surface. Trials: 29·56 kts.

1 *Bath I.W.:* **Wadsworth** (1915). 1060 tons (1174 *full load*). Designed H.P. 17,000 = $29\frac{1}{2}$ kts. Parsons turbines with reduction gear. Machinery weighs 323 tons. Boilers: 4 Normand—21,500 sq. ft. heating surface. Trials: 30·67 kts.

General Notes.—Dimensions: 310 (*w.l.*) × $29\frac{5}{6}$ × $9\frac{3}{8}$ to $9\frac{5}{8}$ feet (*mean* draught). *Full load* draught 10 feet $1\frac{1}{4}$ inches to 10 feet $8\frac{1}{4}$ inches. Armament: 4—4 inch (50 cal.), 8—21 inch tubes in 4 twin-deck mountings. Designed H.P. 17,000 = 29·5 kts. 290 tons oil fuel. Complement: 101, 132 war

War losses:
Jacob Jones was torpedoed and sunk 6 December 1917. Of the rest all but *Wadsworth* were transferred to the Coast Guard in the mid-1920s.

249 boats by various yards, (Flush Deckers—"# *186 Series*.")

WILLIAMSON and boats Nos. 186—347 series. *Photo, 5th March, 1921, Gieves, Ltd.*

HOVEY & LONG HAVE TWIN 4 INCH MOUNTS
BROOKS CLASS HAVE 5 INCH GUNS

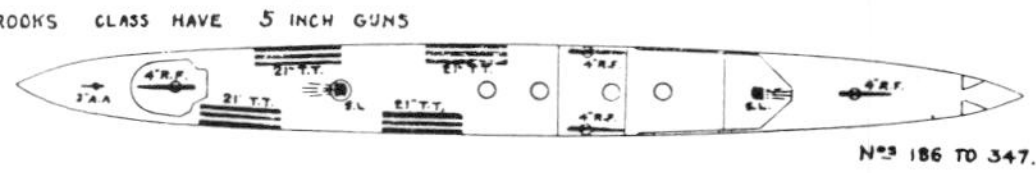

Nos. 186 TO 347.

HERBERT, and boats Nos. 75—185 series. *1920 Photo, by courtesy of Builders.*

FLUSH DECK DESTROYERS—FIRST LINE (DD).

No.	Name	B.	No.	Name	B.
184	Abbot	1	263	Laub	5
211	Alden	2	315	La Vallette	9
258	Aulick	4	250	Lawrence	6
294	Ausburn, Charles	5	118	Lea	2
128	Babbitt	6	158	Leary	6
126	Badger	6	336	Litchfield	8
196	Badger, George F.	1	79	Little	7
185	Bagley	1	209	Long	2
269	Bailey	5	331	Macdonough	9
246	Bainbridge	6	175	Mackenzie	10
267	Ballard	5	220	MacLeish	2
256	Bancroft	4	168	Maddox	9
213	Barker	2	74	Manley	3
149	Barney	2	321	Marcus	9
248	Barry	6	191	Mason	2
251	Belknap	4	253	McCalla	4
95	Bell	7	276	McCawley	5
153	Bernadou	2	252	McCook	4
151	Biddle	2	223	McCormick	2
293	Billingsley	5	262	McDermut	5
150	Blakeley	2	237	McFarland	6
136	Boggs	8	90	McKean	10
215	Borie	2	87	McKee	10
197	Branch	1	264	McLanahan	5
283	Breck	5	274	Meade	5
148	Breckinridge	2	335	Melvin	7
122	Breese	1	165	Meredith	7
232	Brooks	6	322	Mervine	9
210	Broome	2	279	Meyer	5
329	Bruce	9	121	Montgomery	1
131	Buchanan	3	277	Moody	5
222	Bulmer	2	271	Morris	5
299	Burnes, John Francis	9	105	Mugford	10
166	Bush	7	325	Mullany	9
69	Caldwell	8	343	Noa	11
285	Case	5	177	O'Bannon	10
104	Champlin	10	295	Osborne	5
206	Chandler	2	239	Overton	6
323	Chase	9	161	Palmer	7
106	Chew	10	218	Parrott	2
241	Childs	6	238	Paulding, James K.	6
140	Claxton	8	226	Peary	2
186	Clemson	1	298	Percival	9
326	Coghlan	9	340	Perry	8
155	Cole	2	76	Philip	3
85	Colhoun	7	227	Pillsbury	2
72	Conner	2	225	Pope	2
291	Converse	5	345	Preble	3
334	Corry	9	327	Preston	9
167	Cowell	7	344	Preston, William B.	11
109	Crane	10	347	Pruitt	3
70	Craven	11	287	Putnam	5
164	Crosby	7	120	Radford	1
134	Crowninshield	3	124	Ramsay	1
187	Dahlgren	1	113	Rathburne	2
290	Dale	5	292	Reid	5
199	Dallas	1	303	Reno	9
341	Decatur	8	176	Renshaw	10
116	Dent	2	89	Ringgold	10
157	Dickerson	6	88	Robinson	10
117	Dorsey	2	254	Rodgers	4
280	Doyen	5	147	Roper	2
152	Du Pont	2	243	Sands	6
84	Dyer	7	190	Satterlee	1
219	Edsall	2	159	Schenck	6
265	Edwards	5	103	Schley	10
216	Edwards, John D.	2	320	Selfridge	9
146	Elliot	2	189	Semmes	1
154	Ellis	2	281	Sharkey	5
78	Evans	3	318	Shirk	9
93	Fairfax	8	268	Shubrick	5
332	Farenholt	9	346	Sicard	3
304	Farquhar	9	81	Sigourney	7
300	Farragut	9	221	Simpson	2
289	Flusser	5	275	Sinclair	5
169	Foote	7	316	Sloat	9
228	Ford, John D.	2	324	Smith, Robert	9
234	Fox	6	301	Somers	2
123	Gamble	1	207	Southard	2
260	Gillis	4	180	Stansbury	10
233	Gilmer	6	86	Stevens	7
247	Goff	6	224	Stewart	2
188	Goldsborough	1	73	Stockton	2
266	Greene	5	302	Stoddert	9
145	Greer	2	83	Stringham	7
82	Gregory	7	240	Sturtevant	6
92	Gridley	10	333	Sumner	9
71	Gwin	12	273	Swasey	5
133	Hale	3	114	Talbot	8
141	Hamilton	8	156	Talbott, J. Fred	2
307	Hamilton, Paul	9	142	Tarbell	2
183	Haraden	1	125	Tattnall	6
91	Harding	10	94	Taylor	8
231	Hatfield	6	162	Thatcher	7
107	Hazelwood	10	182	Thomas	1
278	Henshaw	5	305	Thompson	9
160	Herbert	6	212	Thompson, Smith	5
198	Herndon	1	270	Thornton	5
178	Hogan	10	135	Tillman	13
181	Hopewell	1	272	Tingey	5
249	Hopkins	6	282	Toucey	5
208	Hovey	2	214	Tracy	2
179	Howard	10	339	Trever	8
342	Hulbert	11	229	Truxtun	2
330	Hull	9	259	Turner	5
236	Humphreys	6	127	Twiggs	6
149	Hunt	1	144	Upshur	2
255	Ingram, Osmond	4	193	Upshur, Abel P.	1
284	Isherwood	5	163	Walker	7
130	James, Reuben	6	139	Ward	8
260	Jones, Jacob	6	132	Ward, Aaron	3
230	Jones, Paul	2	338	Wasmuth	8
308	Jones, William	9	115	Waters	2
170	Kalk	7	257	Welles	4
235	Kane	6	217	Whipple	2
306	Kennedy	6	75	Wickes	2
138	Kennison	8	108	Williams	10
319	Kidder	9	244	Williamson	6
137	Kilty	8	317	Wood	9
80	Kimberly	7	195	Wood, Welborn C.	1
242	King	6	288	Worden	5
119	Lamberton	1	314	Yarborough	9
328	Lamson	9	143	Yarnall	2
286	Lardner	2	337	Zane	8
			313	Zeilin	9

Numerals preceding name are the Official Number which is painted on the bows of each boat.

Number after name = Builder's Name (see list).

Builders :—

1	Newport News S.B. Co.	
2	Wm. Cramp & Sons.	
3	Bath Iron Works.	
4	Bethlehem S.B. Co., Quincy.	
5	„ „ Squantum.	
6	New York S.B. Co.	
7	Fore River S.B. Co.	
8	Navy Yard, Mare Island.	
9	Bethlehem S.B. Co., San Francisco.	
10	Union Iron Works.	
11	Navy Yard, Norfolk.	
12	Seattle Con. and D.D. Co.	
13	Navy Yard, Charleston.	

RINGGOLD (& Union I. W. boats).

Photo, Lieut. H. Reuterdahl, U.S.N.R.F.

STOCKTON CONNER & GWIN.

1919 *Photo.*

Oil fuel supply is about 288—294 tons in earlier boats # 75 series.

BROOKS.

1920 *Photo, by courtesy of Builders.*

General Notes.—Normal displacement: 1215 tons (1308 *full load*). Dimensions: 310 (*w.l.*), 314 ft. 4½ in. (*o.a.*) × 30 ft. 11¼ in. × 9 ft. 4 in. *mean* draught, 9 ft. 9½ in. *full load.* Armament[*]: 4—4 inch, 50 cal., 1—3 inch, 23 cal. AA., 12—21 inch tubes in 4 triple deck mountings. Oil fuel : 375 tons. Complement, 122. In these boats the after 4 inch gun is on deck-house and the A.A. gun is on quarter deck—a modification which will be effected in all other " Flush Deck " T.B.D.

[*] 8—4 inch in *Hovey* (208), *Long* (209); 4—5 inch in *Brooks* (232), *Fox* (234), *Gilmer* (233), *Hatfield* (231), and *Kane* (235). 5—4 inch *Semmes* (189).

Designed S.H.P. 26,000—27,000 = 35 kts. Parsons, Westinghouse or Curtis turbines. 2 Screws. 4 Normand, Yarrow or White-Forster boilers.

Of these ships 36 were converted to fast transports in 1940–44; seven of these were lost and three damaged beyond repair. A further eight became light minelayers and 14 more became seaplane tenders. In September 1940 50 were transferred to the RN and RCN.

8 Farragut Class (*1932 Programme.*)

8 Porter Class (*1933 Programme*).

AYLWIN.   1939.

PHELPS.   1939. *O. W. Waterman.*

DALE.   1937, *O. W. Waterman.*

WINSLOW.   1938. *O. W. Waterman.*

1 Bethlehem S.B. Corpn., Fore River : **Farragut.**
2 New York Navy Yard : **Hull, Dale.**
1 Bath Iron Works Corpn. : **Dewey.**
2 Boston Navy Yard : **MacDonough, Monaghan.**
1 Philadelphia Navy Yard : **Aylwin.**
1 Puget Sound Navy Yard : **Worden.**

Standard displacement : 1,395 tons (except *Farragut*, 1,365 tons ; *Dewey*, 1,345 ; *Aylwin*, 1,375 ; *Worden*, 1410 tons.) Length, (*o.a.*), 341½ feet ; (*w.l.*), 331 feet (except *Farragut*, 330 ; *Dewey*, 329 feet). Beam, 34½ feet. *Mean draught*, 8½ feet (except *Farragut*, 8½ ; *Dewey*, 8½ feet ; *Aylwin*, 8½ feet.) *Maximum* draught, 15½ feet. Complement, 162. Guns : 5—5 inch, 38 cal. (dual purpose), 4 M.G. Tubes : 8—21 inch (quadrupled). Machinery : Geared turbines. S.H.P. 42,800 = 36·5 kts. (Max. trial speed reported to be 41 kts.) Boilers : 4 Yarrow (by Bethlehem), high pressure. Oil fuel : 400 tons. Radius : 6,000 miles. Cost ranges from $3,400,000 to $3,750,000.

4 New York S.B. Corpn. : **Porter, Selfridge, McDougal, Winslow.**
4 Bethlehem S.B. Corpn., Fore River : **Phelps, Clark, Moffett, Balch.**

Displacement : 1,850 tons (*Phelps* and *Clark* as completed, 1,805 tons ; *Balch* and *Moffett*, 1,825 tons). Complement : 175. Dimensions : 371 (*w.l.*), 381 (*o.a.*) × 36½ × 10½ to 10¾ feet (*mean* draught). Guns : 8—5 inch, 38 cal. 8 —1 pdr., 2 M.G. Tubes : 8—21 inch. Machinery : Geared turbines. S.H.P. : 50,000 = 37 kts. (Trials, 39 kts.). 4 Babcock & Wilcox high pressure boilers. Oil fuel : *circa* 500 tons. Cost approaches $4,000,000 each.

Name	No.	Laid down	Launched	Compl.
Farragut	348	20.9.32	15/3/34	18/6/34
Dewey	349	16/12/32	28/7/34	3/10/34
Hull	350	7/3/33	31/1/34	24/5/35
MacDonough	351	15/5/33	22/8/34	28/6/35
Worden	352	29.12.32	27/10/34	1/3/35
Dale	353	10.2.34	23/1/35	19/7/35
Monaghan	354	21.11.33	9/1/35	30/8/35
Aylwin	355	23.9.33	10/7/34	1/5/35

Name	No.	Laid down	Launched	Completed	Name	No.	Laid down	Launched	Completed
Porter	356	18/12/33	12/12/35	2/7/37	*Phelps*	360	2/1/34	18/7/35	26/2/36
Selfridge	357	18/12/33	18/4/36	26.10/37	*Clark*	361	2/1/34	15/10/35	20/5/36
McDougal	358	18/12/33	17/3/36	12/10/37	*Moffett*	362	2/1/34	11/12/35	28/9/37
Winslow	359	18/12/33	21/9/36	19/10/37	*Balch*	363	16/5/34	24/3/36	5/10/37

MACDONOUGH.   1944, *U.S. Navy Official.*

SELFRIDGE   1945, *U.S. Navy Official.*

Appearance Note.—Most of this class now rigged as silhouette, with pole foremast and stump mainmast, but without after fire control or No. 3 turret. Height of funnels has been reduced.

War losses: *Worden* wrecked nr Amchitka Is 12 January 1943; *Hull* and *Monaghan* foundered off Samar 18 December 1944.

War losses: *Porter* torpedoed by Japanese submarine nr Santa Cruz 26 October 1942.

16 Mahan Class (1933 Programme)

PERKINS.

1939, O. W. Waterman.

CUMMINGS.

1938, O.W. Waterman.

2 Bain Iron Works Corpn.: **Drayton, Lamson**
2 Boston Navy Yard: **Case, Conyngham.**
2 United Dry Docks: **Mahan, Cummings.**
2 Federal S.B. and D.D. Co.: **Flusser, Reid**
2 Philadelphia Navy Yard: **Cassin, Shaw.**
2 Norfolk Navy Yard: **Tucker, Downes.**
2 Puget Sound Navy Yard: **Cushing, Perkins.**
2 Mare Island Navy Yard: **Smith, Preston.**

Standard displacement: 1,500 tons (except *Mahan*, 1,450 tons; *Cummings, Cushing, Perkins*, 1,465 tons. *Drayton, Lamson, Flusser, Reid, Smith, Preston*, 1,480 tons). Dimensions: 334 (*w.l.*), 341½ (*o.a.*) × 34⅞ × 9 ft. 8 in. (*Mahan*), 9 ft. 9 in. (1,465 and 1,480-ton ships), 9 ft. 10 in. others, (*mean*): all about 17 feet *max*. Guns: 5—5 inch, 38 cal. (dual purpose), 4 M.G. Tubes: 12—21 inch (quadrupled). Machinery: Geared turbines. S.H.P.: 42,800 = 36·5 kts. Boilers: 4 Express type. Oil fuel: 400 tons. Radius: 6,000 miles. Cost ranges from 83,400,000 to 83,750,000.

Name	No.	Laid down	Launched	Completed	Name	No.	Laid down	Launched	Completed
Mahan	364	12/6/34	15/10/35	16/11/36	Cassin	372	1/10/34	28/10/35	6/4/37
Cummings	365	26/6/34	11/12/35	26/1/37	Shaw	373	1/10/34	28/10/35	20/4/37
Drayton	366	20/3/34	26/3/36	1/6/37	Tucker	374	15/8/34	26/2/36	30/3/37
Lamson	367	20/3/34	17/6/36	4/1/37	Downes	375	15/8/34	22/4/36	26/3/37
Flusser	368	4/6/34	28/9/35	1/12/36	Cushing	376	15/8/34	31/12/35	10/12/36
Reid	369	25/6/34	11/1/36	4/1/37	Perkins	377	15/11/34	31/12/35	10/12/36
Case	370	19/9/34	14/9/35	19/3/37	Smith	378	27/10/34	20/2/36	31/12/36
Conyngham	371	19/9/34	14/9/35	10/4/37	Preston	379	27/10/34	22/4/36	23/1/37

DOWNES.

Added 1944, U.S. Navy Official.

War losses: *Cushing* sunk by gunfire Japanese cruisers SE of Savo Is 13 November 1942; *Mahan* bombed by Japanese aircraft Ormoe Bay 7 December 1944; *Perkins* lost in collision nr Buna 29 November 1943; *Preston* sunk by gunfire Japanese cruiser nr Savo Is 14 November 1942; *Tucker* mined off Espiritu Santo 4 August 1942.

22 Craven Class (1934–35 Programmes)

BLUE.

1937, courtesy "Our Navy."

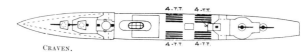

ELLET.

1939.

4 Bethlehem S.B. Corpn., Fore River: **Gridley, Craven, Maury, McCall.**
5 Norfolk Navy Yard: **Bagley, Blue, Helm, Rowan, Stack.**
4 Boston Navy Yard: **Mugford, Ralph Talbot, Mayrant, Trippe.**
1 Mare Island Navy Yard: **Henley.**
3 Puget Sound Navy Yard: **Patterson, Jarvis, Wilson.**
3 Federal S.B. & D.D. Co.: **Benham, Ellet, Lang.**
1 Philadelphia Navy Yard: **Rhind.**
1 Charleston Navy Yard: **Sterett.**

Standard displacement: 1,500 tons. Complement: 172. Dimensions: 334 (*w.l.*), 341½ (*o.a.*) × 34⅞ × 9¼ feet (*mean*) Guns: 4—5 inch, 38 cal. (dual purpose), 4 M.G. Tubes: 16—21 inch (quadrupled). Machinery: Parsons geared turbines. S.H.P.: 42,800 = 36·5 kts. Boilers: 4 Express type (except *Gridley* and *Craven*, 4 Bethlehem Yarrow). Oil fuel: 400 tons. Radius: 6,000 miles. Cost ranges from 83,400,000 to 83,750,000.

CRAVEN.

Notes.—Many of this class have exceeded designed speed on trials. *Ellet* and *Lang* are said to have approached 40 kts. Several ships were delayed in delivery through difficulties with high pressure and superheated installations.

Name	No.	Laid down	Launched	Completed	Name	No.	Laid down	Launched	Completed
Gridley	380	3/6/35	1/12/36	30/6/38	Ellet	398	3/12/36	11/6/38	18/4/39
Craven	382	3/6/35	25/2/37	29/7/38	Lang	399	5/4/37	27/8/38	26/5/39
Bagley	386	31/7/35	3/9/36	10/8/38	McCall	400	17/3/36	20/11/37	19/12/38
Blue	387	25/9/35	27/5/37	10/8/38	Maury	401	24/3/36	14/2/38	17/1/39
Helm	388	25/9/35	27/5/37	16/9/38	Mayrant	402	15/4/37	14/5/38	/39
Mugford	389	28/10/35	31/10/36	23/9/38	Trippe	403	15/4/37	14/5/38	/39
Ralph Talbot	390	28/10/35	31/10/36	23/9/38	Rhind	404	22/9/37	28/7/38	/39
Henley	391	28/10/35	12/1/37	12/9/38	Rowan	405	25/6/37	5/5/38	/39
Patterson	392	22/7/35	6/5/37	11/10/38	Stack	406	25/6/37	5/5/38	/39
Jarvis	393	21/8/35	6/5/37	25/10/38	Sterett	407	2/12/36	27/10/38	/39
Benham	397	1/9/36	16/4/38	18/4/39	Wilson	408	22/3/37	12/4/39	/39

MAYRANT.

1944, U.S. Navy Official.

War losses: *Benham* torpedoed by Japanese warships off Guadalcanal 15 November 1942; *Blue* torpedoed by Japanese destroyer Ironbottom Sound 22 August 1942; *Wenley* torpedoed by Japanese submarine off Finschafen 3 October 1943; *Jarvis* bombed by Japanese aircraft off Guadalcanal 9 August 1942; and *Rowan* torpedoed by German MTB off Salerno 10 September 1943.

2 Dunlap Class (1934 Programme)

DUNLAP.   1937, Mr. James Downey.

2 *United Dry Docks* : **Dunlap, Fanning.**

Standard displacement : 1,490 tons. Dimensions ; 334 (w.l.), 341½ (o.a.) × 34½ × 9½ feet (mean). Guns : 5—5 inch, 38 cal. (dual purpose). 4 M.G. Tubes : 12—21 inch (quadrupled). Machinery : Parsons geared turbines. S.H.P. : 42,800 = 36·5 kts. Boilers : 4 Express type. Oil fuel : 400 tons. Radius : 6,000 miles.

Name	No.	Laid down	Launched	Completed
Dunlap	384	10/4/35	18/4/36	7/7/38
Fanning	385	10/4/35	18/9/36	4/8/38

DUNLAP.   1937 Mr. James Downey.

5 Somers Class. (1934-35 Programmes).

WARRINGTON.   1938, Lieut. L. F. Bowman.

2 *Federal S.B. & D.D. Co.* : **Somers, Warrington.**
3 *Bath Iron Works Corpn.* : **Sampson, Jouett, Davis.**
Displacement ; 1,850 tons. Complement : 198. Dimensions ; 371 (w.l.) × 36½ × 10¼ feet (mean draught). Guns : 8—5 inch, 38 cal. 8—1 pdr., 2 M.G. Tubes : 12—21 inch. Machinery : Geared turbines. S.H.P. : 52,000 = 37 kts. 4 Babcock & Wilcox high pressure boilers. Oil fuel ; circa 500 tons. Cost averages over 85,000,000 each. In the case of *Somers* this includes a special air-conditioning plant.

Name	No.	Laid down	Launched	Completed	Name	No.	Laid down	Launched	Completed
Somers	381	27/6/35	13/3/37	30/6/38	Davis	395	28/7/36	30/7/38	16/12/38
Warrington	383	10/10/35	15/5/37	12/8/38	Jouett	396	26/3/36	24/9/38	7/3/39
Sampson	394	8/4/36	16/4/38	3/10/38					

War loss: *Warrington* foundered off Bahamas 13 September 1944.

SOMERS.   1944, U.S. Navy Official.

7 Anderson Class (1936 Programme)

ROE.   1940, Theo. N. Stone.

MUSTIN.   1940, Official.

2 *Newport News Co.* : **Mustin, Russell,**
2 *Federal S.B. & D.D. Co.* : **Anderson, Hammann.**
2 *Bath Iron Works Corpn.* : **Hughes, Sims.**
2 *Boston Navy Yard* : **O'Brien, Walke.**
2 *Norfolk Navy Yard* : **Morris, Wainwright.**
1 *Charleston Navy Yard* : **Roe.**
1 *Philadelphia Navy Yard* : **Buck.**

SIMS

Standard displacement : 1,570 tons. Dimensions not reported. Guns : 5—5 inch, 38 cal., several smaller. Tubes : 12—21 inch (quadrupled). Machinery : Parsons geared turbines. S.H.P. : 44,000 = 36·5 kts. Boilers : 4 Express. Oil fuel : 400 tons. Cost about $5,500,000 apiece.

Note.—This type combines the most successful features of *Craven* and *Mahan* classes. Reversion to 12 tubes understood to have been due to desire for higher freeboard abaft forecastle. General arrangement similar to *Dunlap* and *Fanning*, but with a single funnel. *Hammann* is reported to have made 39 knots on trials.

War losses: *Benham* torpedoed by Japanese warships off Guadalcanal 15 November 1942; *Blue* torpedoed by Japanese destroyer Ironbottom Sound 22 August 1942; *Henley* torpedoed by Japanese submarine off Finschafen 3 October 1943; *Jarvis* bombed by Japanese aircraft off Guadalcanal 9 August 1942; and *Rowan* torpedoed by German MTB off Salerno 10 September 1943.

27 "Benson" Class.

(1937–39 Programme).

KENDRICK.   1944, U.S. Navy, Official.

7 Bethlehem (Quincy):
BANCROFT
BENSON
BOYLE
CHAMPLIN
MAYO
NIELDS
ORDRONAUX

1 Boston Navy Yard:
MADISON

1 Philadelphia Navy Yard:
HILARY P. JONES

8 Bethlehem (S. Francisco):
CALDWELL
COGHLAN
FRAZIER
GANSEVOORT
GILLESPIE
HOBBY
KALK
WOODWORTH

1 Puget Sound Navy Yard:
CHARLES F. HUGHES

5 Bethlehem (Staten Island):
BAILEY
FARENHOLT
MEADE
MURPHY
PARKER

4 Bethlehem (S. Pedro):
KENDRICK
LAUB
MACKENZIE
McLANAHAN

Displacement:	1,620 tons (2,450 tons full load)
Dimensions:	348½ (o.a.) × 35½ × 18 (max.) feet
Guns:	4—5 inch, 38 cal., etc.
Tubes:	5—21 inch (quintupled)
Machinery:	Geared turbines. 2 shafts. S.H.P. : 50,000 = 37 kts.
Boilers:	4 high pressure
Complement:	250

General Notes.—Built to the design of the Bethlehem Steel Co. All laid up except one in partial commission. War losses: *Barton, Laffey, Lansdale.*

Appearance Note.—Those built by Bethlehem Co. have flat-sided funnels.

HOBBY.   1944, U.S. Navy, Official.

KENDRICK.   1944, U.S. Navy Official.

Name	No.	Laid down	Launched	Completed	Name	No.	Laid down	Launched	Completed
Benson	421	16/5/38	15/11/39	25/7/40	Plunkett	431	1/3/39	9/3/40	{ 16/7/40
Mayo	422	16/5/38	26/3/40	18/9/40	Kearny	432	1/3/39		{ 13/9/40
Gleaves	423	16/5/38	9/12/39	/5/40	Grayson	435	17/7/39	7/8/40	15/4/41
Niblack	424	8/8/38	18/5/40	1/8/40	Woolsey	437	9/10/39	12/2/41	/41
Madison	425	19/12/38	20/10/39	12/40	Ludlow	438	18/12/39	11/11/40	5/3/41
H. P. Jones	427	16/11/38	14/12/39	} 12/40	Edison	439	} 18/3/40	23/11/40	{ 30/1/41
C. F. Hughes	428	3/1/39	16/5/40	}	Ericsson	440			11/3/41
Livermore	429	6/3/39	3/8/40	7/10/40	Wilkes	441	} 1/11/39	31/5/40	
Eberle	430	12/4/39	14/9/40	4/12/40	Nicholson	442			/41
					Swanson	443	15/11/39	2/11/40	/41

Note.— There are probably variations in displacement as well as small differences in appearance in later units of this class. Most are reported to have square sterns. Reversion to 2 funnels is a noteworthy feature; shape of these appears to vary, some being circular and others oval. War losses: *Buck, Gwin, Ingraham, Lansdale, Meredith, Monssen.*

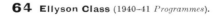

CHARLES F. HUGHES.   (*Benson, Mayo, Madison,* all similar.)   1942, *Keystone.*

64 Ellyson Class (1940–41 *Programmes*).

BANCROFT.   1942, *U.S. Navy Official.*

Standard displacement : 1,700 tons (2,000 tons full load). Guns: 4—5 inch, 38 cal. 4—40 mm. Bofors. 4—20 mm. Oerlikon. Tubes: 5—21 inch. Machinery: Geared turbines. 2 shafts. 4 high pressure watertube boilers. S.H.P.: 50,000 = 36.5 kts. Cost averages $8,814,000 per ship, inclusive. War losses: *Aaron Ward, Beatty, Bristol, Duncan, Laffey, Maddox, Turner.*

Note.—*Kidd* and *Bullard* were both launched Feb. 28, 1943.

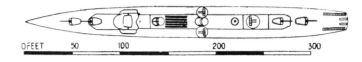

OFEET   50   100   200   300

6 *Boston Navy Yard:* **Forrest, Fitch, Cowie, Knight, Doran, Earle.**

3 *Charleston Navy Yard:* **Corry, Hobson, Tillman.**

2 *Philadelphia Navy Yard:* **Butler, Gherardi.**

2 *Norfolk Navy Yard:* **Herndon, Shubrick.**

2 *Bath Iron Works Corpn.:* **Emmons, Macomb.**

17 *Federal S.B. & D.D. Co.:* **Ellyson, Hambleton, Rodman, Lansdowne, Davison, Edwards, Glennon, Jeffers, Nelson, Stevenson, Stockton, Thorn, Buchanan, Lardner, McCalla, Mervine, Quick.**

5 *Bethlehem (Quincy):* **Bancroft, Boyle, Champlin, Nields, Ordronaux.**

8 *Bethlehem (S. Francisco):* **Woodworth, Caldwell, Coghlan, Frazier, Gansevoort, Gillespie, Hobby, Kalk.**

5 *Bethlehem (Staten Island):* **Farenholt, Bailey, Meade, Murphy, Parker.**

4 *Bethlehem (S. Pedro):* **Kendrick, Laub, Mackenzie, McLanahan.**

10 *Seattle-Tacoma S.B. Corpn., Seattle:* **Carmick, Doyle, Endicott, McCook** (ex-*Farley*)**, Frankford, Baldwin, Harding, Satterlee, Thompson, Welles.**

Butler, Carmick, Cowie, Davison, Doran, Doyle, Ellyson, Endicott, Fitch, Forrest, Gherardi, Hale, Hambleton, Harding, Hobson, Jeffers, Knight, McCook, Macomb, Mervine, Quick, Rodman, Thompson, were fitted out as Fast Minesweepers during war in Pacific. War losses: *Aaron Ward, Beatty, Bristol, Corry, Duncan, Emmons, Glennon, Laffey, Maddox, Turner.* In addition, *Shubrick* was so badly damaged that repairs have been suspended.

This class was variously named in *Jane's Fighting Ships* – Ellyson, Buchanan and Cleaves. The minesweeper conversions (called 'Fitch' class in *Jane's*) were described in following note.

HOBBY.   1941, *U.S. Navy Official.*

WOOLSEY.   Added 1950, U.S. Navy, Official.

Destroyers (DD).

79 "Fletcher" Class.

DD
8 Boston Navy Yard
473 BENNETT
581 CHARETTE
582 CONNER
474 FULLAM
472 GUEST
583 HALL
585 HARADEN
475 HUDSON

6 Charleston Navy Yard
587 BELL
588 BURNS
589 IZARD
590 PAUL HAMILTON
478 STANLEY
479 STEVENS

7 Puget Sound Navy Yard
480 HALFORD
594 HART (ex-Mansfield)
592 HOWORTH
593 KILLEN
595 METCALF
596 SHIELDS
597 WILEY

4 Federal S.B. & D.D. Co.
448 LA VALLETTE
500 RINGOLD
501 SCHROEDER
502 SIGSBEE

DD
11 Bath Iron Works Corpn.
629 ABBOT
515 ANTHONY
630 BRAINE
509 CONVERSE
631 ERBEN
511 FOOTE
642 HALE
643 SIGOURNEY
644 STEMBEL
513 TERRY
516 WADSWORTH

13 Bethlehem (S. Francisco)
527 AMMEN
531 HAZELWOOD
532 HEERMAN
534 McCORD
535 MILLER
528 MULLANY (ex-Beatty)
536 OWEN
538 STEPHEN POTTER
537 THE SULLIVANS (ex-Putnam)
539 TINGEY
530 TRATHEN
540 TWINING
541 YARNALL

4 Bethlehem (S. Pedro)
544 BOYD
545 BRADFORD
546 BROWN
547 COWELL

DD
3 Bethlehem (Staten Island)
519 DALY
520 ISHERWOOD
521 KIMBERLY

11 Seattle-Tacoma S.B. Corpn., Seattle
554 FRANKS
556 HAILEY
561 PRITCHETT
562 ROBINSON
563 ROSS
564 ROWE
565 SMALLEY
566 STODDARD
567 WATTS
568 WREN

9 Consolidated Steel Corpn., Orange, Texas
569 AULICK
570 CHARLES AUSBURN
571 CLAXTON
572 DYSON
573 HARRISON
574 JOHN RODGERS
575 McKEE
578 WICKES
580 YOUNG

3 Gulf S.B. Corpn., Chickasaw, Ala.
550 CAPPS
551 DAVID W. TAYLOR
553 JOHN D. HENLEY

RADFORD. 1944. *U.S. Navy Official.*

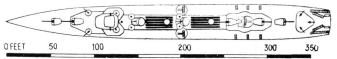

Displacement :	2,050 tons standard (2,750 tons full load)
Dimensions :	376½ (o.a.) × 39½ × 12½ (mean), 18 (max.) feet
Guns :	5—5 inch, 28 cal., 6—40 mm. Bofors, 10—20 mm. Oerlikon (see Conversion Notes)
	Rearmed ships 4—5 inch, 38 cal., 6—3 inch, 50 cal. AA.
Tubes :	5—21 inch (quintupled). Some have two sets of 5 torpedo tubes in active units
A/S weapons :	2 Hedgehogs (D.C. racks and K-guns to be replaced by 2 side-launching torpedo racks)
Machinery :	General Electric geared turbines. 2 shafts. S.H.P.: 60,000 = 35 kts.
Boilers :	4 Babcock & Wilcox
Complement :	350 (war)

General Notes.—Laid down under 1940-41 Programme. Builders above. During the war six units (including *Halford* in 1943) were experimentally fitted with a seaplane and catapult, in place of deckhouse between "Q" and "X" turrets (armament being temporarily reduced by 1—5 inch and 5 T.T.) ; and some, including *Young*, had only one set of tubes. All those with two sets now reduced to one. Eighteen of these ships were modified for duty as escort destroyers (DDE). viz.: *Bache, Beale, Conway, Cony, Eaton, Fletcher, Jenkins, Murray, Nicholas, O'Bannon, Philip, Radford, Renshaw, Saufley, Sproston, Taylor, Walker* and *Waller*—see next page. War losses : *Abner Read, Brownson, Bush, Chevalier, De Haven, Halligan, Hoel, Johnston, Longshaw, Luce, Morrison, Pringle, Spence, Strong, Twiggs, William D. Porter.* Heavily damaged and subsequently scrapped : *Evans, Haggard, Leutze, Newcomb, Thatcher.* Sold : *Hutchins.* Cancelled : *Percival, Watson.*

AMMEN (note new 3-inch AA. guns). 1953, Lieut. Aldo Fraccaroli.

Name	Laid down	Launched	Completed	Name	Laid down	Launched	Completed
Abbot	21 Sep. 1942	17 Feb. 1943	23 Apr. 1943	John Rodgers	25 July 1941	7 May 1942	9 Feb. 1943
Ammen	29 Nov. 1941	17 Sep. 1942	12 Mar. 1943	Killen	26 Nov. 1941	10 Jan. 1943	4 June 1944
Anthony	17 Aug. 1942	20 Dec. 1942	26 Feb. 1943	Kimberly	27 July 1942	4 Feb. 1943	22 May 1943
Aulick	14 May 1941	2 Mar. 1942	27 Oct. 1942	La Vallette	27 Nov. 1941	21 June 1942	12 Aug. 1942
Bell	24 Feb. 1942	24 June 1942	4 Mar. 1943	Laws	19 May 1942	22 Apr. 1943	18 Nov. 1943
Bennett	10 Dec. 1941	16 Apr. 1942	9 Feb. 1943	Metcalf	10 Aug. 1943	25 Sep. 1944	15 Dec. 1944
Boyd	2 Apr. 1942	29 Oct. 1942	8 May 1943	Miller	18 Aug. 1942	7 Mar. 1943	31 Aug. 1943
Bradford	28 Apr. 1942	12 Dec. 1942	12 June 1943	Mullany	15 Jan. 1942	10 Oct. 1942	23 Apr. 1943
Braine	12 Oct. 1942	7 Mar. 1943	11 May 1943	McCord	17 Mar. 1942	10 Jan. 1943	19 Aug. 1943
Brown	27 June 1942	22 Feb. 1943	10 July 1943	McKee	2 Mar. 1942	2 Aug. 1942	31 Mar. 1943
Burns	9 May 1942	8 Aug. 1942	3 Apr. 1943	Owen	17 Sep. 1942	21 Mar. 1943	20 Sep. 1943
Capps	12 June 1941	31 May 1942	23 June 1943	Paul Hamilton	20 Jan. 1943	7 Apr. 1943	15 Nov. 1943
Charles Ausburn	14 May 1941	16 Mar. 1942	24 Nov. 1942	Prichett	20 July 1943	31 July 1943	15 Jan. 1944
Charrette	20 Feb. 1941	3 June 1942	18 May 1943	Ringold	25 June 1942	11 Nov. 1942	23 Dec. 1942
Claxton	25 June 1941	1 Apr. 1942	8 Dec. 1942	Robinson	12 Aug. 1942	28 Aug. 1943	31 Jan. 1944
Conner	16 Apr. 1942	18 July 1942	8 Dec. 1942	Ross	7 Sep. 1942	10 Sep. 1943	21 Feb. 1944
Converse	23 Feb. 1942	30 Aug. 1942	20 Nov. 1942	Rowe	7 Dec. 1942	30 Sep. 1943	13 Mar. 1944
Cowell	7 Sep. 1942	18 Apr. 1943	23 Aug. 1943	Schroeder	25 June 1941	11 Nov. 1942	31 Dec. 1942
Daly	29 Apr. 1942	24 Oct. 1942	9 Mar. 1943	Shields	10 Aug. 1943	25 Sep. 1944	22 Feb. 1945
David W. Taylor	12 June 1941	4 July 1942	18 Sep. 1943	Sigourney	7 Dec. 1942	24 Apr. 1943	29 June 1943
Dyson	25 June 1941	15 Apr. 1942	30 Dec. 1942	Sigsbee	22 July 1942	7 Dec. 1942	22 Jan. 1943
Erben	28 Oct. 1942	21 Mar. 1943	28 May 1943	Smalley	9 Feb. 1943	27 Oct. 1943	31 Mar. 1944
Foote	14 Apr. 1942	11 Oct. 1942	22 Dec. 1942	Stanley	30 Dec. 1941	2 May 1942	15 Oct. 1942
Franks	8 Mar. 1942	7 Dec. 1942	30 July 1943	Stembel	21 Dec. 1942	8 May 1943	16 July 1943
Fullam	10 Dec. 1941	16 Apr. 1942	2 Mar. 1943	Stephen Potter	27 Oct. 1942	28 Apr. 1943	21 Oct. 1943
Guest	27 Sep. 1941	20 Feb. 1942	15 Dec. 1942	Stevens	30 Dec. 1941	24 June 1942	1 Feb. 1943
Hale	23 Nov. 1942	4 Apr. 1943	15 June 1943	Stoddard	10 Mar. 1943	19 Nov. 1943	15 Apr. 1944
Halford	3 June 1941	29 Oct. 1942	1 May 1943	Terry	8 June 1942	22 Nov. 1942	26 Jan. 1943
Hall	16 Feb. 1942	18 July 1942	6 July 1943	The Sullivans	10 Oct. 1942	4 Apr. 1943	30 Sep. 1943
Hailey	11 Apr. 1942	9 Mar. 1943	30 Sep. 1943	Tingey	22 Oct. 1942	28 May 1943	25 Nov. 1943
Haraden	3 June 1942	19 Mar. 1943	16 Sep. 1943	Trathen	8 July 1942	22 Oct. 1942	28 May 1943
Hart	25 July 1941	7 May 1942	25 Jan. 1943	Twining	20 Nov. 1942	11 July 1943	1 Dec. 1943
Harrison	10 Aug. 1943	25 Sep. 1944	1 Dec. 1944	Wadsworth	18 Aug. 1942	10 Jan. 1943	16 Mar. 1943
Hazelwood	1 Apr. 1942	20 June 1942	18 June 1943	Watts	26 Mar. 1943	31 Dec. 1943	29 Apr. 1944
Heerman	8 May 1942	5 Dec. 1942	6 July 1943	Wickes	15 Apr. 1942	13 Sep. 1942	16 June 1943
Howorth	26 Nov. 1941	10 Jan. 1943	1 May 1943	Wiley	10 Aug. 1943	25 Sep. 1944	1 May 1945
Hudson	23 Feb. 1942	3 June 1942	13 Apr. 1943	Wren	24 Apr. 1943	29 Jan. 1944	20 May 1944
Isherwood	12 May 1942	24 Nov. 1942	10 Apr. 1943	Yarnall	5 Dec. 1942	25 July 1943	30 Dec. 1943
Izard	9 May 1942	8 Aug. 1942	15 May 1943	Young	7 May 1942	11 Oct. 1942	31 July 1943
John D. Henley	21 July 1942	15 Nov. 1942	2 Feb. 1944				

Appearance Notes.—All Bethlehem-built ships of this class have flat-sided funnels.

Conversion Notes.—*Cowell, Daly, Isherwood, Hailey, Mullany, Ross, Rowe, Smalley* and others have 4-5 inch (in "A," "B," "X" and "Y" positions), 6-3 inch (twin mounts in "Q" position, and two twins amidships between funnels). 5-21 inch (quintuple bank abaft after funnel) and tripod mast. The forward bank of tubes were suppressed (3 inch now mounted in their place). See photo of *Ross.* All active units rearmed, but over half the class are in reserve and mount their original armament.

TWINING. Added 1957, Ted Stone

ROWE. Added 1957, Skyfctos

Destroyers (DD).

53 Later " Fletcher " Class.

COGSWELL.   1953, Skyfotos.

8 *Bath Iron Works Corpn.*	5 *Bethlehem Steel Co. (S. Pedro)*	2 *Charleston Navy Yard*
DD	DD	DD
650 CAPERTON	793 CASSIN YOUNG	649 ALBERT W. GRANT
651 COGSWELL	681 HOPEWELL	665 BRYANT
652 INGERSOLL	794 IRWIN	
653 KNAPP	682 PORTERFIELD	18 *Federal S.B. & D.D. Co.*
691 MERTZ	795 PRESTON	666 BLACK
690 NORMAN SCOTT		660 BULLARD
688 REMEY	3 *Boston Navy Yard*	667 CHAUNCEY
689 WADLEIGH	662 BENNION	668 CLARENCE K. BRONSON
	663 HEYWOOD L. EDWARDS	669 COTTEN
2 *Bethlehem Steel Co. (S. Francisco)*	664 RICHARD P. LEARY	659 DASHIELL
683 STOCKHAM		670 DORTCH
684 WEDDERBURN	3 *Gulf S.B. Corpn.*	671 GATLING
	654 BEARSS	672 HEALY
8 *Bethlehem Steel Co. (Staten Island)*	655 JOHN HOOD	673 HICKOX
796 BENHAM	656 VAN VALKENBURGH	674 HUNT
657 CHARLES J. BADGER		661 KIDD
658 COLAHAN	4 *Todd Pacific Shipyards*	675 LEWIS HANCOCK
797 CUSHING	802 GREGORY	677 McDERMUT
686 HALSEY POWELL	799 JARVIS	678 McGOWAN
798 MONSSEN	800 PORTER	679 McNAIR
685 PICKING	804 ROOKS	676 MARSHALL
687 UHLMANN		680 MELVIN

Displacement :	2,050 tons (2,750 tons *full load*)
Dimensions :	376½ (o.a.) × 39½ × 18 (max.) feet
Guns :	5—5 inch, 38 cal., 10—40 mm., 8—20 mm. AA. (20 mm. removed from all active units)
	Converted ships : 4—5 inch, 38 cal., 6—3 inch. 50 cal. AA. (see *Conversion Notes*)
Tubes :	5—21 inch (quintupled). Some have two sets of 5 torpedo tubes
A S weapons :	2 Hedgehogs (D.C. racks and K-guns to be replaced by 2 side-launching torpedo racks)
Machinery :	General Electric geared turbines. 2 shafts. S.H.P. : 60,000 = 35 kts.
Boilers :	4 Babcock & Wilcox
Complement :	350 (war)

General Notes.—Laid down under 1942 Programme. Builders above. Except that they have lower fire controls and flat-faced bridges these ships are in most respects like " Fletcher " class, described on the following page. Some of the later units of *Fletcher* class are, in fact, almost indistinguishable from modified type—e.g., *Ammen, Sigourney. Dortch* was built in 158 days. War losses : *Callahan, Colhoun, Little.*

Appearance Notes.—The majority of active units have tripod mast as in *McNair* (see photo top right).

CLARENCE K. BRONSON   1957, R. M. Scott

Name	Launched	Completed	Name	Launched	Completed
Albert W. Grant	29 May 1943	24 Nov. 1943	Irwin	31 Oct. 1943	14 Feb. 1944
Bearss	25 July 1943	12 Apr. 1944	Jarvis	14 Feb. 1944	3 June 1944
Benham	29 Aug. 1943	20 Dec. 1943	John Hood	23 Oct. 1943	7 June 1944
Bennion	4 July 1943	14 Dec. 1943	Kidd	28 Feb. 1943	23 Apr. 1944
Black	28 Mar. 1943	21 May 1943	Knapp	10 July 1943	15 Sep. 1943
Bullard	28 Feb. 1943	9 Apr. 1943	Lewis Hancock	1 Aug. 1943	29 Sep. 1943
Bryant	29 May 1943	4 Dec. 1943	McDermut	17 Oct. 1943	19 Nov. 1943
Caperton	24 July 1943	30 July 1943	McGowan	14 Nov. 1943	20 Nov. 1943
Cassin Young	12 Sep. 1943	31 Dec. 1943	McNair	14 Nov. 1943	30 Dec. 1943
Charles J. Badger	3 Apr. 1943	23 July 1943	Marshall	29 Aug. 1943	16 Oct. 1943
Chauncey	28 Mar. 1943	31 May 1943	Melvin	17 Oct. 1943	24 Nov. 1943
Clarence K. Bronson	18 Apr. 1943	11 June 1943	Mertz	11 Sep. 1943	19 Nov. 1943
Cogswell	5 June 1943	17 Aug. 1943	Monssen	29 Oct. 1943	12 Feb. 1944
Colahan	2 May 1943	23 Aug. 1943	Norman Scott	28 Aug. 1943	5 Nov. 1943
Cotten	12 June 1943	24 July 1943	Picking	31 May 1943	21 Sep. 1943
Cushing	30 Sep. 1943	17 Jan. 1944	Porter	13 Mar. 1944	24 June 1944
Dashiell	6 Feb. 1943	20 Mar. 1943	Porterfield	13 June 1943	30 Oct. 1943
Dortch	20 June 1943	7 Aug. 1943	Preston	12 Dec. 1943	20 Mar. 1944
Gatling	20 June 1943	19 Aug. 1943	Remey	24 July 1943	30 Sep. 1943
Gregory	8 May 1944	29 July 1944	Richard P. Leary	6 Oct. 1943	23 Feb. 1944
Halsey Powell	30 June 1943	25 Oct. 1943	Rooks	6 June 1944	2 Sep. 1944
Healy	4 July 1943	3 Sep. 1943	Stockham	25 July 1943	11 Feb. 1944
Heywood L. Edwards	6 Oct. 1943	26 Jan. 1944	Uhlmann	30 July 1943	22 Nov. 1943
Hickox	4 July 1943	10 Sep. 1943	Van Valkenburgh	19 Dec. 1943	2 Aug. 1944
Hopewell	2 May 1943	30 Sep. 1943	Wadleigh	7 Aug. 1943	19 Oct. 1943
Hunt	1 Aug. 1943	22 Sep. 1943	Wedderburn	1 Aug. 1943	9 Mar. 1944
Ingersoll	28 June 1943	31 Aug. 1943			

COTTEN   Added 1957, U.S. Navy. Official

Conversion Notes.—*Black, Caperton, Cogswell, Dortch, Hopewell, John Hood, McGowan, McNair, Picking, Preston, Uhlmann* and many others have 4—5 inch (two forward, two aft), 6—3 inch, 50 cal. AA. (one pair superfiring aft, two pairs between the funnels), 5 torpedo tubes abaft after funnel. A 3-inch director on a tall pedestal replaces 3rd 5-inch in " Q " position. The forward torpedo bank between the funnels was suppressed. These ships have a tripod mast (see photo of *McNair*). All vessels of the class have been or are being similarly rearmed except *Albert W. Grant, Bennion, Bullard, Heywood L. Edwards, Melvin, Mertz, Norman Scott, Richard P. Leary,* which are in reserve and mount their original battery.

COLAHAN.   1944, Lieut. D. Trimingham, R.N.V.R.

CASSIN YOUNG   Added 1961, Giorgio Arra

Escort Destroyers (DDE).
18 Converted "Fletcher" Class.

MURRAY.   *1955, courtesy Godfrey H. Walker, Esq.*

FLETCHER.   *1954, U.S. Navy, Official.*

NICHOLAS (TT now removed).   *1953, U.S. Navy, Official.*

CONY (before conversion).   *1945, U.S. Navy, Official.*

Bath Iron Works Corpn.	*2 Bethlehem (Staten Island)*	*7 Federal S.B. & D.D. Co.*
DDE	**DDE**	**DDE**
507 CONWAY	470 BACHE	445 FLETCHER
508 CONY	471 BEALE	447 JENKINS
510 EATON		498 PHILIP
449 NICHOLAS		446 RADFORD
450 O'BANNON	*2 Consolidated Steel Corpn., Orange, Texas*	499 RENSHAW
468 TAYLOR	576 MURRAY	465 SAUFLEY
517 WALKER	577 SPROSTON	466 WALLER

Displacement :	2,050 tons *standard* (2,940 tons *full load*)
Dimensions :	376½ (o.a.) × 39½ × 18 (*max.*) feet
Guns :	2 —5 inch, 38 cal., 4—3 inch, 50 cal. in twin mountings
Tubes :	4—23 inch fixed in after deckhouse
A S weapons:	I ahead throwing rocket launcher in place of "B" turret, or trainable Hedgehog (D.C. racks to be replaced by 2 side-launching torpedo racks)
Machinery :	G.E. geared turbines. 2 shafts. S.H.P. : 60,000 = 35 kts.
Boilers :	4 Babcock & Wilcox
Complement :	300 (war)

General Notes.—Former destroyers (DD). Converted to serve as close-support convoy escorts. 9 under 1948 Programme, 3 under 1949 Programme, 6 under 1950 Programme. *Anthony*, DD 515, and *Charles Ausburn*, DD 570 were also to have been converted, but are still DDs (see preceding page.)

CONY (after conversion). TT now removed.   *1952, U.S. Navy, Official.*

Name	Laid down	Launched	Completed	Name	Laid down	Launched	Completed
Bache	19 Nov. 1941	27 June 1942	14 Nov. 1942	O'Bannon	3 Mar. 1941	14 Mar. 1942	26 June 1942
Beale	19 Dec. 1941	25 Aug. 1942	23 Dec. 1942	Philip	7 May 1942	13 Oct. 1942	20 Nov. 1942
Conway	5 Nov. 1941	16 Aug. 1942	9 Oct. 1942	Radford	2 Oct. 1941	3 May 1942	21 July 1942
Cony	24 Dec. 1941	16 Aug. 1942	30 Oct. 1942	Renshaw	7 May 1942	13 Oct. 1942	4 Dec. 1942
Eaton	17 Mar. 1942	20 Sep. 1942	4 Dec. 1942	Saufley	27 Jan. 1942	19 July 1942	28 Aug. 1942
Fletcher	2 Oct. 1941	3 May 1942	30 June 1942	Sproston	1 Apr. 1942	31 Aug. 1942	18 May 1943
Jenkins	22 Nov. 1941	21 June 1942	31 July 1942	Taylor	28 Aug. 1941	7 June 1942	28 Aug. 1942
Murray	16 Mar. 1942	16 Aug. 1942	20 Apr. 1943	Walker	31 Aug. 1942	31 Jan. 1943	2 Apr. 1943
Nicholas	3 Mar. 1942	19 Feb. 1942	4 June 1942	Waller	12 Feb. 1942	15 Aug 1942	30 Sep. 1942

NICHOLAS (before conversion).   *1943, U.S. Navy, Official.*

NICHOLAS (after FRAM II conversion)   *1961, United States Navy, Official*

JENKINS (after FRAM II conversion, equipped with DASH)   *1962, courtesy Mr. W. H. Davis*

66 Allen M. Sumner Class.

HAYNSWORTH.

1944, U.S. Navy Official.

JOHN A. BOLE.

Added 1950, U.S. Navy, Official.

Displacement: 2,200 tons. Dimensions: 376½ × 40⅝ × — feet. Guns: **6**—5 inch, 38 cal. **12**—40 mm. AA. Machinery: Geared turbines. 2 shafts. S.H.P.: 60,000 = over 35 kts. These ships are faster than any destroyers previously constructed, and have a larger radius of action. Type is an enlargement and modification of *Fletcher* design. Cost reported to be $8,000,000 each, exclusive of armament, etc.

Note.—Distinctive numbers are 692/694, 696/709, 722/725, 727/732, 734/740, 744/762, 770/781, 857. Those marked (M) were fitted for minelaying and re-rated as DM 23–34 during war in Pacific. War losses: *Cooper, Drexler, Mannert L. Abele, Meredith.*

17 *Bath Iron Works Corpn.*:

Adams (M) (July 23, 1944)
Barton (Oct. 10, 1943)
Collett (March 5, 1944)
De Haven (Jan. 9, 1944)
Harry F. Bauer (M)
Hyman (April 8, 1944)
Laffey (Nov. 21, 1943)
Lyman K. Swenson
　(Feb. 12, 1944)
Maddox (March 19, 1944)
Mansfield (Jan. 29, 1944)
O'Brien (Dec. 8, 1943)
Purdy (May 7, 1944)
Robert H. Smith (M)
　(May 25, 1944)
Shannon (M) (June 24, 1944)
Thomas E. Fraser (M)
　(June 10, 1944)
Tolman (M) (Aug. 13, 1944)
Walke (Oct. 27, 1943)

6 *Bethlehem Steel Co. (S. Francisco)*:

Buck (March 11, 1945)
Henley (April 8, 1945)
John W. Thomason
　(Sept. 29, 1944)
Lofberg (Aug. 12, 1944)
Putnam (March 26, 1944)
Strong (April 22, 1944)

8 *Bethlehem Steel Co. (S. Pedro)*:

Aaron Ward (M) (May 5, 1944)
Bristol (Oct. 29, 1944)
Gwin (M) (April 9, 1944)
Hugh W. Hadley
　(July 16, 1944)
James C. Owens
Lindsey (M) (March 5, 1944)
Lowry (Feb. 6, 1944)
Willard Keith

13 *Bethlehem Steel Co.*
(Staten Island):

Alfred A. Cunningham
　(Aug. 3, 1944)
Beatty (Nov. 30, 1944)
Blue (Nov. 28, 1943)
Brush (Dec. 28, 1943)
Frank E. Evans (Oct. 3, 1944)
Harry E. Hubbard
　(March 24, 1944)
Henry A. Wiley
　(April 21, 1944)
J. William Ditter (M)
　(July 4, 1944)
John A. Bole (Nov. 1, 1944)
John R. Pierce (Sept. 1, 1944)
Samuel L. Moore
　(Feb. 23, 1944)
Shea (M) (May 20, 1944)
Taussig (Jan. 25, 1944)

17 *Federal S.B. & D.D. Co.*:

Allen M Sumner
　(Dec. 15, 1943)
Ault (March 26, 1944)
Borie (July 4, 1944)
Charles S. Sperry
　(March 13, 1944)
Compton (Sept. 17, 1944)
English (Feb. 27, 1944)
Gainard (Sept. 17, 1944)
Hank (May 21, 1944)
Harlan R. Dickson
　(Dec. 17, 1944)
Haynsworth (April 15, 1944)
Hugh Purvis (Dec. 17, 1944)
Ingraham (Jan. 16, 1944)
John W. Weeks (May 21, 1944)
Moale (Jan. 16, 1944)
Soley (Sept. 8, 1944)
Waldron (March 26, 1944)
Wallace L. Lind
　(June 14, 1944)

5 *Todd Pacific Shipyards*:

Douglas H. Fox (1944)
Massey (Aug. 19, 1944)
Robert K. Huntington
　(Dec. 10, 1944)
Stormes (Jan. 1945)
Zellars

BORIE (note new 3-inch AA. guns)

1953, Lieut. Aldo Fraccaroli.

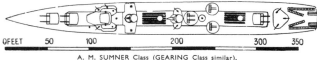

0 FEET　50　100　200　300　350

A. M. SUMNER Class (GEARING Class similar).

Note to Plan.—After set of tubes has been removed.

Notes.—Twelve of this class (two scrapped) were fitted for minelaying and re-rated as DM 23–34 (see a ater page). These ships, as well as those of "Gearing" class, are apt to roll badly when light. They have a larger radius of action than any destroyers previously constructed. Type is an enlargement and modification of *Fletcher* design. Cost reported to be $8,000,000 each, exclusive of armament, etc. *Blue, Alfred A. Cunningham, Frank E. Evans* and *Harry E. Hubbard* used for A.S.W. training. War losses: *Cooper, Drexler, Mannert L. Abele, Meredith.* Sold: *Hugh W. Hadley.*

Special Note.—*Brush* and *Mansfield* struck floating mines off North Korea, Sept. 27, 1950 and Sept. 30, 1950, respectively. Though both ships sustained underwater damage, they made port.

SOLEY

1957, Giorgio Arra

WALDRON

1958, courtesy Ian S. Pearsall, Esq.

33 Destroyers (DD): Modernised "Allen M. Sumner" Class (FRAM II)

		Name	No.	Builder	Launched	Commissioned
Displacement, tons	2 200 standard; 3 320 full load	*ALLEN M SUMNER	DD 692	Federal SB & DD Co	15 Dec 1943	26 Jan 1944
Length, feet (metres)	376·5 (114·8) oa	*MOALE	DD 693	Federal SB & DD Co	16 Jan 1944	26 Feb 1944
Beam, feet (metres)	40·9 (12·4)	*INGRAHAM	DD 694	Federal SB & DD Co	16 Jan 1944	10 Mar 1944
Draft, feet (metres)	19 (5·8)	*CHARLES S. SPERRY	DD 697	Federal SB P DD Co	13 Mar 1944	17 May 1944
Guns	6—5 in (127 mm) 38 calibre dual-purpose	*AULT	DD 698	Federal SB & DD Co	26 Mar 1944	31 May 1944
ASW Weapons	2 triple torpedo launchers (Mk 32)	*WALDRON	DD 699	Federal SB & DD Co	26 Mar 1944	8 June 1944
	2 fixed torpedo tubes (Mk 25)	*WALLACE L. LIND	DD 703	Federal SB & DD Co	14 June 1944	8 Sep 1944
	2 ahead-firing hedgehogs	*BORIE	DD 704	Federal SB & DD Co	4 July 1944	21 Sep 1944
	2 Drone anti-Submarine Helicopters (DASH)	*HUGH PURVIS	DD 709	Federal SB & DD Co	17 Dec 1944	1 Mar 1945
Main engines	2 geared turbines; 60 000 shp; 2 shafts.	*WALKE	DD 723	Bath Iron Works Corp	27 Oct 1943	21 Jan 1944
		*LAFFEY	DD 724	Bath Iron Works Corp	21 Nov 1943	8 Feb 1944
		*O'BRIEN	DD 725	Bath Iron Works Corp	8 Dec 1943	25 Feb 1944
Boilers	4	*DE HAVEN	DD 727	Bath Iron Works Corp	9 Jan 1944	31 Mar 1944
Speed, knots	34	*MANSFIELD	DD 728	Bath Iron Works Corp	29 Jan 1944	14 Apr 1944
Complement	274 (14 officers, 260 enlisted men)	*LYMAN K. SWENSON	DD 729	Bath Iron Works Corp	12 Feb 1944	2 May 1944
		*COLLETT	DD 730	Bath Iron Works Corp	5 Mar 1944	16 May 1944
		*BLUE	DD 744	Bethlehem (Staten Island)	28 Nov 1943	20 Mar 1944
		*TAUSSIG	DD 746	Bethlehem (Staten Island)	25 Jan 1944	20 May 1944
		*ALFRED A. CUNNINGHAM	DD 752	Bethlehem (Staten Island)	3 Aug 1944	23 Nov 1944
		*FRANK E. EVANS	DD 754	Bethlehem (Staten Island)	3 Oct 1944	2 Feb 1945
		*JOHN A. BOLE	DD 755	Bethlehem (Staten Island)	1 Nov 1944	3 Mar 1945
		*PUTNAM	DD 757	Bethlehem (San Francisco)	26 Mar 1944	12 Oct 1944
		*STRONG	DD 758	Bethlehem (San Francisco)	23 Apr 1944	8 Mar 1945
		*LOFBERG	DD 759	Bethlehem (San Francisco)	12 Aug 1944	26 Apr 1945
		*JOHN W. THOMASON	DD 760	Bethlehem (San Francisco)	30 Sep 1944	
		*BUCK	DD 761	Bethlehem (San Francisco)	11 Mar 1945	
		*LOWRY	DD 770	Bethlehem (San Pedro)	6 Feb 1944	23 July 1944
		*JAMES C. OWENS	DD 776	Bethlehem (San Pedro)	1 Oct 1944	17 Feb 1945
		*ZELLARS	DD 777	Todd Pacific Shipyards	19 July 1944	25 Oct 1944
		*MASSEY	DD 778	Todd Pacific Shipyards	19 Aug 1944	24 Nov 1944
		*DOUGLAS H. FOX	DD 779	Todd Pacific Shipyards	30 Sep 1944	26 Dec 1944
		*STORMES	DD 780	Todd Pacific Shipyards	4 Nov 1944	27 Jan 1945
		*ROBERT K. HUNTINGTON	DD 781	Todd Pacific Shipyards	5 Dec 1944	3 Mar 1945

The "Allen M. Sumner" class originally included 57 destroyers and 12 destroyer minelayers (DM). The above 33 ships have been extensively modernised under the FRAM II programme. The unmodernised destroyers of this type which remain as well as the minelayers are listed separately.

ARMAMENT-DESIGN. As built these ships had a pole mast and carried an armament of six 5 inch guns (twin mounts), 12 40 mm AA guns (2 quad, 2 twin), 10 20 mm AA guns (single), and 10 21 inch torpedo tubes (quin). After World War II the after bank of torpedo tubes was replaced by an additional quad 40 mm mount. All 40 mm and 20 mm guns were replaced subsequently by six 3 inch guns (3 twin, 2 single) and a tripod mast was installed to support heavier radar antennas. The 3 inch guns and remaining torpedo tubes were removed during FRAM overhaul.

MODERNISATION. All of these ships have been modernised under the Fleet Rehabilitation and Modernisation (FRAM II) programme. New ASW torpedo launchers were installed as were facilities for operating ASW helicopters and variable depth sonar (VDS). Machinery was overhauled, new electronic equipment was installed, and living and working spaces were rehabilitated.

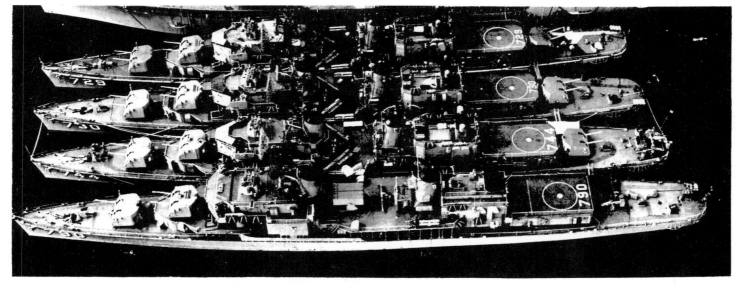

SHELTON (DD 790), BLUE (DD 744), COLLETT (DD 730)   LAYMAN K. SWENSON (DD 729)   *United States Navy*

"ALLEN M. SUMNER" (FRAM II) CLASS

All surviving ships of the 70-destroyer "Allen M. Sumner" class have been stricken or transferred to other navies. Between 1943 and 1945, 58 destroyers and 12 minelayers were completed to this design. See 1974-1975 and earlier editions for characteristics.

Ships of this class serve in the navies of Argentina, Brazil, Chile, Colombia, Greece, Iran, South Korea, Taiwan, Turkey and Venezuela.

MASSEY (DD 778) (see previous page)   *Evelyne Kayne*

HARRY F BAUER

Added 1957, U.S. Navy, Official

10 "Smith" Class
Modified "Allen M. Sumner" Class

DM		DM	
27 ADAMS (ex-DD 739)		23 ROBERT H. SMITH	
33 GWIN (ex-DD 772)		(ex-DD 735)	
26 HARRY F. BAUER		25 SHANNON	
(ex- DD 738)		(ex-DD 737)	
29 HENRY A. WILEY		30 SHEA (ex-DD 750)	
(ex-DD 749)		24 THOMAS E. FRASER	
32 LINDSEY (ex-DD 771)		(ex-DD 736)	
		28 TOLMAN (ex-DD 740)	

General

Modified Destroyers of the "Allen M. Sumner" class. Later fitted with tripod masts. All out of commission. in reserve.

Reclassification

Formerly classified at Light Minelayers (DM). Reclassified as Destroyer Minelayers (DM) in Feb. 1955.

Displacement:	2,250 tons standard (3,375 tons full load)
Dimensions:	376½×41×19 (max.) feet
Guns:	6—5 inch, 38 cal., 12—40 mm. AA., 11—20 mm. AA., (some were rearmed with 6—3 inch, 50 cal. in place of 40 mm.)
Mines:	80 (capacity)
Machinery:	Geared turbines. 2 shafts. S.H.P.: 60,000 = 34 kts.
Boilers:	4 Babcock & Wilcox
Oil fuel:	650 tons
Radius:	6,000 miles at 15 kts.
Complement:	275 (15 officers, 260 men). Accommodation for 22 officers, 300 men

Building

DM 23-28 were built by Bath Iron Works, DM 29-30 by Bethlehem Steel Co., Staten Island, N.Y., and DM 32-33 by Bethlehem Steel Co., San Pedro, California.

Photograph

A port broadside view of *Gwin* appears in the 1956-57 to 1960-61 editions.

Disposals

J. Wm. Ditter, DM 31, and Aaron Ward, DM 24 were scrapped.

Name	Launched	Completed
Adams	23 July 1944	10 Oct. 1944
Gwin	9 Apr. 1944	30 Sep. 1944
Harry F. Bauer	9 July 1944	22 Sep. 1944
Henry A . Wiley	21 Apr. 1944	31 Aug. 1944
Lindsey	5 Mar. 1944	20 Aug. 1944
Robert H. Smith	25 May 1944	4 Aug. 1944
Shannon	24 June 1944	8 Sep. 1944
Shea	20 May 1944	30 Sep. 1944
Thomas E. Fraser	10 June 1944	22 Aug. 1944
Tolman	13 Aug. 1944	27 Oct. 1944

Destroyers (DD).

57 + 5 "Gearing" Class.

13 Bath Iron Works

DD
826 AGERHOLM
845 BAUSSELL
838 ERNEST G. SMALL
(June 9, 1945)
842 FISKE (Sept. 8, 1945)
836 GEORGE K. MACKENZIE
(May 13, 1945)
840 GLENNON (July 14, 1945)
841 NOA (July 30, 1945)
846 OZBOURN
844 PERRY (Nov. 25, 1945)
839 POWER (June 30, 1945)
837 SARSFIELD (May 27, 1945)
843 WARRINGTON (Sept. 27, 1945)
848 WITEK (Feb. 2, 1946)

4 Bethlehem, Quincy
853 CHARLES H. ROAN
(March 15, 1946)
850 JOSEPH P. KENNEDY JR.
(July 26, 1945)
852 LEONARD F. MASON
851 RUPERTUS (Sept. 21, 1945)

3 Bethlehem, S. Francisco
*766 LANSDALE
*767 SEYMOUR D. OWENS
763 WILLIAM C. LAWE
(Feb. 25, 1945)

10 Bethlehem, Staten Island

DD
869 ARNOLD J. ISBELL
(Aug. 6, 1945)
868 BROWNSON (July 7, 1945)
865 CHARLES R. WARE
(April 12, 1945)
866 CONE (May 10, 1945)
870 FECHTELER (Sept. 19, 1945)
872 FOREST ROYAL (Jan. 17, 1946)
864 HAROLD J. ELLISON
(March 14, 1945)
863 STEINAKER (Feb. 13, 1945)
867 STRIBLING (June 8, 1945)
862 VOGELGESANG (Jan. 15, 1945)

11 Consolidated Steel Corpn.
887 BRINKLEY BASS (May 26, 1945)
817 CORRY (July 28, 1945)
884 FLOYD B. PARKS
(March 31, 1945)
885 JOHN R. CRAIG (April 14, 1945)
821 JOHNSTON (Oct. 19, 1945)
890 MEREDITH (June 28, 1945)
889 O'HARE (June 22, 1945)
886 ORLECK (May 12, 1945)
822 ROBERT H. McCARD
(Nov. 9, 1945)
823 SAMUEL B. ROBERTS
888 STICKELL (June 16, 1945)

11 Federal S.B. & D.D. Co.

DD
*720 CASTLE
711 EUGENE A. GREENE
(March 18, 1945)
710 GEARING (Feb. 18, 1945)
712 GYATT (April 15, 1945)
718 HAMNER (Nov. 24, 1945)
713 KENNETH D. BAILEY
(June 17, 1945)
717 THEODORE E. CHANDLER
(Oct. 20, 1945)
715 WILLIAM M. WOOD
(July 29, 1945)
714 WILLIAM R. RUSH
(July 8, 1945)
716 WILTSIE (Aug. 31, 1945)
*721 WOODROW R. THOMPSON

10 Todd Pacific Shipyards
789 EVERSOLE (Dec. 7, 1945)
783 GURKE (ex-John A. Bole,
Feb. 15, 1945)
785 HENDERSON (May 28, 1945)
788 HOLLISTER (Oct. 9, 1945)
787 JAMES E. KYES (Aug. 4, 1945)
784 McKEAN (March 31, 1945)
786 RICHARD B. ANDERSON
(July 7, 1945)
782 ROWAN (Dec. 29, 1944)
*791 SEAMAN
790 SHELTON

*No expenditure authorised on *Castle, Seaman, Lansdale, Seymour D. Owens,* or *Woodrow R. Thompson* during current financial year. Construction of all 5 units was suspended in June 1946, so that some might be completed to modified design.

Displacement:	2,425 tons (3,300 tons full load)
Dimensions:	390½ (o.a.) × 40¾ × 19 (max.) feet
Guns:	6—5 inch, 38 cal. (Witek and Sarsfield, 4—5 inch, with super-imposed twin 5-inch turret forward replaced by ahead throwing weapon), 12 to 16—40 mm. AA., 4 to 11—20 mm. AA.
Tubes:	5—21 inch (quintupled)
Machinery:	Geared turbines. 2 shafts. S.H.P.: 60,000 = 35 kts.
Boilers:	4
Complement:	350 (war)

CHARLES H. ROAN.

1950, U.S. Navy, Official.

General Notes.—These ships are enlarged editions of "Allen M. Sumner" type, with extra 14 feet length, necessitated by additional installations of various kinds. 24 units converted to Radar Picket Destroyers (DDR), 8 to Hunter-killer Destroyers (DDE formerly DDK) and 7 to Escort Destroyers (DDE) I being completed to a new design (DD), and I re-designated (AG)—see preceding and following pages. Cancellations: 809–816, 854–856, 891–926, *Abner Read* (769), *Hoel* (768).

Constructional Notes.—It is reported that heavy weights carried on forecastle have resulted in cracks developing in hulls in way of forward turrets. There are also reports of "A" turret face being stove in by heavy seas and having to be reinforced.

105 Gearing Class.

GEARING.

1944, U.S. Navy Official.

GEORGE K. MACKENZIE.

1950, U.S. Navy, Official.

GEARING

1964, *United States Navy, Official* (direct from U.S.S. *Gearing*, courtesy Commanding Officer)

STRIBLING (FRAM conversion, ASROC)

1962, *Mr. W. H. Davis*

SAMUEL B. ROBERTS

1964, *A. & J. Pavia*

Escort Destroyers (DDE).
8 "Carpenter" Class.

CARPENTER.

1950, courtesy Newport News Shipbuilding & Dry Dock Co.

ROBERT A. OWENS.

1950, *U.S. Navy, Official.*

KEPPLER.

1953, *Skyfotos.*

1 Bath Iron Works Corpn.	4 Bethlehem, S. Pedro	1 Consolidated Steel Corpn. (Completed by Newport News)
DDE	**DDE**	**DDE**
827 ROBERT A. OWENS (15 July 1946)	**858 FRED T. BERRY** (28 Jan. 1945)	**825 CARPENTER** (30 Dec. 1945)
	861 HARWOOD (24 May 1945)	
2 Bethlehem, S. Francisco	**860 McCAFFERY** (12 April 1945)	
765 KEPPLER (24 June 1946)	**859 NORRIS** (25 Feb. 1945)	
764 LLOYD THOMAS (5 Oct. 1945)		

Displacement :	2,425 tons, *Carpenter* and *Robert A. Owens* 2,500 tons (over 3,300 tons *full load*)
Dimensions :	390½ (o.a.) × 40½ × 19 (max.) feet
Guns :	4 to 6—3 inch (twin-automatic), 2 large ahead throwing A/S weapons, 2 or 3 hedgehogs or zebras in *Carpenter* and *Robert A. Owens*; 4—5 inch, 8—3 inch, 1 large A/S weapon in others
Tubes :	5—21 inch (none in *Carpenter* and *Robert A. Owens*)
Machinery :	Geared turbines. 2 shafts. S.H.P. : 60,000 = 35 kts.
Boilers :	4
Complement :	350

Notes.—Originally designed as units of the "Gearing" class. *Robert A. Owens* and *Carpenter*, towed to Newport News in 1947, were completed as Hunter-killer Destroyers on Nov. 5, 1949 and Dec. 15, 1949, respectively. The remaining six were converted under the 1949 Programme. Launch dates above. They were rated as DDKs until March 4, 1950, when the DDE and DDK types merged. *Robert A. Owens* had six 3-inch guns. In *Carpenter* the forward 5-inch twin turret was removed, a pair of twin 3-inch automatic weapons substituted, and a bandstand containing a large weapon of the hedgehog type in place of the superimposed 5-inch turret. It is understood that additional multiple A/S mortars have been installed amidships and aft, and a number of Sono-buoys are included in the equipment. These are dropped in a diamond shaped pattern of five (one in the middle) outlining an area in which a submarine is suspected to be in operation. They contain microphones, and by keeping track of which picks up the loudest sound the destroyer can determine in which direction and at what speed and depth the submarine is moving. Once this is detected the destroyer moves in rapidly for the kill, laying down a pattern of depth bombs.

General Note on DDEs (former DDKs).—Vessels have been completed as such and converted from existing DDs in order to form groups for the purpose of long- and short-range interception of submarines before they can attack convoys,

LLOYD THOMAS.

1953, *U.S. Navy, Official.*

2 "CARPENTER (FRAM I)" CLASS: DESTROYERS (DD)

Name	No.	Builders	Laid down	Launched	Commissioned	F/S
CARPENTER	DD 825	Consolidated Steel Corporation, Orange, Texas	30 July 1945	30 Dec 1945	15 Dec 1949	NRF
ROBERT A. OWENS	DD 827	Bath Iron Works Corporation	29 Oct 1945	15 July 1946	5 Nov 1949	NRF

Displacement, tons: 2 425 standard; 3 540 full load
Dimensions, feet (metres): 390·5 × 41 × 20·9
(119 × 12·5 × 6·4)
Guns: 2—5 in (127 mm) 38 (twin Mk 38)
A/S weapons: 1 ASROC 8-tube launcher;
2 triple torpedo tubes (Mk 32)
Main engines: 2 geared turbines (General Electric)
60 000 shp; 2 shafts
Boilers: 4 (Babcock & Wilcox)
Speed, knots: 33
Complement: 282 (12 officers, 176 enlisted active duty; 8 officers, 86 enlisted reserve)

These ships were laid down as units of the "Gearing" class. Their construction was suspended after World War II until 1947 when they were towed to the Newport News Shipbuilding and Dry Dock Co for completion as DDK. As specialised ASW ships they mounted 3-in (76 mm) guns in place of 5-in mounts and were armed with improved ahead-firing anti-submarine weapons (Hedgehogs and Weapon Able/Alfa); special sonar equipment installed. The DDK and DDE classifications were merged in 1950 with both of these ships being designated DDE on 4 March 1950. Upon being modernised to the FRAM I configuration they were reclassified DD on 30 June 1962. Both of these ships are assigned to Naval Reserve training;

they are manned by composite active duty and reserve crews. *Carpenter* is to be deleted in FY 1981.

Electronics: These ships have electronic warfare antennas on a smaller tripod mast forward of their second funnel.

Fire control: One Mk 56 gunfire control system, one Mk 114 ASW FCS, Mk 1 target designation system and one SPG 35 fire control radar.

Radar: Search: SPS 10 and 40.

Sonar: SQS 23.

CARPENTER

CARPENTER   Added 1957, U.S. Navy, Official

ROBERT A. OWENS (DD 827)   1964, United States Navy

ROBERT A. OWENS (DD 827)   1969, A. & J. Pavia

Escort Destroyers (DDE).

8 Converted " Gearing " Class.

BASILONE.   1954, A. & J. Pavia.

BASILONE.   1950, U.S. Navy, Official.

EPPERSON.   Added 1954, U.S. Navy, Official.

Bath Iron Works Corpn.

837 SARSFIELD
847 ROBERT L. WILSON

4 Consolidated Steel Corpn.

DDE
824 BASILONE
819 HOLDER
818 NEW
820 RICH

1 Bethlehem, Staten Island

DDE
871 DAMATO

1 Federal S.B. & D.D. Co.

DDE
719 EPPERSON

Displacement :	2,425 tons (*standard*) (3,300 tons *full load*)
Dimensions :	390½ (*o.a.*) × 40⅝ × 19 (*max.*) feet
Guns :	4—5 inch, 38 cal., 4 to 10—3 inch, 50 cal. (*Basilone* 4—3 inch, others 6—3 inch)
A/S weapons :	Ahead throwing A/S weapon in place of forward superimposed 5-inch twin turret
Tubes :	Removed in *Basilone* and *Epperson*. Others 5—21 inch
Machinery :	Geared turbines. 2 shafts. S.H.P. : 60,000 = 35 kts.
Boilers :	4
Complement :	350 (war)

Notes.—Former destroyers (DD). Builders above. *Basilone* and *Epperson*, both completed at Bath, were two long suspended units of the " Gearing " class. They were converted to ASW (for anti-submarine warfare) and completed as escort destroyers. They are armed with new weapons and equipped with improved sonar and other electronic gear. Five other units were 4-gun " Gearings " redesignated DDEs on 4 March, 1950. The remaining 4-gun " Gearing " (*Sarsfield*) was redesignated DDE in 1953.

Name	Launched	Completed	Name	Launched	Completed
Basilone	21 Dec. 1945	21 July 1949	*New*	18 Aug. 1945	4 Apr. 1946
Damato	21 Nov. 1945	26 Apr. 1946	*Rich*	5 Oct. 1945	2 July 1946
Epperson	22 Dec. 1945	18 Mar. 1949	*Robert L. Wilson*	5 Jan. 1946	28 Mar. 1946
Holder	25 Aug. 1945	17 May 1946	*Sarsfield*	27 May 1945	31 July 1945

HOLDER.   1953, Skyfotos

ROBERT L. WILSON (before conversion)   Added 1963, Skyfotos

DAMATO   Added 1957, U.S. Navy, Official

Radar Picket Destroyers (DDR).
36 Converted " Gearing " Class.

WILLIAM R. RUSH (note radar aft).   1954, A. & J. Pavia.

VESOLE.   1954, A. & J. Pavia.

15 Bath Iron Works Corpn. DDR	14 Consolidated Steel Corpn. DDR	2 Bethlehem, Staten Island DDR
807 BENNER	881 BORDELON	870 FECHTELER
835 CHARLES P. CECIL	817 CORRY	863 STEINAKER
805 CHEVALIER	874 DUNCAN	
808 DENNIS J. BUCKLEY	880 DYESS	4 Federal S.B. & D.D. Co.
838 ERNEST G. SMALL	882 FURSE	711 EUGENE A. GREENE
830 EVERETT F. LARSON	873 HAWKINS	713 KENNETH D. BAILEY
842 FISKE	875 HENRY W. TUCKER	715 WILLIAM M. WOOD
742 FRANK KNOX	879 LEARY	714 WILLIAM R. RUSH
831 GOODRICH	883 NEWMAN K. PERRY	
832 HANSON	889 O'HARE	1 Todd Pacific Shipyards
833 HERBERT J. THOMAS	877 PERKINS	784 McKEAN
806 HIGBEE	876 ROGERS	
829 MYLES C. FOX	888 STICKELL	
743 SOUTHERLAND	878 VESOLE	
834 TURNER		

NEWMAN K. PERRY.   1953, A. & J. Pavia.

Displacement :   2,425 tons (3,300 tons full load)
Dimensions :   390½ (o.a.) × 40½ × .19 (max.) feet
Guns :   6—5 inch, 38 cal., 12—40 mm. AA. (or 6—3 inch, 50 cal. AA. in place of 40 mm.)
A S weapons :   2 Hedgehogs (Depth Charge Racks and K-guns to be replaced with 2 side-'aunchir.g torpedo racks)
Machinery :   Geared turbines, 2 shafts. S.H.P. : 60,000 = 35 kts.
Boilers :   4
Complement :   305 (peace), 350 (war)

General Notes.—Builders see above. Similar to " Gearing " class. Main differences are that the torpedo tubes are removed. Tripod radar mainmast tower removed and radar located aft of No. 2 stack in most ships (see photos of Vesole and William R. Rush above). All converted from DDs to DDRs and fitted with early warning radar to serve as long-range-warning picket vessels against aircraft.

Gunnery Notes.—Twin mounted 3-inch guns have replaced 40 mm. and 20 mm. guns in Bordelon, Chevalier, Corry, Dyess, Herbert J. Thomas, Southerland.

TURNER.   Added 1953, U.S. Navy, Official.

Name	Launched	Completed	Name	Launched	Completed
Benner	20 Nov. 1944	13 Feb. 1945	Henry W. Tucker	8 Nov. 1944	12 Mar. 1945
Bordelon	3 Mar. 1945	5 June 1945	Herbert J. Thomas	25 Mar. 1945	29 May 1945
Charles P. Cecil	22 Apr. 1945	29 June 1945	Higbee	12 Nov. 1944	27 Jan. 1945
Chevalier	29 Oct. 1944	9 Jan. 1945	Kenneth C. Bailey	17 June 1945	31 July 1945
Corry	28 July 1945	26 Feb. 1946	Leary	20 Jan. 1945	7 May 1945
Dennis J. Buckley	20 Dec. 1944	2 Mar. 1945	McKean	31 Mar. 1945	9 June 1945
Duncan	27 Oct. 1944	25 Feb. 1945	Myles C. Fox	13 Jan. 1945	20 Mar. 1945
Dyess	26 Jan. 1945	21 May 1945	Newman K. Perry	17 Mar. 1945	26 July 1945
Ernest G. Small	9 June 1945	21 Aug. 1945	O'Hare	22 June 1945	29 Nov. 1945
Eugene A. Greene	18 Mar. 1945	8 June 1945	Perkins	7 Dec. 1944	5 Apr. 1945
Everett F. Larson	28 Jan. 1945	6 Apr. 1945	Rogers	20 Nov. 1944	26 Mar. 1945
Fechteler	19 Sep. 1945	2 Mar. 1946	Southerland	5 Oct. 1944	22 Dec. 1944
Fiske	8 Sep. 1945	28 Nov. 1945	Steinaker	13 Feb. 1945	26 May 1945
Frank Knox	17 Sep. 1944	11 Dec. 1944	Stickell	16 June 1945	26 Sep. 1945
Furse	9 Mar. 1945	10 July 1945	Turner	8 Apr. 1945	12 June 1945
Goodrich	25 Feb. 1945	24 Apr. 1945	Vesole	29 Dec. 1944	23 Apr. 1945
Hanson	11 Mar. 1945	11 May 1945	William M. Wood	29 July 1945	23 Nov. 1945
Hawkins	7 Oct. 1944	10 Feb. 1945	William R. Rush	8 July 1945	21 Sep. 1945

BORDELON (broadside silhouette) note mainmast   1957, Captain Aldo Fraccaroli

TURNER (after FRAM II conversion)   1962, courtesy Mr. W. H. Davis

17 "GEARING (FRAM I)" CLASS: DESTROYERS (DD)

Name	No.	Builders	Laid down	Launched	Commissioned	F/S
SOUTHERLAND*	DD 743	Bath Iron Works Corporation	27 May 1944	5 Oct 1944	22 Dec 1944	NRF
WILLIAM C. LAWE*	DD 763	Bethlehem, San Francisco	12 Mar 1944	21 May 1945	18 Dec 1946	NRF
McKEAN*	DD 784	Todd Pacific Shipyards	15 Sep 1944	31 Mar 1945	9 June 1945	NRF
HENDERSON	DD 785	Todd Pacific Shipyards	27 Oct 1944	28 May 1945	4 Aug 1945	NRF
CORRY*	DD 817	Consolidated Steel Corporation	5 Apr 1945	28 July 1945	26 Feb 1946	NRF
JOHNSTON*	DD 821	Consolidated Steel Corporation	6 May 1945	19 Oct 1945	10 Oct 1946	NRF
ROBERT H. McCARD*	DD 822	Consolidated Steel Corporation	20 June 1945	9 Nov 1945	26 Oct 1946	NRF
FISKE*	DD 842	Bath Iron Works Corporation	9 Apr 1945	8 Sep 1945	28 Nov 1945	NRF
VOGELGESANG	DD 862	Bethlehem, Staten Island	3 Aug 1944	15 Jan 1945	28 Apr 1945	NRF
STEINAKER	DD 863	Bethlehem, Staten Island	1 Sep 1944	13 Feb 1945	26 May 1945	NRF
HAROLD J. ELLISON*	DD 864	Bethlehem, Staten Island	3 Oct 1944	14 Mar 1945	23 June 1945	NRF
CONE*	DD 866	Bethlehem, Staten Island	30 Nov 1944	10 May 1945	18 Aug 1945	NRF
DAMATO*	DD 871	Bethlehem, Staten Island	10 May 1945	21 Nov 1945	27 Apr 1946	NRF
ROGERS*	DD 876	Consolidated Steel Corporation	3 June 1944	20 Nov 1944	26 Mar 1945	NRF
DYESS*	DD 880	Consolidated Steel Corporation	17 Aug 1944	26 Jan 1945	21 May 1945	NRF
NEWMAN K. PERRY	DD 883	Consolidated Steel Corporation	10 Oct 1944	17 Mar 1945	26 July 1945	NRF
ORLECK	DD 886	Consolidated Steel Corporation	28 Nov 1944	12 May 1945	15 Sep 1945	NRF

* To be deleted in FY 1981

Displacement, tons: 2 425 standard; 3 480 to 3 520 full load
Dimensions, feet (metres): 390·5 × 41·2 × 19
(119 × 12·6 × 5·8)
Guns: 4—5 in (127 mm)/38 (twin Mk 38)
A/S weapons: 1 ASROC 8-tube launcher;
2 triple torpedo tubes (Mk 32)
Main engines: 2 geared turbines (General Electric; Westinghouse in DD 743, 822, 871, 880);
60 000 shp; 2 shafts
Boilers: 4 (Babcock & Wilcox)
Speed, knots: 32·5
Range, miles: 5 800 at 15 knots
Complement: 307 (12 officers, 176 enlisted active duty; 7 officers, 112 enlisted reserve)

WILLIAM C. LAWE   *1978, L. and L. van Ginderen*

The US Navy survivors of the several hundred destroyers constructed in the USA during World War II.
The "Gearing" class initially covered hull numbers DD 710-721, 742, 743, 763-769, 782-791, 805-926. Forty-nine of these ships were cancelled in 1945 (DD 768, 769, 809-816, 854-856, and 891-926); four ships were never completed and were scrapped in the 1950s; *Castle* (DD 720), *Woodrow R. Thompson* (DD 721), *Lansdale* (DD 766), and *Seymour D. Owens* (DD 767).
Two similar ships completed to a modified design after World War II are listed separately as the "Carpenter" class.
All ships are assigned to Naval Reserve training and are manned by composite active duty-reserve crews.

Armament-Design: As built, these ships had a pole mast and carried an armament of six 5-in guns (twin mounts), 12—40 mm guns (2 quad, 2 twin), 11—20 mm guns (single), and ten 21-in torpedo tubes (quin). After World War II, the after bank of tubes was replaced by an additional quad 40 mm mount. All 40 mm and 20 mm guns were replaced subsequently by six 3-in guns (2 twin, 2 single) and a tripod mast was installed to support heavier radar antennae. The 3-in guns and remaining anti-ship torpedo tubes were removed during FRAM modernisation.

Electronics: Electronic warfare equipment fitted to most ships.

Engineering: During November 1974 *Johnston* conducted experiments using liquefied coal as fuel in one boiler (Project Seacoal).

Fire control: Single Mk 37 gunfire control system, Mk 114 ASW FCS (Mk 111 in DD 763 and 785) and Mk 5 target designation system.

CHARLES R. WARE (DD 865)   *1967, United States Navy*

Helicopters: Fitted to operate the Drone Anti-Submarine Helicopter (DASH) during FRAM modernisation—never carried.

Modernisation: All of these ships underwent extensive modernisation under the Fleet Rehabilitation and Modernisation (FRAM I) programme between 1961 and 1965.
There are two basic FRAM I configurations: Some ships had twin 5-in mounts in "A" and "B" positions and Mk 32 torpedo launchers abaft second funnel; others have twin 5-in mounts in "A" and "Y" positions and Mk 32 launchers on 01 level in "B" position.

Radar: SPS 10, 37 or 40.

Sonar: SQS 23.

Transfers: Ships of this class serve with Argentina, Brazil, Ecuador, Greece, South Korea, Pakistan, Peru Taiwan and Turkey.

WILSON (DD 847)   *1964, United States Navy*

2 Frigates (DL)
2 Guided Missile Destroyers (DDG)

"Mitscher" Class

Name	No.	Builder	Laid down	Launched	DL Comm.	DDG Comm.
*MITSCHER	DDG 35 (ex-DL 2)	Bath Iron Works	3 Oct 1949	26 Jan 1952	16 May 1953	20 Apr 1968
*JOHN S. McCAIN	DDG 36 (ex-DL 3)	Bath Iron Works	24 Oct 1949	12 July 1952	12 Oct 1953	Oct 1968
*WILLIS A. LEE	DL 4	Bethlehem Steel Co. (Quincy)	1 Nov 1949	26 Jan 1952	28 Sep 1954	
*WILKINSON	DL 5	Bethlehem Steel Co (Quincy)	1 Feb 1950	23 Apr 1952	29 July 1954	

Displacement, tons	3675 standard; 4 730 full load
Length, feet (metres)	493 (150·3) oa
Beam, feet (metres)	50 (15·2)
Draft, feet (metres)	26 (7·9)
Missiles DDG	1 single Tartar surface-to-air launcher
Guns DDG	1—5 in (127 mm) 54 calibre dual-purpose
DD	2—5 in (127 mm) 54 calibre dual-purpose (see Gunnery notes)
ASW Weapons DDG	1 ASROC 8-tube launcher
DL/DDG	2 triple torpedo launchers
Main engines	2 geared turbines (General Electric in DDG 35 and DDG 36; Westinghouse in DL 4 and DL 5); 80 000 shp; 2 shafts
Speed, knots	35
Boilers DDG	4—1 225 psi (86·1 kg/cm²) (Combustion Engineering)
DL	4—1 200 psi (84·4 kg/cm²) Foster Wheeler

CLASSIFICATION. These ships were originally classified as Destroyers (DD 927-930, respectively); reclassified as Destroyer Leaders (DL 2-5) on 9 Feb 1951 while under construction; the symbol DL was changed to Frigate on 1 Jan 1955. The Mitscher and John S. McCain were reclassified as the DDG 35 and DDG 36 on 15 Mar 1967.

DESIGN. The "Mitscher" class was the first group of destroyer-type ships built by the United States after World War II. The design provided for potent anti-air and anti-submarine capabilities in a ship which could accompany fast carrier task forces. Accommodations and communications equipment provided for a destroyer flotilla or squadron commander.

CONVERSION. The Mitscher and John S. McCain were converted to guided missile destroyers at the Philadelphia Naval Shipyard. The Mitscher began her conversion in March 1966 and the John S. McCain in June 1966. At this writing the Willis A. Lee and Wilkinson have not been scheduled for missile conversion.

GUNNERY. As built these ships each mounted two 5 inch/54 calibre guns and four 3 inch/50 calibre guns (plus two 12·75 inch Weapons Able ASW rocket launchers and four fixed 21 inch ASW torpedo tubes). Rapid-fire 3 inch/70 calibre guns were mounted in place of the original 3 inch weapons in 1957-58. After twin 3 inch mount subsequently removed to provide helicopter platform.

ELECTRONICS. SQS-26 bow-mounted sonar installed.

JOHN S. McCAIN   1962, courtesy Mr. W. H. Davis

WILKINSON   1964, United States Navy, Official

JOHN S. McCAIN (DDG 36)   1969, United States Navy

MITSCHER (DDG 35)   1969, United States Navy

10 "COONTZ" CLASS: GUIDED MISSILE DESTROYERS (DDG)

Name	No.	Builders	Laid down	Launched	Commissioned	F/S
FARRAGUT	DDG 37 (ex-DLG 6)	Bethlehem Co, Quincy, Mass	3 June 1957	18 July 1958	10 Dec 1960	AA
LUCE	DDG 38 (ex-DLG 7)	Bethlehem Co, Quincy, Mass	1 Oct 1957	11 Dec 1958	20 May 1961	AA
MACDONOUGH	DDG 39 (ex-DLG 8)	Bethlehem Co, Quincy, Mass	15 Apr 1958	9 July 1959	4 Nov 1961	AA
COONTZ	DDG 40 (ex-DLG 9)	Puget Sound Naval Shipyard	1 Mar 1957	6 Dec 1958	15 July 1960	AA
KING	DDG 41 (ex-DLG 10)	Puget Sound Naval Shipyard	1 Mar 1957	6 Dec 1958	17 Nov 1960	AA
MAHAN	DDG 42 (ex-DLG 11)	San Francisco Naval Shipyard	31 July 1957	7 Oct 1959	25 Aug 1960	AA
DAHLGREN	DDG 43 (ex-DLG 12)	Philadelphia Naval Shipyard	1 Mar 1958	16 Mar 1960	8 Apr 1961	AA
WILLIAM V. PRATT	DDG 44 (ex-DLG 13)	Philadelphia Naval Shipyard	1 Mar 1958	16 Mar 1960	4 Nov 1961	AA
DEWEY	DDG 45 (ex-DLG 14)	Bath Iron Works, Maine	10 Aug 1957	30 Nov 1958	7 Dec 1959	AA
PREBLE	DDG 46 (ex-DLG 15)	Bath Iron Works, Maine	16 Dec 1957	23 May 1959	9 May 1960	PA

Displacement, tons: 4 150/4 580 standard; 5 709/5 907 full load
Dimensions, feet (metres): 512·5 × 52·5 × 23·4
(156·2 × 16 × 7·1)
Missiles: SSM; Harpoon to be fitted (already in DDG 37, 40 and 41); SAM; 40 Standard-ER (SM2) (1 twin Mk 10 Launcher)
Gun: 1—5 in (127 mm)/54 (Mk 42) (see Gunnery note)
A/S weapons: 1 ASROC 8-tube launcher;
2 triple torpedo tubes (Mk 32)
Main engines: 2 geared turbines; 85 000 shp; 2 shafts
Boilers: 4 (Foster-Wheeler in DDG 37-39; Babcock & Wilcox in DDG 40-46)
Speed, knots: 33
Fuel, tons: 900
Range, miles: 5 000 at 20 knots
Flag accommodations: 19 (7 officers, 12 enlisted men)
Complement: 377 (21 officers, 356 enlisted men)

DDG 37-42 were authorised in the FY 1956 programme; DDG 43-46 in the FY 1957 programme. Average cost per ship was $52 million.
Although now classified as "destroyers", these ships have many of the capabilities of the larger US cruiser classes, including the Terrier/Standard-ER missile system and Naval Tactical Data System (NTDS).

Classification: *Farragut, Luce* and *MacDonough* were initially classified as frigates (DL 6-8, respectively); changed to guided missile frigate (DLG) 6-8 on 14 November 1956. The first ship ordered as a missile frigate was *Coontz* which became the name ship for the class. All ten ships were classified as guided missile frigates (DLG 6-15) from completion until 30 June 1975 when reclassified as guided missile destroyers (DDG 37-46).

Design: These ships were the only US guided missile "frigates" with separate masts and funnels. They have aluminium superstructures to reduce weight and improve stability. Early designs for this class had a second 5-in gun mount in the "B" position; design revised when ASROC launcher was developed.
Helicopter landing area on stern, but no hangar and limited support capability.

Electronics: *King* and *Mahan* along with the aircraft carrier *Oriskany* (CV 34) were the first ships fitted with the Naval Tactical Data System (NTDS), conducting operational evaluation of the equipment in 1961-62. NTDS now in all ships.
Fitted with OE-82 satellite communications antenna, SSR-1 receiver and WSC-3 transceiver.

Engineering: De Laval turbines in DDG 37-39 and DDG 46; Allis-Chalmers turbines in DDG 40-45.

Fire control: Two Mk 76 missile fire control systems, one Mk 68 gunfire control system, one SPG 53A and two SPG-55B weapon control radars (plus two SPG 50—*Macdonough* only). One Mk 11 WDS and one Mk 111 ASW FCS.

Gunnery: The original four 3-in/50 guns were removed during modernisation.
King was fitted with the 20 mm Phalanx Mk 15 CIWS for at-sea evaluation from August 1973 to March 1974.
Two 40 mm saluting guns fitted.

Modernisation: These ships have been modernised to improve their Anti-Air Warfare (AAW) capabilities. Superstructure enlarged to provide space for additional electronic equipment, including NTDS (previously fitted in *King* and *Mahan*); improved Tacan installed, improved guidance system for Standard missiles (SPG 55 fire control radar), and larger ship's service turbo generators fitted. *Farragut* also had improved ASROC reload capability provided (with additional structure forward of bridge) and second mast increased in height. (Other ships do not carry ASROC reloads).
All ships modernised at Philadelphia Naval Shipyard, except *Mahan* at Bath Iron Works, Bath, Maine, and *King* at Boland Machine & Manufacturing Co, New Orleans, Louisiana between 1969 and 1977.
Cost of modernisation was $39 million per ship in the FY 1970 conversion programme.

Radar: (After modernisation).
3D search: SPS 48 (SPS 52 in *King* and *Pratt*).
Search: SPS 10 and 37.

Rockets: Mk 36 Chaffroc (RBOC) system to be fitted.

Sonar: SQS 23.

FARRAGUT (DLG 6)   1970, United States Navy, PHC F. W. Gotavco

PREBLE   3/1980, Dr. Giorgio Arra

COONTZ (with Harpoon)   3/1979, Michael D. J. Lennon

14 Destroyers (DD) / 4 Guided Missile Destroyers (DDG) — "Forrest Sherman" Class

Name	No.	Builder	Laid down	Launched	DD Comm.	DDG Comm
*FORREST SHERMAN	DD 931	Bath Iron Works	27 Oct 1953	5 Feb 1955	9 Nov 1955	
*BARRY	DD 933	Bath Iron Works	15 Mar 1954	1 Oct 1955	31 Aug 1956	
*DAVIS	DD 937	Bethlehem Steel Co (Quincy)	1 Feb 1955	28 Mar 1956	28 Feb 1957	
*JONAS INGRAM	DD 938	Bethlehem Steel Co (Quincy)	15 June 1955	8 July 1956	19 July 1957	
*MANLEY	DD 940	Bath Iron Works	10 Feb 1955	12 Apr 1956	1 Feb 1957	
*DU PONT	DD 941	Bath Iron Works	11 May 1955	8 Sep 1956	1 July 1957	
*BIGELOW	DD 942	Bath Iron Works	6 July 1955	2 Feb 1957	8 Nov 1957	
*BLANDY	DD 943	Bethlehem Steel Co (Quincy)	29 Dec 1955	19 Dec 1956	26 Nov 1957	
*MULLINNIX	DD 944	Bethlehem Steel Co (Quincy)	5 Apr 1956	18 Mar 1957	7 Mar 1958	
*HULL	DD 945	Bath Iron Works	12 Sep 1956	10 Aug 1957	3 July 1958	
*EDSON	DD 946	Bath Iron Works	3 Dec 1956	1 Jan 1958	7 Nov 1958	
*MORTON	DD 948	Ingalls Shipbuilding Corp	4 Mar 1957	23 May 1958	26 May 1959	
*RICHARD S. EDWARDS	DD 950	Puget Sound Bridge & DD Co	20 Dec 1956	24 Sep 1957	5 Feb 1959	
*TURNER JOY	DD 951	Puget Sound Bridge & DD Co.	30 Sep 1957	5 May 1958	3 Aug 1959	
*DECATUR	DDG 31 (ex-DD 936)	Bethlehem Steel Co (Quincy)	13 Sep 1954	15 Dec 1955	7 Dec 1956	29 Apr 1967
*JOHN PAUL JONES	DDG 32 (ex-DD 932)	Bath Iron Works	18 Jan 1954	7 May 1955	5 Apr 1956	23 Sep 1967
*PARSONS	DDG 33 (ex-DD 949)	Ingalls Shipbuilding Corp	17 June 1957	19 Aug 1958	29 Oct 1959	3 Nov 1967
*SOMERS	DDG 34 (ex-DD 947)	Bath Iron Works	4 Mar 1957	30 May 1958	3 Apr 1959	10 Feb 1968

Displacement tons
DD 931-944   2 780 standard ; 3 950 full load
DD 945-951   2 850 standard ; 4 050 full load
Length, feet (metres)
DD 931-944   418·4 (127·5) oa
DD 945-951   418 (127·4) oa
Beam, feet (metres)
DD 931-944   45·2 (13·8)
DD 945-951   45 (13·7)
Draft, feet (metres)   20 (6·1)
Missiles DDG   1 single Tartar surface-to-air launcher
Guns   DD   2—5 in (127 mm) 54 calibre dual-purpose ; 2—3 in (76 mm) 50 calibre anti-aircraft (see *Armament* notes)
DDG   1—5 in (127 mm) 54 calibre dual-purpose
ASW Weapons   1 ASROC 8-tube launcher
2 triple torpedo launchers (Mk 32)
Main engines   2 geared turbines (Westinghouse in DD 931-933 ; General Electric in others) ; 70 000 shp ; 2 shafts
Boilers   4 (Babcock & Wilcox in DD 931-933, 940-942, 945-947, 950-195 ; Foster Wheeler in others)
Speed   33 knots

These ships were the first US destroyers of post-World War II design and construction. They have all had their anti-submarine capabilities improved and four have been fitted with an anti-aircraft missile system (see below). They were authorised in the Fiscal Year 1952-1956 new construction programmes.
(The hull number DD 934 was reserved for the ex-Japanese *Hanazuki*, DD 935 for the ex-German *T 35*, and DD 939 for the ex-German *Z-39*, all 1945 war prizes which were discarded).

ARMAMENT. As built all 18 ships of this class had three single 5 inch guns, two twin 3 inch mounts, four fixed 21 inch ASW torpedo tubes (amidships), two ASW hedgehogs (forward of bridge), and depth charge racks.

CONVERSION. Four of these ships have been converted to guided missile destroyers, the *Decatur* beginning conversion at the Boston Naval Shipyard on 15 June 1965, the *John Paul Jones* at the Philadelphia Naval Shipyard on 2 Dec 1965, the *Parsons* at the Long Beach (California) Naval Shipyard on 30 June 1965, and the *Somers* at the San Francisco Bay Naval Shipyard on 30 Mar 1966. During conversion all existing armament was removed except forward 5 inch gun ; two triple ASW torpedo launchers installed forward of bridge ; two heavy lattice radar masts fitted ; ASROC mounted aft of second stack ; single Tartar Mk. 13 launcher installed aft (system weighs approximately 135 000 pounds). Plans for additional "Forrest Sherman" class DDG conversions were dropped ; *Turner Joy* was to be the next DDG. Original DDG conversion plans provided for Drone Anti-Submarine Helicopter (DASH) facilities ; however, ASROC substituted in all four ships as DASH lost favour with Navy.

CLASSIFICATION. The *Decatur* was reclassified as DDG 31 on 15 Sep 1966 ; the *John Paul Jones, Somers*, and *Parsons* as DDGs on 6 Mar 1967.

DESIGN. The entire superstructures of these ships are of aluminium to obtain maximum stability with minimum displacement. All living spaces are air conditioned. The *Decatur* and later ships have higher bows ; the *Hull* and later ships have slightly different bow designs. The *Barry* had her sonar dome moved forward in 1959 and a stem anchor fitted.

ELECTRONICS. SQS-23 sonar installed.

GUNNERY. With original armament of one 5 inch mount forward and two 5 inch mounts aft, these were the first US warships with more firepower aft than forward.

Modernisation: Eight ships of this class were extensively modified in 1967-1971 to improve their anti-submarine capabilities: *Barry, Davis, Du Pont* at the Boston Naval Shipyard ; *Jonas Ingram, Manley, Blandy* at the Philadelphia Naval Shipyard ; and *Morton, Richard S. Edwards* at the Long Beach (California) Naval Shipyard. During modernisation the anti-submarine torpedo tubes installed forward of bridge (on 01 level), deckhouse aft of second funnel extended to full width of ship, ASROC launcher installed in place of after gun mounts on 01 level, and variable depth sonar fitted at stern. Six ships of this class were not modernised because of increased costs.

Radar: Search: SPS 10, 37 or 40.

Sonar: SQS-23 (bow mounted in *Barry*, the first US ship so fitted).
VDS in ASW ships.

FORREST SHERMAN (as completed)   *United States Navy*

SOMERS (as DD 947)   *1965, United States Navy*

MANLEY (DD 940)   *United States Navy*

JOHN PAUL JONES (see next page)   1957, *Wright & Logan*

HULL with 8 inch gun forward   4/1975, *USN*

DU PONT (ASW modernisation)   1976, *Wright and Logan*

DECATUR (DDG 31)   1972, *United States Navy, PH3 D. L. Pierce*

PARSONS (DDG 33)   1968 *United States Navy*

PARSONS   8/1979, *Dr. Giorgio Arra*

23 "CHARLES F. ADAMS" CLASS: GUIDED MISSILE DESTROYERS (DDG)

Name	No.	Builders	Laid down	Launched	Commissioned	F/S
CHARLES F. ADAMS	DDG 2	Bath Iron Works, Bath, Maine	16 June 1958	8 Sep 1959	10 Sep 1960	AA
JOHN KING	DDG 3	Bath Iron Works, Bath, Maine	25 Aug 1958	30 Jan 1960	4 Feb 1961	AA
LAWRENCE	DDG 4	New York Shipbuilding Corporation	27 Oct 1958	27 Feb 1960	6 Jan 1962	AA
CLAUDE V. RICKETTS	DDG 5	New York Shipbuilding Corporation	18 May 1959	4 June 1960	5 May 1962	AA
BARNEY	DDG 6	New York Shipbuilding Corporation	18 May 1959	10 Dec 1960	11 Aug 1962	PA
HENRY B. WILSON	DDG 7	Defoe Shipbuilding Co	28 Feb 1958	23 Apr 1959	17 Dec 1960	PA
LYNDE McCORMICK	DDG 8	Defoe Shipbuilding Co	4 Apr 1958	9 Sep 1960	3 June 1961	PA
TOWERS	DDG 9	Todd Shipyards Inc, Seattle	1 Apr 1958	23 Apr 1959	6 June 1961	PA
SAMPSON	DDG 10	Bath Iron Works, Bath, Maine	2 Mar 1959	9 Sep 1960	24 June 1961	AA
SELLERS	DDG 11	Bath Iron Works, Bath, Maine	3 Aug 1959	9 Sep 1960	28 Oct 1961	AA
ROBISON	DDG 12	Defoe Shipbuilding Co	23 Apr 1959	27 Apr 1960	9 Dec 1961	PA
HOEL	DDG 13	Defoe Shipbuilding Co	1 June 1959	4 Aug 1960	16 June 1962	PA
BUCHANAN	DDG 14	Todd Shipyards Inc, Seattle	23 Apr 1959	11 May 1960	7 Feb 1962	PA
BERKELEY	DDG 15	New York Shipbuilding Corporation	1 June 1960	29 July 1961	15 Dec 1962	PA
JOSEPH STRAUSS	DDG 16	New York Shipbuilding Corporation	27 Dec 1960	9 Dec 1961	20 Apr 1963	PA
CONYNGHAM	DDG 17	New York Shipbuilding Corporation	1 May 1961	19 May 1962	13 July 1963	AA
SEMMES	DDG 18	Avondale Marine Ways Inc	18 Aug 1960	20 May 1961	10 Dec 1962	AA
TATTNALL	DDG 19	Avondale Marine Ways Inc.	14 Nov 1960	26 Aug 1961	13 Apr 1963	AA
GOLDSBOROUGH	DDG 20	Puget Sound Bridge & Dry Dock Co	3 Jan 1961	15 Dec 1961	9 Nov 1963	PA
COCHRANE	DDG 21	Puget Sound Bridge & Dry Dock Co	31 July 1961	18 July 1962	21 Mar 1964	PA
BENJAMIN STODDERT	DDG 22	Puget Sound Bridge & Dry Dock Co	11 June 1962	8 Jan 1963	12 Sep 1964	PA
RICHARD E. BYRD	DDG 23	Todd Shipyards Inc, Seattle	12 Apr 1961	6 Feb 1962	7 Mar 1964	AA
WADDELL	DDG 24	Todd Shipyards Inc, Seattle	6 Feb 1962	26 Feb 1963	28 Aug 1964	PA

Displacement, tons: 3 370 standard; 4 500 full load
Dimensions, feet (metres): 437 × 47 × 20 *(133·2 × 14·3 × 6·1)*
Missiles: SSM; Harpoon to be fitted;
  DDG 2-14; SAM; 42 Tartar (1 twin Mk 11 launcher)
  DDG 15-24; SAM; 40 Tartar (1 single Mk 13 launcher) (see *Missile* note)
Guns: 2—5 in *(127 mm)*/54 (single Mk 42)
A/S weapons: 1 ASROC 8-tube launcher;
  2 triple torpedo tubes (Mk 32)
Main engines: 2 geared steam turbines (General Electric in DDG 2, 3, 7, 8, 10-13, 15-22; Westinghouse in DDG 4-6, 9, 14, 23, 24); 70 000 shp; 2 shafts
Boilers: 4 (Babcock & Wilcox in DDG 2, 3, 7, 8, 10-13, 20-22; Foster-Wheeler in DDG 4-6, 9, 14, 23, 24; Combustion Engineering in DDG 15-19)
Speed, knots: 30
Complement: 354 (24 officers, 330 enlisted men)

DDG 2-9 were authorised in FY 1957 new construction programme, DDG 10-14 in FY 1958, DDG 15-19 in FY 1959, DDG 20-22 in FY 1960, DDG 23-24 in FY 1961.

Classification: The first eight ships were to be a continuation of "Hull" class DDs and carried hull numbers DD 952-959. Redesigned as Guided Missile Destroyers and assigned DDG numbers.

Design: These ships were built to an improved "Forrest Sherman" class design with aluminium superstructures and a high level of habitability including air conditioning in all living spaces. DDG 20-24 have stem anchors because of sonar arrangement.
Several ships have been modified with an extension of the bridge structure on the starboard side on the 02 level.

Electronics: Fitted with OE-82 satellite communications antenna, SSR-1 receiver and WSC-3 transceiver.

Fire control: Two Mk 74 MFCS, one Mk 68 GFCS (to be replaced by Mk 86), one Mk 4 weapon system (to be replaced by Mk 13 which is already fitted in DDG 9, 12, 15 and 21), one SPG 51C, one SPG 53A weapon control radars and one Mk 114 ASW FCS.

Missiles: Ships equipped with either launcher can load, direct, and fire about six missiles per minute. *Lawrence* and *Hoel* fitted in 1972-1973 with multiple launcher for Chaparral (MIM-72A) for operational testing, in addition to their Tartar launcher.

Modernisation: Beginning in FY 1980 it was planned to give certain ships of this class a mid-life modernisation, officially known as "DDG upgrade". This modernisation was to include installation of the Harpoon SSM/Standard ARM missile system replacing the existing EW arrangements with the Anti-Ship Missile Defense (ASMD) EW system (including SLQ 31/32 (V) systems), replacing the radar with SPS 40C/D and SPS 52B, installing SPS 58 radar installation of an Integrated Automatic Detection and Tracking System (SYS 1), replacing the radar receivers in the CIC with UYA 4 consoles for real-time tactical data processing, replacing the Mk 4 WDS by Mk 13, installing Mk 86 FCS for the Standard ARM missiles and gun armament and fitting two SQQ 23 sonar domes with control units.
Originally all twenty three ships of the class were to be modernised but the programme was cut to only ten. These were to be DDG 3, 10, 16-22 and 24 under FY 1980-83. Congress rejected the whole of this programme but the navy plans to carry out this modernisation in DDG 15-24 during two overhauls using "Fleet Maintenance" funds. The remaining thirteen ships are due to be deleted beginning in the late 1980s.
Each modernisation will take 20-24 months and cost $125·7 to 178·5 million (1979$). $167 million for advance procurement was authorised under the FY 1979 programme.

Radar: 3D search: SPS 39 (SPS 52 being fitted).
Search: SPS 10 and 37 (DDG 2-14).
SPS 10 and 40 (DDG 15-24); SPS 39.

Rockets: Mk 36 Chaffroc (RBOC) will be fitted.

Sonar: SQS 23 (bow-mounted) (DDG 20-24).
SQS 23 (hull-mounted) (remainder).

LYNDE McCORMICK (DDG 8)   *United States Navy*

HENRY B. WILSON (DDG 7)   *1969, United States Navy*

BARNEY (DDG 6)   *1971, United States Navy*

BUCHANAN (DDG 14)

United States Navy

TATTNALL

1976, Michael D. J. Lennon

BUCHANAN

9/1979, Dr. Giorgio Arra

HENRY B. WILSON

1/1980, Dr. Giorgio Arra

26 + 5 "SPRUANCE" CLASS: DESTROYERS (DD)

Name	No.	Builders	Laid down	Launched	Commissioned	F/S
SPRUANCE	DD 963	Ingalls Shipbuilding Corporation	17 Nov 1972	10 Nov 1973	20 Sep 1975	AA
PAUL F. FOSTER	DD 964	Ingalls Shipbuilding Corporation	6 Feb 1973	23 Feb 1974	21 Feb 1976	PA
KINKAID	DD 965	Ingalls Shipbuilding Corporation	19 Apr 1973	25 May 1974	10 July 1976	PA
HEWITT	DD 966	Ingalls Shipbuilding Corporation	23 July 1973	24 Aug 1974	25 Sep 1976	PA
ELLIOTT	DD 967	Ingalls Shipbuilding Corporation	15 Oct 1973	19 Dec 1974	22 Jan 1976	PA
ARTHUR W. RADFORD	DD 968	Ingalls Shipbuilding Corporation	14 Jan 1974	1 Mar 1975	16 Apr 1977	AA
PETERSON	DD 969	Ingalls Shipbuilding Corporation	29 Apr 1974	21 June 1975	9 July 1977	AA
CARON	DD 970	Ingalls Shipbuilding Corporation	1 July 1974	24 June 1975	1 Oct 1977	AA
DAVID R. RAY	DD 971	Ingalls Shipbuilding Corporation	23 Sep 1974	23 Aug 1975	19 Nov 1977	PA
OLDENDORF	DD 972	Ingalls Shipbuilding Corporation	27 Dec 1974	21 Oct 1975	4 Mar 1978	PA
JOHN YOUNG	DD 973	Ingalls Shipbuilding Corporation	17 Feb 1975	7 Feb 1976	20 May 1978	PA
COMTE DE GRASSE	DD 974	Ingalls Shipbuilding Corporation	4 Apr 1975	26 Mar 1976	5 Aug 1978	AA
O'BRIEN	DD 975	Ingalls Shipbuilding Corporation	9 May 1975	8 July 1976	3 Dec 1977	PA
MERRILL	DD 976	Ingalls Shipbuilding Corporation	16 June 1975	1 Sep 1976	11 Mar 1978	PA
BRISCOE	DD 977	Ingalls Shipbuilding Corporation	21 July 1975	15 Dec 1976	3 June 1978	AA
STUMP	DD 978	Ingalls Shipbuilding Corporation	25 Aug 1975	29 Jan 1977	19 Aug 1978	AA
CONOLLY	DD 979	Ingalls Shipbuilding Corporation	29 Sep 1975	19 Feb 1977	14 Oct 1978	AA
MOOSBURGGER	DD 980	Ingalls Shipbuilding Corporation	3 Nov 1975	23 July 1977	16 Dec 1978	AA
JOHN HANCOCK	DD 981	Ingalls Shipbuilding Corporation	16 Jan 1976	29 Oct 1977	1 Mar 1979	AA
NICHOLSON	DD 982	Ingalls Shipbuilding Corporation	20 Feb 1976	11 Nov 1977	12 May 1979	AA
JOHN RODGERS	DD 983	Ingalls Shipbuilding Corporation	12 Aug 1976	25 Feb 1978	14 July 1979	AA
LEFTWICH	DD 984	Ingalls Shipbuilding Corporation	12 Nov 1976	8 Apr 1978	25 Aug 1979	PA
CUSHING	DD 985	Ingalls Shipbuilding Corporation	27 Dec 1976	17 June 1978	21 Sep 1979	PA
HARRY W. HILL	DD 986	Ingalls Shipbuilding Corporation	3 Jan 1977	10 Aug 1978	11 Nov 1979	PA
O'BANNON	DD 987	Ingalls Shipbuilding Corporation	21 Feb 1977	25 Sep 1978	15 Dec 1979	AA
THORN	DD 988	Ingalls Shipbuilding Corporation	29 Aug 1977	14 Nov 1978	16 Feb 1980	AA
DEYO	DD 989	Ingalls Shipbuilding Corporation	14 Oct 1977	27 Jan 1979	1980	Bldg
INGERSOLL	DD 990	Ingalls Shipbuilding Corporation	5 Dec 1977	10 Mar 1979	1980	Bldg
FIFE	DD 991	Ingalls Shipbuilding Corporation	6 Mar 1978	1 May 1979	1980	Bldg
FLETCHER	DD 992	Ingalls Shipbuilding Corporation	24 Apr 1978	16 June 1979	1980	Bldg
—	DD 997	Ingalls Shipbuilding Corporation	1980	1981	1983	Ord

Displacement, tons: 5 830 light; 7 810 full load
Dimensions, feet (metres): 563·2 × 55·1 × 29, sonar—19 keel
(171·7 × 16·8 × 8·8—5·8)
Aircraft: 1 SH-3 Sea King or 2 SH-2D LAMPS helicopters
Missiles: SSM; Harpoon being fitted (already in DD 965 973, 975-977, 981 and 988);
SAM; one NATO Sea Sparrow; Mk 29 launcher
Guns: 2—5 in (127 mm)/54 (single Mk 45)
A/S weapons: 1 ASROC 8-tube launcher
2 triple torpedo tubes (Mk 32)
Main engines: 4 General Electric LM2500 gas turbines; 80 000 shp; 2 shafts
Speed, knots: 33
Oil fuel, tons: 1 400
Range, miles: 6 000 at 20 knots
Complement: 296 (24 officers, 272 enlisted men)

According to official statements, ''the primary mission of these ships is anti-submarine warfare including operations as an integral part of attack carrier task forces.''
The FY 1969 new construction programme requested funding for the first five ships of this class, although, funds were denied by Congress. In the FY 1970 programme Congress approved funds for five ships, but increasing costs forced the Department of Defense to construct only three ships under the FY 1970 programme (DD 963-965); six ships were authorised in the FY 1971 programme (DD 966-971); seven ships (DD 972-978) in the FY 1972 programme; seven ships (DD 979-985) in the FY 1974 programme, and seven ships (DD 986-992) in the FY 1975 programme.
DD 997 was added to the Navy's FY 1978 programme by Congress and is not Navy initiated. Known as an ''air capable'' *Spruance*, she was to have an enlarged hangar and flight deck and be able to accommodate up to four LAMPS III ASW helicopters.

Originally two of this class were added by the US Senate. The House of Representatives failed to approve funds for any of this class. During the House-Senate Conference about the FY 1978 Military Budget, agreement was reached to provide $310 million for one ship. This sum was authorised with the proviso that no more than this should be spent on this ship. When bids were solicited from shipbuilders should they be over the $310 million, weapons, electronics and other equipment would have to be deleted to bring the cost under the limit.
Since the 1978-79 edition of Jane's the cost of constructing this ship has escalated beyond the $310 million limit imposed by Congress. As a result, to cut costs, the ''air capable'' portions of the design have been reduced and the ship will be constructed as a 31st ''Spruance'' class DD—ordered 27 September 1979 (see 1978-79 edition for illustration of ''air capable'' design).

A/S weapons: The ASROC reload magazine is located under the launcher with the twin-cell launcher nacelles depressing to a vertical position. Capacity 24 rounds. 14 torpedoes carried for Mk 32 tubes.

Design: Extensive use of the modular concept is used to facilitate initial construction and block modernisation of the ships. The ships are highly automated, resulting in about 20 per cent reduction in personnel over a similar ship with conventional systems.

Electronics: Fitted with OE-82 satellite communications antenna, SSR-1 receiver and WSC-3 transceiver.

Engineering: These ships are the first large US warships to employ gas turbine propulsion. Each ship has four General Electric LM2500 marine gas turbine engines, a shaft-power version of the TF39 turbofan aircraft engine, and cp propellers, because gas turbine engines cannot use a reversible shaft. Fitted with advanced self-noise reduction features.
Three gas turbine generators each of 2 000 kW.

Fire control: Mk 116 digital underwater fire control system and one Mk 86 gunfire control system, one Mk 91 missile FCS, one SPG 60 and one SPQ 9 radars.

Gunnery: An improved 5-in/54 (Mk 65) gun is being considered for use in later ships of the class. The ''Spruance'' design can accommodate the 8-in Major Calibre Light-Weight Gun (MCLWG) (Mk 71). There were plans to install that weapon in DD 963, 965, 973, 974, 977, 985-7, 991 during each overhaul after 1980. This plan was cancelled in 1979 when it was decided not to produce this gun owing to its low priority.
600 rounds per gun carried (5-in).
Two 20 mm Phalanx Mk 15 CIWS are planned for installation.

Helicopters. Full helicopter facilities are provided to accommodate the Light Airborne Multi-Purpose System (LAMPS), now the SH-2D helicopter. However, the ship can handle the larger SH-3 Sea King series.

Radar: Search: SPS 40 and SPS 55.
Fire control: SPG 60 and SPQ 9.

Rockets: Mk 36 Chaffroc system is to be fitted in place of Mk 33.

Sonar: SQS 53 (bow-mounted).

Torpedoes: The triple Mk 32 torpedo tubes are inside the superstructure to facilitate maintenance and reloading; they are fired through side ports.

OLDENDORF

3 1980, Dr. Giorgio Arra

HEWITT

10/1975, Litton Industries

PAUL F. FOSTER

4/1976, USN

COMTE DE GRASSE

9/1979, USN (PH3 C. E. Fritz)

ELLIOTT

5/1978, USN (PHC W. E. Kendall)

0 + 4 "KIDD" CLASS GUIDED MISSILE DESTROYERS (DDG)

Name	No.	Builders	Laid down	Launched	Commissioned	F/S
KIDD (ex-Iranian *Kouroosh*)	DDG 993 (ex-US DD 993)	Ingalls Shipbuilding Corp	26 June 1978	11 Aug 1979	Dec 1980	Bldg
CALLAGHAN (ex-iranian *Daryush*)	DDG 994 (ex-US DD 994)	Ingalls Shipbuilding Corp	23 Oct 1978	19 Jan 1980	Apr 1981	Bldg
SCOTT (ex-iranian *Nader*)	DDG 995 (ex-US DD 995, US DD 996)	Ingalls Shipbuilding Corp	12 Feb 1979	Mar 1980	July 1981	Bldg
CHANDLER (ex-Iranian *Anoushirvan*)	DDG 996 (ex-US DD 996, US DD 998)	Ingalls Shipbuilding Corp	7 May 1979	May 1980	Dec 1981	Bldg

Displacement, tons: 8 300 full load, 6 210 light
Dimensions, feet (metres): 563 × 55 × 30 (Sonar)
   (171·6 × 16·8 × 9·1)
Missiles: SAM/ASW; 52 Standard-ER (SM-1)/16 ASROC;
   twin Mk 26 launchers) (see *Missile* notes)
Guns: 2—5 in (127 mm)/54 (single Mk 45)
A/S weapons: 2 triple Mk 32 torpedo tubes; ASROC
Main engines: 4 General Electric LM-2500 gas turbines;
   80 000 shp; 2 shafts
Speed: 30+ knots
Range, miles: 3 300 at 30 knots; 6 000 at 20 knots;
   8 000 at 17 knots
Complement: 338 total (20 officers, 318 enlisted)

Under the approved FY 1979 supplemental budget request the US Navy took over the contracts of four destroyers originally ordered by the Iranian government on 23 April 1978, but cancelled on 3 February 1979 (DDG 995 and 996) and 31 March 1979 (DDG 993 and 994). The four were officially acquired on 25 July 1979 with the signing of the supplemental budget request and the issuing of an Executive Order. These ships are optimised for general warfare instead of anti-submarine warfare as are the "Spruance" class. They will be the most powerful destroyers in the fleet. Originally, it had been planned to build the entire "Spruance" class to this design, but because of "costs" the design was altered to the current plan.

Classification: This class was sometimes referred to as the "DD 993" or "Improved Spruance" class. Originally six were ordered by the Imperial Iranian Government. They were assigned the hull numbers DD 993/998 for accounting purposes. In June 1976, DD 995 and 997 were cancelled. On 23 April 1978, DD 996 and 998 were reclassified DD 995 and 996. On 8 August 1979 DD 993/996 were reclassified DDG 993/996.

Design: The modular concept will be used extensively to facilitate construction and future modernisation.

Electronics: Class will be equipped with Automatic Data Action Systems, also SLQ 32 electronic countermeasures set.

Engineering: The plant duplicates that of the "DD 963" and "CG 47" classes.

Fire control: Will be fitted with two Mk 74 missile fire control systems, two Mk 86 gun fire control systems (SPG 51) and one Mk 116 underwater fire control system.

Gunnery: Two 20 mm CIWS (Mk 15) to be fitted on the O4 level fwd (starboard) and aft (port).

Missiles: The Standard missile load is split between two magazines. Harpoon SSM system and Tomahawk cruise missiles will be fitted.

Radar: Navigation/Surface search: SPS 55.
Air Search: SPS 48.

Rockets: Mk 36 CHAFFROC system to be fitted.

Sonar: SQS 53 (bow-mounted).
SQR 19 (TACTAS).

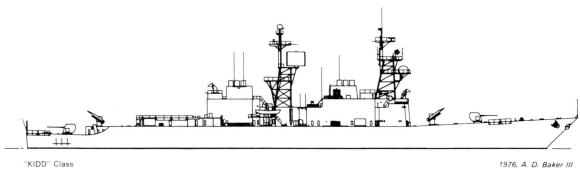

"KIDD" Class   *1976, A. D. Baker III*

65 Evarts Class.

ENGSTROM.
1944, U.S. Navy Official.

21 *Boston Navy Yard :*	31 *Mare Island Navy Yard:*	
10 Bebas	**15** Austin	**30** Martin
260 Cabana	**13** Brennan	**304** Rall
262 Canfield	**19** Burden R. Hastings	**31** Sederstrom
9 Carlson (May, 1943)	**23** Charles R. Greer (Jan. 18, 1943)	**29** Stadtfeld (Sept. 19, 1943)
265 Cloues	**306** Connolly (April 6, 1944)	**33** Tisdale
11 Crouter	**303** Crowley	**24** Whitman (Jan. 10, 1943)
263 Deede	**26** Dempsey (April 22, 1943)	**22** Wileman
261 Dionne (March, 1943)	**14** Doherty	**25** Wintle (April 22, 1943)
264 Elden	**27** Duffy (May, 1943)	
5 Evarts	**16** Edgar G. Chase (Sept. 1942)	5 *Philadelphia Navy Yard :*
7 Griswold	**17** Edward C. Daly	**45** Andres
528 John J. Powers (Feb. 29, 1944)	**34** Eisele	**47** Decker
530 John M. Bermingham (Nov. 17, 1943)	**28** Emery	**48** Dobler
529 Mason (Nov. 17, 1943)	**35** Fair	**49** Doneff
527 O'Toole (Jan. 23, 1944)	**307** Finnegan (ex-H.M.S. Calder, Feb. 22, 1944)	**50** Engstrom
256 Seid	**32** Fleming	
257 Smartt	**18** Gilmore	8 *Puget Sound Navy Yard :*
8 Steele (May 3, 1943)	**305** Halloran	**41** Brackett
258 Walter S. Brown (Feb. 22, 1943)	**21** Harold C. Thomas	**44** Donaldson
259 William C. Miller (Feb. 22, 1943)	**301** Lake	**37** Greiner
6 Wyffels	**20** Le Hardy	**39** Lovering (May 4, 1943)
	302 Lyman	**43** Mitchell (Feb. 8, 1944)
	36 Manlove	**42** Reynolds (June 29, 1943)
		40 Sanders (June 4, 1943)
		38 Wyman

Displacement : 1,150 tons (1,360 tons *full load*). Complement : 260. Dimensions : 283½ (*w.l.*), 289 (*o.a.*), × 35 × — feet. Guns : 3—3 inch, 50 cal., dual purpose, 2—40 mm. AA., 4—20 mm. AA., also D.C.T. (No tubes.) Machinery : Diesel with electric drive. 2 shafts. H.P. 6,000 = 20 kts.

Notes.—This type was built only in Navy Yards. In addition, 32 were delivered to Royal Navy under Lend-lease scheme ; six of these were lost and the remainder returned to U.S.A. for scrapping.

General Notes on Destroyer-Escorts.—Many of these originally ordered were cancelled, i.e., DE 114—128, 28—4300, 373—281, 425—437, 451—507, 511—515, 543—562, 607—632, 645—664, 723—738, 751—762, 772—788, 801—1005. These included *Creamer, Curtis W. Howard, Delbert W. Halsey, Ely, Gaynier, John J. van Buren* also *Myles C. Fox* and *Vogelgesang*, names reallotted to destroyers.

54 Buckley Class.

ROBERT I. PAINE with tubes removed.
1945, U.S. Navy Official.

6 *Bethlehem-Hingham :*	9 *Bethlehem, S. Francisco :*	
575 Ahrens	**643** Damon M. Cummings (April 18, 1944)	**199** Manning (Oct. 1, 1943)
577 Alexander J. Luke (Dec. 28, 1943)	**640** Fieberling	**200** Neuendorf (Oct. 18, 1943)
51 Buckley (Jan. 9, 1943)	**633** Foreman (Aug. 1, 1943)	**210** Otter (Oct. 23, 1943)
57 Fogg (March 20, 1943)	**639** Gendreau (Dec. 12, 1943)	**203** Thomason (Aug. 24, 1943)
59 Foss (April 10, 1943)	**642** Paul G. Baker (March 12, 1944)	**213** William T. Powel (Nov. 27, 1943)
578 Robert I. Paine (Dec. 30, 1943)	**644** Yammen (May 21, 1944)	
	634 Whitehurst (Sept. 5, 1943)	6 *Consolidated Steel Corpn., Orange :*
5 *Bethlehem, Quincy :*	**641** William C. Cole (Dec. 28, 1943)	**795** Gunason (Oct. 17, 1943)
681 Gillette	**638** Willmarth (Nov. 1943)	**800** Jack W. Wilke
679 Greenwood		**796** Major
678 Harmon (July 25, 1943)	8 *Charleston Navy Yard :*	**799** Scroggins
683 Henry R. Kenyon (Oct. 30, 1943)	**202** Eichenberger	**798** Varian
680 Loeser (Sept. 11, 1943)	**201** James E. Craig	**797** Weeden (Oct. 27, 1943)
	204 Jordan (Aug. 24, 1943)	

Buckley Class—*continued.*

10 *Defoe Co. :*	**698** Raby	7 *Philadelphia Navy Yard :*
704 Cronin	**696** Spangler	**217** Coolbaugh (May 29, 1943)
700 Currier		**218** Darby (May 29, 1943)
702 Earl V. Johnson (Jan. 12, 1944)	1 *Dravo Corpn., Pittsburgh :*	**222** Fowler (July 3, 1943)
705 Frybarger	**667** Wiseman	**220** Francis M. Robinson (May 29, 1943)
697 George		**219** J. Douglas Blackwood (May 29, 1943)
703 Holton	2 *Norfolk Navy Yard :*	**221** Solar (May 29, 1943)
699 Marsh	**198** Lovelace (July 4, 1943)	**223** Spangenburg (July 3, 1943)
701 Osmus	**153** Reuben James	

Displacement : 1,400 tons (1,720 tons *full load*). Complement : 220. Dimensions : 306 (*o.a.*) × 36½ × — feet. Guns : 3—3 inch, 50 cal., d.p., 2—40 mm. AA., 6—20 mm. AA., and D.C.T. Tubes : 3—21 inch, in triple mount (removed from some, vide photo of *Robert I. Paine*) Machinery : Turbo-electric. S.H.P. : 12,000 = 28 kts. Fuel : 340 tons. War losses : *Fechteler, Underhill.*

General Notes.—46 ships of this class, originally rated as Destroyer Escorts (DE), were transferred under Lend-Lease scheme to Royal Navy in which they served as frigates. Six of these were lost, and the remainder were returned to U.S.A. for scrapping. Fifty more of "Buckley" class were adapted for duty as Fast Transports or for subsidiary purposes. *Foss, Marsh* and others rigged as power supply ships have two large reels for power cables amidships. *Fechteler* and *Underhill* were lost in the Second World War *Solar* was Destroyed by internal explosion, April 30, 1946.

J. DOUGLAS BLACKWOOD.
Added 1950, U.S. Navy, Official.

FRANCIS M. ROBINSON (3-inch gunned type).
1953, U.S. Navy, Official.

J. DOUGLAS BLACKWOOD (5-inch gunned type).
1952, U.S. Naval Academy,

DARBY (note differences in bridge and superstructure).
1955, courtesy B. L. Devenish-Meares, Esq.

VAMMEN (with mainmast)   1962, courtesy Mr. W. H. Davis

J. DOUGLAS BLACKWOOD   May 1964, Philadelphia, courtesy Dr. Ian S. Pearsall
(5-inch gunned type)

FRYBARGER (3-3inch)   Added 1957, Ted Stone

FRANCIS M. ROBINSON (3-inch gunned type)   1960, courtesy Mr. James Flynn

VAMMEN (A/S)   1959, United States Navy, Official

DARBY (DE 218) (5 inch guns)   1962, United States Navy

MARSH (DE 699) (Power transmission)   United States Navy

177

97 + 2 "Rudderow" Class.

11 Bethlehem-Hingham:

DE
584 CHARLES J. KIMMEL
    (Jan. 15, 1944)
585 DANIEL A. JOY (Jan. 15, 1944)
583 GEORGE A. JOHNSON
580 LESLIE L. B. KNOX
586 LOUGH
581 McNULTY
582 METIVIER
588 PEIFFER
579 RILEY
587 THOMAS F. NICKEL
589 TINSMAN

3 Bethlehem, Quincy:
685 COATES (Dec. 9, 1943)
684 DE LONG
686 EUGENE E. ELMORE
    (Dec. 23, 1943)

10 Boston Navy Yard:
536 BIVIN
531 EDWARD H. ALLEN
533 HOWARD F. CLARK
    (Nov. 8, 1943)
535 LEWIS
538 OSBERG
537 RIZZI
534 SILVERSTEIN (Nov. 8, 1943)
532 TWEEDY
*540 VANDIVIER
*539 WAGNER

20 Brown S.B. Co., Houston:
421 CHESTER T. O'BRIEN
405 DENNIS (Dec. 4, 1943)
422 DOUGLAS A. MUNRO
423 DUFILHO
406 EDMONDS
424 HAAS
410 JACK MILLER
409 LA PRADE
415 LAWRENCE C. TAYLOR
420 LELAND E. THOMAS

DE
414 LE RAY WILSON
416 MELVIN R. NAWMAN
417 OLIVER MITCHELL
403 RICHARD M. ROWELL
    (Nov. 17, 1943)
402 RICHARD S. BULL
419 ROBERT F. KELLER
411 STAFFORD
408 STRAUS
418 TABBERER
412 WALTER C. WANN

1 Charleston Navy Yard:
231 HODGES

33 Consolidated Steel Corpn., Orange:
343 ABERCROMBIE
366 ALVIN C. COCKRELL
368 CECIL J. DOYLE
353 DOYLE C. BARNES
346 EDWIN A. HOWARD
367 FRENCH
349 GENTRY
357 GEORGE E. DAVIS
    (April 8, 1944)
355 JACCARD
347 JESSE RUTHERFORD
339 JOHN C. BUTLER
370 JOHN L. WILLIAMSON
360 JOHNNIE HUTCHINS
    (May 4, 1944)
354 KENNETH M. WILLETT
348 KEY
356 LLOYD E. ACREE
365 McGINTY
358 MACK (April 11, 1944)
351 MAURICE J. MANUEL
352 NAIFEH
340 O'FLAHERTY
363 PRATT (June 1, 1944)
371 PRESLEY
341 RAYMOND
342 RICHARD W. SUESENS

DE
345 ROBERT BRAZIER
    (Jan. 22, 1944)
362 ROLF
364 ROMBACH
369 THADDEUS PARKER
350 TRAW
361 WALTON
372 WILLIAMS
359 WOODSON (April 29, 1944)

3 Defoe Co.:
706 HOLT
707 JOBB
708 PARLE

16 Federal S.B. & D.D. Co., Port Newark:
447 ALBERT T. HARRIS
    (April 16, 1944)
446 CHARLES E. BRANNON
    (April 23, 1944)
439 CONKLIN (Feb. 13, 1944)
438 CORBESIER (Feb. 13, 1944)
448 CROSS (July 4, 1944)
509 FORMOE (April 2, 1944)
508 GILLIGAN (Feb. 22, 1944)
444 GOSS (March 19, 1944)
445 GRADY (April 2, 1944)
449 HANNA (July 4, 1944)
510 HEYLIGER (Aug. 6, 1944)
443 KENDAL C. CAMPBELL
    (March 19, 1944)
450 JOSEPH E. CONNOLLY
    (Aug. 6, 1944)
440 McCOY REYNOLDS
    (Feb. 22, 1944)
442 ULVERT M. MOORE
    (March 7, 1944)
441 WILLIAM SEIVERLING
    (March 7, 1944)

2 Philadelphia Navy Yard:
225 DAY (Oct. 14, 1943)
224 RUDDEROW (Oct. 14, 1943)

EDWARD H. ALLEN. *Added 1950, U.S. Navy, Official.*

EDWARD H. ALLEN. *Added 1950, U.S. Navy, Official.*

RUDDEROW. *1941, U.S. Navy, Official.*

*Completion of *Vandivier* and *Wagner*, laid down at Boston Dec. 27, 1943, was suspended in Aug., 1946.

Displacement:	Turbo-electric ships: 1,450 tons (2,230 tons *full load*)
	Geared turbine ships: 1,350 tons (2,100 tons *full load*)
Dimensions:	306 (o.a.) × 36⅔ × 14 (*max.*) feet (electric ships), 11 (*max.*) feet (turbine ships)
Guns:	2—5 inch, 38 cal., 2—40 mm. AA., 6—20 mm. AA., and D.C.T.
Tubes:	Removed
Machinery:	Geared turbines, except in 20 ships built by Bethlehem and Defoe Companies and by Charleston and Philadelphia Navy Yards, which have turbo-electric propulsion. 2 shafts. S.H.P.: 12,000
	24 kts.
Complement:	220 (war)

Notes.—Reported that some ships of "Rudderow" type have shown signs of structural weakness around forward turret. Fifty-one ships of this class, with turbo-electric propulsion, were converted into Fast Transports. *Oswald A. Powers* and *Sheehan* have been scrapped. War losses: *Eversole, Oberrender, Samuel B. Roberts, Shelton.*

DE LONG *Added 1957, U.S. Navy, Official*

Broadside silhouette *1955, courtesy B. L. Devenish-Meares, Esq.*

PARLE *1962, courtesy Mr. W. H. Davis*

Rated as

Escort Vessels, Radar Picket (DER)

2 Converted "John C. Butler" Class

	DER 540 VANDIVIER	DER 539 WAGNER
Name:	Vandivier	Wagner
Builders:	Boston Naval Shipyard	Boston Naval Shipyard
Laid down:	8 Nov. 1943	8 Nov. 1943
Launched:	27 Dec. 1943	27 Dec. 1943
Completed	1 Dec. 1955	31 Dec. 1955
Displacement:	1,260 tons light, 1,745 tons standard (2,100 tons full load)	
Dimensions:	306 (o.a.) × 36¾ × 8¾ (mean), 11 (max.) feet	
Guns:	2—5 inch 38 cal. d.p.	
A/S weapons:	Hedgehogs and 2 torpedo launchers	
Machinery:	Westinghouse geared turbines. 2 shafts. S.H.P.: 12,000=24 kts.	
Boilers:	2 Babcock & Wilcox water tube	
Oil fuel:	340 tons	
Radius:	5,000 miles at 15 kts.	
Complement:	187	

General Notes

The completion of these two destroyer escorts (DEs) launched in 1943, was suspended in August 1946. Under the 1954 fiscal year new construction and modernisation program they were completed and converted to Radar Picket Escort Vessels (DERs) at Boston Naval Shipyard. Commissioned 11 Oct. 1955, and 22 Nov. 1955, respectively.

Gunnery Notes

The six 20 mm. guns formerly mounted have been removed.

Engineering Notes

These two ships are the only steam driven DERs among all the Radar Picket Destroyer Escorts.

WAGNER.

1957, U.S. Navy, Official

General Notes for DEs

Former Destroyer Escorts are now officially grouped under the generic heading of Patrol Vessels with the specific classi- fication of Escort Vessels, but they approximate to the Frigate category in British and other navies.

---

58 Bostwick Class. (CANNON CLASS)

6 Dravo Corporation, Wilmington,
Del.:

DE
103 BOSTWICK (Aug. 30, 1943)
104 BREEMAN
105 BURROWS
112 CARTER (Feb. 29, 1944)
113 CLARENCE L. EVANS
102 THOMAS (July 31, 1943)

31 Federal S.B. & D.D. Co., Port
Newark:

167 ACREE (May 9, 1943)
168 AMICK (May 26, 1943)
169 ATHERTON (May 26, 1943)
190 BAKER (Nov. 28, 1943)
166 BARON (May 9, 1943)
170 BOOTH (June, 1943)
189 BRONSTEIN (Nov. 14, 1943)
171 CARROLL (June, 1943)
191 COFFMAN (Nov. 28, 1943)
172 COONER (August, 1943)

192 EISNER (Dec. 12, 1943)
173 ELDRIDGE (1943)
193 GARFIELD THOMAS
(Dec. 12, 1943)
182 GUSTAFSON (Oct. 3, 1943)
162 LEVY (March 28, 1943)
163 McCONNELL (March 28, 1943)
176 MICKA (Aug. 22, 1943)
188 O'NEILL (Nov. 14, 1943)
164 OSTERHAUS (April 18, 1943)
165 PARKS (April 18, 1943)
185 RIDDLE (Oct. 17, 1943)
196 RINEHART (Jan. 9, 1944)
197 ROCHE (Jan. 9, 1944)
183 SAMUEL S. MILES (Oct. 3, 1943)
187 STERN (Oct. 31, 1943)
181 STRAUB (Sept. 18, 1943)
186 SWEARER (Oct. 31, 1943)
195 THORNHILL (Dec. 30, 1943)
180 TRUMPETER (Sept. 18, 1943)
184 WESSON (June 20, 1943)
194 WINGFIELD (Dec. 30, 1943)

9 Tampa S.B. Co:

763 CATES (Oct. 10, 1943)
765 EARL K. OLSEN
768 EBERT
764 GANDY (Dec. 12, 1943)
770 MUIR (June 4, 1944)
769 NEAL A. SCOTT (June 4, 1944)
767 OSWALD
766 SLATER (Feb. 13, 1944)
771 SUTTON

12 Western Pipe & Steel Co.:

739 BANGUST (June 6, 1943)
747 BRIGHT (Sept. 26, 1943)
746 HEMMINGER (Sept. 12, 1943)
742 HILBERT (July 18, 1943)
744 KYNE (October, 1943)
743 LAMONS (Aug. 1, 1943)
750 McCLELLAND (Nov. 28, 1943)
749 ROBERTS (Nov. 14, 1943)
745 SNYDER (Aug. 29, 1943)
748 TILLS (Oct. 3, 1943)
740 WATERMAN (June 20, 1943)
741 WEAVER (July 4, 1943)

Displacement: 1,240 tons (1,520 tons *full load*). Complement: 220. Dimensions: 306 (o.a.) × 36¾ × — feet. Guns: 3—3 inch, 50 cal., d.p., 2—40 mm. AA., 4—20 mm. A.A. and D.C.T. Tubes: 3—21 inch, in triple mount. Machinery: Diesel-electric. B.H.P.: 6,000=21 kts.

Note.—Eight ships of this class were transferred to Brazilian Navy and six to French Navy.

ARMAMENT. Designed armament for this class was three 3 inch guns, six 40 mm guns (three twin), several 20 mm guns, and a bank of three 21 inch torpedo tubes. Torpedo tubes removed and light AA guns reduced. (With full armament the designed wartime complement was 15 officers and 201 enlisted men).

EARL K. OLSEN.

1953, U.S. Navy, Official.

Escort Vessels (ex-Destroyer Escorts) DE.

81 "Edsall" Class.

SAVAGE.

Added 1950, U.S. Navy, Official.

37 Brown S.B. Co., Houston:

DE
390 CALCATERRA (Aug. 16, 1943)
251 CAMP
391 CHAMBERS
398 COCKRILL
389 DURANT
393 HAVERFIELD (Aug., 1943)
400 HISSEM
252 HOWARD D. CROW
250 HURST (April, 1943)
396 JANSSEN
243 J. RICHARD WARD
(Jan. 6, 1943)
241 KEITH (Dec. 21, 1942)
388 LANSING (Aug. 3, 1943)
249 MARCHAND
392 MERRILL (Aug., 1943)
383 MILLS
240 MOORE (Dec. 21, 1942)
244 OTTERSTETTER (Jan. 19, 1943)
253 PETTIT
382 RAMSDEN
384 RHODES (June 25, 1943)
385 RICHEY (June 20, 1943)
254 RICKETTS
386 SAVAGE
255 SELLSTROM (May 12, 1943)
245 SLOAT
246 SNOWDEN
247 STANTON

DE
238 STEWART (Nov. 22, 1942)
399 STOCKDALE
239 STURTEVANT
248 SWASEY (March 18, 1943)
394 SWENNING
242 TOMICH
387 VANCE
397 WILHOITE
395 WILLIS

44 Consolidated Steel Corpn.:

147 BLAIR (April, 1943)
327 BRISTER (Aug. 24, 1943)
148 BROUGH
149 CHATELAIN
337 DALE W. PETERSON
335 DANIEL (Nov. 16, 1943)
138 DOUGLAS L. HOWARD
(Jan. 25, 1943)
129 EDSALL (Nov. 1, 1942)
324 FALGOUT
139 FARQUHAR
142 FESSENDEN
328 FINCH (Nov., 1943)
135 FLAHERTY (Jan. 17, 1943)
334 FORSTER (Nov. 13, 1943)
144 FROST (March 21, 1943)
131 HAMMAN (ex-*Langley*)
316 HARVESON
137 HERBERT C. JONES

DE
141 HILL (Feb. 28, 1943)
145 HUSE
146 INCH (April 4, 1943)
130 JACOB JONES
317 JOYCE
140 J. R. Y. BLAKELEY
(March 7, 1943)
318 KIRKPATRICK (June 5, 1943)
331 KOINER
329 KRETCHMER (Aug. 31, 1943)
325 LOWE
338 MARTIN H. RAY
(Dec. 29, 1943)
320 MENGES
321 MOSLEY (June 26, 1943)
150 NEUNZER
322 NEWELL
330 O'REILLY
152 PETERSON
133 PILLSBURY
151 POOLE
134 POPE
332 PRICE (Oct. 30, 1943)
323 PRIDE
132 ROBERT E. PEARY
336 ROY O. HALE
333 STRICKLAND (Nov. 2, 1943)
326 THOMAS J. GARY

Displacement:	1,200 tons (1,850 tons *full load*)
Dimensions:	306 (o.a.) × 36¾ × 11 (max.) feet
Guns:	3—3 inch, 50 cal. (*Camp*, 2—5 inch, 38 cal., d.p.), 8—40 mm. AA., 4—20 mm. AA. and D.C.T.
Tubes:	Removed
Machinery:	Fairbanks-Morse Diesels. 2 shafts. B.H.P.: 6,000 — 21 kts.
Complement:	220 (war)

Note.—War losses: *Fiske, Frederick C. Davis, Holder, Leopold.*

KRETCHMER.

1946, S. C. Heal, Esq.

PETERSON (A/S)

1954, Skyfotos

WILHOITE (DER 397) (see following page)

United States Navy

Rated as **Escort Vessels, Radar Picket** (DER).

16 Converted " Edsall " Class.

JOYCE.

1952, Ted Stone.

FORSTER

1957, U.S. Navy, Official

7 Brown S.B. Co., Houston		9 Consolidated Steel Corporation	
DER	**DER**	**DER**	**DER**
390 CALCATERRA	544 OTTERSTETTER	324 FALGOUT	331 KOINER
391 CHAMBERS	384 RHODES	142 FESSENDEN	325 LOWE
393 HAVERFIELD	385 SAVAGE	316 HARVESON	133 PILLSBURY
	397 WILHOITE	317 JOYCE	333 STRICKLAND
		318 KIRKPATRICK	

Displacement : 1,200 tons (1,850 tons *full load*)
Dimensions : 306 (o.a.) × 36½ × 11 (*max.*) feet
Guns : 2—3 inch, 50 cal., 6—20 mm. AA.
Machinery : Diesels. 2 shafts. B.H.P. : 6,000 = 21 kts.
Complement : 220

Notes.—Originally rated as Destroyer Escorts (DE) but now grouped under the generic heading of Patrol Vessels with the specific designation of Radar Picket Escort Vessels. Six converted to DER 1951. *Haverfield, Pillsbury, Savage* and *Wilhoite* in 1954-55. *Calcaterra, Chambers, Falgout, Koiner, Lowe, Rhodes*, in 1955-56.

Name	Launched	Completed	Name	Launched	Completed
Calcaterra	16 Aug. 1943	17 Nov. 1943	Koiner	5 Sep. 1943	27 Dec. 1943
Chambers	17 Aug. 1943	22 Nov. 1943	Lowe	28 July 1943	22 Nov. 1943
Falgout	24 July 1943	15 Nov. 1943	Pillsbury	10 Jan. 1943	7 June 1943
Fessenden	9 Mar. 1943	25 Aug. 1943	Otterstetter	19 Jan. 1943	6 Aug. 1943
Harveson	22 May 1943	12 Oct. 1943	Savage	15 July 1943	29 Oct. 1943
Haverfield	30 Aug. 1943	29 Nov. 1943	Strickland	2 Nov. 1943	10 Jan. 1944
Joyce	26 May 1943	30 Sep. 1943	Rhodes	29 June 1943	25 Oct. 1943
Kirkpatrick	5 June 1943	23 Oct. 1943	Wilhoite	5 Oct. 1943	16 Dec. 1943

LOWE (DER 325)

United States Navy

77 Asheville Class.

GRAND ISLAND.   1944, U.S. Navy Official.

2 Canadian Vickers:

PF
1 Asheville (ex-H.M.C.S. Nadur,
  ex-H.M.S. Adur)
                (Aug. 22, 1942)
2 Natchez (ex-H.M.S. Annan)
                (Sept. 12, 1942)

7 American S.B. Co., Cleveland:
21 Bayonne (Sept. 11, 1943)
102 Forsyth (May 20, 1944)
101 Greensboro' (1944)
20 Gulfport (1943)
19 Huron (July 3, 1943)
99 Orlando (1943)
100 Racine (1944)

6 American S.B. Co., Lorain:
18 Alexandria (Jan. 15, 1944)
15 Annapolis (Oct. 16, 1943)
16 Bangor (1943)
17 Key West (1943)
93 Lorain (ex-Vallejo)
                (March 18, 1944)
94 Milledgeville (1944)

8 Globe S.B. Co.:
58 Abilene (ex-Bridgeport)
59 Beaufort
60 Charlotte
56 Covington
61 Manitowoc
63 Moberley (ex-Scranton)
57 Sheboygan (July 31, 1943)
65 Uniontown (ex-Worcester)

8 Leathem D. Smith S.B. Co.:
68 Brunswick
69 Davenport
70 Evansville
62 Gladwyne (ex-Chattanooga)
                (Aug. 7, 1943)
64 Knoxville
71 New Bedford (Dec. 29, 1943)
67 Peoria
66 Reading (Aug. 28, 1943)

12 Permanente Metals Corpn.:
7 Albuquerque (Sept. 14, 1943)
10 Brownsville (Nov. 14, 1943)
12 Casper
8 Everett
11 Grand Forks
14 Grand Island (Sept. 23, 1943)
5 Hoquiam (July 31, 1943)
6 Pasco
9 Pocatello (Oct. 17, 1943)
13 Pueblo (Jan. 20, 1944)
4 Sausalito
3 Tacoma

**18 Consolidated Steel Corpn.,
Los Angeles:**
35 Belfast
46 Bisbee (Sept. 8, 1943)
51 Burlington (Dec. 7, 1943)
50 Carson City (Nov. 19, 1943)
38 Coronado (June 17, 1943)
44 Corpus Christi (Aug. 17, 1943)
41 El Páso (July 16, 1943)
40 Eugene (July 6, 1943)
47 Gallup (Sept. 17, 1943)
36 Glendale (May 28, 1943)
45 Hutchinson (Aug. 27, 1943)
34 Long Beach (May 5, 1943)
49 Muskogee (Oct. 18, 1943)
39 Ogden (June 23, 1943)
43 Orange (Aug. 6, 1943)
48 Rockford (Sept. 27, 1943)
37 San Pedro (June 11, 1943)
42 Van Buren (July 27, 1943)

Displacement: 1,100 tons (first 2 ships, 1,000 tons).   Complement: 180.   Dimensions: 304 (o.a.) × 37½ × 12 feet (except *Asheville* and *Natchez*, 301½ × 36½ × 11½ feet).   Guns: 3—3 inch, 50 cal., d.p., 10—20 mm. AA., 4 D.C.T.   Machinery: Triple expansion. 2 shafts.   H.P.: 5,500 = 18 kts.

Notes.—First 2 ships are of the same design as British frigates of the "River" class.   PF 72-92 were transferred to Royal Navy under Lend-Lease scheme, and have since been returned for scrapping.   Contracts for PF 95-98 (*Macon, Roanoke, Sitka, Stamford*) were cancelled.

12 Walter Butler:
25 Charlottesville
33 Dearborn (ex-Toledo)
28 Emporia
22 Gloucester
31 Grand Rapids
29 Groton
30 Hingham
24 Muskegon
27 Newport (Aug. 15, 1943)
26 Poughkeepsie (Aug. 12, 1943)
23 Shreveport
32 Woonsocket

4 Froemming Bros.:
52 Allentown
55 Bath
53 Machias (Aug. 22, 1943)
54 Sandusky

---

13 "Dealey" Class

3 *Bath Iron Works Corpn.*
1006 DEALEY
1014 CROMWELL
1015 HAMMERBERG

2 *Bethlehem-Pacific Coast Steel
Corpn.*
1025 BAUER
1026 HOOPER (ex-Gatch)

2 *Defoe S.B. Co., Bay City,
Mich.*
1021 COURTNEY
1022 LESTER

4 *New York S.B. Corpn.*
1027 JOHN WILLIS
1028 VAN VOORHIS
1029 HARTLEY
**1030 JOSEPH K.
TAUSSIG**

2 *Puget Sound B. & D. Co.*
1023 EVANS
1024 BRIDGET

Displacement:	1,270 to 1,280 tons light, 1,450 tons standard (1,914 tons full load)
Dimensions:	314½ (o.a.) × 36¾ × 9⁷⁄₁₂ to 9¼ (mean) 13¾ (max.) feet
Guns:	4—3 inch, 50 cal., d.p. AA. (all have forward 3 inch in gunhouses)
A/S weapons:	1 Mark 108 Launcher, Weapon Able (except *Dealey* which has 2 British Squids), 1 D.C.T., 8 D.C. Projectors, 2 fixed T.T.
Machinery:	De Laval geared turbine. 1 shaft. S.H.P.: 20,000 = 25 kts.
Boilers:	2 Foster Wheeler
Oil fuel:	400 tons
Radius:	4,500 miles at 15 kts.
Complement:	*Dealey* 149 (9 officers, 140 men), *Evans* and others 170 (11 officers, 159 men)

General Notes
Dealey was the prototype for new and modern anti-submarine vessels. Lavishly equipped with electronic gear. Designed specifically for fast convoy work and constructed in such a manner that in the event of war similar D Es could be built rapidly. Single engine room. Twin rudders. Single screw, all aluminium superstructure saving 40 per cent in weight. The hull number DE 1032 was assigned to the offshore procurement program for the Portuguese *Pero Escobar* built in Italy.

Gunnery Notes
Dealey originally had an open twin 3 inch, 50 cal. mounting forward, other ships forward mount in a gunhouse as in photo of *Dealey*.

Name	Laid down	Launched	Completed
Cromwell	3 Aug. 1953	4 June 1954	24 Nov. 1954
Dealey	15 Oct. 1952	8 Nov. 1953	3 June 1954
Hammerberg	12 Nov. 1953	20 Aug. 1954	28 Feb. 1955
Courtney	2 Sep. 1954	2 Nov. 1955	31 Aug. 1956
Evans	8 Apr. 1955	14 Sep. 1955	14 June 1957
Lester	2 Sep. 1954	5 Jan. 1956	14 June 1957
John Willis	5 July 1955	4 Feb. 1956	21 Feb. 1957
Van Voorhis	29 Aug. 1955	28 July 1956	15 Apr. 1957
Bridget	19 Sep. 1955	25 Apr. 1956	24 Oct. 1957
Hartley	31 Oct. 1955	24 Nov. 1956	30 July 1957
Hooper	4 Jan. 1956	1 Aug. 1957	16 Apr. 1958
J. K. Taussig	3 Jan. 1956	3 Jan. 1957	10 Sep. 1957
Bauer	1 Dec. 1956	4 June 1957	22 Nov. 1957

BAUER   1958, U.S. Navy, Official

HAMMERBERG   1957, courtesy "Our Navy"

HAMMERBERG (DE 1015)
1972, United States Navy

COURTNEY (DE 1021)
1970, US Navy, PHCS Walter H. Long

LESTER (DE 1022)
1970, US Navy, J. R. Andrews

BAUER (DE 1025)
1969, US Navy, PH1 D. Nichols

4 "Claud Jones" Class

4 Avondale Marine Ways

DE	DE
1035 CHARLES BERRY	**1033 CLAUD JONES**
1036 McMORRIS	**1034 JOHN R. PERRY**

Displacement:	1,315 tons *light*, 1,450 tons *standard* (1,930 tons *full load*)
Dimensions:	312 (o.a.) × 38½ × 9½ (mean), 14¼ (max.) feet.
Guns:	2—3 inch, 50 cal. d.p. AA. with forward 3 inch in gunhouse
A/S weapons:	2 hedgehog launchers forward, 1 D.C.T.
Machinery:	4 Fairbanks-Morse diesels with reduction drive. 1 shaft.
Complement:	175

General Notes

Claud Jones and *John R. Perry* were provided under the 1956 fiscal appropriations and *Charles Berry* and *McMorris* under the 1957 program. The latter two originally ordered from American S.B. Co., Lorain, Ohio, are being completed by Avondale Marine Ways. They embody new features including a unique upper deck arrangement, aluminium masts and deck house.

Engineering Notes

Claud Jones DE 1033 and *John R. Perry* DE 1034, *Charles Berry* DE 1035 and *McMorris* DE 1036, have diesel main propelling machinery plants, which cost less and have increased endurance, and two funnels instead of one as in the "Dealey" type.

Name	Laid down	Launched	Completed
Claud Jones	1 June 1957	27 May 1958	10 Feb. 1959
John R. Perry	1 Oct. 1957	29 July 1958	5 May 1959
Charles Berry	29 Oct. 1958	17 Mar. 1959	5 Nov. 1959
McMorris	5 Nov. 1958	26 May 1959	4 Mar. 1960

CLAUD JONES   *1959. U.S. Navy, Official*

CLAUDE JONES (DE 1033)   *United States Navy*

CHARLES BERRY (DE 1035)   *1971. United States Navy*

McMORRIS (DE 1036)   *1969, United States Navy by PH2 B. M. Laurich*

2 ESCORT SHIPS (DE) : "BRONSTEIN" CLASS

Name	No	Builder	Laid down	Launched	Commissioned
*BRONSTEIN	DE 1037	Avondale Shipyards	16 May 1961	31 Mar 1962	15 June 1963
*McCLOY	DE 1038	Avondale Shipyards	15 Sep 1961	9 June 1962	21 Oct 1963

Displacement, tons 2 360 standard; 2 650 full load
Length, feet (metres) 371·5 (113·2) oa
Beam, feet (metres) 40·5 (12·3)
Draft, feet (metres) 23 (7·0)
Guns 3—3 inch (76 mm) 50 calibre AA (twin forward, single aft)
A/S weapons 1 ASROC 8-tube launcher
2 triple torpedo tubes (Mk 32)
facilities for small helicopter
Main engines 1 geared turbine (De Laval); 20 000 shp; 1 shaft
Boilers 2 (Foster Wheeler)
Speed, knots 26
Complement 220

These two ships may be considered the first of the "second generation" of post-World War II escort ships which are comparable in size and ASW capabilities to conventional destroyers. The *Bronstein* and *McCloy* have several features such as hull design, large sonar and ASW weapons that subsequently were incorporated into the mass-produced "Garcia", "Brooke", and "Knox" classes.
Both ships were built under the Fiscal Year 1960 new construction programme by Avondale Shipyards in Westwego, Louisiana.

DESIGN. These ships have a sharply raked stem, stem anchor, and mast and stacks combined in a "mack" structure. Position of stem anchor and portside anchor (just forward of gun mount) necessitated by large bow sonar dome. Note the deckhouse adjacent to "mack" in photograph of *McCloy*.

ELECTRONICS. SQS-26 bow-mounted sonar installed. SPS-40 and SPS-10 search radars mounted on "mack".

McCLOY (DE 1038)   *1971, United States Navy, PHC F. W. Gotauco*

BRONSTEIN (DE 1037)   *United States Navy*

USS McCLOY (DE 1038)   *1972, United States Navy*

6 "BROOKE" CLASS: GUIDED MISSILE FRIGATES (FFG)

Name	No.	Builders	Laid down	Launched	Commissioned	F S
BROOKE	FFG 1	Lockheed S.B. & Construction Co	10 Dec 1962	19 July 1963	12 Mar 1966	PA
RAMSEY	FFG 2	Lockheed S.B. & Construction Co	4 Feb 1963	15 Oct 1963	3 June 1967	PA
SCHOFIELD	FFG 3	Lockheed S.B. & Construction Co	15 Apr 1963	7 Dec 1963	11 May 1968	PA
TALBOT	FFG 4	Bath Iron Works, Bath, Maine	4 May 1964	6 Jan 1966	22 Apr 1967	AA
RICHARD L. PAGE	FFG 5	Bath Iron Works, Bath, Maine	4 Jan 1965	4 Apr 1966	5 Aug 1967	AA
JULIUS A. FURER	FFG 6	Bath Iron Works, Bath, Maine	12 July 1965	22 July 1966	11 Nov 1967	AA

Displacement, tons: 2 640 standard; 3 426 full load
Dimensions, feet (metres): 414·5 × 44·2 × 24·2 (sonar);
15 (keel) *(126·3 × 13·5 × 7·4; 4·6)*
Aircraft: 1 SH-2D LAMPS helicopter
Missiles: SAM; 16 Tartar/Standard-MR (1 single Mk 22
launcher)
Gun: 1—5 in *(127 mm)*/38 (Mk 30)
A/S weapons: 1 ASROC 8-tube launcher;
2 triple torpedo tubes (Mk 32)
Main engines: 1 geared turbine (Westinghouse in FFG 1-3,
General Electric in others); 35 000 shp; 1 shaft
Boilers: 2 (Foster-Wheeler)
Speed, knots: 27·2
Complement: 248 (17 officers, 231 enlisted men)

These ships are identical to the "Garcia" class escorts except
for the Tartar missile system in lieu of a second 5-in gun mount
and different electronic equipment. Authorised as DEG 1-3 in
the FY 1962 new construction programme and DEG 4-6 in the
FY 1963 programme. Plans for ten additional DEGs in the FY
1964 and possibly three more DEGs in a later programme were
dropped because of the $11 million additional cost of a DEG
over FF. In 1974-75 *Talbot* was reconfigured as test and evaluation ship for systems being developed for the "Oliver Hazard
Perry" class (FFG 7) frigates and "Pegasus" class (PHM 1)
hydrofoil missile combatants, but returned to original state in
1976-77.

Classification: Reclassified as FFG 1-6 on 30 June 1975.

Fire control: One Mk 74 MFCS, one Mk 56 GFCS, one Mk 114
ASW FCS, one Mk 4 weapon direction system, one SPG 51 and
one SPG 35 fire control radars.

Helicopters: These ships were designed to operate Drone
Anti-Submarine Helicopters (DASH), but the programme was
cut back before helicopters were provided. They were fitted to
operate the Light Airborne Multi-Purpose System (LAMPS),
currently the SH-2D helicopter during 1972-75 refits.

Missiles: These ships have a single Tartar Mk 22 launching
system which weighs 92 395 lb. Reportedly, the system has a
rate of fire similar to the larger Mk 11 and Mk 13 systems
installed in guided missile destroyers, but the FFG system has a
considerably smaller magazine capacity (16 missiles according
to unofficial sources).
FFG 4-6 have automatic ASROC loading system (note angled
base of bridge structure aft of ASROC in these ships).

Radar: 3D search: SPS 52.
Search: SPS 10.
Missile control: SPG 51C.

Rockets: Mk 33 Chaffroc RBOC. Mk 36 to replace Mk 33 in FFG 1
and 3.

Sonar: SQS 26 AX (bow-mounted).
(SQS 56 evaluated in *Talbot*.)

TALBOT (DEG 4)   *1967 United States Navy by PHI A. E. Gilless*

RAMSEY (DEG 2)   *1967, Lockheed SB & Construction Co*

BROOKE (DEG 1)   *United States Navy*

SCHOFIELD (DEG 3)   *1969, US Navy,*

BROOKE (DEG 1) .   *1969, United States Navy,*

SCHOFIELD   *1/1980, Dr. Giorgio Arra*   RAMSEY   *9/1979, Dr. Giorgio Arra*

BROOKE   *4/1979, Dr. Giorgio Arra*

10 "GARCIA" CLASS: FRIGATES (FF)

Name	No.	Builders	Laid down	Launched	Commissioned	F/S
GARCIA	FF 1040	Bethlehem Steel, San Francisco	16 Oct 1962	31 Oct 1963	21 Dec 1964	AA
BRADLEY	FF 1041	Bethlehem Steel, San Francisco	17 Jan 1963	26 Mar 1964	15 May 1965	PA
EDWARD McDONNELL	FF 1043	Avondale Shipyards	1 Apr 1963	15 Feb 1964	15 Feb 1965	AA
BRUMBY	FF 1044	Avondale Shipyards	1 Aug 1963	6 June 1964	5 Aug 1965	AA
DAVIDSON	FF 1045	Avondale Shipyards	20 Sep 1963	2 Oct 1964	7 Dec 1965	PA
VOGE	FF 1047	Defoe Shipbuilding Co	21 Nov 1963	4 Feb 1965	25 Nov 1966	AA
SAMPLE	FF 1048	Lockheed S.B. & Construction Co	19 July 1963	28 Apr 1964	23 Mar 1968	PA
KOELSCH	FF 1049	Defoe Shipbuilding Co	19 Feb 1964	8 June 1965	10 June 1967	AA
ALBERT DAVID	FF 1050	Lockheed S.B. & Construction Co	29 Apr 1964	19 Dec 1964	19 Oct 1968	PA
O'CALLAHAN	FF 1051	Defoe Shipbuilding Co	19 Feb 1964	20 Oct 1965	13 July 1968	PA

Displacement, tons: 2 620 standard; 3 403 full load
Dimensions, feet (metres): 414·5 × 44·2 × 24 (sonar)
(126·3 × 13·5 × 7·3)
Aircraft: 1 SH-2D LAMPS helicopter (except *Sample* and *Albert David*)
Guns: 2—5 in *(127 mm)* 38 (single Mk 30)
A/S weapons: 1 ASROC 8-tube launcher;
2 triple torpedo tubes (Mk 32)
Main engines: 1 geared turbine (Westinghouse in 1040, 1041, 1043-1045; GE in others); 35 000 shp; 1 shaft
Boilers: 2 (Foster-Wheeler)
Speed, knots: 27·5
Complement: 239 (13 officers, 226 enlisted men (1040, 1041, 1043, 1044)
247 (16 officers, 231 enlisted men) (remainder)

These ships exceed some of the world's destroyers in size and ASW capability, but are designated as frigates by virtue of their single propeller shaft and limited speed. The FF 1040 and FF 1041 were authorised in the FY 1961 new construction programme, FF 1043-1045 in FY 1962, and FF 1047-1051 in FY 1963.

Classification: Originally classified as ocean escorts (DE); reclassified as frigates (FF) on 30 June 1975. The hull numbers DE 1039, 1042, and 1046 were assigned to frigates built overseas for Portugal to US "Dealey" design.

Design: Anchors are mounted at stem and on portside, just forward of 5-in gun. Hangar structure of this class modified during the early 1970s to handle LAMPS except in *Sample* and *Albert David*.

Electronics: *Voge* and *Koelsch* are fitted with a specialised ASW Naval Tactical Data System (NTDS).
Fitted with OE-82 satellite communications antenna, SSR-1 receiver and WSC-3 transceiver.

Fire control: One Mk 56 gunfire control system, one Mk 114 ASW FCS and one Mk 1 target designation system, one SPG 35 fire control radar.

Helicopters: The Drone Anti-Submarine Helicopter (DASH) programme was cut back before these ships were provided with helicopters. Reportedly only *Bradley* actually operated with DASH. All but two of these ships were fitted to operate the Light Airborne Multi-Purpose System (LAMPS), now the SH-2D helicopter between FY 1972-75.

Missiles: *Bradley* was fitted with a Sea Sparrow Basic Point Defense Missile System (BPDMS) in 1967-68; removed for installation in the carrier *Forrestal* (CV 59).

Radar: Search: SPS 10 and 40.

Sonar: SQS 26 AXR (bow-mounted) in FF 1040-1041, 1043-1045. SQS 26 BR (bow-mounted) in FF 1047-1051.

Torpedoes: Most of these ships were built with two Mk 25 torpedo tubes built into their transom for launching wire-guided ASW torpedoes. However, they have been removed from the earlier ships and deleted in the later ships. *Voge* and later ships have automatic ASROC reload system (note angled base of bridge structure behind ASROC in these ships).

BRUMBY

10/1979, L. and L. van Ginderen

DAVIDSON

3/1979, Dr. Giorgio Arra

GARCIA (DE 1040)

1965, United States Navy

SAMPLE (DE 1048)   *1970, United States Navy*

GARCIA   *1975*   O'CALLAHAN about to refuel from *Kitty Hawk*   *1975, USN*

EDWARD McDONNELL   *3/1975, Wright and Logan*

BRADLEY   *2/1979, Dr. Giorgio Arra*

46 "KNOX" CLASS (FRIGATES (FF))

Name	No.	Builders	Laid down	Launched	Commissioned
*KNOX	FF 1052	Todd Shipyards (Seattle)	5 Oct 1965	19 Nov 1966	12 April 1969
*ROARK	FF 1053	Todd Shipyards (Seattle)	2 Feb 1966	24 April 1967	22 Nov 1969
*GRAY	FF 1054	Todd Shipyards (Seattle)	19 Nov 1966	3 Nov 1967	4 April 1970
*HEPBURN	FF 1055	Todd Shipyards (San Pedro)	1 June 1966	25 Mar 1967	3 July 1969
*CONNOLE	FF 1056	Avondale Shipyards	23 Mar 1967	20 July 1968	30 Aug 1969
*RATHBURNE	FF 1057	Lockheed SB & Constn Co	8 Jan 1968	2 May 1969	16 May 1970
*MEYERKORD	FF 1058	Todd Shipyards (San Pedro)	1 Sep 1966	15 July 1967	28 Nov 1969
*W. S. SIMS	FF 1059	Avondale Shipyards	10 Apr 1967	4 Jan 1969	3 Jan 1970
*LANG	FF 1060	Todd Shipyards (San Pedro)	25 Mar 1967	17 Feb 1968	28 Mar 1970
*PATTERSON	FF 1061	Avondale Shipyards	12 Oct 1967	3 May 1969	14 Mar 1970
*WHIPPLE	FF 1062	Todd Shipyards (Seattle)	24 April 1967	12 April 1968	22 Aug 1970
*REASONER	FF 1063	Lockheed SB & Constn Co	6 Jan 1969	1 Aug 1970	31 July 1971
*LOCKWOOD	FF 1064	Todd Shipyards (Seattle)	3 Nov 1967	5 Sep 1964	5 Dec 1970
*STEIN	FF 1065	Lockheed SB & Constn Co	1 June 1970	19 Dec 1970	8 Jan 1972
*MARVIN SHIELDS	FF 1066	Todd Shipyards (Seattle)	12 Apr 1968	23 Oct 1969	10 April 1971
*FRANCIS HAMMOND	FF 1067	Todd Shipyards (San Pedro)	15 July 1967	11 May 1968	25 July 1970
*VREELAND	FF 1068	Avondale Shipyards	20 Mar 1968	14 June 1969	13 June 1970
*BAGLEY	FF 1069	Lockheed SB & Constn Co	22 Sep 1970	24 April 1971	6 May 1972
*DOWNES	FF 1070	Todd Shipyards (Seattle)	5 Sep 1968	13 Dec 1969	28 Aug 1971
*BADGER	FF 1071	Todd Shipyards (Seattle)	17 Feb 1968	7 Dec 1968	1 Dec 1970
*BLAKELY	FF 1072	Avondale Shipyards	3 June 1968	23 Aug 1969	18 July 1970
*ROBERT E. PEARY	FF 1073	Lockheed SB & Constn Co	20 Dec 1970	23 June 1971	23 Sep 1972
*HAROLD E. HOLT	FF 1074	Todd Shipyards (San Pedro)	11 May 1968	3 May 1969	26 Mar 1971
*TRIPPE	FF 1075	Avondale Shipyards	29 July 1968	1 Nov 1969	19 Sep 1970
*FANNING	FF 1076	Todd Shipyards (San Pedro)	7 Dec 1968	24 Jan 1970	23 July 1971
*OUELLET	FF 1077	Avondale Shipyards	15 Jan 1969	17 Jan 1970	12 Dec 1970
*JOSEPH HEWES	FF 1078	Avondale Shipyards	15 May 1969	7 Mar 1970	24 April 1971
*BOWEN	FF 1079	Avondale Shipyards	11 July 1969	2 May 1970	22 May 1971
*PAUL	FF 1080	Avondale Shipyards	12 Sep 1969	20 June 1970	14 Aug 1971
*AYLWIN	FF 1081	Avondale Shipyards	13 Nov 1969	29 Aug 1970	18 Sep 1971
*ELMER MONTGOMERY	FF 1082	Avondale Shipyards	23 Jan 1970	21 Nov 1970	30 Oct 1971
*COOK	FF 1083	Avondale Shipyards	20 Mar 1970	23 Jan 1971	18 Dec 1971
*McCANDLESS	FF 1084	Avondale Shipyards	4 June 1970	20 Mar 1971	18 Mar 1972
*DONALD B. BEARY	FF 1085	Avondale Shipyards	24 July 1970	22 May 1971	22 July 1972
*BREWTON	FF 1086	Avondale Shipyards	2 Oct 1970	24 July 1971	8 July 1972
*KIRK	FF 1087	Avondale Shipyards	4 Dec 1970	25 Sep 1971	9 Sep 1972
*BARBEY	FF 1088	Avondale Shipyards	5 Feb 1971	4 Dec 1971	11 Nov 1972
*JESSE L. BROWN	FF 1089	Avondale Shipyards	8 April 1971	18 Mar 1972	17 Feb 1973
*AINSWORTH	FF 1090	Avondale Shipyards	11 June 1971	15 Apr 1972	31 Mar 1973
*MILLER	FF 1091	Avondale Shipyards	6 Aug 1971	3 June 1972	30 June 1973
*THOMAS C. HART	FF 1092	Avondale Shipyards	8 Oct 1971	12 Aug 1972	28 July 1973
*CAPODANNO	FF 1093	Avondale Shipyards	12 Oct 1971	21 Oct 1972	17 Nov 1973
*PHARRIS	FF 1094	Avondale Shipyards	11 Feb 1972	16 Dec 1972	26 Jan 1974
*TRUETT	FF 1095	Avondale Shipyards	27 Apr 1972	3 Feb 1973	1 June 1974
*VALDEZ	FF 1096	Avondale Shipyards	30 June 1972	24 Mar 1973	27 July 1974
*MOINESTER	FF 1097	Avondale Shipyards	25 Aug 1972	12 May 1973	2 Nov 1974

ROBERT E. PEARY (DE 1073)

1972, United States Navy

Displacement, tons: 3 011 standard; 3 877 (1052-1077) 3 963 (remainder) full load
Length, feet (metres): 438 *(133·5)* oa
Beam, feet (metres): 46·75 *(14·25)*
Draught, feet (metres): 24·75 *(7·55)*
Helicopter: 1 SH-2 LAMPS (except 1061 and 1070)
Missile launchers: 1 Sea Sparrow BPDMS multiple launcher (Mk 25) in 1052-1069 and 1071-1083; 1 NATO Sea Sparrow multiple launcher (Mk 29) in *Downes*; Harpoon in *Downes* and *Ainsworth* (see Missile note)
Guns: 1—5 inch *(127 mm)* 54 calibre (Mk 42)
A/S weapons: 1 ASROC 8-tube launcher; 4 fixed torpedo tubes (Mk 32)
Main engines: 1 geared turbine (Westinghouse) 35 000 shp; 1 shaft
Boilers: 2
Speed, knots: 27+
Complement: 245 (17 officers, 228 enlisted men); increased to 283 (22 officers, 261 enlisted men) with BPDMS and LAMPS installation; (as built 12 ships had accommodation for 2 staff officers)

The 46 frigates of the "Knox" class comprise the largest group of destroyer or frigate type warships built to the same design in the West since World War II. These ships are similar to the previous "Garcia" and "Brooke" classes, but slightly larger because of the use of non-pressure-fired boilers.
Although now classified as frigates they were authorised as DE 1052-1061 (10 ships) in the Fiscal Year 1964 new construction programme, DE 1062-1077 (16 ships) in FY 1965, DE 1078-1087 (10 ships) in FY 1966, DE 1088-1097 (10 ships) in FY 1967, and DE 1098-1107 (10 ships) in FY 1968. However, construction of six ships (DE 1102-1107) was deferred in 1968 as US Navy emphasis shifted to the more versatile and faster DX/DXG ships; three additional ships (DE 1098-1100) were cancelled on 24 Feb 1969 to finance cost overruns of FY 1968 nuclear-powered attack submarines and to comply with a Congressional mandate to reduce expenditures; the last ship of the FY 1968 programme (DE 1101) was cancelled on 9 April 1969.
The DEG 7-11 guided missile "frigates" constructed in Spain are similar to this design.

Classification: Originally classified as ocean escorts (DE); reclassified as frigates (FF) on 30 June 1975.

Design: A 4 000 lb lightweight anchor is fitted on the port side and an 8 000 lb anchor fits into the after section of the sonar dome.

Electronics: Fitted with OE-82 satellite communications antenna, SSR-1 receiver and WSC-3 transceiver.

Engineering: DE 1101 was to have had gas turbine propulsion; construction of the ship was cancelled when decision was made to provide gas turbine propulsion in the "Spruance" class (DD 963) destroyers.
These ships can steam at 22 knots on one boiler. They have a single 5-blade, 15 ft diameter propeller.

Fire control: One Mk 68 gunfire control with SPG 53A radar, one Mk 115 MFCS, one Mk 114 ASW FCS and one Mk 1 target designation system.

Fiscal: These ships have cost considerably more than originally estimated. Official programme cost for the 46 ships as of January 1974 was $1 424 million an average of $30·959 million per ship not including the LAMPS, Standard missile, VDS, or BPDMS installation.

AYLWIN (DE 1081)   *PH1 James A. Warren*

1972, United States Navy

Gunnery: All ships of the class are to be fitted with 20 mm Phalanx CIWS Mk 16 on the fantail. In those ships with Sea Sparrow the CIWS will replace it.

Helicopters: These ships were designed to operate the now-discarded DASH unmanned helicopter. From FY 1972 to FY 1976 they were modified to accommodate the Light Airborne Multi-Purpose System, the SH-2D anti-submarine helicopter; hangar and flight deck are enlarged. Cost approximately $1 million per ship for LAMPS modification.

Missiles: Sea Sparrow Basic Point Defence Missile System (BPDMS) launcher installed in 31 ships from 1971-75 (FF 1052-1069, 1071-1083).
Modified NATO Sea Sparrow installed in *Downes* for evaluation.
In addition, some ships are being fitted with the Standard interim surface-to-surface missile which is fired from the ASROC launcher forward of the bridge. Two of the eight "cells" in the launcher are modified to fire a single Standard.
Cost was approximately $400 000 per ship for BPDMS and $750 000 for Standard missile modification.

Downes and *Lockwood* have been used in at-sea firing tests and shipboard compatability for the Harpoon ship-to-ship missiles.
Harpoon fitted in *Ainsworth* in August 1976 (first production model in US Navy) followed by *Thomas C. Hart.* Being fitted in all other ships in immediate future.

Modifications: In 1979 a programme was initiated to fit 3.5 ft bow bulwarks and spray strakes to all ships of the class adding 9.1 tons to the displacement. By early 1980 FF 1067, 1069, 1077, 1090 had been fitted with FF 1053, 1059, 1062, 1064, 1072, 1095, 1097 being fitted. The remainder will be fitted at their next overhaul.

Names: DE 1073 originally was named *Conolly;* changed on 12 May 1971.

Radar: Search: SPS 10 and 40.
(**Note:** *Downes* has SPS 58 threat detectio.. radar, and Improved Point Defence/Target Acquisition System (IPD/TAS) radar).

Rockets: Mk 36 Chaffroc RBOC to be fitted in near future replacing Mk 33 system in FF 1052, 1055, 1061, 1065, 1068, 1072, 1074-76, 1078-1085 and 1087.

Sonar: SQS 26 CX (bow-mounted).
SQS 35 (Independent VDS) (except FF 1053-55, 1057-62, 1072 and 1077).
In FY 1980 funds were approved to retro-fit twelve sets of SQR 18-A TACTAS towed array sonar in twelve "Knox" class ships. In FY 1981 programme funds were requested to retro-fit four more ships with SQR 18A. Nineteen more ships equipped with SQS 35 (IVDS) will be so fitted in the next few years.

Torpedoes: Improved ASROC-torpedo reloading capability as in some ships of earlier "Garcia" class (note slanting face of bridge structure immediately behind ASROC). Four Mk 32 torpedo tubes are fixed in the midships structure, two to a side, angled out at 45 degrees. The arrangement provides improved loading capability over exposed triple Mk 32 torpedo tubes.

LANG

1976, Michael D. J. Lennon

JESSE L. BROWN

1976, Michael D. J. Lennon

BOWEN (DE 1079) with BPDMS and LAMPS

1972, United States Navy

RATHBURNE (with LAMPS helicopter)

1/1977, Dr. Giorgio Arra

LOCKWOOD

2/1977, Dr. Giorgio Arra

HEPBURN (with Sea Sparrow)

11/1979, Ron Wright

HAROLD E. HOLT (DE 1074)—with BPDMS and LAMPS

1972, US Navy

BAGLEY (DE 1069)

1972, United States Navy

MEYERKORD (with Sea Sparrow)

7/1979, Dr. Giorgio Arra

1 "GLOVER" CLASS: FRIGATE (FF)

Name	No.	Builders	Laid down	Launched	Commissioned	F/S
GLOVER	FF 1098 (ex-AGFF 1, ex-AGDE 1, ex-AG 163)	Bath Iron Works, Bath, Maine	29 July 1963	17 Apr 1965	13 Nov 1965	AA

Displacement, tons: 2 643 standard; 3 426 full load
Dimensions, feet (metres): 414·5 × 44·2 × 24 (sonar)
(126·3 × 13·5 × 7·3)
Gun: 1—5 in (127 mm)/38 (Mk 30)
A/S weapons: 1 ASROC 8-tube launcher;
2 triple torpedo tubes (Mk 32);
facilities for small helicopter
Main engines: 1 geared turbine (Westinghouse); 35 000 shp;
1 shaft
Boilers: 2 (Foster-Wheeler)
Speed, knots: 27
Complement: 248

The ship was originally authorised in the FY 1960 new construction programme, but was postponed and re-introduced in

the FY 1961 programme. Estimated construction cost was $29·33 million.
Glover was built to test an advanced hull design and propulsion system. She was classed as an auxiliary but retained a full combat capability.
On 1 October 1979 Glover ceased her experimental role and assumed the status of a Frigate (FF). She will have capabilities updated by having facilities for LAMPS II installed and her electronic equipment modernised during her next overhaul.

Classification: Glover was originally classified as a miscellaneous auxiliary (AG 163); completed as an escort research ship (AGDE 1). Subsequently changed to frigate research ship on 30 June 1975 and reclassified as a regular frigate on 1 October 1979.

Design: Glover has a massive bow sonar dome integral with her hull and extending well forward underwater.

Electronics: The prototype sonar and equipment originally installed when she was an AGFF was removed in the summer of 1979.
Fitted with OE-82 satellite communications antenna.

Fire control: Mk 56 GFCS with SPG 35; one Mk 114 ASW FCS and one Mk 1 target designation system.

Radar: Search: SPS 10 and 40.

Sonar: Bow-mounted SQS 26 AXR active sonar, hull-mounted SQR 13 Passive/Active Detection and Location (PADLOC) sonar, and SQS 35 Independent Variable Depth Sonar (IVDS) lowered from the stern originally mounted.

GLOVER (AGDE 1)   1968. United States Navy

GLOVER (AGDE 1)   United States Navy

GLOVER (AGDE 1)   1969. United States Navy PHAN T. R. Hearsum

GLOVER (Old hull number as AGFF 1)   1974, USN

3 + 31 + (21) "OLIVER HAZARD PERRY" CLASS: GUIDED MISSILE FRIGATES (FFG)

Name	No.	Builders	Laid down	Launched	Commissioned	F/S
OLIVER HAZARD PERRY	FFG 7 (ex-PF 109)	Bath Iron Works, Bath, Maine	12 June 1975	25 Sep 1976	17 Dec 1977	AA
McINERNEY	FFG 8	Bath Iron Works, Bath, Maine	7 Nov 1977	4 Nov 1978	19 Nov 1979	AA
WADSWORTH	FFG 9	Todd Shipyards Corporation, San Pedro	13 July 1977	29 July 1978	8 Mar 1980	PA
DUNCAN	FFG 10	Todd Shipyards Corporation, Seattle	29 Apr 1977	1 Mar 1978	1980	Bldg
CLARK	FFG 11	Bath Iron Works, Bath, Maine	17 July 1978	24 Mar 1979	1980	Bldg
GEORGE PHILIP	FFG 12	Todd Shipyards Corporation, San Pedro	14 Dec 1977	16 Dec 1978	1980	Bldg
SAMUEL ELIOT MORISON	FFG 13	Bath Iron Works, Bath, Maine	4 Dec 1978	14 July 1979	1980	Bldg
SIDES	FFG 14	Todd Shipyards Corporation, San Pedro	7 Aug 1978	19 May 1979	1980	Bldg
ESTOCIN	FFG 15	Bath Iron Works, Bath, Maine	2 Apr 1979	3 Nov 1979	1981	Bldg
CLIFTON SPRAGUE	FFG 16	Bath Iron Works, Bath, Maine	30 Sep 1979	16 Feb 1980	1981	Bldg
JOHN A. MOORE	FFG 19	Todd Shipyards Corporation, San Pedro	19 Dec 1978	20 Oct 1979	1981	Bldg
ANTRIM	FFG 20	Todd Shipyards Corporation, Seattle	21 June 1978	27 Mar 1979	1981	Bldg
FLATLEY	FFG 21	Bath Iron Works, Bath, Maine	13 Nov 1979	1980	1981	Bldg
FAHRION	FFG 22	Todd Shipyards Corporation, Seattle	1 Dec 1978	24 Aug 1979	1981	Bldg
LEWIS B. PULLER	FFG 23	Todd Shipyards Corporation, San Pedro	23 May 1979	29 Mar 1980	1981	Bldg
JACK WILLIAMS	FFG 24	Bath Iron Works, Bath, Maine	25 Feb 1980	1980	1981	Bldg
COPELAND	FFG 25	Todd Shipyards Corporation, San Pedro	24 Oct 1979	1980	1982	Bldg
GALLERY	FFG 26	Bath Iron Works, Bath, Maine	1980	1980	1981	Ord
MAHLON S. TISDALE	FFG 27	Todd Shipyards Corporation, San Pedro	1980	1980	1982	Ord
BOONE	FFG 28	Todd Shipyards Corporation, Seattle	27 Mar 1979	16 Jan 1980	1982	Bldg
—	FFG 29	Bath Iron Works, Bath, Maine	1980	1981	1982	Ord
REID	FFG 30	Todd Shipyards Corporation, San Pedro	1980	1981	1982	Ord
STARK	FFG 31	Todd Shipyards Corporation, Seattle	24 Aug 1979	1980	1982	Bldg
—	FFG 32	Bath Iron Works, Bath, Maine	1981	1981	1982	Ord
—	FFG 33	Todd Shipyards Corporation, San Pedro	1981	1981	1983	Ord
—	FFG 34	Bath Iron Works, Bath, Maine	1981	1981	1982	Ord
—	FFG 36	Bath Iron Works, Bath, Maine	1981	1982	1983	Ord
CROMMELIN	FFG 37	Todd Shipyards Corporation, Seattle	1980	1981	1983	Ord
—	FFG 38	Todd Shipyards Corporation, San Pedro	1981	1982	1983	Ord
—	FFG 39	Bath Iron Works, Bath, Maine	1981	1982	1983	Ord
—	FFG 40	Todd Shipyards Corporation, Seattle	1980	1981	1982	Ord
—	FFG 41	Todd Shipyards Corporation, San Pedro	1981	1982	1983	Ord
—	FFG 42	Bath Iron Works, Bath, Maine	1982	1982	1983	Ord
—	FFG 43	Todd Shipyards Corporation, San Pedro	1982	1982	1984	Ord
Six ships	FFG 44/49	Approved FY 1980 programme				Ord
Four ships	FFG 50/53	Requested FY 1981 programme				Proj
Four ships	FFG 54/57	Proposed FY 1982 programme				Proj
Three ships	FFG 58/60	Proposed FY 1983 programme				Proj
Four ships	FFG 61/64	Proposed FY 1984 programme				Proj

Displacement, tons: 3 605 full load
Dimensions, feet (metres): 445 × 45 × 24·5 (sonar); 14·8 (keel) (135·6 × 13·7 × 5·7; 4·5)
Aircraft: 2 SH-2 LAMPS helicopters (see note)
Missiles: SSM/SAM; 40 Harpoon/Standard (1 single Mk 13 launcher)
Gun: 1—76 mm/62 (Mk 75)
A/S weapons: 2 triple torpedo tubes (Mk 32)
Main engines: 2—LM 2500 gas turbines (General Electric); 41 000 shp; 1 shaft (cp propeller)
Speed, knots: 29
Range, miles: 4 500 at 20 knots
Complement: 164 (11 officers, 153 enlisted men)

They are follow-on ships to the large number of frigates (formerly DE) built in the 1960s and early 1970s, with the later ships emphasising anti-ship/aircraft/missile capabilities while the previous classes were oriented primarily against submarines (eg, larger SQS 26 sonar and ASROC).

The lead ship (FFG 7) was authorised in the FY 1973 shipbuilding programme; three ships (FFG 8-10) in the FY 1975 programme; and six ships (FFG 11-16) in the FY 1976 programme. Congress authorised nine ships in the FY 1976, but cost escalation permitted the construction of only six ships; eight ships in the FY 1977 (FFG 19-26); eight ships in the FY 1978 (FFG 27-34), nine ships in the FY 1979 (FFG 36-43) and six ships in FY 1980 (FFG 44-49).

The three additional ships of this class under construction at the Todd-Seattle shipyard for the Royal Australian Navy are assigned US Navy hull numbers FFG 17, 18 and 35 for accounting purposes. In addition to the three Australian ships, three other ships (with no US Navy hull numbers assigned) are to be built for Spain in El Ferrol. The order for a fourth Australian frigate announced in February 1980.

Aircraft: LAMPS III is scheduled to enter service about 1985. Starting in FY 1985 FFG 7-34 (excluding FFG 17 and 18) will be retro-fitted to support LAMPS III which includes the installation of the Rapid Hauldown and Traversing System (RAST) which is equipment designed for safe helicopter operations in high seas. At the same time the SQR 19 (TACTAS) sonar will be fitted on FFG 7-34. The entire retro-fit will cost $13 million (1979$) per unit. LAMPS III support facilities, RAST and the TACTAS sonar will be fitted in all ships authorised from FY 1979 onwards, during construction.

Classification: These ships were originally classified as "patrol frigates" (PF) at a time when the term "frigate" was used in the US Navy for the DL/DLG/DLGN. *Oliver Hazard Perry* was designated PF 109 at time of keel laying and designated FFG 7 on 30 June 1975.
The name of FFG 13 was changed from *Samuel E. Morison* to *Samuel Eliot Morison* on 17 August 1979.

Design: These ships are slightly longer but lighter than the earlier "Knox" class. The original single hangar has been changed to two adjacent hangars, each to house an SH-2 or follow-on LAMPS helicopters.
Several weapon and sensor systems for this class were evaluated at sea in the guided missile frigate *Talbot* (FFG 4). Fin stabilisers may be fitted at a later date (space and weight reserved).

Electronics: Fitted with OE-82 satellite communications antenna, SSR-1 receiver and WSC-3 transceiver.

Engineering: Two auxiliary retractable propeller pods are provided aft of the sonar dome to provide "get home" power in the event of a casualty to the main engines or propeller shaft. Each pod has a 325 hp engine to provide a ship speed of 3 to 5 knots.

Fire control: The Mk 92 weapons control system is installed with a dome-shaped antenna atop the bridge. (The Mk 92 is the Americanised version of the WM-28 system developed by NV Hollandse Signaalapparaten). Mk 13 weapon direction system.

Fiscal: The design-to-cost estimate of $45·7 million in the FY 1973 dollars based on a 49-ship programme has increased to $55·3 million in the same dollars due to design and cost estimating changes. However, adding the estimated inflation and contract escalation factors brings the estimated cost per ship in the FY 1980 programme to $200·6 million.

Gunnery: The principal gun on this ship is the single 76 mm OTO Melara with a 90-round-per-minute firing rate (designated Mk 75 in US service). Space and weight are reserved for one 20 mm Phalanx Mk 15 CIWS.

Missiles: The single-arm Tartar-type missile launcher will be capable of firing both Standard-MR surface-to-air and Harpoon surface-to-surface missiles. "Mixed" missile magazines provided.

Radar: Long-range search: SPS 49.
Search and navigation: SPS 55.
Weapons control: STIR (modified SPG 60).

Rockets: Mk 36 Chaffroc RBOC launcher fitted.

Sonar: SQS 56 (hull-mounted).
To be fitted with SQR 19 TACTAS starting in mid-1980s.

OLIVER HAZARD PERRY   *12/1977, USN*

SUBMARINES

AFTER the customary delays, enquiries and trials, USS *Holland* SS 1 was accepted into the Navy on 11 April 1900 and for the next 14 years private designs held sway. The dived speeds of the classes from 1911 onwards were in excess of their foreign contemporaries. The British and, particularly, the Germans, had earlier opted for larger designs with improved surface performance, the operational theory being that submarines should dive only when necessary for an attack or for safety.

In the immediate post-war years submarine designs were as irrational in the US Navy as they were in Britain and France. Luckily only six USN boats were launched between 1924 and 1932. By then sanity was prevailing and such requirements as long range, a good torpedo load, improved habitability and manoeuvrability were taking precedence, with a possible war in the Western Pacific as the target. With the "Porpoise" class (launched in 1935) diesel-electric propulsion was introduced which, from a biassed submariner's viewpoint, was an admirable move. There were periods of back-sliding, but, on 21 August 1941, USS *Gato* was launched by the Electric Boat Company, the first of the true American 'fleet boats'. These were magnificent submarines for their day and their task. From Pearl Harbor to Japan is the best part of 3,500 miles. However, with a maximum surface speed of 20 knots and a range of 11,500 miles at ten knots, such distances presented few problems. Getting on patrol was one thing, sinking ships was quite another. The American torpedoes were, if possible, worse than those in the U-boats in the early days of World War II.

Despite such problems the success of the Pacific submariners is proved by some stark figures – Japanese merchant ship losses totalled 8,897,393 gross tons, of which submarines accounted for 4,859,634.

While post-war Guppy conversion activity was underway new construction was also in hand. The three small "Barracuda (ex-K)" class were designed as cheap ASW boats and were not a success. The six much larger "Tangs" and *Darter* were the first attempts to apply German Type XXI principles and were reasonably successful. By now the diving depth requirement had been increased from 400 to 700 feet.

On 14 June 1952 the world's first nuclear propelled warship was laid down, USS *Nautilus*. On 17 January 1955 she made her historic signal 'Underway on nuclear power'.

In December 1953 the diesel submarine USS *Albacore* had been commissioned, a design with a revolutionary beam/length ratio of 7.5, producing the first whale-shaped hull. In her final configuration, she was capable of 33 knots dived. Her trials were sufficiently convincing for a modified form of the "Albacore" hull to be adopted in the later nuclear boats after the "Skipjack" class.

After the "Skipjacks" came the 41 boats of the "Thresher" and "Sturgeon" classes. *Los Angeles*, commissioned in November 1976, proved to be much larger, nearly 7,000 tons dived and 360 feet long. Great efforts went into quieting this class and from the 40th boat, SSN 751 *San Juan*, onwards, acoustic tile cladding was added to the hull. By the end of 1991 forty seven of this class should be completed.

SSN-21 *Seawolf* is due for completion in May 1995. With a designed dived displacement of 9,150 tons, 34 feet shorter than the "Los Angeles" class at 326 feet, her beam is 9.3 feet greater at 42.3 feet. *Seawolf*'s single reactor and single shaft are due to provide an increased speed of 35 knots and she is to be tile cladded. Whereas the later "Los Angeles" class has a load of 26 tube-launched weapons plus 12 missiles in a vertical launch system external to the hull, *Seawolf* has eight internal tubes and a choice of 50 missiles or torpedoes. Proposed appropriation for the next two in FY 1991 totals $3,482 billion.

In 1949 the converted fleet boat *Carbonero* ushered in a new era, that of the missile firing submarine. But the cruise missile of the 1950s was being rapidly out-dated by the development of the Polaris ballistic missile which Admiral Raborn had started in 1955. The whole "George Washington" class of five entered service between December 1959 and March 1961. It was a triumph of planning and construction never exceeded in the West. Next came the five "Ethan Allens" and the 31 boats of the "Lafayette/Benjamin Franklin" classes; by 1967 the target of 41 Polaris boats was reached.

The planned building rate of the 18,700 ton "Ohio" class to carry the "Trident" weapons was delayed by financial constraints, SALT considerations and problems at the builders. The first was not commissioned until 11 November 1981. By mid-1991 twelve of these submarines, each carrying 24 missiles, are to be in service, number nine onwards carrying the 6,500-mile Trident 2 (D-5).

J.M.
May 1991

No.	Type	Date	Displacement	H.P. Surface	*Max.* speed	Fuel	Complement	T. Tubes	*Max.* draug't
			tons		kts.				feet
4	*new* boats	'14-'16	/710	...	...	...	...	...	...
1	M 1 (H)	'13-'15	...	...	...	...	...	...	...
7	L 5—7 (L)	'13-'15	/575	...	...	For 4500 at 11 kts.	...	...	15
	L 1—4 (H)	'13-'15	...	...	...	...	...	...	...
8	K 1—K 8 (H)	'12-'13	390/520	950	14·5/10·5	For 2500 at 11 kts.	.	...	...
3	H 1—H 3 (H)	'11-'13	/430	800	14/11	For 2500 at 11 kts.	...	4	...
1	G 4 (Li)	'11-'12	358/458	1000	14/9.5	Surface for 1680 at 8 kts. 40 at 5 kts.	...	4	...
3	G 1—G3 (L)	'10-'11	/510	1200	14/10	...	...	6	...
4	F 1—F 4 (H)	'10-'11	350/430	...	14/9·5	For 2500 at 11 kts.	...	2	...
2	E 1, E 2 (H)	1910	350/430	...	14/11	Petrol for 2500 at 11 kts.	...	2	...
3	D 1—D 3 (H)	1909	280/345	600	13/9	Petrol	15	2	14¾
5	C 1—C 5 (H)	1909	238/275	500	11/10	For 1050 surface 60 kts. sub.	10	2	14¾
3	B 1—B 3 (H)	'06-'07	/170	250	9½/8½	Petrol for 1000 kts.	10	2	13
7	A 1—A 7 (H)	'01-'03	/120	160	9/7	Petrol for 400 kts.	7	1	12

(H)=Holland. (L)=Lake. (Li)=Laurenti.

No.	Type	Date	Displacement	H.P.	*Max.* speed	Fuel	Complement	T. Tubes	*Max.* draug't
			tons		kts.				kts.
8	New boats (L)	*bldg.*	...	...	...	..	...	...	...
1	Semi-submerged	...	..	...	22	...	...	...	...
2	Semi-submerged	...	..	...	16	...	...	...	...
1	*Turbot* (L)	1910	...	...	...	...	.	...	...
2	*Skipjack* (H)	1910	...	...	...	...	...	..	...
1	*Tuna* (L)	'10-'11	435	...	..	...	...	...	...
1	*Carp* (H)	'10-'11	...	...	...	...	...	...	...
1	*Thrasher* (Li)	'10-'11	...	...	...	...	...	...	...
1	*Seal* (L)	1910	500	...	16/9½	Petrol for 3000 kts. Endurance 70 hours	...	6	...
3	*Narwhal* (H)	1909	280/345	...	13/9	...	15	4	14¾
4	*Bonita* (H)	1909	238/275	500	10/9	...	10	2	14¾
1	*Octopus* (H)	1909							
3	*Viper* (H)	'06-'07	/170	250	9½/8½	Petrol for 1000 kts.	10	2	13
7	*Adder* (H)	'01-'03	/120	160	9/7	Petrol for 400 kts.	7	1	12

(H)=Holland. (L)=Lake. (Li)=Laurenti.

(1) The first submarine in the US Navy was *Holland*. Her data was as follows: Built 1896, 74 tons, 4 cylinder petrol engine, electricm otor, horse power 45/160, speed 8/5 knots, dimensions 54 × 10.75 × 10.5 feet, endurance 18 hours at 3 knots, armament 3 torpedoes – originally carried a dynamite gun which was very soon removed.

(2) The original names allocated to submarines were superseded by the numbers as given in the Table above.

A1—A7. Radii, 300 at 8.5 kts. surface, 28 at 7 kts. submerged. Dimensions : 63½ × 12 × 12 feet

A-1 SOLD

OTHERS USED AS TARGETS

E1, E2. Radii, 2500 at 11 kts. surface, 100 at 5 kts. submerged.

Photo, H. Reuterdahl, Esq.

ALL SOLD

G 4 (1912). Dimensions: 157½ × 17½ feet. Armament: 4—18 inch tubes. H.P. 1000 11 / 110 9.5 Radius: 12 hours submerged. Fitted with a 10 ton drop keel.

SOLD

C1 C5. Nominal radius, 300 at 9 kts. surface, 80 at 5 kts. submerged. — SOLD

Photo, Müller.

B1 B3. Radii about same as C class.

USED AS TARGET

SUNK AS TARGET

G1 G3. SOLD

H 2.

1921 *Photo.*

2 *Holland* type : **H 2** (ex-*Nautilus*), and **H 3** (ex-*Garfish*). (1913.) *H 2* by Union I. W., *H 3* by Moran Co. Dimensions : 150 ft. 3½ in. × 15 ft. 9½ in. × 12½ feet. 4—18 inch torpedo tubes. 8 torpedoes carried. Engines : 2 sets of 240 B.H.P. (350 r.p.m.) 8-cyl., 4-cycle N1seco Diesel. Fuel : 5520/9593 gallons. Motors : 2—300 H.P. Electric Dynamic Co., with Electric Boat Co. knife-switch control. Gould storage batteries, 27-WL type. Radii of action : about 2300 miles at 11 kts. on surface, 30 miles at 5 kts. submerged. H 1 (ex-*Seawolf*) wrecked, March, 1920. All three authorized 1909, as Nos. 28—30. Other details as Table.

Notes.—One of the most successful submarine types ever evolved. The British, Chilean and Italian H classes and Russian AG class, built or assembled during the War of 1914-18, were all slightly improved editions of this design.

D1—D3. Dimensions: 134 × 14 × 11½ feet.

Photo, Boston News Co.

ALL SOLD

H 5.

1921 *Copyright Photo, O. W. Waterman.*

6 *Holland* type : **H 4—H 9** (1918), assembled by Bremerton N. Yd., Puget Sound. Dimensions : 150¼ × 15¾ × 12½ feet. 4 bow 18 inch tubes (8 torpedoes carried). Engines : 2 sets of 240 B.H.P. (350 r.p.m.) 8-cyl., 4-cycle N1seco Diesel engines. Fuel : 5275/11530 gallons. Motors : 2—300 H.P. Electric Dynamic Co., with Electric Boat Co. knife-switches. Other details as Table.

Notes.—Ordered for Russian Government, but bought in knock-down condition by U.S. Government and assembled in 8½ months.

ALL SCRAPPED

K 5 *Photo, U. S. Navy Recruiting Bureau.*

8 *Holland* type: **K 1** (ex-*Haddock*), **K 2** (ex-*Cachalot*), **K 3** (ex-*Orca*), **K 4** (ex *Walrus*) and **K 5—K 8.** (1913-14.) *K* 2, 5, 6, by Fore River. *K* 3, 7, 8, by Union I. W., *K* 4 by Moran Co. Dimensions: about 153 × 16¾ × 12 feet 4 bow torpedo tubes. 8 torpedoes carried. Machinery: 2 sets 6-cylinder 500 B.H.P. Nlseco Diesel engines. Radius of action: 4500 miles at 10 kts. *on surface*, 120 miles at 5 kts. *submerged*.

ALL SCRAPPED

L 3. *Photo, U. S. Navy Recruiting Bureau.*

7 *Holland* type: **L 1—4, L 9—11** (1914-15), viz., Electric Boat Co. Dimensions: about 169 × 17½ feet. 1—3 inch AA. gun. 4 torpedo tubes. Machinery: 2 sets of 650 H.P. Nlseco Diesel engines in *L 1—4* and *9—11*. Radius of action: about 4500 miles *on surface* at cruising speed, and 150 miles at 5 kts. *submerged*. Cost £650,000 each.

Note.—*L 6* and *L 7* contracted for by Lake Co., but were built by the California S. B. Co., Long Beach, Cal.

L 6. *By courtesy of Bureau C. & R.*, 1921.

4 *Lake* type: **L 5** (Lake T. B. Co., 1915), **L 6, L 7** (Craig S. B. Co., Long Beach, Cal., 1916), **L 8** (Portsmouth N. Yd., 1917). Dimensions: 165 × 14¾ × 13¼ feet. 1—3 inch, 23 cal. AA. gun.* 4—18 inch torpedo tubes (8 torpedoes carried). Engines: 2 sets of 600 B.H.P. (375 r.p.m.) 6-cyl., 2-cycle Busch Sulzer Diesel engines. Fuel: 11925/18892 gallons. Motors: 2—400 H.P. Diehl Mfg. Co., with Cutler-Hammer Co. magnetic controllers. Batteries: Electric Storage Co., Type 29-U. Radius of action: *about* 4500 miles *on surface* at cruising speed, —— miles at 5 kts. *submerged*. Other details as Table.

*In *L 8* only.

Note.—*L 6* and *L 7* contracted for by Lake Co., and built by the Craig S. B. Co., Long Beach, Cal. When in European waters, during the War, were marked as "AL" boats, to distinguish them from the British "L" Class Submarines. *L 5—7* authorized 1912, as *Nos. 44—46*, *L 8*, 1913, as *No. 48*. Owing to the engines having given unsatisfactory results in service, these 4 boats have been laid up, and their sale is contemplated, 1924.

ALL SOLD & SCRAPPED

Photo, copyright by E. Muller, Junr.

1 *Holland* type: ***M 1.*** (Electric Boat Co., 1915.) Dimensions: 165 × 16 × 13½ feet. Armament: 1—3 inch, 50 cal. gun (high angle anti-aircraft model) and 4 torpedo tubes. Machinery: 2 sets of 8 cylinder 900 H.P. Nlseco Diesel engines. Radius of action: 3000 miles at 14 kts. *on surface*. Has three periscopes.

SOLD

T1. *1921 Photo, courtesy of Bureau C. & R.*

3 *Holland type:* **T1** (ex-*AA* 1, ex-*Schley*, Fore River Co., 1918), **T2** (ex-*AA 2*, 1919), **T3** (ex-*AA 3*, 1919), both by Fore River Co.). Dimensions: *about* 264 (*w.l.*), 269¾ (*o.a.*) × 23 × 14 feet. Machinery: 4 sets of 1100 H.P. Nelseco Diesel engines *on surface*, arranged in tandem pairs to 2 screws. *On trials* all exceeded surface designed speed of 20 kts. by ½ to ¾ kts. Armament: 1—4 inch gun and 6—21 inch tubes (4 bow and 2 deck aft). 16 torpedoes carried. For other details *v.* Table. Authorised: *T 1* (1914, as No. 52). *T 2, T 3* (1915, as Nos. 60, 61). Designed 1914. Completed 1920-21. *Surface* endurance: 7000/9000 miles. Although designed as Fleet Submarines, these vessels are officially admitted to be incapable of manœuvring with the fleet under all conditions, the tandem arrangement of engines having proved unsatisfactory.

SCRAPPED

N 1. 1921 *Photo.*

3 *Holland* type: **N 1—N 3** (1916-17) designs by Electric Boat Co., built by Seattle Con. and D. D. Co. Dimensions: 147¼ × 15¾ × 12½ feet. 4 bow 18 inch torpedo tubes (to carry 8 torpedoes). Engines: 2 sets 240 B.H.P. (375 r.p.m.) 8-cyl., 4-cycle Nelseco Diesel engines. Fuel: 6068/6068 gallons. Motors: 2—280 H.P. Electric Dynamic Co., with E.B.C. Knife Control Switch. Gould storage batteries, Type 23-WL. Radius of action: 1500 miles at cruising speed *on surface*, and —— miles at 5 kts. *submerged*. Authorized 1914, as Nos. 53—55. Other details as Table.

SCRAPPED

1925 *Photo, by courtesy of the Navy Dept.*

3 *Electric Boat Co. design*: **N 1—N 3** (1916-17) designs by Electric Boat Co., built by the Moran Co., of Settle. Dimensions: 147¼ × 15¾ × 12½ feet. 4 bow 18 inch torpedo tubes (to carry 8 torpedoes). Engines: 2 sets 240 B.H.P. (375 r.p.m.) 8-cyl., 4-cycle Nelseco Diesel engines. Fuel: 6068/6068 gallons. Motors: 2—280 H.P. Electric Dynamic Co., with E.B.C. Knife Control Switch. Gould storage batteries, Type 23-WL. Radius of action: 1500 miles at cruising speed *on surface*, and —— miles at 5 kts. *submerged*. Authorized 1914, as Nos. 53—55. Other details as Table.

SOLD

O3. *Photo, N. G. Moser.*

10 *Holland* type: **O 1—O 10** (1917-18), viz., *O 1* by Portsmouth N. Y., *O 2* by Bremerton, Pugent Sound, N. Y., *O 3—O 10* by Electric Boat Co. and Fore River Co. Dimensions: about 175 × 17 × feet. 1—3 inch AA. gun. 4 torpedo tubes. Machinery: 2 sets of 4-cycle Nlesco Diesel engines. Electric batteries weigh 65 tons. Radius of action: 5000-6000 miles, at 11-12 kts. *on surface*. Completed 1918.

SCRAPPED

O 5. 1920 *Photo.*

9 *Electric Boat Co. design*: **O 1—O 4** and **O 6—O 10** (1917-18), viz.: *O 1* by Portsmouth N. Y.; *O 2* by Bremerton Puget Sound, N. Y.; *O 3*, *O 4* and *O 6—O 10* by Fore River Co. Dimensions: 172⅓ × 18 × 14 ft. 5 in. 1—3 inch, 23 cal. AA. gun. 4 torpedo tubes (8 torpedoes). Engines: 2 sets of 440 B.H.P. (400 r.p.m.) 6-cyl. 4-cycle Nelseco Diesel engines. Fuel: 10089/21897 gallons. Motors: 2—370 H.P. in *O 1*, *O 2*, by New York Navy Yard; in others, by Electric Dynamic Co., all with Cutler-Hammer Co. magnetic controller. Gould storage batteries, Type 29-WLL in *O 1* and *O 2*. Electric Storage Co., Type 49-WL in others. Electric batteries weigh 65 tons. Radius of action: 3500-3000 miles, at 11 kts. *on surface*. Authorized 1915, as Nos. 62—71. Completed 1918. Other details as Tables.

Note.—*O 5* wrecked, Oct. 28, 1923, and not considered worth repair after salvage.

O-9 LOST SCRAPPED

1924, *Official Photo.*

6 *Lake* type: **O 11—O 16** (1917-18), viz., *O 11—O 13* by Lake T. B. Co., *O 14—O 16* by Mare Island, N.Y. Dimensions: 175 × 16¼ × 13⅝ feet. 1—3 inch, 23 cal. AA. gun. 4 torpedo tubes (8 torpedoes). Engines: 2 sets of 500 B.H.P. (410 r.p.m.) 6-cyl. 4-cycle Sulzer Diesel engines. Fuel: 10,094/18588 gallons. Motors: 2—440 H.P. Diehl Mfg. Co., with Cutler-Hammer Co. magnetic controllers. Electric Storage Co. batteries, Type 29-WL. Radius of action as *O 1—O 10*, below. Authorized 1915, as Nos. 72—77. Completed 1918. Other details as Table.

O-12 SCUTTLED SCRAPPED

S 3 (gun not mounted).

1920 Photo.

10 "*Bureau design*" boats: **S3,** (1918), **S4, S6—S13** (1919-21); all by Portsmouth Ny. Yd. Dimensions: 231 × 21½ × 13½ feet. Guns: 1—4 inch, 50 cal. Torpedo tubes: 4—bow, 21 inch (12 torpedoes carried). *S* 10—S 13, 5 tubes (14 torpedoes carried). Engines: *S* 3—9, 2 sets of 4-cycle Nelseco Diesels, each 700 B.H.P. (8 cyl); *S* 10—13, 2 sets of 4-cycle "Bureau Design" M.A.N. (6 cyl) type, each 1000 B.H.P. Motors: 2 sets 600 H.P. Westinghouse. Oil: 19,271/36,950 gallons. Authorised: *S* 3 (1916, as No. 107), *S* 4—13 (1916-17, as Nos. 109—118). *S* 5 lost, 1920. Completed 1919-23. Other details as Table.

1 *Lake* type: **S2** (1919). Dimensions: 207 × 19½ × 16 feet = 830/977 tons. Guns: 1—4 inch, 50 cal. Tubes: 4—21 inch (12 torpedoes carried). Engines: 2 sets Busch-Sulzer, total B.H.P. 1,800. Motors: 2—600 H.P. Diehl Mfg. Co. Speed, 15.11 kts. Complement, 38. Oil, 17,491/26,458 gallons. *Special Note.*—In 1921, S 2 was fitted with an experimental type of flexible clutch, which permits change-over of drive when surfacing or diving to be made without reduction of speed. This type of clutch proved so successful that it is understood to have been fitted to all submarines under construction since.

S 4 (gun not mounted).

Courtesy Bureau C. & R., 1921.

4 *Lake* type: **S14—S17** (1919—20). All by Lake T.B. Co. Dimensions: 231 × 21⅝ × 13 feet = 876/1092 tons. Guns: 1—4 inch, 50 cal. Tubes: 4—21 inch (12 torpedoes carried). Engines: Busch-Sulzer, B.H.P. 1,000. Motors: 2—600 H.P. Westinghouse. Speed, 14/12.25 kts. Complement, 38. Oil, 19271/36950 gallons.

S 45.

1926 Official Photo.

6 *Electric Boat Co.* design: **S 42—S 47** (1923-24). All contracted for by Electric Boat Co., and built by Bethlehem S. B. Co., Quincy. Authorized 1916-18, as Nos. 155—158. Dimensions: 225½ × 20¼ × 16 feet = 906/1126 tons. Guns: 1—4 inch, 50 cal. Tubes: 4—21 inch. 12 Torpedoes carried. Engines: Two sets 600 B.H.P., 8 cylinder, 4 cycle Nelseco. Motors: 2 sets 750 H.P. Elect. Dy. Co. Oil: 11463—46363 gallons.

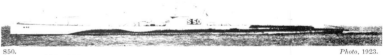

S 50.

Photo, 1923.

3 *Lake* type: **S48—S50** (1921). All by Lake T. B. Co. Dimensions: 240 × 21½ × 13½ feet. Guns: 1—4 inch, 50 cal. Tubes: 5—21 inch (4 bow, 1 stern). 14 torpedoes carried. Engines: 2 sets of 900 B.H.P. Busch-Sulzer. Motors: 2 sets 750 h.p. Ridgeway. Crash dive in 60 secs. *Max.* dive limit: 200 feet. Divided into 6 watertight compartments. Double hull amidships, single hull at ends. 3 periscopes. Oil: 23,411 gallons normal, 44,505 max. For any other details, v. Table. Authorized 1916-18 as Nos. 159—161. *Note.*—S 51, of this type, was sunk by collision, Sept. 25th, 1925. She was salved and brought into port July, 1926, and scrapped.

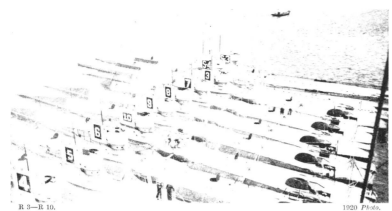

R 3—R 10.

1920 Photo.

20 *Electric Boat Co. design*: **R 1—R 20** (1917-19), viz., R 1—R 11 by Fore River S.B. Co., R 15—R 20 by Union I. W. San Francisco. Dimensions: 186 ft. 11 in. × 18 × 14½ feet. Guns: 1—3 inch, 50 cal. gun. 4 torpedo tubes (8 torpedoes carried). Engines: 2 sets of 440 B.H.P. (400 r.p.m.) 6-cyl, 4-cycle Nelseco Diesel. Fuel: 7691/18880 gallons. Motors: 2—467 H.P. Electric Dynamic Co., with Cutler-Hammer Co. magnetic controllers. Batteries: Electric Storage Co. Type 31-WLL. Other details as Table. Authorized 1916, as Nos. 78—97. Completed 1918-19.

R-3 SCRAPPED   R-8 SCUTTLED   R-12 LOST   R-17 SCRAPPED   R-19 LOST
ALL OTHERS SOLD

R 23.

1920 Photo.

7 *Lake* type: **R21—R27** (1918-19) all built by Lake T. B. Co. Dimensions: 175 × 16⅝ × 14 feet. Guns: 1—3 inch, 50 cal. Torpedo tubes: 4 (8 torpedoes carried). Engines: 2 sets of 500 H.P. (410 r.p.m.) 6-cyl, 4-cycle Busch-Sulzer. Fuel: 9715/17922 gallons. Motors: 2—400 H.P. Diehl Mfg. Co., with Cutler Hammer Co. magnetic controllers. Batteries: Electric Storage Co. Type 31-W.L. Authorized 1916, as Nos. 98—104. Completed 1919. Other details as Table.

ALL SCRAPPED

S 30.

1921 Copyright Photo, O. W. Waterman.

25 *Electric Boat Co.* design: **S 1** (1918), **S 18—41** (1918-22), viz., S 1 by Fore River S. B. Co., S 18—S 29 by Bethlehem S.B. Co., Quincy, S 30—S 41 by Bethlehem S. B. Co., San Francisco. Dimensions: 219½ × 20¼ × 16 feet. Machinery: 2 sets of 600 B.H.P. Nelseco Diesel engines. Motors: 2 sets 750 H.P. Ridgeway or Electric Dynamic Co. (S 1). Oil: 11,511/41,921 gallons. Have large radius of action *on surface*. Armament: 1—4 inch gun and 4—21 inch bow tubes (12 torpedoes carried). Authorized: S 1 (1916, as No. 105), S 18—29 (1916-17 as Nos. 125—136), S 30—41 (1916-17, as Nos. 137—148). S 1 experimentally fitted, 1923, to carry a small seaplane in a cylindrical tank abaft C.T.

General Note to all "S" boats.—Special attention given to constructional strength against depth charge attack. S 33 was immersed to a depth of 208 feet for 65 minutes without inconvenience. S 1—4, S 6—8, S 14—35, all have Cutler-Hammer system of electric control. S 9—13, S 36—51, all fitted with Westinghouse or G. E. Co. pneumatic controllers, considered to be a decided improvement.

Note.—S 30 built at expense of Phillippines Government.

S 19 reached a depth of 200 feet during special diving trials, Dec., 1925.

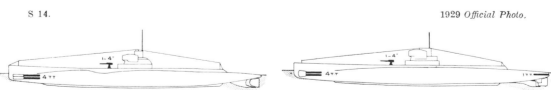

S 14.

1929 Official Photo.

BARRACUDA.   1935, *Bear Photo Service.*

3 *Bureau* design : **Barracuda** (ex-*V*.1), **Bass** (ex-*V*.2), **Bonita** (ex-*V*.3). Built at Portsmouth Navy Yard. Displacement : 2,000/2,506 tons. Complement : 75. Dimensions : 326 (*w.l.*), 341¼ (*o.a.*) × 27⅜ × 14½ feet. Guns : 1—3 inch AA., 2 M.G. Tubes : 6—21 inch, 16 torpedoes carried. Machinery : 2 sets Busch-Sulzer Diesels aft for main drive, H.P. : 6,700 = 18·75 kts. on *surface.* Also 2 sets M.A.N. auxiliary Diesels forward driving generators supplying current to electric motors, H.P. : 2,400 = 8 kts. *submerged.* Latter combination can be used for cruising on surface with electric drive. Radius of action : 12,000 miles. Designed speed never realised in service.

Name & No.	Laid down	Launched	Compl.		Name & No.	Laid down	Launched	Compl.
Barracuda (B 1)	20/10/21	17/7/24	1/11/24		Bonita (B 3)	16/11/21	9/6/25	17/6/26
Bass (B 2)	20/10/21	27/12/24	26/9/25					

BARRACUDA.   1925 *Official Photo.*

BONITA.   1935, *O. W. Waterman.*

BASS.   1930 *Photo.*

V 4.   1928 *Official Photo.*

V 4.   1929 *Official Photo.*

Argonaut (ex *V*.4) (Portsmouth Navy Yard, Nov. 10th, 1927). Machinery by Brooklyn Navy Yd. Displacement : 2660/4080 tons. Dimensions : 381 × 33½ × 15½ feet. Armament : 2—6 inch gun, 4—21 inch tubes, 60 mines. Diesels of 3175 S.H.P. Speed 14·6/8 kts. Complement, 86. Is an improved edition of V1 type in other respects. Estimated cost : Hull and machinery, $5,300,000 ; armament, etc., $850,000. Authorised 1916, as *No.* 166, and completed April, 1928.

DOLPHIN.   1935, *O. W. Waterman.*

Dolphin (**D.1** ex-*V*.7) Portsmouth Navy Yard. Laid down June 14, 1930. Launched March 8, 1932. Completed Oct. 14th, 1932.

Displacement : 1,540/2,215 tons, Complement, 63. Dimensions : 307 (*w.l.*), 319 (*o.a.*) × 27⅜ ×13 feet. M.A.N. Diesels, H.P. : 4,200 = 17 kts. *surface.* Electric motors, H.P. : 875 = 8 kts. *submerged.* Guns : 1—4 inch, 50 cal. Tubes : 6—21 inch + 3 Torpedoes stowed externally.

NAUTILUS.   *Added,* 1938, *Wide World Photos.*

Narwhal (**N.1** ex-*V*.5) (Dec. 17, 1929), **Nautilus** (**N.2** ex-*V*.6) (March 15, 1930). Laid down at Portsmouth and Mare Island Navy Yards, respectively, May 10 and August 2, 1927. Machinery for both vessels built at New York Navy Yard. Displacement : 2,730/3,960 tons. Dimensions : 371 (*o.a.*), 349 (*w.l.*) × 33⅜ × 15½ feet (*mean*). Armament : 2—6 inch, 6—21 inch tubes. M.A.N. Diesels, H.P. 5,450 = 17 kts. *surface.* Westinghouse electric motors, H.P. 2,540 = 8·5 kts. *submerged.* Complement, 88. Estimated cost : Hull and machinery, $5,350,000 armament, $1,020,000. Authorised 1916 as Nos. 167–168. Completed in July and Oct., 1930, respectively.

Note.—Also carry eight external Torpedo Stowage Tubes, two each side fore and aft under the half-deck amidships. Neither vessel can exceed 14 kts. with present engines, which it is proposed to replace in 1939–40.

CUTTLEFISH.   1935, *O. W. Waterman.*

Cachalot (**C.1** ex-*V*.8) Portsmouth Navy Yard. Laid down Oct. 21, 1931. Launched Oct. 19, 1933. Completed March 1, 1934. **Cuttlefish** (**C.2** ex-*V*.9) Electric Boat Co. Laid down Oct. 7, 1931. Launched Nov. 21, 1933. Completed June, 1934.

Respective displacements : 1,110 and 1,120/1,650 tons Complement, 45. Dimensions : 260 (*w.l.*), 271¾ (*o.a.*) × 24¼ × 12 feet (*Cachalot*) ; 25 × 12¾ (*Cuttlefish*). Machinery : 2 sets Winton Diesels. H.P. : 3,100 800 = 17·9 kts. Armament : 1—3 inch AA. Tubes : 6—21 inch. All-welded construction. Guns mounted abaft CT. No external torpedo stowage.

Note.—Owing to design of original engines (with direct drive) having proved unsatisfactory, *Cachalot* and *Cuttlefish* were given new machinery under 1936 Programme.

4 Pike Class.

PORPOISE. 1937, *O. W. Waterman.*

2 *Portsmouth Navy Yard :* **Pike, Porpoise.**
Displacement : 1,310/1,934 tons. Dimensions : 283 (*w.l.*), 301 (*o.a.*) × 25 × 13 feet (*mean*). Winton Diesels. Elliott motors.

2 *Electric Boat Co. :* **Shark, Tarpon.**
Displacement : 1,315/1,968 tons. Dimensions : 287 (*w.l.*), 298 (*o.a.*) × 25 × 13¾ feet (*mean*). Winton Diesels, with electric drive. Elliott motors. First all-welded submarines in U.S. Navy.

Both types : Complement : 50. Guns : **1**—3 inch, 50 cal. Tubes : **6**—21 inch. Speed reported to exceed 20 kts.

Name and No.	Laid down	Launched	Compl.
Porpoise (*P*1)	27/10/33	20/6/35	15/1/36
Pike (*P*2)	20/12/33	12/9/35	17/4/36
Shark (*P*3)	24/10/33	21/5/35	25/1/36
Tarpon (*P*4)	22/12/33	4/9/35	12/3/36

6 Perch Class.

PLUNGER. 1938, *O. W. Waterman.*

3 *Electric Boat C[illegible] :* **Perch, Pickerel, Permit** (ex-*Pinna*).
2 *Portsm[illegible] Navy Yard :* **Plunger, Pollack,** 1 *Mare Island Yard :* **Pompano.**
Di[illegible]cement : 1,330/1,998 tons (except *Plunger* and *Pollack*, 1,335 tons). Complement : 50. Dimensions : 290 (*w.l.*), 300½ (*o.a.*) × 25 × 13¾ feet (*mean* draught). Guns : **1**—3 inch, 50 cal., **1** M.G.A.A. Tubes : **6**—21 inch. Winton Diesels in first 3, with G.E. motors ; Fairbanks-Morse Diesels and Elliott motors in *Plunger* and *Pollack* ; H.O.R. (modified M.A.N.) Diesels and Allis-Chambers motors in *Pompano*. Cost averages $2,400,000 each.

Name and No.	Laid down	Launched	Completed
Perch (*P*5)	25/2/35	9/5/36	4/6/37
Pickerel (*P*6)	25/3/35	7/7/36	26/1/37
Permit (*P*7)	6/6/35	5/10/36	17/3/37
Plunger (*P*8)	17/7/35	8/7/36	31/3/37
Pollack (*P*9)	1/10/35	15/9/36	28/4/37
Pompano (*P*10)	14/1/36	11/3/37	4/12/37

6 Salmon Class.

SEAL. 1938, *Official.*

3 *Electric Boat Co. :* **Salmon, Seal, Skipjack.**
2 *Portsmouth Navy Yard :* **Snapper, Stingray.**
1 *Mare Island Navy Yard :* **Sturgeon.**
Displacement : 1,450/2,198 tons (first 3), 1,445 tons (others). Dimensions : 298 (*w.l.*) × 26 × 14¼ feet (*mean*). Guns: **1**—3 inch, 50 cal., **1** M.G. AA. Tubes: **8**—21 inch (4 bow, 4 stern). H.O.R. Diesels (except *Snapper*). Complement 55.

Name and No.	Laid down	Launched	Completed
Salmon (*S*1)	15/4/36	12/6/37	/38
Seal (*S*2)	25/5/36	25/8/37	/38
Skipjack (*S*3)	22/7/36	23/10/37	/38
Snapper (*S*4)	23/7/36	24/8/37	1/3/38
Stingray (*S*5)	1/10/36	6/10/37	30/6/38
Sturgeon (*S*6)	27/10/36	15/3/38	2/9/38

SNAPPER. *Added* 1940, *O. W. Waterman.*

8 Sargo Class (1936–37 Programmes).

SAILFISH. 1940, *courtesy "The Motor Boat".*

4 *Electric Boat Co. :* **Sargo, Saury, Seadragon, Spearfish.**
3 *Portsmouth Navy Yard :* **Searaven, Seawolf, Sailfish** (ex-*Squalus*).
1 *Mare Island Navy Yard :* **Swordfish.**

Displacement : 1,475 tons. Complement : 62. Dimensions : 299 (*w.l.*), 310 (*o.a.*) × 27 × 13¾ feet (*mean*). Guns : **1**—4 inch, 2—20 mm. Oerlikon. Tubes : **8**—21 inch (4 bow, 4 stern). Machinery : H.O.R. Diesels in first 5, G.M. (Winton) in others. B.H.P. : 6,140 = 20 kts.

Name and No.	Laid down	Launched	Completed
Sargo (188)	12/5/37	6/6/38	26/8/39
Saury (189)	28/6/37	20/8/38	17/7/39
Spearfish (190)	9/9/37	29/10/38	17/7/39
Sailfish (192)	18/10/37	14/9/38	12/5/40
Swordfish (193)	27/10/37	1/4/39	20/9/39
Seadragon (194)	18/4/38	21/4/39	1940
Searaven (196)	9/8/38	21/6/39	1940
Seawolf (197)	27/9/38	17/8/39	1940

Notes.—Cost about $5,000,000 each. *Squalus* foundered May 23, 1939, but was salved and renamed *Sailfish* in Feb. 1940. Repairs cost about $1,000,000. War losses : *Sculpin, Sealion.*

5 Tambor Class (1938 Programme).

THRESHER. 1941, *U.S. Navy, official*

3 *Electric Boat Co. :* **Tambor, Tautog, Thresher.**
1 *Portsmouth Navy Yard :* **Trout.**
1 *Mare Island Navy Yard :* **Tuna.**

Displacement : 1,475 tons. Dimensions : 299 × 27 × 13¾ feet. Guns : **1**—4 inch, 2—20 mm. Oerlikon. Tubes : **10**—21 inch (6 bow, 4 stern). Machinery : G.M. Diesels in first 3, Fairbanks-Morse in others, with all-electric drive. B.H.P. : 6,400 = 21 kts. (22 kts. reached on trials). Complement : 65. Differ from *Sargo* type in silhouette, hull form, and internal lay-out. Double-hull construction, with external control room as in German submarines. Bilge keels are fitted.

Name & No.	Laid down	Launched	Completed
Tambor (198)	16/1/39	20/12/39	3/6/40
Tautog (199)	1/3/39	27/1/40	3/7/40
Thresher (200)	27/4/39	27/3/40	27/8/40
Trout (202)	28/8/39	21/5/40	40
Tuna (203)	19/7/39	2/10/40	41

War loss : *Triton* (201).

2 Mackerel Class.

MACKEREL. 1941, *U.S.N. official.*

1 *Electric Boat Co. :* **Mackerel.** (204). (Sept. 28, 1940).
1 *Portsmouth Navy Yard :* **Marlin.** (205). (Jan. 29, 1941).

Displacement : 800 tons. Dimensions : 231 (*pp.*), 253 (*o.a.*) × 21½ × 12 feet. Guns : **1**—3 inch, **2** M.G. T.T., **6**—21 inch (4 bow, 2 stern). Machinery : Nelseco Diesels in *Mackerel*. American Locomotive Co. Diesels in *Marlin*. Electric Dynamic motors. B.H.P. : 1,600 = 14·5 kts. Provided for under 1939 Programme as Nos. 204, 205. *Mackerel* laid down Oct. 6, 1939, *Marlin*, May 28, 1940. Both completed in 1941. Trials gave a speed of 16 knots. Submerged speed reported to be 11 kts. (?)

54 Gato Class (*1939–41 Programmes*).

ROCK. 1944, *U.S. Navy, Official.*

31 *Electric Boat Co. :* **Angler, Barb, Bashaw, Blackfish, Bluefish, Bluegill, Bream, Cavalla, Cero, Cobia, Cod, Croaker, Dace, Flasher, Flounder, Gabilan, Gato, Greenling, Grouper, Guardfish, Gunnel, Gurnard, Haddo, Hake, Hoe, Jack, Lapon, Mingo, Muskallonge, Paddie, Pargo.**

9 *Portsmouth Navy Yard :* **Drum, Finback, Flying Fish, Haddock, Halibut, Kingfish, Sawfish, Shad, Steelhead.**

5 *Mare Island Navy Yard :* **Silversides, Sunfish, Tinosa, Tunny, Whale.**

9 *Manitowoc S.B. Co. :* **Peto, Pogy, Pompon, Puffer, Rasher, Raton, Ray, Redfin, Rock.**

Displacement : 1,525 tons. Dimensions : 307 × 27 × 14 feet. Guns : **1**—3 inch, 50 cal., d.p., **2**—20 mm. Oerlikon. Tubes : **10—21** inch (6 bow, 4 stern). Machinery : G.M. Diesels in some ; *Gar*, Fairbanks-Morse. Have 2 engine-rooms instead of 1 as in *Tambor* class, to reduce size of compartments. B.H.P. : 6,500 = 21 kts. Complement : 65. Otherwise slightly improved editions of *Tambor* class. Inclusive cost per ship officially estimated at $6,288,200. War losses : *Albacore, Amberjack, Bonefish, Corvina, Darter, Dorado, Flier, Growler, Grunion, Harder, Herring, Robalo, Runner, Scamp, Scorpion, Snook, Trigger, Tullibee, Wahoo.*

(Missing numbers have been lost.)

No.	Name	Laid down	Launched	Completed
212	*Gato*	5/10/40	21/8/41	42
213	*Greenling*	12/11/40	20/9/41	42
214	*Grouper*	28/12/40	27/10/41	42
217	*Guardfish*	1/4/41	20/1/42	42
220	*Barb*	7/6/41	2/4/42	42
221	*Blackfish*	7/41	18/4/42	42
222	*Bluefish*	8/41	21/2/43	43
224	*Cod*	42	21/3/43	43
225	*Cero*	42	4/4/43	43
228	*Drum*	11/9/40	12/5/41	11/41
229	*Flying Fish*	6/12/40	9/7/41	12/41
230	*Finback*	5/2/41	25/8/41	42
231	*Haddock*	31/3/41	20/10/41	42
232	*Halibut*	41	3/12/41	42
234	*Kingfish*	8/41	2/3/42	42
235	*Shad*	10/41	15/4/42	42
236	*Silversides*	4/11/40	26/8/41	42
239	*Whale*	28/6/41	14/3/42	42
240	*Angler*	42	4/7/43	43
241	*Bashaw*	42	25/7/43	43
242	*Bluegill*	42	8/8/43	43
243	*Bream*	43	17/10/43	44
244	*Cavalla*	43	14/11/43	44
245	*Cobia*	43	28/11/43	44
246	*Croaker*	43	19/12/43	44
247	*Dace*	22/7/42	25/4/43	43

No.	Name.	Laid down	Launched	Completed
249	*Flasher*		20/6/43	43
251	*Flounder*		22/8/43	43
252	*Gabilan*		19/9/43	43
253	*Gunnel*	21/7/41	17/5/42	42
254	*Gurnard*	9/41	1/6/42	42
255	*Haddo*	10/41	21/6/42	42
256	*Hake*	11/41	7/42	42
258	*Hoe*	42	17/9/42	42
259	*Jack*	42	16/10/42	43
260	*Lapon*	42	27/10/42	
261	*Muskallonge*	42	13/12/42	
262	*Paddie*	42	30/12/42	
263	*Mingo*	42	30/11/42	
264	*Pargo*	42	24/1/43	
265	*Peto*	18/6/41	30/4/42	21/11/42
266	*Pogy*	10/41	22/6/42	43
267	*Pompon*	11/41	8/42	43
268	*Puffer*	42	22/11/42	43
269	*Rasher*			
270	*Raton*			
271	*Ray*	42	43	43
272	*Redfin*			
274	*Rock*			
276	*Sawfish*	41	23/6/42	42
280	*Steelhead*	42	11/9/42	43
281	*Sunfish*	41	2/5/42	42
282	*Tunny*	10/11/41	1/7/42	42
283	*Tinosa*	42	8/10/42	43

122 Balao Class.

13 Cramp S.B. Co.:
- **Devilfish** (May 30, 1943)
- **Dragonet** (April 18, 1943)
- **Hackleback** (May 30, 1943)
- **Lancetfish** (Aug. 18, 1943)
- **Ling** (Aug. 18, 1943)
- **Lionfish** (Nov. 7, 1943)
- **Manta** (Nov. 7, 1943)
- **Moray** (May 14, 1944)
- **Roncador** (May 14, 1944)
- **Sabalo** (June 4, 1944)
- **Sablefish** (June 4, 1944)
- **Trumpetfish** (Feb. 19, 1944)
- **Tusk** (July 8, 1945)

42 Electric Boat Co.
- **Apogon** (1943)
- **Archerfish** (May 29, 1943)
- **Aspro** (April 7, 1943)
- **Barbero** (Dec. 12, 1943)
- **Batfish** (May 3, 1943)
- **Baya** (Jan. 2, 1944)
- **Becuna** (Jan. 30, 1944)
- **Bergall** (Feb. 16, 1944)
- **Besugo** (Feb. 27, 1944)
- **Blackfin** (March 12, 1944)
- **Blenny** (April 9, 1944)
- **Blower** (April 23, 1944)
- **Blueback** (May 7, 1944)
- **Boarfish** (May 21, 1944)
- **Brill** (June 25, 1944)
- **Bugara** (July 2, 1944)
- **Bumper** (Aug. 6, 1944)
- **Burrfish** (June 18, 1943)
- **Cabezon** (Aug. 27, 1944)
- **Caiman** (March 30, 1944)
- **Capitaine** (Oct. 1, 1944)
- **Carbonero** (Oct. 15, 1944)
- **Carp** (Nov. 12, 1944)
- **Catfish** (Nov. 19, 1944)
- **Charr** (May 28, 1944)
- **Chivo** (Jan. 14, 1945)
- **Chopper** (Feb. 14, 1945)

- **Chub** (June 18, 1944)
- **Clamagore** (Feb. 23, 1945)
- **Cobbler** (April 1, 1945)
- **Cochino** April 16, 1945)
- **Corporal** (June 10, 1945)
- **Cubera** (June 17, 1945)
- **Cusk** (July 28, 1945)
- **Dentuda** (Sept. 10, 1944)
- **Diodon**
- **Dogfish**
- **Entemedor** (Dec. 17, 1944)
- **Greenfish**
- **Halfbeak**
- **Perch** (Sept. 12, 1943)
- **Sealion** (Oct. 31, 1943)

15 Manitowoc S.B. Co.:
- **Guavina**
- **Guitarro**
- **Hammerhead** (Oct. 27, 1943)
- **Hardhead**
- **Hawkbill**
- **Icefish** (Feb. 20, 1944)
- **Jallao**
- **Kraken**
- **Lamprey**
- **Lizardfish**
- **Loggerhead**
- **Macabi**
- **Mapiro**
- **Menhaden** (Dec. 20, 1944)
- **Mero**

9 Mare Island Navy Yard:
- **Seahorse** (Jan. 9, 1943)
- **Skate** (March 4, 1943)
- **Spadefish** (Jan. 8, 1944)
- **Spot** (May 20, 1944)
- **Springer** (1944)
- **Stickleback** (Jan. 1, 1944)
- **Tilefish** (Oct. 25, 1943)
- **Tiru** (1944)
- **Trepang** (March 23, 1944)

43 Portsmouth Navy Yard:
- **Atule** (March 6, 1944)
- **Balao** (Nov. 1942)
- **Bang** (Aug. 30, 1943)
- **Billfish** (Nov. 13, 1942)
- **Bowfin** (Dec. 7, 1943)
- **Cabrilla** (Dec. 4, 1942)
- **Crevalle** (Feb. 22, 1943)
- **Pampanito** (1943)
- **Parche** (July 24, 1943)
- **Picuda** (1943)
- **Pilotfish** (Aug. 30, 1943)
- **Pintado** (Sept. 15, 1943)
- **Pipefish** (Oct. 12, 1943)
- **Piper** (June 26, 1944)
- **Piranha** (Oct. 27, 1943)
- **Plaice** (Nov. 15, 1943)
- **Pomfret** (Oct. 27, 1943)
- **Queenfish** (Nov. 30, 1943)
- **Quillback** (Oct. 1, 1944)
- **Razorback** (Jan. 27, 1944)
- **Redfish** (Jan. 27, 1944)
- **Ronquil** (Jan. 27, 1944)
- **Sandlance** (June 25, 1943)
- **Scabbardfish** (Jan. 27, 1944)
- **Seacat** (Feb. 21, 1944)
- **Seadevil** (Feb. 28, 1944)
- **Seadog** (March 28, 1944)
- **Seafox** (March 28, 1944)
- **Sea Owl** (May 7, 1944)
- **Sea Poacher** (May 20, 1944)
- **Segundo** (Feb. 5, 1944)
- **Sennet**
- **Spikefish** (April 26, 1944)
- **Stelret** (Oct. 27, 1943)
- **Tench** (July 7, 1944)
- **Thornback** (July 7, 1944)
- **Threadfin** (June 26, 1944)
- **Tigrone** (July 20, 1944)
- **Tirante**
- **Toro** (Aug. 19, 1944)
- **Torsk** (Sept., 1944)
- **Trutta** (Aug. 18, 1944)

CORPORAL ("Guppy" conversion)   Added 1950, U.S. Navy, Official.

CHOPPER.   1952, A. & J. Pavia.

Displacement:	1,526 tons (2,425 tons *full load*)
Dimensions:	311¼ × 27 × 17 feet (Guppy conversions 309 (o.a.) feet, but length varies)
Guns:	Mostly 1 or 2—5 inch, 25 cal., 2—40 mm. AA. Armament varies (Guppies, no guns)
Tubes:	10—21 inch (6 bow, 4 stern), 24 torpedoes
Machinery:	G.M., Fairbanks-Morse or H.O.R. 2-stroke Diesels. B.H.P.: 6,500 = 20 kts. (surface), H.P.: 2,750 = 10 kts. (submerged). Dogfish, submerged speed, 17·25 kts.
Complement:	85

Notes.—In order to facilitate rapid building, all are of the same general type as *Gato* class, of all-welded construction, and with a high standard of accommodation, including separate messing and sleeping compartments. Average time of construction during war was reduced to about nine months. War losses: *Barbel, Bullhead, Capelin, Cisco, Escolar, Golet, Kete, Lagarto, Shark, Tang.* Eighteen cancelled: *Dugong, Eel, Espada, Garloppa, Garuppa, Goldring, Jawfish, Needlefish* (379), *Nerka, Ono, Turbot, Ulua, Unicorn, Vandace, Walrus* (431), *Whitefish, Whiting, Wolffish.* In addition *Apogon, Pilotfish* and *Skate* were placed on disposal list after being employed as atom bomb targets. *Dentuda* and *Parche* of this class are non-operational submarines assigned to Naval Reserve Training duties. *Cusk* armed with guided missiles; *Barbero* equipped to carry cargo; *Sealion* and *Perch* fitted to carry troops; and *Burrfish* modified for radar picket duties with reduced armament; *Guavina* converted to oiler. *Tiru* altered during construction for higher submerged speed. *Baya* equipped for electronic experiments (see later pages). After two explosions in her battery room, *Cochino* caught fire and sank off the northern coast of Norway, Aug. 26, 1949, while on an Arctic training cruise. *Blower* (325), *Bluejack* (326), *Boarfish* (327), *Chub* (329), *Brill* (330), *Bumper* (333) transferred to Turkey.

REDFISH.   1953, U.S. Navy, Official.

PIPER.   1952, Charles C. Rumsegh.

DOGFISH.   1949, Evening News, Portsmouth, England.

HAWKBILL. (In later units, numbered 408 and above, gun is before C.T.)   1946, Ted Stone.

2 Converted "Balao" Class.

CUSK.   1951, U.S. Navy, Official.

SSG	SSG
337 CARBONERO	348 CUSK

Displacement :	1,526 tons (2,425 tons submerged)
Dimensions :	311¼ × 27 × 17 feet
Machinery :	Diesels : B.H.P. : 6,500 = 20 kts. (surface), H.P. : 2,750 = 10 kts. (submerged)

Notes.—Before conversion were of "Balao" class, see earlier page. *Carbonero* launched a guided missile in 1949. Conversion of *Cusk* for guided missile operation was completed and test carried out in June 1948. " Loon " missile is contained in a watertight **steel** hangar and takes off from a ramp fixed to the submarine's deck.

Submarines (SS)
21 "Gato" Class

10 *Electric Boat Co.*
T CERO
T COBIA
T COD
T GATO
T GREENLING
T GUARDFISH
T GURNARD
T HAKE
T HOE
T PARGO

3 *Mare Island Navy Yard*
T SILVERSIDES
T SUNFISH
T WHALE

6 *Portsmouth Navy Yard*
T DRUM
T HADDOCK
T KINGFISH
T SAWFISH
T SHAD
T STEELHEAD

2 *Manitowoc S.B. Co.*
T PETO
T PUFFER

WHALE   *Added 1956, U.S. Navy, Official*

Displacement:	1,525 tons *surface* (2,425 tons *submerged*)
Dimensions:	311¾ × 27 × 17 feet
Guns:	Vary 1—3 or 5 inch, 50—25 cal., d.p., 2—20 mm. AA.; but some, including *Finback*, had 2—5 inch, 25 cal., 2—40 mm. AA.
Tubes:	10—21 inch (6 bow, 4 stern)
Machinery:	G.M. 2-stroke diesels. B.H.P.: 6,500 =21 kts. (surface). Electric motors. H.P.: 2,750=10 kts. (submerged). Have 2 engine rooms instead of 1 as in previous class, to reduce size of compartments
Oil fuel:	300 tons
Radius:	12,000 miles at 10 kts.
Complement:	85

HAKE   *U.S. Navy, Official*

General Notes

Ordered under the 1939-41 Programs. Are improved editions of " Tambor " class. Inclusive cost per ship officially estimated at $6,288,200. War losses: *Albacore, Amberjack, Bonefish, Corvina, Darter, Dorado, Flier, Growler, Grunion, Harder, Herring, Robalo, Runner, Scamp, Scorpion, Snook, Trigger, Tullibee, Wahoo.* Following units of this class have been assigned to training duties with Naval Reserve units: *Drum, Greenling, Guardfish, Gurnard, Kingfish, Pargo, Puffer, Sawfish, Shad, Silversides, Steelhead, Sunfish.*

No.	Name	Laid down	Launched	Completed
212	Gato	5 Oct. 1940	21 Aug. 1941	31 Dec. 1941
213	Greenling	12 Nov. 1940	20 Sep. 1941	21 Jan. 1942
217	Guardfish	1 Apr. 1941	20 Jan. 1942	8 May 1942
224	Cod	21 July 1942	21 Mar. 1943	21 June 1943
225	Cero	24 Aug. 1942	4 Apr. 1943	3 July 1943
228	Drum	11 Sep. 1940	12 May 1941	23 Dec. 1941
231	Haddock	31 Mar. 1941	20 Oct. 1941	14 Mar. 1942
234	Kingfish	29 Aug. 1941	2 Mar. 1942	16 June 1942
235	Shad	24 Oct. 1941	15 Apr. 1942	15 July 1942
236	Silversides	4 Nov. 1940	26 Aug. 1941	15 Dec. 1942
239	Whale	28 June 1941	14 Mar. 1942	1 June 1942
245	Cobia	17 Mar. 1943	28 Nov. 1943	28 Mar. 1944
254	Gurnard	2 Sep. 1941	1 June 1942	18 Sep. 1942
256	Hake	1 Nov. 1941	17 July 1942	30 Oct. 1942
258	Hoe	2 Jan. 1942	17 Sep. 1942	16 Dec. 1942
264	Pargo	21 May 1942	24 Jan. 1943	26 Apr. 1943
265	Peto	18 June 1941	30 Mar. 1942	21 Nov. 1942
268	Puffer	16 Feb. 1942	22 Nov. 1942	22 Apr. 1943
276	Sawfish	20 Jan. 1942	23 June 1942	26 Aug. 1943
280	Steelhead	1 June 1942	11 Sep. 1942	7 Dec. 1943
281	Sunfish	25 Sep. 1941	2 May 1942	15 July 1942

SILVERSIDES   *1955, U.S. Navy, Official*

Conversion Notes

Grouper was converted to a large submarine hunter-killer (SSK) in 1950 and *Angler, Bashaw, Bluegill, Bream, Cavalla* and *Croaker* were similarly converted to anti-submarine submarines (SSK) in 1951-53. *Pompom, Rasher, Raton, Ray, Redfin* and *Rock* were converted to Radar Picket Submarines (SSR); and *Flying Fish* (scrapped in 1959) was converted to an experimental submarine (AGSS). *Tunny* was converted to a Guided Missile Submarine (SSG) in 1953.

Training Notes

All units marked **T** are non-operational submarines assigned to naval reserve training.

Transfer Notes

In 1954 *Barb*, SS 202, and *Dace*, SS 247, were transferred to Italy, and *Guittaro*, SS 363, and *Hammerhead*, SS 364, were transferred to Turkey (loans extended for five years in 1959). In late August 1955 *Mingo*, SS 261, was transferred to Japan on loan for five years. *Muskallunge* and *Paddle* were loaned to Brazil in Jan. 1957. *Jack* and *Lapon* were loaned to Greece in 1957 (*Jack* transferred on 21 Apr. 1958, *Lapon* transferred on 8 Aug. 1957).

Recent Disposals

Blackfish, SS 221, *Finback*, SS 230, *Gunnel*, SS 253, *Haddo*, SS 255, *Pogy*, SS 266, and *Tinosa*, SS 283, were stricken from the Navy List in early 1959.
Bluefish, SS 222, *Flasher*, SS 249, *Flounder*, SS 251, and *Gabilan*, SS 252, were stricken in late 1959.

4 Converted "Gato" Class

4 *Manitowoc S.B. Co.*

AGSS
269 RASHER
270 RATON

AGSS
272 REDFIN
274 ROCK

Displacement:	1,750 tons *standard*, 1,800 tons *surface* (2,500 tons *submerged*)
Dimensions:	343 × 27 × 17 feet.
Machinery:	G.M. 2-stroke diesels. B.H.P.: 6,500=21 kts. (surface). Electric motors. H.P.: 2,750=10 kts. (submerged)
Oil fuel:	300 tons
Radius:	12,000 miles at 10 kts.
Complement:	85

General

Before conversion into Radar Picket Submarines, SSR, these were conventional submarines of the "Gato" class, see later page. They were cut in two to permit the installation of new electronic equipment. Two new mid-sections lengthened them by 31 feet from their original 311¾ feet and increased their displacement from their original 1,525 tons. *Redfin* re-commissioned 9 Jan. 1953. *Rock* 12 Oct. 1953. *Redfin* was reclassified from SSR to SS in 1959 and to AGSS in June 1963, and *Rasher, Raton,* and *Rock* to AGSS in 1960.

Name	Laid down	Launched	Completed
Rasher	4 May 1942	20 Dec. 1942	8 June 1943
Raton	29 May 1942	24 Jan. 1943	13 July 1943
Redfin	3 Sep. 1942	4 Apr. 1943	31 Aug. 1943
Rock	23 Dec. 1942	20 June 1943	26 Oct. 1943

Disposals

Pompon, SSR 267, and *Ray*, 271, were stricken from the Navy List at the end of 1960.

REDFIN   *1961, United States Navy, Official*

9 Attack Submarines (SS): Guppy III Type

Name	No.	Builder	Laid down	Launched	Commissioned
*CLAMAGORE	SS 343	Electric Boat Co	16 Mar 1944	25 Feb 1945	21 Oct 1944
*COBBLER	SS 344	Electric Boat Co	3 Apr 1944	1 Apr 1945	8 Aug 1945
*CORPORAL	SS 346	Electric Boat Co	27 Apr 1944	10 June 1945	9 Nov 1945
*GREENFISH	SS 351	Electric Boat Co	29 June 1944	21 Dec 1945	7 June 1946
*TIRU	SS 416	Mare Island Navy Yard	17 Apr 1944	16 Sep 1947	1 Sep 1948
*TRUMPETFISH	SS 425	Cramp Shipbuilding Co	23 Aug 1943	13 May 1945	29 Jan 1946
*REMORA	SS 487	Portsmouth Navy Yard	5 Mar 1945	12 July 1945	3 Jan 1946
*VOLADOR	SS 490	Portsmouth Navy Yard	15 June 1945	17 Jan 1946	10 Jan 1948
*PICKEREL	SS 524	Boston Navy Yard	8 Feb 1944	15 Dec 1944	4 Apr 1949

Displacement, tons	1 975 standard ; 2 540 submerged
Length, feet (metres)	326·5 (99·4) oa
Beam, feet (metres)	27 (8·2)
Draft, feet (metres)	17 (5·2)
Torpedo tubes	10—21 in (533 mm) ; 6 fwd, 4 aft
Main engines	4 diesels ; 6 400 shp/2 electric motors ; 5 400 shp ; 2 shafts
Speed, knots	20 surface ; 15 submerged
Complement	approx 86

Nine submarines of the "Balao" and "Tench" classes were modernised under the GUPPY III programme in 1960-1962 (see *Design* notes). All previously were GUPPY II submarines. Plans for 15 additional GUPPY III modernisations were dropped in favour of new construction, nuclear-powered submarines.

DESIGN. The Greater Underwater Propulsion Programme (GUPPY) evolved after World War II as a method to improve underwater performance of existing US submarines. The GUPPY concept was based on the German Type XXI submarines which were mass produced in 1944-1945. The Type XXI characteristics included a streamlined hull and superstructure, snorkel, and increased battery power.
The US Navy's GUPPY conversions have similar features, with resulting increases in underwater speed and endurance, plus improved fire control and electronic equipment over their unmodernised sister submarines.

ELECTRONICS. GUPPY submarines are fitted with BQR-2 array sonar.

ENGINEERING. The GUPPY III submarines have two 126-cell electric batteries; all GUPPY submarines are fitted with snorkel to permit operation of diesel engines to charge batteries and for propulsion while at Periscope depth. The *Tiru* has only three diesel engines (4 800 shp).

PHOTOGRAPHS. Small, fin-like structures on submarines are hydrophones (referred to as PUFFS—acronym for Passive Underwater Fire Control Feasibility Study, an anti-submarine targeting system). GUPPY conversions have rounded bows as opposed to "ship" bows in streamlined fleet-type submarines.

PICKEREL (SS 524) with P-3 Orion   *Lockheed Aircraft*

CORPORAL (SS 346)   *1967, United States Navy*

COBBLER (SS 344)   *1970, Anthony & Joseph Pavia*

GREENFISH (SS 351)   *1969, United States Navy*

14 Attack Submarines (SS): GUPPY II Type

Displacement, tons	1 870 standard; 2 420 submerged				
Length, feet (*metres*)	307·5 (*93·6*) oa				
Beam, feet (*metres*)	27·2 (*8·3*)				
Draft, feet (*metres*)	18 (*5·5*)				
Torpedo tubes	10—21 in (*533 mm*); 6 fwd, 4 aft				
Main engines	3 diesels; 4 800 shp/2 electric motors; 5 400 shp; 2 shafts				
Speed, knots	18 surface; 15 submerged				
Complement	Approx 82				

Name	No.	Builder	Laid down	Launched	Commissioned
*CATFISH	SS 339	Electric Boat Co	6 Jan 1944	19 Nov 1944	19 Mar 1945
*CUBERA	SS 347	Electric Boat Co	11 May 1944	17 June 1945	19 Dec 1945
*DIODON	SS 349	Electric Boat Co	1 June 1944	10 Sep 1945	18 Mar 1946
*DOGFISH	SS 350	Electric Boat Co	22 June 1944	27 Oct 1945	29 Apr 1946
*HALFBEAK	SS 352	Electric Boat Co	6 July 1944	19 Feb 1946	22 July 1946
*TUSK	SS 426	Cramp Shipbuilding Co	23 Aug 1943	8 July 1945	11 Apr 1946
*CUTLASS	SS 478	Portsmouth Navy Yard	22 July 1944	5 Nov 1944	17 Mar 1945
*SEA LEOPARD	SS 483	Portsmouth Navy Yard	7 Nov 1944	2 Mar 1945	11 June 1945
*ODAX	SS 484	Portsmouth Navy Yard	4 Dec 1944	10 Apr 1945	11 July 1945
*SIRAGO	SS 485	Portsmouth Navy Yard	3 Jan 1945	5 May 1945	13 Aug 1945
*POMODON	SS 486	Portsmouth Navy Yard	29 Jan 1945	12 June 1945	11 Sep 1945
*AMBERJACK	SS 522	Boston Navy Yard	8 Feb 1944	15 Dec 1944	4 Mar 1946
*GRAMPUS	SS 523	Boston Navy Yard	8 Feb 1944	15 Dec 1944	26 Oct 1949
*GRENADIER	SS 525	Boston Navy Yard	8 Feb 1944	15 Dec 1944	2 Oct 1951

Fifteen submarines of the "Balao" and "Tench" classes were modernised under the GUPPY II programme in 1948-1950. The *Odax* and *Pomodon* were initially modernised to a GUPPY I configuration; subsequently updated to GUPPY II. The *Cochino* (SS 345) of this type was lost off Norway on a training cruise on 26 Aug 1949 (one civilian on board was lost; no naval personnel killed). General GUPPY notes are found in the GUPPY III listing.

The *Tiru* (now GUPPY III) was completed to the GUPPY configuration.

ENGINEERING. GUPPY II submarines have four 126-cell electric batteries. The *Pomodon* has only two 1 600 hp-diesel and is fitted with a special 1 500-hp diesel for snorkel operations.

CUBERA (SS 347)   *1964. United States Navy*

POMODON (SS 486)   *1961. United States Navy*

AMBERJACK (SS 522)   *1965, United States Navy*

15 Attack Submarines (SS): GUPPY IIA Type

Name	No.	Builder	Laid down	Launched	Commissioned
*ENTEMEDOR	SS 340	Electric Boat Co	3 Feb 1944	17 Dec 1944	6 Apr 1945
*HARDHEAD	SS 365	Manitowoc Shipbuilding Co	7 July 1943	12 Dec 1943	18 Apr 1944
*JALLAO	SS 368	Manitowoc Shipbuilding Co	29 Sep 1943	12 Mar 1944	8 July 1944
*MENHADEN	SS 377	Manitowoc Shipbuilding Co	21 June 1944	20 Dec 1944	22 June 1945
*PICUDA	SS 382	Portsmouth Navy Yard	15 Mar 1943	12 July 1943	16 Oct 1943
*BANG	SS 385	Portsmouth Navy Yard	30 Apr 1943	30 Aug 1943	4 Dec 1943
*POMFRET	SS 391	Portsmouth Navy Yard	14 July 1943	27 Oct 1943	19 Feb 1944
*RAZORBACK	SS 394	Portsmouth Navy Yard	9 Sep 1943	27 Jan 1944	3 Apr 1944
*RONQUIL	SS 396	Portsmouth Navy Yard	9 Sep 1943	27 Jan 1944	22 Apr 1944
*SEA FOX	SS 402	Portsmouth Navy Yard	2 Nov 1943	28 Mar 1944	13 June 1944
*THREADFIN	SS 410	Portsmouth Navy Yard	18 Mar 1944	26 June 1944	30 Aug 1944
*THORNBACK	SS 418	Portsmouth Navy Yard	5 Apr 1944	7 July 1944	13 Oct 1944
*TIRANTE	SS 420	Portsmouth Navy Yard	28 Apr 1944	9 Aug 1944	6 Nov 1944
*TRUTTA	SS 421	Portsmouth Navy Yard	22 May 1944	18 Aug 1944	16 Nov 1944
*QUILLBACK	SS 424	Portsmouth Navy Yard	27 June 1944	1 Oct 1944	29 Dec 1944

Displacement, tons	1 840 standard; 2 445 submerged
Length, feet (metres)	306 (93·2) oa
Beam, feet (metres)	27 (8·2)
Draft, feet (metres)	17 (5·2)
Torpedo tubes	10—21 in (533 mm); 6 fwd; 4 aft
Main engines	3 diesels; 4 800 shp/2 electric motors; 5 400 shp; 2 shafts
Speed, knots	18 surface; 15 submerged
Complement	Approx 84

Sixteen submarines of the "Balao" and "Tench" classes were modernised under the GUPPY IIA programme in 1952-1954. The *Stickleback* (SS 415) of this type was rammed and sunk off Hawaii on 29 May 1958 (no crewmen lost). General GUPPY conversion notes are found in the GUPPY III listing.

ENGINEERING. The GUPPY IIA submarines have two 126-cell electric batteries.

PHOTOGRAPHS. Note differing superstructure designs; stepped structures in some submarines are being replaced with more streamlined structures of light-weight materials as in *Hardhead*.

HARDHEAD (SS 365)   1964. United States Navy

SEAFOX (SS 402)   1961. United States Navy

THREADFIN (SS 410) —to Turkey   1967, United States Navy

GUPPY SUBMARINES

All 52 submarines modernised to the GUPPY (Greater Underwater Propulsion Project) configurations have been deleted or transferred to other navies. The last GUPPY submarines to serve with the US Navy were *Clamagore* (SS 343) deleted on 27 June 1975 and *Tiru* (SS 416) deleted on 1 July 1975. They were not transferred to Turkey, as planned. *Tiru* was converted to a mobile target and sunk in July 1979 while *Clamagore* was transferred to the Patriots' Point Development Authority, Charleston S.C. on 3 August 1979 for preservation as a memorial. Other corrections to the comprehensive list of GUPPY submarine disposals and transfers provided in the 1974-75 edition include: *Blenny* (SS 324) deleted on 15 August 1973 (sunk as target); *Sea Poacher* (SS 406) transferred to Peru on 1 July 1974; *Atule* (SS 403) transferred to Peru on 31 July 1974. *Tench* (SS 417) to Peru 16 September 1976 for spares.

10 Attack Submarines (SS): GUPPY IA Type

Name	No.	Builder	Laid down	Launched	Commissioned
*BECUNA	SS 319	Electric Boat Co	29 Apr 1943	30 Jan 1944	27 May 1944
*BLACKFIN	SS 322	Electric Boat Co	10 June 1943	12 Mar 1944	4 July 1944
*CAIMAN	SS 323	Electric Boat Co	24 June 1943	30 Mar 1944	17 July 1944
*BLENNY	SS 324	Electric Boat Co	8 July 1943	9 Apr 1944	27 July 1944
*CHIVO	SS 341	Electric Boat Co	21 Feb 1944	14 Jan 1945	28 Apr 1945
*CHOPPER	SS 342	Electric Boat Co	2 Mar 1944	4 Feb 1945	25 May 1945
*ATULE	SS 403	Portsmouth Navy Yard	2 Dec 1943	6 Mar 1944	21 June 1944
*SEA POACHER	SS 406	Portsmouth Navy Yard	23 Feb 1944	20 May 1944	31 July 1944
*SEA ROBIN	SS 407	Portsmouth Navy Yard	1 Mar 1944	25 May 1944	7 Aug 1944
*TENCH	SS 417	Portsmouth Navy Yard	1 Apr 1944	7 July 1944	6 Oct 1944

Displacement, tons 1 870 standard ; 2 440 submerged
Length, feet (metres) 308 (93·8) oa
Beam, feet (metres) 27 (8·2)
Draft, feet (metres) 17 (5·2)
Torpedo tubes 10—21 in (533 mm) ; 6 fwd, 4 aft
Main engines 3 diesels ; 4 800 shp/2 electric motors ; 5 400 shp ; 2 shafts
Speed, knots 18 surface ; 15 submerged
Complement approx 84

Ten submarines of the "Balao" and "Tench" classes were modernised under the GUPPY IA programme in 1951. General GUPPY conversion notes are found in the GUPPY III listing.

ENGINEERING. GUPPY IA submarines have two 126-cell electric batteries.

CAIMAN (SS 323)   1964, United States Navy

BLENNY (SS 324)   1966, United States Navy

TENCH (SS 417)   1968, United States Navy

8 Fleet Submarines (AGSS/SS): "Tench" Class

		Name	No.	Builder	Laid down	Launched	Commissioned
Displacement, tons	1 840 standard; 2 400 submerged	TIGRONE	AGSS 419	Portsmouth Navy Yard	8 May 1944	20 July 1944	25 Oct 1944
Length, feet (metres)	312 (95·1) oa	*TORSK	AGSS 423	Portsmouth Navy Yard	7 June 1944	6 Sep 1944	16 Dec 1944
Beam, feet (metres)	27·2 (8·3)	*ARGONAUT	SS 475	Portsmouth Navy Yard	28 June 1944	1 Oct 1944	15 Jan 1945
Draft, feet (metres)	16·5 (5·0)	*RUNNER	SS 476	Portsmouth Navy Yard	10 July 1944	17 Oct 1944	26 Feb 1945
Torpedo tubes	10—21 in (533 mm); 6 fwd, 4 aft	*MEDREGAL	AGSS 480	Portsmouth Navy Yard	21 Aug 1944	15 Dec 1944	14 Apr 1945
Main engines	4 diesels; 6 400 shp/2 electric	*REQUIN	AGSS 481	Portsmouth Navy Yard	24 Aug 1944	1 Jan 1945	28 Apr 1945
	motors; 5 400 shp; 2 shafts	*IREX	SS 482	Portsmouth Navy Yard	2 Oct 1944	26 Jan 1945	14 May 1945
Speed, knots	20 surface; 10 submerged	*SPINAX	SS 489	Portsmouth Navy Yard	14 May 1945	20 Nov 1945	20 Sep 1946
Complement	approx 85						

Twenty-seven "Tench" class submarines were completed as fleet submarines in 1944-1946 and four others were completed to GUPPY configurations in 1949-1950. Fourteen of the older boats subsequently were converted under the various GUPPY programmes. A further 101 submarines of this design were cancelled in 1944-1945 as building programmes were adjusted, Allied victory in the Pacific came closer, and submarine transits to patrol areas became shorter with acquisition of advanced submarine bases (see below)

Only eight non-GUPPY submarines of this class remain on the Navy List, among them three former radar picket submarines (see *Conversion* notes). The *Torsk* is in caretaker status with a skeleton crew on board.

MEDREGAL (SS 480)   *1963, United States Navy*

CANCELLATIONS. Cancelled units were *Unicorn* (SS 429), *Vandace* (SS 430), *Walrus* (SS 431), *Whitefish* (SS 432), *Whiting* (SS 433), *Wolffish* (SS 434), unnamed SS 438-474, 495-515, 517-521, *Dorado* (SS 526), *Comber* (SS 527), *Sea Panther* (SS 528), *Tibourn* (SS 529), unnamed SS 530-544, 548-550, 545-547, *Pompano* (SS 491), *Grayling* (SS 492), *Needlefish* (SS 493), *Sculpin* (SS 494), and *Wahoo* (SS 516). The hulls of the uncompleted *Unicorn* and *Walrus* were not stricken until 1957. Construction of the *Turbot* (SS 427) and *Ulua* (SS 428) were "deferred" in August 1945 and their unfinished hulls were used in machinery experiments.

CLASSIFICATION. *Tigrone* to AGSS on 1 Dec 1963, *Torsk* to AGSS on 1 May 1968, *Medregal* to AGSS on 1 May 1967, *Requin* to AGSS on 29 June 1968.

CONVERSIONS. The *Tigrone*, *Requin*, and *Spinax* were converted to radar picket submarines in 1947-1948 and reclassified SSR, *Tigrone* on 31 Mar 1948 and the others on 19 Jan 1948; fitted with elaborate air search radar and air control centre. All three reclassified SS on 15 Aug 1959 with end of radar picket submarine programme.

SPINAX (SS 489)   *1965, United States Navy*

DESIGN. These ships were originally of an improved "Balao" class design, slightly larger and with a deeper operating capability. As built the fleet types carried deck guns of varying size and number (authorised gun armament was one 5 inch 25 calibre mount and a single 40 mm mount plus MG). Several of the surviving fleet-type have been fitted with streamlined superstructures but can be differentiated from GUPPY conversions by their ship-like prows.

ENGINEERING. Six of the eight surviving submarines of this type have snorkel installations (not in *Tigrone* and *Spinax*).

DISPOSALS AND TRANSFERS
Toro (SS 422) stricken from the Navy List in 1963, **Corsair** (SS 435) and **Conger** (SS 477) stricken in 1963, **Diablo** (SS 479) sold to Pakistan in 1964, and **Sarda** (SS 488) sold to Spain in 1965.

RUNNER   *1961, United States Navy, Official*

13 Fleet Submarines (AGSS/SS): "Balao" Class

Displacement, tons	1 450 standard; 2 400 submerged
Length, feet (metres)	312 (95·1) oa
Beam, feet (metres)	27·2 (8·25)
Draft, feet (metres)	17·2 (5·25)
Torpedo tubes	10—21 in (533 mm); 6 fwd, 4 aft
Main engines	4 diesels; 6 400 shp/2 electric motors; 5 400 shp; 2 shafts
Speed, knots	20 surface; 10 submerged
Complement	approx 85

Name	No.	Builder	Laid down	Launched	Commissioned
*CREVALLE	AGSS 291	Portsmouth Navy Yard	14 Nov 1942	22 Feb 1943	24 June 1943
*SABALO	SS 302	Cramp Shipbuilding (Phila)	5 June 1943	4 June 1944	19 June 1945
*SABLEFISH	SS 303	Cramp Shipbuilding (Phila)	5 June 1943	4 June 1944	18 Dec 1945
*ARCHERFISH	AGSS 311	Portsmouth Navy Yard	22 Jan 1943	28 May 1943	4 Sep 1943
*CHARR	AGSS 328	Electric Boat Company	26 Aug 1943	28 May 1944	23 Sep 1944
*BUGARA	SS 331	Electric Boat Company	21 Oct 1943	2 July 1944	15 Nov 1944
*CARBONERO	SS 337	Electric Boat Company	16 Dec 1943	15 Oct 1944	7 Feb 1945
*CUSK	SS 348	Electric Boat Company	25 May 1944	28 July 1945	5 Feb 1946
*STERLET	SS 392	Portsmouth Navy Yard	14 July 1943	27 Oct 1943	4 Mar 1944
*SEGUNDO	SS 398	Portsmouth Navy Yard	14 Oct 1943	5 Feb 1944	9 May 1944
*SEA CAT	AGSS 399	Portsmouth Navy Yard	30 Oct 1943	21 Feb 1944	16 May 1944
*SEA OWL	SS 405	Portsmouth Navy Yard	7 Feb 1944	7 May 1944	17 July 1944
*SENNET	SS 408	Portsmouth Navy Yard	8 Mar 1944	6 June 1944	22 Aug 1944

One hundred-twenty "Balao" class submarines were completed in 1943-1948, most of which were operational during World War II. Thirty-one submarines were converted to GUPPY configurations. Ten submarines of this type were cancelled in 1944 and the SS 353-355 were renumbered SS 435-437. Numerous war losses, transfers, conversions, and disposals are listed below. Three stricken submarines were used as target ships in the 1946 atomic bomb tests at Bikini (Skate, Apogon, Pilotfish).

Twenty-nine "Balao" class submarines remain on the Navy List: 13 boats listed above, three conversions listed separately, and 13 immobilised dockside trainers (see Training note). The Crevalle is an operational training ship for the Naval Reserve.

CANCELLATIONS. Cancelled units were Jawfish (SS 356), Ono (SS 357), Garlopa (SS 358), Garruda (SS 359), Goldring (SS 360), Needlefish (SS 379), Nerka (SS 380), Dugong (SS 353), Eel (SS 354), and Espada (SS 355). The hull of the uncompleted Lancetfish (SS 296) was stricken in 1957.

CLASSIFICATION. Crevalle to AGSS in 1960, Archerfish to AGSS in 1960, Sea Cat to AGSS on 29 June 1968.

CONVERSIONS. Flying Fish (SS 229) fitted for experimental work and reclassified AGSS in 1950; Manta (SS 299) fitted for research, to AGSS in 1949; Archerfish (SS 311) fitted for surveying and oceanographic research, to AGSS in 1960; Burrfish (SS 312) converted to radar picket configuration, to SSR in 1949 (reverted to SS in 1961); Perch (SS 313) converted to transport submarine, to SSP in 1948, to ASSP in 1950, to APSS in 1956; Sealion (SS 315) converted to transport submarine, to SSP in 1948, to ASSP in 1950, to APSS in 1956; Barbero (SS 317) converted to cargo submarine, to SSA in 1948, to ASSA in 1950; subsequently converted to fire Regulus I missile and reclassified SSG in 1955; Baya (SS 318) converted to electronic research craft, to AGSS in 1949; Carbonero (SS 337) converted to fire guided missiles but not reclassified; Cusk (SS 348) converted to fire guided missiles, to SSG in 1948 (reverted to SS in 1954); Guavina (SS 263) converted to refuel seaplanes, to SSO in 1948, to AGSS in 1951, to AOSS in 1957. Conversion of Picuda (SS 382) to submarine minelayer (SSM) was cancelled.

DESIGN. As built these submarines carried deck guns of varying size and number. Authorised armament included one 5 inch 25 calibre gun and a single 40 mm mount plus 20 mm and ·50 calibre machine guns; several submarines carried two 5 inch guns, two 40 mm guns, and several MG. Original configuration provided for carrying 24 contemporary torpedoes (including ten in tubes). Streamlined superstructures fitted to some fleet boats.

ENGINEERING. All surviving fleet type submarines of this class have snorkel installations except the Crevalle and Archerfish.

TRAINING. Thirteen of the submarines of this type are immobilised dockside training ships for the Naval reserve. Their torpedo tubes are welded shut, propellers removed, berthing spaces converted to classrooms. Bowfin (AGSS 287), Cabrilla (AGSS 288), Ling (AGSS 297), Lionfish (AGSS 298), Roncador (AGSS 301), Perch (APSS 313), Cabezon (AGSS 334), Carp (AGSS 338), Pampanito (AGSS 383), Parche (AGSS 384), Sea Dog (AGSS 401), Piper (AGSS 409).

WAR LOSSES. Ten submarines of this class were lost during World War II: Capelin (SS 289), Cisco (SS 290), Esoclar (SS 294), Tank (SS 306), Shark (SS 314), Barbel (SS 316), Bullhead (SS 332), Golet (SS 361), Kete (SS 369), Lagarto (SS 371).

PIPER (AGSS 409) (now dockside trainer)   1964, United States Navy

SEA CAT (AGSS 399)   1967, A. & J. Pavia

DISPOSALS AND TRANSFERS

Balao (AGSS 286) stricken in 1963, Devilfish (AGSS 292) stricken in 1967 and sunk as targets, Hackleback (AGSS 295) stricken in 1966, Lancetfish (SS 296) stricken in 1958, Manta (AGSS 299), Moray (AGSS 300), and Seahorse (AGSS 304) stricken in 1967, Skate (SS 305) sunk in 1948, Tilefish (SS 307) transferred to Venezuala in 1965, Apogon (SS 308) sunk at Bikini in 1946 (stricken 1947), Aspro (AGSS 309) stricken in 1962, Burrfish (SS 312) to Canada in 1961, Barbero (SSG 317) stricken in 1964, Bergall (SS 320) to Turkey in 1959, Besugo (AGSS 321) to Italy in 1966, Blower (SS 325), Blueback (SS 326), Boarfish (SS 327), Chub (SS 329), and Brill (SS 330) to Turkey in 1948, Bumper (SS 333) to Turkey in 1950, Dentuda (AGSS 335) stricken in 1967, Capitaine (SS 336) to Italy in 1966, Guavina (AOSS 362) stricken in 1967 (expended as target), Guitarro (SS 363) and Hammerhead (SS 364) to Turkey in 1954, Hawkbill (SS 366) and Icefish (SS 367) to Netherlands in 1953, Kraken (SS 370) to Spain in 1959, Lamprey (SS 372) to Argentina in 1960, Lizardfish (SS 373) to Italy in 1960, Loggerhead (AGSS 374) stricken in 1967, Macabi (SS 375) to Argentina in 1960, Mapiro (SS 376) and Mero (SS 378) to Turkey in 1960, Sand Lance (SS 381) to Brazil in 1963, Pilotfish (SS 386) stricken in 1947, Pintado (AGSS 387), Pipefish (AGSS 388), and Piranha (AGSS 389) stricken in 1967, Plaice (SS 390) to Brazil in 1963, Plaice (SS 393) stricken in 1963, Redfish (AGSS 395) stricken in 1965, Scabbardfish (AGSS 397) to Greece in 1965, Sea Devil (AGSS 400) stricken in 1964, Spikefish (AGSS 404) stricken in 1963 Spadefish (AGSS 411) and Trepang (AGSS 412) stricken in 1967, Spot (SS 413) and Springer (SS 414) to Chile in 1962 and 1961, respectively.

1 Transport Submarine (APSS): "Sealion" Type

Name	No.	Builders	Laid down	Launched	Completed
*SEALION	APSS 315	Electric Boat Div, Groton	25 Feb 1943	31 Oct 1943	8 Mar 1944

Displacement, tons	2 145 surface; 2 500 submerged
Length, feet (*metres*)	311·5 (*95·0*)
Beam, feet (*metres*)	27 (*8·2*)
Draft, feet (*metres*)	17 (*5·2*)
Guns, AA	2—40 mm
Main engines	2 GM diesels, 2 305 hp; Electric motors (2 of original 4 diesels removed for additional accommodation for troops)
Speed, knots	13 surface; 10 submerged
Complement	74 (6 officers, 68 men)
Troops	160

The *Sealion* and *Perch* (APSS 313) were converted from "Balao" class submarines to underwater transports used to deliver Marines, commandos, frogmen or other passengers in covert operations or where surface ships would be too vulnerable. The *Perch* was declared unsuitable for underway operations in 1967 and became an immobilised Naval Reserve training ship at San Diego. The former Regulus missile submarine *Tunny* (ex-SSG 282) was quickly modified to provide an interim replacement until conversion of the more-effective *Grayback* (APSS 574) is completed.

CONVERSION. The *Sealion* was converted to a submarine transport at the San Francisco Naval Shipyard in 1948 and the *Perch* at the Mare Island Naval Shipyard. All torpedo tubes and half of diesel propulsion plant were removed to provide berthing for 160 troops; stowage provided for rubber rafts and other equipment.

STATUS. In 1960 the *Sealion* was assigned to operational reserve training duties and the *Perch* was mothballed. Both ships were recommissioned late in 1961.

PHOTOGRAPHS. Note hull bulges abaft conning towers.

PERCH (APSS 313)　　　　　　　　　　　　　　　　*1965, United States Navy*

SEALION (APSS 315)　　　　　　　　　　　　　　　　*United States Navy*

SEALION (LPSS 315)　　　　　　　　　*1965, United States Navy*

PERCH　　　　　　　　　　　*Added 1949, U.S. Navy, Official*

1 Experimental Submarine (AGSS): "Baya" Type

			Name	No.	Builder	Laid down	Launched	Completed
Displacement, tons	1 900 surface; 2 625 submerged		*BAYA	AGSS 318	Electric Boat Division, Groton	9 Apr 1943	2 Jan 1944	20 May 1945

Displacement, tons   1 900 surface; 2 625 submerged
Length, feet (*metres*) 334·8 (*102·0*) oa
Beam, feet (*metres*) 27 (*8·2*)
Draft, feet (*metres*) 17 (*5·2*)
Torpedo tubes   4 aft
Main engines   Diesels, 4 800 hp
               Electric motors, 2 750 hp
Speed, knots   10·5 surface; 8 submerged
Complement   76 (8 officers, 68 men)

RECONSTRUCTION. In 1958-59 *Baya* was converted to a laboratory submarine for electronic experiments. She was cut in two at the San Francisco Naval Shipyard and a 23-ft section inserted amidships between the forward torpedo room and the forward battery room. She was fitted with a bigger and blunter bow to house electronic gear, two booms to act as sonar antennae when extended, a mushroom anchor in the bottom of the submarine in a recess built into the hull, living quarters for 12 research laboratory scientists, and a

LORAD anti-submarine detection system (long range).

BAYA (AGSS 318)   *1960, courtesy "Our Navy"*

BAYA   *Added 1959, United States Navy, Official*

1 Transport Submarine (APSS): "Tunny" Type

		Name	No.	Builder	Laid down	Launched	Completed
Displacement, tons	1 816 surface; 2 425 submerged	*TUNNY	APSS 282 (ex-SSG)	Mare Island Naval Shipyard	10 Nov 1941	1 July 1942	1 Sep 1942

Displacement, tons   1 816 surface; 2 425 submerged
Length, feet (*metres*) 311·8 (*95·0*)
Beam, feet (*metres*) 27 (*8·2*)
Draft, feet (*metres*) 17 (*5·2*)
Main engines   Diesels, 6 500 hp
               Electric motors, 2 750 hp
Speed, knots   21 on surface; 10 submerged
Complement   81 (9 officers, 72 men)

CONVERSION. The *Tunny* was converted to a Regulus missile-launching submarine in 1952 at the Mare Island Naval Shipyard. A hangar was fitted aft of the conning tower to carry two Regulus I missiles and a launching ramp which folded flush with the deck was installed aft of the hangar; related guidance and check-out equipment also installed.

MISSILES. The Regulus I was a surface-to-surface missile which could deliver a nuclear warhead on targets 500 miles from the launching ship or submarine. When the Regulus submarine force was phased out in 1964 there were five Regulus "boats": *Tunny, Barbero* (SSG 317), *Grayback* (SSG 574), *Growler* (SSG 577), and the nuclear-powered *Halibut* (SSGN 587). Four additional nuclear-powered Regulus submarines were planned when the Regulus II programme was cancelled to provide funds for Polaris.

TUNNY (APSS 282)   *United States Navy*

The *Barbero* was stricken from the Navy List on 1 July 1964 and expended as a target.

STATUS. The *Tunny* was reclassified from SSG to SS on 15 May 1965 and to APSS on 10 Oct 1966.

TUNNY (Regulus 1 surface-to-surface guided missile aboard) *Added 1959, United States Navy, Official*

1 Training Submarine (SST): "Barracuda" Type

Displacement, tons	765 surface; 1 160 submerged
Length, feet (*metres*)	196 (*59·7*) oa
Beam, feet (*metres*)	24·8 (*7·5*)
Draft, feet (*metres*)	16 (*4·9*)
Torpedo tubes	4—21 in (*533 mm*), 2 fwd, 2 aft
Main engines	3 GM diesels, GE electric motors 1 050 shp; 2 shafts
Speed, knots	10 surface; 8 submerged
Complement	50 (5 officers, 45 men)

Name	No.	Builders	Laid down	Launched	Completed
*BARRACUDA	SST 3 (ex-K 1)	Electric Boat Co, Groton	1 July 1949	2 Mar 1951	10 Nov 1951

Medium sized, quiet, and handy design specifically built for anti-submarine operations. Had letter and number instead of name until 15 Dec 1955 when "B" name was substituted for "K" number. Originally had an ungainly prow housing listening gear, electronic and sonar detection equipment, short hull, to make her manoeuvrable and suitable for ambushing other submarines. Carried homing torpedoes. By 1959 this class was considered to be wanting as hunter killer craft. They lacked speed, range and endurance.

DISPOSALS
Sister boats *Bass*, SS 551 (ex-K 2) and *Bonita*, SS 552 (ex-K 3) were officially stricken from the Navy List on 1 Apr 1965.

BARRACUDA (SST 3)   *United States Navy*

BARRACUDA   *U.S. Navy, Official*

BONITA   *1954, U.S. Navy, Official*

BASS   *Added 1964, United States Navy, Official*

Attack Submarines (SS)

Ex-Radar Picket Submarines (SSR)

2 "Sailfish" Class

SS 572 SAILFISH	**SS 573 SALMON**
Displacement:	1,990 tons *standard* 2,425 tons (surface), 3,168 tons *submerged*
Dimensions:	350½ (o.a.) × 29 × 16½ feet
Tubes:	6—21 inch (all forward). 12 torpedoes stowed
Machinery:	Fairbanks Morse diesels. 2 shafts. S.H.P.: 6,000=20·5 kts. (surface); Elliott electric motors=15 kts. (*submerged*)
Complement:	96 (11 officers, 85 men)

General
Ordered on 27 Feb. 1952 from Portsmouth Navy Shipyard. Commissioned on 14 Apr. 1956 and 25 Aug. 1956, respectively. Fitted with an air control centre.

Name	Laid down	Launched	Completed
Sailfish	8 Dec. 1953	7 Sep. 1955	Sep. 1956
Salmon	10 Mar. 1954	25 Feb. 1956	Dec. 1956

SALMON   1959, United States Navy, Official

Conversion
In 1959 *Salmon* was modified, at the expense of some search radar, to serve as a missile guidance submarine as well as a radar picket. The deck mounted radar was removed in 1961. Both underwent FRAM II conversion in Fiscal Year 1964.

Reclassification
Both were reclassified from SSR to SS in Mar. 1961.

Photographs
A photograph of *Sailfish* appears in the 1958-59 to 1962-63 editions

SAILFISH   Added 1958, U.S. Navy, Official

SAILFISH (SS 572)   1966, United States Navy

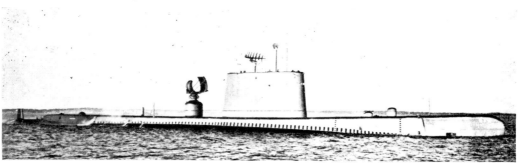

SALMON (SS 573)   United States Navy

SALMON   1/1977, Dr. Giorgio Arra

6 Attack Submarines (SS): "Tang" Class

Displacement, tons	2 100 surface ; 2 400 submerged
Length, feet (metres)	269 or 278 (82·0 or 84·7) oa
Beam, feet (metres)	27·3 (8·3)
Draft, feet (metres)	19 (6·2)
Torpedo tubes	8 - 21 in (533 mm) 6 fwd, 2 aft
Main engines	3 F-M diesels, 4 500 shp
	2 Electric motors ; 5,600 shp
Speed, knots	15 or 20 on surface ; 18 submerged
Complement	83 (8 officers, 75 men)

Name	No.	Builder	Laid down	Launched	Completed
*GUDGEON	SS 567	Portsmouth Naval Shipyard	20 May 1950	11 June 1952	21 Nov 1952
*HARDER	SS 568	Electric Boat Co, Groton	30 June 1950	3 Dec 1951	19 Aug 1952
*TANG	SS 563	Portsmouth Naval Shipyard	18 Apr 1949	19 June 1951	25 Oct 1951
*TRIGGER	SS 564	Electric Boat Co, Groton	24 Feb 1949	14 June 1951	31 Mar 1952
*TROUT	SS 566	Electric Boat Co, Groton	1 Dec 1949	21 Aug 1951	27 June 1952
*WAHOO	SS 565	Portsmouth Naval Shipyard	24 Oct 1949	16 Oct 1951	30 May 1952

This class embodied various improvements to give higher submerged speed, with a development of the Schnorkel. They are streamlined deep-diving vessels but have comparatively short hulls. *Trigger* was the first submarine of the post-war programme to be laid down. *Tang* was the first of the new class to be completed. *Tang* and *Trigger* authorised in Fiscal Year 1947 new construction programme, *Wahoo* and *Trout* in FY 1948, and *Gudgeon* and *Harder* in FY 1949.
The hull is shorter than previous fleet types and this reduction in length is said to contribute to the underwater speed. *Gudgeon* was the first United States submarine to circumnavigate the world during Sep 1957-Feb 1958.

GUDGEON (SS 567)   *1968, United States Navy*

ENGINEERING. *Tang, Trigger, Trout* and *Wahoo* were originally powered by a compact radial type engine produced after five years of development work, comprising a 16-cylinder 2-cycle plant, mounted vertically with four rows of cylinders radially arranged. These new engines were half the weight and two-thirds the size of the engines previously available for submarines. They proved to be unsatisfactory and were replaced by machinery similar to that in *Gudgeon* and *Harder* which have a Fairbanks-Morse high speed lightweight engine mounted horizontally. The electric motors are Elliott in *Tang* and *Trigger*, General Electric in *Wahoo* and *Trout*, Westinghouse in *Gudgeon* and *Harder*.

TROUT (SS 566)   *1965, United States Navy*

RECONSTRUCTION. In 1957 *Tang, Trigger, Trout* and *Wahoo* had extra 9 ft centre section added to accommodate three new Fairbanks-Morse 1 500 shp "in line" diesels to replace the "pancake" type. The vessels were cut in half, the sections inserted, and welded together again. *Tang* had extra 15 ft section added in 1967.

TRIGGER   *1955, U.S. Navy, Official*

TROUT   *1955, courtesy " Our Navy "*

TRIGGER (SS 564)

1969, Anthony & Joseph Pavia

TANG Class

1974, William Whalen Jr

GUDGEON (SS 567)

1970, US Navy, PH3 J. B. Land

WAHOO

1960, United States Navy, Official

WAHOO (SS 565)

1968, United States Navy.

Six submarines of this class were constructed, incorporating improvements based on German World War II submarine developments. *Wahoo* was authorised in FY 1948, and *Gudgeon* in FY 1949. *Gudgeon* was the first US submarine to circumnavigate the world during September 1957-February 1958. Modernised under FRAM II programme.

The three survivors of this class were to be transferred to Iran (see *Transfer* note below) and *Wahoo* was half way through a two year overhaul when Iran cancelled the project on 31 March 1979. The overhaul was cancelled and, still in a dismantled condition, she was finally decommissioned on 31 March 1980 and laid up in reserve at Philadelphia.

Classification: On 1 April 1979 *Gudgeon* reclassified as AGSS for acoustic research as replacement for *Tang*, being later reclassified as SSAG.

Electronics: Mk 106 Mod 18 torpedo fire control system.

Sonar: BQG 4 (PUFFS).

Transfers: *Trigger* (SS 564) was transferred to Italy on 10 July 1973 and *Harder* (SS 568) followed on 15 March 1974. *Trout* (SS 566) was transferred to Iran on 19 December 1978 at New London. Her acquisition was officially cancelled on 3 February 1979. She lay at New London until late 1979, with a token crew, when she was towed to Philadelphia and laid up in reserve. At the time of the cancellation of her acquisition, Iran asked that the USA act as an agent for her resale. As of 1 January 1980 a customer had not been found. *Wahoo* (SS 565) was also to be transferred to Iran, but her acquisition was also cancelled (see above notes). *Tang* (SS 563) was the third submarine to be transferred to Iran, but her acquisition was cancelled on 3 February 1979 and she was later leased to Turkey on 8 February 1980.

GUDGEON

1978, Dr. Giorgio Arra

*DARTER SS 576

1 Attack Submarine (SS): "Darter" Type

Displacement, tons	1 720 surface; 2 388 submerged
Length, feet (*metres*)	268·6 (*81·9*) oa
Beam, feet (*metres*)	27·2 (*8·3*)
Draft, feet (*metres*)	19 (*5·8*)
Main engines	3 Fairbanks Morse diesels, 4 000 shp; Elliott electric motors · 1 shaft
Speed, knots	17 on surface; 25 submerged
Complement	83 (8 officers, 75 men)

DARTER (SS 576)

courtesy Giorgio Ghiglione

Designed for significantly higher submerged speed. An exceptionally quiet submarine. FY 1954 programme. Built by Electric Boat Division, General Dynamics Corporation. Laid down on 10 Nov 1954. Launched on 28 May 1956. Commissioned on 20 Oct 1956.

DARTER

1967, Dr. Giorgio Arra

DARTER

1/1980, Dr. Giorgio Arra

Planned sister submarines *Growler* and *Grayback* were completed to missile-launching configuration.

Basic design of *Darter* is similar to the "Tang" class below. Authorised in the FY 1954 shipbuilding programme. No additional submarines of this type were built because of shift to high-speed hull design and nuclear propulsion.

Home port shifted to Sasebo, Japan in March 1979 making her and *Grayback* the only US submarines homeported overseas.

Electronics: Mk 106 Mod 11 torpedo fire control system.

Sonar: BQG 4 (PUFFS).

1 Experimental Submarine (AGSS): "Albacore" Type

*ALBACORE AGSS 569

Displacement, tons	1 500 surface; 1 850 submerged
Length, feet (*metres*)	204 (*62·2*) oa
Beam, feet (*metres*)	27·5 (*8·4*)
Draft, feet (*metres*)	18·5 (*5·6*)
Torpedo tubes	None
Main engines	2 GM diesels, radial pancake type Westinghouse electric motor, 15 000 shp; 1 shaft
Main engines	2 GM diesels, radial pancake type Westinghouse electric motor, 15 000 shp
Speed, knots	25 on surface; 33 submerged
Complement	52 (5 officers, 47 men)

High speed experimental submarine. Built by Portsmouth Naval Shipyard. Laid down on 15 Mar 1952. Launched on 1 Aug 1953. Completed on 5 Dec 1953. Conventionally powered submarine of radical design with new hull form which makes her faster and more manoeuvrable than any other conventional submarine. Officially described as a hydrodynamic test vehicle. Streamlined, whale-shaped without the naval flat-topped deck. Conning tower modelled on a fish's dorsal fin.

ALBACORE (AGSS 569)

United States Navy

CONVERSION. Phase I (1953): cruciform stern. Phase II (1956): open stern, plastic sonar bow. Phase III (1959): improved sonar system, enlarged dorsal rudder, dive brakes on after sail section. Phase IV (1961): Electrical Drive, contra-rotating motors and 2 propellers contra-rotating about the same axis. A high capacity, long endurance silver zinc battery providing power to drive her at 30+knots submerged (commenced in Dec 1962, completed on 20 Feb 1965). Conversions were carried out at Portsmouth Naval Shipyard.

ALBACORE

1962, United States Navy, Official

1955, U.S Navy, Official

ALBACORE

1 "DOLPHIN" CLASS: AUXILIARY SUBMARINE (AGSS)

Name	No.	Builders	Laid down	Launched	Commissioned	F/S
DOLPHIN	AGSS 555	Portsmouth Naval Shipyard	9 Nov 1962	8 June 1968	17 Aug 1968	PA

Displacement, tons: 800 standard; 930 full load.
Dimensions, feet (metres): 152 × 19·3 × 18 *(46·3 × 5·9 × 5·5)*
Torpedo tubes: Removed
Main machinery: Diesel-electric (2 Detroit 12 V71 diesels), 1 650 hp; 1 shaft
Speed, knots: 15+ dived
Complement: 22 (7 officers, 15 enlisted men) plus 4 to 7 scientists

Specifically designed for deep-diving operations. Authorised in the FY 1961 new construction programme but delayed because of changes in mission and equipment coupled with higher priorities being given to other submarine projects. Fitted for deep-ocean sonar and oceanographic research. She is highly automated and has three computer-operated systems, a safety system, hovering system, and one that is classified. The digital-computer submarine safety system monitors equipment and provides data on closed-circuit television screens; malfunctions in equipment set off an alarm and if they are not corrected within the prescribed time the system, unless over-ridden by an operator, automatically brings the submarine to the surface. There are several research stations for scientists and she is fitted to take water samples down to her operating depth.

Underwater endurance is limited (endurance and habitability were considered of secondary importance in design).

Assigned to Submarine Development Group 1 at San Diego.

Design: Has a constant diameter cylindrical pressure hull approximately 15 ft in outer diameter closed at both ends with hemispherical heads. Pressure hull fabricated of HY-80 steel with aluminium and fibre-glass used in secondary structures to reduce weight. No conventional hydroplanes are mounted, improved rudder design and other features provide manoeuvring control and hovering capability.

Engineering: Fitted with 330 cell silver-zinc battery. Submerged endurance is approximately 24 hours with an at-sea endurance of 14 days.

DOLPHIN

USN

1 NUCLEAR-POWERED OCEAN ENGINEERING AND RESEARCH VEHICLE

Name	Builders	F/S
NR 1	General Dynamics (Electric Boat Div)	ASA

Displacement, tons: 400 submerged
Dimensions, feet (metres): 136·4 × 12·4 × 14·6 *(41·6 × 3·8 × 4·5)*
Reactor: 1 pressurised-water cooled
Machinery: Electric motors; 2 propellers; four ducted thrusters
Complement: 7 (2 officers, 3 enlisted men, 2 scientists)

NR 1 was built primarily to serve as a test platform for a small nuclear propulsion plant; however, the craft additionally provides an advanced deep submergence ocean engineering and research capability.
Laid down on 10 June 1967; launched on 25 January 1969; placed in service 27 October 1969. Commanded by an officer-in-charge vice commanding officer. First nuclear-propelled service craft.

Design: The NR 1 is fitted with wheels beneath the hull to permit "bottom crawling" and she is fitted with external lights, external television cameras, a remote-controlled manipulator, and various recovery devices. No periscopes, but fixed television mast. A surface "mother" ship is required to support her.
Engineering: The NR 1 reactor plant was designed by the Atomic Energy Commission's Knolls Atomic Power Laboratory. She is propelled by two propellers driven by electric motors outside the pressure hull with power provided by a turbine generator within the pressure hull. Four ducted thrusters, two horizontal and two vertical, are provided for precise manoeuvring.

NR 1   *1969, General Dynamics, (Electric Boat Division)*

Fiscal: The final estimated ship construction cost at time of launching was $67 million plus $19·9 million for oceanographic equipment and sensors, and $11·8 million for research and development (mainly related to the nuclear propulsion plant), for a total estimated cost of $99·2 million.

1 "GRAYBACK" CLASS (LPSS/SS)

Name	No.	Builders	Laid down	Launched	Commissioned
*GRAYBACK	SS 574 (ex-LPSS 574, ex-SSG 574)	Mare Island Naval Shipyard	1 July 1954	2 July 1957	7 Mar 1958

Displacement, tons: 2 670 standard; 3 650 dived
Length, feet (metres): 334 *(101·8)* oa
Beam, feet (metres): 27 *(8·2)*
Draught, feet (metres): 19 *(5·8)*
Torpedo tubes: 8—21 inch *(533 mm)* 6 bow; 2 stern
Main machinery: 3 diesels (Fairbanks Morse); 4 500 bhp; 2 electric motors (Elliott); 5 500 shp; 2 shafts
Speed, knots: 20 surfaced; 16·7 dived
Complement: 88 (10 officers, 78 enlisted men)
Troops: 85 (10 officers, 75 enlisted men)

The *Grayback* has been fully converted to a transport submarine and is officially classified as an amphibious warfare ship. She was originally intended to be an attack submarine, being authorised in the Fiscal Year 1953 new construction programme, but redesigned in 1956 to provide a Regulus missile launching capability; completed as SSG 574 in 1958, similar in design to the *Growler* (SSG 577). See *Growler* listing for basic design notes.

Classification: The *Grayback* was reclassified as an attack submarine (SS) on 30 June 1975 although she retains her transport configuration and capabilities. The reclassification was an administrative change associated with funding support.

Conversion: She began conversion to a transport submarine at Mare Island in November 1967. The conversion was originally estimated at $15 200 000 but was actually about $30 000 000. She was reclassified from SSG to LPSS on 30 Aug 1968 (never officially designated APSS).
During conversion she was fitted to berth and mess 67 troops and carry their equipment including landing craft or swimmer delivery vehicles (SDV). Her torpedo tubes and hence attack capability are retained. As completed (SSG) she had an overall length of 322 ft 4 in; lengthened 12 ft during LPSS conversion. Conversion was authorised in Fiscal Year 1965 programme and completed with her new commissioning on 9 May 1969; delayed because of higher priorities being allocated to other submarine projects.

Electronics: Mk 106 Mod 12 torpedo fire control system.

Sonar: BQS-2; BQS-4 (PUFFS).

GRAYBACK   *1958, USN*

GRAYBACK   *1959, United States Navy, Official*

GRAYBACK

GRAYBACK (LPSS 574)

1 "GRAYBACK" CLASS (SSG)

Name	No.	Builders	Laid down	Launched	Commissioned
GROWLER	SSG 577	Portsmouth Naval Shipyard	15 Feb 1955	5 April 1958	30 Aug 1958

Displacement, tons: 2 540 standard; 3 515 dived
Length, feet (metres): 317·6 *(96·8)* oa
Beam, feet (metres): 27·2 *(8·2)*
Draught, feet (metres): 19 *(5·8)*
Torpedo tubes: 6—21 inch *(533 mm)* 4 bow; 2 stern
Main machinery: 3 diesels (Fairbanks Morse); 4 600 bhp; 2 electric motors (Elliott); 5 500 shp; 2 shafts
Speed, knots: 20 surfaced; approx 12 dived
Complement: 87 (9 officers, 78 enlisted men)

The *Growler* was authorised in the Fiscal Year 1955 new construction programme; completed as a guided missile submarine to fire the Regulus surface-to-surface cruise missile (see *Halibut*, SSN 587, for *Missile* notes).

When the Regulus submarine missile programme ended in 1964, the *Growler* and her near-sister *Grayback* were withdrawn from service, *Growler* being decommissioned on 25 May 1964. The *Grayback* was subsequently converted to an amphibious transport submarine (LPSS). The *Growler* was scheduled to undergo a similar conversion when the *Grayback* was completed, but the second conversion was deferred late in 1968 because of rising ship conversion costs.
The *Growler* is in reserve as an SSG.

Design: The *Grayback* and *Growler* were initially designed as attack submarines similar to the *Darter*. Upon redesign as missile submarines they were cut in half on the building ways and were lengthened approximately 50 feet, two cylindrical hangars, each 11 feet high and 70 feet long, were superimposed on their bows, a missile launcher was installed between the hangars and sail structure, and elaborate navigation and fire control systems were fitted. The height of the sail structure on the *Growler* is approximately 30 feet above the deck; the *Grayback's* lower sail structure was increased during LPSS conversion.

Electronics: Mk 106 Mod 13 torpedo fire control system.

Sonar: BQS-4.

GROWLER

3 "BARBEL" CLASS (SS)

Name	No.	Builders	Laid down	Launched	Commissioned
*BARBEL	SS 580	Portsmouth Naval Shipyard	18 May 1956	19 July 1958	17 Jan 1959
*BLUEBACK	SS 581	Ingalls Shipbuilding Corporation	15 April 1957	16 May 1959	15 Oct 1959
*BONEFISH	SS 582	New York Shipbuilding Corp	3 June 1957	22 Nov 1958	9 July 1959

Displacement, tons: 2 146 surfaced; 2 894 dived
Length, feet (metres): 219·5 *(66·8)* oa
Beam, feet (metres): 29 *(8·8)*
Draught, feet (metres): 28 *(8·5)*
Torpedo tubes: 6—21 inch *(533 mm)* Mk 58 bow
Main machinery: 3 diesels; 4 800 bhp (Fairbanks Morse); 2
electric motors (General Electric); 3 150 shp; 1 shaft
Speed, knots: 15 on surfaced; 21 dived
Complement: 77 (8 officers, 69 men)

These submarines were the last non-nuclear combatant submarines built by the US Navy. All three were authorised in the Fiscal Year 1956 new construction programme.

Construction: The *Blueback* was the first submarine built by the Ingalls Shipbuilding Corp at Pascagoula, Mississippi, and the *Bonefish* was the first constructed at the New York Shipbuilding Corp yard in Camden, New Jersey. None of the three shipyards that built this class is now employed in submarine construction.

Design: These submarines have the "tear drop" hull design which was tested in the experimental submarine *Albacore*. As built, their fore planes were bow-mounted; subsequently moved to the sail.
They introduced a new concept in centralised arrangement of controls in an "attack centre" to increase efficiency; which has been adapted for all later US combat submarines.

Electronics: Mk 101 Mod 20 torpedo fire control system.

Sonar: BQS-4.

BLUEBACK

1967, USN

BONEFISH (SS 582)

1952, Unites Stated Navy

BARBEL

9/1979, Dr. Giorgio Arra

BARBEL

1959, United States Navy, Official

BONEFISH (SS 582)

1969, United States Navy

1 "NAUTILUS" CLASS: SUBMARINE (nuclear-powered) (SSN)

Name	No.	Builders	Laid down	Launched	Commissioned	F/S
NAUTILUS	SSN 571	General Dynamics (Electric Boat Div)	14 June 1952	21 Jan 1954	30 Sep 1954	PR

Displacement, tons: 3 764 surfaced; 4 040 dived
Dimensions, feet (metres): 319·4 × 27·6 × 22 *(97·4 × 8·4 × 6·7)*
Torpedo tubes: 6—21 in *(533 mm)* bow (Mk 50)
Main machinery: 1 pressurised-water cooled S2W (Westinghouse) reactor; 2 steam turbines (Westinghouse), approx 15 000 shp; 2 shafts
Speed, knots: 20+ surfaced; 20+ dived
Complement: 105 (13 officers, 92 enlisted men)

Nautilus was the world's first nuclear-propelled vessel. She predated the first Soviet nuclear-powered submarine by an estimated five years.

The funds for her construction were authorised in the FY 1952 budget. She put to sea for the first time on 17 January 1955 and signalled the historic message: "Underway on nuclear power".

On her shakedown cruise in May 1955 she steamed submerged from London, Connecticut, to San Juan, Puerto Rico, travelling more than 1 300 miles in 84 hours at an average speed of almost 16 knots; she later steamed submerged from Key West, Florida, to New London, a distance of 1 397 miles, at an average speed of more than 20 knots.

During 1958 she undertook extensive operations under the Arctic ice pack and in August she made history's first polar transit from the Pacific to the Atlantic, steaming from Pearl Harbour to Portland, England. Under the ice she passed the geographic North Pole on 3 August 1958.

During 1972-74 she underwent a 30 month overhaul and modification at the Electric Boat yard in Groton, Connecticut, where the submarine was built. Modified for submarine communications research.

When it was announced that *Nautilus* was to begin decommissioning in FY 1979, the plan was to preserve her as a memorial at the United States Naval Academy, Annapolis, Maryland. Shortly after the announcement, the Submarine Memorial Association Inc, Groton, Connecticut, which has custody of *Croaker* (SS 246) decided to ask that they be given the *Nautilus* for preservation at "her birthplace" alongside *Croaker*. The resultant uncertainty was resolved on 30 October 1979 when Secretary of the Navy, Edward Hidalgo, announced that the Old Marine Railway Slip at the Washington Navy Yard would be *Nautilus*'s final berthing place. The fact that the reactor and its components will be retained in *Nautilus*, "in a defuelled and mothballed state", means a need for proper security of the

NAUTILUS   1975, General Dynamics, (Electric Boat Division)

reactor area and other compartments; she was decommissioned on 3 March 1980 at Mare Island and it is planned to prepare her for public exhibit in FY 1981. Cost will be about $5 million. Preparations will include breaching the pressure hull to create a public entrance way. Current plans call for her arrival at the Washington Navy Yard in the spring of 1982. After preparation, it will cost about $600 000 each year to maintain the submarine who will have a token crew of 2 officers and 24 enlisted men.

Electronics: Mk 101 Mod 6 torpedo fire control system.

Engineering: In January 1948 the Department of Defense requested the Atomic Energy Commission to undertake the design, development, and construction of a nuclear reactor for submarine propulsion. Initial research and conceptual design of the Submarine Thermal Reactor (STR) was undertaken by the Argonne National Laboratory. Subsequently the Atomic Energy Commission's Bettis Atomic Power Laboratory, operated by the Westinghouse Electric Corporation, undertook development of the first nuclear propulsion plant.

Nautilus STR Mark II nuclear plant (redesignated S2W) was first operated on 20 December 1954 and first developed full power on 3 January 1955.

After more than two years of operation, during which she steamed 62 562 miles, she began an overhaul which included refuelling in April 1957. She was again refuelled in 1959 after steaming 91 324 miles on her second fuel core, and again in 1964 after steaming approximately 150 000 miles on her third fuel core.

Sonar: BQS 4.

NAUTILUS   Added 1958, Arcadian Photos

NAUTILUS (SSN 571)   United States Navy

1 "SEAWOLF" CLASS: SUBMARINE (nuclear-powered) (SSN)

Name	No.	Builders	Laid down	Launched	Commissioned	F/S
SEAWOLF	SSN 575	General Dynamics (Electric Boat Div)	15 Sep 1953	21 July 1955	30 Mar 1957	PA

Displacement, tons: 3 765 surfaced; 4 200 dived
Dimensions, feet (metres): 337·5 × 27·7 × 23 (102·9 × 8·4 × 7)
Torpedo tubes: 6—21 in (533 mm) bow
Main machinery: 1 pressurised-water cooled S2Wa (Westinghouse) reactor;
  2 steam turbines (General Electric), 15 000 shp; 2 shafts
Speed, knots: 20+ surfaced; 20+ dived
Complement: 101 (11 officers, 90 enlisted men)

SEAWOLF

1974, William Whalen, Jr.

Seawolf was the world's second nuclear-propelled vehicle; she was constructed almost simultaneously with *Nautilus* to test a competitive reactor design. Funds for *Seawolf* were authorised in the FY 1952 new construction programme.
She is no longer considered a "first line" submarine and has been engaged primarily in research work since 1969.

Design: GUPPY-type hull with stepped sail.

Electronics: Mk 101 Mod 8 torpedo fire control system.

Engineering: Initial work in the development of naval nuclear propulsion plants investigated a number of concepts, two of which were of sufficient interest to warrant full development: the pressurised water and liquid metal (sodium). *Nautilus* was provided with a pressurised-water reactor plant and *Seawolf* was fitted initially with a liquid-metal reactor. Originally known as the Submarine Intermediate Reactor (SIR), the liquid-metal plant was developed by the Atomic Energy Commission's Knolls Atomic Power Laboratory.
The SIR Mark II/S2G reactor in *Seawolf* achieved initial criticality on 25 June 1956. Steam leaks developed during the dockside testing. The plant was shut down and it was determined that the leaks were caused by sodium-potassium alloy which had entered the super-heater steam piping. After repairs and testing *Seawolf* began sea trials on 21 January 1957. The trials were run at reduced power and after two years of operation *Seawolf* entered the Electric Boat yard for removal of her sodium-cooled plant and installation of a pressurised-water plant similar to that installed in *Nautilus* (designated S2Wa). When the original *Seawolf* plant was shut down in December 1958 the submarine had steamed a total of 71 611 miles. She was recommissioned on 30 September 1960. The pressurised-water reactor was refuelled for the first time between May 1965 and August 1967, having propelled *Seawolf* for more than 161 000 miles on its initial fuel core.

Sonar: BQS 4.

SEAWOLF (at speed)

1957, U.S. Navy, Official

SEAWOLF (SSN 575)

1967, United States Navy

SEAWOLF

1963, Electric Boat Division, General Dynamics Corporation

4 "SKATE" CLASS: SUBMARINES (nuclear-powered) (SSN)

Name	No.	Builders	Laid down	Launched	Commissioned	F/S
SKATE	SSN 578	General Dynamics (Electric Boat Div)	21 July 1955	16 May 1957	23 Dec 1957	PA
SWORDFISH	SSN 579	Portsmouth Naval Shipyard	25 Jan 1956	27 Aug 1957	15 Sep 1958	PA
SARGO	SSN 583	Mare Island Naval Shipyard	21 Feb 1956	10 Oct 1957	1 Oct 1958	PA
SEADRAGON	SSN 584	Portsmouth Naval Shipyard	20 June 1956	16 Aug 1958	5 Dec 1959	PA

Displacement, tons: 2 310 light; 2 360 full load (578-9);
2 384 light; 2 547 full load (583-4)
Dimensions, feet (metres): 267·7 × 25 × 22 *(81·5 × 7·6 × 6·7)*
Torpedo tubes: 8—21 in *(533 mm)* 6 bow; 2 stern (short)
Main machinery: 1 pressurised-water cooled S3W (Westinghouse) reactor in *Skate* and *Sargo*, 1 pressurised-water cooled S4W (Westinghouse) in *Swordfish* and *Seadragon*; 2 steam turbines (Westinghouse); 6 600 shp; 2 shafts
Speed, knots: 20+ surfaced; 25+ dived
Complement: 87 (11 officers, 76 enlisted men)

The first production model nuclear-powered submarines, similar in design to *Nautilus* but smaller. *Skate* and *Swordfish* were authorised in the FY 1955 new construction programme and *Sargo* and *Seadragon* in FY 1956.
Skate was the first submarine to make a completely submerged transatlantic crossing. In 1958 she established a (then) record of 31 days submerged with a sealed atmosphere, on 11 August 1958 she passed under the ice at the North Pole during a polar cruise, and on 17 March 1959 she became the first submarine to surface at the North Pole. *Sargo* undertook a polar cruise during January-February 1960 and surfaced at the North Pole on 9 February 1960.
Seadragon sailed from the Atlantic to the Pacific via the Northwest Passage (Lancaster Sound, Barrow and McClure Straits) in August 1960. *Skate,* operating from New London, Connecticut and *Seadragon,* based at Pearl Harbour, rendezvoused under the ice at the North Pole on 2 August 1962 and then conducted anti-submarine exercises under the polar ice pack and surfaced together at the North Pole.
Skate also operated in the Arctic Ocean during April-May 1969, conducting exercises under the Arctic ice pack with the later nuclear-powered attack submarines *Pargo* and *Whale;* and again during the spring of 1971 with the nuclear attack submarine *Trepang.*

Electronics: Fitted with Mk 101 Mod 19 torpedo fire control system.

Engineering: The reactors for this class were developed by the Atomic Energy Commission's Bettis Atomic Power Laboratory, the new propulsion system was similar to that of *Nautilus* but considerably simplified with improved operation and maintenance. The propulsion plant developed under this programme had two arrangements, the S3W configuration in *Skate*, *Sargo* and *Halibut* and the S4W configuration in *Swordfish* and *Sea-* *dragon.* Both arrangements proved satisfactory. *Skate* began her first overhaul and refuelling in January 1961 after steaming 120 862 miles on her initial reactor core during three years of operation. *Swordfish* began her first overhaul and refuelling in early 1962 after more than three years of operation in which time she steamed 112 000 miles.

Sonar: BQS 4.

SARGO   1959 *United States Navy, Official*

SWORDFISH   1959, *United States Navy, Official*

SARGO   6/1979, *Dr. Giorgio Arra*

SKATE (first production model nuclear powered submarine)   1963, *Electric Boat Division, General Dynamics Corporation*

1 "TRITON" CLASS: SUBMARINE (nuclear-powered) (SSN)

Name	No.	Builders	Laid down	Launched	Commissioned	F/S
TRITON	SSN 586 (ex-SSRN 586)	General Dynamics (Electric Boat Div)	29 May 1956	19 Aug 1958	10 Nov 1959	AR

Displacement, tons: 5 940 surfaced; 6 670 dived
Dimensions, feet (metres): 447 × 37 × 24 (136·2 × 11·3 × 7·3)
Torpedo tubes: 6—21 in (533 mm) 4 bow; 2 stern (Mk 60)
Main machinery: 2 pressurised-water cooled S4G (General Electric) reactors;
2 steam turbines (General Electric); 34 000 shp; 2 shafts
Speed, knots: 27+ surfaced; 20+ dived
Complement as SSRN: 170 (14 officers, 156 enlisted men)

Triton was designed and constructed to serve as a radar picket submarine to operate in conjunction with surface carrier task forces.

Authorised in the FY 1956 new construction programme and built for an estimated cost of $109 million.

Triton circumnavigated the globe in 1960, remaining submerged except when her sail structure broke the surface to enable an ill sailor to be taken off near the Falkland Islands. The 41 500 mile cruise took 83 days and was made at an average speed of 18 knots.

Reclassified as an attack submarine (SSN) on 1 March 1961 as the Navy dropped the radar picket submarine programme. She is no longer considered a "first line" submarine and was decommissioned on 3 May 1969 to become the first US nuclear submarine placed in preservation. Laid up at Norfolk.

There had been proposals to operate the Triton as an underwater national command post afloat, but no funds were provided.

Design: Triton was fitted with large radar antenna which retracted into the sail structure and an elaborate combat information centre. Until the Trident SSBN programme Triton was the longest US submarine ever constructed.

Electronics: Mk 101 Mod 11 torpedo fire control system.

Engineering: Triton is the only US submarine with two nuclear reactors. The Atomic Energy Commission's Knolls Atomic Power Laboratory was given prime responsibility for development of the power plant. After 2½ years of operation, during which she steamed more than 110 000 miles, Triton was overhauled and refuelled from July 1962 to March 1964.

Sonar: BQS 4.

TRITON   1959, USN

TRITON (looking down into the "sail")   Added 1961, courtesy General Electric Company, Schenectady (Engineers)

TRITON (SSN 586)   United States Navy

5 "SKIPJACK" CLASS: SUBMARINES (nuclear-powered) (SSN)

Name	No.	Builders	Laid down	Launched	Commissioned	F/S
SKIPJACK	SSN 585	General Dynamics (Electric Boat Div)	29 May 1956	26 May 1958	15 Apr 1959	AA
SCAMP	SSN 588	Mare Island Naval Shipyard	23 Jan 1959	8 Oct 1960	5 June 1961	AA
SCULPIN	SSN 590	Ingalls Shipbuilding Corp	3 Feb 1958	31 Mar 1960	1 June 1961	AA
SHARK	SSN 591	Newport News S.B. & D.D. Co	24 Feb 1958	16 Mar 1960	9 Feb 1961	AA
SNOOK	SSN 592	Ingalls Shipbuilding Corp	7 Apr 1958	31 Oct 1960	24 Oct 1961	PA

Displacement, tons: 3 075 surfaced; 3 513 dived
Dimensions, feet (metres): 251·7 × 31·5 × 29·4
(76·7 × 9·6 × 8·9)
Torpedo tubes: 6—21 in (533 mm) bow (Mk 59)
A/S weapons: A/S torpedoes
Main machinery: 1 pressurised-water-cooled S5W (Westing-house) reactor; 2 steam turbines (Westinghouse in *Skipjack*; General Electric in others); 15 000 shp; 1 shaft
Speed, knots: 16+ surfaced; 30+ dived
Complement: 93 (8 officers, 85 enlisted men)

Combine the high-speed endurance of nuclear propulsion with the high-speed "tear-drop" "Albacore" hull design. *Skipjack* was authorised in the FY 1956 new construction programme and the five other submarines of this class were authorised in FY 1957. These submarines are still considered suitable for "first line" service. Each cost approximately $40 million. *Scorpion* (SSN 589) of this class was lost some 400 miles south-west of the Azores while *en route* from the Mediterranean to Norfolk, Virginia, in May 1968. She went down with 99 men on board.

Construction: *Scorpion*'s keel was laid down twice; the original keel, laid down on 1 November 1957, was renumbered SSBN 598 and became the Polaris submarine *George Washington*; the second SSN 589 keel became *Scorpion*. *Scamp*'s keel laying was delayed when materiel for her was diverted to SSBN 599. This class introduced the Newport News Shipbuilding and Dry Dock Company and the Ingalls Shipbuilding Corporation to nuclear submarine construction. Newport News had not previously built submarines since before World War I.

Design: *Skipjack* was the first US nuclear submarine built to the "tear-drop" design. These submarines have a single propeller shaft (vice two in earlier nuclear submarines) and their diving planes are mounted on sail structures to improve underwater manoeuvrability. No after torpedo tubes are fitted because of their tapering sterns.

Electronics: Fitted with Mk 101 Mod 17 TFCS.

Engineering: The "Skipjack" class introduced the S5W fast attack submarine propulsion plant which has been employed in all subsequent US attack and ballistic missile submarines except the "Los Angeles" class (SSN 688) *Narwhal* (SSN 671) and *Glenard P. Lipscomb* (SSN 685). The plant was developed by the Bettis Atomic Power Laboratory.

Sonar: Modified BQS 4

SCAMP   *12/1976, Dr. Giorgio Arra*

SCAMP   *12/1976, Dr. Giorgio Arra*

SCORPION (SSN 589) Lost at sea, May 1968   *United States Navy*

SHARK (SSN 591)—See previous page   *1968, United States Navy*

SKIPJACK

1959, United States Navy, Official

SNOOK (SSN 592)

1964 United States Navy

SCAMP

12/1976, Dr. Giorgio Arra

1 "TULLIBEE" CLASS: SUBMARINE (nuclear-powered) (SSN)

Name	No.	Builders	Laid down	Launched	Commissioned	F/S
TULLIBEE	SSN 597	General Dynamics (Electric Boat Div)	26 May 1958	27 Apr 1960	9 Nov 1960	AA

Displacement, tons: 2 317 standard; 2 640 dived
Dimensions, feet (metres): 273 × 23·3 × 21 (83·2 × 7·1 × 6·4)
Torpedo tubes: 4—21 in (533 mm) Mk 64 amidships
A/S weapons: A/S torpedoes
Main machinery: 1 pressurised-water cooled S2C (Combustion Engineering) reactor; turbo-electric drive with steam turbine (Westinghouse); 2 500 shp; 1 shaft
Speed, knots: 15+ surfaced; 20+ dived
Complement: 56 (6 officers, 50 enlisted men)

Tullibee was designed specifically for anti-submarine operations and was the first US submarine with the optimum bow position devoted entirely to sonar. No additional submarine of

this type was constructed because of the success of the larger, more-versatile "Thresher" class. *Tullibee* was authorised in the FY 1958 new construction programme. She is no longer considered a "first line" submarine.

Design: She has a modified, elongated "tear-drop" hull design. Originally she was planned as a 1 000 ton craft, but reactor requirements and other considerations increased her size during design and construction.
Her four amidships torpedo tubes are angled out from the centreline two to port and two to starboard. Not fitted to fire SUBROC.

Electronics: Mk 112 torpedo fire control system.

Engineering: She has a small nuclear power plant designed and developed by the Combustion Engineering Company. The propulsion system features turbo-electric drive rather than conventional steam turbines with reduction gears in an effort to reduce operating noises.

Navigation: Fitted with Ship's Inertial Navigation System (SINS).

Sonar: BQQ 2 system (BQS 6 active and BQR 7 passive) the first submarine so fitted.
BQG 4 passive (PUFFS—Passive Underwater Fire Control Feasibility System) with three (originally two) domes on top of hull.

TULLIBEE

1968, USN

TULLIBEE (SSN 597)

1960, United States Navy

TULLIBEE (SSN 597)

United States Navy

13 "THRESHER" CLASS: SUBMARINES (nuclear-powered) (SSN)

Name	No.	Builders	Laid down	Launched	Commissioned	F/S
PERMIT	SSN 594	Mare Island Naval Shipyard	16 July 1959	1 July 1961	29 May 1962	PA
PLUNGER	SSN 595	Mare Island Naval Shipyard	2 Mar 1960	9 Dec 1961	21 Nov 1962	PA
BARB	SSN 596	Ingalls Shipbuilding Corp	9 Nov 1959	12 Feb 1962	24 Aug 1963	PA
POLLACK	SSN 603	New York Shipbuilding Corp	14 Mar 1960	17 Mar 1962	26 May 1964	PA
HADDO	SSN 604	New York Shipbuilding Corp	9 Sep 1960	18 Aug 1962	16 Dec 1964	PA
JACK	SSN 605	Portsmouth Naval Shipyard	16 Sep 1960	24 Apr 1963	31 Mar 1967	PA
TINOSA	SSN 606	Portsmouth Naval Shipyard	24 Nov 1959	9 Dec 1961	17 Oct 1964	AA
DACE	SSN 607	Ingalls Shipbuilding Corp	6 June 1960	18 Aug 1962	4 Apr 1964	PA
GUARDFISH	SSN 612	New York Shipbuilding Corp	28 Feb 1961	15 May 1965	20 Dec 1966	AA
FLASHER	SSN 613	General Dynamics (Electric Boat Div)	14 Apr 1961	22 June 1963	22 July 1966	PA
GREENLING	SSN 614	General Dynamics (Electric Boat Div)	15 Aug 1961	4 Apr 1964	3 Nov 1967	PA
GATO	SSN 615	General Dynamics (Electric Boat Div)	15 Dec 1961	14 May 1964	25 Jan 1968	AA
HADDOCK	SSN 621	Ingalls Shipbuilding Corp	24 Apr 1961	21 May 1966	22 Dec 1967	PA

Displacement, tons: 3 750 standard; *Flasher, Greenling* and *Gato* 3 800; 4 300 dived except *Jack* 4 470 dived, *Flasher, Greenling* and *Gato* 4 242 dived

Length, feet (metres): 278·5 *(84·9)* oa except *Jack* 297·4 *(90·7)* oa, *Flasher, Greenling* and *Gato* 292·2 *(89·1)*

Beam, feet (metres): 31·7 *(9·6)*

Draught, feet (metres): 28·4 *(8·7)*

Missiles: To be fitted for Harpoon

Torpedo tubes: 4—21 in *(533 mm)* Mk 63 amidships

A/S weapons: SUBROC and A/S torpedoes

Main machinery: 1 pressurised-water cooled S5W (Westinghouse) reactor; 2 steam turbines, 15 000 shp; 1 shaft

Speed, knots: 20+ surfaced; 30+ dived

Complement: 103 (12 officers, 91 enlisted men)

They have a greater depth capability than previous SSNs and are the first to combine the SUBROC anti-submarine missile capability with the advanced BQQ 2 sonar system. The lead ship of the class, *Thresher* (SSN 593), was authorised in the FY 1957 new construction programme, the SSN 594-596 in FY 1958, SSN 603-607 in FY 1959, SSN 612-615 in FY 1960, and SSN 621 in FY 1961.

Thresher (SSN 593) was lost off the coast of New England on 10 April 1963 while on post-overhaul trials. She went down with 129 men on board (108 crewmen plus four naval officers and 17 civilians on board for trials).

Construction: *Greenling* and *Gato* were launched by the Electric Boat Division of the General Dynamics Corp (Groton, Connecticut); towed to Quincy Division (Massachusetts) for lengthening and completion.

Design: *Jack* was built to a modified design to test a modified power plant (see *Engineering* notes).

Flasher, Gato and *Greenling* were modified during construction; fitted with SUBSAFE features, heavier machinery, and larger sail structures.

These submarines have a modified "tear-drop" hull design. Their bows are devoted to sonar and their four torpedo tubes are amidships, angled out, two to port and two to starboard. The sail structure height of the earlier submarines is 13 ft 9 in to 15 ft above the deck, with later submarines of this class having a sail height of 20 ft.

Electronics: Mk 113 torpedo fire control system which is being replaced by Mk 117 (already in SSN 594 and 621).

All fitted with WSC-3 satellite communications transceiver.

Engineering: *Jack* was fitted with two propellers on one shaft (actually a single shaft within a sleeve-like shaft) and a contrarotating turbine without a reduction gear. Both innovations

HADDOCK

7/1979, Dr. Giorgio Arra

TINOSA

10/1979, Michael D. J. Lennon

were designed to reduce operating noises. To accommodate the larger turbine, the engine spaces were lengthened by 10 ft and the shaft structure was lengthened 7 ft to mount the two propellers. The propellers were of different size and smaller than in the other submarines of this class. Also eliminated in *Jack* was a clutch and secondary-propulsion electric motor. *Jack's* propulsion arrangement provided a 10 per cent increase in power efficiency, but no increase in speed. The arrangement was not a success and was removed.

Names: Names changed during construction: *Plunger* ex-*Pollack; Barb* ex-*Pollack* ex-*Plunger; Pollack* ex-*Barb.*

Sonar: BQQ 2 (BQS 6 active and BQR 7 passive). The positioning of the conformal array for BQR 7 in the bow dictates the use of midships tubes.

GUARDFISH (SSN 612)   1968, United States Navy

PLUNGER (SSN 595)   United States Navy

BARB   1973, USN

PERMIT   1963, United States Navy, Official

PERMIT   1963, United States Navy, Official

37 "STURGEON" CLASS: SUBMARINES (nuclear-powered) (SSN)

Name	No.	Builders	Laid down	Launched	Commissioned	F/S
STURGEON	SSN 637	General Dynamics (Electric Boat Div)	10 Aug 1963	26 Feb 1966	3 Mar 1967	AA
WHALE	SSN 638	General Dynamics (Quincy)	27 May 1964	14 Oct 1966	12 Oct 1968	AA
TAUTOG	SSN 639	Ingalls Shipbuilding Corp	27 Jan 1964	15 Apr 1967	17 Aug 1968	PA
GRAYLING	SSN 646	Portsmouth Naval Shipyard	12 May 1964	22 June 1967	11 Oct 1969	AA
POGY	SSN 647	Ingalls Shipbuilding Corp	4 May 1964	3 June 1967	15 May 1971	PA
ASPRO	SSN 648	Ingalls Shipbuilding Corp	23 Nov 1964	29 Nov 1967	20 Feb 1969	PA
SUNFISH	SSN 649	General Dynamics (Quincy)	15 Jan 1965	14 Oct 1966	15 Mar 1969	AA
PARGO	SSN 650	General Dynamics (Electric Boat Div)	3 June 1964	17 Sep 1966	5 Jan 1968	AA
QUEENFISH	SSN 651	Newport News S.B. & D.D. Co	11 May 1964	25 Feb 1966	6 Dec 1966	PA
PUFFER	SSN 652	Ingalls Shipbuilding Corp	8 Feb 1965	30 Mar 1968	9 Aug 1969	PA
RAY	SSN 653	Newport News S.B. & D.D. Co	1 Apr 1965	21 June 1966	12 Apr 1967	AA
SAND LANCE	SSN 660	Portsmouth Naval Shipyard	15 Jan 1965	11 Nov 1969	25 Sep 1971	AA
LAPON	SSN 661	Newport News S.B. & D.D. Co	26 July 1965	16 Dec 1966	14 Dec 1967	AA
GURNARD	SSN 662	San Francisco NSY (Mare Island)	22 Dec 1964	20 May 1967	6 Dec 1968	PA
HAMMERHEAD	SSN 663	Newport News S.B. & D.D. Co	29 Nov 1965	14 Apr 1967	28 June 1968	AA
SEA DEVIL	SSN 664	Newport News S.B. & D.D. Co	12 Apr 1966	5 Oct 1967	30 Jan 1969	AA
GUITARRO	SSN 665	San Francisco NSY (Mare Island)	9 Dec 1965	27 July 1968	9 Sep 1972	PA
HAWKBILL	SSN 666	San Francisco NSY (Mare Island)	12 Sep 1966	12 Apr 1969	4 Feb 1971	PA
BERGALL	SSN 667	General Dynamics (Electric Boat Div)	16 Apr 1966	17 Feb 1968	13 June 1969	AA
SPADEFISH	SSN 668	Newport News S.B. & D.D. Co	21 Dec 1966	15 May 1968	14 Aug 1969	AA
SEAHORSE	SSN 669	General Dynamics (Electric Boat Div)	13 Aug 1966	15 June 1968	19 Sep 1969	AA
FINBACK	SSN 670	Newport News S.B. & D.D. Co	26 June 1967	7 Dec 1968	4 Feb 1970	AA
PINTADO	SSN 672	San Francisco NSY (Mare Island)	27 Oct 1967	16 Aug 1969	11 Sep 1971	PA
FLYING FISH	SSN 673	General Dynamics (Electric Boat Div)	30 June 1967	17 May 1969	29 Apr 1970	AA
TREPANG	SSN 674	General Dynamics (Electric Boat Div)	28 Oct 1967	27 Sep 1969	14 Aug 1970	AA
BLUEFISH	SSN 675	General Dynamics (Electric Boat Div)	13 Mar 1968	10 Jan 1970	8 Jan 1971	AA
BILLFISH	SSN 676	General Dynamics (Electric Boat Div)	20 Sep 1968	1 May 1970	12 Mar 1971	AA
DRUM	SSN 677	San Francisco NSY (Mare Island)	20 Aug 1968	23 May 1970	15 Apr 1972	PA
ARCHERFISH	SSN 678	General Dynamics (Electric Boat Div)	19 June 1969	16 Jan 1971	17 Dec 1971	AA
SILVERSIDES	SSN 679	General Dynamics (Electric Boat Div)	13 Oct 1969	4 June 1971	5 May 1972	AA
WILLIAM H. BATES (ex-Redfish)	SSN 680	Ingalls Shipbuilding (Litton)	4 Aug 1969	11 Dec 1971	5 May 1973	PA
BATFISH	SSN 681	General Dynamics (Electric Boat Div)	9 Feb 1970	9 Oct 1971	1 Sep 1972	AA
TUNNY	SSN 682	Ingalls Shipbuilding (Litton)	22 May 1970	10 June 1972	26 Jan 1974	PA
PARCHE	SSN 683	Ingalls Shipbuilding (Litton)	10 Dec 1970	13 Jan 1973	17 Aug 1974	PA
CAVALLA	SSN 684	General Dynamics (Electric Boat Div)	4 June 1970	19 Feb 1972	9 Feb 1973	PA
L. MENDEL RIVERS	SSN 686	Newport News S.B. & D.D. Co	26 June 1971	2 June 1973	1 Feb 1975	AA
RICHARD B. RUSSELL	SSN 687	Newport News S.B. & D.D. Co	19 Oct 1971	12 Jan 1974	16 Aug 1975	AA

Displacement, tons: 3 640 standard; 4 640 dived
Dimensions, feet (metres): 292·2 × 31·7 × 26 *(89 × 9·5 × 7·9)* *(see Design* notes)
Missiles: Being fitted for Harpoon (already in SSN 638, 662, 663, 686, 687)
Torpedo tubes: 4—21 in *(533 mm)* Mk 63 amidships
A/S weapons: SUBROC and A/S torpedoes
Main machinery: 1 pressurised-water cooled S5W (Westing-house) reactor; 2 steam turbines; 15 000 shp; 1 shaft
Speed, knots: 20+ surfaced; 30+ dived
Complement: 107 (12 officers, 95 enlisted men)

The 37 "Sturgeon" class attack submarines were the largest US Navy group of nuclear-powered ships built to the same design until the advent of the "Los Angeles" class.
SSN 637-639 were authorised in the FY 1962 new construction programme. SSN 646-653 in FY 1963, SSN 660-664 in FY 1964, SSN 665-670 in FY 1965, SSN 672-677 in FY 1966, SSN 678-682 in FY 1967, SSN 683-684 in FY 1968, and SSN 686-687 in FY 1969.

Construction: *Pogy* was begun by the New York Shipbuilding Corp (Camden, New Jersey), contract with whom was terminated on 5 June 1967; contract for completion awarded to Ingalls Shipbuilding Corp on 7 December 1967.
Guitarro sank in 35 ft of water on 15 May 1969 while being fitted out at the San Francisco Bay Naval Shipyard. According to a congressional report, the sinking, caused by shipyard workers, was "wholly avoidable". Subsequently raised; damage estimated at $25 million. Completion delayed more than two years.

Design: These submarines are slightly larger than the previous "Thresher" class and can be identified by their taller sail structure and the lower position of their diving planes on the sail (to improve control at periscope depth). Sail height is 20 ft, 6 in above deck. Sail-mounted diving planes rotate to vertical for breaking through ice when surfacing in arctic regions.
These submarines probably are slightly slower than the previous "Thresher" and "Skipjack" classes because of their increased size with the same propulsion system as in the earlier classes.
SSN 678/684, 686 and 687 are ten feet longer than remainder of class to accommodate extra sonar and electronic gear.

Electronics: Mk 113 torpedo fire control system is being replaced by Mk 117 (already in SSN 638, 639, 646-9, 652, 662-3, 665 668-9, 673).
Fitted with WSC-3 satellite communications transceiver.

Name: *William H. Bates* (SSN 680) previously *Redfish* renamed 25 June 1971.

Operational: *Whale, Pargo,* and older nuclear submarine *Sargo* conducted exercises in the Arctic ice pack during March-April 1969. *Whale* surfaced at the geographic North Pole on 6 April, the 60th anniversary of Rear-Admiral Robert E. Peary's reaching the North Pole. This was the first instance of single-screw US nuclear submarines surfacing in the Arctic ice.

Radar: BPS 14 Search.

DRUM   3/1980, Dr. Giorgio Arra

LAPON   7/1979, Wright and Logan

Sonar: BQQ 2 sonar system. Principal components of the BQQ 2 include the BQS 6 active sonar, with transducers mounted in a 15 ft diameter sonar sphere, and BQR 7 passive sonar, with hydrophones in a conformal array on sides of forward hull. The active sonar sphere is fitted in the optimum bow position, requiring placement of torpedo tubes amidships. These submarines also have BQS 8 under-ice sonar and BQS 12 (first 16 boats) or BQS 13 active/passive sonars. Transducers for the BQS 8, intended primarily for under-ice navigation, are in two small domes aft of the sail structure.
Sonar suites of the *Guitarro* and *Cavalla* have been modified. All "Sturgeon" class submarines are to be refitted with replacement of the BQQ 2 by BQQ 5 during regular overhauls.

Submersibles: *Hawkbill* and *Pintado* have been modified to carry and support the Navy's Deep Submergence Rescue Vehicles (DSRV). See section on Deep Submergence Vehicles for additional DSRV details.

QUEENFISH (SSN 651)

1967, US Navy, by PH3 A. R. Foss

RICHARD B. RUSSELL

1975, Newport News SB & DD Co

RICHARD B. RUSSELL

6/1975, USN

POGY (SSN 647)

1971, Ingalls Shipbuilding

BLUEFISH (SSN 675)   1970, General Dynamics, Electric Boat Division

HAWKBILL   2/1977, Dr. Giorgio Arra

RAY (SSN 653)   1967, Newport News by B. T. Nixon

CAVALLA   8/1976, JLM van der Burg

WILLIAM H. BATES   3/1979, Dr. Giorgio Arra

POGY   1973, USN

1 "HALIBUT" CLASS: SUBMARINE (nuclear-powered) (SSN)

Name	No.	Builders	Laid down	Launched	Commissioned	F/S
HALIBUT	SSN 587 (ex-SSGN 587)	Mare Island Naval Shipyard, Vallejo, Calif	11 Apr 1957	9 Jan 1959	4 Jan 1960	PR

Displacement, tons: 3 850 standard; 5 000 dived
Dimensions, feet (metres): 350 × 29·5 × 21·5 *(106·6 × 9 × 6·5)*
Torpedo tubes: 6—21 in *(533 mm)* 4 bow (Mk 61); 2 stern (Mk 62)
Main machinery: 1 pressurised-water cooled S3W (Westinghouse) reactor; 2 steam turbines (Westinghouse); 6 600 shp; 2 shafts
Speed, knots: 15+ surfaced; 20+ dived
Complement: 98 (10 officers, 88 enlisted men)

Halibut is believed to have been the first submarine designed and constructed specifically to fire guided missiles.
She was originally intended to have diesel-electric propulsion but on 27 February 1956 the Navy announced she would have nuclear propulsion. She was the US Navy's only nuclear-powered guided missile submarine (SSGN) to be completed. Authorised in the FY 1956 new construction programme and built for an estimated cost of $45 million.

She was reclassified as an attack submarine on 25 July 1965 after the Navy discarded the Regulus submarine-launched missile force. Her missile equipment was removed. Reportedly she has been fitted with a ducted bow thruster to permit precise control and manoeuvring, when active employed on research duties.
She can carry the 50 ft Deep Submergence Rescue Vehicle (DSRV) and other submersibles on her after deck and operate these while dived.
Decommissioned on 30 June 1976 and laid up at Bremerton.

Design: Built with a large missile hangar faired into her bow (see *picture*). Her hull was intended primarily to provide a stable surface launching platform rather than for speed or manoeuvrabilty.

Electronics: Mk 101 Mod 11 torpedo fire control system (removed 1977).

Missiles: Designed to carry two Regulus II surface-to-surface missiles. The Regulus II was a transonic missile which could carry a nuclear warhead and had a range of 1 000 miles. The Regulus II was cancelled before becoming operational and *Halibut* operated from 1960 to 1964 carrying five Regulus I missiles, subsonic cruise missiles which could deliver a nuclear warhead on targets 575 n. miles from launch.
During this period the US Navy operated a maximum of five Regulus guided (cruise) missile submarines, *Halibut*, the post-war constructed *Grayback* (SSG 574 now SS 574) and *Growler* (SSG 577), and the World War II-built *Tunny* (SSG 282 subsequently LPSS 282) and *Barbero* (SSG 317).
As SSGN *Halibut* carried a complement of 11 officers and 108 enlisted men.

Navigation: Fitted with Ship's Inertial Navigation System (SINS).

Sonar: BQS 4.

HALIBUT (with DSRV embarked)   *1970, USN*

HALIBUT (SSN 587)   *1968, United States Navy*

HALIBUT (SSN 587)   *United States Navy*

1 "GLENARD P. LIPSCOMB" CLASS: SUBMARINE (nuclear-powered) (SSN)

Name	No.	Builders	Laid down	Launched	Commissioned	F/S
GLENARD P. LIPSCOMB	SSN 685	General Dynamics (Electric Boat Div)	5 June 1971	4 Aug 1973	21 Dec 1974	AA

Displacement, tons: 5 813 standard; 6 480 dived
Dimensions, feet (metres): 365 × 31·7 × 31 *(111·3 × 9·7 × 9·5)*
Missiles: To be fitted for Harpoon
Torpedo tubes: 4—21 in *(533 mm)* amidships
A/S weapons: SUBROC and A/S torpedoes
Main machinery: 1 pressurised-water cooled S5Wa (Westinghouse) reactor. Turbine-electric drive (General Electric); 1 shaft
Speed, knots: approx 25+ dived
Complement: 120 (12 officers, 108 enlisted men)

Studies of a specifically "quiet" submarine were begun in October 1964. After certain setbacks approval for the construction of this submarine was announced on 25 October 1968 and the contract awarded to General Dynamics on 14 October 1970. The Turbine-Electric Drive Submarine (TEDS) was constructed to test "a combination of advanced silencing techniques" involving "a new kind of propulsion system, and new and quieter machinery of various kinds", according to the Department of Defense. The TEDS project will permit an at-sea evaluation of improvements in ASW effectiveness due to noise reduction.

No further class of turbine-electric nuclear submarines has been proposed. Rather, quieting features developed in *Glenard P. Lipscomb* which do not detract from speed have been incorporated in the "Los Angeles" design.

Authorised in the FY 1968 new construction programme, estimated construction cost was approximately $200 million.

Electronics: Mk 113 Mod 8 TFCS. To be replaced by Mk 117 Mod 3.
Fitted with WSC-3 satellite communications transceiver.

Engineering: Turbine-electric drive eliminates the noisy reduction gears of standard steam turbine power plants. The turbine-electric power plant is larger and heavier than comparable geared steam turbine submarine machinery.
Tullibee (SSN 597) was an earlier effort at noise reduction through a turbine-electric nuclear plant.

GLENARD P. LIPSCOMB
1974, General Dynamics, Electric Boat Division

1 "NARWHAL" CLASS: SUBMARINE (nuclear-powered) (SSN)

Name	No.	Builders	Laid down	Launched	Commissioned	F/S
NARWHAL	SSN 671	General Dynamics (Electric Boat Div)	17 Jan 1966	9 Sep 1967	12 July 1969	AA

Displacement, tons: 4 450 standard; 5 350 dived
Dimensions, feet (metres): 314·6 × 37·7 × 27 *(95·9 × 11·5 × 8·2)*
Missiles: To be fitted for Harpoon
Torpedo tubes: 4—21 in *(533 mm)* amidships
A/S weapons: SUBROC and A/S torpedoes
Main machinery: 1 pressurised water-cooled S5G (General Electric) reactor. 2 steam turbines; 17 000 shp; 1 shaft
Speed, knots: 20+ surfaced; 30+ dived
Complement: 107 (12 officers, 95 enlisted men)

Authorised in the FY 1964 new construction programme.

Design: *Narwhal* is similar to the "Sturgeon" class submarines in hull design.

Electronics: Mk 113 Mod 6 torpedo fire control system. To be replaced by Mk 117 system.
Fitted with WSC-3 satellite communications transceiver.

Engineering: *Narwhal* is fitted with the prototype sea-going S5G natural circulation reactor plant. According to Admiral H. G. Rickover the natural circulation reactor "offers promise of increased reactor plant reliability, simplicity, and noise reduction due to the elimination of the need for large reactor coolant pumps and associated electrical and control equipment by taking maximum advantage of natural convection to circulate the reactor coolant".
The Atomic Energy Commission's Knolls Atomic Power Laboratory was given prime responsibility for development of the power plant. Construction of a land-based prototype plant began in May 1961 at the National Reactor Testing Station in Idaho. The reactor achieved initial criticality on 12 September 1965.

Sonar: BQS 8 upward-looking sonar for under-ice work (photo). BQQ 2 system (BQS 6 active and BQR 7 passive). BQS 6 is fitted in a 15 ft sphere and BQR 7 with conformal hydrophone array forward.

NARWHAL
2 1974, USN

11 + 22 + (7) "LOS ANGELES" CLASS: SUBMARINES (nuclear-powered) (SSN)

Name	No.	Builders	Laid down	Launched	Commissioned	F/S
LOS ANGELES	SSN 688	Newport News S.B. & D.D. Co	8 Jan 1972	6 Apr 1974	13 Nov 1976	PA
BATON ROUGE	SSN 689	Newport News S.B. & D.D. Co	18 Nov 1972	26 Apr 1975	25 June 1977	AA
PHILADELPHIA	SSN 690	General Dynamics (Electric Boat Div)	12 Aug 1972	19 Oct 1974	25 June 1977	AA
MEMPHIS	SSN 691	Newport News S.B. & D.D. Co	23 June 1973	3 Apr 1976	17 Dec 1977	AA
OMAHA	SSN 692	General Dynamics (Electric Boat Div)	27 Jan 1973	21 Feb 1976	11 Mar 1978	PA
CINCINNATI	SSN 693	Newport News S.B. & D.D. Co	6 Apr 1974	19 Feb 1977	10 June 1978	AA
GROTON	SSN 694	General Dynamics (Electric Boat Div)	3 Aug 1973	9 Oct 1976	8 July 1978	AA
BIRMINGHAM	SSN 695	Newport News S.B. & D.D. Co	26 Apr 1975	29 Oct 1977	16 Dec 1978	AA
NEW YORK CITY	SSN 696	General Dynamics (Electric Boat Div)	15 Dec 1973	18 June 1977	3 Mar 1979	AA
INDIANAPOLIS	SSN 697	General Dynamics (Electric Boat Div)	19 Oct 1974	30 July 1977	5 Jan 1980	PA
BREMERTON	SSN 698	General Dynamics (Electric Boat Div)	8 May 1976	22 July 1978	23 Feb 1980	AA
JACKSONVILLE	SSN 699	General Dynamics (Electric Boat Div)	21 Feb 1976	18 Nov 1978	1980	Bldg
DALLAS	SSN 700	General Dynamics (Electric Boat Div)	9 Oct 1976	28 Apr 1979	1980	Bldg
LA JOLLA	SSN 701	General Dynamics (Electric Boat Div)	16 Oct 1976	11 Aug 1979	1980	Bldg
PHOENIX	SSN 702	General Dynamics (Electric Boat Div)	30 July 1977	8 Dec 1979	1981	Bldg
BOSTON	SSN 703	General Dynamics (Electric Boat Div)	11 Aug 1978	1980	1981	Bldg
BALTIMORE	SSN 704	General Dynamics (Electric Boat Div)	21 May 1979	1980	1982	Bldg
—	SSN 705	General Dynamics (Electric Boat Div)	4 Sep 1979	1981	1982	Bldg
—	SSN 706	General Dynamics (Electric Boat Div)	8 Dec 1979	1981	1982	Bldg
—	SSN 707	General Dynamics (Electric Boat Div)	1980	1981	1983	Ord
—	SSN 708	General Dynamics (Electric Boat Div)	1980	1982	1983	Ord
—	SSN 709	General Dynamics (Electric Boat Div)	1981	1982	1984	Ord
—	SSN 710	General Dynamics (Electric Boat Div)	1981	1983	1984	Ord
SAN FRANCISCO	SSN 711	Newport News S.B. and D.D. Co	26 May 1977	1979	1980	Bldg
ATLANTA	SSN 712	Newport News S.B. and D.D. Co	17 Aug 1978	1980	1981	Bldg
HOUSTON	SSN 713	Newport News S.B. and D.D. Co	29 Jan 1979	1980	1982	Bldg
—	SSN 714	Newport News S.B. and D.D. Co	1 Aug 1979	1981	1982	Bldg
—	SSN 715	Newport News S.B. and D.D. Co	1980	1981	1983	Ord
—	SSN 716	Newport News S.B. and D.D. Co	1980	1982	1983	Ord
—	SSN 717	Newport News S.B. and D.D. Co	1981	1982	1984	Ord
—	SSN 718	Newport News S.B. and D.D. Co	1981	1983	1984	Ord
—	SSN 719	General Dynamics (Electric Boat Div)	1981	1983	1984	Ord
—	SSN 720	General Dynamics (Electric Boat Div)	1982	1983	1985	Ord
—	SSN 721	Approved FY 1980 programme				
—	SSN 722	Approved FY 1980 programme				
—	SSN 723	Proposed FY 1981 programme				
—	SSN 724	Proposed FY 1982 programme				
—	SSN 725	Proposed FY 1983 programme				
—	SSN 742	Proposed FY 1984 programme				
—	SSN 743	Proposed FY 1984 programme				

Displacement, tons: 6 000 standard; 6 900 dived
Dimensions, feet (metres): 360 × 33 × 32·3 *(109 7 × 10·1 × 9·9)*
Missiles: Tube launched Harpoon
Torpedo tubes: 4—21 in *(533 mm)* amidships
A/S weapons: SUBROC and Mk 48 A/S torpedoes
Main machinery: 1 pressurised-water cooled S6G (GE) reactor; 2 geared turbines; 1 shaft; approx 35 000 shp
Speed, knots: 30+ dived
Complement: 127 (12 officers, 115 enlisted men)

SSN 688-690 were authorised in the FY 1970 new construction programme, SSN 691-694 in the FY 1971, SSN 695-699 in the FY 1972, SSN 700-705 in the FY 1973, SSN 706-710 in the FY 1974, SSN 711-713 in the FY 1975, SSN 714-715 in the FY 1976, SSN 716-718 in the FY 1977, SSN 719 in the FY 1978, SSN 720 and SSN 721 and 722 in the FY 1980 programmes. Five more of this class are planned, these being the last of the

"Los Angeles" class which will be succeeded by the new SSN class.
Detailed design of the "SSN 688" class as well as construction of the lead submarine was contracted to the Newport News Shipbuilding & Dry Dock Company, Newport News, Virginia. Due to controversy in Washington, strikes and other shipyard problems these submarines are considerably behind schedule with the lead ship being completed over two years behind the original date. Thus, *Los Angeles* was nearly five years from keel laying to commissioning while *Birmingham* took only three years.

Design: Every effort has been made to improve sound quieting and the trials of *Los Angeles* have shown success in this area.

Electronics: UYK-7 computer is installed to assist command and control functions: Mk 113 Mod 10 torpedo fire control system fitted in SSN 688-699 (to be replaced by Mk 117 in near future); Mk 117 in later submarines.

Fitted with WSC-3 satellite communications transceiver.

Engineering: The S6G reactor is reportedly a modified version of the D2G type fitted in *Bainbridge* and *Truxtun*. The D2G reactors each produce approximately 35 000 shp. Reactor core life between refuellings is estimated at ten years.

Fiscal: The costs of these submarines have increased in every fiscal year programme. In FY 1976 an average cost of $221·25 million per boat was estimated for a 38-submarine class. However, FY 1977 boats are estimated to cost approximately $330 million each, the single FY 1979 boat is estimated at $325·6 million and the two in FY 1980, $809·6 million.

Radar: BPS 15.

Sonar: BQQ 5 long range acquisition; BQS 15 close range; Towed array fitted.

LOS ANGELES

6/1979, Dr, Giorgio Arra

OMAHA   *9|1979, Dr. Giorgio Arra*

LOS ANGELES   *8|1976, Newport News SB and DD Co*

5 "GEORGE WASHINGTON" CLASS (BALLISTIC MISSILE SUBMARINES (SSBN))

Name	No.	Builders	Laid down	Launched	Commissioned	F/S
GEORGE WASHINGTON	SSBN 598	General Dynamics (Electric Boat Div)	1 Nov 1957	9 June 1959	30 Dec 1959	PA
PATRICK HENRY	SSBN 599	General Dynamics (Electric Boat Div)	27 May 1958	22 Sep 1959	9 Apr 1960	PA
THEODORE ROOSEVELT	SSBN 600	Mare Island Naval Shipyard	20 May 1958	3 Oct 1959	13 Feb 1961	PA
ROBERT E. LEE	SSBN 601	Newport News Shipbuilding & D.D. Co	25 Aug 1958	18 Dec 1959	16 Sep 1960	PA
ABRAHAM LINCOLN	SSBN 602	Portsmouth Naval Shipyard	1 Nov 1958	14 May 1960	11 Mar 1961	PR

Displacement, tons: 6 019 standard surfaced; 6 888 dived
Dimensions, feet (metres): 381·7 × 33 × 29
   (116·3 × 10·1 × 8·8)
Missiles: 16 tubes for Polaris A-3 SLBM
Torpedo tubes: 6—21 in *(533 mm)* Mk 59 (bow)
Main machinery: 1 pressurised-water cooled S5W (Westinghouse) reactor;
   2 geared turbines (General Electric); 15 000 shp; 1 shaft
Speed, knots: 20 surfaced; 31 dived
Complement: 112 (12 officers, 100 enlisted men) (operated by two crews)

George Washington was the West's first ship to be armed with ballistic missiles. A supplement to the FY 1958 new construction programme signed on 11 February 1958 provided for the construction of the first three SSBNs. The Navy ordered the just-begun attack submarine *Scorpion* (SSN 589) to be completed as a missile submarine on 31 December 1957. The hull was redesignated SSGN 598 and completed as *George Washington*. *Patrick Henry* similarly was re-ordered on the last day of 1957, her materials having originally been intended for the not-yet-started SSN 590. These submarines and three sister ships (two authorised in FY 1959) were built to a modified "Skipjack" class design with almost 130 ft being added to the original design to accommodate two rows of eight missile tubes, fire control and navigation equipment, and auxiliary machinery. All are depth limited compared with later designs. *Theodore Roosevelt* (SSBN 600) and *Abraham Lincoln* (SSBN 602) are scheduled to be decommissioned in FY 1980 and laid up at Bremerton in reserve. *Abraham Lincoln* will begin inactivation in June 1980 and *Theodore Roosevelt* will follow in October 1980. Current plans call for the missile compartment to be cut out and scrapped and the hull put back together during this process. This is being done as a result of SALT I provisions. *Abraham Lincoln* has not made any deployments since 1978 and has had her operations severely restricted.

The FY 1981 budget includes funds for the retention of *George Washington* (SSBN 598), *Patrick Henry* (SSBN 599) and *Robert E. Lee* (SSBN 601) as SSNs. This will be done by decommissioning the missile compartment and removing the associated electronics along with one of the two Ships Inertial Navigation Systems (SINS). The missile compartment itself will remain. As SSNs they will be primarily used for training, ASW exercises and other secondary duties which will free the more modern SSNs currently employed in this role for "front-line" duties. Due to their short-life cores and material condition it is planned to retain SSBN 598, 599 and 601 in an active status for only two to three years and then they too will be laid up. It is not known whether the three ships will be reclassified SSNs.

THEODORE ROOSEVELT
7/1979, Dr. Giorgio Arra

Appearance: Note that "hump" of hull extension for housing missile tubes is more pronounced in these submarines than later classes.

Designation: Originally classified SSGN 598-600. Reclassified SSBN 598-600 on 26 June 1958.

Electronics: Fitted with WSC-3 satellite communications transceiver.

Engineering: *George Washington* was the first FBM submarine to be overhauled and "refuelled". During her 4½ years of operation on her initial reactor core she carried out 15 submerged missile patrols and steamed more than 100 000 miles.

Missiles: These ships were initially armed with the Polaris A-1 missile (1 200 n. mile range). *George Washington* successfully fired two Polaris A-1 missiles while submerged off Cape Canaveral on 20 July 1960 in the first underwater launching of a ballistic missile from a US submarine. She departed on her initial patrol on 15 November 1960 and remained submerged for 66 days, 10 hours. All five submarines of this class have been refitted to fire the improved Polaris A-3 missile (2 500 n. mile range). Missile refit and first reactor refuelling were accomplished simultaneously during overhaul. *George Washington* from 20 June 1964 to 2 February 1966, *Patrick Henry* from 4 January 1965 to 21 July 1966, *Theodore Roosevelt* from 28 July 1965 to 14 January 1967, *Robert E. Lee* from 23 February 1965 to 2 July 1966, and *Abraham Lincoln* from 25 October 1965 to 3 June 1967, four at Electric Boat yard in Groton, Connecticut, and *Robert E. Lee* at Mare Island Naval Shipyard (California). These submarines all have Mk 84 fire control systems and gas-steam missile ejectors (originally fitted with Mk 80 fire control systems and compressed air missile ejectors, changed during A-3 missile refit).

These submarines will not be modified to carry and launch the advanced Poseidon ballistic missile.

Navigation: Fitted with three Mk 2 Mod 4 Ship's Inertial Navigation System (SINS) and navigational satellite receiver.

ROBERT E. LEE
1961, United States Navy, Official

ABRAHAM LINCOLN
1961, United States Navy, Official

THEODORE ROOSEVELT (SSBN 600)   *United States Navy*

THEODORE ROOSEVELT   *1963, United States Navy, Official*

ABRAHAM LINCOLN   *USN*

GEORGE WASHINGTON   *1960, Electric Boat Division, General Dynamics Corporation*

GEORGE WASHINGTON (SSBN 598)   *United States Navy*

ROBERT E. LEE   *USN*

POSEIDON CONVERSION SCHEDULE

SSBN No.	FY Programme	Conversion Yard	Start	Complete
616	1973	General Dynamics Corp (Electric Boat Div)	15 Oct 1972	7 Nov 1974
617	1973	Newport News S.B. & D.D. Co	15 Jan 1973	11 Apr 1975
619	1973	General Dynamics Corp (Electric Boat Div)	19 Mar 1973	15 Aug 1975
620	1974	Portsmouth Naval Shipyard	1 Feb 1974	15 Apr 1976
622	1975	Newport News S.B. & D.D. Co	15 Jan 1975	14 May 1977
623	1973	Puget Sound Naval Shipyard	15 June 1973	27 June 1975
624	1974	Newport News S.B. & D.D. Co	1 Oct 1973	23 Oct 1975
625	1975	Portsmouth Naval Shipyard	29 Apr 1975	29 July 1977
626	1975	General Dynamics Corp (Electric Boat Div)	1 Dec 1975	21 Feb 1978
627	1968	General Dynamics Corp (Electric Boat Div)	3 Feb 1969	28 June 1970
628	1970	Newport News S.B. & D.D. Co	10 Nov 1969	18 Feb 1971
629	1968	Newport News S.B. & D.D. Co	11 May 1969	11 Aug 1970
630	1969	Mare Island Naval Shipyard	4 Aug 1969	22 Feb 1971
631	1970	Puget Sound Naval Shipyard	3 Oct 1969	16 Dec 1970
632	1969	General Dynamics Corp (Electric Boat Div)	11 July 1969	19 Nov 1970
633	1970	General Dynamics Corp (Electric Boat Div)	10 Jan 1970	30 Apr 1971
634	1971	General Dynamics Corp (Electric Boat Div)	15 July 1970	29 Oct 1971
635	1970	Portsmouth Naval Shipyard	19 Jan 1970	2 Sep 1971
636	1971	Newport News S.B. & D.D. Co	22 July 1970	21 Sep 1971
640	1971	General Dynamics Corp (Electric Boat Div)	25 Feb 1971	15 May 1972
641	1971	Newport News S.B. & D.D. Co	15 Feb 1971	12 May 1972
642	1972	General Dynamics Corp (Electric Boat Div)	15 July 1971	27 Oct 1972
643	1971	Portsmouth Naval Shipyard	28 Apr 1971	31 July 1972
644	1971	Puget Sound Naval Shipyard	30 Apr 1971	21 July 1972
645	1972	Newport News S.B. & D.D. Co	15 July 1971	17 Nov 1972
654	1972	Puget Sound Naval Shipyard	14 Sep 1971	8 Feb 1973
655	1972	Newport News S.B. & D.D. Co	15 Nov 1971	22 Mar 1973
656	1972	General Dynamics Corp (Electric Boat Div)	12 Nov 1971	7 Apr 1973
657	1972	Puget Sound Naval Shipyard	20 Feb 1972	17 May 1973
658	1973	Newport News S.B. & D.D. Co	21 Aug 1972	19 Dec 1973
659	1973	Portsmouth Naval Shipyard	16 Oct 1972	8 Feb 1974

TENTATIVE TRIDENT CONVERSION SCHEDULE

SSBN No.	FY Programme	Occasion	Start	Complete
627	1979	During overhaul at Portsmouth Naval Shipyard	3 Aug 1979	4 Dec 1980
629	1980	During tender availability	3 Apr 1980	22 June 1980
630	1980	During tender availability	28 June 1980	16 Sep 1980
632	1980	During ship overhaul	12 Jan 1980	15 May 1981
633	1980	During ship overhaul	1 July 1980	4 Nov 1981
634	1982	During tender availability	27 Oct 1981	20 Jan 1982
640	1980	During ship overhaul	Nov 1979	2 Apr 1981
641	1979	During overhaul at Newport News S.B. and D.D. Co	2 Mar 1979	3 Sep 1980
643	1980	During ship overhaul	June 1980	1 Nov 1981
655	1980	During tender availability	4 Dec 1979	23 Feb 1980
657	1979	During tender availability	2 Oct 1978	20 Dec 1979
658	1979	During tender availability	1 Sep 1979	19 Nov 1980

Note: Completion dates in Trident conversion include the conducting of sea and missile firing trials and in the case of SSBN 657 her service as a test platform for the missile.

5 "ETHAN ALLEN" CLASS (BALLISTIC MISSILE SUBMARINES (SSBN))

Name	No.	Builders	Laid down	Launched	Commissioned	F/S
ETHAN ALLEN	SSBN 608	General Dynamics (Electric Boat Div)	14 Sep 1959	22 Nov 1960	8 Aug 1961	PA
SAM HOUSTON	SSBN 609	Newport News Shipbuilding & D.D. Co	28 Dec 1959	2 Feb 1961	6 Mar 1962	PA
THOMAS A. EDISON	SSBN 610	General Dynamics (Electric Boat Div)	15 Mar 1960	15 June 1961	10 Mar 1962	PA
JOHN MARSHALL	SSBN 611	Newport News Shipbuilding & D.D. Co	4 Apr 1960	15 July 1961	21 May 1962	PA
THOMAS JEFFERSON	SSBN 618	Newport News Shipbuilding & D.D. Co	3 Feb 1961	24 Feb 1962	4 Jan 1963	PA

Displacement, tons: 6 955 surfaced; 7 880 dived
Dimensions, feet (metres): 410 × 33 × 32 *(125 × 10·1 × 9·8)*
Missiles: 16 tubes for Polaris A-3 SLBM
Torpedo tubes: 4—21 in *(533 mm)* bow
Main machinery: 1 pressurised-water cooled S5W (Westinghouse) reactor;
2 geared turbines (General Electric); 15 000 shp; 1 shaft
Speed, knots: 20 surfaced; 30 dived
Complement: 142 (15 officers, 127 enlisted men) (operate with two separate crews) (see note under "Lafayette" class)

These submarines were designed specifically for the ballistic missile role and are larger and better arranged than the earlier "George Washington" class submarines. The first four ships of this class were authorised in the FY 1959 programme; *Thomas Jefferson* was in the FY 1961 programme. These submarines and the previous "George Washington" class will not be converted to carry the Poseidon missile because of material limitations and the age they would be after conversion.

In the FY 1981 budget, funds are included to remove this class from the SLBM force and convert them to SSNs. The conversion will be more extensive than that done to the "George Washington" class. However, the missile compartment will be retained in a decommissioned state. The conversion is being undertaken because each has recently been refuelled with long-life cores and overhauled. The first to be converted will be *Ethan Allen*. They will have the same type of duties as the three remaining boats of the "George Washington" class. It is unknown whether the ships will be reclassified SSNs. It is planned to retain this class on the active list a minimum of five years as "SSNs".

Design: These submarines and the subsequent "Lafayette" class have a depth capability similar to the "Thresher" class attack submarines; pressure hulls of HY-80 steel.

Electronics: Fitted with WSC-3 satellite communications transceiver.

Missiles: These ships were initially armed with the Polaris A-2 missile (1 500 n. mile range). *Ethan Allen* launched the first A-2 missile fired from a submarine on 23 October 1961. She was

THOMAS JEFFERSON

9/1977, USN

the first submarine to deploy with the A-2 missile, beginning her first patrol on 26 June 1962. *Ethan Allen* fired a Polaris A-2 missile in the Christmas Island Pacific Test Area on 6 May 1962 in what was the first complete US test of a ballistic missile including detonation of the nuclear warhead. All five of these submarines have been modified to fire the A-3 missile (2 500 n. mile range).

Navigation: Fitted with two Mk 2 Ship's Inertial Navigation Systems (SINS) and navigational satellite receiver.

THOMAS EDISON

1962, Electric Boat Division, General Dynamics Corporation, Groton, Conn. (Builders)

JOHN MARSHALL (SSBN 611)

1967, United States Navy

ETHAN ALLEN (SSBN 608)

1966, General Dynamics Electric Boat

ETHAN ALLEN

1962, courtesy Mr. W. H. Davis

ETHAN ALLEN (SSBN 608)

United States Navy

JOHN MARSHALL   1964, United States Navy, Official

ETHAN ALLEN   1971, USN

THOMAS JEFFERSON   5 1976, USN

SAM HOUSTON (SSBN 609)   1967, United States Navy

ETHAN ALLEN   1971, USN

31 "BENJAMIN FRANKLIN" and "LAFAYETTE" CLASSES (BALLISTIC MISSILE SUBMARINES (SSBN))

Name	No.	Builders	Laid down	Launched	Commissioned	F S
LAFAYETTE	SSBN 616	General Dynamics (Electric Boat Div)	17 Jan 1961	8 May 1962	23 Apr 1963	AA
ALEXANDER HAMILTON	SSBN 617	General Dynamics (Electric Boat Div)	26 June 1961	18 Aug 1962	27 June 1963	AA
ANDREW JACKSON	SSBN 619	Mare Island Naval Shipyard	26 Apr 1961	15 Sep 1962	3 July 1963	AA
JOHN ADAMS	SSBN 620	Portsmouth Naval Shipyard	19 May 1961	12 Jan 1963	12 May 1964	AA
JAMES MONROE	SSBN 622	Newport News Shipbuilding & D.D. Co	31 July 1961	4 Aug 1962	7 Dec 1963	AA
NATHAN HALE	SSBN 623	General Dynamics (Electric Boat Div)	2 Oct 1961	12 Jan 1963	23 Nov 1963	AA
WOODROW WILSON	SSBN 624	Mare Island Naval Shipyard	13 Sep 1961	22 Feb 1963	27 Dec 1963	AA
HENRY CLAY	SSBN 625	Newport News Shipbuilding & D.D. Co	23 Oct 1961	30 Nov 1962	20 Feb 1964	AA
DANIEL WEBSTER	SSBN 626	General Dynamics (Electric Boat Div)	28 Dec 1961	27 Apr 1963	9 Apr 1964	AA
JAMES MADISON	SSBN 627	Newport News Shipbuilding & D.D. Co	5 Mar 1962	15 Mar 1963	28 July 1964	AA
TECUMSEH	SSBN 628	General Dynamics (Electric Boat Div)	1 June 1962	22 June 1963	29 May 1964	AA
DANIEL BOONE	SSBN 629	Mare Island Naval Shipyard	6 Feb 1962	22 June 1963	23 Apr 1964	AA
JOHN C. CALHOUN	SSBN 630	Newport News Shipbuilding & D.D. Co	4 June 1962	22 June 1963	15 Sep 1964	AA
ULYSSES S. GRANT	SSBN 631	General Dynamics (Electric Boat Div)	18 Aug 1962	2 Nov 1963	17 July 1964	AA
VON STEUBEN	SSBN 632	Newport News Shipbuilding & D.D. Co	4 Sep 1962	18 Oct 1963	30 Sep 1964	AA
CASIMIR PULASKI	SSBN 633	General Dynamics (Electric Boat Div)	12 Jan 1963	1 Feb 1964	14 Aug 1964	AA
STONEWALL JACKSON	SSBN 634	Mare Island Naval Shipyard	4 July 1962	30 Nov 1963	26 Aug 1964	AA
SAM RAYBURN	SSBN 635	Newport News Shipbuilding & D.D. Co	3 Dec 1962	20 Dec 1963	2 Dec 1964	AA
NATHANAEL GREENE	SSBN 636	Portsmouth Naval Shipyard	21 May 1962	12 May 1964	19 Dec 1964	AA
BENJAMIN FRANKLIN	SSBN 640	General Dynamics (Electric Boat Div)	25 May 1963	5 Dec 1964	22 Oct 1965	AA
SIMON BOLIVAR	SSBN 641	Newport News Shipbuilding & D.D. Co	17 Apr 1963	22 Aug 1964	29 Oct 1965	AA
KAMEHAMEHA	SSBN 642	Mare Island Naval Shipyard	2 May 1963	16 Jan 1965	10 Dec 1965	AA
GEORGE BANCROFT	SSBN 643	General Dynamics (Electric Boat Div)	24 Aug 1963	20 Mar 1965	22 Jan 1966	AA
LEWIS AND CLARK	SSBN 644	Newport News Shipbuilding & D.D. Co	29 July 1963	21 Nov 1964	22 Dec 1965	AA
JAMES K. POLK	SSBN 645	General Dynamics (Electric Boat Div)	23 Nov 1963	22 May 1965	16 Apr 1966	AA
GEORGE C. MARSHALL	SSBN 654	Newport News Shipbuilding & D.D. Co	2 Mar 1964	21 May 1965	29 Apr 1966	AA
HENRY L. STIMSON	SSBN 655	General Dynamics (Electric Boat Div)	4 Apr 1964	13 Nov 1965	20 Aug 1966	AA
GEORGE WASHINGTON CARVER	SSBN 656	Newport News Shipbuilding & D.D. Co	24 Aug 1964	14 Aug 1965	15 June 1966	AA
FRANCIS SCOTT KEY	SSBN 657	General Dynamics (Electric Boat Div)	5 Dec 1964	23 Apr 1966	3 Dec 1966	AA
MARIANO G. VALLEJO	SSBN 658	Mare Island Naval Shipyard	7 July 1964	23 Oct 1965	16 Dec 1966	AA
WILL ROGERS	SSBN 659	General Dynamics (Electric Boat Div)	20 Mar 1965	21 July 1966	1 Apr 1967	AA

Displacement, tons: 6 650 light surfaced; 7 250 standard surfaced; 8 250 dived
Dimensions, feet (metres): 425 × 33 × 31·5
(129·5 × 10·1 × 9·6)
Missiles: 16 tubes for Poseidon C-3 SLBM (see *Missile* notes)
Torpedo tubes: 4—21 in (533 mm) Mk 65 (bow)
Main machinery: 1 pressurised-water cooled S5W (Westinghouse) reactor; 2 geared turbines; 15 000 shp; 1 shaft
Speed, knots: 20 surfaced; approx 30 dived
Complement: 168 (20 officers, 148 enlisted men) (SSBN 640 onward); 140 (14 officers, 126 enlisted men) (remainder)

These submarines were the largest undersea craft to be completed in the West. The first four submarines (SSBN 616, 617, 619, 620) were authorised in the FY 1961 shipbuilding programme with five additional submarines (SSBN 622-626) authorised in a supplemental to the FY 1961 programme; SSBN 627-636 (ten) in the FY 1962, SSBN 640-645 (six) in the FY 1963, and SSBN 654-659 (six) in the FY 1964. Cost for the earlier ships of this class was approximately $109·5 million per submarine.

Design: *Benjamin Franklin* and later submarines are officially considered a separate class; however, differences are minimal (eg, quieter machinery).

Electronics: Fitted with Mk 113 Mod 9 torpedo fire control system, and WSC-3 satellite communication transceiver.

Engineering: *Benjamin Franklin* and subsequent submarines of this class have been fitted with quieter machinery. All SSBNs have diesel-electric stand-by machinery, snorts, and "outboard" auxiliary propeller for emergency use.
The nuclear cores inserted in refuelling these submarines during the late 1960s and early 1970s cost approximately $3·5 million and provide energy for approximately 400 000 miles.

SIMON BOLIVAR

9/1975, Dr. Giorgio Arra

Missiles: Polaris; The first eight ships of this class were fitted with the Polaris A-2 missile (1 500 n. mile range) and the 23 later ships with the Polaris A-3 missile (2 500 n. mile range). SSBN 620 and SSBN 622-625 (five ships) were rearmed with the Polaris A-3 missile during overhaul-refuellings from 1968 to 1970. *Andrew Jackson* launched the first Polaris A-3 missile on 26 October 1963. *Daniel Webster* was the first submarine to deploy with the A-3 missile, beginning her first patrol on 28 September 1964. *Daniel Boone* was the first SSBN to deploy to the Pacific, beginning her first patrol with the A-3 missile on 25 December 1964.
Poseidon (C3); *James Madison* was the first submarine to undergo conversion to carry the Poseidon missile. She launched the first Poseidon missile on 3 August 1970 and began the first Poseidon patrol on 31 March 1971. Poseidon conversion, overhaul, and reactor refuelling are conducted simultaneously. In addition to changes in missile tubes to accommodate larger Poseidon, the conversion provides replacement of Mk 84 fire control system with Mk 88 system (see Poseidon Conversion Schedule following).

Trident I (C4); Current planning provides for 12 units of these two classes to be fitted with the Trident I missile. *Francis Scott Key* is the first SSBN to be converted to fire the Trident I missile. Six of the conversions, namely those of SSBN 627, 632, 633, 640/641 and 643 will take place during the regularly scheduled overhauls of the submarines (hence the longer conversion periods) and the remainder during tender availabilities alongside an AS (FBM) (hence the shorter conversion periods). The actual industrial time spent on the conversion package is about one month. The conversion includes minor modifications to the launcher and to the ballasting of the submarine to accommodate the greater weight of the Trident missile as well as extensive modifications to the installed fire control, instrumentation and missile checkout subsystems to support the increased sophistication of the longer range missile. A tentative conversion schedule is indicated on the following page. *Francis Scott Key* received her Trident conversion during her tender availability and served as a sea-going test bed for the sea testing phase of the Trident I missile. *Francis Scott Key* completed her trials role and returned to her deterrent mission on 20 October 1979 as the first SSBN to deploy with the Trident I missile. All Trident equipped SSBNs of this class will be based at Kings Bay, Georgia beginning in early 1980.

Navigation: These submarines are equipped with an elaborate Ship's Inertial Navigation System (SINS), a system of gyroscopes and accelerometers which relates movement of the ship in all directions, true speed through the water and over the ocean floor, and true north to give a continuous report of the submarine's position. Navigation data produced by SINS can be provided to each missile's guidance package until the instant the missile is fired.
As converted, all Poseidon submarines have three Mk 2 Mod 4 SINS; all fitted with navigational satellite receivers.

Personnel: Each submarine is assigned two alternating crews designated "Blue" and "Gold". Each crew mans the submarine during a 60 day patrol and partially assists during the intermediate 28 day refit alongside a Polaris tender.

HENRY CLAY (see photograph in Frontispiece of Polaris missile being launched)   1964, United States Navy, Official

LAFAYETTE   1963, United States Navy, Official

WOODROW WILSON (SSBN 624)   United States Navy   DANIEL WEBSTER (SSBN 626)   United States Navy

MARIANO G. VALLEJO   *1974, USN*

JOHN C CALHOUN (SSBM 630)   *1970, United States Navy, PH1 T. Milton Putray*

WILL ROGERS in Holy Loch, Scotland   *1972, USN*

ALEXANDER HAMILTON (SSBN 617)   *United States Navy*

GEORGE C. MARSHALL (SSBN 654)   *1967, United States Navy*

DANIEL BOONE (SSBN 629)

1970, United States Navy

DANIEL BOONE (SSBN 629)

United States Navy

HENRY L. STIMSON (SSBN 655)

1967, United States Navy

DANIEL WEBSTER (SSBN 626)

United States Navy

BENJAMIN FRANKLIN (SSBN 640)

1966, United States Navy

BATON ROUGE

10/1979, J. L. M. van der Burg

LOS ANGELES

6/1979, Dr, Giorgio Arra

OMAHA

9 1979, Dr. Giorgio Arra

0 + 7 + 9 "OHIO" CLASS (BALLISTIC MISSILE SUBMARINES (SSBN))

Name	No.	Builders	Laid down	Launched	Commission	F/S
OHIO	SSBN 726	General Dynamics (Electric Boat Div)	10 Apr 1976	7 Apr 1979	early 1981	Building
MICHIGAN	SSBN 727	General Dynamics (Electric Boat Div)	4 Apr 1977	Apr 1980	early 1982	Building
—	SSBN 728	General Dynamics (Electric Boat Div)	9 June 1977	early 1981	late 1982	Building
GEORGIA	SSBN 729	General Dynamics (Electric Boat Div)	7 Apr 1979	late 1981	mid-1983	Building
	SSBN 730	General Dynamics (Electric Boat Div)	—	late 1982	early 1984	Ord
	SSBN 731	General Dynamics (Electric Boat Div)	—	mid-1983	late 1984	Ord
	SSBN 732	General Dynamics (Electric Boat Div)	—	early 1984	mid-1985	Ord
	SSBN 733	Approved FY 1980 programme				Proj
	SSBN 734	Requested FY 1981 programme				Proj
	SSBN 735	Proposed FY 1982 programme				Proj
	SSBN 736	Proposed FY 1983 programme				Proj
	SSBN 737	Proposed FY 1984 programme				Proj
	SSBN 738	Proposed FY 1985 programme				Proj
	SSBN 739-741	Proposed FY 1986-89 programmes				

Displacement, tons: 16 600 surfaced; 18 700 dived
Dimensions, feet (metres): 560 × 42 × 35·5
(170·7 × 12·8 × 10·8)
Missiles: 24 tubes for Trident I Submarine-Launched Ballistic Missile (SLBM)
Torpedo tubes: 4—21 in *(533 mm)* Mk 68 (bow)
Main machinery: 1 pressurised-water cooled S8G (General Electric) reactor; geared turbines; 1 shaft; 60 000 shp
Complement: 133 (16 officers, 117 enlisted men)

These submarines will be the largest undersea craft yet constructed, being significantly larger than the Soviet "Delta" class missile submarines which are now the largest afloat. The lead submarine was contracted to the Electric Boat Division of the General Dynamics Corp (Groton, Connecticut) on 25 July 1974. The only other US shipyard currently capable of building submarines of this class is the Newport News S.B. & D.D. Co in Virginia.
A series of problems both in Washington and in the shipbuilding yards has resulted in progressive delays to this class.
Ohio herself is scheduled to begin deployment from the Trident base at Bangor, Washington in 1981. As each "Ohio" class is commissioned a Polaris-armed SSBN ("SSBN 598" and "608" classes) will be withdrawn from service.
Contract for long term lead-items on SSBN 733 and 734 awarded to General Dynamics on 6 February 1980.

Design: The size of the Trident submarine is dictated primarily by the larger size missile required for 4 or 6 000 mile range and the larger reactor plant to drive the ship. The submarine will have 24 tubes in a vertical position.
The principal characteristics of the Trident concept as proposed were: (1) long-range missile (eventually of 6 000 miles (Trident II)) to permit targeting the Soviet Union while the submarine cruises in remote areas, making effective ASW virtually impossible for the foreseeable future, (2) extremely quiet submarines, (3) a high at-sea to in-port ratio.

Designation: Initially the hull number SSBN 711 was planned for the first Trident submarine. However, on 21 February 1974 the designation SSBN 1 was assigned, confusing the Navy's submarine designation system which goes back to USS *Holland* (SS 1), commissioned in 1900. Subsequently, the designation was again changed on 10 April 1974, with the "block" SSBN 726-735 being reserved for the Trident programme. Six more 736-741 now added.

Electronics: UYK-7 computer is provided to support electronic and weapon systems. Mk 118 digital torpedo fire control system is installed. To be fitted with WSC-3 satellite communication transceiver.

Engineering: These submarines will have a nuclear core life of about nine years between refuellings. A prototype of the S8G reactor plant has been constructed at West Milton, New York.

Fiscal: Costs of the first four SSBNs have increased over the initial appropriations. See 1975-76 edition for initial costs. SSBNs 731 and 732 in FY 1978 are funded at $1 703 million for the pair.

Originally requested under FY 1979 was $911·9 million for SSBN 733 construction and $274·8 million for advance procurement of SSBN 734. However, because of construction delays, design problems, settlement claims, etc, with previously authorised SSBNs, Congress refused to authorise the $911·9 million to build SSBN 733. Instead it approved $198 million for further advance procurement of SSBN 733 and the money for SSBN 734. The FY 1980 budget approved $1 121 million to construct SSBN 733 and $64 million for further advance procurement of SSBN 734.

Missiles: The Trident submarines will be armed initially with the Trident I missile, which became operational late in 1979. This missile has a range of 4 000 n. miles, a range already exceeded by the SS-N-8 missile in the Soviet "Delta" class submarines. However, the US missile will have a MIRV warhead, which at present is not fitted to SS-N-8, although SS-N-6 (Mod III) has an MRV head.
The Trident missile is expected to carry more than the 10 to 14 re-entry vehicles that the Poseidon can lift. In addition, the Mk 500 MARV (Manoeuvring Re-entry Vehicle) is under development for the purpose of demonstrating its compatability with the Trident I missile. This re-entry vehicle intended to evade ABM interceptor missiles and is not terminally guided to increase its accuracy.

Navigation: Each submarine will have two Mk 2 Ships Inertial Navigation Systems; to be fitted with satellite navigation receivers.

Sonar: BQQ 5 (passive only).

MICHIGAN (rear on the pier), OHIO (in the dock), "keel" of GEORGIA (circular section, to right between cranes)   7/1979, USN (P. H. I. William Wickham)

AMPHIBIOUS FORCES

AMPHIBIOUS landings have been carried out for more than 2,000 years, but the majority, typified by the British assaults at Gallipoli, have been *ad hoc* affairs.

The Gallipoli landings pointed out some of the needs of an amphibious operation – beach survey, mine clearance, rapid debarkation and landing, efficient navigation, good communications, gunfire support, air reconnaissance and support and thorough tri-service training. Amphibiosity is a tricky affair at the best of times but leave any essential element out of the equation and the endeavour is probably doomed.

A brilliant Marine officer, Earl Hancock Ellis, delivered a series of lectures in 1913 foretelling the Pacific war. Further work in the early 1920s led, eventually, in 1932, to the publication of the doctrinal volume *Marine Corps Landing Operations*, followed by the *Tentative Manual for Landing Operations*, a manual which dealt with all aspects, as then known, of amphibious operations. What was needed was a form of craft capable of delivering the Marines to their target beach and the Landing Craft Vehicle and Personnel (LCVP) and Landing Craft Mechanized (LCM), both products of Andrew Higgins, became available at the same time as the amphibious Alligator (Amtrac) was converted for Marine operations.

At the time of Pearl Harbor the USMC was 65,000 strong, with 18,000 at various stations abroad, 4,000 with the navy and 20,000 in training, leaving 23,000 immediately available. There were no specialized assault ships so the LCVPs and LCMs had to be carried in converted merchant ships, although The Maritime Commission had designs in hand which resulted in the attack transports *Doyen* and *Feland* in 1942. Across the Atlantic, the Royal Marines had found themselves at a similar disadvantage when Britain went to war in September 1939, and a considerable number of merchant ships were converted as Landing Ships Infantry; each carrying several LCAs, LCPs and LCSs. America's involvement brought a spate of designs which ranged from ships with an oceanic capability (LST and LSD) to craft (LCT, LCI, LCV, LCM etc), many of which were able to be carried in the LSTs and LSDs on long haul operations. All manner of modifications took place but there were never enough amphibious ships and craft, particularly as landings on defended beaches caused heavy losses.

With this as a background, the US Navy's amphibious forces have been developed since World War II. Command and communications ships such as *Northampton* and the "Blue Ridges" were completed while steady improvements were made to the wartime designs of LSTs and LSDs. In 1957 the "Iwo Jima" class of LPHs was designed to provide the helicopters needed for 'vertical envelopment' by Marine forces. Then came the "Tarawas" of 39,300 tons full load. Their facilities included a large flight deck, a big hangar with space for twenty six Sea Knight helicopters or Harriers, a well deck with stern doors for launching craft of LCV/LCM size and below, plus accommodation for 1,700 Marines with their kit and vehicles. A range of 10,000 miles at 20 knots made these most valuable ships.

In 1989 the first of the new "Wasp" class was commissioned. Larger than the "Tarawas", these ships are very aptly described as Amphibious Assault Ships (multi-purpose) LHD. With a capacity to operate eight Harriers and thirty helicopters simultaneously, they can also carry three Landing Craft Air Cushion (LCAC), which have a range of 220 miles at 40 knots and can accommodate 25 Marines and a main battle tank. Amphibious warfare has come a very long way in fifty years.

J.M.
May 1991

Cargo Ships, Attack type.

Achernar (Dec. 22, 1943)	Southampton
Alamance	Starr
Algol (ex-*James Baines*)	Stokes
Alshain (Jan. 26, 1944)	Suffolk
Andromeda (Dec. 22, 1942)	Tate
Aquarius (July 23, 1943)	Theenim (Oct. 31, 1944)
Arneb (ex-*Mischief*)	Thuban (April 26, 1943)
Capricornus (ex-*Spitfire*)	Todd
Caswell	Tolland (June 26, 1944)
Centaurus (Sept. 3, 1943)	Torrance
Cepheus (Oct. 27, 1943)	Towner
Chara (March 15, 1944)	Trego (June 19, 1944)
Diphda (May 11 1944)	Trousdale
Duplin	Tyrrell
Lenoir	Union
Leo (June 29, 1944)	Uvalde (May 20, 1944)
Marquette (April 29, 1945)	Valencia
Mathews (Dec. 29, 1944)	Venango
Merrick (Jan. 28, 1945)	Vermilion
Montague	Vinton
Muliphen (Aug. 26, 1944)	Virgo (June 4, 1943)
New Hanover	Warrick
Oglethorpe (April 15, 1945)	Washburn
Ottawa	Waukesha
Prentiss	Wheatland
Rankin	Whiteside
Rolette (March 11, 1945)	Whitley
Seminole	Winston (Nov. 30, 1944)
Sheliak (Oct. 17, 1944)	Woodford
Shoshone	Wyandot
Skagit	

Average 6,000 tons *gross*. Dimensions: 459 (*o.a.*) × 63 × 24½ feet (*max.*). Machinery: Geared turbines. S.H.P. 6,000 = 15.5 kts. (AKA 15–20, 53–108).

Artemis	Roxane
Athene	Sappho
Aurelia	Sarita
Birgit	Scania
Circe	Selinur
Corvus	Sidonia
Devosa	Sirona
Hydrus (Oct. 28, 1944)	Sylvania
Lacerta	Tabora
Lumen	Troilus
Medea	Turandot
Mellena	Valeria
Ostara	Vanadis
Pamina	Veritas
Polana	Xenia
Renate	Zenobia

Average 5,800 tons *gross*. Dimensions: 426 (*o.a.*) × 58 × 15½ feet (*max.*). Machinery: Turbo-electric. 2 shafts. S.H.P. 6,600 = 16.5 kts. (AKA 21–52).

1944, U.S. Navy Official.

LIBRA (ex-*Jean Lykes*, 1941), **OBERON** (ex-*Delalba*, March 18, 1942), **TITANIA** (ex-*Harry Culbreath*, Feb. 28, 1942). 6,085 tons *gross*. Dimensions: 439 (*w.l.*), 459 (*o.a.*) × 63 × 25¾ feet (*max.*) Guns: 4—5 inch, etc. Machinery: Geared turbines. S.H.P. 6,000 = 15.5 kts. (AKA 12, 13 & 15).

ALMAACK (ex-*Executor*, 1940). 6,200 tons *gross*. Dimensions: 473 (*o.a.*) × 66 × 27 feet (*max.*). Guns: 4—5 inch, etc. Machinery: Geared turbines. S.H.P. 8,000 = 16.5 kts. (AKA 10).

ALCHIBA (ex-*Mormacdove*, July 6, 1939), **ALCYONE** (ex-*Mormacgull*, 1939), **ALGORAB** (ex-*Mormacwren*, June 15, 1939), **ALHENA** (ex-*Robin Kettering*, Jan. 18, 1941), **ARCTURUS** (ex-*Mormachawk*, May 18, 1939), **BELLATRIX** (ex-*Raven*, 1941), **BETELGEUSE** (ex-*Mormaclark*, Sept. 18, 1939), **ELECTRA** (ex-*Meteor*, 1941), **PROCYON** (ex-*Sweepstakes*, Nov. 14, 1940). 6,200 tons *gross*. Dimensions: 435 (*w.l.*), 459 (*o.a.*) × 63 × 25¾ feet (*max.*). Guns: 4—5 inch, etc. Machinery: Diesel. B.H.P. 6,000 = 15.5 kts. (AKA 1–4, 6–9, 11).

Allendale (Sept. 9, 1944.)	Broadwater (Nov. 5, 1944).
Arenac (Sept. 14, 1944)	Brookings
Attala (Sept. 27, 1944)	Bronx
Audubon	Buckingham
Bandera (Oct. 6, 1944)	Clearfield (Jan. 12, 1945)
Barnwell (Sept. 30, 1944)	Colbert
Beckham (Oct. 15, 1944)	Collingsworth
Bergen	Cottle
Bexar	Crockett
Bingham	Dane
Bland (Oct. 26, 1944)	Darke
Bollinger (Nov. 19, 1944)	Deuel
Bosque (Oct. 28, 1944)	Dickens
Botetourt (Oct. 19, 1944)	Drew
Bottineau	Eastland
Bowie (Oct. 31, 1944)	Edgecombe
Braxton (Nov. 3, 1944)	Effingham

Fond du Lac	Meriwether
Freestone	Mifflin
Gage	Missoula
Gallatin	Montrose
Glynn	Mountrail
Gosper	Napa
Granville	Natrona
Grimes	Navarro
Haskell (June 13, 1944)	Neshoba
Hendry (June 25, 1944)	Newberry
Highlands (July 8, 1944)	New Kent
Hinsdale (July 24, 1944)	Noble
Hocking (Aug. 6, 1944)	Oconto
Hyde	Okaloosa
Jerauld	Okanogan
Karnes	Olmsted
Kenton (Aug. 21, 1944)	Oneida
Kershaw	Oxford
Kingsbury	Pickaway
Kittson	Pickens
Lagrange (Sept. 1, 1944)	Pitt
Lander	Pondera
Lanier (Aug. 29, 1944)	Randall
La Porte	Rawlins
Latimer	Renville
Lauderdale	Rockbridge
Laurens	Rockingham
Lavaca	Rockwall
Lenawee	Rutland
Logan	St. Croix
Lowndes	St. Mary's (Sept 4, 1944)
Lubbock	Sanborn
Lycoming	Sandoval
McCracken	San Saba
Magoffin	Sarasota
Marathon	Sevier
Marvin H. McIntyre (ex-*Arlington*, Sept. 21, 1944)	Sherburne
	Sibley
Mellette	Talladega
Menard	Tazewell
Menifee	Telfair

Mostly county names. Displacement: 6,700 tons. Dimensions: 436½ (*o.a.*) × 62 × 28 feet (*max.*). Machinery: Geared turbines. S.H.P. 8,500 = 17 kts. (APA 117–239).

Appling (April 9 1944)	Carteret
Audrain (April 21 1944)	Catron
Banner (May 3, 1944)	Clarendon
Barrow	Cleburne
Berrien	Colusa
Bladen	Cortland
Bracken	Crenshaw
Briscoe	Crittenden
Brule	Cullman
Burleson	Dawson
Butte	Elkhart
Carlisle	Fallon

SHERBURNE. 1944, *U.S. Navy Official.*

Transports, Attack type—*continued.*

Fergus	***Geneva***
Fillmore	***illiam*** (March 28, 1944)
Garrard	***agara*** (Feb. 10, 1945)
Gasconade	***residio***

All county names. Displacement: 4,100 tons. Dimensions 426 (*o.a.*) × 58 × 15½ feet. Machinery: Turbo-electric. 2 shafts. S.H.P. 6,600 = 16.5 kts. (APA 57–88.)

BAXTER (ex-*Antinous*), **SUMTER** (ex-*Iberville*), **WARREN** (ex-*Jean Lafitte*), **WAYNE** (ex-*Afoundria*) (all 1943). Displacement: 7,700 tons. Dimensions: 468¾ (*o.a.*) × 63 × 26 feet (*max.*). Machinery: Geared turbines. S.H.P. 6,300 = 16 kts. (APA 94, 52–54).

ORMSBY (ex-*Twilight*), **PIERCE** (ex-*Northern Light*), **SHERIDAN** (ex-*Messenger*), (all 1943). Displacement: 6,550 tons. Dimensions: 459 (*o.a.*) × 63 × 25¾ feet (*max.*) Machinery: Geared turbines. S.H.P. 6,000 = 15.5 kts. (APA 49–51).

Adair (ex-*Exchester*)	***Hampton***
Dauphin (June 10, 1944)	***Hanover***
Dutchess (Aug. 26 1944)	***Leedstown*** (ex-*Wood*, ex-*Exchequer*, Feb. 13, 1943)
Griggs	***Shelby***
Grundy	***Sitka***
Guilford	***Windsor*** (ex-*Excelsior*, Dec. 28, 1942)
Hamblen	

Mostly county names. Displacement: 7,550 tons. Dimensions: 473 (*o.a.*) × 66 × 20 feet (*max.*). Machinery: Geared turbines. S.H.P. 8,000 = 16.5 kts. (APA 55, 56, 91, 97, 98, 105, 110–116).

pine (ex-*Sea Arrow*)	***Fayette*** (ex-*Sea Hawk*)
Barnstaple (ex-*Sea Snapper*)	***Fremont*** (ex-*Sea Corsair*, March 31, 1943)
Bayfield (ex-*Sea Bass*)	***Gladwin***
Bolivar (ex-*Sea Angel*, 1942)	***Goodhue*** (ex-*Sea Wren*)
Burleigh (Dec. 3, 1943)	***Goshen*** (ex-*Sea Hare*)
Callaway (ex-*Sea Mink*)	***Grafton*** (ex-*Sea Sparrow*)
Cambria (ex-*Sea Swallow*)	***Henrico*** (ex-*Sea Darter*)
Cavalier	***Knox*** (July 17, 1943)
Cecil (ex-*Sea Angler*)	***Lamar***
Chilton (ex-*Sea Needle*, Dec. 24 1942)	***Leon*** (ex-*Sea Dolphin*)
Clay (ex-*Sea Carp* Jan. 23, 1943)	***Mendocino***
Custer (ex-*Sea Eagle*, Nov. 6, 1942)	***Montour*** (Dec. 9, 1944)
Dade (ex-*Lorain*)	***Queen's*** (Sept. 12, 1944)
Du Page (ex-*Sea Hound*, Dec. 19, 1942)	***Riverside*** (April 13, 1944)
Elmore (ex-*Sea Panther*, Jan. 29, 1943)	***Westmoreland***

All county names. Displacement: 7,650 tons. Dimensions: 492 (*o.a.*) × 69½ × 28½ feet (*max.*) Machinery: Geared turbines. S.H.P. 8,500 = 16.5 kts. (APA 33–48, 92, 93, 95, 96, 99–104, 106–109).

CALVERT (ex-*Delorleans*, May 29, 1943), **CHARLES CARROLL** (ex-*Deluruguay*, 1941), **CRESCENT CITY** (ex-*Delorleans*, 1940), **MONROVIA** (ex-*Delargentino*, 1942). About 8,000 tons *gross*. Dimensions: 468 (*pp.*), 491 (*o.a.*) × 65½ × 25½ feet (*max.*) Machinery: Geared turbines. S.H.P. 7,800 = 16 kts. (APA 21, 28, 31, 32).

FREDERICK FUNSTON (Sept. 27, 1941), **JAMES O'HARA** (1942). Displacement: 7,500 tons. Dimensions: 492 (*o.a.*) × 69½ × 27¼ feet (*max.*). Machinery: Geared turbines. S.H.P. 8,500 = 16.5 kts. (APA 89, 90).

DOYEN (July 9, 1942), **FELAND** (Nov. 10, 1942). Built by Consolidated Steel Co., Los Angeles. 6,510 tons *gross*. Dimensions: 389 × 56 × 19 feet. Machinery: Geared turbines. S.H.P. 8,000 = 18 kts. (APA 1, 11.)

1944, *U.S. Navy Official.*

ARTHUR MIDDLETON (ex-*African Comet*, ex-*American Banker*, 1941), **GEORGE CLYMER** (ex-*African Planet*, ex-*American Farmer*, 1941), **PRESIDENT ADAMS** (1941), **PRESIDENT HAYES** (1940), **PRESIDENT JACKSON** (1940), **SAMUEL CHASE** (ex-*African Meteor*, ex-*American Shipper*, 1941), **THOMAS JEFFERSON** (ex-*President Garfield*, 1941). 9,255 tons *gross*. Dimensions: 465 × 69¾ × 29½ feet. Machinery: Geared turbines. S.H.P.: 8,500 = 16·5 kts. (APA 25, 27, 19, 20, 18, 26, 30.)

1944, *U.S. Navy Official.*

HARRY LEE (ex-*Exochorda*, 1931). 9,359 tons *gross*. Dimensions: 453 × 61¾ × 28½ feet. Machinery: Geared turbines. S.H.P.: 7,200 = 16 kts. Capacity: 1,800. (APA 10.)

BARNETT. 1940, *courtesy Grace Lines.*

BARNETT (ex-*Santa Maria*), (1928). 7,712 tons *gross*. Dimensions: 466 × 64 × 25¼ feet. Guns: 1—5 inch, 3—3 inch, some smaller. Machinery: Sulzer Diesel. 2 shafts. B.H.P.: 8,000 = 16 kts. Complement: 197. Capacity: 1,800. (APA 5.)

HUNTER LIGGETT. 1944, *U.S. Navy Official.*

AMERICAN LEGION (1920), **HARRIS** (ex-*President Grant*, ex-*Pine Tree State*, 1921), **HUNTER LIGGETT** (ex-*Pan America*, ex-*Palmetto State*, 1922), **J. FRANKLIN BELL** (ex-*President McKinley*, ex-*American Mail*, 1921), **JOSEPH T. DICKMAN** (ex-*President Roosevelt*, ex-*Peninsula State*, 1922), **LEONARD WOOD** (ex-*Western World*, ex-*Nutmeg State*, 1921), **ZEILIN** (ex-*President Jackson*, ex-*Silver State*, 1921). Displacement: 10,000 tons. Dimensions: 517 × 72¼ × 30½ feet. Machinery: 4 sets geared turbines. 2 shafts. S.H.P.: 12,000 = 18 kts. 8 watertube boilers. Oil fuel: 3,315 tons. Capacity: 2,500. (APA 17, 2, 15, 14, 16, 13, 12, 3.)

HEYWOOD. 1942, *U.S. Navy Official.*

(HEYWOOD Class—4 Ships)

FULLER (ex-*City of Newport News*, ex-*Archer*, 1919), **HEYWOOD** (ex-*City of Baltimore*, ex-*Steadfast*, 1919), **NEVILLE** (ex-*City of Norfolk*, ex-*Independence*, 1918), **WILLIAM P. BIDDLE** (ex-*City of San Francisco*, ex-*City of Hamburg*, ex-*Eclipse*, 1919). 8,378 tons *gross*. Dimensions: 487 (*w.l.*), 495½ (*o.a.*) × 56 × 25¼ feet. Guns: 1—5 inch, 3—3 inch, some smaller. Machinery: Geared turbines. 1 shaft. S.H.P.: 9,500 = 16 kts. Oil fuel: 1,905 tons. Capacity: 1,700. (APA 7, 6, 9, 8.)

Amphibious Force Flagships.

MOUNT MCKINLEY. 1945, *U.S. Navy Official.*

OSAGE. 1944, *U.S. Navy Official.*

Adirondack	***Mount Olympus*** (ex-*Eclipse*)
Appalachian (Jan. 29, 1943)	***Panamint***
Auburn (ex-*Kathay*)	***Pocono***
Blue Ridge (March 7, 1943)	***Rocky Mount*** (March 7, 1943)
Catoctin (ex-*Mary Whitridge*)	***Taconic***
Eldorado (ex-*Monsoon*)	***Teton***
Estes (ex-*Morning Star*)	***Wasatch*** (ex-*Fleetwing*)
Mount McKinley (ex-*Cyclone*)	

Displacement: 6,500 tons. Dimensions: 459¼ (*o.a.*) × 63 × 25¾ feet (*max.*) Machinery: Geared turbines. S.H.P. 6,000 = 15.5 kts. (AGC 1–3, 5, 7–17).

ANCON. 1944, *U.S. Navy Official.*

ANCON (1939). 10,021 tons *gross*. Dimensions: 474½ (*pp.*), 493 (*o.a.*) × 64 × 26½ feet. Machinery: Geared turbines. 2 shafts. Guns: 2—5 inch, etc. S.H.P. 9,000 = 18 kts. (AGC 4).

BISCAYNE (July, 1941). Ex-Seaplane Tender, built at Puget Sound Navy Yard. Displacement: 1,695 tons. Dimensions: 310¾ (*o.a.*) × 41 × 12 feet. Guns: 2—5 inch, etc. Machinery: 2 sets Diesels with electric drive. 2 shafts. B.H.P. 6,000 = 20 kts. (AGC 18).

General Note.—Originally rated as Combined Operations Communications H.Q. Ships, these vessels are fitted as flagships for Chiefs of Combined Forces, with accommodation for Marine or Army units attached. Radar and radio equipment is exceptionally elaborate.

Landing Ships.

Note.—Attack Cargo Ships and Attack Transports, recorded on earlier pages, are in fact other species of Landing Ships.

OZARK. 1944, *U.S. Navy Official.*

CATSKILL (May, 1942), **OZARK** (June 15, 1942). Both built by Willamette Iron & Steel Corpn., Portland, Oregon, under 1940 Programme. Designed as large Minelayers, but have been converted into Landing Ships (Vehicle). Displacement: 5,875 tons. Dimensions: 453⅔ × 60¼ feet. Guns: 4—5 inch, 38 cal., etc. Machinery: Geared turbines. 2 shafts. S.H.P.: 11,000 = 18·5 kts. (LSV 1, 2)

MONITOR, MONTAUK, OSAGE, SAUGUS, built by Ingall's S.B. Corpn., Pascagoula, Miss. Designed as Netlayers, but converted into Landing Ships (Vehicle). Displacement: 5,625 tons. Dimensions: $451\frac{1}{3} \times 60\frac{1}{4}$ feet. Guns: 4—5 inch, 38 cal., etc. Machinery: Geared turbines. 2 shafts. S.H.P.: 11,000 = 18·5 kts. (LSV 3–6)

BELLE GROVE. 1944, *U.S. Navy Official.*

Ashland
Belle Grove
Carter Hall (March 4, 1943)
Epping Forest (April 2, 1943)
Gunston Hall
Lindenwald
Oak Hill (June 25, 1943)
White Marsh

All built by Moore Dry Dock Co. Displacement: 4,500 tons. Dimensions: $457\frac{3}{4}$ (*o.a.*) × 72 × — feet. Machinery: Skinner Unaflow reciprocating. 2 shafts. I.H.P. 7,000 = 15 kts. (LSD 1–8).

Cabildo
Casa Grande
Catamount
Colonial
Comstock
Donner
Fort Mandan
Fort Marian
Fort Snelling
Point Defiance
Rushmore
San Marcos (Jan. 10, 1945)
Shadwell
Tortuga (Jan. 29, 1945)
Whetstone

All built by Navy Yards. Of same type as *Ashland* class, above, but propelled by geared turbines. S.H.P. 7,000 = 15 kts. (LSD 13–27).

Note.—These Landing Ships (Dock) serve as parent ships to landing craft and to coastal craft.

Fast Transports.

BEVERLY W. REID. 1945, "*Ships and Aircraft*"

Amesbury (June 5, 1943)
Arthur L. Bristol
Balduck
Barber (1943)
Barr (Dec. 28, 1943)
Bassett
Begor
Belet (March 3, 1944)
Beverly W. Reid
Blessman (June 19, 1943)
Borum
Bowers (Oct. 31, 1943)
Bray (April 15, 1944)
Brock (Jan. 1944)
Bull (March 27, 1943)
Bunch (Oct. 1943)
Burdo
Burke (April 3, 1943)
Carpellotti
Cavallaro (July, 1944)
Charles Lawrence
Chase
Cofer (Jan. 1944)
Cook (Aug. 26, 1944)
Cread (Feb. 12, 1944)
Crosley (Feb. 12, 1944)
Daniel T. Griffin (Feb. 22, 1943)
[illegible]
Donald W. Wolf
Don O. Woods
Durik
Earhart
Earle B. Hall
England (Sept. 26, 1943)
Enright (May 29, 1943)
Frament
Francovich (June 5, 1945)
Gantner (April 17, 1943)
George W. Ingram
Gosselin
Haines (June, 1943)
Harry L. Corl
Hayter
Hollis
Hopping (March 9, 1943)
Horace A. Bass
Hunter Marshall
Ira Jeffery (May 15, 1943)
Jack C. Robinson
Jenks (Sept. 11, 1943)
John P. Gray
John Q. Roberts
Joseph C. Hubbard
Joseph E. Campbell
Joseph M. Auman
Julius A. Raven (March 3, 1944)
Kephart
Kinzer
Kirwin (June 15, 1944)
Kleinsmith
Kline (June, 1944)
Knudson
Laning
Lee Fox (May 29, 1943)
Liddle
Lloyd
Loy
Maloy (Aug. 18, 1943)
Myers (Feb. 15, 1944)
Newman (Aug. 9, 1943)
Odum
Pavlic
Ray K. Edwards
Raymond W. Herndon (July 15, 1944)
Rednour (Feb. 12, 1944)
Reeves (April 22, 1943)
Register (January, 1944)
Ringness
Rogers Blood
Ruchamkin (June 15, 1944)
Runels (Sept. 7, 1943)
Schmitt (May 29, 1943)
Scott (April 3, 1943)
Scribner
Tatum
Tollberg (Feb. 1944)
Truxton
Upham
Walsh (April 28, 1945)
Walter S. Gorka
Walter X. Young
Wantuck
Weber (May 1, 1943)
Weiss
William J. Pattison (April 18, 1944)
William M. Hobby
Witter (Oct. 17, 1943)
Yokes

Ex-destroyer escorts. Displacement: 1,315 tons. Dimensions: 306 (*o.a.*) × 36 × — feet. Guns: Sundry 40 mm. and 20 mm. AA. Machinery: Turbo-electric. S.H.P. 12,000 = 28 kts. (APD 37–46, 48–136). War loss: *Bates.*

MANLEY. 1940, *O. A. Tunnell, courtesy "Our Navy."*

BELKNAP, BROOKS, CLEMSON, DALLAS, GEORGE E. BADGER, GILMER, GOLDSBOROUGH, GREENE, HULBERT, HUMPHREYS, KANE, McFARLAND, OSMOND INGRAM, OVERTON, SANDS, WILLIAMSON (1918–19). Displacement: 1,190 tons. Dimensions: 311 (*w.l.*) × $30\frac{2}{3}$ × $9\frac{1}{4}$ feet (*mean*). (APD 34, 10, 31, 16, 33, 11, 32, 36, 28, 12, 18, 26, 35, 23, 13.)

BERNADOU (1918), **DENT** (1918), **HERBERT** (1919), **TALBOT** (1918), **TATTNALL** (1918), **WATERS** (1918). Displacement: 1,090 tons. Dimensions: 309 (*w.l.*) × $30\frac{1}{2}$ × $8\frac{2}{3}$ feet (*mean*). (APD 5, 6, 9, 22, 20, 7, 19, 8.)

CROSBY, KILTY, SCHLEY (all 1918). Displacement: 1,060 tons. Dimensions: 309 (*w.l.*) × $30\frac{1}{2}$ × $8\frac{1}{2}$ feet (*mean*). (APD 17, 15, 14, 6.)

MANLEY (1917). Displacement: 1,020 tons. Dimensions: 308 (*w.l.*) × $30\frac{2}{3}$ × $7\frac{1}{2}$ feet (*mean*). (APD 1.)

Ex-destroyers, refitted in 1940–44. Guns: 2—4 inch, 50 cal., some smaller. Machinery: Geared turbines (either Parsons, Westinghouse or Curtis). 2 shafts. S.H.P.: 13,500 = 25 kts. Boilers: 2 White-Forster (except *Manley*, 2 Normand). Each can carry landing craft and $\frac{1}{3}$ battalion of Marines. War losses: *Colhoun, Dickerson, Gregory, Little, McKean, Noa, Ward.* Badly damaged and not worth repairing: *Rathburne, Roper, Stringham.*

Landing Craft.

L S T 332. 1943, *U.S. Navy Official.*

LST (Landing Ship, Tank). Originally this category comprised LST 1/510, 1,490 tons; and LST 511/1152, 1,653 tons, but many have been transformed into fleet-auxiliaries. When equipped with a portable landing strip, the LST can carry 8 reconnaissance aircraft. Dimensions: $327\frac{3}{4}$ × 50 feet. Machinery: Diesel. 2 shafts. B.H.P.: 1,800 = over 10 kts. Complement: 64. Following launchings have been reported: LST 943 (Sept. 9, 1944), LST 970 (Dec. 16, 1944), LST 978 (Jan. 20, 1945), all from Bethlehem-Hingham Shipyard; LST 968 (Dec. 9, 1944), from Norfolk Navy Yard.

LSM 201. 1944, *U.S. Navy Official.*

LSM (Landing Ship, Medium). Comprised LSM 1–558. Displacement: 490 tons. Dimensions: $203\frac{1}{2}$ × 34 feet. Machinery: Diesel. 2 shafts. Following launchings have been reported: LSM 212 (June 10, 1944), LSM 223 (Aug. 15, 1944), LSM 224 (Aug. 22, 1944), LSM 232 (Oct. 14, 1944), LSM 419 (Nov. 18, 1944), LSM 421 (Nov. 30, 1944), LSM 431 (Feb. 2, 1945), LSM 437 (March 10, 1945), LSM 440 (March 24, 1945), LSM 445 (April 24, 1945), LSM 446 (April 28, 1945), all by Dravo Corporation; LSM 190, 191 (both Nov. 21, 1944), LSM 296, 297 (both Dec. 18, 1944), LSM 389, 390 (both Dec. 12, 1944), LSM 391, 392 (both Jan. 1, 1945), LSM 395, 396 (both Jan. 2, 1945), all by Charleston Navy Yard; LSM 283 (Nov 15, 1944), LSM 293 (Feb. 2, 1945), both by Federal S.B. & D.D. Co.

1944, *U.S. Navy Official.*

LCI (Landing Craft, Infantry). Comprised LCI 1/350, 216 tons; LCI 351/1109, 246 tons. Dimensions: 157 × $23\frac{1}{3}$ feet. Machinery: Diesel. 2 shafts. B.H.P.: 1,600 = 15 kts. Complement: 25. LCI (a) fires rockets.

LCS (Landing Craft, Support). Comprised LCS 1/130. 227 tons. Dimensions: 157 × $23\frac{1}{3}$ feet. This type is armed with rocket guns and carries smoke-screen apparatus, and resembles LCI in appearance. Machinery: Diesel. 2 shafts. B.H.P.: 1,600 = 15 kts.

1944, *U.S. Navy Official.*

LCT (Landing Craft, Tank). Comprised LCT (5) 1/500, 126 tons. Dimensions: $112\frac{1}{3}$ × 32 feet; LCT (6) 501/1405, 132 tons. Dimensions: $120\frac{1}{3}$ × 32 feet. Machinery: Diesel. 3 shafts. B.H.P.: 675 = over 10 kts.

1944, *U.S. Navy Official.*

LCM (Landing Craft, Mechanised). Comprised LCM (3), 20 tons. Dimensions: 50 × 14 feet. LCM (6), 22 tons. Dimensions: 56 × 14 feet. Machinery: Diesel. 2 shafts. B.H.P.: 450 = 12 kts.

LCP (Landing Craft, Personnel). Comprised LCP (L) and LCP (R). Both 7 tons. Dimensions: 36 × $10\frac{3}{4}$ feet. Machinery: Diesel. B.H.P.: 225 = over 10 kts.

1944, *U.S. Navy Official.*

LCVP (Landing Craft, Vehicle, Personnel), 8 tons. Dimensions: $36\frac{1}{3}$ × 11 feet. Machinery: Diesel. B.H.P.: 225 = over 10 kts.

LVT (Landing Vehicle, Tracked). Length: 26 feet. Another amphibious type is the DUKW, length 30 feet.

At the outbreak of the Korean War a large number of the preceding classes had been scrapped or returned to mercantile duties although such types as the AKAs, APAs, LSDs and LSTs remained to give valuable service. The succeeding lists trace the development of the amphibious forces from 1953.

4 AMPHIBIOUS COMMAND SHIPS (LCC): "MOUNT McKINLEY" CLASS

Name	No	Builder	Launched	Commissioned
MOUNT McKINLEY	LCC 7	North Carolina SB Co	27 Sep 1943	1 May 1944
ESTES	LCC 12	North Carolina SB Co	1 Nov 1943	9 Oct 1944
POCONO	LCC 16	North Carolina SB Co	25 Jan 1945	29 Dec 1945
TACONIC	LCC 17	North Carolina SB Co	10 Feb 1945	17 Jan 1946

Displacement, tons	7 510 light ; 12 560 full load
Length, feet (metres)	435 (132 2) wl ; 495 3 (150 5) oa
Beam, feet (metres)	63 (19 2)
Draft, feet (metres)	28 2 (8 5)
Draft, feet (metres)	28 2 (8 5)
Guns	1—5 inch (127 mm) 38 cal DP 4—40 mm AA (twin)
Helicopters	Utility helicopter carried
Main engines	1 turbine (General Electric) 6 000 shp ; 1 shaft
Boilers	2 (Babcock & Wilcox in AGC 7 ; Combustion Engineering in others)
Speed, knots	16 4
Complement (ship)	517 (36 officers, 486 enlisted men)

Acquired by the Navy in 1943-1944 while under construction to Maritime Commission C2-S-AJ1 design. After 5 inch gun and two twin 40 mm mounts replaced by helicopter platform. The *Pocono* and *Taconic* have a single mast aft in lieu of after king post in earlier ships. All survivors transferred to Maritime Administration reserve (remain on Navy List).

CLASSIFICATION. Originally referred to as Auxiliary Combined Operations and Communications Headquarters Ships, but designated Amphibious Force Flagships (AGC) ; five surviving ships redesignated Amphibious Command Ships (LCC) on 1 Jan 1969.

ELECTRONICS. The *Mount McKinley* and *Estes* had an SPS-37 search radar antenna on the forward king post, SPS-30 and SPS-10 antennas on the lattice mast atop the superstructure, and a TACAN antenna installed on the after king post ; the *Pocono* and *Taconic* had a TACAN antenna on the forward king post, SPS-30 and SPS-10 antennas on the lattice mast atop the superstructure, and an SPS-37 antenna on the after pole mast.

DISPOSALS
Fourteen World War II amphibious force flagships have been stricken from the Navy List: **Appalachian** (AGC 1) on 1 Mar 1959 ; **Blue Ridge** (AGC 2), **Rocky Mount** (AGC 3) on 1 Jan 1960 ; **Ancon** (AGC 4) on 25 Feb 1946 ; **Catoctin** (AGC 5) on 1 Mar 1959 ; **Mount Olympus** (AGC 8) in 1961 ; **Wasatch** (AGC 9) on 1 Jan 1960 ; **Auburn** (AGC 10), **Panamint** (AGC 13) in late 1960 ; **Teton** (AGC 14), **Adirondack** (AGC 15)

ESTES (LCC 12)

1969, United States Navy

in 1961 ; **Biscayne** (AGC 18, ex-AVP 11) transferred to US Coast Guard on 19 July 1946. **Eldorado** (AGC/LCC 11) stricken on 16 Nov 1972.
The **Duane** (AGC 6) was retained by the Coast Guard. All except the **Ancon, Duane,** and **Biscayne** were converted C2 merchants hull. Several other Coast Guard cutters served as amphibious command ships with WAGC designations (see "Campbell" class)
The yacht **Williamsburg** (ex-*Aras*, ex-PG 56) was designated AGC 369 in 1945, served as presidential yacht until stricken in 1962 (converted to oceanographic research ship, renamed *Anton Bruun*).

POCONO (AGC 16)

United States Navy

MOUNT McKINLEY (helicopter aft)

Added 1964, Giorgio Arra

MOUNT McKINLEY

1957, U.S. Navy, Official

2 AMPHIBIOUS COMMAND SHIPS (LCC): "BLUE RIDGE" CLASS

Name	No	Builder	Laid down	Launched	Commissioned
* BLUE RIDGE	LCC 19	Philadelphia Naval Shipyard	27 Feb 1967	4 Jan 1969	14 Nov 1970
* MOUNT WHITNEY	LCC 20	Newport News SB & DD Co	8 Jan 1969	8 Jan 1970	16 Jan 1971

Displacement, tons	19 290 full load
Length, feet (metres)	620 (188·5) oa
Beam, feet (metres)	82 (25·3)
Main deck width, feet (metres)	108 (33)
Draft, feet (metres)	27 (8·2)
Guns	4—3 in (76 mm) 50 cal AA (twin)
Helicopters	Utility helicopter carried
Main engines	1 geared turbine (General Electric); 22 000 shp; 1 shaft
Boilers	2 (Foster Wheeler)
Speed, knots	20
Complement	732 (52 officers, 680 enlisted men)
Flag accommodation	688 (217 officers, 471 enlisted men)

These are the first amphibious force flagships of post-World War II design. They can provide integrated command and control facilities for sea, air and land commanders in amphibious operations. The *Blue Ridge* was authorised in the Fiscal Year 1965 new construction programme, the AGC 20 in FY 1966. An AGC 21 was planned for the FY 1970 programme but cancelled late in 1968. It was proposed that the last ship combine fleet as well as amphibious force command-control facilities.

CLASSIFICATION. Originally designated Amphibious Force Flagships (AGC); redesignated Amphibious Command Ships (LCC) on 1 Jan 1969.

DESIGN. General hull design and machinery arrangement are similar to the "Iwo Jima" class assault ships.

ELECTRONICS. Fitted with SPS-48 three-dimensional search radar, SPS-40 and SPS-10 search radar, 3 are on "island" structure. After "tower" does not have large antenna sphere originally intended for these ships. (See model photo in 1970-1971 edition.) Tactical Aircraft

BLUE RIDGE (LCC 19)

1971, United States Navy

Navigation (TACAN) pod tops mast.
Both ships fitted with Naval Tactical Data System (NTDS). Antennas adjacent to helicopter landing area swing out for flight operations.

GUNNERY. At one stage of design two additional twin 3 inch mounts were provided on forecastle; subsequently deleted from final designs. Antennas and their supports severely restrict firing arcs of guns.

MOUNT WHITNEY (LCC 20)

1970, Newport News Shipbuilding & Dry Dock Co

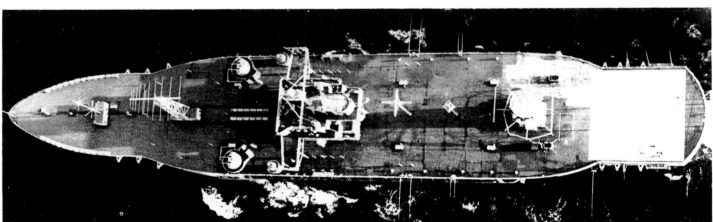

MOUNT WHITNEY (LCC 20)—

1970, United States Navy

150 "LST I—1152" Classes.

LST 511-1152 SERIES

Displacement :	1.653 tons *standard* (4.080 tons *full load*)
Dimensions :	316 (w.l.), 328 (o.a.) × 50 × 14 (*max.*) feet
Guns ;	7—40 mm. AA., 2—20 mm. AA.
Machinery :	Diesel. 2 shafts. B.H.P. : 1.700 = 11 kts.
Cargo capacity :	2,100 tons
Complement :	211

Notes.—LST 526 was the only U.S. ship of her type to serve as an aircraft carrier in the Second World War. Fitted with a plywood flight deck she carried 10 Piper Cubs and their Army Pilots, and operated off the west coast of France in 1945. (Some British LSTs flew off artillery observation aircraft from their upper decks). One Landing Ship Tank (casualty evacuation) remained in the list. the LSTH 731, now reclassified as LST 731 and in the Atlantic Reserve Fleet.

LST 1-510 SERIES

Displacement :	1,625 tons (4,050 tons *full load*)
Dimensions :	328 (o.a.) × 50 × 14¼ (*max.*) feet
Machinery :	Diesel. 2 shafts. B.H.P. : 1,700 = 10 8 kts.

Notes.—Are ocean tank carriers with low doors. In the Second World War LST 32 was fitted with railway lines on the tank deck to enable her to transport trucks from Sicily to the mainland. Seven LSTs were modified as LSTH for casualty evacuation and treatment of wounded, all since stricken from the list of naval vessels. About 90 LST are active (all classes). 38 LSTs are assigned to MSTS and designated USNS.

SNOHOMISH COUNTY (LST 1126)   *1964, United States Navy*

LST 1144.   *1951 Photo.*

SUMNER COUNTY (LST 1148)   *1968, United States Navy*

2 Steam Type

LST 1153 TALBOT COUNTY
LST 1154 TALLAHATCHIE COUNTY

Displacement:	2.324 tons (6,000 tons *full load*)
Dimensions:	368 (w.l.), 382 (o.a.) × 54 × 14½ (17 *max.* feet)
Guns:	2—5 inch, 38 cal., 4—40 mm. AA.
Machinery:	Geared turbines. 2 shafts. S.H.P.: 6,000 = 14 kts.
Complement:	82

Notes
Built by Boston Navy Yard 1153 launched 24 Apr. 1947, completed 3 Sep 1947: 1154 launched 19 July 1946, completed 9 June 1949. They are the only steam powered LSTs. This type can carry 4 small landing craft, and has increased troop accommodation, greater tank, vehicle and cargo capacity and improved arrangements for discharge, compared with " LST 1-1152 " class.

TALBOT COUNTY

INSHORE FIRE SUPPORT SHIP

Amphibious Cruiser Type

IFS
I CARRONADE

Builders:	Puget Sound Bridge and Dredging Co.
Laid down:	19 Nov. 1952
Launched:	26 May 1953
Completed:	25 May 1955

Displacement:	1,040 tons *light* (1,500 tons *full load*)
Dimensions:	245 × 39 × 10 feet
Guns:	1—5 inch; 8 rocket throwers
Machinery:	Fairbanks-Morse diesels: 2 shafts, geared drive, twin screws with variable pitch. B.H.P.: 3,100 = 15 kts.
Complement:	162

Notes
A new type of naval vessel popularly known as the " bob-tailed cruiser ", into which the latest improvements in shipboard habitability have been built. Designed to support troops in amphibious landings. Built by Puget Sound Bridge & Dredging Co. Main armament comprises rapid fire rocket launchers. Keel laid on 19 Nov. 1952. Launched on 26 May 1953. Commissioned on 25 May 1955.

CARRONADE   *1956 U.S. Navy, Official*

15 Tank Landing Ships (LST): "Terrebonne Parish" Class

TERREBONNE PARISH	LST 1156	WALDO COUNTY	LST 1163
TERRELL COUNTY	LST 1157	WALWORTH COUNTY	LST 1164
TIOGA COUNTY	LST 1158	WASHOE COUNTY	LST 1165
TOM GREEN COUNTY	LST 1159	WASHTENAW COUNTY	LST 1166
TRAVERSE COUNTY	LST 1160	WESTCHESTER COUNTY	LST 1167
VERNON COUNTY	LST 1161	WEXFORD COUNTY	LST 1168
WAHKIAKUM COUNTY	LST 1162	WHITFIELD COUNTY	LST 1169
		WINDHAM COUNTY	LST 1170

Displacement, tons	2 590 light; 5 800 full load
Dimensions, feet	384 oa × 55 × 17
Guns	6—3 in. 50 cal (3 twin)
Main engines	4 GM diesels; 2 shafts; controllable pitch propellers; 6 000 bhp = 15 knots
Complement	116
Troops	395

Design is modification of that of two experimental ships constructed after the Second World War. LST 1156 was launched on 9 Aug 1952, 1158 on 11 Apr 1953, 1163 on 17 Mar 1953, 1156-1160 were built by Bath Iron Works, 1166-1170 by Christy Corporation, and 1161-1165 by Ingalls Shipbuilding Corporation.

VERNON COUNTY (LST 1161)   *1965, United States Navy*

TOM GREEN COUNTY (LST 1159)   *United States Navy*

TERRELL COUNTY (LST 1157)   *1969, United States Navy*

WOOD COUNTY (LST 1178)   *1971, J. S. Kinross*

7 Tank Landing Ships (LST): "Suffolk County" Class

Name	LST	Builder	Launched
DE SOTO COUNTY	1171	Avondale, New Orleans	28 Feb 1957
SUFFOLK COUNTY	1173	Boston Navy Yard	5 Sep 1956
GRONT CAUNTY	1174	Avondale, New Orleans	12 Oct 1956
YORK COUNTY	1175	Newport News SB & DD Co	5 Mar 1957
GRAHAM COUNTY	1176	Newport News SB & DD Co	19 Sep 1957
LORAIN COUNTY	1177	American SB Co. Lorrain	22 June 1957
WOOD COUNTY	1178	American SB Co. Lorrain	14 Dec 1957

Displacement, tons	4 164 light; 8 000 full load
Dimensions, feet	445 oa × 62 × 16·5
Guns	6—3 in. 50 cal (3 twin)
Main engines	6 Nordberg diesels (4 larger in *Graham County*); 2 shafts; controllable pitch propellers; 13 700 bhp = 17 knots
Complement	184 (10 officers, 174 men)
Troops	600

DE SOTO COUNTY (LST 1171)   *United States Navy*

Greater speed, size and troop capacity than previous LSTs. Air conditioned. Contract for LST 1172 not awarded. *Suffolk County* commissioned on 15 Aug 1957. *De Soto County* on 10 June 1958. *Graham County* on 14 Apr 1958. *Lorain County* on 30 Aug 1958. *Wood County* on 5 Aug 1959. *Grant County* on 8 Nov 1957.

ENGINEERING. Controllable-pitch propellers provide high degree of maneuvrability

20 "NEWPORT" CLASS: TANK LANDING SHIPS (LST)

Name	No.	Laid down	Launched	Commissioned	F S
NEWPORT	LST 1179	1 Nov 1966	3 Feb 1968	7 June 1969	AA
MANITOWOC	LST 1180	1 Feb 1967	4 June 1969	24 Jan 1970	AA
SUMTER	LST 1181	14 Nov 1967	13 Dec 1969	20 June 1970	AA
FRESNO	LST 1182	16 Dec 1967	28 Sep 1968	22 Nov 1969	PA
PEORIA	LST 1183	22 Feb 1968	23 Nov 1968	21 Feb 1970	PA
FREDERICK	LST 1184	13 Apr 1968	8 Mar 1969	11 Apr 1970	PA
SCHENECTADY	LST 1185	2 Aug 1968	24 May 1969	13 June 1970	PA
CAYUGA	LST 1186	28 Sep 1968	12 July 1969	8 Aug 1970	PA
TUSCALOOSA	LST 1187	23 Nov 1968	6 Sep 1969	24 Oct 1970	PA
SAGINAW	LST 1188	24 May 1969	7 Feb 1970	23 Jan 1971	AA
SAN BERNARDINO	LST 1189	12 July 1969	28 Mar 1970	27 Mar 1971	PA
BOULDER	LST 1190	6 Sep 1969	22 May 1970	4 June 1971	AA
RACINE	LST 1191	13 Dec 1969	15 Aug 1970	9 July 1971	PA
SPARTANBURG COUNTY	LST 1192	7 Feb 1970	11 Nov 1970	1 Sep 1971	AA
FAIRFAX COUNTY	LST 1193	28 Mar 1970	19 Dec 1970	16 Oct 1971	AA
LA MOURE COUNTY	LST 1194	22 May 1970	13 Feb 1971	18 Dec 1971	AA
BARBOUR COUNTY	LST 1195	15 Aug 1970	15 May 1971	12 Feb 1972	PA
HARLAN COUNTY	LST 1196	7 Nov 1970	24 July 1971	8 Apr 1972	AA
BARNSTABLE COUNTY	LST 1197	19 Dec 1970	2 Oct 1971	27 May 1972	AA
BRISTOL COUNTY	LST 1198	13 Feb 1971	4 Dec 1971	5 Aug 1972	PA

Displacement, tons: 8 450 full load
Dimensions, feet (metres): 522.3 (hull) · 69.5 · 17.5 (aft) *(159.2 · 21.2 · 5.9)*
Guns: 4—3 in *(76 mm)*/50 (twin Mk 33)
Main engines: 6 diesels (General Motors in 1179-1181, Alco in others);
  16 000 bhp, 2 shafts, (cp propellers) · 20 knots
Range, miles: 2 500 + (cruising)
Complement: 196 (12 officers, 174 enlisted men)
Troops: 431 (20 officers, 411 enlisted men)

These ships are of an entirely new design, larger and faster than previous tank landing ships. They operate with 20 knot amphibious squadrons to transport tanks, other heavy vehicles, engineer equipment, and supplies which cannot be readily landed by helicopters or landing craft. These are the only recent construction amphibious ships with a pole mast instead of tripod-lattice mast.
Newport was authorised in the FY 1965 new construction programme, LST 1180-1187 in FY 1966, and LST 1188-1198 in FY 1967. LST 1179-1181 built by Philadelphia Naval Shipyard, LST 1182-1198 built by National Steel & S.B. Co, San Diego, California. Seven additional ships of this type that were planned for the FY 1971 new construction programme were deferred.
Ships of this class will be transferred to the Naval Reserve Force from FY 1981 onwards.

Design: These ships are the first LSTs to depart from the bow door design developed by the British early in World War II. The hull form required to achieve 20 knots would not permit bow doors, thus these ships unload by a 112 ft ramp over their bow. The ramp is supported by twin derrick arms. A ramp just forward of the superstructure connects the lower tank deck with the main deck and a vehicle passage through the superstructure provides access to the parking area amidships. A stern gate to the tank deck permits unloading of amphibious tractors into the water, or unloading of other vehicles into an LCU or onto a pier. Vehicle stowage is rated at 500 tons and 19 000 sq ft (5 000 sq ft more than previous LSTs). Length over derrick arms is 562 ft; full load draught is 11.5 ft forward and 17.5 ft aft. Bow thruster fitted to hold position offshore while unloading amphibious tractors.

Electronics: Fitted with OE-82 satellite communications antenna and WSC-3 transceiver.

Gunnery: Two 20 mm Mk 15 CIWS to be fitted.

Rockets: One Mk 36 Chaffroc RBOC to be fitted.

NEWPORT (LST 1179)   1969, United States Navy

BOULDER   1976, Dr. Giorgio Arra

FRESNO   1/1979, USN

SUMTER   6/1979, Michael D. J. Lennon

RACINE (LST 1191)   1971, United States Navy, PH3 D. W. Read

WHITE MARSH.

1952, A. & J. Pavia.

ASHLAND (LSD 1)

A. & J. Pavia

LSD
1 ASHLAND (Dec. 21, 1942)
2 BELLE GROVE (Feb. 17, 1942)
3 CARTER HALL (March 4, 1943)
4 EPPING FOREST (April 2, 1943)

LSD
5 GUNSTON HALL (May 1, 1943)
6 LINDENWALD (June 11, 1943)
7 OAK HILL (June 25, 1943)
8 WHITE MARSH (July 19, 1943)

Displacement :	4,500 tons
Dimensions :	454 (w.l.), 457¾ (o.a.) × 72 × 18 feet
Guns :	1—5 inch, 4—40 mm. AA., 16,—20 mm. AA.
Machinery :	Skinner Unaflow reciprocating. 2 shafts. I.H.P. : 7,400 = 17 kts.
Boilers :	2, of 2-drum type

Notes.—All built by Moore Dry Dock Co. These Landing Ships (Dock) are designed to serve as parent ships to landing craft and to coastal craft. Gunston Hall and Lindenwald have been adapted for Arctic service. Conversion completed March 15 and 1, 1949, respectively. All can carry 18 flat nosed LCMs (Landing Craft Medium) or 3 LCUs in their well-decks running three-quarters of their length. In each LCM is a smaller LCVP (Landing Craft, Vehicle-Personnel).

4 New Construction.

LSD 28   LSD 29   LSD 30   LSD 31

Displacement :	6,500 tons standard
Dimensions :	510 (o.a.) × 84 × — feet

Notes.—Same general design as earlier types, but larger and faster. LSD 28 order 8 Nov. 1951, cancelled, but reordered with LSD 29, 30, 31 from Ingalls Shipbuilding Corporation, Pascagoula, Mississippi.

RUSHMORE.

1952, Harvey Gilston, Esq.

COMSTOCK (LSD 19)

1965, United States Navy

LSD
16 CABILDO (Dec. 28, 1944)
13 CASA GRANDE (ex-Spear, ex-Portway, April 11, 1944)
17 CATAMOUNT (Jan. 27, 1945)
18 COLONIAL (Feb. 28, 1945)
19 COMSTOCK (April 28, 1945)
20 DONNER (April 6, 1945)
21 FORT MANDAN (1945)

LSD
22 FORT MARION (May 22, 1945)
14 RUSHMORE (ex-Sword, ex-Swashway, May 10, 1944)
25 SAN MARCOS (Jan. 10, 1945)
15 SHADWELL (ex-Tomahawk, ex-Waterway, May 24, 1944
26 TORTUGA (Jan. 21, 1945)
27 WHETSTONE (1945)

Displacement:	4,032 tons (9,375 tons full load)
Dimensions :	457¾ (o.a.) × 72½ × 18 (max.) feet
Guns :	1—5 inch, 38 cal., 12—40 mm. AA.
Machinery :	Geared turbines. 2 shafts. S.H.P. : 7,000 = 15·4 kts.
Complement :	240

Notes.—Catamount, Colonial, Comstock and others built by Newport News, some built by Navy Yards. Of same type as "Ashland" class, below, but differently armed and propelled. Can carry 3 LSUs or 18 LCMs.

8 Dock Landing Ships (LSD): "Thomaston" Class

	LSD		LSD
THOMASTON (9 Feb 1954)	28	SPEIGEL GROVE (10 Nov 1955)	32
PLYMOUTH ROCK (7 May 1954)	29	ALAMO (20 Jan 1956)	33
FORT SNELLING (16 July 1954)	30	HERMITAGE (12 June 1956)	34
POINT DEFIANCE (28 Sep 1954)	31	MONTICELLO (10 Aug 1956)	35

Displacement, tons	6 880 light, 11 270 full load; Alamo, Hermitage, Monticello, Spiegel Grove: 12 150 full load
Dimensions, feet	510 oa × 84 × 19 max.
Guns	12—3 in. 50 cal (see gunnery)
Main engines	Steam turbines. 2 shafts; 23 000 shp = 24 knots
Boilers	2
Complement	305 plus 100 marines

Larger and faster than earlier types. Built by Ingalls Shipbuilding Corp. Fitted with helicopter landing platforms, and two 50 ton cranes. 21 LCM (6) or 3 LCU and 6 LCM, and 3 to 8 helicopters can be carried. Launch dates above.

GUNNERY. Two twin 3 inch, 50 cal mountings were removed in 1962.

SPIEGEL GROVE (LSD 32)

courtesy Dr Aldo Fraccaroli

MONTICELLO (LSD 35), LCU 1476

1967, United States Navy

5 "ANCHORAGE" CLASS: DOCK LANDING SHIPS (LSD)

Name	No.	Builders	Commissioned		F/S
ANCHORAGE	LSD 36	Ingalls Shipbuilding Corp	15 Mar	1969	PA
PORTLAND	LSD 37	General Dynamics, Quincy, Mass	3 Oct	1970	AA
PENSACOLA	LSD 38	General Dynamics, Quincy, Mass	27 Mar	1971	AA
MOUNT VERNON	LSD 39	General Dynamics, Quincy, Mass	13 May	1972	PA
FORT FISHER	LSD 40	General Dynamics, Quincy, Mass	9 Dec	1972	PA

Displacement, tons: 8 600 light; 13 600 full load
Dimensions, feet (metres): 553·3 × 84 × 20 *(168·6 × 25·6 × 6)*
Guns: 6—3 in *(76 mm)*/50 (twin Mk 33) (8 (twins) in LSD 38)
Main engines: Steam turbines (De Laval); 24 000 shp; 2 shafts = 20 knots sustained, 22 max
Boilers: 2 (Foster-Wheeler except Combustion Engineering in *Anchorage*)
Complement: 397 (21 officers, 376 enlisted men)
Troops: 376 (28 officers, 348 enlisted men)

ANCHORAGE   *7/1979, Dr. Giorgio Arra*

These ships are similar in appearance to earlier classes but with a tripod mast. Helicopter platform aft with docking well partially open; helicopter platform can be removed. Docking well approximately 430 × 50 ft *(131·1 × 15·2 m)* can accommodate three LCU-type landing craft. Space on deck for one LCM, and davits for one LCPL and one LCVP. Two 50 ton capacity cranes. LSD 36 was authorised in the FY 1965 shipbuilding programme; LSD 37-39 in the FY 1966 programme; LSD 40 in the FY 1967 programme.
Anchorage was laid down on 13 March 1967 and launched in 5 May 1968; *Portland* on 21 September 1967 and 20 December 1969; *Pensacola* on 12 March 1969 and 11 July 1970; *Mount Vernon* on 29 January 1970 and 17 April 1971; and *Fort Fisher* on 15 July 1970 and 22 April 1972.
Estimated minimum construction cost $11·5 million per ship.

Electronics: Fitted with OE-82 satellite communications antenna, SSR-1 receiver and WSC-3 transceiver.

Gunnery: Two 20 mm Mk 15 CIWS to be fitted.

Rockets: One Mk 36 Chaffroc (RBOC) to be fitted.

PENSACOLA (LSD 38)   *1971, General Dynamics Corp*

PORTLAND (LSD 37)   *1971, United States Navy, PH1 Robert L. Varney*

0 + 3 "LSD 41" CLASS DOCK LANDING SHIPS (LSD)

Displacement, tons: 10 976 light; 15 774 full load
Dimensions, feet (metres): 608 × 84 × 19·7 *(185·3 × 25·6 × 6)*
Guns: 2—20 mm Mk 15 CIWS
Main engines: Details not available; about 36 000 shp; 2 shafts = 23 knots
Complement: 423 (22 officers, 401 enlisted men)
Troops: 338 (25 officers, 313 enlisted men)

Originally six of this class were to be constructed as replacements for the "Thomaston" class. Upon examination of the design by Secretary of Defense Harold Brown, construction was cut back to two units as it was considered the technology used in the design was outmoded. The lead ship was originally to be requested in FY 1980 programme and the second unit under the FY 1983 programme. However, the "LSD 41" class was not included "in this year's program and will not until we assess the changes in future amphibious lift requirements . . . ."
But, under Congressional pressure, this class was reinstated on 8 January 1980. A request for one ship is included in FY 1981 budget, a second planned for FY 1983 and a third for FY 1985. A contract for long-lead items for first ship was awarded to Lockheed S.B. and C. Co. Seattle on 14 February 1980.

Design: Based on the previous "Anchorage" class which was designed over ten years ago. Well deck measures 440 ft × 50 ft. The ship will be able to handle the CH-53E helicopter and/or the AV-3A Harrier V/STOL aircraft as well as air cushion landing craft vehicles.

Electronics: Will be fitted with the SPS 55 and SPS 65V radars as well as the SLQ 32V electronic countermeasures systems.

Engineering: The type of propulsion plant to be used in the design is still open to question. Originally it was intended to fit diesel propulsion.

Rockets: To be fitted with Mk 36 Chaffroc (RBOC) system.

MOUNT VERNON   *1/1980, Dr. Giorgio Arra*

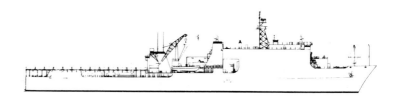

2 "RALEIGH" CLASS: AMPHIBIOUS TRANSPORT DOCKS (LPD)

Name	No.	Builders	Commissioned	F/S
RALEIGH	LPD 1	New York Naval Shipyard	8 Sep 1962	AA
VANCOUVER	LPD 2	New York Naval Shipyard	11 May 1963	PA

Displacement, tons: 8 040 light; 13 600 full load
Dimensions, feet (metres): 521·8 × 100 × 22 *(158·4 × 30·5 × 6·7)*
Aircraft: Up to 6 UH-34 or CH-46 helicopters (see *Aircraft* note)
Guns: 6—3 in *(76 mm)*/50 (twin Mk 33)
Main engines: 2 steam turbines (De Laval); 24 000 shp; 2 shafts
Boilers: 2 (Babcock & Wilcox)
Speed, knots: 21
Complement: 490 (30 officers, 460 enlisted men)
Troops: 1 139 (143 officers, 996 enlisted men)

The amphibious transport dock (LPD) was developed from the dock landing ship (LSD) concept but provides more versatility. The LPD replaces the amphibious transport (LPA) and, in part, the amphibious cargo ship (LKA) and dock landing ship. The LPD can carry a "balanced load" of assault troops and their equipment, has a docking well for landing craft, a helicopter deck, cargo holds and vehicle garages. *Raleigh* was authorised in the FY 1959 new construction programme, *Vancouver* in the FY 1960. *Raleigh* was laid down on 23 June 1960 and launched on 17 March 1962; *Vancouver* on 19 November 1960 and 15 September 1962. Approximate construction cost was $29 million per ship.
A third ship of this class, *La Salle* (LPD 3), was reclassified as a miscellaneous command ship (AGF 3) on 1 July 1972.

Aircraft: These ships are not normally assigned helicopters because they lack integral hangars and maintenance facilities. It is intended that a nearby amphibious assault ship (LHA or LPH) would provide helicopters during an amphibious operation. Telescopic hangars have been fitted.

Design: These ships resemble dock landing ships (LSD) but have fully enclosed docking well with the roof forming a permanent helicopter platform. The docking well is 168 ft long and 50 ft wide *(51·2 × 15·2)*, less than half the length of wells in newer LSDs; the LPD design provides more space for vehicles, cargo and troops. Ramps allow vehicles to be driven between helicopter deck, parking area and docking well, side ports provide roll-on/roll-off capability when docks are available. An overhead monorail in the docking well with six cranes facilitates loading landing craft. The docking well in these ships can hold one LCU and three LCM-6s or four LCM-8s or 20 LVTs (amphibious tractors). In addition, two LCM-6s or four LCPLs are carried on the boat deck which are lowered by crane.

Electronics: Fitted with OE-82 satellite communications antenna, SSR-1 receiver and WSC-3 transceiver.

Gunnery: Two 20 mm Mk 15 CIWS to be fitted.

Rockets: Mk 36 Chaffroc system to be fitted.

RALEIGH   *1/1976, USN*

VANCOUVER   *2/1979, Dr. Giorgio Arra*

VANCOUVER (LPD 2)   *1963. United States Navy*

RALEIGH (showing bridge layout)   *1964. United States Navy, Official*

RALEIGH (LPD 1)   *1969, United States Navy*

12 "AUSTIN" CLASS: AMPHIBIOUS TRANSPORT DOCKS (LPD)

Name	No.	Builders	Commissioned	F/S
AUSTIN	LPD 4	New York Naval Shipyard	6 Feb 1965	AA
OGDEN	LPD 5	New York Naval Shipyard	19 June 1965	PA
DULUTH	LPD 6	New York Naval Shipyard	18 Dec 1965	PA
CLEVELAND	LPD 7	Ingalls Shipbuilding Corp	21 Apr 1967	PA
DUBUQUE	LPD 8	Ingalls Shipbuilding Corp	1 Sep 1967	PA
DENVER	LPD 9	Lockheed S.B. & Construction Co	26 Oct 1968	PA
JUNEAU	LPD 10	Lockheed S.B. & Construction Co	12 July 1969	PA
CORONADO	LPD 11	Lockheed S.B. & Construction Co	23 May 1970	AA
SHREVEPORT	LPD 12	Lockheed S.B. & Construction Co	12 Dec 1970	AA
NASHVILLE	LPD 13	Lockheed S.B. & Construction Co	14 Feb 1970	AA
TRENTON	LPD 14	Lockheed S.B. & Construction Co	6 Mar 1971	AA
PONCE	LPD 15	Lockheed S.B. & Construction Co	10 July 1971	AA

Displacement, tons: 10 000 light;
15 900 (4-6), 16 550 (7-10), 16 900 (11-13), 17 000 (14 and 15) full load
Dimensions, feet (metres): 570 × 100 × 23 (173·3 × 30·5 × 7)
Aircraft: Up to 6 UH-34 or CH-46 helicopters
Guns: 2—3 in (76 mm)/50 (twin Mk 33)
Main engines: 2 steam turbines (De Laval); 24 000 shp; 2 shafts
Boilers: 2 Foster-Wheeler (Babcock & Wilcox in LPD 5 and 12)
Speed, knots: 21
Complement: 473 (27 officers, 446 enlisted men)
Troops: 930 in LPD 4-6 and LPD 14-15; 840 in LPD 7-13
Flag accommodation: Approx 90 in LPD 7-13

JUNEAU
1 1980, Dr. Giorgio Arra

These ships are enlarged versions of the earlier "Raleigh" class; most notes for the "Raleigh" class apply to these ships.

The dates of laying down and launching are: *Austin* and *Ogden* 4 February 1963 and 27 June 1964; *Duluth* 18 December 1963 and 14 August 1965; *Cleveland* 30 November 1964 and 7 May 1966; *Dubuque* 25 January 1965 and 6 August 1966; *Denver* 7 February 1964 and 23 January 1965; *Juneau* 23 January 1965 and 12 February 1966; *Coronado* 3 May 1965 and 30 July 1966; *Shreveport* 27 December 1965 and 25 October 1966; *Nashville* 14 March 1966 and 7 October 1967; *Trenton* 8 August 1966 and 3 August 1968; *Ponce* 31 October 1966 and 20 May 1970. *Duluth* completed at Philadelphia Naval Shipyard.

LPD 4-6 were authorised in the FY 1962 new construction programme, LPD 7-10 in FY 1963, LPD 11-13 in FY 1964, LPD 14 and LPD 15 in FY 1965, and LPD 16 in FY 1966.

Electronics: Fitted with OE-82 satellite communications antenna, SSR-1 receiver and WSC-3 transceiver.

Gunnery: Two 20 mm Mk 15 CIWS to be fitted.

Rockets: Each ship will be fitted with Mk 36 Chaffroc. Mk 28 already fitted in *Coronado* and *Nashville*.

DULUTH
11/1979, John Mortimer

NASHVILLE (LPD 13)
1969, Lockheed SB & Constn Co

AUSTIN (LPD 4)
1969, United States Navy

OGDEN (LPD 5)
United States Navy

7 "IWO JIMA" CLASS: AMPHIBIOUS ASSAULT SHIPS (LPH)

Name	No.	Builders	Laid down	Launched	Commissioned	F/S
IWO JIMA	LPH 2	Puget Sound Naval Shipyard	2 Apr 1959	17 Sep 1960	26 Aug 1961	AA
OKINAWA	LPH 3	Philadelphia Naval Shipyard	1 Apr 1960	14 Aug 1961	14 Apr 1962	PA
GUADALCANAL	LPH 7	Philadelphia Naval Shipyard	1 Sep 1961	16 Mar 1963	20 July 1963	AA
GUAM	LPH 9	Philadelphia Naval Shipyard	15 Nov 1962	22 Aug 1964	16 Jan 1965	AA
TRIPOLI	LPH 10	Ingalls Shipbuilding Corp	15 June1964	31 July 1965	6 Aug 1966	PA
NEW ORLEANS	LPH 11	Philadelphia Naval Shipyard	1 Mar 1966	3 Feb 1968	16 Nov 1968	PA
INCHON	LPH 12	Ingalls Shipbuilding Corp	8 Apr 1968	24 May 1969	20 June 1970	AA

Displacement, tons: 18 000 (2, 3 and 7), 18 300 (9 and 10), 17 706 (11), 17 515 (12) full load
Dimensions, feet (metres): 602·3 × 84 × 26 (183·7 × 25·6 × 7·9)
Flight deck width, feet (metres): 104 (31·7)
Aircraft: For helicopters see *Aircraft* note
4 AV-8A Harriers in place of some troop helicopters
Missiles: 2 Basic Point Defence Missile System (BPDMS) launchers (Mk 25) firing Sea Sparrow missiles
Guns: 4—3 in (76 mm)/50 (twin Mk 33)
Main engines: 1 geared turbine (De Laval in *Tripoli*, GE in *Inchon*, Westinghouse in others); 22 000 shp; 1 shaft
Boilers: 2 Babcock & Wilcox in *Guam*; Combustion Engineering in remainder
Speed, knots: 23
Complement: 609 (47 officers, 562 enlisted men)
Troops: 1 731 (143 officers, 1 588 enlisted men)

Iwo Jima was the world's first ship designed and constructed specifically to operate helicopters. Each LPH can carry a Marine battalion landing team, its guns, vehicles, and equipment, plus a reinforced squadron of transport helicopters and various support personnel.
Iwo Jima was authorised in the FY 1958 new construction programme, *Okinawa* in the FY 1959, *Guadalcanal* in the FY 1960, *Guam* in the FY 1962, *Tripoli* in the FY 1963, *New Orleans* in the FY 1965, and *Inchon* in the FY 1966.
Estimated cost of *Iwo Jima* was $40 million.
Guam was modified late in 1971 and began operations in January 1972 as an interim sea control ship. She operated Harrier AV-8 V/STOL aircraft and SH-3 Sea King A/S helicopters in convoy escort exercises; she reverted to the amphibious role in 1974 but kept 12 AV-8As on board. Several of these ships operated RH-53 minesweeping helicopters to clear North Vietnamese ports in 1973 and the Suez Canal in 1974.

Aircraft: The flight decks of these ships provide for simultaneous take off or landing of seven CH-46 Sea Knight or four CH-53 Sea Stallion helicopters during normal operations. The hangar decks can accommodate 19 CH-46 Sea Knight or 11 CH-53 Sea Stallion helicopters, or various combinations of helicopters.

Design: Each ship has two deck-edge lifts, one to port opposite the bridge and one to starboard aft of island. Full hangars are provided, no arresting wires or catapults. Two small elevators carry cargo from holds to flight deck. Storage provided for 6 500 gallons (US) of vehicle petrol and 405 000 gallons (US) of JP-5 helicopter fuel.

Electronics: Tacan. Advanced electronic warfare equipment fitted.
All except *Tripoli* fitted with OE-82 satellite communications antenna, SSR-1 receiver and WSC-3 transceiver.

Fire control: As rearmed with BPDMS these ships have two Mk 115 missile fire control systems.

Gunnery: As built, each ship had eight 3-in guns in twin mounts, two forward of the island structure and two at stern. Gun battery reduced by half with substitution of BPDMS launchers (see *Missiles* note). Two 20 mm Mk 15 CIWS to be fitted. Two 40 mm saluting guns fitted.

Medical: These ships are fitted with extensive medical facilities including operating room, X-ray room, hospital ward, isolation ward, laboratory, pharmacy, dental operating room, and medical store rooms.

Missiles: One Sea Sparrow launcher forward of island structure and one on the port quarter. *Okinawa* had one BPDMS launcher fitted in 1970 and the second in 1973; *Tripoli* and *Inchon* rearmed in 1972, *Iwo Jima* and *New Orleans* in 1973, *Guam* and *Guadalcanal* in 1974.

Radar: Search: SPS 10 and 40.
Navigation: SPN 10.

Rockets: One Mk 36 Chaffroc (RBOC) to be fitted.

TRIPOLI

11/1979, John Mortimer

GUADALCANAL (CH 53, Sea Stallion on elevator)

5/1978, USN (Lt Cdr. J. Mancias)

OKINAWA (LPH 3)

1965 United States Navy

OKINAWA (LPH 3)   *1970, United States Navy, PH3 De Varold Bengston*   OKINAWA   *1/1977, Dr. Giorgio Arra*

INCHON (LPH 12)   *1972, Stefan Terzibaschitsch*   INCHON (LPH 12)   *1972, Stefan Terzibaschitsch*

OKINAWA   *1/1977, Dr. Giorgio Arra*

4 + 1 "TARAWA" CLASS: AMPHIBIOUS ASSAULT SHIPS G.P. (LHA)

Name	No.	Builders	Erection of First Module	Launched	Commissioned	F/S
TARAWA	LHA 1	Ingalls Shipbuilding Corporation	15 Nov 1971	1 Dec 1973	29 May 1976	PA
SAIPAN	LHA 2	Ingalls Shipbuilding Corporation	21 July 1972	18 July 1974	15 Oct 1977	AA
BELLEAU WOOD	LHA 3	Ingalls Shipbuilding Corporation	5 Mar 1973	11 Apr 1977	23 Sep 1978	PA
NASSAU	LHA 4	Ingalls Shipbuilding Corporation	13 Aug 1973	21 Jan 1978	28 July 1979	AA
PELILEU (ex-Da Nang)	LHA 5	Ingalls Shipbuilding Corporation	12 Nov 1976	25 Nov 1978	21 June 1980	Bldg

Displacement, tons: 39 300 full load
Dimensions, feet (metres): 820 × 106 × 26 *(250 × 32·3 × 7·9)*
Flight deck, feet (metres): 118·1 *(36)*
Aircraft: (See *Aircraft* note for helicopters). Harrier AV-8A V/STOL aircraft in place of some helicopters as required
Missiles: SAM—2 Sea Sparrow launchers (Mk 25) (BPDMS)
Guns: 3—5 in *(127 mm)*/54 (single Mk 45)
   6—20 mm (Mk 67) (single); 2—40 mm saluting
Main engines: 2 geared turbines (Westinghouse); 140 000 shp; 2 shafts
Boilers: 2 (Combustion Engineering)
Speed, knots: 24
Range, miles: 10 000 at 20 knots
Complement: 902 (90 officers, 812 enlisted men)
Troops: 1 903 (172 officers, 1 731 enlisted men)

LHA 1 was authorised in the FY 1969 new construction programme, the LHA 2 and LHA 3 in FY 1970 and LHA 4 and LHA 5 in FY 1971. All ships of this class were built at a new ship production facility known as "Ingalls West". The new yard was developed specifically for multi-ship construction of the same design. LHA 5 renamed 15 February 1978.

Aircraft: The flight deck can operate a maximum of 9 CH-53 Sea Stallion or 12 CH-46 Sea Knight helicopters; the hangar deck can accommodate 19 CH-53 Sea Stallion or 30 CH-46 Sea Knight helicopters. A mix of these and other helicopters and at times AV-8A Harriers could be embarked.

Design: Beneath the full-length flight deck are two half-length hangar decks, the two being connected by an elevator amidships on the port side and a stern lift; beneath the after elevator is a floodable docking well measuring 268 ft in length and 78 ft in width which is capable of accommodating four LCU 1610 type landing craft. Also included is a large garage for trucks and AFVs and troop berthing for a reinforced battalion.
Storage for 10 000 gallons (US) of vehicle petrol and 400 000 gallons (US) of JP-5 helicopter fuel.

Electronics: Helicopter navigation equipment provided. Each ship also will have an Integrated Tactical Amphibious Warfare Data System (ITAWDS) to provide computerised support in control of helicopters and aircraft, shipboard weapons and sensors, navigation, landing craft control, and electronic warfare.
Fitted with OE-82 satellite communications antenna, SSR-1 receiver and WSC-3 transceiver.

TARAWA   6/1979, Dr. Giorgio Arra

Engineering: A 900 hp fixed bow thruster is provided for holding position while unloading landing craft.
Four turbo-alternators, each 2 500 kW; two diesel-alternators, each 2 000 kW.

Fire control: One Mk 86 gunfire control system and two Mk 15 Missile fire control systems; also one SPG 60 and one SPG 9A weapon control radars.

Fiscal: In early 1974 the estimated total cost of the five LHAs was $1 145 million or an average of $229 million per ship.

Gunnery: To be fitted with two 20 mm Mk 15 CIWS

Medical: These ships are fitted with extensive medical facilities including operating rooms, X-ray room, hospital ward, isolation ward, laboratories, pharmacy, dental operating room and medical store rooms.

Radar: 3D search: SPS 52.
Search: SPS 10 and 40.
Air/navigation: SPN 35.

Rockets: One Mk 36 Chaffroc (RBOC) to be fitted.

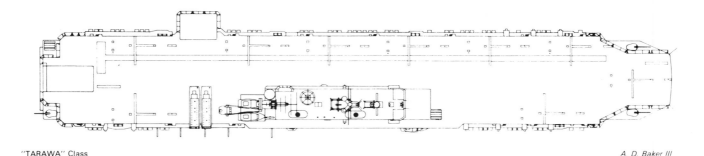

"TARAWA" Class   A. D. Baker III

TARAWA   6/1979, Dr. Giorgio Arra

3 Amphibious Assault Ships (LPH): "Essex" Class (ex-CVA/CVS)

Name	No.	Builder	Laid down	Launched	Commissioned
BOXER	LPH 4 (ex-CVS 21)	Newport News SB & DD Co	13 Sep 1943	14 Dec 1944	16 Apr 1945
PRINCETON	LPH 5 (ex-CVS 37)	Philadelphia Navy Yard	14 Sep 1943	8 July 1945	18 Nov 1945
VALLEY FORGE	LPH 8 (ex-CVS 45)	Philadelphia Navy Yard	7 Sep 1944	18 Nov 1945	3 Nov 1946

Displacement, tons	30 800 standard; 40 600 full load
Length, feet (*metres*)	820 (*249·2*) wl; 888 (*270·7*) oa
Beam, feet (*metres*)	93 (*28·3*)
Draft, feet (*metres*)	31 (*9·4*)
Flight deck width, feet (*metres*)	147·5 (*44·7*) maximum
Helicopters	approx 30
Guns *Boxer*	8—5 in (*127 mm*) 38 cal DP
Princeton, Valley Force	6—5 in (*127 mm*) 38 cal DP
Main engines	4 geared turbines (Westinghouse) 150 000 shp; 4 shafts
Boilers	8—600 psi (Babcock & Wilcox)
Speed, knots	33

Complement	approx 1 000
Troops	approx 1 500

These ships are former "Essex" class attack/ASW carriers, relegated to amphibious warfare. See listing for modified "Essex" class attack carriers for general class notes.

CLASSIFICATION. These ships were initially classified as "aircraft carriers" (CV). All were redesignated Attack Aircraft Carriers (CVA) in October 1952 and subsequently became ASW Support Aircraft Carriers (CVS) and Amphibious Assault Ships (LPH): *Boxer* to CVS on 1 Feb 1956 and LPH on 30 Jan 1959. *Princeton* to CVS in Jan 1954 and LPH on 2 Mar 1959. *Valley Forge* to CVS in Jan 1954 and LPH on 3 June 1961.

GUNNERY. These are the only "Essex" class carriers in service which have 5 inch gun mounts on their flight decks. The *Boxer* has four twin mounts; others have two with two single 5 inch guns on port side of flight deck.

NOMENCLATURE. The *Princeton* was renamed during construction, ex-*Valley Forge*.

BOXER (LPH 4)   *United States Navy*

VALLEY FORGE   *1965, United States Marine Corps*

1 COMMAND SHIP (CC)
1 MAJOR COMMUNICATIONS RELAY SHIP (AGMR) } CONVERTED AIRCRAFT CARRIERS

Name	No.	Builder	Laid down	Launched	CVL Comm	CC-AGMR Comm.
WRIGHT	CC 2 (ex-AVT 7, ex-CVL 49)	New York SB Corp	21 Aug 1944	1 Sep 1945	9 Feb 1947	11 May 1963
ARLINGTON (ex-*Saipan*)	AGMR 2 (ex-CC 3, ex-AVT 6, ex-CVL 48)	New York SB Corp	10 July 1944	8 July 1944	14 July 1945	27 Aug 1966

Displacement, tons	14 500 standard; 19 600 full load
Length, feet (*metres*)	664 (*202·4*) wl; 683·6 (*208·4*) oa
Beam, feet (*metres*)	76·8 (*23·6*)
Draft, feet (*metres*)	28 (*8·5*)
Flight deck width, feet (*metres*)	109 (*33·2*)
Guns	*Wright* 8—40 mm anti-aircraft (twin); *Arlington* 8—3 in (*76 mm*) 50 calibre (twin)
Helicopters	5 or 6 carried by *Wright*
Main engines	4 geared turbines (General Electric); 120 000 shp; 4 shafts
Boilers	4 (Babcock & Wilcox)
Speed, knots	33
Complement	746 plus approx 1 000 on command or communications staff

These ships were built as the light carriers *Saipan* (CVL 48) and *Wright* (CVL 49), respectively. They served as experimental and training carriers for a decade before being mothballed in 1967. Both were reclassified as Auxiliary Aircraft Transports on 15 May 1959, being designated AVT 6 (*Saipan*) and AVT 7 (*Wright*). The *Wright* was converted to a command ship at the Puget Sound Naval Shipyard, 1962-1963; the *Saipan* was to have been similarly converted, but the requirement for an additional ship of this category was cancelled. The *Saipan* subsequently was converted to a major communications relay ship at the Alabama Drydock and Shipbuilding Company in 1953-1965, and renamed *Arlington*. See Conversion and Nomenclature notes. The *Arlington* was decommissioned on 14 Jan 1970 and placed in reserve; the *Wright* was similarly decommissioned on 22 May 1970 and placed in reserve.

CONVERSION. The *Wright* was converted to a command ship under the Fiscal Year 1962 authorisation at a cost of $25 000 000. Like the *Northampton*, she is fitted with elaborate communications, data processing, and display facilities for use by national authorities. The command spaces include presentation theatres similar to those at command posts ashore. The *Wright* has the most powerful transmitting antennas ever installed on a ship. They are mounted on plastic-glass masts to reduce interference with electronic transmissions. The tallest mast is 83 feet high and is designed to withstand 100-mph winds. She was reclassified from AVT 7 to CC 2 on 1 Sep 1962.

The *Saipan* was converted to a major communications relay ship at a cost of $26 886 424. She actually began conversion to a command ship (CC 3) and work was halted in February 1964. Work was resumed for her conversion to a communications ship later that year. She is fitted with elaborate communications relay equipment for the support of major commands afloat or ashore. The *Saipan* was reclassified from AVT 6 to CC 3 on 1 Jan 1964, and to AGMR 2 on 3 Sep 1964; she was renamed *Arlington* in April 1965.

WRIGHT (CC 2)   1968, United States Navy

The flat unencumbered deck of an aircraft carrier-type ship facilitates antenna placement for optimum electro-magnetic wave propagation. The new "Blue Ridge" class of amphibious command ships has a similar appearance.

NOMENCLATURE. The Navy's two communications ships are named for the naval radio stations at Arlington, Virginia; and Annapolis, Maryland.

ARLINGTON (AGMR 2)—See previous page   1967, United States Navy

1 MAJOR COMMUNICATIONS RELAY SHIP (AGMR): CONVERTED ESCORT CARRIER

Name	*No*	*Builder*	*Laid down*	*Launched*	*CVE Comm*	*AGMR Comm*
ANNAPOLIS	AGMR 1 (ex AKV 39, ex-CVE 107)	Todd Shipyards (Tacoma)	29 Nov 1943	20 July 1944	5 Feb 1945	7 Mar 1964

Displacement, tons	11 473 standard, 22 500 full load
Length, feet (*metres*)	525 (*160.0*) wl, 563 (*171.6*) oa
Beam, feet (*metres*)	75 (*22.9*)
Draft, feet (*metres*)	30.6 (*9.3*)
Flight deck width, feet (*metres*)	106 (*32.5*)
Guns	8—3 in (*76 mm*) 50 calibre anti aircraft (twin)
Main engines	2 turbines (Allis Chalmers), 16 000 shp, 2 shafts
Boilers	4 (Combustion Engineering)
Speed, knots	18
Complement	710 (44 officers, 666 enlisted men)

The *Annapolis* was built as the escort aircraft carrier *Gilbert Islands* (CVE 107). She was decommissioned on 21 May 1946 and placed in reserve, again active as a CVE from Sep 1951 to Jan 1955 when she was again decommissioned. While in reserve on 7 May 1959 she was reclassified as a Cargo Ship and Aircraft Ferry (AKV 39). Converted into a communications ship by the New York Naval Shipyard 1962-1964. Decommissioned on 20 Dec 1969 and placed in reserve.

CONVERSION. During conversion the ship was fitted with elaborate communications relay equipment including approximately 30 transmitters providing frequency band coverage from low frequency to ultra high frequency. The power outputs of the transmitters vary from 10 to 10 000 watts. Numerous radio receivers also were installed as were five large antenna towers. The ship was renamed *Annapolis* and reclassified AGMR 1 on 1 June 1963.
The former escort carrier *Vella Gulf* (AKV 11, ex-CVHE 111 ex-CVE 111) was to have been converted to the AGMR 2; her conversion never began because of the availability of the larger carrier *Saipan* for use in this role.

DESIGN. The *Gilbert Islands* was one of 19 "Commencement Bay" class escort carriers built during the latter part of World War II. This ship is the last escort or "jeep" aircraft carrier on the Navy List

ANNAPOLIS (AGMR 1)　　　　　　　　　　*1964, United States Navy*

PHOTOGRAPHS. Note enclosed "hurricane bow" installed during conversion to AGMR to improve rough-sea operation. She has a small helicopter landing area on the port side of the former flight deck

ANNAPOLIS (AGMR 1)　　　　　　　　　　*1966, United States Navy*

1 CONVERTED HEAVY CRUISER (COMMAND SHIP (CC))

Name	No.	Builders	Laid down	Launched	Commissioned
NORTHAMPTON	CC 1 (ex-CLC 1, ex-CA 125)	Bethlehem Steel Co Quincy, Mass	31 Aug 1944	27 Jan 1951	7 Mar 1953

Displacement, tons: 14 700 standard; 17 700 full load
Length, feet (metres): 664 *(202·4)* wl; 676 *(206·0)* oa
Beam, feet (metres): 71 *(21·6)*
Draught, feet (metres): 29 *(8·8)*
Gun: 1—5 inch *(127 mm)* 54 cal (Mk 42) (see *Gunnery* notes)
Helicopters: 3 UH/34
Main engines: 4 geared turbines (General Electric); 120 000 shp; 4 shafts
Boilers: 4 (Babcock & Wilcox)
Speed, knots: 33
Complement: 1 191 (68 officers, 1 123 enlisted men)
Flag accommodations: 328 (191 officers, 137 enlisted men)

NORTHAMPTON   *USN*

The *Northampton* was begun as a heavy cruiser of the "Oregon City" class, numbered CA 125. She was cancelled on 11 Aug 1945 when 56·2 per cent complete. She was re-ordered as a command ship on 1 July 1948 and designated CLC 1 (Task Force Command Ship and later Tactical Command Ship). As CLC 1 she was configured for use primarily by fast carrier force commanders and fitted with an elaborate combat information centre (CIC), electronic equipment, and flag accommodations. She was employed as flagship for Commander Sixth Fleet 1954-55 and Commander Second Fleet 1955-61. Her designation was changed to CC (Command Ship) on 15 April 1961 and she was relieved as Second Fleet flagship in October 1961. Decommissioned on 8 April 1970 and placed in reserve.

Design. The *Northampton* is one deck higher than other US heavy cruisers to provide additional office and equipment space. Her foremast is the tallest unsupported mast afloat (125 feet). All living and working spaces are air-conditioned. Helicopter landing area aft with hangar for three UH/34 type.

Electronics: Advanced communications, electronic data processing equipment, and data displays are installed; tropospheric scatter and satellite relay communications facilities.

Gunnery: As built, the *Northampton* mounted 4—5 inch Mark 42 54 calibre and 8—3 inch weapons. When decommissioned, she was armed with only one 5 inch gun aft.

Radar: Search; SPS-8A and 37.

NORTHAMPTON

1953. U.S. Navy, Official

NORTHAMPTON (CC 1)

United States Navy

1 "TULARE" CLASS: AMPHIBIOUS CARGO SHIP (LKA)

Name	No.	Builders	Commissioned	F S
TULARE (ex Evergreen Mariner)	LKA 112	Bethlehem, San Francisco	13 Jan 1956	MPR

Displacement, tons: 9 050 light; 17 500 full load
Dimensions, feet (metres): 564 × 80 × 28 (171.9 × 24.4 × 8.5)
Guns: 6—3 in (76 mm)/50 (twin Mk 33)
Main engines: Steam turbine (De Laval); 22 000 shp; 1 shaft = 23 knots
Boilers: 2 (Combustion Engineering)
Complement: 393 (10 officers, 154 enlisted active duty; 21 officers, 208 enlisted reserve)
Troops: 319 (18 officers, 301 enlisted men)

Laid down on 16 February 1953; launched on 22 December 1953; acquired by Navy during construction; C4-S-1A type. Has helicopter landing platform and booms capable of lifting 60 ton landing craft. Carries 9 LCM-6 and 11 LCVP landing craft as deck cargo. Designation changed from AKA 112 to LKA 112 on 1 January 1969.
Tulare was assigned to the Naval Reserve Force on 1 July 1975. Decommissioned 15 February 1980 and transferred to Maritime Administration Suisin Bay for lay-up.

TULARE (AKA 112)   *United States Navy*

TULARE   *1969, USN*

Class: Thirty-five "Mariner" design C4-S-1A merchant ships built during the early 1950s; five acquired by Navy, three for conversion to amphibious ships (AKA-APA) and two for support of Polaris-Poseidon programme (designated AG).

2 AMPHIBIOUS TRANSPORTS (LPA): "PAUL REVERE" CLASS

Name	No.	Launched	Commissioned
*PAUL REVERE (ex-Diamond Mariner)	LPA 248	13 Feb 1954	3 Sep 1958
*FRANCIS MARION (ex-Prairie Mariner)	LPA 249	11 Apr 1953	6 July 1961

Displacement, tons	10 709 light; 16 838 full load
Dimensions, feet	563.5 oa × 76 × 27
Guns	8—3 inch 50 cal AA (twin)
Main engines	geared turbines (General Electric); 22 000 shp; 1 shaft = 22 knots
Boiler	2 (Foster Wheeler)
Complement	414 (35 officers, 379 enlisted men)
Troops	1 657 (96 officers, 1 561 enlisted men)

Paul Revere is a C4-S-1 type cargo vessel converted into an Attack Transport by Todd Shipyard Corp, San Pedro, Calif. under the Fiscal Year 1957 Conversion programme. Fitted with helicopter platform. *Francis Marion* was a similar "Mariner" type hull converted into an APA by Bethlehem Steel, Key Highway Yard, Baltimore, Md. under the Fiscal Year 1959 programme. Both ships were built by New York Shipbuilding Corporation, Camden, New Jersey. Designation changed from APA to LPA on 1 Jan 1969.
These are the only attack transports in active US service. Fitted to serve as force flagship.

FRANCIS MARION (LPA 249)   *1969, Anthony and Joseph Pavia*

PAUL REVERE (LPA 248)   *1969, US Navy*

FRANCIS MARION   *1975, Dr. Giorgio Arra*

PAUL REVERE (APA 248)   *United States Navy*

5 "CHARLESTON" CLASS: AMPHIBIOUS CARGO SHIPS (LKA)

Name	No.	Builders	Commissioned	F/S
CHARLESTON	LKA 113	Newport News S.B. & D.D Co	14 Dec 1968	NRF
DURHAM	LKA 114	Newport News S.B. & D.D Co	24 May 1969	NRF
MOBILE	LKA 115	Newport News S.B. & D.D Co	29 Sep 1969	PA
ST. LOUIS	LKA 116	Newport News S.B. & D.D Co	22 Nov 1969	PA
EL PASO	LKA 117	Newport News S.B. & D.D Co	17 Jan 1970	AA

Displacement, tons: 10 000 light; 18 600 full load
Dimensions, feet (metres): 575·5 × 62 × 25·5 *(175·4 × 18·9 × 7·7)*
Guns: 6—3 in *(76 mm)*/50 (twin Mk 33)
Main engines: 1 steam turbine (Westinghouse); 19 250 shp; 1 shaft = 20 knots
Boilers: 2 (Combustion Engineering)
Complement: 334 (24 officers, 310 enlisted men)
Troops: 226 (15 officers, 211 enlisted men)

Charleston laid down 5 December 1966, launched 2 December 1967; *Durham* laid down 10 July 1967, launched 29 March 1968; *Mobile* laid down 15 January 1968, launched 19 October 1968; *St. Louis* 3 April 1968 and 4 January 1969 and *El Paso* 22 October 1968 and 17 May 1969. These ships are designed specifically for the attack cargo ship role; can carry nine landing craft (LCM) and supplies for amphibious operations. Design includes two heavy-lift cranes with a 78·4 ton capacity, two 40 ton capacity booms, and eight 15 ton capacity booms; helicopter deck aft. The LKA 113-116 were authorised in the FY 1965 shipbuilding programme; LKA 117 in the FY 1966 programme. Cost of building was approximately $21 million per ship.
Charleston to NRF on 21 November 1979, *Durham* on 1 October 1979 with *Mobile* to follow 1 September 1980.

Classification: Originally designated Attack Cargo Ship (AKA), *Charleston* redesignated Amphibious Cargo Ship (LKA) on 14 December 1968; others to LKA on 1 January 1969.

Engineering: These are among the first US Navy ships with a fully automated main propulsion plant; control of plant is from bridge or central machinery space console. This automation permitted a 45 man reduction in complement.

Fire control: One Mk 1 Target Designation System (LKA 116 only).

Gunnery: Two 20 mm Mk 16 CIWS to be fitted.

Rockets: One Mk 36 Chaffroc RBOC to be installed.

ST. LOUIS (LKA 116)　　　　　*1969, Newport News SB & DD Co*

ST. LOUIS (LKA 116)　　　　　*1969, Newport News SB & DD Co*

DURHAM　　　　　*2/1979, Dr. Giorgio Arra*

ST. LOUIS　　　　　*1978, Michael D. J. Lennon*

CHARLESTON　　　　　*10/1976, Michael D. J. Lennon*

MOBILE (LKA 115)　　　　　*1960, United States Navy*

MINE WARFARE FORCES

IT was not until the USA became embroiled in World War I that any appreciable numbers of mine planters and minesweepers appeared in the list. The first of these types formed Captain Reginald Belknap's Mining Squadron One in 1918 – two old cruisers along with seven converted merchant ships and their tender *Blackhawk*. The project on which they were engaged consisted of laying an anti-U boat barrage of 100,000 moored mines between the Shetland Islands and Bergen in Norway. Between March and August 1918, over 70,000 mines had been laid, 80 per cent by the US Navy. This vast expenditure of effort resulted in the certain loss of five U-boats although others lost 'cause unknown' may have been sunk here.

Mine clearance also required the acquisition of trawlers, tugs and the like from civilian employment to a total of about 100. The regular force of 54 of the "Bird" class, 1,009-ton minesweepers was hastily constructed in 1918–19. By 1939 the total of the "Birds" had fallen to 41 of which 19 were employed on non-minewarfare duties. By 7 December 1941 there were five minesweepers in Subic Bay and five at Pearl Harbor. The list of minewarfare ships and craft in Samuel Eliot Morison's *History of USN Operations in World War Two* shows how urgent a minewarfare programme becomes when hostilities begin. Totals of 38 minelayers and 796 minesweepers of various kinds built or acquired between 1941 and 1945 prove how vital these operations were considered at that time.

By the outbreak of the Korean War in 1950 these totals had slumped to 4 minelayers and 179 minesweepers. The discovery of a new type of Soviet mine used by the North Koreans sparked an upsurge in awareness of a continuing threat. By 1963 there were still 65 World War II sweepers but there were also 64 of post-Korean construction.

By 1983 the strength of the US Navy's mine countermeasures force had dropped to 19 "Aggressives". Of these 16 were in the Naval Reserve Force, which also contained the two "Acme" class whose modernization had been cancelled. In addition to the ships there were 23 RH-53D Sea Stallion helicopters which, towing MCM sleds, could counter mines in shallow water but had no capability against mines laid in deep water. The aerial aspect of mine-warfare extended to mine-laying. All surface minelayers had long been paid off and only aircraft and submarines still retained this capability.

In FY 1982 funds were requested for the prototype of a new class of MCM vessel, to be known as the "Avenger" class, and the contract was awarded that June. Although laid down on 3 June 1983, commissioning did not take place until 12 September 1987. With a wooden hull coated in fibreglass, the full load displacement is 1,310 tons. Four diesels and 2 electric motors produce a speed of 13.5 knots, there is a full fit of minesweeping/hunting gear and an integrated navigation system. Eight of the class are due in service by late 1991, aiming towards a total of 14.

The second new design was for a coastal minehunter. The original plan for a surface effect ship was cancelled in 1986 when the design failed to withstand shock testing. In August 1986 the Italian company Intermarine received a design contract and in May 1987 a construction contract for a class based on their "Lericis". Construction is now in progress on the 851-ton full load "Osprey" class. The first two are due in 1992 but the usual haggling between the Navy, DoD and Congress has held back any notable advance in numbers although the eventual target is 17 ships.

The helicopter force of 23 RH-53D Sea Stallions has been reinforced by 31 MH-53E Sea Dragons, three-engined machines with improved MCM equipment. The great advantage of this helicopter force is the fact that they can be deployed in any suitable carrier at a far greater speed than the surface MCM vessels but the limitation to shallow water remains.

Finally comes COOP. The Craft of Opportunity Programme is planned to provide five converted fishing vessels on the West coast and 17 YPs on the East. Fitted with a computerized system and side-scan sonar these will provide some augmentation of a most inadequate force.

J.M.
May 1991

Mine Planters.

Note.—The Mine Planting Force during the War consisted of the ex-Cruisers *San Francisco* and *Baltimore*, and Converted Liners *Aroostook*, *Canandaigua*, *Canonicus*, *Housatonic*, *Quinnebaug*, *Roanoke*, *Shawmut*, with *Blackhawk* as Tender. *Aroostook* and *Shawmut* are retained, and *Black Hawk* assigned to new duties; the other vessels have been reconditioned for Mercantile Service. These ships laid the Northern Barrage from Scotland to Norway.

Same as "Shawmut" below

(*Pacific Fleet.*)

AROOSTOOK (Cramps, 1907. Ex-S.S. *Bunker Hill*, of Eastern Steamship Co., purchased 1917 and converted into Mine Planter). All details as *Shawmut*, below. Served as Tender to *NC* Flying Boats during Cross Atlantic Flight.

SCRAPPED

SHAWMUT (AROOSTOOK same) *Photo, O. W. Waterman.*

(*Atlantic Fleet.*)

SHAWMUT (Cramps, 1907. Ex-S.S. *Massachusetts*, of Eastern Steamship Co., purchased 1917 and converted into Mine Planter). 3800 tons. Complement, 314. Dimensions: 395 (*o.a.*) × $52\frac{1}{4}$ × 16 feet (*mean*). Guns: 1—5 inch, 2—3 inch AA., 2 M.G. Reciprocating engines and 8 S. E. boilers. 2 screws. H.P. 7000 = 20 kts. Fuel: 400 tons coal + 160 tons oil. Served as Tender to *NC* Flying Boats during Cross-Atlantic Flight.

OGLALA – SCRAPPED

Mine Planters—*continued.*

Photo, U. S. Navy.

(*Atlantic Fleet.*)

SAN FRANCISCO (1889). Displacement, 4083 tons. Complement, 315. Dimensions: 410 (*w.l.*) × $49\frac{1}{4}$ × $18\frac{3}{4}$ (*mean*) feet. Armament: 4—5 inch, 2—1 pdr., 2 M.G. Carries 300 Mark II mines. 4 searchlights. Designed H.P. 8500 = 19 kts. 8 Babcock boilers. Coal: 663 tons

SOLD

Photo, U. S. Navy

(*Pacific Fleet.*)

BALTIMORE (1888). Displacement, 4413 tons. Complement, 345. Dimensions: $327\frac{1}{2}$ (*w.l.*) × $48\frac{2}{3}$ × $19\frac{1}{2}$ (*mean*) feet. Guns: 4—5 inch, 51 cal., 2—3 inch AA., 2 M.G. Armour: 4" deck. Designed H.P. 8500 = 20 kts. Boilers: 8 Babcock. Coal: *maximum* 1092 tons.

SOLD

Note.—*Condor*, *Plover*, *Goshawk* and *Nos. 55, 56, 57* stopped. Nine boats still unfinished on July 1st, 1919. These craft may also serve as Mine Layers, Tugs, Coastguard Cutters and Salvage Ships.

Mine-Sweepers.

In addition to the vessels described below, about 100 other ships (such as Trawlers, Tugs, etc.) were chartered or purchased for War Duty. It is not definitely known yet how many of these vessels will be retained in the Post-War Fleet Organisation, and so no attempt is made to describe them this year. For Tugs, fitted as Mine Sweepers, see a subsequent page.

1920 *Photo.*

("BIRD" CLASS—44 BOATS.)

LAPWING, OWL, ROBIN, SWALLOW, SANDERLING, AUK, CHEWINK, CORMORANT, GANNET (all built by Todd S. B. Co., Tebo Yacht Basin, Brooklyn, N. Y.).

TANAGER, CARDINAL, ORIOLE, CURLEW, GREBE, MALLARD, ORTOLAN, PEACOCK (all built by Staten Id. S. B. Co., N. Y.).

AVOCET, BOBOLINK, LARK, REDWING, RAVEN, SHRIKE (all built by Baltimore D. D. & S. B. Co.).

PELICAN, FALCON, OSPREY, SEAGULL, TERN (all built by Gas Engine & Power Co., Morris Heights, N. Y.).

TURKEY, WOODCOCK, QUAIL PARTRIDGE (all built by Chester S. B. Co.)

SANDPIPER, WARBLER, VIREO, WILLET (all built by Philadelphia Navy Yard).

SWAN, WHIPPOORWILL, BITTERN (all built by Alabama S. B. & D. D. Co., Mobile).

WIDGEON, TEAL, BRANT (all built by Sun S. B. Co., Chester).

KINGFISHER, RAIL (both built by Puget Sound Navy Yard).

EIDER, THRUSH (both built by Pusey & Jones, Wilmington).

FINCH, HERON (both built by Standard S. B. Co., N. Y.).

FLAMINGO, PENGUIN (both built by New Jersey D. D. & T. Co., Elizabeth Port).

PIGEON. Builder not known. Built 1918-19. 950 tons *normal*, 1009 *full load* at $10\frac{1}{4}$ feet aft. Dimensions: $187\frac{3}{4}$ (*o.a.*) × $35\frac{1}{2}$ × $9\frac{3}{4}$ feet (*mean* draught). Guns: 2—3 inch AA., 2 M.G. Machinery: 1 set triple expansion and 2 B. & W. boilers. Designed I.H.P. 1400 = 14 kts. Oil fuel only

14 Light Mine Layers—DM.

(ex-Flush Deck Destroyers of "# 75 Series.")

MAHAN (3—4 inch guns).　　　　　　　　　　1921 *Photo.*

LANSDALE (4—4 inch guns).　　　　　　　　　1921 *Photo.*

7 *Fore River*: **Israel, Lansdale. Luce** (ex-*Schley*), **Mahan, Maury, Murray, Stribling.** Are ex-Destroyers *Nos. 96—102*; authorized 1916-17.)

7 *Union I. W.*: **Anthony, Burns. Hart, Ingraham, Ludlow, Rizal, Sproston.** (Are ex-Destroyers *Nos. 110–112, 171–174*; authorized 1917.)

Displacements : 1191 tons *normal* (1284 *full load*). Dimensions : 310 (*w.l.*), 314 ft. 4½ in. (*o.a.*) × 30 ft. 11½ in. × 9 ft. 2 in. (*mean* draught), 9 ft. 9½ in. (*full load* draught aft).

Guns : *Ludlow, Mahan* and *Murray*, 3—4 inch, 50 cal. ; rest, 4—4 inch, 50 cal., and (in all) 1—3 inch, 23 cal. AA.

Torpedo tubes : Removed on conversion.

Mines carried : Unofficially reported to carry 80 Mark IV mines, for which magazines, deck rails and chutes have been fitted.

Machinery (*about* 486 tons) : Curtis geared turbines. 4 Yarrow boilers—27,540 sq. ft. heating surface. 2 screws. Designed S.H.P. 27,000 = 35 kts. (only *Lansdale* and *Mahan* made this *on trials*). Fuel : 283 tons oil. Complement, 128.

Notes.—Flush Deck Destroyers converted 1920-21. *Israel* has submarine bell. *Rizal* built at expense of Philippine Government. and manned by Filipino crew.

FORE RIVER BOATS :—				UNION I. W. BOATS :—			
Name.	*Begun.*	*Launch.*	*Comp.*	*Name.*	*Begun.*	*Launch.*	*Comp.*
Israel	26/1/18	22/6/18	20/8/18	Anthony	18/4/18	10/8/18	19/6/19
Lansdale	20/4/18	21/7/18	26/10/18	Burns	15/4/18	4/7/18	7/8/19
Luce	9/2/18	29/6/18	11/9/18	Hart	8/1/18	7/4/18	26/5/19
Mahan	4/5/18	4/8/18	24/10/18	Ingraham	12/1/8	7/7/18	15/5/19
Maury	25/2/18	4/7/18	23/9/18	Ludlow	7/1/18	9/6/18	23/12/18
Murray	22/12/17	3/6/18	20/8/18	Rizal	26/6/18	21/9/18	28/5/19
Stribling	14/12/17	29/5/18	10/8/18	Sproston	20/4/18	10/8/18	11/7/19

Minelayers.

TERROR.　　　　　　　　　　　　　1943, *U.S. Navy Official.*

TERROR (June 6, 1941). Built at Philadelphia Navy Yard, under 1938 Programme. Displacement : 5,875 tons. Complement : 400. Dimensions : 453⅜ (*o.a.*) × 60⅛ × — feet. Guns : 4—5 inch, 38 cal. etc. Machinery : Diesel. B.H.P.: 11,000 = 25 kts. Distinctive number is CM 5.

MONADNOCK.　　　　　　　　　　　1942, *U.S. Navy Official*

MONADNOCK (ex-s.s. *Cavalier*) (1938). Displacement : 3,638 tons. Complement : 350. Dimensions : 280½ × 48½ × 13½ feet. Guns : 2—3 inch, 50 cal., etc. Machinery : Geared turbines. S.H.P. : 5,000 = 17 kts. Distinctive number : CM 9. Sister ship *Miantonomoh* became a war loss.

SHAWMUT (ex-*Salem*, ex-*Joseph R. Parrott*, 1916). **WEEHAWKEN** (ex-*Estrada Palma*, 1920. Displacement : 5,300 tons. Complement : 350. Dimensions : 336½ (*pp.*), 350 (*o.a.*) × 57 × — feet. Guns : 3—3 inch, 50 cal., etc. Machinery : Triple expansion. 2 shafts. I.H.P. : 2,700 = 12 kts. Oil fuel. Distinctive Nos.: are CM 11, 12.

WASSUC (ex-s.s *Yale*, 1923). Acquired 1941 for conversion into a minelayer. 1,670 tons *gross*. Dimensions : 223¾ × 42 × 14 feet. Guns : 2—5 inch, 38 cal. Machinery : Triple expansion. 2 shafts. I.H.P. 2,080 = 12 kts. Distinctive number is CMc 3.

9 Auxiliary Minelayers.

BARBICAN (ex-*Colonel G. Armistead*), **BARRICADE** (ex-*Col. John Storey*), **BASTION** (ex-*Col. H. J. Hunt*), **CHIMO** (ex-*Col. C. W. Bundy*), **OBSTRUCTER** (ex-*Lieut. Sylvester*), **PICKET** (ex-*Gen. Henry Knox*), **PLANTER** (ex-*Col. George Ricker*), **TRAPPER** (ex-*Gen. A. Murray*).

Displacement : 700 tons. Complement : 100. Dimensions : 188 × 37 × 12 feet. Guns : not reported. Machinery : Diesel. B.H.P. : 600 = 10 kts.

Note.—These vessels were taken over from Army and equipped at Charleston Navy Yard in 1944. Numbered ACM 1–3, 5–9.

BUTTRESS (ex-*PCE 878*). Displacement : 795 tons. Dimensions : 184½ × 33 × 9 feet. Guns : 2—3 inch, 50 cal., etc. Machinery : Diesel. B.H.P. : 2,400 = 20 kts.

LINDSEY.　　　　　　　　　　　　1944, *U.S. Navy Official.*

SHEA.　　　　　　　　　　　　　1944, *U.S. Navy Official.*

Following 12 modern Destroyers have been fitted as Minelayers, and were so classed during war in Pacific :

AARON WARD, ADAMS, GWIN, HARRY F. BAUER, HENRY A. WILEY, J. WILLIAM DITTER, LINDSEY, ROBERT H. SMITH, SHANNON, SHEA, THOMAS E. FRASER, TOLMAN. Displacement : 2,200 tons.

All will be found described on an earlier page, under *Allen M. Sumner* class of Destroyers. Numbered DM 23—34.

MONTGOMERY. (Since lost.)　　　　　1940, "*Ships and Aircraft.*"

1 *Cramp*: **TRACY** (Aug. 12, 1919.) Converted to present service in 1937. (DM 19.)

Displacement : 1,190 tons *standard*. Dimensions : 310 (*w.l.*), 314½ (*o.a.*) × 30⅜ × 9¼ feet (*mean* draught), 13½ feet (*max.*). Guns : 4—4 inch, 50 cal. 1—3 inch, 23 cal., AA. Torpedo tubes removed. Machinery : Parsons geared turbines. 2 shafts. S.H.P. : 27,000 = 35 kts. Boilers : 4 White-Forster. Total heating service, 27,500 sq. feet. Oil fuel 375 tons.

1 *Newport News S.B.Co.*: **BREESE** (May 11, 1918). Converted 1920–21. (DM 18.)

Displacement : 1,160 tons *standard* (1,284 *full load*). Dimensions : 309 (*w.l.*), 314 ft. 4 in. (*o.a.*) × 30 ft. 6 in. × 9 ft. (*mean* draught), 9 ft. 10 ins. (*full load* draught aft). Guns : 4—4 inch, 50 cal., 1—3 inch, 23 cal. AA. Topedo tubes removed. Unofficially reported to carry 80 Mark IV mines, for which magazines, deck rails and chutes have been fitted. Machinery : Curtis geared turbines. 2 shafts. Designed S.H.P. : 27,000 = 35 kts. 4 Thornycroft boilers—27,540 sq. ft. heating service. Fuel : 283 tons oil. Complement : 128. War losses : *Gamble, Montgomery.*

Fast Minesweepers (Modified Destroyers.)

Following 23 modern Destroyers have been fitted for minesweeping, and were classed as Fast Minesweepers during war in Pacific :

BUTLER, CARMICK, COWIE, DAVISON, DORAN, DOYLE, ELLYSON, ENDICOTT, FITCH, FORREST, GHERARDI, HALE, HAMBLETON, HARDING, HOBSON, JEFFERS, KNIGHT, McCOOK, MACOMB, MERVINE, QUICK, RODMAN, THOMPSON. Displacement : 1,700 tons.

All will be found described on an earlier page, under *Buchanan* class of Destroyers. Numbered DMS 19—21, 23—30. War loss: *Emmons*.

BOGGS, DORSEY, HOPKINS, LAMBERTON, SOUTHARD (1918-20.)

Displacement : 1,060 to 1,190 tons. Guns : 2—3 inch, 50 cal., 2—40 mm. AA., 5—20 mm. AA., Machinery : Geared turbines. S.H.P. : 25,000 = 35 kts. Numbered DMS 1—3, 10, 13. Will probably be discarded in near future, with other former flush-deck destroyers. War losses : *Hovey, Long, Palmer, Perry, Wasmuth.*

---

65 Raven Class.

RAVEN.   1941, *U.S. Navy Official.*

2 *Norfolk Navy Yard :* **AUK, RAVEN** (Aug. 24, 1940).

14 *American S.B. Co. :* **SEER** (May, 1942), **SPEED** (April, 1942), **SPRIG** (1944), **STAFF, STEADY, STRIVE** (April, 1942), **SURFBIRD** (1944), **SUSTAIN** (June 23, 1942), **TANAGER** (1944), **TERCEL** (Dec. 16, 1944), **TOUCAN** (1944), **TOWHEE** (1945), **WAXWING** (1945), **WHEATEAR** (April 29, 1945).

3 *Associated Shipbuilders :* **SPEAR, TRIUMPH, VIGILANCE**

4 *Defoe Boat & Motor Works :* **BROADBILL, CHICKADEE, NUTHATCH, PHEASANT.**

18 *General Engineering & D. D. Co. :* **ARDENT** (June, 1943), **CHAMPION, CHIEF, COMPETENT, DEFENSE, DEVASTATOR, GLADIATOR, HEED, HERALD, IMPECCABLE, MINEVET, MOTIVE** (Aug. 17, 1942), **MURRELET, ORACLE** (Sept. 30, 1942), **PEREGRINE, PIGEON, SHELDRAKE** (Nov. 1941), **STARLING** (April 11, 1942).

9 *Gulf S.B. Corpn. :* **DEXTROUS, ROSELLE, RUDDY, SCOTER, SHOVELER, TOKEN, TUMULT, VELOCITY, ZEAL.**

2 *John H. Mathis Co. :* **SWAY, SWIFT** (Dec. 6, 1942).

3 *Pennsylvania Shipyard, Inc. :* **PILOT, PIONEER, PREVAIL** (Sept. 13, 1942).

6 *Savannah Machine & Foundry Co. :* **POCHARD, PTARMIGAN, QUAIL, REDSTART, SYMBOL** (July 2, 1942), **THREAT.**

4 *Winslow Marine Ry. & S.B. Co. :* **PURSUIT, REQUISITE, REVENGE** (ex-*Right*), **SAGE** (Nov. 21, 1942).

Steel. Displacement : 890 tons. Dimensions : 220½ × 32 × 9¼ feet. Guns : 2—3 inch, dual purpose, etc. Machinery : 2 sets G.M. or Fairbanks-Morse Diesels with electric drive. 2 shafts. B.H.P. 3,500 = 18 kts. Complement : 100. A number of ships of this class were transferred to Royal Navy, but will be returned. Numbered AM 55, 57—62, 64, 100—105, 107—112, 114, 116—120, 122—124, 126—131, 314—324, 340, 341, 371—390. War losses : *Portent, Sentinel, Skill, Skylark, Swallow, Swerve, Tide.*

131 Admirable Class.

ADMIRABLE (Some of this type have funnel.)   1944, *U.S. Navy Official.*

17 *American S.B. Co. :* **DISDAIN, DOUR, EAGER, ELUSIVE, EMBATTLE** (all 1944), **JUBILANT, KNAVE,** (both 1943), **LANCE, LOGIC** (both April 10, 1943), **LUCID, MAGNET,** (both 1943), **MAINSTAY, MARVEL** (both July 31, 1943), **MEASURE, METHOD, MIRTH, NIMBLE** (all 1943).

10 *Associated Shipbuilders :* **SIGNET, SKIRMISH, SKURRY, SPECTACLE, SPECTER, STAUNCH, STRATEGY, STRENGTH, SUCCESS, SUPERIOR.**

9 *General Engineering & D.D. Co. :* **RANSOM** (Sept. 18, 1943), **REBEL** (Oct. 28, 1943), **RECRUIT** (Dec. 11, 1943), **REFORM, REFRESH** (April 12, 1944), **REIGN** (1944), **REPORT** (1944), **REPROOF** (Aug. 8, 1944), **RISK** (Nov. 7, 1944).

16 *Gulf S.B. Corpn. :* **NOTABLE** (June 12, 1943), **NUCLEUS** (June 27, 1943), **OPPONENT** (June 12, 1943), **PALISADE** (June 27, 1943), **PENETRATE** (1943), **PERIL, PHANTOM** (both July 25, 1943), **PINNACLE, PIRATE, PIVOT, PLEDGE, PRIME, PROJECT, PROWESS, QUEST, RAMPART.**

10 *Puget Sound Bridge Co. :* **DUNLIN, EXECUTE, FACILITY, FANCY, FIXITY, GADWAL, GAVIA, GRAYLAG, HARLEQUIN, HARRIER.**

9 *Savannah Machine & Foundry Co. :* **IMPLICIT, IMPROVE, INCESSANT, INCREDIBLE, INDICATIVE** (Dec. 12, 1943), **INFLICT** (Jan. 16, 1944), **INSTILL, INTRIGUE, INVADE.**

24 *Tampa S.B. Co. :* **ADMIRABLE, ADOPT, ADVOCATE, AGENT** (all 1942), **ALARM, ALCHEMY, APEX, ARCADE, ARCH, ARMADA** (all Dec. 7, 1942), **ASPIRE, ASSAIL, ASTUTE, AUGURY, BARRIER, BOMBARD, CRAIG, CRUISE** (both March 21, 1943), **DEFT, DELEGATE, DESIGN,** (Feb. 6, 1943), **DESTINY** (Feb. 7, 1943), **DEVISE, DIPLOMA.**

24 *Willamette Iron & Steel Corpn :* **ADJUTANT, BITTERN, BOND, BREAKHORN, BUOYANT, CANDID, CAPABLE, CAPTIVATE, CARAVAN, CARIAMA, CAUTION** (Dec. 7, 1942), **CHANGE, CHUKOR, CLAMOUR, CLIMAX, COMPEL, CONCISE, CONTROL, COUNSEL, CREDDOCK, DIPPER, DOTTEREL, DRAKE, DRIVER.**

12 *Winslow Marine Ry. & S.B. Co. :* **GARLAND, GAYETY, HAZARD, HILARITY, INAUGURAL, SAUNTER, SCOUT, SCRIMMAGE, SCUFFLE, SENTRY, SERENE, SHELTER.**

Steel. Displacement : 795 tons. Complement : 100. Dimensions : 180 (*w.l.*), 184½ (*o.a.*) × 33 × 9 feet. Guns : 1—3 inch d.p., some smaller. Machinery : Diesel. 2 shafts. B.H.P. : 1,800 = 15 kts. Numbered AM 136—165, 214—226, 232—235, 238—242, 246—291, 295—311, 351—366. War loss : *Salute.*

19 Bullfinch Class (*ex-Trawlers*).

GOSHAWK.   1941, *Ships and Aircraft.*

BULLFINCH (ex-*Villanova*), **CARDINAL** (ex-*Jeanne d'Arc*) (1937), both 262 tons, H.P. 735 ; **CATBIRD** (ex-*Bittern*) (1937), **CURLEW** (ex-*Kittiwake*) (1937), both 355 tons, H.P. 575 ; **FLICKER** (ex-*Delaware*) (1937), 303 tons, H.P. 735 ; **ALBATROSS** (ex-*Illinois*), **BLUEBIRD** (ex-*Maine*) (1931), both 256 tons, H.P. 550 ; **GRACKLE** (ex-*Notre Dame*), **GOLDFINCH** (ex-*Fordham*) (1929), both 255 tons, H.P. 500 ; **GULL** (ex-*Boston College*) (1928), 241 tons, H.P. 400 ; **KITE** (ex-*Holy Cross*), **LINNET** (ex-*Georgetown*) (1928), both 229 tons, H.P. 400 ; **GOSHAWK** (ex-*Penobscot*) (1919), 522 tons, H.P. 450 ; **GOLDCREST** (ex-*Shawmut*) **CHAFFINCH** (ex-*Trimount*) (1928), both 235 tons, H.P. 380 ; **MERGANSER** (ex-*Ocean*), **EAGLE** (ex-*Wave*), **HAWK** (ex-*Gale*), **IBIS** (ex-*Tide*) (1937-38), all 320 tons, H.P. 650.

All acquired in 1941–42 for conversion into Minesweepers. *Gross* tonnages as given above. Machinery : Diesel, B.H.P. as above. Numbered AM 66—81.

Numerical Type. (*YMS 1–480.*)

YMS 449.   1944, *U.S. Navy Official.*

YMS 260.   1944, *U.S. Navy Official.*

YMS 89 (and others up to 135).   1942, *U.S. Navy Official.*

American Car & Foundry Co : (One launched Sept. 7, 1942.)

Associated Shipbuilders : **YMS 148** (Nov. 29, 1942), **287** (Oct. 27, 1942), **288** (Nov. 28, 1942), **289** (Jan. 26, 1943), **290** (Feb. 27, 1942), **291** (1943), **292** (June 8, 1943), **293** (July 7, 1943).

Astoria Marine Construction Co.: **YMS 100** (April 12, 1942), etc.

Ballard Marine Ways Co.: **YMS 327** (Dec. 5, 1942), **328** (Dec. 19, 1942), **329** (Feb. 23, 1943), **330** (March 27, 1943), **333** (Sept., 1943).

Bellingham Marine Ry. Co.: **YMS 275,** etc.

Burger Boat Co.: **YMS 107-110, 160,** etc.

Colberg Plant : **YMS 95.**

Gibbs Gas Engine Co.: **YMS 57,** etc.

Henry C. Grebe & Co.: **YMS 85, 171, 406.**

Greenport Basin & Construction Co.: **YMS 22** (Dec. 13, 1942), **23** (Dec. 31, 1941), **25** (Jan. 28, 1942), **26** (Feb. 28, 1942), **28** (March 21, 1942), **31** (May 23, 1942), **183** (June 25, 1942), **184** (July 18, 1942), **185** (Aug. 8, 1942), **186** (Aug., 1942), **187** (Sept. 7, 1942), **188** (Sept. 26, 1942), **193** (Jan. 2, 1943), **194** (Jan. 30, 1943), **379** (May 29, 1943), **380** (June 26, 1943), **381** (July, 1943), **382** (Aug. 21, 1943), **456** (Dec. 11, 1943), etc.

Harbor Boat Building Co.: **YMS 117** (Aug. 23, 1942), **118, 119, 120** (April 4, 1942), **315.**

Hubbards' South Coast Co.: **YMS 88-90, 91** (March 7, 1942), **260-263, 264** (Jan. 18, 1943), etc.

Robert Jacob, Inc.: **YMS 38** (1941), **40** (1942), **41** (April 14, 1942), **207, 362** (May 22, 1943), etc.

Al. Larson Boat Shop : **YMS 86** (Feb., 1942), and another.

J. M. Martinac S.B. Corpn.: **YMS 125** (Dec. 18, 1941), **126, 128, 217** (Nov. 21, 1942), etc.

Henry B. Nevins, Inc.: **YMS 1** (Jan. 10, 1942), **2** (Jan. 28, 1942), **3** (April 13, 1942), **4** (1942), **5** (April 13, 1942) etc.

Noank S.B. Co.: (Numbers not reported).

Rice Bros. Corpn.: **YMS 12** (March 14, 1942), etc.

Frank L. Sample, Junr., Inc.: **YMS 106, 318.**

San Diego Marine Construction Co.: **YMS 113** (Feb. 13, 1942), etc.

Seattle S.B. & Dry Dock Corpn.: **YMS 335** (Nov. 21, 1942), **336** (Dec. 19, 1942), **337** (Feb. 20, 1943), **338** (March 20, 1943), etc.

Stadium Yacht Basin : **YMS 235,** etc.

Tacoma Boat Building Co.: **YMS 129, 130** (both Dec. 18, 1941), **245** (Feb. 6, 1943), **246** (March 11, 1943), **288** (Nov. 28, 1942), etc.

Western Boat Building Co.: **YMS 147** (Oct. 24, 1942).

Wheeler S.B. Corpn.: **YMS 42** (March 17, 1942), **44-47 49, 51** (June 22, 1942), **52** (July 14, 1942), **53** (1942).

Wood. Displacement : *YMS 1*—135, 207 tons ; 136—480, 215 tons. Dimensions : 135½ × 24½ × 6 feet. Guns : **1**—3 inch. **2**—20 mm., 2 D.C.T. Machinery : 2 G.M. Diesels. B.H.P. : 1,000 = 12 kts. Complement : 50. (Several of this class transferred to Royal Navy, R. Hellenic Navy, R. Norwegian Navy, French Navy, and Soviet Navy). War losses: *YMS* 14, 19, 21, 24, 30, 39, 48, 50, 70, 71, 84, 103, 127, 133, 304, 350, 365, 378, 385, 409, 481.

10 *Snow Shipyards :* **ROLLER** (May, 1941), **SKIMMER** (June, 1941), **TAPACOLA, TURACO, STALWART, SUMMIT** (Sept. 20, 1941), **TRIDENT** (Oct. 8, 1941), **VALOR, VICTOR** (Dec. 6, 1941), **VIGOR.**
2 *Warren Fish Co., Pensacola :* **CONQUEROR** (Aug. 20, 1941), **CONQUEST** (1941).
2 *Warren Boat Yard, R.I.:* **HEROIC, IDEAL** (Sept. 20, 1941).
6 *F. L. Fulton :* **INDUSTRY, LIBERATOR, LOYAL, MEMORABLE, MERIT, OBSERVER.**
3 *Noank Shipyard, Inc.:* **PLUCK** (April 4, 1942), **POSITIVE, POWER.**
6 *Anderson & Cristofani :* **PRESTIGE, PROGRESS, RADIANT, RELIABLE** (Nov. 1, 1941), **ROCKET, ROYAL.**
2 *Harry G. Marr :* **SECURITY, SKIPPER** (Jan. 16, 1942).

All ordered January and April, 1941, under 1940 Programme. Wood. Length : 97½ feet. Machinery : Diesel. Further particulars wanted. Numbered AMc 36-55, 61-110.

Note.—16 Coastal Minesweepers of a new 105 feet motor type, resembling Canadian motor minesweepers, were ordered Dec. 11, 1941.

70   Accentor Class

INDUSTRY.   1942, *U.S. Navy Official.*

8 *W. A. Robinson :* **ACCENTOR, BATELEUR, BARBET, BRAMBLING** (all 1941), **ENERGY, EXULTANT, FEARLESS, FORTITUDE** (all 1942).
5 *Bristol Yacht Bldg. Co.:* **CARACARA** (May, 1941), **CHACALACA** (June, 1941), **ASSERTIVE, AVENGE, BOLD** (Feb. 14, 1942).
8 *Gibbs Gas Engine Co.:* **CHIMANGO** (March 8, 1941), **COTINGA** (March 25, 1941), **COURLAN** (April 4, 1941), **DEVELIN** (April, 1941), **DEMAND** (May, 1941), **DETECTOR** (May, 1941), **DOMINANT** (June, 1941), **ENDURANCE** (June, 1941).
8 *Greenport Basin & Construction Co.:* **ACME** (May, 1941), **ADAMANT** (June, 1941), **ADVANCE, AGGRESSOR** (July, 1941), **FULMAR** (Feb. 25, 1941), **JACAMAR** (March 10, 1941), **LIMPKIN** (April 5, 1941), **LORIKEET** (April, 1941).
2 *Hodgdon Bros., Goudy & Stevens :* **BULWARK, COMBAT** (both 1941).
2 *Camden S.B. Co.:* **GOVERNOR** (July, 1941), **GUIDE** (Sept. 20, 1941).
2 *Delaware Bay S.B. Co.:* **PARAMOUNT, PEERLESS** (Sept. 6, 1941).
4 *Herreshoff Mfg. Co.:* **MARABOUT** (Feb., 1941), **OSTRICH** (March 29, 1941), **COURIER** (May, 1941), **DEFIANCE** (June, 1941).

38 (or more) Pipit Class (*ex-Seiners*).

PHOEBE.   1943, *courtesy Western Boat Building Co.*

PIPIT (ex-*Spartan*), **MAGPIE** (ex-*City of San Pedro*), **PLOVER** (ex-*Sea Rover*), **KESTREL** (ex-*Chanco*), **HEATH HEN** (ex-*Noreen*), **BUNTING** (ex-*Vagabond*), **COCKATOO** (ex-*Vashon*), **CROSSBILL** (ex-*North Star*), **LONGSPUR** (ex-*New Ambassador*), **SANDERLING** (ex-*New Conte di Savoia*), **GROUSE** (ex-*New Bol*), **HORNBILL** (ex-*J. A. Martinolich*), **CONDOR** (ex-*New Example*), **WAXBILL** (ex-*L. J. Fulton*), **CHATTERER** (ex-*Sea Breeze*), **PINTAIL** (ex-*Three Star*), **GROSBEAK** (ex-*Del Rio*), **CROW** (ex-*Jadran*), **KILDEER** (ex-*Vindicator*), **FLAMINGO** (ex-*H. N. Eldridge*), **BLUEJAY** (ex-*Charles S. Ashley*), **EGRET** (ex-*Julia Eleanor*), **CANARY** (ex-*John G. Murley*), **HUMMING BIRD** (ex-*Whaling City*), **FRIGATE BIRD** (ex-*Star of San Pedro*), **MOCKING BIRD** (ex-*Rio Douro*), **PUFFIN** (ex-*Mary Jane*), **REED BIRD** (ex-*Fearless*), **COURSER** (ex-*Nancy Rose*), **FIRECREST** (ex-*S. C. Giuseppe*), **PARRAKEET** (ex-*Jackie Sue*), **ROAD RUNNER** (ex-*Treasure Island*), **KINGBIRD** (ex-*Governor Saltonstall*), **PHOEBE** (ex-*Western Robin*), **RHEA** (ex-*No. 250*), **RUFF** (ex-*No. 251*), **AGILE** (ex-*No. 3*), **AFFRAY** (ex-*No. 36*).

All acquired 1940-41 for conversion into Coastal Minesweepers. Range from 86 to 170 tons *gross*. Machinery : Diesel. B.H.P. 150 to 400. Further particulars wanted. Numbered AMc 1-17, 19-35, 56-59, 111, 112. War loss : *Nightingale.*

21 Owl Class

1920.

OWL, ROBIN, CORMORANT (all built by Todd S.B. Co., Tebo Yacht Basin, Brooklyn, N.Y.). **ORIOLE, GREBE, PEACOCK** (all by Staten Id. S.B. Co., N.Y.). **BOBOLINK, LARK** (all by Baltimore D.D. & S.B. Co.). **SEAGULL, TERN** (both by Gas Engine & Power Co., Morris Heights, N.Y.). **TURKEY, WOODCOCK, PARTRIDGE** (all by Chester S.B. Co.). **WARBLER, VIREO, WILLET** (all by Philadelphia Navy Yard). **WHIPPOORWILL** (Alabama S.B. & D.D. Co., Mobile). **BRANT** (Sun S.B. Co., Chester). **KINGFISHER, RAIL** (both by Puget Sound Navy Yard). **EIDER** (Pusey & Jones, Wilmington). Numbered AM 2—54.
All built 1918-19. Displacement : 840 tons. Dimensions : 187¾ (*o.a.*) × 35½ × 8¾ to 10½ feet (*mean draught*). Guns : **2**—3 inch AA. Machinery : 1 set triple expansion. Designed I.H.P. : 1,400 = 14 kts. Boilers : 2 Babcock & Wilcox. Oil fuel : 275 tons. Complement : 72 to 90 (according to employment of ship). War losses : *Bittern, Finch, Penguin, Pigeon, Quail, Tanager.*

Auxiliary Minelayers.

ACM 11 (ex-MP 12, Brig. Gen. Royal T. Frank)
ACM 12 (ex-MP 10, Major Gen. Erasmus Weaver)   ACM 13 (ex-MP 14, Col. Horace F. Spurgeon)

Notes.—On 23 Nov., 1949, functions of controlled minelaying were transferred from the army to the Navy, senior planters (MP) and junior planters (JMP) being reclassified.

Minesweepers (AM).

63 "Auk" Class

RANDOLPH.   1948, Mr. W. H. Davis.

RANDOLPH.

Note.—The disposition of Randolph and other Army mineplanters not transferred to Navy is not known at present.

1 Norfolk Navy Yard	14 General Engineering & D.D. Co.	2 John H. Mathis Co.	
AM	**AM**	**AM**	
57 AUK (Aug. 26, 1941)	340 ARDENT (June 22, 1943)	120 SWAY (Sept. 29, 1942)	
	314 CHAMPION (Dec. 12, 1942)	122 SWIFT (Dec. 5, 1942)	
14 American S.B. Co.	315 CHIEF (Jan. 5, 1943)		
112 SEER (May 23, 1942)	316 COMPETENT (Jan. 9, 1943)	3 Pennsylvania Shipyard	
116 SPEED (April 18, 1942)	317 DEFENSE (Feb. 18, 1943)	104 PILOT (July 5, 1942)	
384 SPRIG (Sept. 15, 1944)	318 DEVASTATOR (April 19, 1943)	105 PIONEER (July 26, 1942)	
114 STAFF (June 17, 1942)	319 GLADIATOR (May 7, 1943)	106 PREVAIL (Sept. 13, 1942)	
118 STEADY (June 6, 1942)	100 HEED (June 19, 1942)		
117 STRIVE (May 16, 1942)	101 HERALD (July 4, 1942)	9 Savannah Machine & Foundry Co.	
383 SURFBIRD (Aug. 31, 1944)	320 IMPECCABLE (May 21, 1943)	372 MURRELET (Dec. 29, 1944)	
119 SUSTAIN (June 23, 1942)	102 MOTIVE (Aug. 17, 1942)	373 PEREGRINE (Feb. 17, 1945)	
385 TANAGER (Dec. 9, 1944)	103 ORACLE (Sept. 30, 1942)	374 PIGEON (March 28, 1945)	
386 TERCEL (Dec. 16, 1944)	62 SHELDRAKE (Feb. 12, 1942)	375 POCHARD (June 11, 1944)	
387 TOUCAN (Sept. 15, 1944)	64 STARLING (April 11, 1942)	376 PTARMIGAN (July 15, 1944)	
388 TOWHEE (Jan. 9, 1945)		377 QUAIL (Aug. 20, 1944)	
389 WAXWING (March 10, 1945)	9 Gulf S.B. Corpn.	378 REDSTART (Oct. 18, 1944)	
390 WHEATEAR (April 21, 1945)	341 DEXTROUS (Jan. 17, 1943)	123 SYMBOL (July 2, 1942)	
	379 ROSELLE (Aug. 29, 1945)	124 THREAT (Aug. 15, 1942)	
3 Associated Shipbuilders	380 RUDDY (Oct. 29, 1944)		
322 SPEAR (Feb. 25, 1943)	381 SCOTER (Sept. 26, 1945)	4 Winslow Marine Ry. & S.B. Co.	
323 TRIUMPH (Feb. 25, 1943)	382 SHOVELER (Dec. 10, 1945)	108 PURSUIT (June 12, 1942)	
324 VIGILANCE (April 5, 1943)	126 TOKEN (March 28, 1942)	109 REQUISITE (July 25, 1942)	
	127 TUMULT (April 19, 1942)	110 REVENGE (ex-Right, Nov. 7, 1942)	
4 Defoe S.B. co.	128 VELOCITY (April 19, 1942)	111 SAGE (Nov. 21, 1942)	
58 BROADBILL (May 21, 1942)	131 ZEAL (Sept. 15, 1942)		
59 CHICKADEE (July 20, 1942)			
60 NUTHATCH (Sept. 16, 1942)			
61 PHEASANT (Oct. 24, 1942)			

Displacement:	890 tons (1,250 tons full load)
Dimensions:	215 (w.l.), 221½ (o.a.) × 32¼ × 11 (max.) feet
Guns:	1—3 inch d.p., 2 or 4—40 mm. AA.
Machinery:	Diesel, with electric drive. 2 shafts. B.H.P.: 2,976–3,532 = 18 kts.
Complement:	105 (war)

General Notes.—Following 28 units of above type, transferred to Royal Navy in 1943–44 under Lend-Lease scheme, have been returned or acquired by Allied navies: H.M.S. Antares, Arcturus, Aries, Catherine, Chamois, Chance, Clinton, Combatant, Cynthia, Elfreda, Fairy, Florizel, Foam, Frolic, Friendship, Gazelle, Gorgon, Gozo, Grecian, Jasper, Lightfoot, Persian, Pique (ex-Celerity), Postillion, Steadfast, Strenuous (ex-Vital), Tattoo, Tourmaline (ex-Usage). War losses: Minivet, Portent, Sentinel, Skill, Skylark, Swallow, Swerve, Tide.

Experimental Notes.—In Peregrine the new ship stabilisation system, which has been under study by naval architects and engineers for some time, has been temporarily installed. It comprises two high box-like tanks projecting from each side of the hull amidships and containing electronic controllers and electrically powered impellers or large variable pitch propellers. Water is pumped automatically from one tank to another to counteract the ship's motion. The arrangement is attached outside the hull to minimise structural changes. The stabilisation system is designed to reduce the ship's roll by 80 per cent.

Motor Mine Planters.

YMP I (ex-JMP 70)
YMP 2 (ex-Sgt. Truman O. Olson)

Notes.—These two vessels are ex-Army Junior Mine Planters. Now in Navy List and rated as service craft.

L I   L 2   L 3   L 4

Note.—Small Motor Mine Planters attached to ACM 12.

L 74

Destroyer Minesweepers (DMS). Ex-Destroyers.

13 " Fitch " Class.

DMS	DMS	DMS
33 CARMICK (ex-DD 493)	35 ENDICOTT (ex-DD 435)	36 McCOOK (ex-DD 496)
39 COWIE (ex-DD 632)	25 FITCH (ex-DD 452)	31 MERVINE (ex-DD 489)
37 DAVISON (ex-DD 618)	30 GHERARDI (ex-DD 637)	32 QUICK (ex-DD 490)
41 DORAN (ex-DD 634)	40 KNIGHT (ex-DD 633)	38 THOMPSON (ex-DD 627)
42 EARLE (ex-DD 635)		

Displacement :	1,630 tons (2,575 tons full load)
Dimensions :	341 (w.l.), 348½ (o.a.) × 36 × 10 (mean) 18 (max.) feet
Guns :	3—5 inch, 38 cal., 4—40 mm. AA., 4 to 5—20 mm. AA.
Machinery :	Geared turbines. 2 shafts. S.H.P. : 50,000 = 37 kts.
Boilers :	4 Babcock & Wilcox
Complement :	250

Notes.—Modified Destroyers of " Gleaves " class. DMS 37 built by Federal S.B. & D.D. Co., DMS 25, 39-42 by Boston Navy Yard, DMS 31-33, 35, 36, 38 by Seattle-Tacoma S.B. Corpn. Formerly known as High Speed Minesweepers (DMS). Reclassified as Destroyer Minesweepers (DMS) in Feb. 1955. Butler, Forrest and Harding scrapped. Hobson, DMS 26, sank in mid-Atlantic, 27 April, 1952, after collision with the aircraft carrier Wasp during a night exercise. Ellyson, DMS 19, and Macomb, DMS 23, were reclassified as destroyers DD 454 and DD 458, respectively, in May 1954, and Doyle, Hambleton, Jeffers and Rodman were reclassified as destroyers DD 494, DD 455, DD 621 and DD 456, respectively, on 15 Jan. 1955 (see " Gleaves " class, preceding page). All the remainder of this class are also to revert to destroyers, with their original DD numbers, later in 1955. Second World War loss : Emmons.

Name	Laid down	Launched	Completed	Name	Laid down	Launched	Completed
Carmick	29 May 1941	8 Mar. 1942	28 Dec. 1942	Gerhardi	16 Sep 1941	12 Feb. 1942	15 Sep. 1942
Cowie	18 Mar. 1941	27 Sep. 1941	1 June 1942	Knight	18 Mar. 1941	27 Sep. 1941	23 June 1942
Davison	26 Feb. 1942	19 July 1942	11 Sep. 1942	McCook	1 May 1941	3 May 1942	15 Mar. 1943
Doran	14 June 1941	10 Dec. 1941	4 Aug. 1942	Mervine	3 Nov. 1941	3 May 1942	16 June 1942
Earle	14 June 1941	10 Dec. 1941	1 Sep. 1942	Quick	3 Nov. 1941	3 May 1942	2 July 1942
Endicott	1 May 1941	5 Apr. 1942	25 Feb. 1943	Thompson	22 Sep. 1941	10 Aug. 1942	10 July 1943
Fitch	6 Jan. 1941	14 June 1941	3 Feb. 1942				

AUK type.   Added 1946, U.S. Navy, Official.

FITCH.   1952, Harvey Gilston, Esq.

RODMAN.   1951, U.S. Navy, Official.

WAXWING   Added 1957, Ted Stone

59 "Admirable" Class (AM)

1944, U.S. Navy, Official.
(Appearance varies according to builder; some have a funnel.)

JUBILANT. Funnel type

1955, U.S. Navy, Official

5 American S.B. Co.

AM
223 DOUR (March 25, 1944)
224 EAGER (June 10, 1944)
255 JUBILANT (Feb. 20, 1943)
256 KNAVE (March 13, 1943)
261 MAINSTAY (July 31, 1943)

9 Associated Shipbuilders

304 SCURRY (ex-Skurry, Oct. 11, 1943)
302 SIGNET (Aug. 16, 1943)
303 SKIRMISH (Aug. 16, 1943)
306 SPECTER (Feb. 15, 1944)
307 STAUNCH (Feb. 15, 1944)
308 STRATEGY (March 28, 1944)
309 STRENGTH (March 28, 1944)
310 SUCCESS (May 11, 1944)
311 SUPERIOR (May 11, 1944)

5 General Engineering & D.D. Co.

283 RANSOM (Sept. 18, 1943)
284 REBEL (Oct. 28, 1943)
285 RECRUIT (Dec. 11, 1943)
288 REIGN (May 29, 1944)
289 REPORT (Aug. 8, 1944)

4 Gulf S.B. Corpn.

269 OPPONENT (June 12, 1943)
275 PIRATE (Dec. 16, 1943)
277 PLEDGE (Dec. 23, 1943)
280 PROWESS (Feb. 17, 1944)

2 Puget Sound Bridge Co.

232 EXECUTE (June 22, 1944)
233 FACILITY (June 22, 1944)

4 Savannah Machine & Foundry Co.

249 INCREDIBLE (Nov. 21, 1943)
252 INSTILL (March 5, 1944)
253 INTRIGUE (April 8, 1944)
254 INVADE (Feb. 6, 1944)

6 Tampa S.B. Co.

AM
214 CRAG (ex-Craig, March 21, 1943)
215 CRUISE (March 21, 1943)
218 DENSITY (Feb. 6, 1944)
219 DESIGN (Feb. 6, 1944)
220 DEVICE (May 21, 1944)
221 DIPLOMA (May 21, 1944)

13 Willamette Iron & Steel Corpn.

159 CHANGE (Dec. 15, 1942)
160 CLAMOUR (Dec. 24, 1942)
161 CLIMAX (Jan. 9, 1943)
162 COMPEL (Jan. 16, 1943)
163 CONCISE (Feb. 6, 1943)
164 CONTROL (Jan. 28, 1943)
165 COUNSEL (Feb. 17, 1943)
356 CREDDOCK (July 22, 1944)
357 DIPPER (July 26, 1944)
362 GADWALL (July 15, 1943)
364 GRAYLAG (Dec. 4, 1943)
365 HARLEQUIN (June 3, 1944)
366 HARRIER (June 7, 1944)

11 Winslow Marine Rly. & S.B. Co.

238 GARLAND (Feb. 20, 1944)
239 GAYETY (March 19, 1944)
240 HAZARD (May 21, 1944)
241 HILARITY (July 30, 1944)
242 INAUGURAL (Oct. 1, 1944)
296 SCOUT (May 2, 1943)
297 SCRIMMAGE (May 16, 1943)
298 SCUFFLE (Aug. 8, 1943)
299 SENTRY (Aug. 15, 1943)
300 SERENE (Oct. 31, 1943)
301 SHELTER (Nov. 14, 1943)

Displacement: 650 tons (945 tons full load)
Dimensions: 180 (w.l.), 184½ (o.a.) × 33 × 10 (max.) feet
Guns: 1—3 inch d.p., 4—40 mm. AA.
Machinery: Diesel. 2 shafts. B.H.P.: 1,710   15 kts.
Complement: 104

Notes.—Crag and Cruise, completed by Charleston Navy Yard, are armed only with 2—40 mm. AA. War loss: Salute. Various others cancelled or sold. Transferred to Soviet Navy: Advocate, Agent, Alarm, Alchemy, Apex, Arcade, Arch, Armada, Aspire, Assail; and to Chinese Navy: Lance, Logic, Lucid, Magnet.

VITAL (see previous page)

United States Navy, Official

Minesweepers (AMS).

56 "Albatross" Class.

AMS
1 ALBATROSS (ex-YMS 80)
41 BARBET (ex-YMS 45)
2 BOBOLINK (ex-YMS 164)
42 BRAMBLING (ex-YMS 109)
43 BRANT (ex-YMS 113,
          Feb. 13, 1942)
3 BUNTING (ex-YMS 170)
4 CARDINAL (ex-YMS 179)
40 CHATTERER (ex-YMS 415)
5 CONDOR (ex-YMS 192)
44 COURLAN (ex-YMS 114)
6 COURSER (ex-YMS 201)
45 CROSSBILL (ex-YMS 120,
          April 4, 1942)
7 CROW (ex-YMS 215)
8 CURLEW (ex-YMS 218)
46 EGRET (ex-YMS 136)
10 FIRECREST (ex-YMS 231)
11 FLAMINGO (ex-YMS 238)
9 FLICKER (ex-YMS 219)
47 FULMAR (ex-YMS 193,
          Jan. 2, 1943)
12 GOLDFINCH (ex-YMS 306)
13 GRACKLE (ex-YMS 312)
14 GROSSBEAK (ex-YMS 317)
15 GROUSE (ex-YMS 321)
16 GULL (ex-YMS 324)
17 HAWK (ex-YMS 362,
          May 22, 1943)
18 HERON (ex-YMS 369)
19 HORNBILL (ex-YMS 371)

AMS
20 HUMMER (ex-YMS 372)
21 JACKDAW (ex-YMS 373)
22 KITE (ex-YMS 374)
48 LAPWING (ex-YMS 268)
23 LARK (ex-YMS 376)
24 LINNET (ex-YMS 395)
49 LORIKEET (ex-YMS 271)
26 MERGANSER (ex-YMS 417)
27 MOCKINGBIRD (ex-YMS 419)
50 NIGHTINGALE (ex-YMS 290,
          Feb. 27, 1942)
28 OSPREY (ex-YMS 422)
29 OSTRICH (ex-YMS 430)
31 PARTRIDGE (ex-YMS 437)
32 PELICAN (ex-YMS 441)
33 PLOVER (ex-YMS 442)
34 REDHEAD (ex-YMS 443)
57 REDPOLE (ex-YMS 294)
51 REEDBIRD (ex-YMS 291)
52 RHEA (ex-YMS 299)
53 ROBIN (ex-YMS 311)
54 RUFF (ex-YMS 327, Dec. 5, 1942)
35 SANDERLING (ex-YMS 446)
55 SEAGULL (ex-YMS 402)
58 SISKIN (ex-YMS 425)
36 SWALLOW (ex-YMS 461)
37 SWAN (ex-YMS 470)
56 TURKEY (ex-YMS 444)
38 VERDIN (ex-YMS 471)
39 WAXBILL (ex-YMS 479)

Displacement: 270 to (350 tons full load)
Dimensions: 136 × 24½ × 8 (max.) feet
Guns: 1—3 inch, 2—20 mm. AA., 2 D.C.T.
Machinery: 2 G.M. Diesel. B.H.P.: 1,000 = 15 kts.
Fuel: 16 tons
Complement: 50

Notes.—Wood. Various units of this type will be found in other navies. Parrakeet (AMS 30) is reported to have been stricken from the list.

BRAMBLING (two funnelled type)

1955, U.S. Navy, Official

Special Note.

Magpie (AMS 25) of this class struck a floating mine and sank off the Korean east coast on Oct. 1, 1950.

CURLEW (one funnelled type)

1952, U.S. Navy, Official

Fleet Minesweepers (Non-magnetic) (MSO).

65 "Agile" Class.

DIRECT.

1955, U.S. Navy, Official.

MSO		MSO		MSO	
421	AGILE	443	FIDELITY (21 Aug. 1953)	470	SALUTE (14 Aug. 1954)
422	AGGRESSIVE (4 Oct. 1952)	444	FIRM (15 Apr. 1953)	471	SKILL
423	AVENGE (15 Mar. 1953)	445	FORCE (26 June 1953)	472	VALOR (13 May 1953)
424	BOLD (28 Mar. 1953)	446	FORTIFY (14 Feb. 1953)	473	VIGOR (24 June 1953)
425	BULWARK (28 Mar. 1953)	447	GUIDE (17 Apr. 1954)	474	VITAL (12 Oct. 1953)
426	CONFLICT (16 Dec. 1952)	448	ILLUSIVE (12 July 1952)	488	CONQUEST (20 May 1954)
427	CONSTANT (14 Feb. 1952)	449	IMPERVIOUS (29 Aug. 1952)	489	GALLANT (4 June 1954)
428	DASH (20 Sep. 1952)	455	IMPLICIT (1 Aug. 1953)	490	LEADER (15 Sep. 1954)
429	DETECTOR (5 Dec. 1952)	456	INFLICT (16 Oct. 1953)	491	PERSISTANT
430	DIRECT (27 May 1953)	457	LOYALTY (22 Nov. 1953)	492	PLEDGE
431	DOMINANT (5 Nov. 1953)	458	LUCID (14 Nov. 1953)	493	STALWART
432	DYNAMIC (17 Dec. 1952)	459	NIMBLE (16 Aug. 1954)	494	STURDY
433	ENGAGE (ex-Elusive. 18 June 1953)	460	NOTABLE (15 Oct. 1954)	495	SWERVE
434	EMBATTLE (27 Aug. 1953)	461	OBSERVE (19 Oct. 1954)	496	VENTURE
435	ENDURANCE (9 Aug. 1952)	462	PINNACLE (3 Jan. 1955)	508	
436	ENERGY (13 Feb. 1953)	463	PIVOT (9 Jan. 1954)	409	
437	ENHANCE (11 Oct. 1952)	464	PLUCK (6 Feb. 1954)	510	
438	ESTEEM (20 Dec. 1952)	465	PRESTIGE (30 Apr. 1954)	511	
439	EXCEL (25 Sep. 1953)	466	PRIME (27 May 1954)	519	
440	E. PLOIT (10 Apr. 1953)	467	REAPER (25 June 1954)	52u	
441	EXULTANT (6 June 1953)	468	RIVAL (15 Aug. 1953)	521	
442	FEARLESS (17 June 1953)	469	SAGACITY (20 Feb. 1954)		

Displacement : 665 tons light (750 tons full load)
Dimensions : 165 (w.l.), 171 (o.a.) × 35 × 9½ (11 (max.) feet
Guns : 1—40 mm.
Machinery : 4 Packard diesels. 2 shafts. Controllable pitch propellers. Speed 15·5 kts.
Complement : 72 to 74

Notes.—Wooden hulls and non-magnetic equipment. Range of 2,400 miles at 12 kts. Diesels of non-magnetic stainless steel alloy ; controllable pitch propellers. Aggressive, AM 422, built by Luders Marine Const. Co., Stamford, Conn. $3,500,000, laid down 25 May 1951, commissioned 25 Nov. 1953. Illusive, AM 448, built by Martinlock S.B. Co., San Diego, commissioned 14 Nov. 1953, Bold, AM 424, Bulwark, AM 425, built by Norfolk Navy Shipyard, remainder by private yards. Nos. 450-454, 475-487, 498-507, 512-518 built for foreign countries under MDAP. No U.S. names allocated. 8 to France, 6 to Netherlands, 4 to Portugal. Further new construction for U.S. Navy provides for four 165 foot AMS under 1954 fiscal programme. Three more 165 foot AMS requested in 1955 fiscal appropriations. All above vessels, formerly known as Wooden Minesweepers (AM), were reclassified as Minesweepers, Ocean (Non-magnetic) (MSO) in Feb. 1955. Launch dates above. Following laid down : Agile 22 Feb. 1954, Skill 17 Aug. 1953, Persistent 17 June 1954, Pledge 24 June 1954, Stalwart 22 June 1954, Sturdy 15 Oct. 1954, Swerve 20 Dec. 1954, Venture 11 Jan. 1955. MDAP Nos. 506 and 507 launched 13 Nov. 1954, 19 Feb. 1955, respectively.

Coastal Minesweepers (Non-magnetic) (MSC).

22 "Bluebird" Class.

BLUEBIRD.

1955, U.S. Navy, Official.

MSC		MSC		MSC	
121	BLUEBIRD	195	LIMPKIN	202	SPOONBILL
122	CORMORANT	196	MEADOWLARK	203	THRASHER
190	FALCON	197	PARROT	204	THRUSH
191	FRIGATE BIRD	198	PEACOCK	205	VIREO
192	HUMMING BIRD	199	PHOEBE	206	WARBLER
193	JACANA	200	REDWING	207	WHIPPOORWILL
194	KINGBIRD	201	SHRIKE	208	WIDGEON
				209	WOODPECKER

Displacement : 335 tons light (375 tons full load)
Dimensions : 138 (pp.), 144 (o.a.) × 27 × 8½ feet
Guns : 2—20 mm.
Machinery : General Motors diesels. 2 shafts. B.H.P. : 880 = 14 kts.
Complement : 39

Notes.—Coastal motor minesweepers of wooden construction. Bluebird and Cormorant (commissioned 14 Aug. 1953) built by Mare Island Naval Shipyard, 310 tons light, Packard engines, B.H.P. : 1,200. New type of vessels constructed throughout of materials with the lowest possible magnetic attraction to attain the greatest possible safety factor when sweeping for magnetic mines. Only named vessels AMS 121, 122, 190-209 will be commissioned into U.S. Navy. Remainder 60-120, 123-154, 167-171, 218-221, 255-267 built for NATO to foreign countries under MDAP.

17 to Italy : AMS 72-76, 79-82, 88 90, 133-137. 15 to Belgium : AMS 63-65, 77, 78, 101, 103, 104, 151-154, 169-171. 2 to Denmark : AMS 127, 128. 30 to France : AMS 66-71, 83-87, 93, 94, 96-99, 113-120, 123-126, 141-142. 14 to Netherlands : AMS 100, 105-112, 148-150, 167, 168. 1 to Norway : AMS 102. 8 to Portugal : AMS 60 (ex U.S.S. Adjutant), 61, 62, 91, 92, 145-147. 3 to Spain : AMS 130, 139, 143. 2 to Japan : AMS 95, 144. 1 to Pakistan : AMS 138. 2 to NGRC : AMS 123, 140.

AMS 155 to 166 were reserved for German built vessels but order and numbers were cancelled.

All the above vessels, formerly known as Auxiliary Motor Minesweepers (AMS), were reclassified as Minesweepers, Coastal (MSC). in Feb. 1955.

VITAL

Added 1960, Wright & Logan

ALBATROSS

1962, United States Navy, Official

PINNACLE

1960, Skyfotos

CORMORANT

Added 1958. U.S. Navy, Official

COASTAL MINEHUNTERS (MHC)

1 "Bittern" Class

MHC
43 BITTERN

Displacement:	300 tons *standard* (360 tons *full load*)
Dimensions:	138 (pp.), 144½ (o.a.) × 28 × 8 feet
Guns:	1—40 mm. AA.
Machinery:	Diesels. 2 shafts. B.H.P.: 1,200 = 14 kts.
Complement:	44 (4 officers, 40 men)

Notes

One prototype Mine Hunter (MHC) of wooden construction was built by Consolidated Shipbuilding Corporation, New York City, cost $1,782,107, under the 1954 Fiscal program. Designed to locate mines and other underwater obstacles, rather than to sweep them. To accomplish this she was equipped with various types of electronic instruments in place of minesweeping gear found in coastal minesweepers. To be mass produced in the event of mobilisation. Three more were to have been built under the 1955 Naval Appropriations, but were not started. Built of non-magnetic materials, with bronze, aluminium and stainless steel fittings. *Bittern* was laid down on 18 Aug. 1955, launched on 4 Mar. 1957 and commissioned on 26 Aug. 1957.

BITTERN

1959, *United States Navy, Official*

COASTAL MINEHUNTERS (MHC) Former Coastal Minesweepers

8 Converted Underwater Locator Type YMS Class

MHC
14 MINAH (ex-*AMC* 204, ex-*PCS* 1465)

Displacement:	267 tons *standard* (350 tons *full load*)
Dimensions:	130 (w.l.), 136 (o.a.) × 23⅓ × 8½ (*max.*) feet
Guns:	1—3 inch d.p., 1—40 mm. AA.
Machinery:	G.M. diesel. 2 shafts. B.H.P.: 1,000 = 14 kts.
Complement:	47

General Notes

Formerly a patrol vessel (submarine chaser) of the PCS type. Built by Astoria Marine Construction Co. Launched on 27 Dec. 1943. Similar to AMS (ex-*YMS*) 35 type in appearance. Reclassified *AMCU* 14 in 1952.

MHC
12 HARKNESS (ex-*AGSC* 12, ex-*YMS* 242)
13 JAMES M. GILLIS (ex-*AGSC* 13, ex-*YMS* 262)

Displacement:	270 tons *standard* (350 tons *full load*)
Dimensions:	136 (o.a.) × 24½ × 8 (*max.*) feet
Guns:	1—3 inch
Machinery:	G.M. diesels. 2 shafts. B.H.P.: 1,000 = 15 kts.
Complement:	34

General Notes

Originally coastal motor minesweepers of the YMS type. Reclassified as AMCU in 1952. Formerly classed as Coastal Surveying Vessels (ASGC). Built by Tacoma B.B. and South Coast Co. in 1942-43. All three of the above vessels have the same basic hull design. *Simon Newcomb* was driven aground in Aug. 1949 and scrapped on 31 Jan. 1950. *John Blish* and *Littlehales* were also scrapped.

YMS Type

U.S. Navy, Official

MHC
44 BOBOLINK (ex-*AMS* 2, ex-*YMS* 164)
45 BUNTING (ex-*AMS* 3, ex-*YMS* 170)
48 REDHEAD (ex-*AMS* 34, ex-*YMS* 443)
49 SANDERLING (ex-*AMS* 35, ex-*YMS* 446)
50 WAXBILL (ex-*AMS* 39, ex-*YMS* 479)

Displacement:	270 tons *standard* (350 tons *full load*)
Dimensions:	136 (o.a.) × 24½ × 8 (*max.*) feet
Guns:	1—3 inch
Machinery:	G.M. diesels. 2 shafts. B.H.P.: 1,000 = 15 kts.
Complement:	34

General Notes

Former vessels of "Albatross" class of coastal minesweepers MSC(O), ex-*AMS*, ex-*YMS* (see previous page), converted to coastal minehunters in Aug. 1954 to Mar. 1955.

Recent Disposals

Sister ships *Gull*, MHC 46 (ex-*AMS* 16, ex-*YMS* 324) and *Merganser*, MHC 47 (ex-*AMS* 26, ex-*YMS* 417) were stricken from the Navy List in 1959.

Reclassification Notes

All the above seven vessels, formerly known as Minehunters (AMCU), were reclassified as MHC on 7 Feb. 1955.

COASTAL MINEHUNTERS (MHC) Former Large Infantry Landing Ships

21 Converted Underwater Locator Type LSIL Class

MHC
11 BLACKBIRD (ex-*LCI* (L) 515)

Displacement:	260 tons (393 tons *full load*)
Dimensions:	153 (w.l.), 157 (o.a.) × 23⅓ × 5⅝ (*max.*) feet
Guns:	2—20 mm. AA.
Machinery:	G.M. diesels. 2 shafts. B.H.P.: 1,800 = 14 kts.
Complement:	34

General Notes

Built in 1943-44. Formerly landing craft infantry large. Same type as ships below, but converted earlier. Named *Blackbird* in Jan. 1955.

Disposal Notes

AMC(U) 10 was stricken from the Navy List in 1951.

MHC
16 AVOCET (ex-*LSIL* 653)
17 BLUE JAY (ex-*LSIL* 654)
18 CHAFFINCH (ex-*LSIL* 694)
19 CHEWINK (ex-*LSIL* 701)
20 CHIMANGO (ex-*LSIL* 703)
21 COCKATOO (ex-*LSIL* 709)
22 COTINGA (ex-*LSIL* 776)
24 GOLDCREST (ex-*LSIL* 869)
25 JACAMAR (ex-*LSIL* 870)
26 KESTREL (ex-*LSIL* 874)
28 LONGSPUR (ex-*LSIL* 884)
29 MAGPIE (ex-*LSIL* 944)
30 MALLARD (ex-*LSIL* 963)
33 ORIOLE (ex-*LSIL* 973)
34 ORTOLAN (ex-*LSIL* 976)
37 RAIL (ex-*LSIL* 1022)
38 SANDPIPER (ex-*LSIL* 1008)
39 SENTINEL (ex-*LSIL* 1052)
41 SKIMMER (ex-*LSIL* 1093)
42 SPARROW (ex-*LSIL* 1098)

Displacement:	260 tons *light* (387 tons *full load*)
Dimensions:	153 (w.l.), 159 (o.a.) × 23⅓ × 5⅝ feet
Machinery:	G.M. diesels. 2 shafts. B.H.P. 1,800 = 14 kts.
Complement:	34

General Notes

Former LSIL (Landing Ships Infantry Large). Converted into underwater locator minesweepers and reclassified as AMCU in 1952. Latterly known as Minehunters.

Disposal Notes

Sister ship *Owl*, MHC 35, was stricken from the Navy List in 1958.

On 1 July 1954 names and classification of AMCU were withdrawn from *Accentor* (AMCU 15), restored to designation and number *Dunlin* (AMCU 23) to LSIL 777, *Kildeer* (AMCU 27) to LSIL 883, *Medrick* (AMCU 31) to LSIL 966, *Minivet* (AMCU 32) to LSIL 969, *Partridge* (AMCU 36) to LSIL 1001 and *Shearwater* (AMCU 40) to LSIL 1053. Conversion to minehunters was cancelled, and they are now disposed of.

3 "Ability" Class

MSO	Launched	MSO	Launched
519 ABILITY	29 Dec. 1956	**520 ALACRITY**	8 June 1957
		521 ASSURANCE	31 Aug. 1957

Displacement:	801 tons *light* (963 tons *full load*)
Dimensions:	189 × 36 × 11 feet
Guns:	1—40 mm. A.
Machinery:	2 General Motors diesels. 2 shafts. Controllable pitch propellers. B.H.P.: 2,700＝15 kts.
Complement:	82 (7 officers, 75 men)

General

Non-magnetic, wooden hulled vessels built by Petersen Builders Inc., Sturgeon Bay, Wisc. Last of the Fiscal Year 1955 new construction program to be awarded. Designed to serve as mine division commander's flagships. Equipped to conduct all types of mine countermeasures operations. Laid down on 5 Mar. 1956, 3 May 1956, and 28 Jan. 1957, respectively. Launch dates above. *Assurance* commissioned on 21 Nov. 1958.

ABILITY   *United States Navy, Official*

ABILITY (MSO 519)   *A. & J. Pavia*

ALACRITY   *1964, A. & J. Pavia*

OCEAN MINESWEEPER (MSO): "ABILITY" CLASS

The two surviving minesweepers of this class, **Alacrity** (MSO 520) and **Assurance** (MSO 521), have been allocated to sonar test programmes and redesignated as auxiliary ships AG 520 and AG 521, respectively. See listing under Experimental, Research, and Surveying Ships. **Ability** (MSO 519) of this class stricken on 1 Feb. 1971.

4 OCEAN MINESWEEPERS (MSO): "ACME" CLASS

Name	No.	Launched	Commissioned
ACME	MSO 508	23 June 1955	27 Sep. 1956
***ADROIT**	MSO 509	20 Aug. 1955	4 Mar. 1957
ADVANCE	MSO 510	12 July 1957	16 June 1958
***AFFRAY**	MSO 511	18 Dec. 1956	8 Dec. 1958

Displacement, tons	720 light; 780 full load
Dimensions, feet	173 oa × 35 × 10
Guns	1—40 mm AA; 2—50 cal MG
Main engines	4 Packard diesels; 2 shafts; 2 800 bhp = 14 knots
Complement	70 peacetime; 68 wartime

This class is different from the "Agile" type but has similar basic particulars. All built by Frank L. Sample, Jnr, Inc, Boothbay Harbour, Maine. Plans to modernise these ships were cancelled (see notes under "Agile" class).

Two ships were decommissioned and placed in reserve late in 1970. *Adroit* and *Affray* are assigned to Naval Reserve training, manned partially by active and partially by reserve personnel (see notes under "Agile" class).

AFFRAY (MSO 511)   *1969, United States Navy*

AFFRAY   *1961, United States Navy, Official*

ADVANCE (MSO 510)   *1968, United States Navy*

2 Inshore Minesweepers (MSI): "Cove" Class

COVE MSI 1   **CAPE** MSI 2

Displacement, tons	120 light; 249 full load
Dimensions, feet	111·8 × 23 × 5·5 (10 max)
Main engines	2 GM diesels; 1 shaft; 650 bhp = 12 knots
Complement	21 (3 officers, 18 men)

Provided under the 1956 Naval Appropriations. Prototypes for inshore minesweeping. Cost $750 000 plus $350 000 for equipment. Both built ar Bethlehem Shipyards Co Bellingham, Washington. Laid down on 1 Feb 1957 and 1 May 1957, respectively, launched on 8 Feb 1958 and 5 Apr 1958 and placed in service on 20 Nov 1958 and 27 Feb 1959, respectively. Both active.

MAP TRANSFER PROGRAMME. MSI 3 to MSI 10 were built under off-shore procurement. MSI 13 and MSI 14 were transferred to Iran in 1964. MSI 15 to 19 were built in 1965-67 for transfer.

COVE (MSI 1)   *United States Navy*

44 Minesweeping Boats (MSB)

MSB	MSB	MSB	MSB	MSB	MSB	MSB	MSB
5	11	18	25	31	37	43	49
6	13	19	26	32	38	44	50
7	15	20	27	33	39	46	51
8	16	21	28	34	40	47	52
9	17	22	29	35	41	48	53
10			30	36	42		

Displacement, tons	30 light; 42 full load; except MSB 29, 81 full load
Dimensions, feet	57·2 × 15·5 × 4 (MSB 29, 82 × 19 × 5·5)
Guns	Several MG (Vietnam configuration)
Main engines	Diesel engines; 2 shafts; 600 bhp = 10 knots
Complement	6 to 8

Wooden hulls. Designed to be carried in parent ships to theatre of operations. All built in 1951 and 1952, except MSB 29, launched on 5 Oct 1956. MSB 49 was heavily damaged by gunfire on 15 Feb 1967 in South Vietnam and beached, but was later salvaged.

ENGINEERING. MSB 5 was the first vessel built for the US Navy with gas turbine engines (used to provide the power for the boat's generators), 48 MSBs were fitted with gas turbine generators. MSB 23, destroyed by fire on 2 Feb 1955 while under construction was rebuilt as a plastic hulled vessel and delivered in Aug 1956, but was later reclassified as "equipment". MSB 24 was never built.

CLASS. Class B. MSB 5-22, 25-28, 30-53; Class C: MSB 29 (see *Disposals*).

MSB 17   *1966, United States Navy*

Minesweeping Launches (MSL)

Displacement, pounds	18 500 hoisting; 23 100 full load
Dimensions, feet	36 oa × 11·6 × 3·7
Main engines	Gas turbine; 1 shaft; 200 shp = 12 knots or geared diesel; 1 shaft; 160 shp = 10 knots
Complement	4 to 6 enlisted men

Versatile minesweeping craft intended to sweep for acoustic, magnetic, and moored mines in inshore waters and in advance of landing craft. Twenty MSLs and two minesweeping helicopters are carried by each Mine Countermeasures Support Ship (MCS); MSLs are also carried by large amphibious ships operating in areas where MCS support is not available.

CONSTRUCTION: MSL 1-4 completed in 1946 (wood hull, gas turbine); MSL 5-29 completed in 1948 (wood hull, gas turbine); MSL 30 completed in 1948 (plastic hull, gas turbine); MSL 31-56 completed in 1966 (plastic hull, geared diesel); three wood hull boats converted to geared diesel in 1967.

MSL 11   *1967, United States Navy*

3 Converted Netlayer Type

MCS
5 MONITOR (ex-*AN* 1, 29 Jan. 1943)
3 OSAGE (ex-*AN* 3, 30 June 1943)
4 SAUGUS (ex-*AN* 4,4 Sep. 1943)

Displacement:	5,625 tons *standard* (9,040 tons *full load*)
Dimensions:	440 (w.l.), 451½ (o.a.) × 60¼ × 20 feet
Guns:	2 or 3—5 inch, 38 cal. d.p., 8—40 mm. AA.
Machinery:	Geared turbines. 2 shafts. S.H.P.: 11,000 = 20·3 kts.
Boilers:	4 Combustion Engineering type
Complement:	564

Notes

All built by Ingall's S.B. Corpn., Pascagoula, Miss. Launch dates above. Designed as Netlayers and Net Carriers (see photo below), but converted into Landing Ships (Vehicle),

LSV. Carry 40 LVTs and 800 troops. Out of commission, in reserve. Reclassified as Mine Warfare Command and Support Ships, MCS, in 1955. Again reclassified as Mine Countermeasures and Support Ships in 1958.

1 LST Type

MCS 6

Notes

The tank landing ship *Orleans Parish*, LST 1069, see later page, was reclassified MSC 6 on 19 Jan. 1959

16 Ocean Minesweepers (MSO)

MSO 523	MSO 527	MSO 531	MSO 535
MSO 524	MSO 528	MSO 532	MSO 536
MSO 525	MSO 529	MSO 533	MSO 537
MSO 526	MSO 530	MSO 534	MSO 538

Displacement, tons	1 000 full load
Length, feet	200 oa
Main engines	Diesel

This is a new class of ships combining the capabilities of Ocean Minesweepers (MSO) and Coastal Minehunters (MHC). Similar in design to the "Ability" class but larger. Four ships authorised in the Fiscal Year 1964 shipbuilding programme, five in FY 1967, and seven in FY 1968. Estimated cost per ship is $8 700 000.

2 Mine Countermeasures Support Ships (MCS): "Catskill" Class

Name	No.	Launched	Completed	Conversion
CATSKILL	MCS 1 (ex-LSV 1, ex CM 6, ex-AP 106)	19 May 1942	30 June 1944	Boland Machine & Manufacturing Co, New Orleans, Louisiana
OZARK	MSC 2 (ex-LSV 2, ex-CM 7, ex-AP 107)	15 June 1942	23 Sep 1944	Norfolk Shipbuilding & Dry Dock Corpn, Norfolk, Virginia

Displacement, tons	5 875 standard; 9 040 full load
Length, feet (metres)	440 (134·1) wl; 455·5 (138·8) oa
Beam, feet (metres)	60·2 (18·4)
Draft, feet (metres)	20 (6·1)
Guns, dual purpose	2—5 in (127 mm) 38 cal.
Guns, AA	8—40 mm
Boilers	4 Combustion Eng. "D" type
Main engines	GE geared turbines 11 000 shp; 2 shafts
Speed, knots	20·3
Accommodation	564 (114 officers, 450 men)

OZARK (MCS 2)   1966, United States Navy

Both built by Willamette Iron & Steel Corpn, Portland, Oregon, under the 1940 Programme and laid down on 12 July, 1941. Designed as Large Minelayers, but subsequently converted into Landing Ships (Vehicle), LSV. Reclassified as Mine Warfare Command and Support ships and redesignated MCS in 1955. Again reclassified as Mine Countermeasures and Support Ships in 1958, and as Mine Countermeasures Support Ships on 25 Aug 1960. Stricken from the Navy List on 1 Sep 1961, but reinstated on 1 Oct 1963 (Ozark) and 1 June 1964 (Catskill) and converted into the new conception of Mine Countermeasures Support Ships under the Fiscal Year 1963 (Ozark) and 1964 (Catskill) Shipbuilding and Conversion Programmes. Catskill recommissioned on 6 Oct 1976; Ozark recommissioned on
Two new-construction MCS are planned.

CONVERSION. It is officially stated that each conversion of the former Vehicle Landing Ship (LSV) type will be capable of transporting, maintaining, operating and supporting twenty 36-foot minesweeping launches (MSL) and two helicopter minesweepers. These capabilities will provide a high degree of mobility to minesweeping operations. They will be used mainly in forward areas in support of amphibious landing operations. They will be capable of controlling and providing support for minesweeping ships and boats, and helicopters

DISPOSALS
Of the three vessels of the original netlayer type converted into vehicle landing ships, **Saugus**, MCS 4 (ex-LSV 4, ex-AN 4) was stricken from the Navy List on 1 July 1961.

and **Monitor**, MCS 5 (ex-LSV 5, ex-AN 5) and **Osage**, MCS 3 (ex-LSV 3, ex-AN 3), were stricken on 1 Sep 1961. The netlayer **Galilea** (ex-Montauk), AKN 6 (ex-LSV 6, ex-AN 2, ex-AP 161) was stricken from the Navy List on 1 Sep 1960.

OZARK (MCS 2)   1969, United States Navy

OZARK (wartime photo)   Added 1957, U.S. Navy, Official

OZARK (MCS 2)   1966, United States Navy

10 Destroyers Minelayer (DM): "Smith" Class

Name	No.	Builders	Launched	Completed
ADAMS	DM 27 (ex-DD 739)	Bath Iron Works Corpn	23 July 1944	10 Oct 1944
GWIN	DM 33 (ex-DD 772)	Bethlehem, San Pedro	9 Apr 1944	30 Sep 1944
HARRY F. BAUER	DM 26 (ex-DD 738)	Bath Iron Works Corpn	9 July 1944	22 Sep 1944
HENRY A. WILEY	DM 29 (ex-DD 749)	Bethlehem, Staten Island	21 Apr 1944	31 Aug 1944
LINDSEY	DM 32 (ex-DD 771)	Bethlehem, San Pedro	5 Mar 1944	20 Aug 1944
ROBERT H. SMITH	DM 23 (ex-DD 735)	Bath Iron Works Corpn	25 May 1944	4 Aug 1944
SHANNON	DM 25 (ex-DD 737)	Bath Iron Works Corpn	24 June 1944	8 Sep 1944
SHEA	DM 30 (ex-DD 750)	Bethlehem, Staten Island	20 May 1944	30 Sep 1944
THOMAS E. FRASER	DM 24 (ex-DD 736)	Bath Iron Works Corpn	10 June 1944	22 Aug 1944
TOLMAN	DM 28 (ex-DD 740)	Bath Iron Works Corpn	13 Aug 1944	27 Oct 1944

Displacement, tons — 2 250 standard; 3 375 full load
Length, feet (*metres*) — 376·5 (*114·8*)
Beam, feet (*metres*) — 41 (*12·5*)
Draft, feet (*metres*) — 19 (*5·8*)
Guns, surface — 6—5 in (*127 mm*) 38 cal.
Guns, AA — 12—40 mm; 11—20 mm, (some rearmed with 6—3 in (*76 mm*) in place of 40 mm)
Mines — 80
Boilers — 4 Babcock and Wilcox
Main engines — Geared turbines 60 000 shp; 2 shafts
Speed, knots — 34
Complement — 275 (15 officers, 260 men)

Modified Destroyers of the "Allen M. Sumner" class. Later fitted with tripod masts. All out of commission, in reserve.

RECLASSIFICATION. Formerly classified as Light Minelayers (DM). Reclassified as Destroyer Minelayers (DM) in Feb 1955.

DISPOSALS
J. Wm Ditter, DM 31, and **Aaron Ward**, DM 34 were scrapped.

GWIN (DM 33)   *Godfrey H. Walker Esq*

1 Mine Countermeasures Support Ship (MCS): Modified LSD

Name	No.	Builder	Commissioned
EPPING FORREST	MCS 7 (ex-LSD 4)	Moore Dry Dock Co	5 Jan 1944

Displacement, tons — 4 790 standard
Dimensions, feet — 454 wl; 457·8 oa × 72·1 × 18
Guns — 8—40 mm AA (2 quad)
Main engines — 2 Skinner Unaflow; 7 400 shp; 2 shafts = 15 knots
Boilers — 2

Modified to service and transport minesweeping launches (MSL). Laid down on 23 Nov 1942. Launched on 2 Apr 1943. Employed in that service in the Western Pacific for several years prior to being reclassified MCS 7 on 30 Nov 1962. Limited minelaying capability.

(The mine countermeasures ship *Orleans Parish*, MCS 6, ex-LST 1069, was redesignated as an LST on 1 June 1966 and is operated by the Navy's Military Sea Transportation Service; see Logistic Support Ships).

EPPING FOREST (MCS 7)   *1967, United States Navy*

MSS 1   *1969, United States Navy*

2 Ex-MINESWEEPERS (MSI): RESEARCH SHIPS

Name	No.	Builders	In Service
COVE	MSI 1	Bethlehem Shipyards Co, Bellingham	20 Nov 1958
CAPE	MSI 2	Bethlehem Shipyards Co, Bellingham	27 Feb 1959

Displacement, tons: 120 light; 240 full load
Dimensions, feet (metres): 105 × 22 × 10 *(32 × 6·7 × 3)*
Guns: Removed
Main engine: Diesel (General Motors); 650 bhp; 1 shaft = 12 knots
Complement: 21 (3 officers, 18 men)

These ships were prototype inshore minesweepers (MSI) authorised under the FY 1956 new construction programme. *Cape* laid down on 1 May 1957 and launched on 5 April 1958; *Cove* laid down 1 February 1957 and launched 8 February 1958.
Cape is operated by the Naval Undersea Research Development Center, San Diego, California; neither in service nor in commission. *Cove* transferred to Johns Hopkins Applied Physics Laboratory on 31 July 1970 with the same status. Both conduct Navy research.
Neither ship is now in the Navy List but are rated as "floating equipment". Both active.

COVE   1959, *United States Navy, Official*

CAPE   1960, *courtesy Mr. W. H. Davis*

CAPE   1968, USN

0 + 0 (+ 9) MINE COUNTERMEASURE SHIPS (MCM)

Displacements, tons: 1 640 standard; 2 200 full load
Dimensions, feet (metres): 239·5 × 44·3 × 11·2 *(73 × 13·5 × 3·4)*
Gun: Probably one 20 mm
Main engines: 2 diesels; 6 800 bhp; 2 shafts (cp propellers) = 18 knots
Complement: About 100

At least fifteen ships of a new class of US Mine Warfare vessel are to be constructed over the next 10-15 years. The class is planned as replacements for the "Aggressive", "Dash" and "Acme" classes now some 20-25 years old. One ship was to be requested under the FY 1980 Shipbuilding programme while two ships are planned for the FY 1983 programme and two more for the FY 1984 programme. Cost to be about $100-110 million per ship (FY 1979$). Construction of the first ship delayed to FY 1982 while the design is being altered and new minesweeping gear developed. Prototype to be requested under FY 1982. Four more ships scheduled for FY 1984 and a further four under the FY 1985 programme.

Sonar: Probably SQQ 14.

23 "AGGRESSIVE" and "DASH" CLASSES: OCEAN MINESWEEPERS (MSO)

Name	No.	Launched	Commissioned	F/S
CONSTANT	MSO 427	14 Feb 1952	8 Sep 1954	NRF
DASH	MSO 428	20 Sep 1952	14 Aug 1953	NRF
DETECTOR	MSO 429	5 Dec 1952	26 Jan 1954	NRF
DIRECT	MSO 430	27 May 1953	9 July 1954	NRF
DOMINANT	MSO 431	5 Nov 1953	8 Nov 1954	NRF
ENGAGE	MSO 433	18 June 1953	29 June 1954	NRF
ENHANCE	MSO 437	11 Oct 1952	16 Apr 1955	NRF
ESTEEM	MSO 438	20 Dec 1952	10 Sep 1954	NRF
EXCEL	MSO 439	25 Sep 1953	24 Feb 1955	NRF
EXPLOIT	MSO 440	10 Apr 1953	31 Mar 1954	NRF
EXULTANT	MSO 441	6 June 1953	22 June 1954	NRF
FEARLESS	MSO 442	17 July 1953	22 Sep 1954	NRF
FIDELITY	MSO 443	21 Aug 1953	19 Jan 1955	AA
FORTIFY	MSO 446	14 Feb 1953	16 July 1954	NRF
ILLUSIVE	MSO 448	12 July 1952	14 Nov 1953	AA
IMPERVIOUS	MSO 449	29 Aug 1952	15 July 1954	NRF
IMPLICIT	MSO 455	1 Aug 1953	10 Mar 1954	NRF
INFLICT	MSO 456	6 Oct 1953	11 May 1954	NRF
PLUCK	MSO 464	6 Feb 1954	11 Aug 1954	NRF
CONQUEST	MSO 488	20 May 1954	20 July 1955	NRF
GALLANT	MSO 489	4 June 1954	14 Sep 1955	NRF
LEADER	MSO 490	15 Sep 1954	16 Nov 1955	AA
PLEDGE	MSO 492	20 July 1955	20 Apr 1956	NRF

Displacement, tons: 620 light; 735 full load (428-431); 720 (remainder)
Dimensions, feet (metres): 172 × 36 × 13·6 *(52·4 × 11 × 4·2)*
Gun: 1—20 mm Mk 68 (single); (all modernised ships are unarmed)
Main engines: 4 diesels (Packard) (Waukesha in modernised ships); 2 280 bhp; 2 shafts; cp propellers = 14 knots; *Dash, Detector, Direct* and *Dominant,* have 2 diesels (General Motors); 1 520 bhp (see *Modernisation* note)
Range, miles: 2 400 at 10 knots
Complement: 76 (6 officers, 70 enlisted men); 86 in NRF ships (3 officers, 36 enlisted active duty; 3 officers, 44 enlisted reserve) (see *Modernisation* note)

These ships were built on the basis of mine warfare experience in the Korean War (1950-53); 58 built for US service and 35 transferred upon completion to NATO navies.(One ship cancelled, MSO 497.) They have wooden hulls and non-magnetic engines and other equipment. All surviving ships were built in private shipyards.
Initially designated as minesweepers (AM); reclassified as ocean minesweepers (MSO) in February 1955. Originally fitted with UQS 1 mine detecting sonar. Active MSOs serve as tenders to various research facilities.
Leader (MSO 490) and *Illusive* (MSO 448) deployed to Europe from 14 August 1978 to 6 August 1979 for operations with the NATO STANAVFORCHAN (MCM) and for exercises with various European navies. This is the first deployment made by US Mine Warfare vessels since 1973. One of the prime reasons this year long deployment was undertaken was because the experiences gained will be used in development of the new class of Mine Countermeasures Ships (MCM) (above).

Engineering: Diesel engines are fabricated of non-magnetic stainless steel alloy.

Modernisation: All the ocean minesweepers in commission during the mid-1960s were to have been modernised; estimated cost and schedule per ship were $5 million and ten months in shipyard. However, some of the early modernisations took as long as 26 months which, coupled with changes in mine countermeasures techniques, led to cancellation of programme after 13 ships were modernised: MSO 433, 437, 438. 441-443, 445, 446, 448, 449, 456, 488, and 490. The modernisation provided improvements in mine detection, engines, communications, and habitability: four Waukesha Motor Co diesel engines installed (plus two or three diesel generators for sweep gear), SQQ 14 sonar with mine classification as well as detection capability provided, twin 20 mm in some ships (replacing single 40 mm because of space requirements for sonar hoist mechanism), habitability improved, and advanced communications equipment fitted; bridge structure in modernised ships extended around mast and aft to funnel.
Some MSOs have received SQQ 14 sonar but not full modernisation.

Transfers: Ships of this class serve in the navies of Belgium, France, Italy, Netherlands, Spain, and Uruguay.

LEADER   11/1978, *Leo van Ginderen*

GUNBOATS

THE original gunboats were employed during the Civil War, being in some ways derivatives of the wooden hulked screw sloops which were mostly barque rigged. Most of the gunboats of this period had a good deal less displacement than the sloops which averaged 1,000 to 2,000 tons and were generally schooner rigged. The first two classes were single shaft ships and the following three were side wheel paddlers with speeds rarely exceeding 11 knots. Armament varied greatly; ranging downwards from 9-inch SB guns. The great majority of those 80 ships which were built for the North during the Civil War were deployed in coastal waters or rivers, although some of the 1,370 ton "Mohongo" class made successful passages to Europe and the Far East. One, *Mohongo* herself, made a safe journey through the Straits of Magellan in a full gale.

After the Civil War, the majority of these gunboats were sold. It was not until the Navy Act of 1883, which began the reconstruction of the fleet, that they once more figured in the building lists.

Over the next twenty years, 23 of the larger classes, varying from some 850 tons to the single *Topena* of 2,300 tons, were acquired. Again, armament varied considerably; a battery of six or eight 4-inch guns being generally favoured. Some had two shafts, some only one, although speeds were generally in the range 12–16 knots. The longevity of many of these ships was a tribute to their builders, the most senior being the Newport News built *Wilmington*, who commissioned in 1897 and sold in 1946.

During the period before World War I, the Americans had a new problem – they had become an Imperial Power. New acquisitions in the Pacific had been boosted by the take-over of Spanish colonies in the wake of the Spanish–American War of 1898. The US Navy now had responsibilities in the Caribbean and the South-West Pacific but an alternative had to be found to cruisers (which were expensive both in manpower and money) for the task of patrolling these areas as well as the China Coast.

To deal with this problem, three gunboats were built in 1914 (*Sacramento*, *Monocacy* and *Palos*) – but these were small fry as a major war portended.

World War I made the gunboat unnecessary, since it was essentially a peace-time vessel, and it was not until 1918–22 that two more 1,760 ton ships were launched: *Asheville* and *Tulsa*. Both ships served off the coast of China; the former was sunk off Java by the Japanese on 3 March 1942.

After a long pause the two ships of the "Erie" class were launched in 1936. Taking advantage of the London Treaty of 1930, this was the only pair of ships built to the limits of 2,000 tons, 6.1-inch guns with a speed of 20 knots. Although at that time these two were anachronisms, the six river gunboats built under the FY 1925 programme had a definite task. *Wake*, *Tutuila*, *Panay*, *Oaku*, *Luzon* and *Mindanao* had a ring of destiny about their names and were designed for service on the Yangtze Kiang.

Only one of these six vessels survived the Japanese Wars. In December 1937 *Panay* was sunk in the Yangtze by the Japanese; *Tutuila* ran up-river to Chunking in March 1942 and was transferred to the Chinese; *Wake* was captured by the Japanese in December 1941 and transferred to the Chinese in 1946. The remaining three reached the Philippines where *Luzon* was sunk in February 1942 while *Mindanao* and *Oaku* were scuttled in May.

During World War II the designation P6 was applied to a number of varieties of ships and craft. Many were primarily anti-submarine vessels which were known in other navies as frigates. By the time of the Vietnam War there were no true gunboats; although many craft underwent extemporized conversions to carry guns of various calibres.

J.M.
May 1991

HELENA & WILMINGTON. *Photo, copyright, Rau.*

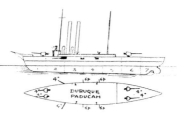

Ram.

KATAHDIN (1893). 2155 tons. Armament: 1 6 pdrs. No torpedoes. Covered with 6"—2½" Harvey armour. 18" Conning tower. Designed speed: 16 kts. Actual speed: much less.

SUNK AS TARGET

SOLD   SCUTTLED

Gunboats, etc.

ATLANTA & BOSTON (1884). 3100 tons. Armament: 2 8", 35 cal., 6 6" (old), 6 6 pdr., 2 3 pdr., 1 1 pdr., 2 machine. Partial 1½" deck. Original speed: 15·5 kts. Boilers: Babcock and cylindrical.

NASHVILLE (1895), WILMINGTON (1895) & HELENA (1896), all of 1370–1392 tons. Armament: 8 4", and some small Q.F. Armour, 2½" deck and 2" on guns. Speed: under 14 kts.

CASTINE, MACHIAS (1891-92), MARIETTA, WHEELING, ANNAPOLIS, VICKSBURG, NEWPORT, PRINCETON, (1896-97), DUBUQUE & PADUCAH (1905), all of *circa* 1000 tons. Armament: 6 4", 1 6 pdr., 2 1 pdr. Speeds: about 12 kts. or less.

BENNINGTON, CONCORD, YORKTOWN (1888-90). 1700 tons. Armament: 6 old 6", 2 6 pdr., 2 3 pdr., 2—1 pdr. Deck: ¾" steel. 2" Conning tower. Original speeds: 17 kts.

Other Craft.

There are also *Bancroft* (1892), 840 tons, 4 4", originally 14 kts.; *Petrel* (1888), 800 tons, 4 old 6", originally 13·5 kts.; *Dolphin* (1884), 1485 tons, 2 4", originally 15·5 kts.; *Isla de Cuba* and *Isla de Luzon* (1886), (ex Spanish), 4 4", 2½" deck, originally 15·9 kts.; *Topeka* (1883), 1880 tons, 6 4", originally 16 kts.; *Don Juan d' Austria* and *General Alcada, circa* 1300 tons, and twenty-two small gunboats, mostly captured from the Spaniards, of from 300 to 40 tons, armed with small Q.F.; five old iron steamers and twelve wood ditto used for training purposes; six wooden sailing ships, thirty-nine tugs, seventeen hulks, and six "auxiliary cruisers" *Buffalo*, 12 5", 1 4"; *Dixie*, 16 kts. (8—5"), *Prairie*, 14·5 kts. (6 5", 2 4"), *Yankee*, 12·5 kts. (no guns), *Yosemite*, 16 kts. (10 5"), all *circa* 6000 tons, and *Panther*, 13 kts. (6 5", 2 4"), of 1260 tons. This carries 175 tons of coal; the others 1000-1300 tons. Also twenty-three converted yachts, speeds 17·85-11 kts.; sixteen colliers, 12-3·5 kts., average capacity 3000 tons, mostly carrying one or two Hotchkiss guns (6 pdr.); and eleven miscellaneous ships.

Old cruiser *Philadelphia* converting into a receiving ship.

KATAHDIN. (1906)

NASHVILLE. *Photo, copyright, Rau.*

BENNINGTON CLASS.

Gunboats. (1919)

NUMBER (22). To be built by Charleston, N.Y., begun June, 1919.
ASHEVILLE (Charleston N.Y.) (July, 1918). *Normal* displacement, 1575 tons. Complement, Length (*waterline*), 225 feet. Beam, 41¼ feet. *Mean* draught, 11½ feet. Guns: 3–4 inch, 50 cal. Machinery: Parsons turbine with reduction gear. 1 screw. Boilers: 3 Bureau (modified Thornycroft). Designed H.P. 800 = 12 kts. Fuel, tons.

LOST

SACRAMENTO (Feb., 1914). *Normal* displacement, 1425 tons. Complement, 163. Length (*waterline*), 210 feet. Beam, 50¾ feet. *Mean* draught, 11½ feet. Guns: 3–4 inch, 50 cal.; 2–3 pdr.; 2–1 pdr. Machinery: 1 set triple expansion. Boilers: 2 Babcock. H.P. (on trials), 1022 = 12·78 kts. Coal: *maximum*, 428 tons. Built by Cramps. Completed, 1914.

MERC FERMINA

SAMOA (ex German s.s. *Staatssekretaer Solf*) (1913, seized 1917). 550 tons. Complement, 32. Dimension: 131 (*waterline*) × 25½ × feet. Guns: 4–3 pdr., 2 M.G. Machinery: 1 set vert. compound. H.P., Speed and Fuel not known.

SOLD

WILMETTE (ex s.s. *Eastland*, 1903, taken over 1918). 2,600 tons. Complement, 181. Length (*waterline*), 265 feet. Beam, 38½ feet. Draught, feet. Guns: 4–4 inch, 2–3 inch A.A., 2–1 pdr. Machinery; 2 sets triple expansion. 2 screws. Boilers: Designed I.H.P. 4000 = 16·5 kts. Fuel, tons.

SCRAPPED

DUBUQUE.   *Photo, Navy Dept.*

DUBUQUE (1904), **PADUCAH** (1904). *Normal* displacement, 1085 tons. Complement, 190 and 176. Length (*waterline*), 174 feet. Beam, 35 feet. *Mean* draught, 12¼ feet. Guns: *Dubuque*, 2–4 inch. *Paducah*, 4–4 inch, and in both, 4–6 pdr., 2–1 pdr. Machinery: 2 sets triple expansion. 2 screws. Boilers: 2 Babcock. Designed H.P. 1000 = 12·9 kts. Coal: *maximum* 252 tons.

SOLD   SCRAPPED

WHEELING.   *Photo, Fons.*

MARIETTA & WHEELING (1897). *Normal* displacement, 990 tons. Complements, 182 and 163. Length (*waterline*), 174 feet. Beam, 34 feet. *Mean* draught, 12 feet. Guns: 4–4 inch, 40 cal.; 2–3 pdr.; 2–1 pdr. (+1–Y in *Wheeling*). Machinery: 2 sets vertical triple expansion. 2 screws. Boilers: *Marietta*, 2 Babcock; *Wheeling*, 2 single-ended. Designed H.P. 1250 = 13 kts. Coal: *maximum*, 234 and 256 tons. *Nominal* radius: 4000 at 10 kts.

ALL SOLD

(Mainmast of *Princeton* removed).   *Photo, Abraham & Sons.*

ANNAPOLIS (1896). **NEWPORT** (1896). **PRINCETON.**
Normal displacement, 1010 tons. Complement, 165—147. Length (*waterline*), 168 feet. Beam, 36 feet. *Mean* draught, 12 feet. Guns: *Annapolis*, 6–4 inch, 4–6 pdr., 1 Y-gun. *Newport*, 1–4 inch, 2–3 inch, 2–6 pdr. *Princeton*, none. Machinery: 1 set vertical triple expansion. 1 screw. Boilers: 2 Babcock. Designed H.P. 800 = 12 kts. Coal: 235 tons.

Notes.—*Vicksburg* now Fisheries Protection Gunboat, Alaska.   *SOLD*

SCRAPPED   STRICKEN

HELENA (1896) & **WILMINGTON** (1895). Displacement, 1392 tons. Complement, 207 *average*. Length (*waterline*), 250¾ feet. Beam, 39⅔ feet. *Mean* draught, 9 feet. Guns: 8–4 inch, 40 cal.; 4–3 pdr. Machinery: 2 sets vertical triple expansion. 2 screws. Designed H.P. 1988 = 13 kts. Coal: *maximum*, 258 tons in *Wilmington*; 307 tons in *Helena*. *Nominal* radius: 2200 miles at 10 kts.   *SCUTTLED*

SOLD

Photo, copyright, Rau.

NASHVILLE (1895). 1371 tons. Guns: 8–4 inch, 4–6 pdr., 2–1 pdr., 2 machine. 2½″ sponsons to 4 inch guns. H.P. 2500 = 16 kts. Coal: 381 tons. Complement 188.

SOLD AS BARGE

MACHIAS.   *Photo, U.S. Navy.*

CASTINE (1892), **MACHIAS** (1891). 1177 tons. Complement, 182—177. Guns: *Castine*, 2–4 inch, 6–6 pdr., 2–1 pdr., 1 Y-gun; *Machias*, 4–4 inch, 2–3 pdr., 2–1 pdr. Speed, 15½ to 16 kts. Coal: *Castine*, 246 tons; *Machias*, 267 tons.

MERC   DISCARDED

Mainmast now removed.

PETREL (1888). Displacement, 890 tons. Complement, 135. Guns: 4—4 inch, (40 cal.), 2—3 pdr., 2—1 pdr. Designed H.P. 1000 = 11.5 kts. Coal: 198 tons.

SOLD

DON JUAN DE AUSTRIA (1887). 1130 tons. Guns: 4—4 inch, 2—1 pdr. H.P. 941 = 12.2 kts. Coal: 204 tons.

MERC DEWEY

YORKTOWN (1888). 1710 tons. Complement, 219. Guns: 6—5 inch, (40 cal.), 4—6 pdr., 2—1 pdr. Original speed, 17 kts. Coal: 336 tons.

SOLD

ISLA DE LUZON (1887). 1030 tons. Guns: 4—3 pdr. Speed: *about* 11 kts. Coal: 159 tons.

SCRAPPED

Photo, Navy Dept.

(Used as Yacht by the Secretary of the Navy.)

DOLPHIN (1884). 1486 tons. Complement, 156. Guns: 2—3 inch, 4—6 pdr. Speed, 15.5 kts. Coal: 255 tons.

TO MEX

NANTUCKET (ex *Rockport,* ex *Ranger,* 1876). 1261 tons. Guns: 1—4 inch, 2—3 inch. I.H.P. 500 = 10 kts. Coal: 182 tons.

MERC EMERY RICE

Mainmast now removed.

ALERT (1875). 1100 tons. Complement: 137. Dimensions: 177½ × 32 × 13 feet (*mean draught*). Guns: 1—6 pdr. H.P. 500 = 10 kts. 2 Babcock boilers. Coal: 202 tons.

SOLD

ESSEX (1874). 1375 tons. Guns: 6—3 pdr. H.P. 800 = 10 kts. Coal: 155 tons.

SCRAPPED

GOPHER (1871). 840 tons. 5—3 pdr., 4—1 pdr. Speed, 9 kts. Coal: 80 tons.

LOST

WOLVERINE (1842). 685 tons. H.P. 365 = 10.5 kts. Paddle wheel. Coal: 115 tons. Guns: 6—3 pdr.

STRICKEN

YANTIC (1864). 900 tons. 4—3 pdr., 2—1 pdr. H.P. 310 = 8.3 kts. Coal: 130 tons.

LOST

Small Gunboats for Service in the Philippines.

SCUTTLED   SOLD

Monocacy.   *Photo, Leslie's Weekly.*

MONOCACY (1914), **PALOS** (1914). 190 tons. Complement, 47. Guns: 2—6 pdr., 6 machine. Machinery: 2 sets vertical compound. Boilers: 2 Babcock. Designed H.P. 800 = 13¼ kts. Coal: 34 tons. Built at Mare Island Navy Yard and re-erected by Shanghai Dock and Engineering Co.

QUIROS (1895), **VILLALOBOS** (1896). 360 tons. Complement, 56. Guns: 4—3 pdr. Designed H.P. 550 = 11 kts. Coal: 70 tons.

ALL SUNK AS TARGET

CALLAO (1888), **PAMPANGA** (1888), **SAMAR** (1888). 243 tons. Guns: *Callao* none; others 4—3 pdr. Speed, 10 to 10½ kts. Coal: 33 tons. Old gunboats captured in Spanish War.

SOLD   SUNK AS TARGET   SOLD

No photo available.

ECLANO (1885). 620 tons. Complement, 99. Guns: 4—4 inch, 4—3 pdr. Speed, 11 kts. Coal: 98 tons. Old gunboat captured in Spanish War.   SUNK AS TARGET

Note.

Romblon, Bobol, Cebu, Jolo, Marie Duque, (Uraga Dock Co, 1902-3), are small gunboats belonging to the War Department, Philippines. 350 tons. Guns: 3 small Q. F. Designed H.P. 450 = 10 kts.

Patrol Vessels—Gunboats (PG). (1931)

TULSA. 1925 *Photo, by courtesy of the Navy Dept.*

TULSA (Charleston, N.Y., 25th August, 1922). **ASHEVILLE** (Charleston, N.Y., July, 1918). *Normal* displacement, 1575 tons (*full load*, 1760 tons). Complement, 185. Length (*p.p.*) 225 feet, (*o.a.*) 241¼ feet. Beam, 41¼ feet. *Mean* draught, 11⅓ feet. Guns: 3—4 inch, 50 cal., 2—3 pdr., 3—1 pdr. Machinery: Parsons turbine with reduction gear. 1 screw. Boilers: 3 Bureau (modified Thornycroft). Designed H.P. 800 = 12 kts. Fuel, 180 tons coal + 440 tons oil.

SOLD   *LOST*

1919 *Photo.*

SACRAMENTO (Feb., 1914). *Normal* displacement, 1425 tons. Complement, 153. Length (*waterline*), 210 feet. Beam, 40⅝ feet. *Mean* draught, 11½ feet. Guns: 3—4 inch, 50 cal. ; 2—3 pdr. ; 2—1 pdr. Machinery: 1 set triple expansion. Boilers: 2 Babcock. H.P. (on trials), 1022 = 12·78 kts. Coal: *maximum*, 428 tons. Built by Cramps. Completed, 1914.

MERC FERMINA

MONOCACY 1927 *Photo.*

(Asiatic Fleet.)

MONOCACY (1914), **PALOS** (1914). 190 tons. Complement, 46. Guns: 2—3 inch 23 cal., 7—30 cal. Machinery: 2 sets vertical compound. Boilers: 2 Babcock. Designed H.P. 800 = 13¼ kts. Coal: 34 tons. Built at Mare Island Navy Yard and re-erected by Shanghai Dock and Engineering Co.

SCUTTLED   *SOLD*

(Asiatic Fleet.)

HELENA (1896). Displacement: 1392 tons. Complement, 193 to 196. Length (*waterline*), 250¾ feet. Beam, 39¾ feet. *Mean* draught, 9 feet. Guns: 8—4 inch, 40 cal. ; 4—3 pdr. Machinery: 2 sets vertical triple expansion. 2 screws. H.P. (*trials*) 1988 = 15·5 kts. Coal: *maximum*, 307 tons. *Nominal* radius 2200 miles at 10 kts.

Note.—*Wilmington*, sister to *Helena*, is still retained in service for training purposes under heading "Unclassified."

SOLD

PANAY. *SUNK* 1929 *Official Photo.*

OAHU, PANAY. Displacement: 385 tons *standard*. *Mean* draught (fresh water), 5½ feet. Freeboard at side (main deck): Forward, 7 ft. 9½ in.; amidships, 3 ft. 9½ in.; aft, 4 ft. 6 in. Triple expansion engines, $\frac{13\frac{1}{2} \times 22 \times 34}{16}$, revs. 320. H.P. 2250 = 15 kts. (Trials, 17.73 kts). Guns: 2—3 inch, 50 cal. AA., 10—30 cal.

LUZON. 1929 *Official Photo.*

LUZON, MINDANAO. Displacement: 500 tons *standard*. *Mean* draught (fresh water), 6 feet. Freeboard at side (main deck): Forward, 10 ft. 7 in.; amidships, 5 ft. 7 in.; aft, 5 ft. 10 in. Triple expansion engines, $\frac{15 \times 23 \times 36\frac{1}{4}}{18}$, revs. 320. H.P. 3150 = 16 kts. Guns: 2—3 inch, 50 cal. AA., 10—30 cal. The following characteristics are common to all six :—2 Thornycroft oil-burning boilers, 250 lbs. working pressure. 2 screws. Lengths of each pair are 150, 180 and 198 feet respectively.

Above 6 gunboats authorised 1924 as *PG 43—48*, and laid down 1926 by Kiangnan Dock and Engineering Works Shanghai. Completed, 1927-28.

Patrol Vessels—Gunboats. (1939)

ERIE. 1936, *R. Perkins.*

CHARLESTON (Feb. 25, 1936). Built at Charleston Navy Yard. **ERIE** (Jan. 29, 1936). Built at New York Navy Yard.

SUNK

Standard displacement: 2,000 tons. Dimensions: 308 (*w.l.*), 328½ (*o.a.*) × 41⅓ × 11½ feet (*mean* draught). Guns: 4—6 inch, 2—quad. M.G. AA., 2—3 pdr. Protection: 1" side at waterline (3" over vital spaces); 3" C.T.; 1" shields and bridge; 2" + 1" decks. Machinery: Geared turbines. 2 shafts. S.H.P.: 6,200 = 20 kts.

Notes.—Ordered 1933 under Emergency Programme. Laid down in Oct. and Dec., 1934, and completed in Oct., 1936. 6 inch guns are 47 cal. new model.

TENDERS

THE later years of the nineteenth century brought an increasing awareness of the role of small craft, such as torpedo boats, in modern warfare. The problem which then faced the planners was how to support this increasing flotilla. Although each ship carried fuel and armaments for a brief foray; they needed support, sustenance and hot baths when they returned to harbour. If the vessel was operating from a fixed base these necessities could be dealt with ashore. If, however, their operating area was removed from such shore-based facilities, their means of support had to be made mobile. The result was that ships with maintenance staffs had to be provided and many of these came from the Merchant Navies of the powers concerned. This was not a problem confined to the US Navy and the demand grew steadily as the smaller ships increased in size and complexity. Various types of vessel had to be catered for; in the early days torpedo-boats, and later destroyers; submarines soon followed and the small torpedo-craft such as the PT boats all needed tenders.

By 1919 the US Navy was operating 12 ships as "Tenders to Torpedo Craft". Four of these were old cruisers, the remainder merchant ships. Seven ships of varying antecedents supported the submarines, while others cared for the sea planes and submarine chasers.

The lessons of World War I were reflected in a more professional approach during the inter-war years. Custom-built seaplane tenders were supported by converted destroyers and minesweepers; while other vessels sprouted large masts as airship tenders. Destroyer tenders such as *Whitney* and *Dobbin* followed four earlier specialized ships until, in 1938, *Dixie* and *Prairie* were laid down. When this pair entered service in 1940 there were nine destroyer tenders, but the submariners were less well served, with only six tenders. *Dixie* continued her distinguished life until 1982, the longest serving ship on active duty in the US Navy.

World War II saw a major increase in the strength of the tender force as operations spread world-wide. Despite the post-war retrenchments, by 1950 their numbers were still considerable. Six classes of seaplane tenders, ranging from the 15,000 ton "Currituck" class to the 2,800 ton "Barnegat" class, provided 26 floating havens. Thirteen submarine tenders included the seven ships of the up-to-date "Fulton" class while the destroyers were served by 18 tenders of which ten had been built in 1944–45. For heavier repair work there were 26 heavy repair ships and 46 "battle damage repair ships".

In 1991 the tenders for seaplanes have disappeared. The submarine tenders are designed to service both ballistic missile and attack submarines. The destroyer/frigate tenders have to cope with everything from the complex electronics of Aegis to the more simple matters of gas-turbine propulsion. The submariners rely on their shore-bases, eight tenders for attack submarines and four for ballistic missile boats. Nine destroyer tenders serve the smaller surface ships. These may seem to be figures adding up to a considerable total but no-one should be led astray by that fact. Should hostilities of any kind take place there will never be enough tenders: the home, haven and hope of those in smaller ships.

J.M.
May 1991

Tenders to Torpedo Craft. (1919)

Third class cruiser, **BIRMINGHAM,** is fitted for and serves as flagship to T.B.D. in full commission, Pacific Fleet. She is described on a previous page.

Third class cruiser, **SALEM,** serves as flagship to T.B.D. in reserve, Pacific Fleet. Is described on a previous page.

First class cruiser, **ROCHESTER,** is flagship to T.B.D. in full commission, Atlantic Fleet. Third class cruiser, **CHESTER,** is flagship to T.B.D. in Reserve, Atlantic. Both ships described on preceding pages.

Two Tenders to Torpedo Craft, Pacific Fleet, and three Tenders to Torpedo Craft, Atlantic Fleet, not selected at the time these pages were prepared; accordingly, they cannot be listed.

WHITNEY, DOBBIN. Both ships authorized but not yet under contract or construction. 10,600 tons. Dimensions: 460 (*w.l.*) $483\frac{5}{8}$ (*o.a.*) × 61 × 21 feet (*mean* draught). Guns: 8—5 inch, 4—3 inch AA. Torpedo tubes: 2—21 inch. Geared turbines. 1 screw. Designed S.H.P. 7000 = 16 kts. Coal: 1107 tons. Complement, —. Generally sister ships to *Holland*, Tender to Submarines.

ALL SCRAPPED

Copyright photo (see Note).

(*Pacific Fleet Reserve Flotillas.*)

BLACK HAWK (Cramp, 1913, ex-Grace Steamship Co. S.S. *Santa Catalina*, taken over 1917). 13,500 tons. Dimensions: $404\frac{1}{2} \times 53\frac{3}{4} \times 28\frac{1}{2}$ feet. Guns: 4—5 inch, 2 M.G. I.H.P. 3400 = 13 kts. Oil: 2108 tons. Complement, 442. Served 1917-18 as Repair Ship to Mine Force.

Note.—Above illustration from "The Northern Barrage," prepared by U.S. Mine Force, and published by U.S. Naval Institute, Annapolis.

SCRAPPED

BRIDGEPORT (Vegesack, Germany, 1901, ex-North German Lloyd S.S. *Breslau*, seized 1917). 8600 tons. Dimensions: $429\frac{1}{3} \times 54\frac{1}{3} \times 28\frac{1}{4}$ feet. Guns: 8—5 inch, 2 M.G. I.H.P., 3600 = 12.5 kts. Coal: 1060 tons. Complement, 386.

HOSPITAL SHIP LARKSPUR

(*Pacific Fleet.*)

BUFFALO (*ex El Cid*), (1892). 6000 tons. Complement: 424. Dimensions: $391 \times 48\frac{1}{4} \times 19\frac{1}{2}$ feet. Armament: 6—4 inch, 4—3 pdr., 2—1 pdr., 2 M.G. H.P. 3600 = 14·5 kts. Coal: 1408 tons.

MERC SIRUS

PRAIRIE. *Official Photo, U. S. Naval Air Service.*

(*Pacific Fleet*).

PRAIRIE (*ex El Sol*), (1890). 6620 tons. Complement: 350. Dimensions: $404\frac{3}{4} \times 48\frac{1}{4} \times 20\frac{3}{4}$ feet (*mean* draught). Armament: 10—3 inch, 2—1 pdr., 2 M.G. H.P. 3800 = 14·5 kts. Coal: 1331 tons.

SCRAPPED

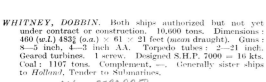

Photo, C. E. Waterman.

(*Pacific Fleet.*)

MELVILLE (1915). 7150 tons. Complement, 397. Dimensions: $400 \times 54\frac{1}{2} \times 20$ feet (*mean* draught). Guns: 8—5 inch (51 cal.), 1—3 inch AA., 2—3 pdr. Torpedo tubes: 1—18 inch. Machinery: Parsons turbines and Westinghouse reduction gear. 2 Babcock and Wilcox boilers. H.P. (*on trials*) 4006 = 15.09 kts. Fuel: 900 tons *oil*.

SCRAPPED

(*Atlantic Fleet.*)

DIXIE (ex *El Sud*), (1893). 6114 tons. Complement, 448. Dimensions: $391 \times 48\frac{1}{4} \times 20$ feet (*mean* draught). Armament: 10—3 inch, 2—6 pdr., 2—1 pdr., 2 M.G. H.P. 3800 = 14.5 kts. Coal: 1100 tons.

SOLD

(*Atlantic Fleet*).

PANTHER (1889). 3380 tons. Complement: 242. Dimensions: $304\frac{2}{3} \times 40\frac{2}{3} \times 15\frac{3}{4}$ feet (*mean* draught). Guns: 4—3 inch. H.P. 3200 = 13·5 kts. Coal, 691 tons.

SOLD

Tenders to Torpedo Craft—*Continued.*

(Asiatic Fleet.)

POMPEY (1888). Ex-Collier, 3085 tons. Complement: 121. Dimensions: $234 \times 33\frac{1}{2} \times 15\frac{5}{6}$ feet (*mean* draught). Guns: 4 6 pdr. Speed: 10·5 kts. Coal: 205 tons.

LOST

Tenders to Submarine. (1919)

Projected.

HOLLAND. Authorized; not yet under contract or construction. 10,600 tons. Dimensions: 460 (*w.l.*), $483\frac{5}{6}$ (*o.a.*) × 61 (*extreme* × 21 feet (*mean* draught). Guns: 4—5 inch, 2—3 inch AA. Geared turbines. 1 screw. Designed S H P. 7000 = 16 kts. Oil: 1107 tons. Complement. . Generally sister ship to *Whitney* and *Dobbin*, Tenders to Torpedo Craft.

BUSHNELL.   *U.S. Navy Photo.*

(Atlantic Fleet.)

BUSHNELL (1915). 3580 tons. Complement: 194. Dimensions: $300 \times 45\frac{3}{4} \times 15$ feet (*mean* draught). Guns: 4—5 inch (51 cal.), 2—3 pdr. (saluting). Machinery: Turbines with reducing gear. H.P. (on trials) 2617 = 14·15 kts. Fuel: 660 tons oil.

SCRAPPED

Tenders to Submarines—*Continued.*

Photo, Copyright, E. Muller, Jr.

FULTON (ex-*Niagara*) (1914). 1408 tons. Complement: 173. Dimensions: $216 \times 35 \times 13$ feet (*mean* draught). Guns: 2—3 inch (50 cal.), 1—1 pdr. auto anti-aircraft. Torpedo tubes: None officially listed, but from published plans and photos 4 tubes appear to be mounted on foc's'le in two twin deck-mountings. Machinery: 1100 B.H.P. 6-cyl. 2-cycle Nlseco Diesel engine. 1 screw. Designed speed: 12·25 kts.; 12·34 on trials. Fuel: 234 tons oil.

SOLD

(Pacific Fleet.)

BEAVER (Newport News, 1910, purchased 1918). 5970 tons. Dimensions: 380 (*o.a.*) × 47 × 21 feet (*max.* draught). Guns: 4—5 inch, 2—3 inch AA., 2—1 pdr., 2 M.G. 1 screw. I.H.P. 4500 = 16·5 kts. Fuel: 2350 barrels oil fuel. Complement, 373.

SCRAPPED

(Atlantic Fleet.)

CAMDEN (Flensburg, Germany, 1900, ex-German-Australian ss. *Kiel*, seized 1917). 9000 tons (estimated). Dimensions: $403\frac{3}{4}$ (*o.a.*) × 48 × feet. Guns: 4—4 inch, 2—3 inch AA., 2—1 pdr., 4 M.G. I.H.P. 2550 = 12 kts. Coal: 975 tons. Complement, 345.

SCRAPPED

Tenders to Submarines—*continued.*

(Pacific Fleet.)

SAVANNAH (Flensburg, Germany, 1899, ex-Hamburg-American S.S. *Saxonia*, seized 1917). 10,800 tons. Dimensions: $414 \times 46 \times 26\frac{1}{2}$ feet. Guns: 1—5 inch, 2 M.G. I.H.P. 2000 = 10·5 kts. Coal: 743 tons + 531 tons additional stowage = 1274 tons. Complement, 412.

SCRAPPED

(Atlantic Fleet.)

RAINBOW (1890, purchased 1898). 4300 tons. Dimensions: $351\frac{3}{4} \times 41 \times 17\frac{1}{4}$ feet. Guns: 4—5 inch, 2 M.G. I.H.P. 1800 = 12 kts. Coal: 1166 tons. Complement, 274.

SCRAPPED

MONADNOCK (1883). 3990 tons. Guns: 4—10 inch, 2—4 inch, 4—6 pdr., 2—1 pdr. Armour: Iron belt 9″, steel turrets $11\frac{1}{2}″-7\frac{1}{2}″$. H.P. (on trials) 2163 = 11·63 kts. Coal: 395 tons. Complement, 228.

Note.—Above Old Monitor Submarine Depot Ship, Asiatic Fleet, with *Mohican* as Tender. She is to be withdrawn from service and placed out of commission.

SOLD

Tenders to Seaplanes. (1919)

U.S. Dreadnoughts now carry and fly off small aeroplanes from barbette crowns, in the same way as British Ships.

Armoured Cruisers, **NORTH CAROLINA** and **SEATTLE** were specially equipped to serve as Seaplane Carriers and Depot Ships. Doubtful if these Armoured Cruisers are still on this duty. *ALL SCRAPPED*

Mine Layers, **AROOSTOOK** and **SHAWMUT**, acted as Tenders to the *NC* Flying Boats on Cross-Atlantic Flight.

Kite Balloons worked by nearly all classes of warships.

Up to the present, no special Aircraft Carriers, like British *Argus*, *Furious*, *Nairana*, etc., have been added to U.S. Navy.

ALL SCRAPPED

Tenders to Submarine Chasers. (1919)

SCRAPPED   *STRICKEN*   *SCRAPPED*

Cruisers, **SALEM** and **CHICAGO**, Auxiliary **PRAIRIE**, Coastguard Cruiser **SNOHOMISH**, Armed Yacht *Yacona* and various Tugs have been used for convoying Submarine Chasers across the Atlantic. They will be released from this duty when all SC-boats have been withdrawn from European waters.

Gunboat, **VICKSBURG**, listed as Fisheries Protection Vessel, Alaska, also serves as Parent Ship to four Submarine Chasers.

SOLD

Photo, Lieut. H. Reuterdahl, U.S.N.R.F.

LEONIDAS (1898). Ex-Fuel Ship. 4023 tons. Dimensions: $274 \times 39\frac{1}{4} \times 17\frac{3}{4}$ feet. Complement, 167. Guns: 1—6 inch, 2—3 inch, 2 M.G. H.P. 1100 = 8½ kts. Coal: 205 tons.

SOLD

HANNIBAL (1898). Ex-Fuel Ship. 4000 tons. Dimensions: $274 \times 39\frac{1}{4} \times 17\frac{3}{4}$ feet. Complement, 295. Guns: 1—6 inch, 2—3 inch, 2 M.G. H.P. 1100 = 9 kts. Coal: 491 tons.

SUNK AS TARGET

Destroyer Tenders (AD). (1924)

Cruiser (Second Line) **CHARLESTON**, serving as flagship to T.B.D. in full commission, Pacific Fleet. She is described on a previous page. *SCRAPPED*

WHITNEY (Boston N.Yd., 1923), **DOBBIN** (Philadelphia N.Yd., May 5th, 1921). 10,600 tons. Dimensions: 460 (*p.p.*), $483\frac{5}{8}$ (*o.a.*) × 61 × 21 feet (*mean* draught). Guns: 8—5 inch, 4—3 inch AA., 2—6 pdr. Torpedo tubes, for testing purposes: 2—21 inch. Parsons geared turbines. Boilers: 2 Bureau Modified Thornycroft. 1 screw. Designed S.H.P. 7000 = 16 kts. Oil: 1107 tons. Complement, ·372. Equipped to serve as Depot, Repair and Hospital Ship for 18 Destroyers. To have special anti-torpedo protection. Generally sister ships to *Holland*, Tender to Submarines.

ALL SCRAPPED

ALTAIR (1919), **DENEBOLA** (1919), **RIGEL** (1918). 13,925 tons. Dimensions: $423\frac{5}{8} \times 54 \times 27\frac{1}{4}$ feet. Guns: 4—5 inch, 51 cal., 2—3 inch A.A. Curtis geared turbines. Cylindrical boilers. S.H.P. 2500 = 10.5 kts. Oil: 1097 tons. Complement, 481. All three built by Skinner & Eddy Corporation, Seattle.

ALL SCRAPPED

1919 Photo, C. E. Waterman.

(Battle Fleet.)

MELVILLE (1915). 7150 tons. Complement, 480. Dimensions: 400 (*p.p.*) × $54\frac{1}{4}$ × 20 feet (*mean* draught). Guns: 8—5 inch (51 cal.), 1—3 inch AA., 2—3 pdr. Torpedo tubes: 1—18 inch. Machinery: Parsons turbines and Westinghouse reduction gear. 2 Babcock and Wilcox boilers. H.P. (on trials) 4006 = 15.09 kts. Fuel: 900 tons oil.

SCRAPPED

(Asiatic Fleet.)
1920 Photo.

BLACK HAWK (Cramp, 1913, ex-Grace Steamship Co. S.S. *Santa Catalina*, taken over 1917). 13,500 tons. Dimensions: $404\frac{1}{4}$ (*p.p.*) × $53\frac{3}{4}$ × $28\frac{1}{2}$ feet. Guns: 4—5 inch, 2—3 pdr., 2 M.G. I.H.P. 3400 = 13 kts. Oil: 2108 tons. Complement, 471.

SCRAPPED

Destroyer Tenders (AD)—*Continued.*

1920 Photo, Seward, Weymouth.

(Scouting Fleet.)

BRIDGEPORT (Vegesack, Germany, 1901, ex-North German Lloyd S.S. *Breslau*, seized 1917). 8600 tons. Dimensions: $429\frac{1}{2}$ (*p.p.*) × $54\frac{1}{4}$ × $28\frac{1}{4}$ feet. Guns: 8—5 inch. I.H.P. 3600 = 12.5 kts. Coal: 1060 tons. Complement, 552.

HOSP. LARKSPUR

(Pacific Fleet.)

BUFFALO (ex s.s. *Nictheroy*, 1892, bought during War with Spain, 1898). 6525 tons. Complement, 431. Dimensions: 391 (*p.p.*) × $48\frac{1}{4}$ × $20\frac{3}{4}$ feet. Armament: 6—4 inch, 4—3 pdr., 2—1 pdr., 2 M.G. H.P. 3600 = 14.5 kts. Coal: 1048 tons.

MERC SIRUS

Auxiliaries—Submarine Tenders (AS). (1929)

Note.—Obsolete Cruiser *Chicago*, Submarine Barracks at Pearl Harbour. Various Minesweepers of "Bird" class serve as Submarine Tenders at New London, Hampton Roads; Coco Solo; San Pedro and Pearl Harbour.

Completing.

HOLLAND (Puget Sound N. Yd. Begun April 11th, 1921, to be completed 1924). 10,600 tons. Dimensions: 506 (*o.a.*) × 61 (*extreme*) × 20 feet (*mean* draught). Guns: 8—5 inch, 4—3 inch AA., 2—6 pdr. Parsons geared turbines. 1 screw. Boilers: 2 Bureau Modified Thornycroft. Designed S.H.P. 7000 = 16 kts. Oil: 1050 tons. Complement, 388. Generally sister ship to *Whitney* and *Dobbin*, Destroyer Tenders.

SCRAPPED

CANOPUS (New York S.B. Co., 1919). 9325 tons. Dimensions: 373¾ × 51½ × 24½ feet. Guns: 2—5 inch, 51 cal., 4—3 inch AA. Machinery: Quadruple expansion. 1 screw. Cylindrical boilers. H.P. 3850 = 13 kts. Oil: 1277 tons. Complement, 314.

SCUTTLED (LOST)

BUSHNELL. 1919 *U. S. Navy Photo.*

(*Atlantic Fleet.*)

BUSHNELL (Seattle Constrn. and D.D. Co., 1915). 3580 tons. Complement: 314. Dimensions: 350½ × 45⅔ × 15 feet (*mean* draught). Guns: 4—5 inch (51 cal.). Machinery: Parsons turbines with reduction gear. Boilers: Water-tube. H.P. (*on trials*) 2617 = 14·15 kts. Fuel: 660 tons *oil*.

SCRAPPED

Photo, Copyright, E. Muller, Jr.

(*Atlantic Fleet.*)

FULTON (ex-*Niagara*) (1914). 1408 tons. Complement: 157. Dimensions: 226½ × 35 × 13 feet (*mean* draught). Guns: 2—3 inch (50 cal.). Torpedo tubes: None officially listed, but from published plans and photos 4 tubes appear to be mounted on foc's'le in two twin deck-mountings. Machinery: 1100 B.H.P. 6-cyl. 2-cycle Nlseco Diesel engines. 1 screw. Designed speed: 12·25 kts.; 12·34 *on trials*. Fuel: 234 tons *oil*.

SOLD

1920 *Photo.*

(*Pacific Fleet.*)

BEAVER (Newport News, 1910, purchased 1918). 5970 tons. Dimensions: 380 (*o.a.*) × 47 × 21 feet (*max.* draught). Guns: 4—5 inch, 2 M.G. 1 screw. I.H.P. 4500 = 16·5 kts. Fuel: 2350 tons oil fuel. Complement, 291.

SCRAPPED

1924 *Official Photo.*

(*Atlantic Fleet.*)

CAMDEN (Flensburg, Germany, 1900, ex-German-Australian s.s. *Kiel*, seized 1917). 9000 tons (estimated). Dimensions: 403⅔ (*o.a.*) × 48 × 24 feet. Guns: 4—4 inch, 4 M.G. I.H.P. 2550 = 12 kts. Coal: 975 tons. Complement, 301.

SCRAPPED

(*Atlantic Fleet.*) 1920 *Photo.*

SAVANNAH (Flensburg, Germany, 1899, ex-Hamburg-American S.S. *Saxonia*, seized 1917). 10,800 tons. Dimensions: 414½ × 46 × 26½ feet. Guns. 4—5 inch, 2 M.G. I.H.P. 2000 = 10·5 kts. Coal: 743 tons + 531 tons additional stowage = 1274 tons. Complement, 354.

SCRAPPED

(*Asiatic Fleet.*) 1920 *Photo.*

RAINBOW (ex s.s. *Norse King*, 1890, purchased 1898). 4360 tons. Dimensions: 351¾ × 41 × 17¼ feet. Guns: 2—5 inch, 2 M.G. I.H.P. 1800 = 12 kts. Coal: 1166 tons. Complement, 312.

SCRAPPED

Heavier-than-Air Aircraft Tender (AV). (1924)

1924, *Official Photo.*

WRIGHT (ex-Emergency Fleet Corporation Hull *No. 180*, "Type B," launched at Hog Island, April 28th, 1920). Conversion effected by Tietjen & Lang Dry Dock Co., Hoboken, 1920-22. 11,000 tons. Dimensions: 448 (*p.p.* and *o.a.*) × 58 × 31 feet. Guns: 2—5 inch, 51 cal., 2—3 in. 50 cal. AA. Designed S.H.P. 6000 = 15 kts. G.E geared turbines and 6 Babcock & Wilcox boilers. Oil: 1630 tons. Complement, 313.

Special Notes.—This ship now serves as Tender to Seaplanes, a large space forward with a big hatchway in weather deck being provided for stowage of spare seaplane wing sections. Other spare parts also carried for Seaplanes. Conversion work carried out allows besides for stowage of 6 Kite Balloons, with all necessary gear for inflation and handling in a balloon well, aft. Large hydrogen generator (using salt water for cooling), hydrogen compressor and flasks, air blower and 2 balloon winches for inflation and flying of Kite Balloons. Foundry, smithy, carpentry, and machine shops, motor erecting shop, fabric and dope shops for repairs and maintenance of aircraft material.

Note.—Minesweepers *Gannet*, *Teal* and *Sandpiper*, have been serving for some time past as Tenders to Seaplanes.

Aircraft Tenders. (1939)

Note.—Minesweepers *Avocet*, *Heron*, *Lapwing*, *Swan*, *Thrush*, *Gannet*, *Pelican*, *Teal* and *Sandpiper*, are now officially rated as Aircraft Tenders (small type) for Patrol Planes.

CURTISS, ALBEMARLE. Laid down April 25, 1938, and 1939, by New York S.B. Corpn. under 1937 and 1938 Programmes respectively. Displacement: 8,625 tons.

4 smaller Seaplane Tenders, **BARNEGAT, BISCAYNE, CASCO, MACKINAC,** of 1,695 tons displacement are to be built under 1938 and 1939 Programmes at Puget Sound Navy Yard.

CHILDS (1920), **WILLIAMSON** (1919). Ex-destroyers. Displacement: 1,190 tons. Dimensions: 310 (*w.l.*), 314⅓ (*o.a.*) × 30⅔ × 9¼ feet (*mean* draught). Guns: 2—4 inch, 50 cal., 2 M.G. AA. Machinery: Westinghouse geared turbines. S.H.P.: 26,000 = 35 kts. Boilers: 4 White-Forster.

Note: These 2 vessels are distinguished by numerals 14 and 15 painted on bows.

PATOKA. 1924 *Official Photo, U.S. Navy Dept.*

PATOKA (1919). Displacement: 5,375 tons. Dimensions: 463¼ (*p.p.*) × 60 × 26¼ feet (*mean* draught). Complement: 156. Guns: 2—5 inch, 2—3 inch AA. Machinery: Quadruple expansion. I.H.P.: 2,900 = 10·5 kts. Boilers: 3 S.E. Oil fuel: 1,109 tons. *Patoka*, though classed as an oiler, is fitted with a mooring mast for airships. Equipment includes workshops for repair of aircraft and storage for petrol.

SCRAPPED

Auxiliaries—Destroyer Tenders. (1939)

DIXIE (May 27, 1939). Laid down March 17, 1938, by New York S.B. Corpn., under 1937 Programme.

PRAIRIE. Laid down Dec. 7, 1938, by same builders, under 1938 Programme. Displacement: 9,450 tons. Dimensions: 520 (*w.l.*) × 73⅓ × — feet.

ALTAIR. 1927 *Official Photo.*

ALTAIR (1919), **DENEBOLA** (1919), **RIGEL** (1918). 6,250 tons. Dimensions: 423¾ × 54 × 20 feet. Guns: 4—5 inch, 51 cal., 4—3 inch AA., 2—6 pdr. Curtis geared turbines. Boilers: 3 single-ended. S.H.P. 2500 = 10·5 kts. Oil: 1097 tons. Complement, 284 to 590. All three built by Skinner & Eddy Corporation, Seattle.

Destroyer Tenders (1939)—*continued.*

DOBBIN.   1925 *Official Photo, U.S. Navy Dept.*

WHITNEY (Boston N.Yd., Oct. 12th, 1923), **DOBBIN** (Philadelphia N.Yd., May 5th, 1921). 8,325 tons. Dimensions: 460 (*p.p.*), 483⅝ (*o.a.*) × 61 × 24½ feet (*mean draught*). Guns: 8—5 inch, 4—3 inch AA., 2—6 pdr. Torpedo tubes, for testing purposes: 2—21 inch. Parsons geared turbines. Boilers: 2 Bureau Modified Thornycroft. 1 screw. Designed S.H.P. 7000 = 16 kts. Oil: 1107 tons. Complement, 589. Equipped to serve as Depot, Repair and Hospital Ship for 18 Destroyers. Possess special anti-torpedo protection. Generally sister ships to *Holland*, Tender to Submarines. Both fitted as flagships.

ALL SCRAPPED

Official, added 1935.

MELVILLE (1915). 5,250 tons. Complement, 574. Dimensions: 400 (*p.p.*) × 54½ × 20 feet (*mean draught*). Guns: 8—5 inch (51 cal.), 1—3 inch AA., 2—3 pdr. Torpedo tubes: 1—18 inch. Machinery: Parsons geared turbines. 2 Thornycroft boilers H.P. (estimated) 4006 = 15·09 kts. Fuel: 930 tons *oil*. Built by New York S.B. Co.

SCRAPPED

1920 Photo, Seward, Weymouth.

BRIDGEPORT (Vegesack, Germany, 1901, ex-North German Lloyd S.S *Breslau*, seized 1917). 7,175 tons. Dimensions: 429½ (*p.p.*) × 54½ × 24⅔ feet. Guns: 8—5 inch, 4—3 inch 50 cal. AA. Machinery: Quadruple expansion. Boilers: 2 double-ended and 2 single-ended. I.H.P. 3600 = 12·5 kts. Coal: 1060 tons. Complement, 552.

HOSP. LARKSPUR

1934 Photo.

BLACK HAWK (Cramp, 1913, ex-Grace Steamship Co. S.S. *Santa Catalina*, taken over 1917). 5,600 tons. Dimensions: 404½ (*p.p.*) × 53¾ × 19¾ feet. Guns: 4—5 inch, 2—3 pdr., 2—1 pdr. Machinery: Quadruple expansion. Boilers: 3 single-ended. I.H.P. 3400 = 13 kts. Oil: 2108 tons. Complement, 685.

SCRAPPED

Auxiliaries—Submarine Tenders. (1939)

FULTON. Displacement: 9,250 tons. Laid down July 19, 1939 at Mare Island Navy Yard, under 1938 Programme.

Note.—Obsolete Cruiser *Alton, ex-Chicago*, Submarine Barracks at Pearl Harbour. Various Minesweepers of "Bird" class serve as Submarine Tenders at New London, Hampton Roads; Coco Solo, and Pearl Harbour.

1937, O. W. Waterman.

HOLLAND (Puget Sound N. Yd., April 12, 1926). Begun April 11th, 1921, completed 1926. 8,100 tons. Dimensions: 460 (*p.p.*), 513 (*o.a.*) × 61 (*extreme*) × 22⅔ feet (*mean draught*). Guns: 8—5 inch, 4—3 inch AA., 2—6 pdr. Torpedo tubes: 1—21 inch, *submerged*. Parsons geared turbines. 1 screw. Boilers: 2 Bureau Modified Thornycroft. Designed S.H.P. 7.000 = 16 kts. Oil: 1050 tons. Complement, 398. Generally sister ship to *Whitney* and *Dobbin*, Destroyer Tenders.

SCRAPPED

ARGONNE.   1930 Photo, Lt.-Com. H. A. Gosnell, U.S.N.

ARGONNE (Hog Island, 1920). 8,400 tons. Dimensions: 448 × 58 × 24⅔ feet *max.* draught. Guns: 4—5 inch, 51 cal., 4—3 inch, 50 cal. AA., 2—6 pdr. Curtis geared turbines. 1 screw. Boilers: 6 Babcock. S.H.P. 6000 = 15 kts. Oil fuel: 1473 tons. Complement, 344.

1935, Bear Photo Service.

CAMDEN (Flensburger S.B. Co., 1900, ex-German-Australian s.s. *Kiel*, seized 1917). Displacement: 6,075 tons. Dimensions: 403⅔ (*o.a.*) × 48 × 22½ feet. Guns: 4—4 inch, 2—3 pdr., 2—1 pdr. Boilers: 4 Babcock. I.H.P. 2550 = 12 kts. Coal: 975 tons. Complement, 378.

SCRAPPED

1926 Official Photo.

CANOPUS (New York S.B. Co., 1919). 5,975 tons. Dimensions: 373¾ × 51½ × 21½ feet. Guns: 2—5 inch, 51 cal., 4—3 inch AA., 2—3 pdr. Machinery: Quadruple expansion. 1 screw. Boilers: 4 single-ended. H.P. 3858 = 13 kts. Oil: 1277 tons. Complement, 317.

SCUTTLED (LOST)

BEAVER.   *1935, courtesy of U.S. Naval Institute, Annapolis, Md.*

BEAVER (Newport News, 1910, purchased 1918). 4,670 tons. Dimensions: 380 (*o.a.*) × 47 × 22⅔ feet (*max. draught*). Guns: 4—5 inch, 2—1 pdr. 1 screw. Boilers: 6 single-ended. I.H.P. 4500 = 16·5 kts. Fuel: 530 tons oil fuel. Complement, 350.

SCRAPPED

Seaplane Tenders—(AV). (1950)

4 "Currituck" Class.

NORTON SOUND. *Added 1949, Tomitch.*

CURRITUCK (Sept. 11, 1943)
NORTON SOUND (Nov. 28, 1943)
PINE ISLAND (Feb. 26, 1944)
SALISBURY SOUND (ex-*Puget Sound*, June 18, 1944)

Displacement:	9,106 tons (15,092 tons *full load*)
Dimensions:	520 (*w.l.*), $540\frac{1}{2}$ (*o.a.*) × $69\frac{1}{4}$ × 26 (*max.*) feet
Guns:	4—5 inch, 38 cal., 20—40 mm. AA.
Machinery:	Geared turbines (Parsons in *Currituck*, Allis-Chalmers in others). 2 shafts. S.H.P.: 12,000 = 19·2 kts.
Complement:	1,247 (*war*)

Notes.—First ship built by Philadelphia Navy Yard, others by Todd Shipyards, Los Angeles. Nos.: *AV* 7, 11, 12, 13. *Norton Sound* has been adapted as the Navy's seagoing rocket laboratory ship and equipped for experiments with guided missiles. Two forward 5-inch guns removed to make space for helicopter platform. Ship has carried out experiments in the Pacific, making practice firings with "loon" missiles, American versions of the wartime V-1 "buzz" bombs, and with shipboard launching of the Navy's "Aerobee", a true rocket which has attained altitudes up to 78 miles and speeds estimated at about 2,000 miles an hour.

4 "Whiting" Class.

CUMBERLAND SOUND (Feb. 23, 1944)
HAMLIN (Jan. 11, 1944)
KENNETH WHITING (Dec. 15, 1943)
ST. GEORGE (Feb. 14, 1944)

Displacement:	8,510 tons (14,000 tons *full load*)
Dimensions:	492 (*o.a.*) × $69\frac{1}{2}$ × 26 (*max.*) feet
Guns:	2—5 inch, 38 cal., 12—40 mm. AA.
Machinery:	Allis-Chalmers geared turbines. 2 shafts. S.H.P.: 8,500 = 18·7 kts.
Boilers:	2 Foster-Wheeler

Notes.—All are modified C 3 (Todd-Pacific) type conversions. Distinctive Nos. AV 17, 15, 14, 16, respectively. *Townsend*, AV 18, cancelled.

1 "Chandeleur" Class.

CHANDELEUR (Nov. 29, 1941)

Displacement:	9,031 tons (14,200 tons *full load*)
Dimensions:	492 (*o.a.*) × $69\frac{1}{2}$ × $23\frac{3}{4}$ (*max.*) feet
Guns:	1—5 inch, 38 cal., 4—3 inch, 50 cal.
Machinery:	General Electric geared turbines. 2 shafts. S.H.P.: 8,500 = 18·4 kts.
Boilers:	2 Foster Wheeler

Notes.—Maritime Commission type C3–S1–B1. Distinctive No. AV 10.

2 "Curtiss" Class.

CURTISS. *Added 1950, U.S. Navy, Official.*

CURTISS (April 20, 1940)
ALBEMARLE (July 13, 1940)

Displacement:	8,671 tons (13,475 tons *full load*)
Dimensions:	508 (*w.l.*), $527\frac{1}{3}$ (*o.a.*) × $69\frac{1}{4}$ × $21\frac{1}{3}$ (*max.*) feet
Guns:	4—5 inch, 38 cal., 14—40 mm. AA.
Aircraft:	25
Machinery:	Parsons geared turbines. 2 shafts. S.H.P.: 12,000 = 19·7 kts.
Boilers:	4 Babcock & Wilcox Express
Complement:	1,195 (*war*)

Notes.—Built as large seaplane tenders by New York S.B. Corpn., under 1937 and 1938 Programmes, respectively, with space for Flag and Fleet Air Wing staffs. Nos. AV 4, 5.

2 "Tangier" Class.

TANGIER. *1944, U.S. Navy, Official.*

POCOMOKE (ex-*Exchequer*, June 8, 1940)
TANGIER (ex-*Sea Arrow*, 1939)

Displacement:	8,560 tons (14,800 tons *full load*)
Dimensions:	465 (*pp.*), 492 (*o.a.*) × $69\frac{3}{4}$ × $24\frac{3}{4}$ (*max.*) feet
Guns:	1—5 inch, 38 cal., 4—3 inch, 50 cal., 8—40 mm. AA.
Machinery:	2 sets geared turbines (General Electric in *Pocomoke*; De Laval in *Tangier*). S.H.P.: 8,500 = 18·4 kts.
Boilers:	2 Foster-Wheeler
Oil fuel:	1,417 tons
Complement:	857

Notes.—Both are modified C 3–Cargo (S) type mercantile conversions. Distinctive Nos., AV 9, 8, respectively.

Seaplane Tenders (Small). (1950)

13 "Barnegat" Class.

SUISUN. *1946, Mr. W. H. Davis.*

BARNEGAT
CORSON
DUXBURY BAY
FLOYDS BAY
GARDINERS BAY
GREENWICH BAY
ONSLOW
ORCA
SAN CARLOS
SHELIKOF
SUISUN
TIMBALIER
VALCOUR

Displacement:	1,766 tons (2,800 tons *full load*)
Dimensions:	300 (*w.l.*), $310\frac{2}{3}$ to $311\frac{3}{4}$ (*o.a.*) × 41 × $13\frac{1}{2}$ (*max.*) feet
Guns:	1—5 inch, 38 cal., 5—40 mm. AA.
Machinery:	2 sets Diesels. 2 shafts. B.H.P.: 6,080 = 18·2 kts.
Complement:	215

Notes.—Original main armament of 4—5 inch was severely reduced to save top weight. *Absecon*, *Barataria*, *Bering Strait*, *Casco*, *Castle Rock*, *Chincoteague*, *Cook Inlet*, *Coos Bay*, *Half Moon*, *Humboldt*, *Mackinac*, *Matagorda*, *Rockaway*, *Unimak*, *Yakutat* lent to Coast Guard for duty as weather ships. *Rehoboth* and *San Pablo* fitted for oceanographical surveying. Other ships of this class have been adapted for various duties.

No.	*Name*	*Builders*	*Launched*
AVP 10	*Barnegat*	Puget Sound	25 May '41
37	*Corson*		15 July '44
38	*Duxbury Bay*	Lake Washington Shipyard	2 Oct. '44
40	*Floyds Bay*		28 Jan. '45
39	*Gardiners Bay*		2 Dec. '44
41	*Greenwich Bay*		18 Mar. '45
48	*Onslow*		20 Sept. '42
49	*Orca*		4 Oct. '42
51	*San Carlos*		20 Dec. '42
52	*Shelikof*		31 Jan. '43
53	*Suisun*		14 Mar. '43
54	*Timbalier*		18 Apr. '43
55	*Valcour*		5 June '43

Submarine Tenders. (1950)

1 "Euryale" Class.

EURYALE. *1947, U.S. Navy, Official.*

EURYALE

Displacement:	8,282 tons (15,400 tons *full load*)
Dimensions:	$492\frac{1}{2}$ (*o.a.*) × $69\frac{1}{2}$ × 25 feet
Guns:	1—5 inch, 38 cal., 4—3 inch, 50 cal.
Machinery:	Geared turbine. S.H.P.: 8,500 = 16·5 kts.

Note.—No. AS 22. Modified C2 type.

7 "Fulton" Class.

ORION. *1950, U.S. Navy, Official.*

4 Mare Island Navy Yard

FULTON (Dec. 17, 1940)
SPERRY (Dec. 17, 1941)
BUSHNELL (Sept. 14, 1942)
HOWARD W. GILMORE (ex-*Neptune*, Sept. 16, 1943)

1 Puget Sound Navy Yard

NEREUS (Feb. 12, 1945)

2 Moore Dry Dock Co., Oakland, Calif.

ORION (Oct. 14, 1942)
PROTEUS (Nov. 12, 1942)

Displacement:	9,734 tons (18,000 tons *full load*)
Dimensions:	$530\frac{1}{2}$ (*o.a.*) × $73\frac{1}{3}$ × $25\frac{1}{2}$ (*max.*) feet
Guns:	4—5 inch, 10—40 mm. AA., 20—20 mm. AA.
Machinery:	G.M. Diesels with electric drive. B.H.P.: 11,200 = 15·4 kts.
Complement:	1,300

Notes.—*Fulton* authorised by 1938 Programme, others by 1940. (AS 11, 12, 15–19.) Vary in detail.

Submarine Tenders (1950)—*continued.*

4 "Ægir" Class.

ÆGIR	ANTHEDON	APOLLO	CLYTIE

Displacement: 8,100 tons (16,100 tons *full load*)
Dimensions: 492 (o.a.) × 69½ × 26½ (*max.*) feet
Guns: 1—5 inch, 38 cal., 4—3 inch, 50 cal.
Machinery: Turbine. S.H.P.: 8,500 — 18·4 kts.

Note.—Nos. 23–26. C3–S–A2 type.

2 "Griffin" Class.

PELIAS.   1944, U.S. Navy, Official.

GRIFFIN (ex-*Mormacpenn*, Nov. 10, 1939)
PELIAS (ex-*Mormacyork*, Nov. 14, 1939)

Displacement: 8,600 tons (14,500 tons *full load*)
Dimensions: 492 × 69½ × 24½ (*max.*) feet
Guns: 4—3 inch, 50 cal.
Machinery: 4 sets Busch-Sulzer Diesels. B.H.P.: 8,500 — 16·5 kts.
Complement: 1,513

Notes.—C3 Cargo type. Nos. AS 13, 14.

Motor Torpedo Boat Tender.

OYSTER BAY (1942)

Displacement: 1,766 tons (2,800 tons *full load*)
Dimensions: 310¾ (o.a.) × 41 × 13½ feet
Guns: 2—5 inch, 38 cal., 8—40 mm. AA.
Machinery: 2 shafts. Diesel. B.H.P.: 2,400 — 18 kts.
Complement: 215

Notes.—AVP 28 (AGP 6). Built by Lake Washington Shipyard.

Destroyer Tenders. (1950)

10 "Everglades" Class.

GRAND CANYON.   1947, U.S. Navy, Official.

ARCADIA (Nov. 19, 1944)	**ISLE ROYAL**
BRYCE CANYON	**KLONDIKE** (Aug. 12, 1944)
EVERGLADES (Jan. 28, 1945)	**SHENANDOAH** (March 29, 1945)
FRONTIER (March 25, 1945)	**TIDEWATER** (June 30, 1945)
GRAND CANYON (April 27, 1945)	**YELLOWSTONE** (April 12, 1945)

Displacement: 8,165 tons (16,635 tons *full load*)
Dimensions: 465 (w.l.), 492 (o.a.) × 69½ × 27½ feet
Guns: 1—5 inch, 4—3 inch, 4—40 mm. AA.
Machinery: Geared turbines. S.H.P.: 8,500 — 18·4 kts.
Boilers: 2 Foster-Wheeler or Babcock & Wilcox
Complement: 826

Notes.—By Todd Shipyards, and other builders. Nos. AD 23, 36, 24, 25, 28, 29, 22, 26, 31, 27. Three other ships (*Arrowhead, Canopus, New England*) were cancelled in 1945, and a fourth (*Great Lakes*) sold. *Frontier* commissioned March 2, 1946. *Bryce Canyon* completed Dec. 20, 1949.

PRAIRIE.   1941, U.S. Navy, Official.

2 *New York S.B. Corpn.*	3 *Tampa S.B. Co.*
DIXIE (May 27, 1939)	**PIEDMONT** (Dec. 7, 1942)
PRAIRIE (Dec. 9, 1939)	**SIERRA** (Feb. 23, 1943)
	YOSEMITE (May 16, 1943)

Displacement: 9,450 tons (17,176 tons *full load*)
Dimensions: 520 (w.l.), 530½ (o.a.) × 73½ × 25½ feet
Guns: 4—5 inch, 38 cal., 8—40 mm. AA.
Machinery: Geared turbines. 2 shafts. S.H.P.: 11,000 –19·6 kts.
Complement: 1,262 (war)

Notes.—Nos. AD 14, 15, 17, 18, 19 respectively. *Piedmont* commissioned Jan. 5, 1944.

Destroyer Tenders (1950)—*continued.*

CASCADE (June 7, 1942)

Displacement: 9,800 tons (16,600 tons *full load*)
Dimensions: 492 (o.a.) × 69½ × 27½ (*max.*) feet
Guns: 2—5 inch, 38 cal., 6—40 mm. AA.
Machinery: Turbines. S.H.P.: 8,500 — 18·4 kts.
Complement: 860

Note.—Nc. AD 16.

2 "Hamul" Class.

HAMUL.   1947, Wright & Logan.

HAMUL (ex-*Dr. Lykes*, April 6, 1940)   **MARKAB** (ex-*Mormacpenn*, Dec. 21, 1940)

Displacement: 8,560 tons (14,800 tons *full load*)
Dimensions: 465 (pp.), 492 (o.a.) × 69½ × 24½ feet
Guns: 1—5 inch, 4—3 inch, 4—40 mm. AA.
Machinery: Geared turbines. S.H.P.: 8,500 — 18·4 kts.
Boilers: 2 Foster-Wheeler
Complement: 857

Note.—AD 20, 21.

FLEET SUPPORT SHIPS (1973)

3 DESTROYER TENDERS (AD): "GOMPERS" CLASS

Name	No	Laid down	Launched	Commissioned
• **SAMUEL GOMPERS**	AD 37	9 July 1964	14 May 1966	1 July 1967
• **PUGET SOUND**	AD 38	15 Feb 1965	16 Sep 1966	27 Apr 1968

AD 40 (Fiscal year 1973 programme)

Displacement, tons	22 260 full load
Dimensions, feet	643 oa × 85 × 22·5
Guns	1—5 inch (127 mm) 38 cal DP in *Samuel Gompers* and *Puget Sound*
Missile launchers	1 Basic Point Defence Missile System (BPDMS) launcher firing Sea Sparrow missiles planned for AD 40
Main engines	Geared turbines (De Laval); 20 000 shp; 1 shaft = 20 knots
Boilers	2 (Combustion Engineering)
Complement	1 806 (135 officers, 1 671 enlisted men)

These are the first US destroyer tenders of post-World War II design; capable of providing repair and supply services to new destroyer-type ships which have advanced missile, anti-submarine, and electronic systems. The tenders also have facilities for servicing nuclear power plants. Services can be provided simultaneously to six guided-missile destroyers moored alongside. Basic hull design similar to "L. Y. Spear" and "Simon Lake" submarine tenders. Provided with helicopter platform and hangar; two 7 000-pound capacity cranes.

Samuel Gompers authorised in Fiscal Year 1964 new construction programme and *Puget Sound* in FY 1965 programme. Both ships built by Puget Sound Naval Shipyard, Bremerton, Washington.

AD 39 of FY 1969 programme cancelled prior to start of construction to provide funds for overruns in other new ship programmes.

AD 40 of this class authorised in FY 1973 new construction programme; estimated cost of this ship $86 900 000. NATO Sea Sparrow missile system planned for AD 40.

NOMENCLATURE Destroyer tenders generally are named for geographic areas. Samuel Gompers was an American labour leader.

PUGET SOUND (AD 38)   1972, United States Navy

6 DESTROYER TENDERS (AD) : "KLONDIKE" CLASS

Name	No.	Launched	Commissioned
ARCADIA	AD 24	19 Nov 1944	13 Sep 1951
EVERGLADES	AD 24	28 Jan 1945	25 May 1951
*SHENANDOAH	AD 26	29 Mar 1945	13 Aug 1945
*YELLOWSTONE	AD 27	12 Apr 1945	15 Jan 1946
ISLE ROYAL	AD 29	19 Sep 1945	9 June 1962
*BRYCE CANYON	AD 36	7 Mar 1946	15 Sep 1950

Displacement, tons	8 165 standard ; 16 635 to 16 900 full load
Dimensions, feet	465 wl ; 492 oa × 69·5 × 27·2
Guns	1—5 inch (127 mm) 38 cal DP
Main engines	Geared turbines ; 8 500 shp 1 shaft = 18·4 knots
Boilers	2 (Foster-Wheeler or Babcock & Wilcox)
Complement	778 to 918

These ships are of modified C-3 design completed as destroyer tenders. Officially considered two classes (see below). *Arcadia, Shenandoah Yellowstone* built by Todd Shipyards, Los Angeles, Calif ; *Bryce Canyon* by Charleston Navy Yard ; *Everglades* by Los Angeles SB & DD Co ; and *Isle Royal* by Todd Pacific Shipyards, Seattle, Wash. *Isle Royal* first commissioned on 26 Mar 1946 and placed in reserve before being completely outfitted ; recommissioned for service on 9 June 1962 and commenced operations in January 1963.
Originally 14 ships of two similar designs, the "Klondike" class of AD 22-25 and "Shenandoah" class of AD 26-33, 35, and 36. *Great Lakes* (AD 30), *New England* (AD 32), *Canopus* (AD 33, ex-AS 27), *Arrow Head* (AD 35, ex-AV 19) cancelled before completion ; *Klondike* (AD 22) reclassified AR 22 ; *Grand Canyon* (AD 28) reclassified AR 28. Also see *Disposals and Transfers.*
Three ships remain in active service ; others in reserve. (*Arcadia* remains on Navy List in Maritime Administration reserve fleet).

ARMAMENT. Original armament for "Klondike" class was 1—5 in gun, 4—3 in guns. and 4—40 mm guns ; for "Shenandoah" class was 2—5 in guns and 8—40 mm guns.

MODERNISATION. Most of these ships have been modernised under the FRAM II programme to service modernised destroyers fitted with ASROC improved electronics helicopters etc.

DISPOSALS AND TRANSFERS
Tidewater AD 31 transferred to Indonesia in Jan 1971 for use as tender to off-shore oil operations (Navy manned) ; **Frontier** AD 25 stricken on 1 Dec 1972.

ISLE ROYAL (AD 29)   1970, United States Navy

1 DESTROYER TENDER (AD) : "CASCADE" TYPE

Name	No.	Launched	Commissioned
*CASCADE	AD 16	7 June 1942	12 Mar 1943

Displacement, tons	9 800 standard ; 16 600 full load
Dimensions, feet	492 oa × 69·5 × 27·2
Guns	1—5 inch (127 mm) 38 cal DP
Main engines	Turbines (General Electric) ; 1 shaft ; 8 500 shp = 18·4 knots
Boilers	2 (Foster-Wheeler)
Complement	857

Built by Western Pipe & Steel Co. San Francisco, C3-S1-N2 type. Modernised to service FRAM destroyers.
The *Cascade* is in active service.

CASCADE (AD 16)   1971, United States Navy

5 DESTROYER TENDERS (AD) : "DIXIE" CLASS

Name	No.	Launched	Commissioned
* DIXIE	AD 14	27 May 1939	25 Apr 1940
* PRAIRIE	AD 15	9 Dec 1939	5 Aug 1940
* PIEDMONT	AD 17	7 Dec 1942	5 Jan 1944
* SIERRA	AD 18	23 Feb 1943	20 Mar 1944
* YOSEMITE	AD 19	16 May 1943	25 May 1944

Displacement, tons	9 450 standard ; 17 176 full load
Dimensions, feet	520 wl ; 530·5 oa × 73·3 × 25·5
Guns	1 or 2—5 inch (127 mm) 38 cal DP
Main engines	Geared turbines ; 2 shafts ; 11 000 shp = 19·6 knots
Boilers	4 (Babcock & Wilcox "A")
Complement	1 076 to 1 698 (total accommodation)

Dixie and *Prairie* built by New York Shipbuilding Corp. Camden, New Jersey ; others by Tampa Shipbuilding Co. Florida. All five ships are active. The two after 5 inch guns and the eight 40 mm AA guns were removed.
All five ships are active, amongst the oldest ships remaining in service with the US Navy.

MODERNISATION. All of these ships have been modernised under the FRAM II programme to service destroyers fitted with ASROC, improved electronics, helicopters, etc. Two or three 5 inch guns and eight 40 mm guns removed during modernisation.

FLEET SUPPORT SHIPS (1973)

SHENANDOAH (AD 26)   1964, United States Navy

PIEDMONT (AD 17)   1970, United States Navy

ISLE ROYAL (AD 29)   1970, United States Navy

YOSEMITE (AD 19)   1968, United States Navy

4 SUBMARINE TENDERS (AS): "L. Y. SPEAR" CLASS

Name	No.	Laid down	Launched	Commissioned
*L. Y. SPEAR	AS 36	5 May 1966	7 Sep 1967	28 Feb 1970
*DIXON	AS 37	7 Sep 1967	20 June 1970	7 Aug 1971
	AS 39	(Fiscal Year 1972 programme)		
	AS 40	(Fiscal Year 1973 programme)		

Displacement, tons	13 000 standard; AS 36 and AS 37 23 350 full load; AS 39 and AS 40 24 000 full load
Dimensions, feet	643·6 oa × 85 × 25·3 (AS 39 and AS 40 28·6)
Guns	2—5 inch (127 mm) 38 cal DP in L. Y. Spear and Dixon; 4—20 mm AA planned for AS 39 and AS 40
Missile launchers	1 Basic Point Defence Missile System (BPDMS) launcher firing Sea Sparrow missiles planned for AS 39 and AS 40
Main engines	Geared turbines (General Electric); 20 000 shp; 1 shaft = 20 knots
Boilers	2 (Foster Wheeler)
Complement	1 072 (42 officers, 1 030 enlisted men)

L. Y. SPEAR (AS 36)   1969, General Dynamics (Quincy)

These ships are the first US submarine tenders designed specifically for servicing nuclear-propelled attack submarines with latter ships built to a modified design to support SSN-688 class submarines. (Four previous submarine tenders of post-World War II construction are configured to support ballistic missile submarines.) Basic hull design similar to "Samuel Gompers" class destroyer tenders. Provided with helicopter deck but no hangar. Each ship can simultaneously provide services to four submarines moored alongside.

L. Y. Spear authorised in Fiscal Year 1965 new construction programme and Dixon in FY 1966 programme. Both ships built by General Dynamics Corp, Quincy, Massachusetts.

AS 38 of FY 1969 programme cancelled prior to start of construction to provide funds for overruns in other new ship programmes.

AS 39 authorised in FY 1972 new construction programme and AS 40 in FY 1973 programme; estimated cost of latter ship $79 900 000. Later ships will have NATO Sea Sparrow missile system.

NOMENCLATURE. Submarine tenders generally are named after pioneers in submarine development and mythological characters.

L. Y. SPEAR (AS 36)   1970, United States Navy

2 SUBMARINE TENDERS (AS): "SIMON LAKE" CLASS

Name	No.	Laid down	Launched	Commissioned
•SIMON LAKE	AS 33	7 Jan 1963	8 Feb 1964	7 Nov 1964
•CANOPUS	AS 34	2 Mar 1964	12 Feb 1965	4 Nov 1965

Displacement, tons	21 450 to 22 250 full load
Dimensions, feet	643·7 × 85 × 30
Guns	4—3 inch (76 mm) 50 cal AA (twin)
Main engines	Geared turbines; 20 000 shp; 1 shaft = 18 knots
Boilers	2 (Combustion Engineering)
Complement	1 075 (55 officers, 1 020 men)

These ships are designed specifically to service Fleet Ballistic Missile Submarines (SSBN), with as many as three submarines alongside being supported simultaneously. The Simon Lake was authorised in the Fiscal Year 1963 new construction programme and built by the Puget Sound Naval Shipyard; the Canopus was authorised in FY 1964 and built by Ingalls Shipbuilding Corp. AS 35 was authorised in FY 1965 programme, but her construction was deferred. The last ship would have permitted one tender to be assigned to each of five FBM submarine squadrons with a sixth ship available to rotate when another was in overhaul, however, only four SSBN squadrons were established.

Note cranes amidships, funnel location (flanked by gun mounts and helicopter platform).

SIMON LAKE (AS 33)   1965 United States Navy

7 "FULTON" and "PROTEUS" CLASSES: SUBMARINE TENDERS (AS)

Name	No.	Builders	Commissioned	F/S
FULTON	AS 11	Mare Island Navy Yard	12 Sep 1941	AA
SPERRY	AS 12	Moore S.B. & D.D. Co, Oakland	1 May 1942	PA
BUSHNELL	AS 15	Mare Island Navy Yard	10 Apr 1943	AR
HOWARD W. GILMORE (ex-*Neptune*)	AS 16	Mare Island Navy Yard	24 May 1944	AR
NEREUS	AS 17	Mare Island Navy Yard	27 Oct 1945	PR
ORION	AS 18	Moore S.B. & D.D. Co, Oakland	30 Sep 1943	AA
PROTEUS	AS 19	Moore S.B. & D.D. Co, Oakland	31 Jan 1944	PA

Displacement, tons 9 734 standard; 16 230-17 020 full load (19 200, AS 19)
Dimensions, feet (metres): 530·5 (except *Proteus* 574·5) × 73·3 × 25·5 *(161·7 (Proteus 175·1) × 22·3 × 7·8)*
Guns: 2—5 in *(127 mm)*/38 in AS 15 and 17; 4—20 mm (Mk 67) (single) in active ships; 2—20 mm (Mk 24) (twin) in AS 17 only
Main engines: Diesel-electric (General Motors) (Allis Chalmers in AS 19); 11 200 bhp; 2 shafts = 15·4 knots
Complement: 1 286-1 937 (except *Proteus* 1 300 (86 officers, 1 214 enlisted men))

These venerable ships are contemporaries of the similar-design "Dixie" class destroyer tenders and the "Vulcan" class repair ships. Launched on 27 December 1940, 17 December 1941, 14 September 1942, 16 September 1943, 12 February 1945, 14 October 1942 and 12 November 1942 respectively. As built, they carried the then-standard large auxiliary armament of four 5-in guns plus eight 40 mm guns (twin). The original 20 ton capacity cylinder cranes have been replaced in *Howard W. Gilmore*, who was decommissioned 30 September 1980 and replaced by *Emory S. Land* (AS 39).

Conversion: *Proteus* AS 19 was converted at the Charleston Naval Shipyard, under the Fiscal Year 1959 conversion programme, at a cost of $23 million to service nuclear-powered fleet ballistic missile submarines (SSBN). Conversion was begun on 19 January 1959 and she was recommissioned on 8 July 1960. She was lengthened by adding a 44 ft section amidships, and the bare hull weight of this six-deck high insertion was approximately 500 tons. Three 5-in guns were removed and her upper decks extended aft to provide additional workshops. Storage tubes for Polaris missiles installed; bridge crane amidships loads and unloads missiles for alongside submarines.

Electronics: AS 11, 12, 18 and 19 fitted with OE-82 satellite communications antenna, SSR-1 receiver and WSC-3 transceiver.

Modernisation: All except *Proteus* have undergone FRAM II modernisation to service nuclear-powered attack submarines. Additional maintenance shops provided to service nuclear plant components and advanced electronic equipment and weapons. After two 5-in guns and eight 40 mm guns (twin) removed.

NEREUS (AS 17)   *United States Navy*

PROTEUS (AS 19)   *1963, United States Navy*

2 Submarine Tenders (AS): "Griffin" Class

GRIFFIN (ex- *Marmacpenn*, 10 Nov 1939) AS 13
PELIAS (ex-*Mormacyork*, 14 Nov 1939)   AS 13

Displacement, tons	8 600 standard; 14 500 full load
Dimensions, feet	492 × 69·5 × 24·2 max
Guns	4—3 in, 50 cal
Main engines	4 sets Busch-Sulzer diesels; 8 500 bhp = 16·5 knots

C3 Cargo type. Launch dates above. Completed on 31 July 1941 and 5 Sep 1941, respectively. Both in the Pacific Reserve Fleet. *Pelias* is Accommodation/Berthing ship at Mare Island, California. *Griffin* is Headquarters ship at Stockton, California.

2 "HUNLEY" CLASS: SUBMARINE TENDERS (AS)

Name	No.	Builders	Commissioned	F.S
HUNLEY	AS 31	Newport News S.B. & D.D. Co	16 June 1962	PA
HOLLAND	AS 32	Ingalls S.B. Co, Pascagoula	7 Sep 1963	AA

Displacement, tons: 10 500 standard; 19 000 full load
Dimensions, feet (metres): 599 × 83 × 27 *(182·6 × 25·3 × 8·2)*
Guns: 4—20 mm (singles)
Main engines: Diesel-electric (6 Fairbanks-Morse diesels); 15 000 bhp; 1 shaft = 19 knots
Complement: 2 568 (144 officers, 2 424 enlisted men)

These are the first US submarine tenders of post-World War II construction; they are designed specifically to provide repair and supply services to fleet ballistic missile submarines (SSBN). Have 52 separate workshops to provide complete support. Helicopter platform fitted aft but no hangar. Both ships originally fitted with a 32 ton capacity hammerhead crane; subsequently refitted with two amidships cranes as in "Simon Lake" class.
Hunley authorised in the FY 1960 shipbuilding programme, laid down on 28 November 1960 and launched on 28 September 1961; *Holland* authorised in the FY 1962 programme, laid down on 5 March 1962 and launched on 19 January 1963. Former ship cost $24 359 800.

Conversions: Conversions to provide for Poseidon C-3 missile handling and repairing and support of related systems carried out at Puget Sound Navy Yard as follows: *Hunley,* completed 22 January 1974; *Holland,* completed 20 June 1975.

Electronics: Fitted with OE-82 satellite communications antenna, SSR-1 receiver and WSC-3 transceiver.

HOLLAND   *USN*

HUNLEY (AS 31)   *United States Navy*

HOLLAND   *1964, United States Navy, Official*

2 + 4 "YELLOWSTONE" and "SAMUEL GOMPERS" CLASSES: DESTROYER TENDERS (AD)

Name	No.	Builders	Laid down	Launched	Commissioned	F/S
SAMUEL GOMPERS	AD 37	Puget Sound Naval S.Y., Bremerton	9 July 1964	14 May 1966	1 July 1967	PA
PUGET SOUND	AD 38	Puget Sound Naval S.Y., Bremerton	15 Feb 1965	16 Sep 1966	27 Apr 1968	AA
YELLOWSTONE	AD 41	National Steel and S.B. Co, San Diego	2 June 1977	27 Jan 1979	May 1980	AA
ACADIA	AD 42	National Steel and S.B. Co, San Diego	14 Feb 1978	28 July 1979	early1981	Bldg
CAPE COD	AD 43	National Steel and S.B. Co, San Diego	27 Jan 1979	—	mid-1981	Bldg
—	AD 44	National Steel and S.B. Co, San Diego	Aug 1980	—	1983	Bldg

Displacement, tons: 20 500 full load
Dimensions, feet (metres): 644 × 85 × 22·5 *(196·3 × 25·9 × 6·9)*
Guns: 1—5 in *(127 mm)*/38 (Mk 30) *(Puget Sound* only); 4—20 mm (Mk 67) (see notes)
Missiles: 1 NATO Sea Sparrow system planned for AD 41 and later ships
Main engines: Steam turbines (De Laval); 20 000 shp; 1 shaft = 18 knots
Boilers: 2 (Combustion Engineering)
Complement: 1 803 (135 officers, 1 668 enlisted men including 4 officers and 96 enlisted ladies)

These are the first US destroyer tenders of post-World War II design; capable of providing repair and supply services to new destroyer classes. The tenders also have facilities for servicing nuclear power plants. Services can be provided simultaneously to six guided-missile destroyers moored alongside. Basic hull design similar to "L. Y. Spear" and "Simon Lake" submarine tenders. Provided with helicopter platform and hangar; two 7 000 lb capacity cranes.
Samuel Gompers authorised in the FY 1964 new construction programme and *Puget Sound* in the FY 1965 programme.
Two sisters of *Samuel Gompers* were cancelled—AD 39 of the FY 1960 programme on 11 December 1965 prior to start of construction to provide funds for overruns in other new ship programmes and AD 40, authorised in the FY 1973 programme, in April 1974 AD 41 was authorised in the FY 1975 programme and AD 42 in the FY 1976 programme, AD 43 in the FY 1977 programme and AD 44 in the FY 1979 programme. (AD 41 and later ships of a slightly modified design.)
Estimated cost of AD 43 (ordered 30 September 1977) is $260·4 million and estimated cost of AD 44 is $318 million.
Puget Sound replaced *Albany* as 6th Fleet Fleet flagship in July 1980 after suitable conversion.

Electronics: Fitted with OE-82 satellite communications antenna and WSC-3 transceiver.

Gunnery: Proposed armament of AD 41-43 is two 40 mm Mk 14 (singles), two 20 mm Mk 67 (singles). Two 40 mm saluting guns (AD 37 and 38).

Particulars: Apply only to "Samuel Gompers" class.

SAMUEL GOMPERS   *8/1978, Dr. Giorgio Arra*

3 "KLONDIKE" and "SHENANDOAH" CLASSES: DESTROYER TENDERS (AD)

Name	No.	Builders	Commissioned	F/S
EVERGLADES	AD 24	Los Angeles S.B. & D.D. Co	25 May 1951	AR
SHENANDOAH	AD 26	Todd Shipyards, Los Angeles	13 Aug 1945	AA
BRYCE CANYON	AD 36	Charleston NY	15 Sep 1950	PA

Displacement, tons: 8 165 standard; 14 700 full load (15,460 AD 24)
Dimensions, feet (metres): 492 × 69·5 × 27·2 *(150 × 21·2 × 8·3)*
Guns: 1—5 in *(127 mm)*/38 (Mk 37) (AD 36)
 2—3 in *(76 mm)*/50 (Mk 26) (AD 24)
 4—20 mm (Mk 68) (AD 26)
Main engines: Steam turbines (Westinghouse); (General Electric in AD 24);
 8 500 shp; 1 shaft = 18·4 knots
Boilers: 2 Foster-Wheeler; (Babcock & Wilcox in AD 24)
Complement: 825 to 899

These ships are of modified C-3 design completed as destroyer tenders. *Everglades* launched 28 January 1945, *Shenandoah* 29 March 1945; *Bryce Canyon* 7 March 1946.
Two ships remain in active service with *Everglades* in reserve as accommodation and depot ship at Philadelphia Navy Yard.
Shenandoah planned for deletion 1 April 1980.

Gunnery: Original armament for "Klondike" class was one 5-in gun, four 3-in guns, and four 40 mm guns; for "Shenandoah" class was two 5-in guns and eight 40 mm guns. One Mk 52 FCS and one Mk 26 FC radar fitted in AD 36.
Two 40 mm saluting guns in AD 24 and 26.

Modernisation: These ships have been modernised under the FRAM II programme to service modernised destroyers fitted with ASROC, improved electronics, helicopters etc.

BRYCE CANYON   7/1979, *Dr. Giorgio Arra*

1 "POINT BARROW" CLASS: AUXILIARY DEEP SUBMERGENCE SUPPORT SHIP (AGDS)

Name	No.	Builders	Commissioned	F/S
POINT LOMA	AGDS 2	Maryland S.B. & D.D. Co	28 Feb 1958	PA
(ex-*Point Barrow*)	(ex-AKD 1)			

Displacement, tons: 9 415 standard; 14 000 full load
Dimensions, feet (metres): 492 × 78 × 22 *(150 × 23·8 × 6·7)*
Guns: None
Main engines: Steam turbines (Westinghouse); 6 000 shp; 2 shafts = 15 knots
Boilers: 2 (Foster-Wheeler)
Complement: 160 (Including scientific personnel and submersible operators)

A docking ship designed to carry cargo, vehicles, and landing craft (originally designated AKD). Launched on 25 May 1957, commissioned in USN as above. Decommissioned and delivered to Military Sea Transportation Service (now Military Sealift Command) on 29 May 1958. Maritime Administration S2-ST-23A design; winterised for arctic service. Fitted with internal ramp and garage system.
Subsequently refitted with hangar over docking well and employed in transport of large booster rockets to Cape Kennedy Space Center. Primarily used to carry the second stage of the Saturn V moon rocket and Lunar Modules. Placed out of service in reserve on 28 September 1972.
Transferred from Military Sealift Command to Navy on 28 February 1974 for modification to support deep submergence vehicles, especially the bathyscaph *Trieste II*. Placed in commission "special" on 28 February 1974 as the AGDS 2; renamed *Point Loma* for the location of the San Diego submarine base where Submarine Development Group 1 operates most of the Navy's submersibles. *Point Loma* was placed in commission on 30 April 1975. Aviation gas capacity increased to approximately 100 000 gallons (US) to support *Trieste II* which uses lighter-than-water avgas for flotation.

Classification: The designation AGDS was established on 3 January 1974; originally it was a service craft designation rather than a ship designation. AGDS 1 was assigned briefly to the floating dry dock *White Sands* (ARD 20), the previous *Trieste II* support ship. *Point Loma* renamed and reclassified AGDS 2 on 28 February 1974.

Electronics: Fitted with OE-82 satellite communications antenna and SSR-1 receiver.

POINT LOMA   7/1979, *Dr. Giorgio Arra*

THE COAST GUARD

THE origins of the US Coast Guard date back over 200 years. The Revenue Cutter Service was formed in 1790, and 58 years later, with a more reasonable balance between the use of government funds and concern for human survival at sea, the Life Saving Service was founded in 1848. On 28 January 1915, the two were amalgamated by Act of Congress to form the US Coast Guard which was described as: "a military force and a branch of the armed forces of the USA at all times. The Coast Guard shall be a service in the Treasury Department except when operating as a service in the Navy."

In 1939 the duties of the lighthouse service were assumed by the Coast Guard and, on 1 November 1941, the whole force was placed under naval command. The Bureau of Navigation and Steamboat Inspection was added to the Coast Guard in 1942.

Between January 1915 and 1919 the Coast Guard increased its fleet to a total of 22 sea-going cutters, 15 harbour cutters and 11 launches. During World War I the force lost 3 cutters, one torpedoed by a U-Boat while escorting a convoy in the English Channel. But a new war was awaiting the Coast Guard. On 16 January 1920, Congress approved an amendment to the US Constitution and Prohibition was in force. In its Treasury role the Coast Guard was soon embroiled with the rum-runners and expanded its fleet very rapidly during the 1920s.

In 1924 there were 20 destroyers transferred from the Navy, 5 more followed in 1926 and a further 6 in 1930, replacing a similar number from the 1924 group. Over the same period 216 cutters (13 of 100 feet and 203 of 75 feet) were built. With the end of Prohibition in December 1933 over 50 of these craft were transferred to the Navy and, after the expenditure of a vast amount of time, energy and money, the Coast Guard returned to more fruitful and sensible occupations.

After completion of the four large "Tampa" class cutters in the early 1920s, there were no real developments until the ten ships of the "Lake" class were launched in 1927–31. Displacing 2,075 tons full load and with a speed of 17 knots, all ten were transferred to Britain in mid-1941. Before the USA's involvement in World War II, eight more cutters were completed; one ice-reinforced and seven of the successful "Treasury" class of 2,350 tons and 327 feet overall. These were probably the first non-specialist ships of this size designed to carry an aircraft, although this was removed in war-time to make room for a third 5.1-inch gun. One of the class was sunk in January 1942 – the remainder continued with convoy duties until, in 1944, all were converted as amphibious force flagships.

The 13 ships of the "Owasco" class were not completed until after the war, although three of the "Wind" class icebrakers were finished in time for temporary transfer to the USSR, being returned in 1949. The remaining pair were completed post-war for the Navy, but currently all ice-breakers serve in the Coast Guard.

Three classes of smaller cutters (two of 165 feet and one of 125 feet) totalling 55 ships, were built from 1926 onwards, all taking an active role in World War II during which one cutter sank a U-boat single-handed. Further Coast Guard contributions were the 230 craft of the 83 feet design which succeeded the nine 80 feet and six 78 feet launches.

In 1991 the fleet had an impressive list of active ships and craft, although these were severely stretched to carry out the many dutues imposed on them. The Coast Guard budget is quite separate from the Navy, the former having been transferred from the Treasury to the Department of Transportation in 1967. The major vessels are either modern – like the 13 members of the 1,780 ton "Famous Cutter" class – or recently modernized like the 12 vessels of the 3,000 ton "High Endurance" cutters. This latter class, with a speed of 29 knots and a full range of naval equipment and armament, are fully capable of undertaking the tasks of a modern frigate. With a helicopter, 8 harpoon missiles and a full set of modern radars one cannot help wondering how the rum-runners would have coped with them.

J.M.
May 1991

U.S. COASTGUARD SERVICE. (1919) (Alphabetically arranged.)

Revised 1919 from "Ships' Data," U.S. Naval Vessels.   Armaments listed those mounted during War, when ships served on Patrol and Distant Service with the Regular Navy.   Proposed 1919, that the Coastguard Service should be merged into the Regular Navy.

5 CUTTERS building and completing by Norway Con. Co., Everett, Wash.   1600 tons.   240 × 39 × 14 feet.   S.H.P. 2600 = 16 kts. (These details unofficial.)

ACUSHNET.   Steel, 1 screw.   800 tons.   Dimensions: 152 × 29 × 13¾ feet   Speed, 12·5 kts.   Guns: 2—1 pdr., 1 Y-gun.

SOLD

ALGONQUIN (1898).   Steel, 1 screw.   1181 tons.   Dimensions: 205 × 32 × 13½ feet.   Speed, 16 kts.   Guns: 4—3 inch, 2 M.G.

YAG-29

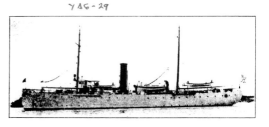

ANDROSCOGGIN (1908).   Wood, 1 screw.   1605 tons.   Dimensions: 210 × 35 × 17½ feet.   Speed, 13·2 kts.   Guns: 3—3 inch, 1—6 pdr., 2 M.G., 1 Y-gun.   Usually on Grand Banks for Fisheries Duty.

SOLD

APACHE (1891).   Iron, 1 screw.   708 tons.   Dimensions: 175 × 29 × 9¼ feet.   Speed, 12 kts.   Guns: 3—3 inch, 2 M.G., 1 Y-gun.

SOLD

BEAR (1874).   Wood, 1 screw.   1700 tons.   Dimensions: 198 × 28½ × 18¼ feet.   Speed not known.   Guns: 3—6 pdr.

STRICKEN

(Depot Ship.)

COLFAX (1871).   Iron, 610 tons.   Dimensions: 179¼ × 25 × 9 feet. No other details known.

SOLD

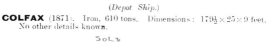

COMANCHE (1896).   Steel, 2 screw.   670 tons.   Dimensions: 169 × 27 × 9 feet.   Guns: 1—3 inch, 2—6 pdr.

MERC TORQUINA (See Windom)

GRESHAM (1897).   Steel, 1 screw.   1090 tons.   Dimensions: 205 × 32 × 11 feet.   Speed, 13 kts.   Guns: 4—3 inch, 2 M.G.

WPG   TRADE WINDS

Photo, Seward, Weymouth.

ITASCA (*ex Bancroft*, 1893).   Steel, 2 screws.   980 tons.   Dimensions: 189 × 32 × 13 feet.   Speed, 14·37 kts.   Guns: 2—3 inch, 2—6 pdr., 1 Y-gun.

SOLD

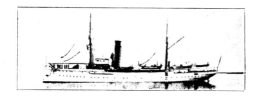

MANNING (1897).   Composite, 1 screw.   1155 tons.   Dimensions: 205 × 32 × 13 ft.   Speed, 14 kts.   Guns: 4—4 inch, 2 M.G.

SOLD

Cruising Cutters—*Continued.*

MORRILL (1889). Iron, 1 screw. 420 tons. Dimensions 145 × 24 × 9 ft. Speed : 13·2 kts. Guns : 1—3 inch, 2—6 pdr., 2 M.G.

MERC EVANGELINE

ONONDAGA (1898). Steel, 1 screw. 1192 tons. Dimensions : 205 × 32 × 13 feet. Speed : 14·5 kts. Guns : 4—6 pdr.

MERC BARGE

OSSIPEE (1915). Steel, 1 screw. 908 tons. Dimensions : 165¾ × 32 × 11¾ feet. Speed : 12·6 kts. Oil fuel only. Guns : 2—3 inch. 2 M.G.

SOLD

PAMLICO (1907). Steel, twin screw. 451 tons. Dimensions : 158 × 30 × 5 ft. Speed : 11·2 kts. Guns : 2—6 pdr.

MERC C.W. CURLETT

SEMINOLE (1900). Steel, 1 screw. 860 tons. Dimensions : 188 × 29 × 11 feet. Speed : 14·7 kts. Guns : 4—3 inch, 2 M.G., 1 Y-gun.

MERC

SENECA (1908). Steel, 1 screw. 1445 tons. Dimensions : 204 × 34 × 17 feet. Speed : 13·2 kts. Guns : 4—4 inch, 2 M.G., 1 Y-gun.

SCRAPPED

SNOHOMISH. Steel, 1 screw. 879 tons. Dimensions : 152 × 29 × 15 feet. Speed : 12·5 kts. Guns : 1—3 inch. 2—6 pdr., 2 M.G.

MERC

TALLAPOOSA (1915). Steel, 1 screw. 912 tons. Dimensions 165¾ × 32 × 11¾ feet. Speed : 12·7 kts. Oil fuel only. Guns : 1—4 inch, 2—6 pdr., 2 M.G., 1 Y-gun. Derelict Destroyer for Gulf of Mexico.

MERC SANTA MARIA

TUSCARORA (1902). Steel, 1 screw. 739 tons. Speed : 11·2 kts Dimensions : 178 × 30 × 11 feet. Guns : 1—3 inch, 2—6 pdr.. 1 Y-gun.

MERC

Photo, U.S. Navy Publicity Bureau.

UNALGA (1912). Steel, 1 screw. 1180 tons. Dimensions : 190 × 32 × 13 feet. Speed 13 kts. 3—6 pdr.

MERC ULUA

WINDOM (1896). Steel, twin screw. 670 tons. Dimensions : 170 × 27 × 9 ft. Speed 12 kts.

MERC TORQUINA

YAMACRAW (1909). Steel, 1 screw. 1082 tons. Dimensions : 191 × 32 × 14 feet. Speed. 13 kts. 2—4 inch, 2—3 inch, 2 M.G.

MERC PEMEX XV

Harbour Cutters.

ARCATA (1903). Wood, 1 screw. 130 tons. Dimensions : 85 × 17 × 10 ft.

MERC PATRICIA FOSS

ARUNDEL (ex *Manhattan*) (1873). Iron, 1 screw. 174 tons. Dimensions : 102 × 20 × 8 feet.

MERC EXPRESS

CALUMET (1894). Iron, 1 screw. 169 tons. Dimensions : 94 × 20 × 8 feet. 2—6 pdr., 2 M.G.

MERC JOHN F DREWS

DAVEY (1908). Steel, 1 screw. 153 tons. Dimensions : 92 × 19 × 10 ft. 1—1 pdr.

MERC DAVID

EMMA KATE ROSS (1882). Iron, 1 screw. 350 tons. Dimensions : 104 × 20 × 10 feet.

GOLDEN GATE (1896). Steel, 1 screw. 220 tons. Dimensions : 110 × 20 × 9 feet.

SOLD

GUTHRIE (1895). Iron, 1 screw. 126 tons. Dimensions : 88 × 17 × 9 feet.

SOLD

Harbour Cutters *continued*.

HARTLEY (1875). Wood, 1 screw. 48 tons. Dimensions: 64 × 11 × 6 feet.

SOLD

HUDSON (1893). Iron, 1 screw. 174 tons. Dimensions: 96 × 20 × 9 feet. Guns: 1—1 pdr.

SOLD

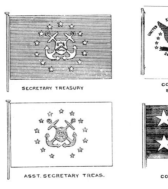

MACKINAC (1903). Steel, 1 screw. 220 tons. Dimensions: 110 × 20 × 10 feet. *Sig.*: GVHB. Guns: 1—6 pdr., 1 M.G.

MERC WILLIAM T. MOORE

Harbour Cutters *continued*.

VERGANA ——, 128 tons. No other details.

Photo, "Syren & Shipping."

MANHATTAN (1918). Steel, 1 screw. Ice Breaker, Salvage Vessel, Tug and Fire Float. 379 tons. 120½ × 24 × 10½ feet. 12 kts.

MERC HAZEL

WINNISIMMET (1903). Steel, 1 screw. 174 tons. Dimensions: 96 × 20 × 9 feet. Guns: 2—1 pdr.

MERC SOPHIA

Harbour Cutters *continued*.

WISSAHICKON (1904). Steel, 1 screw. 174 tons. Dimensions: 96 × 20 × 8 feet. Guns: 1—1 pdr.

MERC ATLAS

LEVI
WOODBURY (1864). Wood, 1 screw. 500 tons. Dimensions: 146 × 28 × 11 feet. 1 gun.
Note.—Above probably re-named or scrapped as there is a new T.B.D. *Woodbury.*

MERC LAKSCO

---

11 Launches.

ACTIVE (—) — tons. ADVANCE (1917), 11 tons. ALERT (1907), 17 tons. GUARD (1913), 52 tons. GUIDE (1907), 32 tons. MAGOTHY (1895), 83 tons. PATROL (1899), 15 tons. PENROSE (1883), 30 tons. SCOUT (1896), 30 tons. SEARCH (1907), — tons. TYBEE (1895), 40 tons.

COAST GUARD. (1931)

Notes.

Officially Revised, 1931, from materials furnished by courtesy of the Commandant, U.S. Coast Guard, Treasury Department, Washington, D.C. Photos also official unless otherwise acknowledged.

SECRETARY TREASURY

COAST GUARD STANDARD.

ASST. SECRETARY TREAS.

COMMANDANT'S FLAG.

Red ▦ White ☐ Blue ▦

I.—ADMINISTRATION.

The U.S. Coast Guard forms part of the Military Forces of the United States, operating under the Secretary of the Treasury in peace, and as part of the Navy, subject to the orders of the Secretary of the Navy, in time of war or when the President shall so direct. (Act of January 28th, 1915.)

Secretary of the Treasury .. The Hon. A. W. Mellon.

*Assistant Secretary of the Treasury** The Hon. Seymour Lowman

Commandant .. .. .. Rear-Admiral F. C. Billard.

8 Chief of Divisions (Inspection, Operations, Personnel, Supplies and Accounts, Intelligence, Construction and Repair, Engineering, Communications).

2 Boards (Life-Saving Apparatus, Inter-Departmental Board on International Service of Ice Observation, Ice Patrol and Ocean Derelict Destruction).

* The Assistant Secretary has immediate supervision of the Coast Guard.

II.—ORGANIZATION (SHIPS).

The vessels of the service are for the most part grouped in divisions, each of which is under the command of a Division Commander, who is one of the ranking officers of the service. The Divisions are as follows :—

				Headquarters.
1.	North-Western Division, Pacific Coast			Seattle, Wash.
2.	California ,,		,,	San Francisco, Cal.
3.	Eastern ,,	Atlantic	,, ..	Boston, Mass.
4.	New York ,,	,,	,, ..	New York, N.Y.
5.	Norfolk ,,	,,	,, ..	Norfolk, Va.
6.	Gulf ,,	Gulf	,, ..	Mobile, Ala.
7.	Lakes ,,		Great Lakes ..	Saulte Ste. Marie, Mich.

8. Bering Sea Fleet, composed of vessels detailed from Northern and Southern Divisions from May to October each year.

Other ships, unattached to the Divisions perform independent duty.

IIa. ORGANIZATION (DISTRICTS, &c.).

Headquarters of Coast Guard at Washington, D.C.

The Coast (and Great Lakes) of the United States are divided into 13 Districts, each being under a District Commander. (*Note.*—These Coast Guard Districts extend over areas different to those of the "Naval Districts" of the Regular Navy.) 1st—9th District extend along Atlantic and Gulf seaboard; 10th, 11th, 12th Districts on Great Lakes; 13th District Pacific Coast and includes Station at Nome, Alaska. Number of C.G. Stations in each District varies between 8 and 41.

III.—TRAINING, REPAIR, STORE ESTABLISHMENTS.

Coast Guard Academy (Fort Trumbull, New London, Conn.). Four years' course for Cadets. Entry by Competitive Examination.

Coast Guard Training Station (Fort Trumbull, New London, Conn.). Receives and trains recruits.

Coast Guard Depot (Arundel Cove, South Baltimore, Md.). For overhaul and repair of vessels stationed on Atlantic Coast, boat-building, &c.

Coast Guard Stores. At Brooklyn N.Y. and San Francisco, Cal. for purchase and issue of supplies to ships and stations.

Coast Guard Radio Repair and Supply Base. At Philadelphia N.Y. Issue and repair radio supplies to ships and stations.

IV. PERSONNEL.

(Total authorized complement, 12,277).

Uniforms similar to U.S. Navy, but C.G. Shield replaces Naval Star on sleeve and shoulder.

Ranks :—Rear-Admiral (1).
Engineer-in-Chief (1).

		Line.	Engineering.	Constructor.	District
					Commander.
Captain	.. ..	21	8	..	..
Commander	..	42	12	1	..
Lieut.-Commander		50	24	1	4
Lieut.	.. ..	106	..	3	10
Lieut. (j.g.)..	} 130				
Ensign	}	..	..	..	..
Chief Warrant Officers	89	..	..	..	..

Warrant Officers total 848.* Pay of Commissioned and W.O. as equivalent grades U.S.N. Age limit, 64.

Petty Officers and Men, 11,137. Enlist for 1, 2 or 3 years; pay as U.S.N.

* Excluding temporary entries.

V.—AVIATION.

10 Aviation Stations authorized and 3 stations in operation, 1 being built. Additional stations to be put in operation each year. 4 Seaplanes in active operation.

5 Twin Motor (engine above wing), large type flying boats under contract, all radio equipped and fitted for life-saving and rescue work.

Notes on subsequent description of Vessels.

Re-classified 1924, as (*a*) Cruising Cutters, 1st Class; (*b*) Cruising Cutters, 2nd Class; (*c*) Coast Guard Destroyers; (*d*) Harbour Cutters and Harbour Launches; (*e*) Patrol Boats.

Ships arranged alphabetically. Classes comprising several ships inserted under earliest name in alphabetical order.

Length is *o.a.* Beam is *moulded.* Draught is *max.* Tonnages are *displacement.*

Stations in italics and Signal Letters in leaded type, usually after description of ships, e.g., *Acushnet* stationed at *Woods Hole, Mass.*, Signal Letters **GVHP.**

11 COAST GUARD DESTROYERS (Transferred from Navy Department).

4 Conyngham Class.

ABEL P. UPSHUR. 1931 *Photo.*

5 *Newport News*: transferred 1930. **Geo. E. Badger, Herndon, Hunt, Abel P. Upshur, Welborn C. Wood.** All built 1920. Displacement: 1215 tons (1318 *full load*). Dimensions: 314½ ×31 ×9¾ feet. S.H.P. 28,000 = 35 kts. Westinghouse geared turbines. 4 White-Forster boilers, 27,500 square feet heating surface. 2 screws. Guns: 3—4 inch, 50 cal., 1—1 pdr.

2 Aylwin Class. 2 Cushing Class.

PORTER. 1931 *Photo*

2 *Cramp*: **Conyngham** (1915). **Porter** (1915). 1090 tons (1205 *full load*.) Designed H.P. 18,000 = 29½ kts. Parsons geared (cruising on starboard shaft only) turbines. Machinery weighs 375 tons. Boilers: 2 White-Forster—24,000 sq. ft. heating surface. Oil: 308 tons. Trials: *Conyngham*, 29·63 kts.; *Porter*, 29·58 kts.
1 *New York S. B. Co.*: **Wainwright** (1915). 1050 tons (1265 *full load*.) Designed H.P. 17,000 = 29½ kts. Parsons geared (cruising on port shaft only) turbines. Machinery averages 369 tons. Boilers: 4 Normand—21,500 sq. ft. heating surface. Trials: 29·67 kts. Oil: 308 tons. (*Jacob Jones* of this type lost during war.)
1 *Fore River*: **Tucker** (1915). Displacements as *Conyngham*. Designed H.P. 17,000 = 29½ kts. Curtis geared (cruising on both shafts) turbines. Machinery weighs 369 tons. Boilers: 4 Yarrow—21,500 sq. ft. heating surface. Oil: 309 tons. Trials: 29·56 kts.
Guns (all four): 3—4 inch, 50 cal., 1—1 pdr. (All other particulars as given under *Conyngham* Class in U.S. Navy Section.)

3 Allen Class.

CASSIN. 1931 *Photo.*

SHAW. 1928 *Photo, Lieut.-Com. G. Finlay, U.S.C.G.*

1 *New York S. B. Co.*: **Ericsson*** (1914). 1090 tons (1211 *full load*). Parsons geared turbines with reciprocating engine (port shaft only) weighs 364 tons. Boilers: 4 Thornycroft—26,936 sq. ft. heating surface. Trials: 29·29 kts.
1 *Bath I.W.*: **McDougal** (1914). 1025 tons (1139 *full load*). Two sets Parsons turbines and two reciprocating. Machinery weighs 325 tons. Boilers: 4 Normand—21,509 sq. feet heating surface. Trials: 30·7 kts. Guns (both): 3—4 inch, 50 cal., 1—1 pdr.
*Has very low mainmast.
(All other particulars as given under *Cushing* Class, in U.S. Navy Section.)
2 *Bath I.W.*: **Cassin, Cummings** (1913). 1020 tons (1139 *full load*) Parsons turbines and reciprocating engines (on port shaft only). Machinery: 329 tons. Boilers: 4 Normand—21,509 sq. feet heating surface. Oil fuel: 312 tons. Trials: *Cassin* 30·14. *Cummings* 30·57 kts.
Guns: 3—4 inch 50 cal., 1—1 pdr. (All other particulars as given under *Aylwin* Class, in U.S. Navy Section.)

1 *Bath I.W.*: **Davis** (1916). Details as *Allen*, in U.S. Navy Section.
1 *Mare Island Navy Yard*: **Shaw** (1916). Displacement, H.P. and speed as *Rowan*. Parsons geared (cruising on port shaft only) turbines. Boilers: 4 Thornycroft. Trials: 29·5 kts. During War, cut in two by R.M.S. *Aquitania*, steamed stern first to Portland (England) and rebuilt by H.M. Dockyard, Plymouth.
1 *Cramp*: **Wilkes** (1916). 1110 tons (1124 *full load*). Designed H.P. 17,000 = 29·5 kts. Parsons geared (cruising on starboard shaft only) turbines. Machinery weighs 367 tons. Boilers: 4 White-Forster. Trials: 29·58 kts.
Guns (all three): 3—4 inch, 50 cal., 1—1 pdr. (All other particulars as given under *Allen* Class in U.S. Navy Section.)

Cruising Cutters

Cruising Cutters—*continued.*

Cruising Cutters—*continued.*

CHELAN. 1929 *Photo.*

TAMPA.

NORTHLAND. *Photo added* 1927.

Name.			Station.	Signal Letters.
ITASCA	..	..	*Honolulu T.H.*	**GVDM.**
SEBAGO	..	..	*Stapleton N.Y.*	**GNDT.**
SARANAC	..	..	*Galveston Texas*	**GVDN.**
SHOSHONE	..	..	*Unalaska Alaska*	**GVFM.**
CAYUGA	..	..	*Building.*	

Built 1930 by Gen. Eng. & Dry Dock Co., Oakland.

CHELAN	..	..	*Seattle, Wash.*	**GYKN.**
CHAMPLAIN	..	..	*Stapleton, N.Y.*	**GNDR.**
MENDOTA	..	..	*Norfolk, Va.*	**GNDS.**
PONTCHARTRAIN	..	..	*Mobile, Ala.*	**GVKP.**
TAHOE	..	..	*San Francisco, Calif.*	**GNDQ.**

All built 1928-29 by Bethlehem Shipbuilding Corporation at Quincy, Mass. Steel, 1 Screw. 1975 tons. Dimensions: 250 (o.a.) × 42 × 16 feet. Turbine-Electric engines (1 main, 2 auxiliary). H.P. 3220 = 16 kts. Guns: 1—5 inch, 1—3 inch, AA., 2—6 pdr. Radius 8,000 miles.

Name.			Station.	Signal Letters.
HAIDA	..	..	*Port Townsend, Wash.*	**GVKW.**
MODOC	..	..	*Wilmington, N.C*	**GVBR.**
MOJAVE	..	..	*Boston. Mass.*	**GVBT.**
TAMPA	..	..		**GVKT.**

All built 1921. Steel, 1 screw. 1780 tons. Dimensions: 240 × 39 × 16½ feet. Guns: 2—5 inch, 1—3 inch AA., 2—6 pdr. S.H.P. 2600 = 16 kts. Machinery: Turbo-electric (General Electric Curtis Turbine).

NORTHLAND (Newport News Shipbuilding Co., 1927). Built of steel, hull being of exceptionally massive construction, to withstand ice pressure. Forefoot cut away to above w.l. Displacement: 2050 tons. Dimensions: 216 (o.a.) × 39 × 15 feet (*mean* draught). Two 6-cyl. 4-cycle Diesel engines with electric drive. Total B.H.P. 1200 = 11 kts. 1 screw. Guns: 2—4 inch, 50 cal., 2—6 pdr. For Bering Sea Patrol. (*San Francisco, Cal.*, **GNDP.**)

Cruising Cutters 1931—*continued.*

GRESHAM (1897). Steel, 1 screw. 1090 tons. Dimensions : 205½ × 32 × 12½ feet. Speed : 14 kts. Guns : 2—3 inch, 50 cal., 2—6 pdr., 1—1 pdr. (*Mobile Ala.* **GVFD.**)

OSSIPEE (1915). Steel, 1 screw. 908 tons. Dimensions : 165¾ × 32 × 11¾ feet. Speed : 12 kts. Guns : 2—3 inch, 2—6 pdr. (*Portland, Me.* **GVBW.**)

REDWING (1919.) Ex-Navy Minesweeper, taken over 1924. Steel, 1 screw. 1210 tons. Dimensions : 187⅝ × 35½ × 13 feet (*mean* draught). Speed : 14 kts. Guns : 2—3 inch, 23 cal., 2—1 pdr. (**GVKM.**) (*Astoria, Oregon*).

SEMINOLE (1900). Steel, 1 screw. 860 tons. Dimensions : 188 × 29½ × 12 feet. Speed : 14 kts. Guns : 2—1 pdr. (*Sault St. Marie, Mich.* **GVFP.**)

SENECA (1908). Steel, 1 screw. 1445 tons. Dimensions : 204 × 34 × 17½ feet. Speed : 13 kts. Guns : 2—4 inch, 50 cal., 2—1 pdr. (*Stapleton, N.Y.,* **GVHL.**)

TALLAPOOSA (1915) Steel, 1 screw. 912 tons. Dimensions : 165¾ × 32 × 11¾ feet. Speed : 12 kts. Oil fuel only. Guns : 2—3 inch, 50 cal., 2—6 pdr. (*Juneau Alaska*).

Cruising Cutters—*continued*

TUSCARORA (1902). Steel, 1 screw. 739 tons. Speed : 14 kts. Dimensions : 178 × 30 × 11 feet. Guns : 2—6 pdr. (*St. Petersburg, Fla,* **GVFS.**)

1919 *Photo, U.S. Navy Publicity Bureau.*

UNALGA (1912). Steel, 1 screw. 1181 tons. Dimensions : 190 × 32½ × 14 feet. Speed : 13 kts. Guns : 2—6 pdr. (**GVHS.**)

Note to Photo.—Additional searchlights are now carried and boats removed from poop.

YAMACRAW (1909). Steel, 1 screw. 1082 tons. Dimensions : 191⅞ × 32½ × 13 feet. Speed : 13 kts. Guns : 2—3 inch, 50 cal., 2—6 pdr. (*Savannah, Ga.,* **GVHR.**)

15 Cruising Cutters. Second Class.

ACUSHNET (1908). Steel, 1 screw. 800 tons. Dimensions : 152 × 29 × 13¾ feet. Speed : 12 kts. Guns : 2—1 pdr. (*Woods Hole, Mass.* **GVHP.**)

1929 *Photo.*

APACHE (1891). Iron, 1 screw. 740 tons. Dimensions : 185½ × 29 × 9¼ feet. Speed : 12 kts. Guns : 3—6 pdr. (*Baltimore, Md.* **GVBS.**)

Cruising Cutters—*continued*

Name.	Station.	Signal Letters.
CAHOKIA	Eureka, Calif.	GVDK.
KICKAPOO	Rockland, Maine.	GVFQ.
MASCOUTIN	Norfolk Va.	GVFB.
SAUKEE	Key West	GVFR.
TAMAROA	San Diego, Calif.	GVCF.

Built 1919-1920 as seagoing tugs ; transferred from U.S. Shipping Board 1921. Steel, 1 screw. 729-767 tons. Dimensions : 151½ × 27½ × 15 feet. Speed : 11 kts. Guns : 2—1 pdr. *Kickapoo* fitted as Ice Breaker. *Cahokia* and *Tamaroa* are oil-fired ; others coal.

CARRABASSET. Photo added 1927.

CARRABASSET (1919). Ex-Fleet Tug taken over from Navy Dept., 1924. Steel, 1 screw. 1133 tons. Dimensions : 155¾ × 30 × 17½ feet. Speed : 13½ kts. Guns : 2—1 pdr. (**GVKL.**)

TAMAROA. 1931 *Photo.*

KANKAKEE. 1929 *Photo.*

KANKAKEE ... Evansville, Ind. ... Built 1919. Steel hull, wood deckhouses. 383 tons. Dimensions : 182 × 34 × 3½ feet. Guns : none. Speed : 12 kts. River Steamer for flood relief.

Cruising Cutters 1931—continued.

1931 Photo.

MANHATTAN (1918). Steel, 1 screw. Ice Breaker, Salvage Vessel, Tug and Fire Float. 406 tons. Dimensions : 120¼ × 24 × 11¾ feet. Speed : 12 kts. Guns : 2—1 pdr. (*New York, N.Y.* **GVCL.**)

PAMLICO (1907). Steel, twin screw. 451 tons. Dimensions : 158 × 30 × 5⅝ feet. Speed : 11 kts. Guns : 2—6 pdr. (*Newbern, N.C.* **GVHJ**).

PEQUOT. Photo added 1927.

PEQUOT (ex-Minelayer *General Samuel M. Mills*, built 1909, transferred from War Department 1922). Steel, 1 screw. 950 tons. Dimensions : 166½ × 32½ × 11½ feet. (*Curtis Bay, Md.* **GVCM**.)
(For *Saukee v. Cahokia*.)

SHAWNEE (1921). Steel. 900 tons. Dimensions : 158¼ × 30 × 14 feet. Guns : 2—1 pdr. Built by Union Con. Co., Oakland, Cal. (*S. Francisco, Calif.* **GVCB.**)

1920 Photo.

SNOHOMISH (1908). Steel, 1 screw. 879 tons. Dimensions : 152 × 29 × 15½ feet. Speed : 12 kts. Guns : 1—3 inch, 50 cal. (*Port Angeles, Wash.* **GVHN.**)
(For *Tamaroa v. Cahokia*.)

Harbour Cutters and Harbour Launches.

Detailed to larger Maritime Ports to enforce Customs and Navigation Laws and the regulation of the anchorage and movements of vessels.

Arcata (1903). Wood. 1 screw. 138 tons. Dimensions : 85 × 17½ × 10½ feet. Speed : 11 kts. Guns : 1—1 pdr. (*Port Townsend, Wash.*, **GVHC.**)

Calumet (1894). Iron. 1 screw. 170 tons. Dimensions : 94½ × 20½ × 9 feet. Guns : None. Speed : 12 kts. (*New York, N.Y.*, **GVDR.**)

Name.	Station.	Signal Letters.
Chautauqua	New York N.Y.	GVJM.
Chicopee	Portland, Maine	GVJL.
Chippewa	Sault Ste. Marie, Mich.	GVJK
Chulahoma	S. Baltimore, Md.	....

All built 1919. Wood. 215 tons. Dimensions : 88 × 20 × 8¾ feet. Speed : 10 kts. Are Ex-Navy Tugs taken over by Coastguard. *Chincoteague* and *Choptank* of this class, sold 1925.

Davey (1908). Steel, 1 screw. 182 tons. Dimensions : 92½ × 19 × 10½ feet. Guns : *Nil.* Speed : 10 kts. (*New Orleans, La.*, **GVHM.**)

Golden Gate (1896). Steel, 1 screw. 240 tons. Dimensions : 110 × 20½ × 9⅝ feet. Speed : 12 kts. (**GVFH.**)

Guard (1914). Wood. 52 tons. Dimensions : 67 ft. 7 in. × 12½ × 6¼ feet. Speed : 9 kts. (*Friday Harb., Wash.*, **GVHW.**)

Guthrie (1895). Iron, 1 screw. 149 tons. Dimensions : 88 × 17½ × 9 feet. Speed : 11 kts. (*Philadelphia, Pa.*, **GVBQ.**)

Hudson (1893). Iron, 1 screw. 179 tons. Dimensions : 96½ × 20 × 9 feet. Speed : 12 kts. (*New York, N.Y.*, **GVDQ.**)

Leopard (1920). Wood. Dimensions : 94 × 24 × 12 feet. (*Curtis Bay, Md.*)

Mackinac (1903). Steel, 1 screw. 241 tons. Dimensions : 110 × 20½ × 10½ feet. Guns : None. Speed : 12 kts. (*Boston, Mass.*, **GVHB.**)

Raritan (1905). Steel. 1 screw. 220 tons *gross*. Dimensions : 103 × 22 ft. 8 in. (*New York, N.Y.*)

Winnisimmet (1903). Steel, 1 screw. 182 tons. Dimensions : 96½ × 20½ × 9 feet. Speed : 12 kts. (*Norfolk, Va.*, **GVFW.**)

Wissahickon (1904). Steel, 1 screw. 194 tons. Dimensions : 96½ × 20½ × 9½ feet. Speed : 12 kts. (*New York, N.Y.*, **GVHD.**)

Harbour Cutters and Harbour Launches—continued.

(Ex-Submarine Chasers.)

Name (late *SC*).		Station.	Signal Letters.
Cook	(438)	New London Conn.	GVKC.
Cygan	(335)	Ketchikan, Alaska	GVKR.
Smith	(155)	Oakland, Cal.	GVKQ.
Tingard	(183)	San Pedro, Cal.	GVJT.

Built 1917-18, taken over 1919-20. Wood. 75 tons. Dimensions : 110 × 14¾ × 6 feet. Speed : 11 kts. Guns : 1—1 pdr. (Twin screw, petrol.)

17 Launches.

Numbered between AB.1. and AB.25.
Displ: 45 tons gross average.
Length from 63ft. to 41ft.

1931 Photo

33—125 ft. steel Patrol Boats: **Active, Agassiz, Alert, Antietam, Bonham, Boutwell, Cahoone, Cartigan, Crawford, Cuyahoga, Diligence, Dix, Ewing, Faunce, Frederick Lee, General Greene, Harriet Lane, Jackson, Legare, Marion, McLane, Montgomery, Morris, Nemaha, Pulaski, Reliance, Rush, Tiger, Travis, Vigilant, Winona, Woodbury, Yeaton.** 220 tons. Dimensions : 125 × 23½ × 6¾ feet. Guns : 1—3 inch, 23 cal.

Swift (1917). Wood Dimensions : 66 × 13½ × 3⅓ feet. Speed : 16 kts. (Twin screw, petrol.) (*San Francisco, Cal.*, **GVHT.**)

Patrol (1917). Wood, 23 tons. Dimensions : 68¾ × 14 × 3¾ feet. Speed : 9 kts.

PETREL. 1929 Photo.

13 steel Patrol Boats: **Corwin, Dallas, Dexter, Eagle, Forward, Gallatin, Mahoning, Nansemond, Naugatuck, Patriot, Perry, Petrel, Wolcott.** 210 tons displacement. 99′ 8″ × 23′ × 8′. Diesel engines. Guns : 1—3 inch, 23 cal.

CG 182. Photo added 1927.

194 wooden Patrol Boats: **CG—100** to **CG—302.** (1924-25) 37 tons displacement. Dimensions : 74′ 11″ × 13′ 7½″ × 4′. Gasoline engine. Guns : 1—1 pdr. 16 boats lost or disposed of.

COAST GUARD. (1939)

Notes.

Officially Revised, 1939, from materials furnished by courtesy of the Commandant, U.S. Coast Guard, Treasury Department, Washington, D.C. Photos also official unless otherwise acknowledged.

SECRETARY TREASURY.

COAST GUARD STANDARD.

ASST SECRETARY TREAS.

UNDER SECRETARY TREASURY.

ENSIGN

COMMANDANT'S FLAG.

Red ▦   White □   Blue ▤

I.—ESTABLISHMENT.

The U.S. Coast Guard was established by the consolidation of the Revenue-Cutter Service and the Life Saving Service by the Act of Congress approved 28 January, 1915. This act constituted the Coast Guard as a part of the military forces of the United States, " which shall operate under the Treasury Department in time of peace and operate as a part of the Navy in time of war or when the President shall so direct."

II.—DUTIES.

1. The Principal duties of the Coast Guard are the enforcement of the maritime laws of the United States and the saving of life and assistance to vessels in distress.

2. Law enforcement duties, performed for all departments of the government, include those relating to customs, movements and anchorage of vessels, immigration, quarantine, neutrality, navigation and other laws governing merchant vessels and motor boats, safety of life on navigable waters during regattas, oil pollution, sponge fisheries, protection of game and the seal and other fisheries in Alaska, protection of bird reservations established by Executive Order and the suppression of mutinies.

3. Life saving and assistance duties include the maintenance of coastal stations and communication lines on the continental coasts of the United States, the work of the International Ice Patrol, derelict destruction, winter cruising on the Atlantic coast, the extension of medical aid to fishing vessels, the Bering Sea Patrol, and flood relief work. In its humanitarian duties the Coast Guard renders aid and assistance to vessels in distress irrespective of nationality and extends its protection, if needed, to all shipping within the scope of its operations.

4. In time of war the Coast Guard operates as a part of the Navy. A military organization was adopted at the time the service was established in 1790, before the establishment of the Navy Department. This organization has been continued since that date for the purpose of maintaining the general efficiency of the operation of the service in its law enforcement duties in time of peace. The executive action under which the Coast Guard operates as a part of the Navy in time of war is similar in effect to a measure of mobilization. In this respect the Coast Guard is a potential reserve force for the Navy. No personnel are normally assigned or equipped as land troops. Vessels are prepared in emergencies to equip landing forces with small arms and machine guns; stations are similarly prepared to undertake emergency police duties in a more limited sense, because of the smaller units involved, but in both cases these duties would be incidental to the primary purpose of the service, the enforcement of civil law and the saving of life and property.

III.—ADMINISTRATION.

Secretary of the Treasury : The Honorable Henry Morgenthau, Jun.
Assistant Secretary of the Treasury* : The Honorable Stephen B. Gibbons.
Headquarters : (Washington, D.C.)
Commandant : Rear-Admiral R. R. Waesche.
* The Assistant Secretary has immediate supervision of the Coast Guard.

IV.—ORGANIZATION.

(a) The United States and its coastal waters are divided into nine divisions, each being under the command of a division commander operating directly under Coast Guard Headquarters in Washington. These divisions in turn include thirteen districts for the operation of 241 Coast Guard (Life Saving) Stations and the vessels and shore establishments assigned.

(b) The following training, repair, and supply establishments are maintained :

(1) Coast Guard Academy, New London, Connecticut. Four year course for cadets (entry by competitive examination).

(2) Coast Guard Receiving Unit and the Coast Guard Institute, New London, Connecticut. Training and educational courses for enlisted ratings.

(3) Coast Guard Depot, Curtis Bay, Maryland. Construction of life-boats, etc. Repair of vessels.

(4) Coast Guard Stores, Brooklyn, New York, and San Francisco, California. Supply depots for ships and stations.

V.—PERSONNEL.

(Total authorised complement : 10,188.)
Ranks : Rear Admiral (2).
Engineer-in-Chief (Ranks as Captain) (1).

	Line	Engineering	Constructor	District Commander
Captain	23	8	—	—
Commander	46	13	1	—
Lieutenant Commander	87	—	2	12
Lieutenant	173	—	2	4
Lieut. (j.g.) & Ensign	372	—	—	—

Professors : 5 (ranks from Lieut. to Commander)
Chief Warrant Officers : 393. Warrant Officers : 148.
Petty Officers and Men : 8,896. (Enlist for three years ; pay as U.S. Navy.)
Uniforms of officers and men are similar to those of U.S. Navy, but commissioned officers wear a gold shield on the sleeve instead of a star, and cap device is a gold spread-eagle, the talons grasping a horizontal foul anchor. A silver shield is mounted on the eagle's breast. Men of C.G. wear a shield on the sleeve.

VI.—VESSELS.

The vessels in commission on 1 July, 1939, consisted of 36 cruising cutters, 12 harbour tugs, 17 165-ft. patrol boats, 32 125-ft. patrol boats, 1 100-ft. patrol boat, 9 80-ft. patrol boats, 46 75-ft. patrol boats, 2 72-ft. patrol boats, 2 65-ft. patrol boats, 8 miscellaneous patrol boats, 8 special craft, 100 picket boats and about 1,800 life, station and small boats of various types.

VII.—AVIATION.

Air Stations in commission : 8. Location : Salem, Mass. ; Charleston, S.C. ; New York, N.Y. ; Miami, Fla. ; St. Petersburg, Fla. ; Biloxi, Miss. ; San Diego, Calif. ; Port Angeles, Wash. ; Elizabeth City, N.C. ; San Francisco, Calif.

VIII.—U.S. MARITIME SERVICE.

The establishment of the U.S. Maritime Service was authorized in June, 1938, as a part of the U.S. Maritime Commission. The administration of the Service is under the immediate supervision of the Commandant of the Coast Guard. The organization maintains training stations for unlicensed personnel at New York City and Oakland, California, and for licensed personnel at New London, Conn. and Oakland, California.

The training ships *American Seaman, Northland, Joseph Conrad,* and *Tusitala* are operated by the Service, the latter two being square-rigged ships.

Enrolment in the Maritime Service is limited to licensed and unlicensed personnel of the merchant marine who have been at least two years on American vessels.

Cruising Cutters.

GEO. W. CAMPBELL   1938, *Official.*

Observe seaplane   1939, *Official.*

Name	Station
GEORGE W. CAMPBELL	Stapleton, N.Y.
SAMUEL D. INGHAM	Port Angeles, Wash.
WILLIAM J. DUANE	Oakland, Calif.
ROGER B. TANEY	Honolulu, T.H.

All laid down May 1, 1935 at Philadelphia Navy Yard and launched June 3, 1936.

ALEXANDER HAMILTON	Oakland, Calif.
JOHN C. SPENCER	Cordova, Alaska

Both laid down at New York Navy Yard, Sept. 11, 1935, and launched Nov. 10, 1936, and Jan. 6, 1937, respectively.

Cruising Cutters—*continued.*

GEORGE M. BIBB   .. *Norfolk, Va.*
Laid down at Charleston Navy Yard, Aug. 15, 1935 and launched Jan. 14, 1937.
Standard displacement : 2,000 tons. Dimensions : 308 (*w.l.*), 327 (*o.a.*) × 41 × 11½ feet (*mean* draught), 12¼ feet (*max.*). Guns : 2—5 inch, 2 quad. M.G. AA., 2—6 pdr. (with provision for mounting 2 extra 5 inch if needed). 1 Seaplane carried in some, with only one 5 inch gun. Westinghouse geared turbines. 2 shafts. S.H.P. : 6,200 = 20 kts. 2 wt. boilers. Fuel : 572 tons. Feed water : 143 tons, fresh water : 109 tons. Cruising radius : 8,000 miles at 12·5 kts.

COMANCHE.   1935, *Official.*

Name.	Station.	Name.	Station.
ALGONQUIN	Portland, Me.	**ONONDAGA**	Astoria, Oregon
COMANCHE	Stapleton, N.Y.	**TAHOMA**	Cleveland, Ohio
MOHAWK	Cape May, N.J.	**ESCANABA**	Grand Haven, Mich.

All launched 1934 except *Escanaba*, 1932. Steel, strengthened for icebreaking. First 3 built by Pusey & Jones Corpn., Wilmington, Del., second 3 by Defoe Works, Bay City, Mich. Displacement : 1,005 tons. Complement : 60. Dimensions : 165 (*o.a.*) × 36 × 13½ feet. Guns : 2—3 inch, 50 cal., 2—6 pdr. Machinery : Turbines with double reduction gear. S.H.P. : 1,500 = 13·5 kts. Radius : 5,000 miles. Approximate average inclusive cost, $584,000 each. These ships are reported to be very successful in service, making good headway through ice nearly 2 feet thick.

Cruising Cutters—*continued*

CAYUGA.   1937, *Hr. Registrator Ossi Janson.*

CAYUGA (Oct. 8, 1931). *Boston, Mass.* Built by United D.D. Co., Staten Island, N.Y. Steel. Displacement : 1,975 tons. Dimensions : 250 (*o.a.*) × 42 × 16 feet. Turbo-Electric engines (1 main, 2 auxiliary). H.P. : 3,220 = 16 kts. 2 Babcock & Wilcox boilers. Oil fuel : 335 tons. Guns : 2—5 inch, 2—6 pdrs. Radius : 8,000 miles.

1938, *Official.*

SHAWNEE (1922). Steel. 900 tons. Dimensions : 158½ × 30 × 14 feet. Guns : 2—1 pdr. Built by Union Con. Co., Oakland, Cal. Refitted completely, 1938. (*Eureka, Calif.*)

Cruising Cutters—continued.

CHELAN.   1929 *Photo.*

Name.	Station.	Name.	Station.
ITASCA	*San Diego, Calif.*	**CHELAN** ..	*Boston, Mass.*
SEBAGO ..	*Norfolk, Va.*	**CHAMPLAIN**	*Stapleton, N.Y.*
SARANAC	*Galveston, Texas*	**MENDOTA** ..	*Norfolk, Va.*
SHOSHONE	*Oakland, Calif.*	**PONTCHARTRAIN**	
			Stapleton, N.Y.

Built 1930 by Gen. Eng. & Dry   **TAHOE** *New Bedford, Mass.*
Dock Co., Oakland.   Built 1928–29 by Bethlehem Shipbuilding Corporation at Quincy, Mass.

All similar to *Cayuga* above, but *Pontchartrain* has only 2—6 pdrs.

NORTHLAND. (Rig modified).   1936.

NORTHLAND (Newport News Shipbuilding Co., 1927). Built of steel, hull being of exceptionally massive construction, to withstand ice pressure. Forefoot cut away to above w.l. Displacement: 2065 tons. Dimensions: 216 (o.a.) × 39 × 15 feet (*mean* draught). Two 6-cyl. 4-cycle Diesel engines with electric drive. Total B.H.P. 1200 = 11 kts. 1 screw. Guns: 2—6 pdr. Built for Bering Sea Patrol, but now used as a seagoing training ship. (*Oakland, Calif.*).

TAMPA.

Name.			Station.
HAIDA	..	..	*Juneau, Alaska*
MODOC	..	..	*Wilmington, N.C.*
MOJAVE	..	..	*Miami, Fla.*
TAMPA	..	..	*Mobile, Ala.*

All built 1921. Steel, 1 screw. 1780 tons. Dimensions: 240 × 39 × 16¼ feet. Guns: 2—5 inch, 1—3 inch AA., 2—6 pdr. S.H.P. 2600 = 15 kts. Machinery: Turbo-electric (General Electric Curtis Turbine).
All built by Gen. Eng. & Dry Dock Co., Oakland, Cal.

1920 *Photo.*

TALLAPOOSA (1915). Steel, 1 screw, 964 tons. Dimensions: 165⅞ × 32 × 11 feet. Speed: 11·8 kts. Oil fuel only. Guns: 2—3 inch, 50 cal., 2—6 pdr. (*Savannah, Ga.*).

Cruising Cutters—continued.

1920 *Photo.*

REDWING (1919.) Ex-Navy Minesweeper, taken over 1924. Steel, 1 screw. Standard displacement: 840 tons. Dimensions: 187⅞ × 35½ × 12½ feet (*mean* draught). Speed: 12·8 kts. Guns: 2—3 inch, 23 cal., 2—1 pdr. (*Port Angeles, Wash.*).

1919 *Photo, U.S. Navy Publicity Bureau.*

OSSIPEE (1915). Steel, 1 screw. 997 tons. Dimensions: 165⅝ × 32 × 11¾ feet. Speed: 12 kts. Guns: 2—3 inch, 2—6 pdr., 2—1 pdr. Strengthened for ice navigation. (*Sault Ste. Marie, Mich.*).

UNALGA (1912). Steel, 1 screw. 1181 tons. Dimensions 190 × 32½ × 14 feet. Speed: 12 kts. Guns: 2—6 pdr. (*San Juan, Puerto Rico.*).

PAMLICO (1907). Steel, twin screw. 451 tons. Dimensions: 115 × 30 × 5¾ feet. Speed: 9·3 kts. Guns: 2—6 pdr. (*Newbern, N.C.*)

Special Craft.

1938, *Official.*

PEQUOT (ex-Minelayer *General Samuel M. Mills*, built 1909, transferred from War Department 1922). Steel, 1 screw. 950 tons. Dimensions: 166½ × 32½ × 11½ feet. 12 kts. (*Boston, Mass.*)

Harbour Craft—Tug Type (14).

Detailed to larger Maritime Ports to enforce Customs and Navigation Laws and the regulation of the anchorage and movements of vessels.

NAUGATUCK   1939, *Official.*

ARUNDEL (June 24, 1939), **MAHONING** (July 22, 1939), **NAUGATUCK, RARITAN** (both March 23, 1939). Former pair built by Gulfport Works, Port Arthur, Texas; latter pair by Defoe Works, Bay City, Mich. Displacement: 328 tons. Dimensions: 110 × 26½ × 10½ feet (*mean* draught). Machinery: Diesel-electric. S.H.P.: 1,000 = 12 kts. Strengthened for icebreaking. Respective Stations: *New York* (former pair), *Boston* and *Philadelphia*.

Note.—These 4 vessels are an improvement on design of *Hudson* class. Reported to be better sea boats.

TUCKAHOE.   1935, *Official.*

Calumet, Navesink, Tuckahoe, (Built at Charleston Navy Yard.) *Hudson* (Built at Portsmouth Navy Yard). All launched 1934. Steel. Displacement: 290 tons. Dimensions: 110½ × 24 × 10½ feet. Diesel engines. 1 shaft. H.P.: 800 = 12 kts. Radius: 2,000 miles. (*New York*).

MANHATTAN.   1938, *Official.*

Manhattan (1918). Steel, 1 Screw. Ice Breaker, Salvage Vessel, Tug and Fire Float. 406 tons. Dimensions: 120½ × 24 × 11¾ feet. Speed: 9·5 kts. Guns: 2—1 pdr. (*New York, N.Y.*)

Winnisimmet (1903). Steel, 1 screw. 182 tons. Dimensions: 96½ × 20½ × 9 feet. Speed: 12 kts. (*Baltimore*).

AB 26.   1937 *Official.*

A.B. 25, 26 (Boston, Mass., 1936). Wood, sheathed. Displacement: 72 tons. Dimensions: 63½ × 19 × 5 feet. Diesel engine. 1 shaft. H.P.: 300 = 10 kts.
There are also 40 anchorage and boarding vessels, known as AB. boats and bearing numbers with the prefix AB, from 1 to 68, employed on harbour duties.

Patrol Boats.

ARGO. (AURORA, CALYPSO, DAPHNE, PERSEUS have only one funnel.)   1933 *Photo.*

17—165 ft. steel Patrol Boats.

						Station.
Argo	..	..	..	..	..	Newport, R.I.
Aurora	..	..	..	..	..	San Pedro, Cal.
Calypso	..	..	..	..	..	Baltimore, Md.
Daphne	..	..	..	..	..	Oakland, Cal.
Galatea	..	..	..	..	..	Stapleton, N.Y.
Hermes	..	..	..	..	..	San Pedro, Cal.
Icarus	..	..	..	..	..	Stapleton, N.Y.
Perseus	..	..	..	..	..	San Diego, Cal.
Thetis	..	..	..	..	..	Boston, Mass.
Ariadne	..	..	..	..	..	Oakland, Cal.
Atalanta	..	..	..	..	..	Seattle, Wash.
Cyane	..	..	..	..	..	Ketchikan, Alaska
Dione	..	..	..	..	..	Norfolk, Va.
Nemesis	..	..	..	..	..	St. Petersburg, Fla.
Nike	..	..	..	..	..	Pascagoula, Miss.
Pandora	..	..	..	..	..	Key West, Fla.
Triton	..	..	..	..	..	Gulfport, Miss.

Built during 1931–34. 337 tons. Dimensions : 165 × 25½ × 8½ feet. Guns : 1—3 inch, 23 cal., 2—1 pdr. Winton Diesel engines. 2 shafts in some, 1 in others. H.P. : 1,300 = 16·5 kts.
Note.—Electra, of this class, renamed *Potomac* and converted into Presidential Yacht.

Patrol Boats—*continued.*

1939. *Official.*

32—125 ft. steel Patrol Boats: ***Active, Alert, Antietam, Cahoone, Colfax, Crawford, Diligence, Dix, Ewing, Faunce, Frederick Lee, General Greene, Harriet Lane, Jackson, Kimball, Legare, Marion, McLane, Morris, Pulaski, Reliance, Rush, Tiger, Travis, Vigilant, Woodbury, Yeaton, Agassiz, Bonham, Boutwell, Cartigan, Nemaha*** (1926-27). Displacement : 220 tons. Dimensions : 125 × 23½ × 6¾ feet. Guns : 1—3 inch, 23 cal., 23 cal. H.P. 300 = 14 kts. All being re-engined, and after refit vary considerably from original appearance.

Kimball and *Yeaton* employed on training duties.

Patrol Boats—*continued.*

FORWARD.   1934 *Photo, Official.*

2—100 ft. steel Patrol Boats: ***Forward, Nansemond.*** (Defoe Boat & Motor Works, Bay City, Mich., 1925-26). Displacement : 210 tons. Dimensions : 99⅔ × 23 × 8 feet. Guns : 1—3 inch, 23 cal. Diesel engines. 2 shafts. Speed : 10 kts.

UNITED STATES COAST GUARD. (1950)

Flags.

ENSIGN

STANDARD

Colour Key

Red

White

Blue

SECRETARY OF THE TREASURY

UNDER SECRETARY OF THE TREASURY

ASSISTANT SECRETARY OF THE TREASURY

ADMIRAL

VICE-ADMIRAL

REAR-ADMIRAL

COMMODORE

SENIOR OFFICER PRESENT

BROAD COMMAND PENDANT

BURGEE COMMAND PENDANT

AUXILIARY

ANCHORAGE

PENDANT

Administration.

Commandant, U.S.C.G.: Admiral Joseph F. Farley.
Assistant Commandant: Rear-Admiral Merlin O'Neill.
Engineer-in-Chief: Rear-Admiral Ellis Reed-Hill.

Personnel.

19,000 officers and men.

I.—ESTABLISHMENT.

The United States Coast Guard was established by the Act of Congress approved January 28, 1915, which consolidated the Revenue Cutter Service founded in 1790 and the Life Saving Service founded in 1878. The act of establishment as amended provides that "the Coast Guard, which shall be a military service and constitute a branch of the land and naval forces of the United States at all times, shall operate under the Treasury Department in time of peace and operate as a part of the Navy, subject to the orders of the Secretary of the Navy, in time of war or when the President shall so direct". The Lighthouse Service, founded in 1789, was transferred to the Coast Guard on July 1, 1939, as a result of the President's Reorganization Plan No. II. On February 28, 1942, the President transferred temporarily from the Secretary of Commerce to the Commandant of the Coast Guard certain safety-at-sea functions of the former Bureau of Marine Inspection and Navigation. The President's Reorganization Plan III, which became effective July 16, 1946, made this temporary transfer of functions permanent.

II.—DUTIES.

1. The peacetime duties of the Coast Guard have as their principal objective safety and security at sea through enforcement of the navigation laws, saving life and assistance to vessels in distress, maintenance of aids to navigation, and marine inspection.

2. Law enforcement duties, performed for all departments of the government, include those relating to customs, movements and anchorage of vessels, immigration, quarantine, neutrality, navigation and other laws governing merchant vessels and motor boats, safety of life on navigable waters during regattas, oil pollution, sponge fisheries, protection of game, seal and fisheries in Alaska, protection of bird reservations established by Executive Order and suppression of mutinies.

3. Life saving and assistance duties include maintenance of coastal stations and communication lines on the continental coasts of the United States, conduct of the International Ice Patrol, icebreaking, weather patrol, derelict destruction, winter cruising on the Atlantic coast, extension of medical aid to fishing vessels, Bering Sea Patrol and flood relief work. In its humanitarian duties the Coast Guard renders aid and assistance to vessels in distress irrespective of nationality and extends its protection, if needed, to all shipping within the scope of its operations.

4. The Coast Guard establishes and maintains navigation aids, consisting of lighthouses, lightships, radio beacons, buoys, and unlighted beacons on the sea and lake coasts of the United States, on the rivers of the United States as authorized by law, and on the coasts of all other territory under United States jurisdiction, with the exception of the Philippine Islands and Panama.

5. In time of war the Coast Guard operates as a part of the Navy. A military organization was adopted at the time the service was established in 1790, before the establishment of the Navy Department. This organization has been continued since that date for the purpose of maintaining the general efficiency of the operation of the service in its law enforcement duties in time of peace. The executive action under which the Coast Guard operates as a part of the Navy in time of war is similar in effect to a measure of mobilisation. In this respect the Coast Guard is a potential reserve force for the Navy. No personnel are normally assigned or equipped as land troops. Vessels are prepared in emergencies to equip landing forces with small arms and machine guns; stations are similarly prepared to undertake emergency police duties in a more limited sense, because of the smaller units involved, but in both cases these duties would be incidental to the primary purpose of the service, the enforcement of civil law and the saving of life and property.

III.—ORGANIZATION.

For the administration and operation of the Coast Guard, the United States, including its territories and insular possessions (except the Philippine Islands), and the waters adjacent thereto are divided into 10 districts, each under the command of a district commander operating directly under the Commandant of the Coast Guard.

IV.—PERSONNEL.

Uniforms of officers and men are similar to those of U.S. Navy, but commissioned officers wear a gold shield on the sleeve instead of a star, and cap device is a gold spread-eagle, the talons grasping a horizontal foul anchor. A silver shield is mounted on the eagle's breast. Men of the Coast Guard wear a shield on the sleeve.

V.—VESSELS.

Coast Guard vessels are designated Coast Guard cutters. Those of 110 feet tug type and below are detailed to the larger maritime ports to enforce Customs and Navigation laws and the regulation of the anchorage and movement of vessels.

VI.—AVIATION.

Air Stations in commission number nine. Location: Salem, Mass.; New York, N.Y.; Miami, Fla.; St. Petersburg, Fla.; San Diego, California; Port Angeles, Washington; Elizabeth City, N.C.; San Francisco, California; Traverse City, Michigan.

Gunboats.
13 "Owasco" Class (WPG).

MENDOTA.   1948, Official.

ANDROSCOGGIN	OWASCO
CHATAUQUA	PONTCHARTRAIN (ex-Okeechobee)
ESCANABA (ex-Otsego, March 25, 1945)	SEBAGO (ex-Wachusett)
IROQUOIS	WACHUSETT (ex-Huron, Nov. 5,
KLAMATH	1944)
MENDOTA (Feb. 29, 1944)	WINNEBAGO
MINNETONKA (ex-Sunapee)	WINONA

Displacement: 1,563 tons (1,913 tons full load)
Dimensions: 254 (o.a.) × 43 × 15 (mean), 16½ (max.) feet
Guns: 2—5 inch, 38 cal., 4—40 mm. AA., 4—20 mm. AA.
Machinery: Geared turbines with electric drive by Westinghouse Co. S.H.P.: 4,000 – 18 kts.

Notes.—All built by Western Pipe & Steel Co., Los Angeles, except Mendota and Pontchartrain, by the Coast Guard Shipyard, Curtis Bay, Md. Cost over $2,300,000 each without armament. WPG 68, 41, 64, 43, 66, 69, 67, 39, 70, 42, 44, 40, 65, respectively.

Patrol Craft (Large) (WPC).

AURORA.   1948, Official.

14—165 ft. steel Cutters

ARGO	CALYPSO	HERMES	PANDORA
ARIADNE	CYANE	NEMESIS	PERSEUS
ATALANTA	DAPHNE	NIKE	TRITON
AURORA	DIONE		
(Built 1931–34)			

Displacement: 334–337 tons
Dimensions: 165 × 25½ × 9½ feet
Guns: 1—3 inch, 23 cal., 2—1 pdr.
Machinery: Winton Diesels. 2 shafts. H.P.: 1,340 – 16 kts.

Note.—WPC 100, 101, 102, 103, 104, 105, 106, 107, 109, 111, 112, 113, 114, 116.

Patrol Craft (Small) (WPC).

GENERAL GREENE.   1948, Official.

22—125 ft. steel Cutters

ACTIVE	CARTIGAN	FREDERICK LEE	McLANE
AGASSIZ	COLFAX	GENERAL	MORRIS
ALERT	CRAWFORD	GREENE	TRAVIS
BONHAM	CUYAHOGA	KIMBALL	VIGILANT
BOUTWELL	DILIGENCE	LEGARE	YEATON
CAHOONE	EWING	MARION	
(1926–27)			

Displacement: 220 tons
Dimensions: 125 (o.a.) × 23½ × 9 (max.) feet
Guns: 1—40 mm. AA., 1—20 mm. AA.
Machinery: Diesel. 2 shafts. B.H.P.: 800 – 13 kts.

Notes.—All re-engined in 1939–42. WPC 125, 126, 127, 129, 130, 131, 132, 133, 134, 157, 135, 137, 139, 140, 143, 144, 145, 146, 147, 153, 154, 156. Active, Colfax, Crawford, Diligence, Ewing, Legare, McLane, Vigilant recently employed as buoy tenders. Kimball and Yeaton employed on training duties.

18 Seaplane Tender Type (WAVP).

McCULLOCH.   1948, Official.

CASCO	UNIMAK
MACKINAC	YAKUTAT
HUMBOLT	BARATARIA
MATAGORDA	BERING STRAIT
ABSECON	CASTLE ROCK
CHINCOTEAGUE	COOK INLET
COOS BAY	DEXTER (ex-Biscayne)
ROCKAWAY	McCULLOCH (ex-Wachapreague)
HALF MOON	GRESHAM (ex-Willoughby)

Displacement: 1,766 tons (2,800 tons full load)
Dimensions: 310½ (o.a.) × 41 × 13½ (max.) feet
Guns: 1—5 inch, 38 cal., 2 or 4—40 mm. AA., 4—20 mm. AA.
Machinery: Diesel. B.H.P.: 6,080 – 18·2 kts.

Notes.—All completed 1941–44. WAVP 370–387, respectively.

6 "Campbell" Class (WPG).

SPENCER.   1943, Official.

4 Philadelphia Navy Yard	1 New York Navy Yard
CAMPBELL (ex-George W. Campbell)	SPENCER (ex-John C. Spencer,
DUANE (ex-William J. Duane)	Jan. 6, 1937)
INGHAM (ex-Samuel D. Ingham)	
TANEY (ex-Roger B. Taney)	1 Charleston Navy Yard
(All June 3, 1936)	BIBB (ex-George M. Bibb, Jan. 14, 1937)

Standard displacement: 2,216 tons
Dimensions: 308 (w.l.) 327 (o.a.) × 41 × 13 (mean), 14½ (max.) feet
Guns: 1—5 inch, 38 cal., 2—40 mm. AA., 4—20 mm. AA.
Machinery: Westinghouse geared turbines. 2 shafts. S.H.P.: 6,200 20·5 kts.
Boilers: 2 Babcock & Wilcox
Oil fuel: 572 tons
Cruising radius: 8,000 miles at 12 kts., 12,300 at 11 kts.

Notes.—War loss: Alexander Hamilton. WPG 32, 33, 35, 37, 36, 31.

Icebreakers (WAGB).
1 "Mackinaw" Type.

MACKINAW.   1948, Official.

MACKINAW (ex-Manitowoc, March 6, 1944)

Displacement: 5,090 tons
Dimensions: 290 (o.a.) × 75 × 19 (max.) feet
Guns: M.G.
Machinery: Diesel, with electric drive. 3 shafts. (1 forward, 2 aft.) B.H.P.: 10,000   16 kts.
Radius: 6,000 miles at cruising speed

Notes.—WAGB 83. Built by Toledo S.B. Co. Cost over $10,000. Of similar type to "Wind" class in next column. Constructed with 1⅝ plating for service as icebreaker on Great Lakes. Completed Jan., 1945.

2 "Mokoma" Type (WPG).

MOKOMA.   1948, Mr. Paul H. Silverstone.

MOKOMA (ex-H.M.S. Totland, ex-Cayuga, Oct. 8, 1931)
TAMPA (ex-Sebec, ex-H.M.S. Banfi, ex-Saranac, 1930)

Displacement: 1,546 tons
Dimensions: 250 (o.a.) × 42 × 16 feet
Guns: 1—3 inch, 50 cal., 2—40 mm. AA., 4—20 mm. AA.
Machinery: Turbo-electric. H.P.: 3,220 – 16 kts.
Boilers: 2 Babcock & Wilcox
Oil fuel: 335 tons

Notes.—WPG 163, 164. Itasca (ex-H.M.S. Gorleston) for sale 1950.

2 "Tahoma" Type (WPG).

ONON_DAGA (1934)   TAHOMA (1934)

Displacement: 1,005 tons
Dimensions: 165 (o.a.) × 36 × 13½ feet
Guns: 2—3 inch, 50 cal., 6 M.G.
Machinery: Geared turbines. S.H.P.: 1,500 – 13 kts.
Radius: 5,000 miles
Complement: 60

Notes.—Steel. Strengthened for icebreaking. Built by Defoe Works, Bay City, Mich. Very successful in service, making good headway through ice nearly 2 feet thick. WPG 79, 80.

Icebreakers—continued.
2 "Wind" Class.

EASTWIND.   1948, Official.

EASTWIND (WAGB 279, Feb. 6, 1943)
NORTHWIND (WAGB 282, Feb. 25, 1945)

Displacement: 3,500 tons (6,500 tons full load)
Dimensions: 250 (pp.), 269 (o.a.) × 63½ × 25¾ feet
Guns: 2—5 inch, 38 cal., 4—40 mm. AA.
Machinery: Diesel, with electric drive. 3 shafts (1 forward, 2 aft.) B.H.P.: 13,300   16 kts.

Notes.—Built by Western Pipe & Steel Co. Now have twin 5-inch turret forward and helicopter platform aft. Construction entirely welded, with double hull and exceptionally heavy plating, designed to crush 9 ft. ice. Cost reported as $10,003,000 each. Northwind (first ship of that name), Southwind and Westwind. were lent to Soviet Navy in 1945. Southwind returned 1950 (see page 470). Eastwind severely damaged in collision with the tanker Gulfstream, Jan. 19, 1949, recommissioned May 17, 1950, after repairs costing $1,300,000 at Newport News.

Tender (WAGL).

STORIS (ex-*Eskimo*, 1942).   Added 1948, *Official.*

Displacement:	1,715 tons
Dimensions:	230 (*o.a.*) × 43 × 14 (*mean*), 15 (*max.*) feet
Machinery:	Diesel, with electric drive. B.H.P.: 1,800 — 13.5 kts.

Notes.—WAGL 38. Built by Toledo S.B. Co. Strengthened for ice navigation, and employed on Greenland service.

Buoy Tenders (WAGL).
38 "Cactus and Iris" Classes.

BASSWOOD.   1948, *Official.*

JONQUIL.   1947, *Official.*

| HEATHER | JONQUIL | WILLOW |
| IVY | MAGNOLIA | |

Displacement:	1,250 tons (*full load*)
Dimensions:	188¼ (*o.a.*) × 37 × 12 (*max.*) feet
Machinery:	Triple expansion. I.H.P.: 1,200 — 12 kts.

Notes.—Ex-Army minelayers, 1942. WAG 331, 329, 330, 328, 332, respectively.

JUNIPER (May 18, 1940)

Displacement:	794 tons
Dimensions:	177 × 32⅔ × 9¼ feet
Machinery:	Diesel, with electric drive. 2 shafts. B.H.P.: 900 — 13 kts.

| MAPLE | NARCISSUS | ZINNIA |
| All 1939 | | |

Displacement:	342 tons (*Maple*, 350 tons)
Dimensions:	122 × 27 × 6½ feet
Machinery:	Diesel. 2 shafts. B.H.P.: 400 — 10 kts.

HEMLOCK (1934)

Displacement:	1,005 tons
Dimensions:	175 × 32 × 12½ feet
Machinery:	Reciprocating. 2 shafts. I.H.P.: 1,000 — 12 kts.

TAMARACK (1934)

Displacement:	400 tons
Dimensions:	124 × 29 × 7½ feet
Machinery:	Diesel, with electric drive. B.H.P.: 600 — 10 kts.

ARBUTUS (1933)

Displacement:	960 tons
Dimensions:	175 × 32 × 12½ feet
Machinery:	Reciprocating. 2 shafts. I.H.P.: 1,000 — 11 kts.

Buoy Tenders—continued.

CLOVER.   Added 1948, *Official.*

20 Marine Iron & S.B. Co., Duluth
BASSWOOD
BLACKHAW (June 18, 1943)
BLACKTHORN (July 20, 1943)
BUTTONWOOD (Nov. 28, 1942)
CACTUS (Nov. 25, 1941)
CITRUS (Aug. 15, 1942)
CLOVER (1942)
CONIFER (Oct. 3, 1942)
COWSLIP (1942)
EVERGREEN
HORNBEAM (Aug. 15, 1943)
MESQUITE (Nov. 14, 1942)
PAPAW
PLANETREE
SASSAFRAS (1943)
SEDGE (1943)
SPAR (Nov. 2, 1943)
SUNDEW (Feb. 8, 1944)
SWEETBRIAR (Dec. 30, 1943)
SWEETGUM (1943)

17 Zenith Dredge Co., Duluth
ACACIA (ex-*Thistle*, April 7, 1944)
BALSAM (1942)
BITTERSWEET (1943)
BRAMBLE (1943)
FIREBUSH (1943)
GENTIAN (1942)
IRIS (March 10, 1944)
LAUREL (Aug. 4, 1942)
MADRONA (Nov. 11, 1942)
MALLOW (1943)
MARIPOSA (Jan. 7, 1944)
SAGEBRUSH (Sept. 30, 1943)
SALVIA (Sept. 15, 1943)
SORREL (Sept. 28, 1942)
TUPELO (Nov. 28, 1942)
WOODBINE
WOODRUSH (1944)

1 Coast Guard Shipyard, Curtis Bay
IRONWOOD (March, 1943)

Displacement:	935 tons
Dimensions:	180 (*o.a.*) × 37 × 12 (*mean*), 14 (*max.*) feet
Machinery:	Diesel, with electric drive. B.H.P.: 1,200 — 14 kts. (except *Citrus, Clover, Conifer, Cowslip, Evergreen, Tupelo, Woodbine,* which are B.H.P.: 1,000 — 13 kts.)

Note.—*Redbud* transferred to Navy as AKL (Cargo Ship Light).

HICKORY (1933)

Displacement:	400 tons
Dimensions:	131¼ × 24½ × 9¼ feet
Machinery:	Reciprocating. I.H.P.: 500 — 12 kts.

MISTLETOE.   1948, *Official.*

MISTLETOE (1939)

Displacement:	1,040 tons
Dimensions:	173 × 34 × 11 feet
Machinery:	Reciprocating. 2 shafts. I.H.P.: 1,000 — 12 kts.

LILAC (1933)

Displacement:	770 tons
Dimensions:	172 × 32 × 8½ feet
Machinery:	Reciprocating. 2 shafts. I.H.P.: 1,000 — 11.5 kts.

| COLUMBINE (1931) | LINDEN (1931) | WISTARIA (1933) |

Displacement:	323 tons
Dimensions:	121½ × 25 × 6½ feet
Machinery:	Diesel, with electric drive. B.H.P.: 240 — 9 kts.

VIOLET (1930)

Displacement:	1,012 tons
Dimensions:	173½ × 32 × 10½ feet
Machinery:	Reciprocating. 2 shafts. I.H.P.: 1,000 — 12 kts.

Buoy Tenders—continued.

WHITE HEATH.   1948, *Official.*

WHITE ALDER	WHITE HOLLY	WHITE SAGE
WHITE BUSH	WHITE LUPINE	WHITE SUMAC
WHITE HEATH	WHITE PINE	
(1943)		

Displacement:	435 tons
Dimensions:	133 (*o.a.*) × 30 × 10 (*max.*) feet
Machinery:	Diesel-electric. B.H.P.: 300 — 10 kts.

1947, *Official.*

SPRUCE (ex-~~Army~~ craft FS 222, 1945)

Displacement:	812 tons (*full load*)
Dimensions:	180 (*o.a.*) × 32 × 9 (*max.*) feet
Machinery:	Diesel. B.H.P.: 1,000 — 13 kts.

| ASTER | THISTLE |
| Both 1943. Wood | |

Displacement:	500 tons (*full load*)
Dimensions:	105 (*o.a.*) × 30½ × 8 (*max.*) feet
Machinery:	Diesel-electric

BARBERRY (Nov. 14, 1942)	COSMOS (Nov. 11, 1942)	SMILAX
BLUEBELL	PRIMROSE	VERBENA
BRIER	RAMBLER	

Displacement:	178 tons
Dimensions:	100 × 24 × 4½ feet
Machinery:	Diesel, with electric drive. B.H.P.: 330 — 8.5 kts.

| HAWTHORN (1921) | OAK (1921) |

Displacement:	875 tons
Dimensions:	160 × 30 × 9½ feet
Machinery:	Reciprocating. I.H.P.: 750 — 8 kts.

CEDAR (1917)

Displacement:	1,370 tons
Dimensions:	201 × 36 × 14 feet
Machinery:	Reciprocating. I.H.P.: 1,300 — 12 kts.

Smaller buoy tenders include the following:

CLEMATIS (1944), 93 tons	DAHLIA (1933), 160 tons
SHADBUSH (1944), 93 tons	CHERRY (1932), 202 tons
BLACKROCK (1942), 160 tons	MYRTLE (1932), 186 tons
BIRCH (1939), 76 tons	ALTHEA (1930), 120 tons
BLUEBONNET (1935–39), 184 tons	POINCIANA (1930), 120 tons
JASMINE (1935–39), 184 tons	BEECH (1928), 255 tons
ELM (1937), 69 tons	PALMETTO (1916), 170 tons
RHODODENDRON (1935), 140 tons	

WALNUT.   1940, *Official.*

| FIR (1939) | HOLLYHOCK (1937) | WALNUT (1939) |

Displacement:	885 tons
Dimensions:	175 × 32 × 11 feet
Machinery:	Reciprocating. 2 shafts. I.H.P.: 1,000 — 12 kts.

Buoy Tenders—continued.

River Types.

SUMAC. 1948, *Official.*

FERN (Nov. 6, 1942)   **FOXGLOVE** (1944)   **SUMAC** (1944)

Displacement: 350 tons
Dimensions: 114½ × 30 × 8 feet
Machinery: Diesel. B.H.P.: 960 = 9.5 kts.

LANATNA (1943)

Displacement: 273 tons
Dimensions: 80 × 30 × 5½ feet
Machinery: Diesel. B.H.P.: 600 = 9.5 kts.

DOGWOOD (1942)   **FORSYTHIA** (1940)   **SYCAMORE** (1940)

Displacement: 230 tons
Dimensions: 114 × 26½ × 5 feet
Machinery: Diesel. B.H.P.: 400 = 10.5 kts.

OLEANDER (1940)

Displacement: 80 tons
Dimensions: 73 × 17½ × 4½ feet
Machinery: Diesel. B.H.P.: 330 = 10 kts.

GOLDENROD (1938)   **POPLAR** (1939)

Displacement: 193 tons
Dimensions: 103¾ × 24½ × 4 feet
Machinery: Diesel. B.H.P.: 300 = 9 kts.

WAKEROBIN (1927)

Displacement: 575 tons
Dimensions: 182 × 43 × 4 feet
Machinery: Paddle. I.H.P.: 550 = 6 kts.

Oceangoing Tugs (WAT).

ACUSHNET. 1948, *Official.*

ACUSHNET (ex-*Shackle*, April 1, 1943)   **YOCONA** (ex-*Seize*, April 8, 1944)

Displacement: 1,557 tons
Dimensions: 207 (w.l.), 213½ (o.a.) × 39 × 13 (mean), 15½ (max.) feet
Machinery: Diesel-electric. 2 shafts. H.P.: 3,000 = 14 kts.

Note.—WAT 167, 168.

Oceangoing Tugs—continued.

CHEROKEE (Nov. 10, 1939)

Displacement: 1,170 tons
Dimensions: 195 (w.l.), 205½ (o.a.) × 38½ × 12 (mean), 16 (max.) feet
Guns: 1—3 inch, 50 cal., 2—20 mm. AA.
Machinery: Diesel-electric. H.P.: 3,000 = 16 kts.

Note.—WAT 165.

Harbour Tugs (WYT).

TUCKAHOE. 1935, *Official.*

3 Charleston Navy Yard, 1934   1 Portsmouth Navy Yard, 1934
CALUMET   **HUDSON**
NAVESINK
TUCKAHOE

Displacement: 290 tons
Dimensions: 110½ × 24 × 10½ (mean), 11½ (max.) feet
Machinery: Diesel, with electric drive. B.H.P.: 800 = 12 kts.

Note.—Strengthened for icebreaking.

NAUGATUCK. 1939, *Official.*

ARUNDEL (June 24, 1939)   **MOHICAN** (July, 1943)
MAHONING (July 22, 1939)   **OJIBWA** (Aug., 1943)
NAUGATUCK (March 23, 1939)   **SAUK** (Aug. 10, 1943)
RARITAN (March 23, 1939)   **SNOHOMISH** (Aug. 10, 1943)
KAW (1942)   **APALACHEE** (1943)
MANITOU (Sept. 29, 1942)   **YANKTON** (1943)
CHINOOK (July, 1943)

Displacement: 328 tons
Dimensions: 110 (o.a.) × 26½ × 10½ (mean), 12½ (max.) feet
Machinery: Diesel-electric. S.H.P.: 1,000 = 12 kts.

Notes.—First pair built by Gulfport Works, Port Arthur, Texas; second pair by Defoe Works, Bay City, Mich.; third pair by Coast Guard Yard, Curtis Bay, Md.; remaining 7 by Ira S. Bushey & Son, Brooklyn, N.Y. Strengthened for icebreaking.

Cable Layer (WARC).

YAMACRAW. 1947, *Official.*

YAMACRAW (1943)

Displacement: 1,054 tons
Dimensions: 188½ × 37 × 12 feet
Machinery: Triple expansion. 2 shafts. I.H.P.: 1,200 = 11 kts.

Notes.—WARC 333. Ex-Army minelayer.

Cargo Ships (WAK).

KUKUI. 1947, *Official.*

KUKUI (1944)   **UNALGA** (1944)

Displacement: 4,900 tons
Dimensions: 338½ (o.a.) × 50 × 21 (max.) feet
Machinery: Diesel. B.H.P.: 1,700 = 12 kts.

Note.—WAK 186, 185.

NETTLE (ex-*FS 396*, 1944)   **TRILLIUM** (ex-*FS 397*, 1944)

Displacement: 728 tons
Dimensions: 176½ × 32 × 10 (max.) feet
Machinery: Diesel. B.H.P.: 1,000 = 13 kts.

Notes.—Ex-Army craft. WAK 169, 170.

Patrol Boats (WYP).

Note.—All now have figure of length prefixed to official number on bows for ready recognition of type, e.g., CG 83444.

No. 312. 1948, *Mr. W. H. Davis.*

WYP. 83-ft. design: Total number in service, 95. 1938–42. Wood

Displacement: 45 tons
Dimensions: 83 × 16 × 4½ feet
Guns: 20 mm. Oerlikons and D.C.
Machinery: 2 petrol engines. H.P.: 1,200 = 20.5 kts
Complement: 10
Cost: ≈42,450 ≈58,000 each

Note.—A number of these vessels have been transferred to the Cuban, Dominican, Ecuadorian, Mexican and Peruvian Navies.

A large number of the following vessels are also in service:

WYP. 80 feet
WYP. 64 feet
WYP. 63 feet
WYP. 56 feet
Pickets. 38 feet

Training Ship.

(Auxiliary Barque) WIX.

EAGLE. Added 1949.

EAGLE (ex-*Horst Wessel*, June 13, 1936)

Displacement: 1,634 tons
Dimensions: 265¾ (pp.), 295½ (o.a.) × 39½ × 15½ (mean), 16½ (max.) feet
Sail area: 21,530 sq. ft.
Machinery: 2 M.A.N. auxiliary Diesels. B.H.P.: 700 = 10 kts
Oil fuel: 48 tons

Note.—Sister ship, *Albert Leo Schlageter*, also fell into American hands, but was sold to Brazil.

COAST GUARD (1980)

Senior Officers

Commandant:
Admiral John B. Hayes
Vice Commandant:
Vice-Admiral Robert H. Scarborough
Chief of Staff:
Rear-Admiral James P. Stewart
Commander, Atlantic Area:
Vice-Admiral Robert I. Price
Commander, Pacific Area:
Vice-Admiral James S. Gracey

Establishment

The United States Coast Guard was established by an Act of Congress approved 28 January 1915, which consolidated the Revenue Cutter Service (founded in 1790) and the Life Saving Service (founded in 1848). The act of establishment stated the Coast Guard "shall be a military service and a branch of the armed forces of the USA at all times. The Coast Guard shall be a service in the Treasury Department except when operating as a service in the Navy".
Congress further legislated that in time of national emergency or when the President so directs, the Coast Guard operates as a part of the Navy. The Coast Guard did operate as a part of the Navy during the First and Second World Wars and the Viet-Nam War.
The Lighthouse Service (founded in 1789) was transferred to the Coast Guard on 1 July 1939 and the Bureau of Navigation and Steamboat Inspection on 28 February 1942. The Coast Guard was transferred to the newly established Department of Transportation on 1 April 1967.

Missions

The current missions of the Coast Guard are to (1) enforce or assist in the enforcement of applicable Federal laws upon the high seas and waters subject to the jurisdiction of the USA including environmental protection; (2) administer all Federal laws regarding safety of life and property on the high seas and on waters subject to the jurisdiction of the USA, except those laws specifically entrusted to other Federal agencies; (3) develop, establish, maintain, operate, and conduct aids to maritime navigation, ocean stations, icebreaking activities, oceanographic research, and rescue facilities; and (4) maintain a state of readiness to function as a specialised service in the Navy when so directed by the President.

Personnel

30 Sep 1979: 4 908 officers, 1 427 warrant officers, 31 274 enlisted men.

Aviation

Only the larger "Hamilton" class cutters and certain classes of icebreakers can support helicopters at sea.
As of 15 February 1980 the Coast Guard's aviation strength consisted of 51 fixed-wing aircraft and 116 helicopters:

25	HC-130	Hercules
17	HC-131	Convair
7	HU-16	Albatross
1	VC-4A	Gulfstream I
1	VC-11A	Gulfstream II
37	HH-3F	Pelican
79	HH-52A	Sea Guard

The Coast Guard has on order 41 land-based patrol and rescue aircraft (Falcon 20G) in the period 1980-84 to replace the long-serving HU-16 Albatross amphibians, now being phased out.

Cutter Strength

All Coast Guard vessels are referred to as "cutters". Cutter names are preceded by USCGC. Cutter serial numbers are prefixed with letter designations similar to the US Navy classification system with the prefix letter "W". The first two digits of serial numbers for cutters less than 100 ft in length indicate their approximate length overall. All Coast Guard cutters are active unless otherwise indicated.
Approximately 600 small rescue and utility craft also are in service.

The following table provides a tabulation of the ship strength of the United States Coast Guard. Ship arrangement is based on function and employment. Numbers of ships listed are actual as of 1 January 1979. Some projections of changes are also included.

Category/Classification		Active*	Reserve	New Construction
Cutters				
WHEC	High Endurance Cutters	17	1	—
WMEC	Medium Endurance Cutters	23	—	9
Icebreakers				
WAGB	Icebreakers	6	—	—
WTGB	Icebreaking Tugs	4	—	2
Patrol Craft				
WPB	Patrol Craft, Large	76	1	—
Training Cutters				
WIX	Training Cutter	1	—	—
WTR	Reserve Training Cutter	1	—	—
Oceanographic Cutters				
WAGO	Oceanographic Cutters	2	—	—
Buoy Tenders				
WLB	Buoy Tender, Seagoing	30	1	—
WLM	Buoy Tender, Coastal	15	—	—
WLI	Buoy Tender, Inland	13	—	—
WLR	Buoy Tender, River	22	—	—
Construction Tenders				
WLIC	Construction Tender, Inland	14	—	—
Lightships				
WLV	Lightships	1	1	—
Harbour Tugs				
WYTM	Harbour Tugs, Medium	14	—	—
WYTL	Harbour Tugs, Small	15	—	—

Shipbuilding Programmes

Approved FY 1979 Programme

2 WMEC ("270 ft" class)
2 WTGB ("140 ft" class)

Approved FY 1980 Programme

3 WMEC ("270 ft" class)

DELETIONS

Icebreakers

1976   *Edisto* (WAGB 284) and *Staten Island* (WAGB 278) (both sold)
1978   9 May *Burton Island* (WAGB 283) (sold)

High Endurance Cutters

1976   *Chautauqua* (WHEC 41) (scrapped), *Mendota* (WHEC 69), *Minnetonka* (WHEC 67), *Ponchartrain* (WHEC 70) and *Winona* (WHEC 65), (all pending for sale)

Medium Endurance Cutters

1980   *Comanche, Modoc* (latter transferred to Maritime Administration for disposal)

Patrol Craft

1976   *Cape Gull* (WPB 95304), *Cape Upright* (WPB 95303) (hulks stripped; sold)
1978   18 Sep *Flagstaff* (WPGH 1) (pending)
1979   15 June *Cape Morgan* (WPB 95313); 6 July *Cape Fox* (WPB 95316) (both retained for spares)

Buoy Tenders

1976   30 Sep *Loganberry* (WLI 65305) (sold); 12 Nov *Clematis* (WLI 74286) (sold), *Shadbush* (WLI 74287) and *Blueberry* (WLI 65302) (both sold)
1977   1 June *Oleander* (WLR 73264) (sold); 30 June *Sycamore* (WLR 268) (sold); 1 July *Tern* (WLI 80801) (sold); 8 July *Foxglove* (WLR 285) (sold); 12 Aug *Forsythia* (WLR 63) (sold); 1 Sep *Verbena* (WLI 317) (sold)
1978   31 Oct *Azalea* (WLI 641) (sunk as target by USN), *Juniper* (WLM 224) (sold), *Balsam* (WLB 62) (sold)
1979   *Tupelo* (WLB 303) (sold)
1980   28 Jan *Blackthorn* (sunk in collision in Tampa Bay)

Training Cutter

1978   3 Nov *Cuyahoga* (WIX 157) (sunk in collision 20 Oct 1978; raised; scuttled 19 Mar 1979 off Cape Charles as a fishing reef)

Tugboats

1979   15 June *Kaw* (WYTM 61) and *Naugatuck* (WYTM 92) both sold

Lightship

1979   13 Dec *Columbia River* (WLV 604) (sold)

"Campbell" Class

"Wind" Class

"Hamilton" Class

POLAR STAR

GLACIER

"Reliance" Class

Drawings, A. D. Baker III

HIGH ENDURANCE CUTTERS

12 "HAMILTON" and "HERO" CLASSES: HIGH ENDURANCE CUTTERS (WHEC)

Name	No.	Builders	Laid down	Launched	Commissioned	F/S
HAMILTON	WHEC 715	Avondale Shipyards Inc, New Orleans, Louisiana	Jan 1965	18 Dec 1965	20 Feb 1967	AA
DALLAS	WHEC 716	Avondale Shipyards Inc, New Orleans, Louisiana	7 Feb 1966	1 Oct 1966	1 Oct 1967	AA
MELLON	WHEC 717	Avondale Shipyards Inc, New Orleans, Louisiana	25 July 1966	11 Feb 1967	22 Dec 1967	PA
CHASE	WHEC 718	Avondale Shipyards Inc, New Orleans, Louisiana	15 Oct 1966	20 May 1967	1 Mar 1968	AA
BOUTWELL	WHEC 719	Avondale Shipyards Inc, New Orleans, Louisiana	12 Dec 1966	17 June 1967	14 June 1968	PA
SHERMAN	WHEC 720	Avondale Shipyards Inc, New Orleans, Louisiana	13 Feb 1967	23 Sep 1967	23 Aug 1968	AA
GALLATIN	WHEC 721	Avondale Shipyards Inc, New Orleans, Louisiana	17 Apr 1967	18 Nov 1967	20 Dec 1968	AA
MORGENTHAU	WHEC 722	Avondale Shipyards Inc, New Orleans, Louisiana	17 July 1967	10 Feb 1968	14 Feb 1969	PA
RUSH	WHEC 723	Avondale Shipyards Inc, New Orleans, Louisiana	23 Oct 1967	16 Nov 1968	3 July 1969	AA
MUNRO	WHEC 724	Avondale Shipyards Inc, New Orleans, Louisiana	18 Feb 1970	5 Dec 1970	10 Sep 1971	PA
JARVIS	WHEC 725	Avondale Shipyards Inc, New Orleans, Louisiana	9 Sep 1970	24 Apr 1971	30 Dec 1971	PA
MIDGETT	WHEC 726	Avondale Shipyards Inc, New Orleans, Louisiana	5 Apr 1971	4 Sep 1971	17 Mar 1972	PA

Displacement, tons: 3 050 full load
Dimensions, feet (metres): 378 × 42·8 × 20
(115·2 × 13·1 × 6·1)
Guns: 1—5 in *(127 mm)*/38 (Mk 30); 2—40 mm; 2—20 mm
A/S weapons: 2 triple topedo tubes (Mk 32)
Helicopters: 1 HH-52A or HH-3 helicopter
Main engines: Combined diesel and gas turbine (CODAG):
2 diesels (Fairbanks-Morse) 7 000 bhp; 2 gas turbines (Pratt
& Whitney FT-4A), 36 000 shp; 2 shafts; (cp propellers)
Speed, knots: 29, 20 cruising
Oil fuel: 800 tons
Range, miles: 14 000 at 11 knots (diesels);
2 400 at 29 knots (gas)
Complement: 164 (15 officers, 149 enlisted)

In the autumn of 1977 *Gallatin* and *Morgenthau* were the first of
the Coast Guard ships to have women assigned as permanent
members of the crew.

Anti-submarine armament: Hedgehog anti-submarine
weapons have been removed during overhaul and Mk 309 fire
control system for Mk 32 torpedo tubes installed. *Hamilton* was
first to be so modernised.

Design: These ships have clipper bows, twin funnels enclosing
a helicopter hangar, helicopter platform aft. All are fitted with
oceanographic laboratories, elaborate communications
equipment, and meteorological data gathering facilities.
Superstructure is largely of aluminium construction. Bridge
control of manoeuvring is by aircraft-type joy-stick rather than
wheel.

Engineering: The "Hamilton" class were the largest US "military" ships with gas turbine propulsion prior to the Navy's
"Spruance" class destroyers. The Fairbanks-Morse diesels are
12-cylinder.
Engine and propeller pitch consoles are located in wheelhouse
and at bridge wing stations as well as engine room control
booth.
A retractable bow propulsion unit is provided for station keeping and precise manoeuvring (unit is located directly forward
of bridge, immediately aft of sonar dome).

Gunnery: Mk 56 GFCS and SPG 35 fire control radar.

Radar: Search: SPS 29, 51 and 64.

Sonar: SQS 38.

GALLATIN

1978, USCG

MUNRO

1978, USCG

6 "CAMPBELL" (327 ft) CLASS: HIGH ENDURANCE CUTTERS (WHEC)

Name	No.	Builders	Laid down	Launched	Commissioned	F/S
BIBB (ex-George M. Bibb)	WHEC 31	Charleston Navy Yard	10 May 1935	14 Jan 1937	10 Mar 1937	AA
CAMPBELL (ex-George W. Campbell)	WHEC 32	Philadelphia Navy Yard	1 May 1935	3 June 1936	16 June 1936	PA
DUANE (ex-William J. Duane)	WHEC 33	Philadelphia Navy Yard	1 May 1935	3 June 1936	16 Aug 1936	AA
INGHAM (ex-Samuel D. Ingham)	WHEC 35	Philadelphia Navy Yard	1 May 1935	3 June 1936	12 Sep 1936	AA
SPENCER (ex-John C. Spencer)	WHEC 36	New York Navy Yard	11 Sep 1935	3 Jan 1936	1 Mar 1937	AR
TANEY (ex-Roger B. Taney)	WHEC 37	Philadelphia Navy Yard	1 May 1935	3 June 1936	20 Nov 1936	AA

Displacement, tons: 2 216 standard; 2 656 full load
Dimensions, feet (metres): 327 × 41 × 15 *(99·7 × 12·5 × 4·6)*
Guns: 1—5 in *(127 mm)*/38 (Mk 30); 2—40 mm;
2—20 mm (WHEC 35)
A/S weapons: Removed
Main engines: Geared turbines (Westinghouse); 6 200 shp;
2 shafts
Boilers: 2 (Babcock & Wilcox)
Speed, knots: 19·8
Range, miles: 4 000 at 19 knots; 8 000 at 10·5 knots
Complement: 144 (13 officers, 131 enlisted men)

These were the Coast Guard's largest cutters until *Hamilton* was completed in 1967.
Duane served as an amphibious force flagship during the invasion of Southern France in August 1944 and was designated AGC 6; the other ships of this class, except the lost *Alexander Hamilton* (PG 34), were similarly employed but retained Coast Guard number with WAGC prefix (amidships structure built up and one or two additional masts installed); all reverted to gunboat configuration after war (WPG). Redesignated WHEC on 1 May 1966.
All of these cutters remain in active service except *Spencer*, decommissioned on 1 February 1974 and placed in reserve at the Coast Guard Yard, Curtis Bay, Maryland. *Spencer* is employed as a stationary engineering school ship.

Anti-submarine armament: During the 1960s these ships each had an ASW armament of one ahead-firing fixed hedgehog and two Mk 32 triple torpedo tube mounts; subsequently removed from all ships.

Gunnery: As built these ships had two 5-in/51 guns (single mounts forward) and two 6 pdr guns; rearmed during World War II with an additional single 5-in/51 gun installed aft plus two or three 3-in/50 anti-aircraft guns, and several 20 mm anti-aircraft guns (depth charge racks installed); *Taney* was experimentally armed with four 5-in/38 guns in single mounts. Present armament fitted after World War II.

Radar: SPS 64.

TANEY
1975, USCG

INGHAM
6/1976, C. and S. Taylor

1 "CASCO" (311 ft) CLASS: HIGH ENDURANCE CUTTER (WHEC)

Name	No.	Builders	Laid down	Launched	Commissioned	F/S
UNIMAK	WHEC 379 (ex-WTR 379, ex-WHEC 379, ex-AVP 31)	Associated Shipbuilders, Seattle, Wash	15 Feb 1942	27 May 1942	31 Dec 1943	AA

Displacement, tons: 1 766 standard; 2 800 full load
Dimensions, feet (metres): 310·75 × 41 × 13·5
(94·7 × 12·5 × 4·1)
Guns: 1—5 in *(127 mm)*/38 (Mk 30); 2—40 mm
A/S weapons: Removed
Main engines: Diesels (Fairbanks-Morse); 6 080 bhp; 2 shafts
Speed, knots: 18
Range, miles: 8 000 at 18 knots
Complement: 150 (13 officers; 137 enlisted men)

Unimak is the sole survivor of 18 former Navy seaplane tenders (AVP) transferred to the Coast Guard in 1946-48 (WAVP/WHEC 370-387). *Unimak* operated as a training cutter (WTR) from 1969 until decommissioned on 30 May 1975 at Baltimore. Replaced by *Reliance* WTR 615. Towed to Boston in January 1977 for reactivation which was delayed by a serious engine-room fire. Recommissioned 15 August 1977 to assist in patrolling the 200 mile EEZ. To remain in commission until the first three or four new 270 ft WMECs are commissioned.

Classification: The former Navy AVPs were designated WAVP by the Coast Guard until changed to high endurance cutters (WHEC) on 1 May 1966. *Unimak* subsequently became a training cutter (WTR) on 28 November 1969. Reclassified WHEC on 15 August 1977.

Transfers: Ships of this class (originally "Barnegat" class) serve in the navies of Ethiopia, Italy, Philippines and Viet-Nam and commercially.

UNIMAK
1977, USCG

MEDIUM ENDURANCE CUTTERS

0 + 4 + 6 (6) "BEAR" (270 ft) CLASS: MEDIUM ENDURANCE CUTTERS (WMEC)

Name	No.	Builders	Laid down	Launched	Commissioned	F/S
BEAR	WMEC 901	Tacoma Boatbuilding Co, Tacoma	23 Aug 1979	11 May 1980	1 Aug 1981	Bldg
TAMPA	WMEC 902	Tacoma Boatbuilding Co, Tacoma	26 May 1980	27 Jan 1981	1 Sep 1981	Bldg
HARRIET LANE	WMEC 903	Tacoma Boatbuilding Co, Tacoma	25 Sep 1980	31 May 1981	1 Jan 1982	Bldg
NORTHLAND	WMEC 904	Tacoma Boatbuilding Co, Tacoma	4 Feb 1981	6 Oct 1981	1 May 1982	Bldg
SENECA	WMEC 905	Approved FY 1978 programme	—	—	—	Ord
PICKERING	WMEC 906	Approved FY 1978 programme	—	—	—	Ord
ESCANABA	WMEC 907	Approved FY 1979 programme	—	—	—	Proj
LEGARE	WMEC 908	Approved FY 1979 programme	—	—	—	Proj
ARGUS	WMEC 909	Approved FY 1979 programme	—	—	—	Proj
TAHOMA	WMEC 910	Requested FY 1981 programme	—	—	—	Proj
ERIE	WMEC 911	Planned FY 1982 programme	—	—	—	—
McCULLOCH	WMEC 912	Planned FY 1982 programme	—	—	—	—
EWING	WMEC 913	Planned future programmes	—	—	—	—
Three ships (minimum)	WMEC 914-916	Planned future programmes	—	—	—	—

Displacement, tons: 1 780 full load
Dimensions, feet (metres): 270 × 38 × 13·5 *(82·3 × 11·6 × 4·1)*
Aircraft: 1 HH-52A or 1 LAMPS III helicopter
Missiles: (see note)
Gun: 1—3 in *(76 mm)*/62 (Mk 75) (see note)
A/S weapons: (see note)
Main engines: Diesels; 7 000 bhp; 2 shafts = 19·5 knots
Range, miles: 6 800 at 13·5 knots
Complement: 95 (13 officers, 82 enlisted men)

The Coast Guard plans to construct up to 25 medium endurance cutters of this class over a seven year period. They will replace the "Campbell" class and other older medium and high endurance cutters when they become operational from about 1981 onwards.

A/S weapons: These ships will have no shipboard A/S weapons, but will rely on helicopters to deliver torpedoes against submarines detected by the ships' towed sonar array.

Design: They will be the only medium endurance cutters with helicopter hangars, and the first cutters with automated command and control centre. Fin stabilisers to be fitted.

Electronics: Fitted with Mk 92 weapons control system, easily identified by radome above the bridge. These ships will not have hull-mounted sonar, but instead the tactical Towed Array Sonar System (TASS), capable of providing long-range targeting data for A/S helicopter attack.

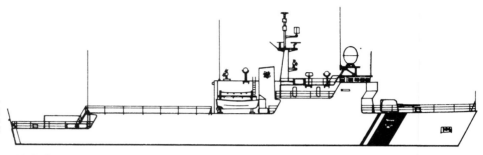

"BEAR" Class

1978, A. D. Baker III

Engineering: Diesels were selected over gas turbine propulsion because of the Coast Guard requirement for long on-station time at slow speeds as opposed to high-speed naval operations.

Fiscal: The Coast Guard's FY 1977 programme provided $49 million for the first two ships of this class.

Gunnery: Weight and space for CIWS. Mk 92 FCS to be fitted.

Helicopters: The plans are designed to accommodate the HH-52 Sea Guard helicopter or its Coast Guard successor, or the Navy's planned LAMPS III (Light Airborne Multi-Purpose System) helicopter. The helicopter hangar is extendable. Weight and space reserved for helicopter landing and traversing system.

Missiles: Weight and space reserved for Harpoon.

Radar: SPS 64 (V) 6.

Rockets: Mk 36 super RBOC to be fitted.

16 "RELIANCE" (210 ft) CLASS: 15 MEDIUM ENDURANCE CUTTERS (WMEC) and 1 TRAINING CUTTER (WTR)

Name	No.	Builders	Commissioned	F/S	Name	No.	Builders	Commissioned	F/S
RELIANCE	WTR 615	Todd Shipyards	20 June 1964	AA	STEADFAST	WMEC 623	American Shipbuilding Co	25 Sep 1968	AA
DILIGENCE	WMEC 616	Todd Shipyards	26 Aug 1964	AA	DAUNTLESS	WMEC 624	American Shipbuilding Co	10 June 1968	AA
VIGILANT	WMEC 617	Todd Shipyards	3 Oct 1964	AA	VENTUROUS	WMEC 625	Coast Guard Yard, Curtis Bay, Baltimore	16 Aug 1968	PA
ACTIVE	WMEC 618	Christy Corp	17 Sep 1966	AA					
CONFIDENCE	WMEC 619	Coast Guard Yard, Curtis Bay, Baltimore	19 Feb 1966	PA	DEPENDABLE	WMEC 626	American Shipbuilding Co	22 Nov 1968	AA
					VIGOROUS	WMEC 627	American Shipbuilding Co	2 May 1969	AA
RESOLUTE	WMEC 620	American Shipbuilding Co	8 Dec 1966	PA	DURABLE	WMEC 628	Coast Guard Yard, Curtis Bay, Baltimore	8 Dec 1967	AA
VALIANT	WMEC 621	American Shipbuilding Co	28 Oct 1967	AA					
COURAGEOUS	WMEC 622	American Shipbuilding Co	10 Apr 1968	AA	DECISIVE	WMEC 629	Coast Guard Yard, Curtis Bay, Baltimore	23 Aug 1968	AA
					ALERT	WMEC 630	American Shipbuilding Co	4 Aug 1969	AA

Displacement, tons: 950 standard; 1 007 full load (except WTR and WMEC 616-619, 970 full load)
Dimensions, feet (metres): 210·5 × 34 × 10·5
(64·2 × 10·4 × 3·2)
Aircraft: 1 HH-52A helicopter embarked as required
Guns: 1—3 in *(76 mm)*/50; 2—40 mm (Mk 19)
Main engines: 2 turbo-charged diesels (ALCO 251B); 2 shafts; 5 000 bhp = 18 knots (WTR 615 and WMEC 616-619 have 2 Solar gas turbines in addition (4 000 shp))
Range, miles: 6 100 at 13 knots (615-619); 6 100 at 14 knots (remainder); 2 700 at 18 knots (all)
Complement: 61 (7 officers, 54 enlisted men)

Designed for search and rescue duties. Design features include 360 degree visibility from bridge; helicopter flight deck (no hangar); and engine exhaust vent at stern in place of conventional funnel. Capable of towing ships up to 10 000 tons. Air-conditioned throughout except engine room; high degree of habitability.
Launched, respectively, on the following dates: 25 May 1963, 20 July 1963, 24 December 1963, 21 July 1965, 8 May 1965, 30 April 1966, 14 January 1967, 18 March 1967, 24 June 1967, 21 October 1967, 11 November 1967, 16 March 1968, 4 May 1968, 29 April 1967, 14 December 1968.
All these cutters are active. *Reliance* is the Coast Guard's reserve training cutter based at Yorktown, Virginia, and retains full search, rescue, and patrol capabilities.

Designation: These ships were originally designated as patrol craft (WPC); changed to WMEC on 1 May 1966.

Helicopters: *Alert* was the first US ship fitted with the Canadian-developed "Beartrap" helicopter hauldown system. No further procurement of this system has been funded.

Radar: SPS 64.

RELIANCE

1979, Dr. Giorgio Arra

ICEBREAKERS

2 "POLAR STAR" CLASS: ICEBREAKERS (WAGB)

Name	No.	Builders	Commissioned	F/S
POLAR STAR	WAGB 10	Lockheed Shipbuilding Co, Seattle, Washington	19 Jan 1976	PA
POLAR SEA	WAGB 11	Lockheed Shipbuilding Co, Seattle, Washington	23 Feb 1978	PA

Displacement, tons: 12 087 full load
Dimensions, feet (metres): 399 × 86 × 31 *(121·6 × 26·2 × 9·5)*
Aircraft: 2 HH-52A helicopters
Guns: 2—40 mm (Mk 19)
Main engines: Diesel-electric; 6 ALCO diesels; 18 000 shp; 3 gas turbines (Pratt & Whitney FT4A-12); 60 000 shp; 3 shafts; (cp propellers) = 18 knots
Range, miles: 28 000 at 13 knots
Complement: 163 (13 officers, 125 enlisted men plus 10 scientists and 15 flight crew)

These ships are the first icebreakers built for US service since *Glacier* was constructed two decades earlier. The programme is intended to replace the World War II-built "Wind" class icebreakers. *Polar Star* authorised in the Fiscal Year 1971 budget of the Department of Transportation; *Polar Sea* in the FY 1973 budget. *Polar Star* was laid down on 15 May 1972 and launched on 17 November 1973; *Polar Sea* was laid down on 27 November 1973 and launched on 24 June 1975. No additional ships are planned for the near future. *Polar Star* based at Seattle.

Design: The "Polar Star" class icebreakers are the largest ships operated by the US Coast Guard. At a continuous speed of 3 knots these ships can break ice 6 ft thick and by riding on the ice they can break 21 ft pack.
These ships have a conventional icebreaker hull form with cutaway bow configuration and well rounded body sections to prevent being trapped in ice. Two 15 ton capacity cranes fitted aft; hangar and flight deck aft; extensive research laboratories provided for arctic and oceanographic research.

Engineering: This CODOG design provides for conventional diesel engines for normal cruising in field ice and gas turbines for heavy icebreaking. The diesel engines drive generators producing AC power; the main propulsion DC motors draw power through rectifiers permitting absolute flexibility in the delivery of power from alternate sources. The use of cp propellers on three shafts will permit manoeuvring in heavy ice without the risk to the propeller blades caused by stopping the shaft while going from ahead to astern.
The Coast Guard had given consideration to the use of nuclear power for an icebreaker; however, at this time the gas turbine-diesel combination can achieve the desirable power requirements without the added cost and operating restrictions of a nuclear powerplant. From January 1976 until November 1977 (her first deployment) *Polar Star* had serious engineering problems which resulted in her being alongside for most of that period. *Polar Star* was still experiencing problems with her propellers in 1979.

Radar: SPS 64.

POLAR STAR   1978, USCG

1 "GLACIER" CLASS: ICEBREAKER (WAGB)

Name	No.	Builders	USN Commissioned	F/S
GLACIER	WAGB 4 (ex-AGB 4)	Ingalls Shipbuilding Corp, Pascagoula, Mississippi	27 May 1955	PA

Displacement, tons: 8 449 full load
Dimensions, feet (metres): 309·6 × 74 × 29 *(94·4 × 22·6 × 8·8)*
Aircraft: 2 helicopters normally embarked
Main engines: Diesel-electric (10 Fairbanks-Morse diesels and 2 Westinghouse electric motors); 21 000 hp; 2 shafts = 17·6 knots
Range, miles: 29 200 at 12 knots; 12 000 at 17·6 knots
Complement: 241 (15 officers, 226 enlisted men)

The largest icebreaker in US service prior to the "Polar Star" class; laid down on 3 August 1953 and launched on 27 August 1954. Transferred from Navy (AGB 4) to Coast Guard on 30 June 1966. During 1972 *Glacier* and assigned helicopters were painted red to improve visibility in Arctic regions. All other icebreakers except *Mackinaw* painted red during 1973.

Engineering: When built *Glacier* had the largest capacity single-armature DC motors ever built and installed in a ship.

Gunnery: As built *Glacier* was armed with two 5-in guns (twin), six 3-in guns (twin), and four 20 mm guns; lighter weapons removed prior to transfer to Coast Guard; 5-in guns removed in 1969. Two single 40 mm guns to be fitted.

Radar: SPS 64.

GLACIER   1976, John A. Jedrlinic

2 "WIND" CLASS: ICEBREAKERS (WAGB)

Name	No.	Builders	Launched	F/S
WESTWIND	WAGB 281 (ex-AGB 6)	Western Pipe & Steel Co, San Pedro, California	31 Mar 1943	GLA
NORTHWIND	WAGB 282	Western Pipe & Steel Co, San Pedro, California	25 Feb 1945	AA

Displacement, tons: 3 500 standard; 6 515 full load
Dimensions, feet (metres): 269 × 63·5 × 29 *(82 × 19·4 × 8·8)*
Aircraft: 2 helicopters normally embarked (HH 52 A)
Guns: 2—40 mm (Mk 19)
Main engines: Diesel-electric; 4 diesels (Enterprise); 10 000 bhp; 2 shafts = 16 knots
Range, miles: 38 000 at 10·5 knots; 16 000 at 16 knots
Complement: 135

Originally seven ships in this class built. Five ships were delivered to the US Coast Guard during World War II and two to the US Navy in 1946. *Westwind* served in the Soviet Navy from 1945 to 1951 (named *Severni Polus* in Soviet service) and with *Northwind* are last of the class. *Westwind* operates on the Great Lakes. Crews of *Northwind* and *Westwind* reduced from 181 to approximately 135 during 1975.

Engineering: These ships were built with a bow propeller shaft in addition to the two stern shafts; bow shaft removed from all units because it would continually break in heavy ice. *Westwind* re-engined in 1973-74, and *Northwind* in 1974-75.

Radar: SPS 64.

NORTHWIND   12/1976, V. H. Young

1 "MACKINAW" CLASS: ICEBREAKER (WAGB)

Name	No.	Builders	Commissioned	F/S
MACKINAW (ex-*Manitowac*)	WAGB 83	Toledo Shipbuilding Co, Ohio	20 Dec 1944	GLA

Displacement, tons: 5 252
Dimensions, feet (metres): 290 × 74 × 19 *(88·4 × 22·6 × 5·8)*
Aircraft: 1 helicopter
Main engines: 2 diesels (Fairbanks-Morse); with electric drive (Elliot); 3 shafts (1 fwd, 2 aft); 10 000 bhp = 18·7 knots
Range, miles: 60 000 at 12 knots; 10 000 at 18·7 knots
Complement: 127 (10 officers, 117 enlisted men)

Laid down on 20 March 1943; launched 6 March 1944. Specially designed and constructed for service as icebreaker on the Great Lakes. Equipped with two 12 ton capacity cranes. Clear area for helicopter is provided on the quarterdeck.

Radar: SPS 64.

MACKINAW   1978, USCG

1 "STORIS" CLASS: MEDIUM ENDURANCE CUTTER (WMEC)

Name	No.	Builders	Commissioned	F/S
STORIS (ex-*Eskimo*)	WMEC 38 (ex-WAGB 38, ex-WAGL 38)	Toledo Shipbuilding Co, Ohio	30 Sep 1942	PA

Displacement, tons: 1 715 standard; 1 925 full load
Dimensions, feet (metres): 230 × 43 × 15 *(70·1 × 13·1 × 4·6)*
Guns: 1—3 in/50; 2—40 mm (single Mk 64)
Main engines: Diesel-electric; 1 shaft; 1 800 bhp = 14 knots
Range, miles: 22 000 at 8 knots; 12 000 at 14 knots
Complement: 106 (10 officers, 96 enlisted men)

Laid down on 14 July 1941; launched on 4 April 1942 as ice patrol tender. Strengthened for ice navigation and sometimes employed as icebreaker. Employed in Alaskan service for search, rescue and law enforcement.
Designation changed from WAG to WAGB on 1 May 1966; redesignated as medium endurance cutter (WMEC) on 1 July 1972.

Radar: SPS 64.

STORIS   1975, USCG

5 + 1 + 3 (5) "KATMAI" CLASS: ICEBREAKING TUGS (WTGB)

Name	No.	Laid down	Commissioned	F/S
KATMAI BAY	WTGB 101	7 Nov 1977	6 Dec 1978	GLA
BRISTOL BAY	WTGB 102	13 Feb 1978	16 Apr 1979	GLA
MOBILE BAY	WTGB 103	13 Feb 1978	19 Aug 1979	GLA
BISCAYNE BAY	WTGB 104	29 Aug 1978	1 Oct 1979	GLA
NEAH BAY	WTGB 105	6 Aug 1979	22 July 1980	GLA
MORRO BAY	WTGB 106	6 Aug 1979	20 Oct 1980	Bldg
PENOBSCOT BAY	WTGB 107	—	—	Proj
THUNDER BAY	WTGB 108	—	—	Proj
STURGEON BAY	WTGB 109	—	—	Proj
—	WTGB 110-114	—	—	Proj

Displacement, tons: 662 full load
Dimensions, feet (metres): 140 × 37·6 × 12·5 *(42·7 × 11·4 × 3·8)*
Main engines: Diesel-electric; 2 500 bhp; 1 shaft =14·7 knots
Endurance: 14 days
Complement: 17 (3 officers, 14 enlisted men)

This class is designed to replace the "110 ft" class WYTMs. Originally classified as WYTMs. Reclassified WTGBs on 5 February 1979. The size, manoeuvrability and other operational characteristics of these new vessels are tailored for operations in harbours and other restricted waters and for fulfilling present and anticipated multi-mission requirements. All units are ice strengthened for operation on the Great Lakes, coastal waters and in rivers. Painted white. WTGB 101 authorised in the FY 1976 programme, WTGB 102-104 in the FY 1977 programme, WTGB 105-106 in the FY 1978 programme, WTGB 108 approved FY 1979 programme, WTGB 109 requested FY 1981 programme, WTGB 110-114 planned FY 1982-83 programme. First seven built at Tacoma Boatbuilding Co, Tacoma.

Radar: SPS 64.

KATMAI BAY   1/1979, USCG

PATROL CRAFT

22 "CAPE" CLASS: PATROL CRAFT—LARGE (WPB)

Name	No.	Builders	F/S
"A" Series			
CAPE SMALL	95300	Coast Guard Yard, Curtis Bay, Maryland	PA
CAPE CORAL	95301	Coast Guard Yard, Curtis Bay, Maryland	PA
CAPE HIGGON	95302	Coast Guard Yard, Curtis Bay, Maryland	AA
CAPE HATTERAS	95305	Coast Guard Yard, Curtis Bay, Maryland	AA
CAPE GEORGE	95306	Coast Guard Yard, Curtis Bay, Maryland	AA
CAPE CURRENT	95307	Coast Guard Yard, Curtis Bay, Maryland	AA
CAPE STRAIT	95308	Coast Guard Yard, Curtis Bay, Maryland	AA
CAPE CARTER	95309	Coast Guard Yard, Curtis Bay, Maryland	PA
CAPE WASH	95310	Coast Guard Yard, Curtis Bay, Maryland	PA
CAPE HEDGE	95311	Coast Guard Yard, Curtis Bay, Maryland	PA
"B" Series			
CAPE KNOX	95312	Coast Guard Yard, Curtis Bay, Maryland	AA
CAPE FAIRWEATHER	95314	Coast Guard Yard, Curtis Bay, Maryland	AA
CAPE JELLISON	95317	Coast Guard Yard, Curtis Bay, Maryland	AA
CAPE NEWAGEN	95318	Coast Guard Yard, Curtis Bay, Maryland	PA
CAPE ROMAIN	95319	Coast Guard Yard, Curtis Bay, Maryland	PA
CAPE STARR	95320	Coast Guard Yard, Curtis Bay, Maryland	AA
"C" Series			
CAPE CROSS	95321	Coast Guard Yard, Curtis Bay, Maryland	AA
CAPE HORN	95322	Coast Guard Yard, Curtis Bay, Maryland	AA
CAPE SHOALWATER	95324	Coast Guard Yard, Curtis Bay, Maryland	AA
CAPE CORWIN	95326	Coast Guard Yard, Curtis Bay, Maryland	PA
CAPE HENLOPEN	95328	Coast Guard Yard, Curtis Bay, Maryland	AA
CAPE YORK	95332	Coast Guard Yard, Curtis Bay, Maryland	AA

Displacement, tons: 105
Dimensions, feet (metres): 95 × 20 × 6 *(29 × 6·1 × 1·8)*
Guns: 2—·5 MGs
Main engines: 4 diesels (Cummings); 2 324 bhp; 2 shafts = 20 knots (21 knots, "C" series)
Range, miles: 2 600 ("A" series); 3 000 ("B" series); 2 800 ("C" series); all at 9 knots (economical); 460 at 20 knots ("C" series 500 at 21 knots)
Complement: 14 (1 officer, 13 enlisted)

Designed for port security, search, and rescue. Steel hulled. "A" series built in 1953; "B" series in 1955-56, and "C" series in 1958-59.
Plans to dispose of this class from 1974-75 onward in favour of new WPB construction have been cancelled; instead all 23 remaining craft will be modernised (see below). Some ships carry women as officers or enlisted personnel as part of the crew. Eight "Cape" class cutters serve in the South Korean Navy.
Cape Higgon and *Hatteras*, paid-off in December 1972, reinstated in 1980-81 after reconstruction.

Modernisation: All 23 craft will be modernised to extend their service life for an estimated ten years. Cost in 1976 was estimated at $500 000 per cutter and by FY 1980 $2 million per cutter. They will receive new engines, electronics, and deck equipment; superstructure will be modified or replaced; and habitability will be improved. The programme began in July 1977 and will be complete by 1981. Each craft will take five months to modernise.

Radar: SPS 64.

CAPE FAIRWEATHER   7/1976, A. D. Baker III

CAPE GEORGE   1976, USCG

53 "POINT" CLASS: PATROL CRAFT—LARGE (WPB)

Name	No.	Builders	F/S
"A" Series			
POINT HOPE	82302	Coast Guard Yard, Curtis Bay, Maryland	AA
POINT VERDE	82311	Coast Guard Yard, Curtis Bay, Maryland	AA
POINT SWIFT	82312	Coast Guard Yard, Curtis Bay, Maryland	AA
POINT THATCHER	82314	Coast Guard Yard, Curtis Bay, Maryland	AA
"C" Series			
POINT HERRON	82318	Coast Guard Yard, Curtis Bay, Maryland	AA
POINT ROBERTS	82332	Coast Guard Yard, Curtis Bay, Maryland	AA
POINT HIGHLAND	82333	Coast Guard Yard, Curtis Bay, Maryland	AA
POINT LEDGE	82334	Coast Guard Yard, Curtis Bay, Maryland	PA
POINT COUNTESS	82335	Coast Guard Yard, Curtis Bay, Maryland	PA
POINT GLASS	82336	Coast Guard Yard, Curtis Bay, Maryland	PA
POINT DIVIDE	82337	Coast Guard Yard, Curtis Bay, Maryland	PA
POINT BRIDGE	82338	Coast Guard Yard, Curtis Bay, Maryland	PA
POINT CHICO	82339	Coast Guard Yard, Curtis Bay, Maryland	PA
POINT BATAN	82340	Coast Guard Yard, Curtis Bay, Maryland	AA
POINT LOOKOUT	82341	Coast Guard Yard, Curtis Bay, Maryland	AA
POINT BAKER	82342	Coast Guard Yard, Curtis Bay, Maryland	AA
POINT WELLS	82343	Coast Guard Yard, Curtis Bay, Maryland	AA
POINT ESTERO	82344	Coast Guard Yard, Curtis Bay, Maryland	AA
POINT JUDITH	82345	Martinac S.B., Tacoma, Washington	PA
POINT ARENA	82346	Martinac S.B., Tacoma, Washington	AA
POINT BONITA	82347	Martinac S.B., Tacoma, Washington	AA
POINT BARROW	82348	Martinac S.B., Tacoma, Washington	PA
POINT SPENCER	82349	Martinac S.B., Tacoma, Washington	AA
POINT FRANKLIN	82350	Coast Guard Yard, Curtis Bay, Maryland	AA
POINT BENNETT	82351	Coast Guard Yard, Curtis Bay, Maryland	PA
POINT SAL	82352	Coast Guard Yard, Curtis Bay, Maryland	AA
POINT MONROE	82353	Coast Guard Yard, Curtis Bay, Maryland	AA
POINT EVANS	82354	Coast Guard Yard, Curtis Bay, Maryland	PA
POINT HANNON	82355	Coast Guard Yard, Curtis Bay, Maryland	AA
POINT FRANCIS	82356	Coast Guard Yard, Curtis Bay, Maryland	AA
POINT HURON	82357	Coast Guard Yard, Curtis Bay, Maryland	AA
POINT STUART	82358	Coast Guard Yard, Curtis Bay, Maryland	PA
POINT STEELE	82359	Coast Guard Yard, Curtis Bay, Maryland	AA
POINT WINSLOW	82360	Coast Guard Yard, Curtis Bay, Maryland	PA
POINT CHARLES	82361	Coast Guard Yard, Curtis Bay, Maryland	AA
POINT BROWN	82362	Coast Guard Yard, Curtis Bay, Maryland	AA
POINT NOWELL	82363	Coast Guard Yard, Curtis Bay, Maryland	AA
POINT WHITEHORN	82364	Coast Guard Yard, Curtis Bay, Maryland	AA
POINT TURNER	82365	Coast Guard Yard, Curtis Bay, Maryland	AA
POINT LOBOS	82366	Coast Guard Yard, Curtis Bay, Maryland	AA
POINT KNOLL	82367	Coast Guard Yard, Curtis Bay, Maryland	AA
POINT WARDE	82368	Coast Guard Yard, Curtis Bay, Maryland	AA
POINT HEYER	82369	Coast Guard Yard, Curtis Bay, Maryland	PA
POINT RICHMOND	82370	Coast Guard Yard, Curtis Bay, Maryland	AA
"D" Series			
POINT BARNES	82371	Coast Guard Yard, Curtis Bay, Maryland	AA
POINT BROWER	82372	Coast Guard Yard, Curtis Bay, Maryland	PA
POINT CAMDEN	82373	Coast Guard Yard, Curtis Bay, Maryland	PA
POINT CARREW	82374	Coast Guard Yard, Curtis Bay, Maryland	PA
POINT DORAN	82375	Coast Guard Yard, Curtis Bay, Maryland	PA
POINT HARRIS	82376	Coast Guard Yard, Curtis Bay, Maryland	PA
POINT HOBART	82377	Coast Guard Yard, Curtis Bay, Maryland	PA
POINT JACKSON	82378	Coast Guard Yard, Curtis Bay, Maryland	AA
POINT MARTIN	82379	Coast Guard Yard, Curtis Bay, Maryland	AA

Displacement, tons: "A" series 67; "C" series 66; "D" series 69
Dimensions, feet (metres): 83 × 17·2 × 5·8 *(25·3 × 5·2 × 1·8)*
Guns: 1—5 MG or 2—5 MGs; some boats unarmed
Main engines: 2 diesels; 1 600 bhp; 2 shafts = 23·5 knots except "D" series 22·6 knots
Range, miles: 1 500 at 8 knots (1 200 "D" series)
Complement: 8 (1 officer, 7 enlisted) (see notes)

Designed for search, rescue, and patrol. Of survivors, "A" series built 1960-61; "C" series in 1961-67; and "D" series in 1970.
26 cutters of the "A" and "B" series were transferred to South Viet-Nam in 1969-70.

Personnel: Most of these units now have an officer assigned; a few still operate with an all-enlisted crew. Some carry women as officers or enlisted personnel.

Radar: SPS 64.

POINT BENNETT   *1979, USCG*

SEAGOING TENDERS

Note: *Acushnet* WAGO 167 serves as Oceanographic cutter with *Evergreen* WAGO 295 from class below. *Acushnet* operates from Gulfport, Miss and *Evergreen* from New London, Conn.

30 "BALSAM" CLASS: BUOY TENDERS (SEAGOING) (WLB)/ OCEANOGRAPHIC CUTTER (WAGO)/ MEDIUM ENDURANCE CUTTERS (WMEC)

Name	No.	Launched	F/S	Name	No.	Launched	F/S
LAUREL	WLB 291	1942	PA	BLACTHAW*	WLB 390	1944	AA
CLOVER	WMEC 292	1942	PA	BRAMBLE*	WLB 392	1944	GLA
EVERGREEN	WAGO 295	1943	AA	FIREBUSH	WLB 393	1944	AA
SORREL*	WLB 296	1943	AR	HORNBEAM	WLB 394	1944	AA
IRONWOOD	WLB 297	1944	PA	IRIS	WLB 395	1944	PA
CITRUS*	WMEC 300	1943	PA	MALLOW	WLB 396	1944	PA
CONIFER	WLB 301	1943	AA	MARIPOSA	WLB 397	1944	GLA
MADRONA	WLB 302	1943	AA	SAGEBRUSH	WLB 399	1944	AA
MESQUITE	WLB 305	1943	GLA	SALVIA	WLB 400	1944	AA
BUTTONWOOD	WLB 306	1943	PA	SASSAFRAS	WLB 401	1944	AA
PLANETREE	WLB 307	1943	PA	SEDGE*	WLB 402	1944	PA
PAPAW	WLB 308	1943	AA	SPAR*	WLB 403	1944	AA
SWEETGUM	WLB 309	1943	AA	SUNDEW*	WLB 404	1944	AA
BASSWOOD	WLB 388	1944	PA	SWEETBRIER	WLB 405	1944	AA
BITTERSWEET	WLB 389	1944	AA	WOODRUSH	WLB 407	1944	GLA

Displacement, tons: 935 standard; 1 025 full load
Dimensions, feet (metres): 180 × 37 × 13 *(54·9 × 11·3 × 4)*
Guns: 1—3 in *(76 mm)*/50 in *Citrus,* (original armament); 2—20 mm guns in *Ironwood, Bittersweet, Firebush, Sedge* and *Sweetbrier;* rest unarmed
Main engines: Diesel-electric; 1 000 bhp in tenders numbered WLB 62-303 series, except *Ironwood;* 1 shaft = 12·8 knots; others 1 200 bhp; 1 shaft = 15 knots
Complement: 53 (6 officers, 47 enlisted men)

Seagoing buoy tenders. *Ironwood* built by Coast Guard Yard at Curtis Bay, Maryland; others by Marine Iron & Shipbuilding Co, Duluth, Minnesota, or Zeneth Dredge Co, Duluth, Minnesota. Completed 1943-45. Eight ships indicated by asterisks are strengthened for icebreaking. Three ships, *Cowslip, Bittersweet,* and *Hornbeam,* have cp bow-thrust propellers to assist in manoeuvring. All WLBs have 20 ton capacity booms. *Evergreen* has been refitted as an oceanographic cutter (WAGO) and is painted white.
Citrus reclassified WMEC in place of *Modoc* (WMEC 194) in June 1979 and *Clover* in place of *Comanche* (WMEC 20) in February 1980.

Modernisation: All of this class have completed modernisation. This has involved a rebuilding of the main engines and overhaul of the propulsion motors, improvement of habitability, installation of hydraulic cargo-handling equipment and the addition of a bow thruster.

Radar: SPS 64.

MADRONA   *6/1979, Dr. Robert Scheina*

COASTAL TENDERS

5 "RED" CLASS: BUOY-TENDERS COASTAL (WLM)

Name	No.	Launched	F/S	Name	No.	Launched	F/S
RED WOOD	WLM 685	1965	AA	RED CEDAR	WLM 688	1971	AA
RED BEECH	WLM 686	1965	AA	RED OAK	WLM 689	1972	AA
RED BIRCH	WLM 687	1966	AA				

Displacement, tons: 471 standard; 512 full load
Dimensions, feet (metres): 157 × 33 × 6 *(47·9 × 10·1 × 1·8)*
Main engines: 2 diesels; 2 shafts; 1 800 hp = 12·8 knots
Range, miles: 3 000 at 11·6 knots
Complement: 31 (4 officers, 27 enlisted men)

All built by Coast Guard Yard, Curtis Bay, Maryland. WLM 685-7 completed 1965-66 and other pair 1971-72. Fitted with cp propellers and bow thrusters; steel hulls strengthened for light icebreaking. Steering and engine controls on each bridge wing as well as in pilot house. Living spaces are air conditioned. Fitted with 10 ton capacity boom.

RED CEDAR   *1976, Dr. Giorgio Arra*

3 "HOLLYHOCK" CLASS: BUOY-TENDERS COASTAL (WLM)

Name	No.	F/S
FIR	WLM 212	PA
HOLLYHOCK	WLM 220	AA
WALNUT	WLM 252	PA

Displacement, tons: 989
Dimensions, feet (metres): 175 × 34 × 12 (53·4 × 10·4 × 3·7)
Main engines: 2 diesels; 2 shafts; 1 350 bhp = 12 knots
Complement: 40 (5 officers, 35 enlisted men)

Launched in 1937 (Hollyhock) and 1939 (Fir and Walnut). Walnut was re-engined by Williamette Iron & Steel Co, Portland, Oregon, in 1958. Redesignated coastal tenders, (WLM), instead of buoy tenders, (WAGL) on 1 January 1965. Fitted with 20 ton capacity boom.

FIR _1977, USCG_

7 "WHITE SUMAC" CLASS: BUOY-TENDERS COASTAL (WLM)

Name	No.	F/S	Name	No.	F/S
WHITE SUMAC	WLM 540	AA	WHITE HEATH	WLM 545	AA
WHITE BUSH	WLM 542	PA	WHITE LUPINE	WLM 546	AA
WHITE HOLLY	WLM 543	AA	WHITE PINE	WLM 547	AA
WHITE SAGE	WLM 544	AA			

Displacement, tons: 435 standard; 600 full load
Dimensions, feet (metres): 133 × 31 × 9 (40·5 × 9·5 × 2·7)
Main engines: Diesels; 2 shafts; 600 bhp = 9·8 knots
Complement: 21 (1 officer, 20 enlisted men)

All launched in 1943. All seven ships are former US Navy YFs, adapted for the Coast Guard Fitted with 10 ton capacity boom.

WHITE SAGE _1976, USCG_

BUOY-TENDERS (INLAND) (WLI)

Name	No.	F/S
BLUEBELL	WLI 313	AA
AZALEA	WLI 641	AA
BUCKTHORN	WLI 642	GLA

Displacement, tons: 200 full load (178 Bluebell)
Dimensions, feet (metres): 100 × 24 × 5 (30·5 × 7·3 × 1·5) (Buckthorn draught 4 ft (1·2))
Main engines: Diesels; 2 shafts; 440 bhp (Azalea) 600 bhp (others) = 9 knots (10·5 Bluebell)
Complement: 14 (1 officer, 13 enlisted men) 15 (Bluebell)

Azalea fitted with large pile driver.
Bluebell completed 1945, Azalea in 1958 and Buckthorn in 1963.

BUCKTHORN _1975, USCG_

Name	No.	F/S
BLACKBERRY	WLI 65303	AA
CHOKEBERRY	WLI 65304	AA

Displacement, tons: 68 full load
Dimensions, feet (metres): 65 × 17 × 4 (19·8 × 5·2 × 1·2)
Main engines: Diesels; 1 shaft; 220 hp = 9 knots
Complement: 5 (enlisted men)

Completed in 1946.

Name	No.	F/S
BAYBERRY	WLI 65400	PA
ELDERBERRY	WLI 65401	AA

Displacement, tons: 68 full load
Dimensions, feet (metres): 65 × 17 × 4 (19·8 × 5·2 × 1·2)
Main engines: Diesels; 2 shafts; 400 hp = 11·3 knots
Complement: 5 (enlisted men)

Completed in 1954.

BAYBERRY _2/1979, USCG_

BUOY TENDERS (RIVER) (WLR)

Notes: (a) All are based on rivers of USA especially the Mississippi and the Missouri and its tributaries.
(b) A new class of WLR is requested in the FY 1981 programme.

SUMAC WLR 311

Displacement, tons: 404 full load
Dimensions, feet (metres): 115 × 30 × 6 (35·1 × 9·1 × 1·8)
Main engines: Diesels; 3 shafts; 960 hp = 10·6 knots
Complement: 23 (1 officer, 22 enlisted men)

Built in 1943.

GASCONADE	WLR 75401	CHEYENNE	WLR 75405
MUSKINGUM	WLR 75402	KICKAPOO	WLR 75406
WYACONDA	WLR 75403	KANAWHA	WLR 75407
CHIPPEWA	WLR 75404	PATOKA	WLR 75408
		CHENA	WLR 75409

Displacement, tons: 145 full load
Dimensions, feet (metres): 75 × 22 × 4 (22·9 × 6·7 × 1·2)
Main engines: Diesels; 2 shafts; 600 hp = 10·8 knots
Complement: 12 (enlisted men)

Built 1964-71.

OUACHITA	WLR 65501		SCIOTO	WLR 65504
CIMARRON	WLR 65502		OSAGE	WLR 65505
OBION	WLR 65503		SANGAMON	WLR 65506

Displacement, tons: 139 full load
Dimensions, feet (metres): 65·6 × 21 × 5 *(20 · 6·4 × 1·5)*
Main engines: Diesels; 2 shafts; 600 hp = 12·5 knots
Complement: 10 (enlisted men)

Built in 1960-62.

OBION pushing barge   *1/1978, USCG*

DOGWOOD WLR 259

Displacement, tons: 230 full load
Dimensions, feet (metres): 114 × 26 × 4 *(34·8 × 7·9 × 1·2)*
Main engines: Diesels; 2 shafts; 2 800 hp = 11 knots
Complement: 21 (1 officer, 20 enlisted men)

Built in 1940.

LANTANA WLR 80310

Displacement, tons: 235 full load
Dimensions, feet (metres): 80 × 30 × 6 *(24·3 × 9·1 × 1·8)*
Main engines: Diesels; 3 shafts; 10 000 hp = 10 knots
Complement: 20 (1 officer, 19 enlisted men)

Built in 1943.

TRAINING CUTTER

1 "EAGLE" CLASS: SAIL TRAINING CUTTER (WIX)

Name	No.	Builders	F/S
EAGLE (ex-*Horst Wessel*)	WIX 327	Blohm & Voss, Hamburg	AA

Displacement, tons: 1 784 full load
Dimensions, feet (metres): 231 wl; 295·2 oa × 39·1 × 17 *(70·4; 90 × 11·9 × 5·2)*
Sail area, square feet: 25 351
Height of masts, feet (metres): fore and main 150·3 *(45·8)*; mizzen 132 *(40·2)*
Main engine: Auxiliary diesel (MAN); 700 bhp; 1 shaft = 10·5 knots (as high as 18 knots under full sail alone)
Range, miles: 5 450 at 7·5 knots (diesel only)
Complement: 245 (19 officers, 46 enlisted men, 180 cadets)

Former German training ship. Launched on 13 June 1936. Taken by the USA as part of reparations after the Second World War for employment in US Coast Guard Practice Squadron. Taken over at Bremerhaven in January 1946; arrived at home port of New London, Connecticut, in July 1946. (Sister ship *Albert Leo Schlageter* was also taken by the USA in 1945 but was sold to Brazil in 1948 and re-sold to Portugal in 1962. Another ship of similar design, *Gorch Foch*, transferred to the USSR in 1946 and survives as *Tovarisch*).

Appearance: When the Coast Guard added the orange-and-blue marking stripes to cutters in the 1960s *Eagle* was exempted because of their affect on her graceful lines; however, in early 1976 the stripes and words "Coast Guard" were added in time for the July 1976 Operation Sail in New York harbour.

Radar: SPS 64.

EAGLE   *5/1978, (PH1 L. H. Sallions)*

CONSTRUCTION TENDERS, (INLAND) (WLIC)

Name	No.	F/S		Name	No.	F/S
PAMLICO	WLIC 800	AA		KENNEBEC	WLIC 803	AA
HUDSON	WLIC 801	AA		SAGINAW	WLIC 804	AA

Displacement, tons: 413 light
Dimensions, feet (metres): 160·9 × 30 × 4 *(49 × 9·1 × 1·2)*
Main engines: 2 diesels = 11·5 knots
Complement: 15

Built in 1975-78 at the Coast Guard Yard, Curtis Bay, Maryland. *Saginaw* completed as last of class 6 February 1978.

Name	No.	F/S
COSMOS	WLIC 293	AA
RAMBLER	WLIC 298	AA
SMILAX	WLIC 315	AA
PRIMROSE	WLIC 316	AA

Displacement, tons: 178 full load
Dimensions, feet (metres): 100 × 24 × 5 *(30·5 × 7·3 × 1·5)*
Main engines: Diesels; 2 shafts; 600 bhp = 10·5 knots
Complement: 15 (1 officer, 14 enlisted men)

Cosmos completed in 1942, others in 1944. *Primrose* fitted with pile driver.

PRIMROSE (with pile driver)   *1976, John A. Jedrlinic*

Name	No.	F/S	Name	No.	F/S	Name	No.	F/S
ANVIL	WLIC 75301	AA	MALLET	WLIC 75304	AA	WEDGE	WLIC 75307	AA
HAMMER	WLIC 75302	AA	VISE	WLIC 75305	AA	SPIKE	WLIC 75308	AA
SLEDGE	WLIC 75303	AA	CLAMP	WLIC 75306	AA	HATCHET	WLIC 75309	AA
						AXE	WLIC 75310	

Displacement, tons: 145 full load
Dimensions, feet (metres): 75 (76—WLIC 75306-75310) × 22 × 4 *(22·9 × 6·7 × 1·2)*
Main engines: Diesels; 2 shafts; 600 hp = 10 knots
Complement: 9 or 10 (1 officer in *Mallet*, *Sledge* and *Vise*; 9 enlisted men in all)

Completed 1962-65.

ANVIL   *2/1979, USCG*

OCEANGOING TUGS

2 "DIVER" CLASS: MEDIUM ENDURANCE CUTTER (WMEC)/ OCEANOGRAPHIC CUTTER (WAGO)

Name	No.	Builders	USN Comm.	F/S
ACUSHNET	WAGO 167	Basalt Rock Co,	5 Feb 1944	AA
(ex-USS *Shackle*)	(ex-WAT 167, ARS 9)	Napa, California		
YOCONA	WMEC 168	Basalt Rock Co,	3 Nov 1944	PA
(ex-USS *Seize*)	(ex-WAT 168, ARS 26)	Napa, California		

Displacement, tons: 1 557 standard; 1 745 full load
Dimensions, feet (metres): 213·5 × 39 × 15 *(65·1 × 11·9 × 4·6)*
Guns: Removed
Main engines: Diesels (Cooper Bessemer); 3 000 bhp; 2 shafts = 15·5 knots
Complement: *Acushnet* 64 (7 officers, 57 enlisted men); *Yocona* 72 (7 officers, 65 enlisted men)

Large, steel-hulled salvage ships transferred from the Navy to the Coast Guard after World War II and employed in tug and oceanographic duties. Launched 1 April 1943 and 8 April 1944 respectively. *Acushnet* modified for handling environmental data buoys and reclassified WAGO in 1968; *Yocona* reclassified as WMEC in 1968.

Radar: SPS 64.

ACUSHNET   12/1978, V. H. Young

3 "CHEROKEE" CLASS: MEDIUM ENDURANCE CUTTERS (WMEC)

Name	No.	Builders	USN Comm.	F/S
CHILULA	WMEC 153	Charleston Shipbuilding & Drydock	5 Apr 1945	AA
	(ex-WAT 153, ATF 153)	Co, Charleston, South Carolina		
CHEROKEE	WMEC 165	Bethlehem Steel Co, Staten Island,	26 Apr 1940	AA
	(ex-WAT 165, ATF 66)	New York		
TAMAROA	WMEC 166	Commercial Iron Works, Portland,	9 Oct 1943	AA
(ex-*Zuni*)	(ex-WAT 166, ATF 95)	Oregon		

Displacement, tons: 1 731 full load
Dimensions, feet (metres): 205 × 38·5 × 17 *(62·5 × 11·7 × 5·2)*
Guns: 1—3 in/50; 2—40 mm
Main engines: Diesel-electric (General Motors diesel); 3 000 bhp; 1 shaft = 16·2 knots
Complement: 72 (7 officers, 65 enlisted men)

Steel-hulled tugs transferred from the Navy to the Coast Guard on loan in 1946; transferred permanently 1 June 1969. Classification of all three ships changed to WMEC in 1968. Launched on 1 December 1944, 10 November 1939, and 13 July 1943, respectively.

Radar: SPS 64.

TAMAROA   6/1979, Dr. Robert Scheina

HARBOUR TUGS

11 "110 ft" CLASS: HARBOUR TUGS MEDIUM (WYTM)

MANITOU	WYTM 60	**ARUNDEL**	WYTM 90	**OBJIBWA**	WYTM 97
APALACHEE	WYTM 71	**MAHONING**	WYTM 91	**SNOHOMISH**	WYTM 98
YANKTON	WYTM 72	**RARITAN**	WYTM 93	**SAUK**	WYTM 99
MOHICAN	WYTM 73	**CHINOOK**	WTYM 96		

Displacement, tons: 370 full load
Dimensions, feet (metres): 110 × 27 × 11 *(33·5 × 8·2 × 3·4)*
Main engines: Diesel-electric; 1 shaft; 1 000 hp = 11·2 knots
Complement: 20 (1 officer, 19 enlisted men)

Built in 1943 except WYTM 90 and 93 built in 1939. WYTM 60, 71-73, 91, 96, 98, 99 active in the Atlantic Fleet. Remainder active on inland waterways. Class to be phased out in early 1980s.

MOHICAN   7/1979, Dr. Giorgio Arra

1 "85 ft" CLASS: HARBOUR TUG MEDIUM (WYTM)

MESSENGER   WYTM 85009

Displacement, tons: 230 full load
Dimensions, feet (metres): 85 × 23 × 9 *(25·9 × 7 × 2·7)*
Main engine: Diesel; 1 shaft; 700 hp = 9·5 knots
Complement: 10 (enlisted)

Built in 1944. Active in the Atlantic Fleet.

15 "65 ft" CLASS: HARBOUR TUGS SMALL (WYTL)

CAPSTAN	WYTL 65601	**CATENARY**	WYTL 65606	**LINE**	WYTL 65611
CHOCK	WYTL 65602	**BRIDLE**	WYTL 65607	**WIRE**	WYTL 65612
SWIVEL	WYTL 65603	**PENDANT**	WYTL 65608	**BITT**	WYTL 65613
TACKLE	WYTL 65604	**SHACKLE**	WYTL 65609	**BOLLARD**	WYTL 65614
TOWLINE	WYTL 65605	**HAWSER**	WYTL 65610	**CLEAT**	WYTL 65615

Displacement, tons: 72 full load
Dimensions, feet (metres): 65 × 19 × 7 *(19·8 × 5·8 × 2·1)*
Main engine: Diesel; 1 shaft; 400 hp = 9·8 knots except WYTL 65601-65606 10·5 knots
Complement: 10 (enlisted men)

Built from 1961 to 1967. All active in the Atlantic Fleet.

CAPSTAN *(Mount Vernon behind)*   6/1979, Dr. Robert Scheina

LIGHTSHIPS (WLV)

WLV 612 (Nantucket)
WLV 613 (Relief)

Displacement, tons: 607 full load
Dimensions, feet (metres): 128 × 30 × 11 *(39 × 9·1 × 3·4)*
Main engine: Diesel; 550 bhp; 1 shaft = 11 knots

Both launched 1950. Assigned to Boston, Massachusetts.
Coast Guard lightships exchange names according to assignment; hull numbers remain constant.

INDEX

ONLY THOSE SHIPS THAT ARE ILLUSTRATED HAVE BEEN INCLUDED IN THE INDEX.